Edward A. Bell

numerical constants

c	Velocity of light	2.998×10^{8} m/sec
ϵ_0	Permittivity of free space	8.854×10^{-12} farad/m
μ_0	Permeability of free space	$4\pi \times 10^{-7}$ henry/m
$\sqrt{\mu_0/\epsilon_0}$	Intrinsic impedance of free space	376.7 ohms
e	Charge of an electron	-1.6008×10^{-19} coul
m	Mass of an electron	9.1066×10^{-31} kg
e/m	Electronic charge-to-mass ratio	-1.7578×10^{11} coul/kg
M	Mass of a proton	1.6725×10^{-27} kg

introduction to modern electromagnetics

introduction to modern electromagnetics

Carl H. Durney
Associate Professor of Electrical Engineering
University of Utah

Curtis C. Johnson
Associate Professor of Electrical Engineering
University of Washington

McGraw-Hill Book Company
New York St. Louis San Francisco London
Sydney Toronto Mexico Panama

introduction to modern electromagnetics

Library of Congress Catalog Card Number 69-13605

18388

234567890 MAMM 7654321069

To Marie
To Katharine and Wilma

preface

Electromagnetics continues to be one of the most fundamental subjects in an engineering curriculum because it provides a basic physical and mathematical understanding of electric, magnetic, and propagation phenomena. The principles of electromagnetics have been applied in an increasing number of research areas in recent years, placing an emphasis on soundness, breadth, and the dynamic aspects of an undergraduate course in electromagnetic field theory. For example, the microwave interest with its base in devices, antennas, and propagation, has moved into microwave phenomena in solid-state materials and gaseous plasmas, where statistical and quantum-mechanical effects are prominent. Interest in the optical spectrum has grown rapidly in step with laser advances into new material interactions, acoustic interactions, propagation, and nonlinear effects. These new research and development interests require a concise and modern undergraduate introduction to electromagnetics.

A survey was conducted recently to determine the present-day needs for an electromagnetics textbook. The results indicated a need for mathematical and physical clarity, the use of examples and applications, and a problem-solutions manual to reduce the time required by the instructor. This textbook was prepared with these objectives in mind.

The book is designed for a first course in engineering electromagnetics at the junior or senior level. There is enough material for a full year's course, and some of the more difficult sections, which have been marked with a star at their beginnings and endings, are optional and can be omitted with no loss of continuity. This makes the text somewhat adaptable to courses of varying difficulty and length. Problems at the end of each chapter are numbered according to the section to which they are pertinent. Thus Problem 1.5-1 is the first problem of Section 1.5. A number of problems are designed to be solved by computer.

We have assumed that students using this book have been introduced to vector analysis. Although an extensive review of vector analysis is given in Chapter 1 and the text is mathematically self-contained, the reader who has not had some previous experience with vector analysis will have difficulty learning the mathematics fast enough. Chapter 1 is meant to be a complete but compact discussion of vector analysis. Since many students have had little experience with cylindrical and spherical coordinate systems, these are discussed in some detail. Physical interpretations of operations such as the divergence and curl are emphasized.

We have tried to make the mathematical level high enough to prepare the student for graduate courses in electromagnetism, while at the same time emphasizing concepts and physical understanding.

Our approach differs principally from some of the more traditional approaches in that dynamics is emphasized over statics. Since field concepts are more easily introduced in terms of statics, the basic electrostatic and magnetostatic concepts are developed first in Chapter 2. The extension to time-varying fields is made, and Maxwell's equations are developed in Chapter 3. The remainder of the text is devoted to understanding, solving, and applying Maxwell's equations. The rationalized mks system of units is used throughout the text.

In Chapter 4 energy and power concepts are discussed. This is followed in Chapter 5 by a description of the interaction of electromagnetic fields with charges in materials. The purpose of Chapter 5 is to show in a detailed way how the interaction between the charges in materials and electromagnetic fields can be described in terms of permittivity and permeability. Since the interaction is easier to understand in the case of dielectrics and conductors than magnetic materials, dielectrics and conductors are emphasized; they are treated from a common base and in terms of time-varying fields.

Chapter 6 contains a discussion of the wave equations, potentials, and planewaves. This chapter presents the fundamental concepts of wave propagation. Refraction and reflection at dielectric boundaries, reflection at conducting boundaries, skin effect, radiation from antennas, and propagation between parallel conducting plates are some of the topics considered. Some examples involving laser beams are given.

The connection between field theory and circuit theory is discussed in Chapter 7. The quasi-static approximation is used to show how Kirchhoff's laws are related to Maxwell's equations. This helps to show the connection between planewave propagation, described in Chapter 6, and the wave propagation on two-conductor systems, described in Chapter 8. Transmission-line concepts such as impedance, reflection coefficient, and standing-wave ratio are discussed in Chapter 8. Also included are the Smith chart and optional sections on tapered transmission lines and transients on transmission lines.

The last chapter is on boundary-value problems. In this chapter mathematical techniques for solving the wave equations are discussed. Propagation in wave guides is treated as a boundary-value problem. An optional section describes how a partial separation of variables in Maxwell's equations leads to a description of wave-guide propagation in terms of transmission-line equations. Then wave-guide propagation is discussed in terms of transmission-line concepts, including the use of the Smith chart.

The development of this text was influenced by many sources. We are grateful to the students who worked through the text when it was in the form of course notes and offered corrections and valuable suggestions. Our colleague, Professor Om P. Gandhi, and several reviewers have also offered many valuable suggestions. We appreciate the excellent work of Mrs. Marian Swenson and her staff in typing and reproducing the manuscript through several revisions.

Carl H. Durney
Curtis C. Johnson

contents

CHAPTER 9 BOUNDARY-VALUE PROBLEMS

introduction to modern electromagnetics

CHAPTER

1

mathematical introduction

1.1 INTRODUCTION

Vector calculus is not strictly necessary to the study of electromagnetic field theory, but without it the presentation of the principles of electromagnetic theory would be awkward and cumbersome. Vector calculus not only provides compact and meaningful expression, it also provides a powerful means of comprehension. Hence the use of vector calculus in field theory has become standard.

It is assumed that the reader has previously obtained a basic understanding of vector analysis. Consequently, this chapter is not meant to be a rigorous mathematical development of the principles of vector calculus. Rather, it is meant to provide a review of important principles which are used repeatedly throughout the text, and to provide a common basis and point of departure for the study of the remainder of the text. Hence application and interpretation rather than rigorous mathematical proofs are stressed. Some of the very elementary principles are included for convenience of the reader and for completeness.

Since it is difficult to provide a good physical interpretation of the mathematical relations before the corresponding physical principles are introduced, the reader may not feel at first that he has gained a good appreciation for all the points developed in this chapter. It is hoped, however, that this chapter will provide a good foundation and that a deeper understanding and appreciation will be obtained as the relevant physical principles are encountered.

1.2 REVIEW OF BASIC PROPERTIES OF VECTORS

In contrast to a *scalar*, which is characterized by only a magnitude, a *vector* is characterized by both a magnitude and a direction. A familiar example of a vector quantity is velocity. It is convenient to represent a vector quantity graphically as a directed line segment, as shown in Fig. 1.1. The length of the line segment represents the magnitude of the vector, and the arrow represents the direction of the vector. It is sometimes also convenient to think of the displacement of a point as representing a vector quantity. The magnitude and direction of the displacement then represent the magnitude and direction of the vector. In this book vectors are denoted by boldface type, as indicated in Fig. 1.1.

The basic vector operations, which are only briefly reviewed here, are addition, subtraction, and two kinds of multiplication—the dot and cross products. It is important to note that these operations are independent of any coordinate system which might be used to locate the vectors in space. A detailed discussion of the representation of vectors in several coordinate systems is given in Sec. 1.4, but the basic operations are defined independently of any coordinate system.

Before discussing the basic operations, we need the definition of "equal" vectors. Any two vectors which have the same directions and the same magnitudes are *equal vectors*. Because of this definition, we are free to "slide" a vector to any position in space if we do not change its direction or magnitude. For example, the vector **A** in Fig. 1.1 may be used to denote the velocity of a projectile. Although it is customary to locate the base of the vector at the projectile, it is not necessary to do so. The length and direction of the vector specify the velocity, not the location of the vector in space. Thus any of the vectors **A** shown in Fig. 1.2 may be used to denote the projectile velocity. In some instances, the idea of being able to slide a vector is confusing. For example, suppose the wind velocity in some region of space is to be represented by vectors. This could be accomplished by assigning a vector to each point in space

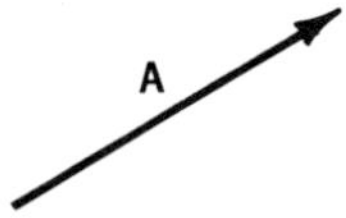

Fig. 1.1 A graphical representation of a vector: a directed line segment.

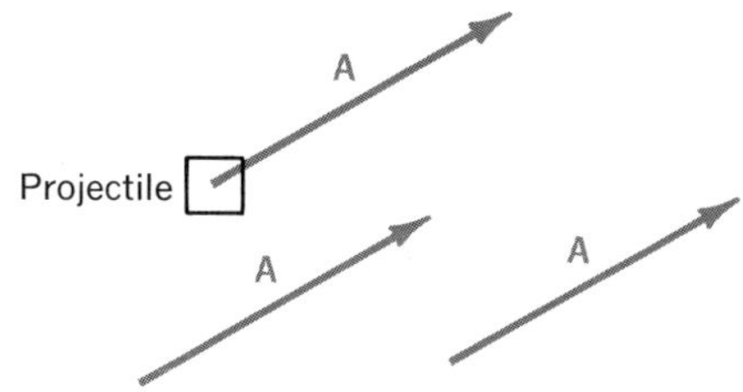

Fig. 1.2 Any of the vectors **A** shown may be used to denote the projectile velocity.

(see Sec. 1.3). The vector at a given point would then represent the wind velocity at that point. In this case it would be confusing to think of sliding the vector from one point to another because it is important to associate one certain vector with a given point. In cases like these we do not usually think of sliding vectors, although we could if we were careful somehow to keep track of which vector belongs to which point.

VECTOR ADDITION AND SUBTRACTION

The addition of two vectors may be conveniently defined in terms of the displacement of a point. Thus, if **A** represents the displacement from point 1 to point 2 and **B** the displacement from point 2 to point 3, as shown in Fig. 1.3, then **C** represents the displacement from point 1 to point 3. It is obvious that **C** is equivalent to **A** + **B**; that is, **A** + **B** = **C**. The sum of two vectors may thus be found by a graphic construction. It is easy to show by such graphical construction that

$$\mathbf{A} + \mathbf{B} = \mathbf{B} + \mathbf{A} \tag{1.1}$$

and

$$\mathbf{A} + (\mathbf{B} + \mathbf{C}) = (\mathbf{A} + \mathbf{B}) + \mathbf{C} \tag{1.2}$$

These two characteristics of vector addition are called the *commutative law* and the *associative law* of vector addition, respectively.

The negative of a vector is defined as a vector with the same magnitude but opposite direction. With this definition, vector subtraction is easily defined in terms of vector addition,

$$\mathbf{A} - \mathbf{B} = \mathbf{A} + (-\mathbf{B}) \tag{1.3}$$

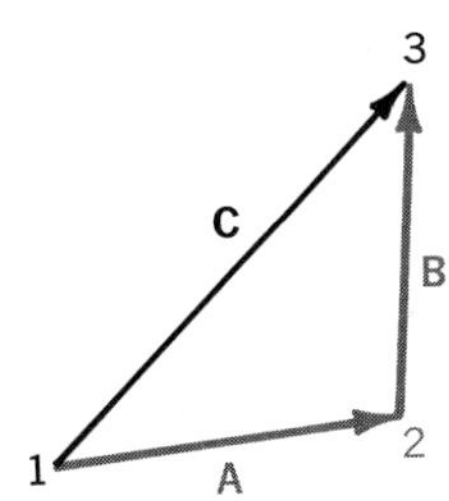

Fig. 1.3 The sum of two vectors.

VECTOR PRODUCTS

As constrasted with a single kind of scalar mutilplication, two kinds of vector multiplication are defined. They are the *dot* and *cross products*, also called the *scalar* and *vector products* of two vectors.

The dot product of two vectors is a scalar quantity and is defined as

$$\mathbf{A} \cdot \mathbf{B} \equiv AB \cos \theta \tag{1.4}$$

where θ is the smaller angle between the two vectors, as indicated in Fig. 1.4. The notation A means the magnitude of the vector **A**. The dot product is commutative and distributive; that is,

$$\mathbf{A} \cdot \mathbf{B} = \mathbf{B} \cdot \mathbf{A} \tag{1.5}$$

$$\mathbf{A} \cdot (\mathbf{B} + \mathbf{C}) = \mathbf{A} \cdot \mathbf{B} + \mathbf{A} \cdot \mathbf{C} \tag{1.6}$$

The cross product of two vectors, written $\mathbf{A} \times \mathbf{B}$, is a vector whose magnitude is $AB \sin \theta$ and whose direction is perpendicular to the plane defined by **A** and **B** and is in the direction a right-hand screw would travel when turned in the same direction as **A** turned into **B** through the angle θ. The graphical representation of

$$\mathbf{A} \times \mathbf{B} = \mathbf{C}$$

is shown in Fig. 1.5. It is easy to show from the definition that the cross product is not commutative, but that it is distributive; that is,

$$\mathbf{A} \times \mathbf{B} \neq \mathbf{B} \times \mathbf{A}$$

but

$$\mathbf{A} \times (\mathbf{B} + \mathbf{C}) = \mathbf{A} \times \mathbf{B} + \mathbf{A} \times \mathbf{C}$$

Some vector identities involving dot and cross products of more than two vectors are listed in the Appendix.

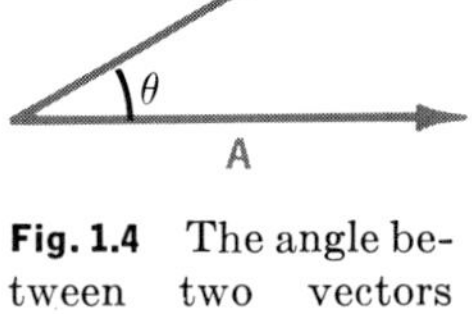

Fig. 1.4 The angle between two vectors used in the dot product.

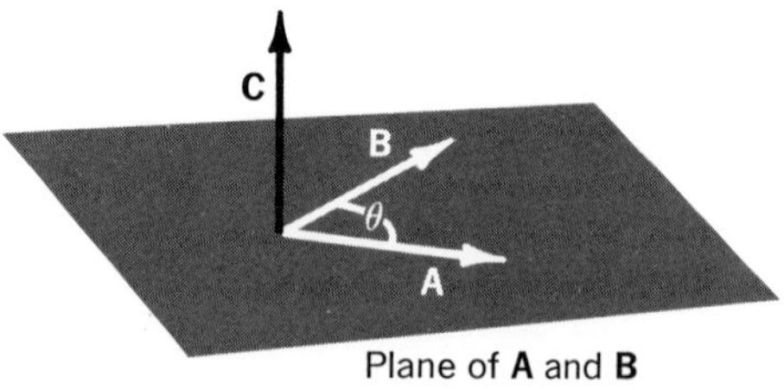

Fig. 1.5 The vector cross product $\mathbf{A} \times \mathbf{B} = \mathbf{C}$, where **C** is perpendicular to **A** and **B**.

UNIT VECTORS

A unit vector is defined as a vector of unit magnitude. We can easily obtain a unit vector in the direction of any given vector by dividing that vector by its magnitude. Thus the unit vector $\hat{\mathbf{A}}$ in the direction of $\mathbf{A}$ is given by

$$\hat{\mathbf{A}} = \frac{\mathbf{A}}{A}$$

In general, unit vectors will be designated in this book by carets. We can also write any vector in terms of its magnitude and a unit vector,

$$\mathbf{A} = \mathrm{A}\hat{\mathbf{A}}$$

It will often be convenient to represent vectors in this manner; this idea is extended in Sec. 1.4, where vectors are written in terms of three unit vectors called *base vectors*. These base vectors are useful because of their convenient relations to coordinate systems. It is also convenient, as discussed in Sec. 1.4, to write addition, subtraction, and dot and cross products in terms of these base vectors.

As a final definition in this section, let us consider the multiplication of a vector by a scalar. The product of a vector and a scalar is defined as a vector whose direction is the same as that of the vector being multiplied and whose magnitude is the product of the scalar and the magnitude of the vector; that is, if $\mathbf{A} = A\hat{\mathbf{A}}$ then

$$\Phi\mathbf{A} = \Phi A\hat{\mathbf{A}} \tag{1.7}$$

1.3 SCALAR AND VECTOR FIELDS

Since the concepts of vector and scalar fields are used frequently in this book, a careful discussion of these concepts is given in this section. Let us first review the definition of a scalar point function. Consider a given set of points, such as all the points in space. Suppose there is a certain scalar value corresponding to each point. The class of points is called the *domain of definition*, and the correspondence of scalar values to each point is called a *scalar point function*. The scalar values corresponding to the points are said to be the *range of values* of the scalar point function. A scalar point function is written as $f(P)$, where P stands for any point in the domain of definition and f is the scalar value at the point P. An example of a scalar point function is the temperature at each point in space. A scalar point function is often called a *scalar field*.

An often-used graphical representation of a scalar field is one in which the equal values of the scalar point function are connected by lines, as

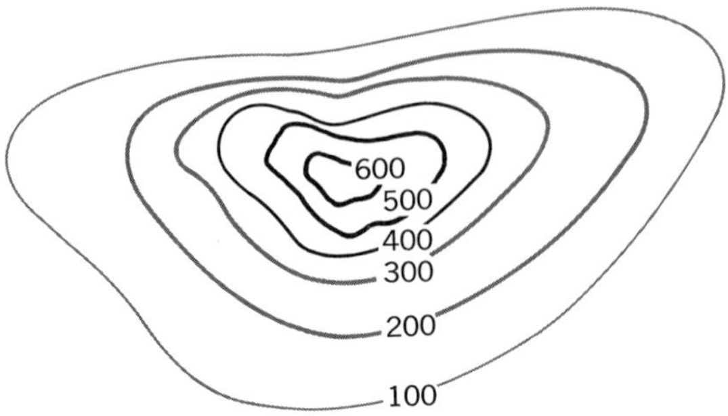

Fig. 1.6 Graphical representation of a scalar field. The lines are constant values of the scalar point function.

shown in Fig. 1.6. In the representation of a temperature field, the lines of constant temperature are called *isotherms*. Geographical contour maps are representations of the scalar point function whose range of values consist of the distances above sea level. A scalar field we shall be often concerned with in this book is the potential field. The lines of constant potential are called *equipotentials*.

A *vector point function* is a point function whose range of values is a class of vectors. Thus to each point in the domain of definition there corresponds a vector. We write a vector point function as $\mathbf{F}(P)$, where P stands for any point in the domain of definition, and $\mathbf{F}$ is the vector at the point P. As you have probably already guessed, a vector point function is often called a *vector field*. Wind velocity is an example of a vector field. If a fan generates a continuous flow of air in a room, the magnitude and direction of the wind at each point P may be determined. The resultant vector wind velocity $\mathbf{v}(P)$ is a vector field function describing the magnitude and direction of the wind velocity at every point in the room. The vector fields we shall be most concerned with in this book are the electric and magnetic fields.

The graphical representation of vector fields is not as easy as that of scalar fields. One representation of a vector field is shown in Fig. 1.7. The vectors represent the magnitude and direction of the vector field at

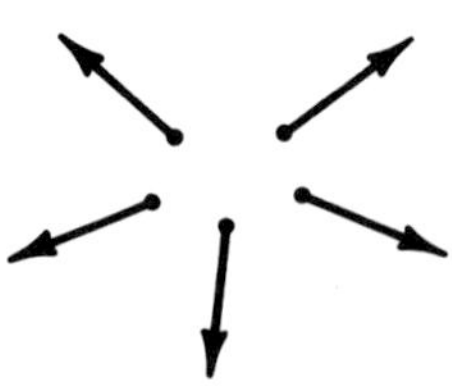

Fig. 1.7 One method of representing a vector field.

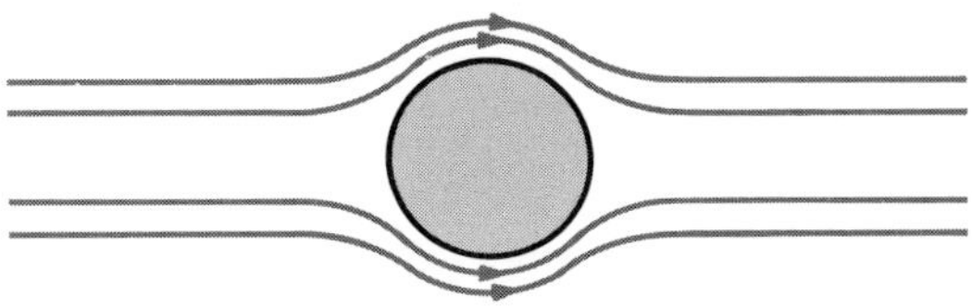

Fig. 1.8 Fluid flow around a cylinder. This illustrates another, probably better, method of graphically representing vector fields.

points P located at the base of each vector. As noted in Sec. 1.2, we do not usually think of "sliding" a vector in connection with vector fields, because it is important to maintain the correlation between each point and the one vector which has been assigned to that point. Hence, when a vector is part of a vector field, we usually think of it as "bound" to a given point. It turns out that the kind of representation shown in Fig. 1.7 is not as convenient as might be expected, because the symmetry of the field is often obscured and the field is indicated only at discrete points. A more commonly used method is one in which continuous lines are drawn, with arrowheads indicating a direction. The direction of the field at each point is then tangent to the line, which is called a *flow line*, or a *flux line*. The magnitude of the field is indicated by the separation between lines. If the lines are far apart, the vector magnitude is small. An example of this is the velocity field of fluid flow around a cylinder, as illustrated in Fig. 1.8.

Although many kinds of vector fields represent the flow of particles, such as fluid molecules or charged particles, there are many vector fields which do not represent an actual physical flow of particles. It is often convenient, however, to think of these fields as representing fluid flow, even though there is no physical motion involved. The field lines are therefore quite generally called flux lines, and the field is spoken of as being a *flux density*. The total flux (flow) through a surface would then be found by an integration procedure. This kind of integration is discussed in Sec. 1.7.

1.4 COORDINATE SYSTEMS

As was pointed out in Sec. 1.2, vectors and the basic vector operations are defined independently of any coordinate system. It becomes very convenient, however, to use coordinate systems in solving practical problems and for the understanding of physical principles.

A coordinate system serves two purposes: one is to locate points in space, and the other is to furnish a convenient way to represent the magnitudes and directions of vectors at points in space, that is, to represent vector fields. This is done in terms of a set of three unit vectors which are called *base vectors*. The expression for a vector field in terms of these base vectors of a coordinate system is called a *representation* of the vector field. For convenience, the base vectors are usually chosen to be mutually orthogonal (mutually perpendicular), but it is not necessary that they be so. We shall first discuss in detail the three most commonly used coordinate systems—rectangular, cylindrical, and spherical—and then discuss the general orthogonal curvilinear coordinate system. The choice of coordinate system depends upon the symmetry of the problem at hand. For example, in cases where cylindrical symmetry is present, the use of a cylindrical coordinate system rather than a rectangular system greatly simplifies the mathematics.

RECTANGULAR COORDINATE SYSTEM

The rectangular coordinate system is the most familiar of the three standard coordinate systems. It should be used whenever possible because of its simplicity and, as we shall see later, because the base unit vectors are constants. Figure 1.9 shows the three mutually orthogonal axes, which we have labeled the x, y, and z axes. Also shown are the three base vectors, labeled $\hat{\mathbf{x}}$, $\hat{\mathbf{y}}$, and $\hat{\mathbf{z}}$, which lie along the x, y, and z axes, respectively. Since these base vectors have constant magnitude and direction, they are constant vectors. In some other coordinate systems, some of the base vectors are not constant because their directions are variable.

A right-handed system is defined as one in which $\hat{\mathbf{x}} \times \hat{\mathbf{y}} = \hat{\mathbf{z}}$. Any point in space is located by its values of x, y, and z. For example, point 1 in Fig. 1.9 is located at $x = x_1$, $y = y_1$, and $z = z_1$, as indicated. We say that x, y, and z are the *independent variables*, and any function, such as a scalar or vector point function, which in general depends on x, y, and z (is a function of x, y, and z) is called a *dependent variable*.

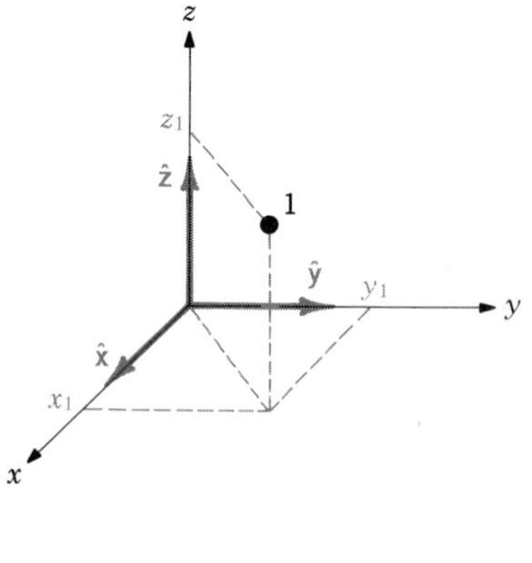

Fig. 1.9 Rectangular coordinate system.

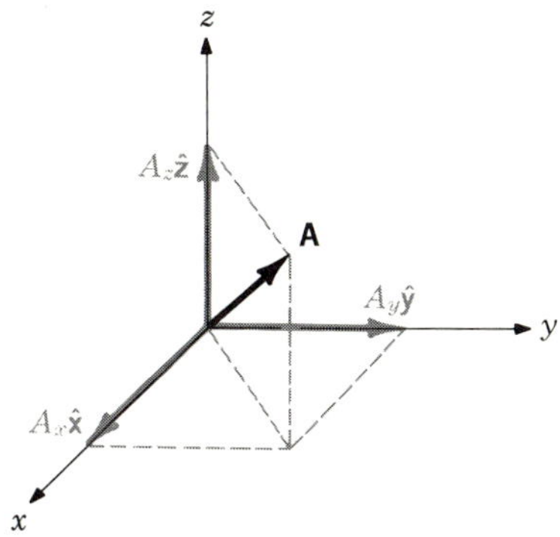

Fig. 1.10 Rectangular components of **A**.

In general, vector or scalar point functions vary from point to point in space. Since each point in space can be located by its x, y, and z coordinate, a vector or scalar point function can be written as a function of x, y, and z. It is easy to see how a scalar field can be expressed in terms of x, y, and z. For example, the temperature scalar point function $T(P)$ is simply $T(x,y,z)$ when (x,y,z) corresponds to the point P. A vector field is more complicated, since both the *magnitude and direction* may be functions of x, y, and z. However, a vector field can be conveniently expressed in terms of its components along the base vectors. If a known vector field **A** is a function of x, y, and z, we may write

$$\mathbf{A}(x,y,z) = A_x(x,y,z)\hat{\mathbf{x}} + A_y(x,y,z)\hat{\mathbf{y}} + A_z(x,y,z)\hat{\mathbf{z}} \tag{1.8}$$

where $A_x(x,y,z)$, $A_y(x,y,z)$, and $A_z(x,y,z)$, which are the scalar components of **A** along the x, y, and z axes, respectively, are to be determined. Equation (1.8) is called the *representation* of the vector **A** in a rectangular coordinate system. Since the base vectors are constants, the dependence of both magnitude and direction of **A** on x, y, and z is completely contained in the dependence of A_x, A_y, and A_z on x, y, and z. Expressing **A** by Eq. (1.8) is commonly called "writing a vector as a sum of its components along the base vectors." A geometric representation based on the addition of vectors is shown in Fig. 1.10.

Since the direction and magnitude of **A** are known, A_x, A_y, and A_z can be obtained by scalar multiplication of Eq. (1.8) in turn by $\hat{\mathbf{x}}$, $\hat{\mathbf{y}}$, and $\hat{\mathbf{z}}$. Because $\hat{\mathbf{x}}$, $\hat{\mathbf{y}}$, and $\hat{\mathbf{z}}$ are mutually orthogonal, the results are

$$\hat{\mathbf{x}} \cdot \mathbf{A} = A_x(x,y,z) \tag{1.9}$$

$$\hat{\mathbf{y}} \cdot \mathbf{A} = A_y(x,y,z) \tag{1.10}$$

$$\hat{\mathbf{z}} \cdot \mathbf{A} = A_z(x,y,z) \tag{1.11}$$

The advantage of having orthogonal base vectors is obvious here.

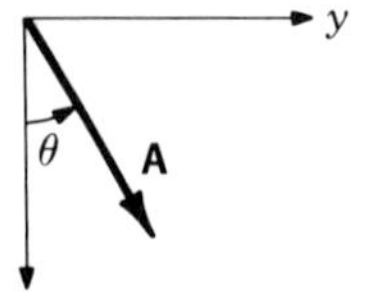

Fig. 1.11 A vector in the xy coordinate system.

Example 1.1 Finding the components of a vector A nearly trivial example which illustrates these principles is illustrated in Fig. 1.11. A known vector $\mathbf{A}$ lies in the xy plane at an angle θ from the x axis. Using (Eq. 1.4), we immediately find that

$$\begin{aligned} A_x &= \hat{\mathbf{x}} \cdot \mathbf{A} \\ &= A \cos \theta \\ A_y &= \hat{\mathbf{y}} \cdot \mathbf{A} \\ &= A \cos \left(\frac{\pi}{2} - \theta \right) \\ &= A \sin \theta \end{aligned}$$

Here A_x and A_y are constants, but in general they may be functions of x, y, and z. A less formal way of obtaining A_x and A_y is simply to resolve $\mathbf{A}$ into components along the x and y directions by finding two vectors in the direction of $\hat{\mathbf{x}}$ and $\hat{\mathbf{y}}$ which add up to $\mathbf{A}$. The two methods are equivalent.

In connection with integration, which is discussed in detail in Sec. 1.5, we need the differential arc length expressed in rectangular coordinates. A differential length results when one of the coordinates is increased by a differential amount. In rectangular coordinates the differential lengths are dx, dy, and dz. The total differential arc length dl is the result of increasing each coordinate by a differential amount. It is given by $(dl)^2 = (dx)^2 + (dy)^2 + (dz)^2$, where dl corresponds to the length of the diagonal of the box shown in Fig. 1.12.

Another quantity of interest is the differential volume, $dV = dx\,dy\,dz$, which is illustrated in Fig. 1.12.

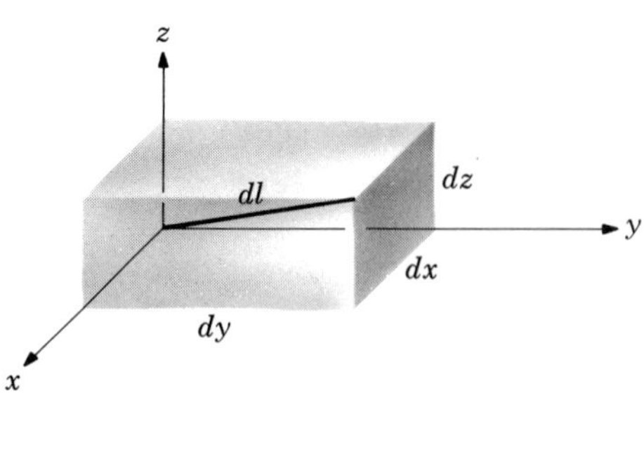

Fig. 1.12 Differential lengths and volume in rectangular coordinates.

As a prelude to the definitions of the unit vectors in the cylindrical and spherical coordinate systems, note that a more general definition of $\hat{\mathbf{x}}$, $\hat{\mathbf{y}}$, and $\hat{\mathbf{z}}$ can be made in terms of the surfaces of constant coordinate value. Thus $\hat{\mathbf{x}}$ is defined as a unit vector perpendicular to the surface x = constant and in the direction of increasing x. Similar definitions are made for $\hat{\mathbf{y}}$ and $\hat{\mathbf{z}}$. It should also be noted that the point (x_1,y_1,z_1) is defined as the intersection of the three mutually orthogonal surfaces $x = x_1$, $y = y_1$, and $z = z_1$.

CYLINDRICAL COORDINATE SYSTEM

The independent variables of the cylindrical coordinate system are r, φ, and z. For convenience, the cylindrical coordinate system is shown in Fig. 1.13 with respect to a rectangular coordinate system. The cylindrical coordinate system is used in place of the standard rectangular coordinate system for problems with cylindrical symmetry. When cylindrical structures, such as a round pipe or rod, are analyzed, the mathematics is much simpler in cylindrical coordinates. The r = constant surface is a cylinder concentric with the z axis, the φ = constant surface is a plane passing through the z axis, and the z = constant surface is a plane perpendicular to the z axis. The intersection of these three surfaces defines the point (r,φ,z). The unit base vectors are $\hat{\mathbf{r}}$, $\hat{\boldsymbol{\varphi}}$, and $\hat{\mathbf{z}}$. Each base vector is defined at a coordinate point as being perpendicular to the constant coordinate surface and in the direction of increasing coordinate. These vectors are shown in Fig. 1.14. Since the three constant coordinate surfaces are mutually orthogonal, it follows from the definitions that the three base vectors are mutually orthogonal. A right-handed coordinate system is

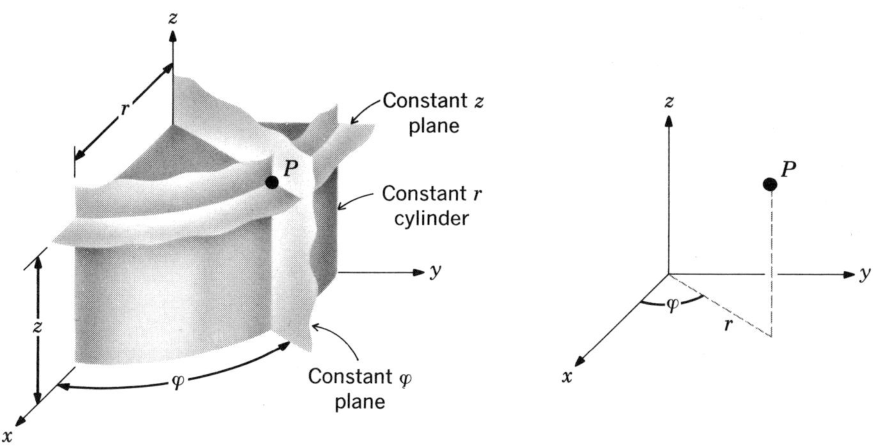

Fig. 1.13 The cylindrical coordinate system.

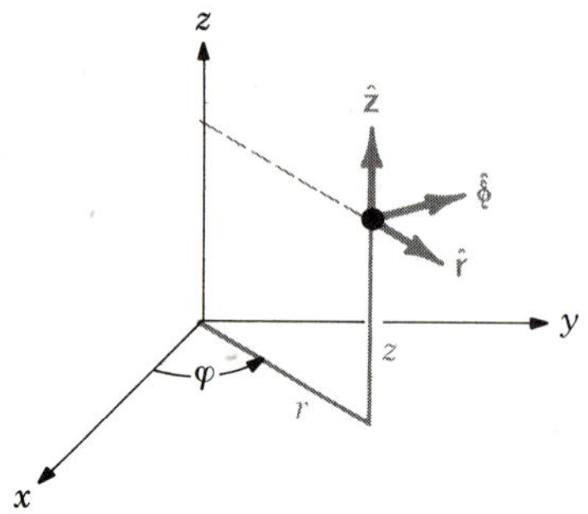

Fig. 1.14 The base vectors of the cylindrical coordinate system at the coordinate point (r,φ,z).

defined by $\hat{\mathbf{r}} \times \hat{\boldsymbol{\phi}} = \hat{\mathbf{z}}$. Note that $\hat{\mathbf{r}}$ and $\hat{\boldsymbol{\phi}}$ are always parallel to the xy plane.

A very important characteristic of $\hat{\mathbf{r}}$ and $\hat{\boldsymbol{\phi}}$ is that their directions are functions of φ (their magnitudes, of course, are constant). This is in contrast to $\hat{\mathbf{x}}$, $\hat{\mathbf{y}}$, and $\hat{\mathbf{z}}$, which are constant vectors. It is essential that this φ dependence of $\hat{\mathbf{r}}$ and $\hat{\boldsymbol{\phi}}$ be kept in mind, especially in integrating and differentiating vectors. The fact that $\hat{\mathbf{r}}$ and $\hat{\boldsymbol{\phi}}$ vary with φ is a nuisance which may be eliminated, of course, by using rectangular coordinates.

Vectors are expressed in the cylindrical coordinate system in a way similar to that used for a rectangular system. The representation of $\mathbf{A}$ in a cylindrical coordinate system is

$$\mathbf{A}(r,\varphi,z) = A_r(r,\varphi,z)\hat{\mathbf{r}} + A_\varphi(r,\varphi,z)\hat{\boldsymbol{\phi}} + A_z(r,\varphi,z)\hat{\mathbf{z}}$$

The differential lengths are dr, $r\,d\varphi$, and dz. Since φ is an angle, the differential length obtained by increasing φ by $d\varphi$ is given by $r\,d\varphi$, as illustrated in Fig. 1.15. The total differential arc length is

$$(dl)^2 = (dr)^2 + (r\,d\varphi)^2 + (dz)^2$$

The differential volume, shown in Fig. 1.16, has the shape of a truncated wedge and is given by

$$dV = r\,dr\,d\varphi\,dz \tag{1.12}$$

because the truncated wedge approaches a rectangular parallelpiped as dr, $r\,d\varphi$, and dz become very small.

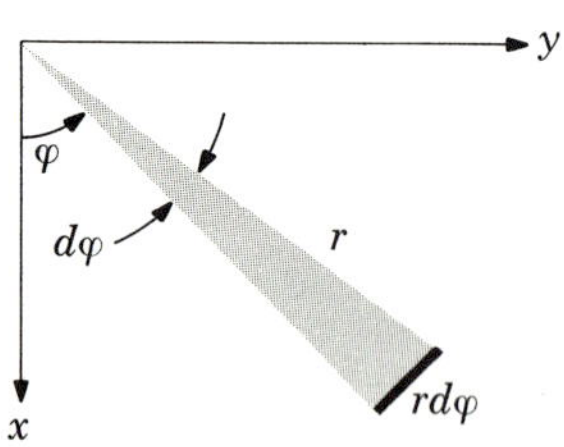

Fig. 1.15 The differential length $r\,d\varphi$ in a cylindrical coordinate system.

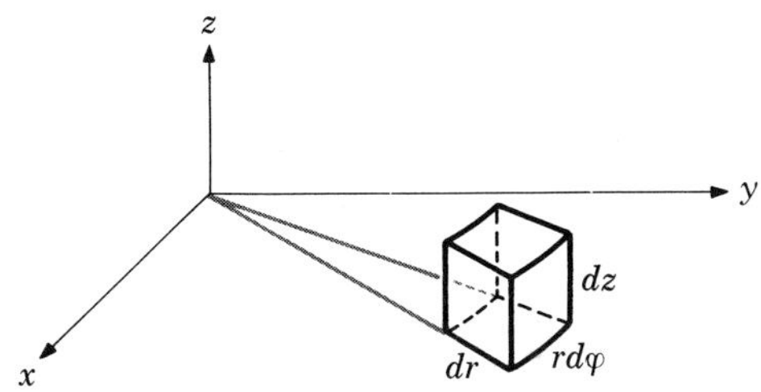

Fig. 1.16 The differential volume in cylindrical coordinates.

SPHERICAL COORDINATE SYSTEM

In the spherical coordinate system, the independent variables are r, θ, and φ. Unfortunately, it has become common practice to use the same symbol r for both the cylindrical and spherical coordinate systems, even though the variable is not the same in the two systems. In most practical situations, however, there is little doubt as to the intended meaning of the symbol r. Since the reader will be faced with this problem in other literature, it seems useless to try to improve the notation, and so we shall follow the common practice. The spherical coordinate system is used for problems with spherical symmetry and in radiation problems, where its use greatly simplifies the mathematics.

The spherical coordinate system is shown in Fig. 1.17, with the rectangular coordinate system as a reference. Let O represent the origin and P the point (r,θ,φ). Then r is the length of the line OP. The angle θ is the angle between the z axis and OP, and the angle φ is the angle between the projection of OP on the xy plane and the x axis.

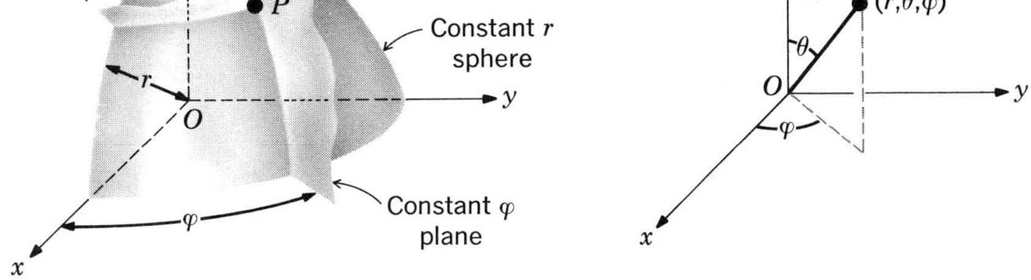

Fig. 1.17 The spherical coordinate system.

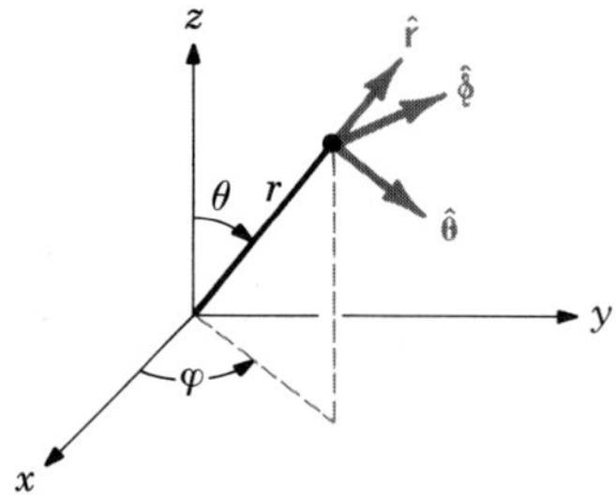

Fig. 1.18 Base vectors of the spherical coordinate system.

The r = constant surface is a sphere centered at the origin, the θ = constant surface is a cone, and the φ = constant surface is a plane. As in the other coordinate systems, the base vectors $\hat{\mathbf{r}}$, $\hat{\boldsymbol{\theta}}$, and $\hat{\boldsymbol{\varphi}}$ are defined as unit vectors perpendicular to the constant r, θ, and φ surfaces, respectively, and pointing in the direction of increasing coordinate value. These base vectors, which are illustrated in Fig. 1.18, are mutually orthogonal, as they are in the other two coordinate systems. A right-handed spherical coordinate system is defined by $\hat{\mathbf{r}} \times \hat{\boldsymbol{\theta}} = \hat{\boldsymbol{\varphi}}$.

In the spherical coordinate system the differential lengths are dr, $r\,d\theta$, and $r \sin\theta\,d\varphi$. These are the differential lengths resulting when r, θ, and φ, respectively, are increased by differential amounts. Since θ and φ are angles, the differential lengths are not simply $d\theta$ and $d\varphi$. Figure 1.19 illustrates the $r\,d\theta$ and $r \sin\theta\,d\varphi$ differential lengths. The total differential arc length resulting when all three coordinates are increased by differential amounts is

$$(dl)^2 = (dr)^2 + (r\,d\theta)^2 + (r \sin\theta\,d\varphi)^2$$

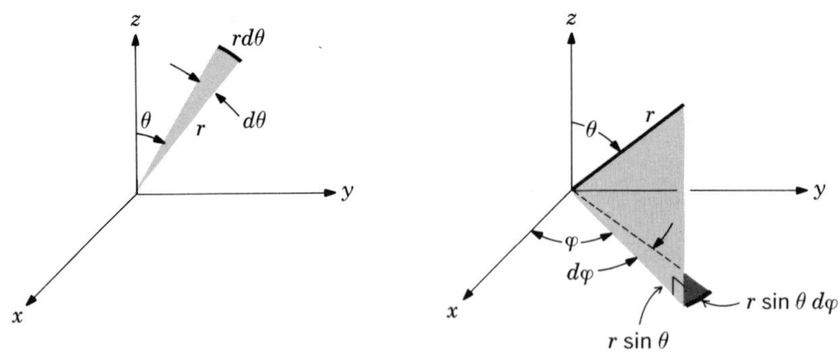

Fig. 1.19 The differential lengths $r\,d\theta$ and $r \sin\theta\,d\varphi$.

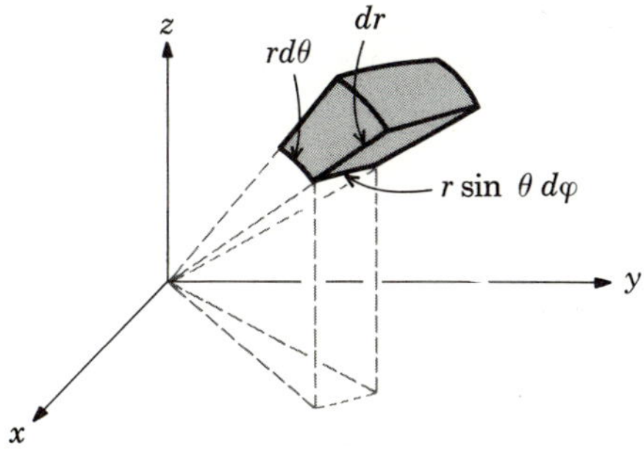

Fig. 1.20 The differential volume in spherical coordinates.

The differential volume is given by

$$\begin{aligned} dV &= dr\; r\, d\theta\; r \sin\theta\, d\varphi \\ &= r^2 \sin\theta\, dr\, d\theta\, d\varphi \end{aligned} \tag{1.13}$$

as shown in Fig. 1.20. And, of course, a vector may be represented in the spherical coordinate system by the form

$$\mathbf{A}(r,\theta,\varphi) = A_r(r,\theta,\varphi)\hat{\mathbf{r}} + A_\theta(r,\theta,\varphi)\hat{\boldsymbol{\theta}} + A_\varphi(r,\theta,\varphi)\hat{\boldsymbol{\varphi}}$$

which is similar to the representation in the other two coordinate systems.

Note that the base vectors change their directions with θ and φ. This variation must be kept in mind in integrating and differentiating the base vectors in spherical coordinates. Because of this difficulty, it is not desirable to use spherical coordinates in certain types of problems unless there are powerful symmetry arguments to the contrary.

1.5 ADDITION AND MULTIPLICATION OF VECTORS REPRESENTED IN THE THREE STANDARD COORDINATE SYSTEMS

There is an obvious similarity in the relationships between the variables and base vectors in the three coordinate systems. For example, $\hat{\mathbf{x}} \times \hat{\mathbf{y}} = \hat{\mathbf{z}}$, $\hat{\mathbf{r}} \times \hat{\boldsymbol{\varphi}} = \hat{\mathbf{z}}$, and $\hat{\mathbf{r}} \times \hat{\boldsymbol{\theta}} = \hat{\boldsymbol{\varphi}}$ are similar relations. Also notice the similarity of the expressions

$$\begin{aligned} \mathbf{A} &= A_x(x,y,z)\hat{\mathbf{x}} + A_y(x,y,z)\hat{\mathbf{y}} + A_z(x,y,z)\hat{\mathbf{z}} \\ \mathbf{A} &= A_r(r,\varphi,z)\hat{\mathbf{r}} + A_\varphi(r,\varphi,z)\hat{\boldsymbol{\varphi}} + A_z(r,\varphi,z)\hat{\mathbf{z}} \\ \mathbf{A} &= A_r(r,\theta,\varphi)\hat{\mathbf{r}} + A_\theta(r,\theta,\varphi)\hat{\boldsymbol{\theta}} + A_\varphi(r,\theta,\varphi)\hat{\boldsymbol{\varphi}} \end{aligned}$$

A little reflection shows that there are similarities in all the expressions we have discussed.

Let us take advantage of these similarities by defining three new generalized independent variables, u_1, u_2, and u_3, which stand for either x, y, and z; r, φ, and z; or r, θ, and φ. In addition, let us define $\hat{\mathbf{u}}_1$, $\hat{\mathbf{u}}_2$, and $\hat{\mathbf{u}}_3$ as being three new generalized unit base vectors which stand for either $\hat{\mathbf{x}}$, $\hat{\mathbf{y}}$, and $\hat{\mathbf{z}}$; $\hat{\mathbf{r}}$, $\hat{\boldsymbol{\varphi}}$, and $\hat{\mathbf{z}}$; or $\hat{\mathbf{r}}$, $\hat{\boldsymbol{\theta}}$, and $\hat{\boldsymbol{\varphi}}$. Then a vector represented in any of the three coordinate systems may be written in the generalized form

$$\mathbf{A} = A_1(u_1,u_2,u_3)\hat{\mathbf{u}}_1 + A_2(u_1,u_2,u_3)\hat{\mathbf{u}}_2 + A_3(u_1,u_2,u_3)\hat{\mathbf{u}}_3$$

where A_1 stands for A_x, A_r, or A_r, and so on. Then we have the relations

$$\hat{\mathbf{u}}_1 \cdot \hat{\mathbf{u}}_1 = 1 \qquad \hat{\mathbf{u}}_1 \cdot \hat{\mathbf{u}}_2 = 0 \qquad \hat{\mathbf{u}}_1 \cdot \hat{\mathbf{u}}_3 = 0 \qquad \cdots$$

$$\hat{\mathbf{u}}_1 \times \hat{\mathbf{u}}_2 = \hat{\mathbf{u}}_3$$

and

$$A_1 = \hat{\mathbf{u}}_1 \cdot \mathbf{A} \qquad \cdots$$

Since u_2 and u_3 may be angles, additional definitions are required in order to represent differential lengths and differential volumes. Let us define

$$\begin{aligned} dl_1 &= h_1\, du_1 \\ dl_2 &= h_2\, du_2 \\ dl_3 &= h_3\, du_3 \end{aligned} \tag{1.14}$$

where dl_1, dl_2, and dl_3 are the differential *lengths* resulting when u_1, u_2, and u_3, respectively, are increased by du_1, du_2, and du_3, respectively. The quantities h_1, h_2, and h_3 are scale factors needed to make Eqs. (1.14) valid. There will be a different set of h's for each coordinate system. From the discussion of differential lengths given previously, it is apparent, for example, that in cylindrical coordinates,

$$\begin{aligned} dl_1 &= dr && \text{and} && h_1 = 1 \\ dl_2 &= r\, d\varphi && \text{and} && h_2 = r \\ dl_3 &= dz && \text{and} && h_3 = 1 \end{aligned}$$

Table 1.1 summarizes the scale factors for the three coordinate systems.

Table 1.1 Summary of the scale factors

Rectangular coordinates	*Cylindrical coordinates*	*Spherical coordinates*
$h_1 = 1$	$h_1 = 1$	$h_1 = 1$
$h_2 = 1$	$h_2 = r$	$h_2 = r$
$h_3 = 1$	$h_3 = 1$	$h_3 = r \sin \theta$

The total differential arc length is given by

$$\begin{aligned}(dl)^2 &= (dl_1)^2 + (dl_2)^2 + (dl_3)^2 \\ &= (h_1\,du_1)^2 + (h_2\,du_2)^2 + (h_3\,du_3)^2\end{aligned}$$

It follows easily that the differential volume is given by

$$dV = h_1\,du_1\,h_2\,du_2\,h_3\,du_3$$

Vector addition may be conveniently discussed in terms of the representations in any of the three coordinate systems. Suppose we wish to add two vectors **A** and **B** with the general representations

$$\begin{aligned}\mathbf{A} &= A_1\hat{\mathbf{u}}_1 + A_2\hat{\mathbf{u}}_2 + A_3\hat{\mathbf{u}}_3 \\ \mathbf{B} &= B_1\hat{\mathbf{u}}_1 + B_2\hat{\mathbf{u}}_2 + B_3\hat{\mathbf{u}}_3\end{aligned}$$

where, for brevity, the functional dependence of the vector components on u_1, u_2, and u_3 has not been written explicitly. Then

$$\mathbf{A} + \mathbf{B} = A_1\hat{\mathbf{u}}_1 + A_2\hat{\mathbf{u}}_2 + A_3\hat{\mathbf{u}}_3 + B_1\hat{\mathbf{u}}_1 + B_2\hat{\mathbf{u}}_2 + B_3\hat{\mathbf{u}}_3$$

Since vector addition is associative, this may be written as

$$\mathbf{A} + \mathbf{B} = (A_1\hat{\mathbf{u}}_1 + B_1\hat{\mathbf{u}}_1) + (A_2\hat{\mathbf{u}}_2 + B_2\hat{\mathbf{u}}_2) + (A_3\hat{\mathbf{u}}_3 + B_3\hat{\mathbf{u}}_3)$$

From the graphical method of vector addition shown in Fig. 1.3, it follows that

$$A_1\hat{\mathbf{u}}_1 + B_1\hat{\mathbf{u}}_1 = (A_1 + B_1)\hat{\mathbf{u}}_1$$

and therefore

$$\mathbf{A} + \mathbf{B} = (A_1 + B_1)\hat{\mathbf{u}}_1 + (A_2 + B_2)\hat{\mathbf{u}}_2 + (A_3 + B_3)\hat{\mathbf{u}}_3 \tag{1.15}$$

It is apparent from Eq. (1.15) how the representation of vectors in coordinate systems simplifies addition.

Next consider the dot product of **A** and **B**,

$$\mathbf{A}\cdot\mathbf{B} = (A_1\hat{\mathbf{u}}_1 + A_2\hat{\mathbf{u}}_2 + A_3\hat{\mathbf{u}}_3)\cdot(B_1\hat{\mathbf{u}}_1 + B_2\hat{\mathbf{u}}_2 + B_3\hat{\mathbf{u}}_3)$$

Since the dot product is distributive [see Eq. (1.6)], we write

$$\begin{aligned}\mathbf{A}\cdot\mathbf{B} = A_1\hat{\mathbf{u}}_1\cdot(B_1\hat{\mathbf{u}}_1 + B_2\hat{\mathbf{u}}_2 + B_3\hat{\mathbf{u}}_3) + A_2\hat{\mathbf{u}}_2\cdot(B_1\hat{\mathbf{u}}_1 + B_2\hat{\mathbf{u}}_2 + B_3\hat{\mathbf{u}}_3) \\ + A_3\hat{\mathbf{u}}_3\cdot(B_1\hat{\mathbf{u}}_1 + B_2\hat{\mathbf{u}}_2 + B_3\hat{\mathbf{u}}_3)\end{aligned}$$

which can be expanded again to obtain terms such as $A_1\hat{\mathbf{u}}_1\cdot B_1\hat{\mathbf{u}}_1$. From Eq. (1.4) it can be shown that

$$A_1\hat{\mathbf{u}}_1\cdot B_1\hat{\mathbf{u}}_1 = A_1B_1\hat{\mathbf{u}}_1\cdot\hat{\mathbf{u}}_1$$

Because the unit vectors are mutually orthogonal, $\mathbf{A}\cdot\mathbf{B}$ reduces to the very important result

$$\mathbf{A}\cdot\mathbf{B} = A_1B_1 + A_2B_2 + A_3B_3 \tag{1.16}$$

The distributive property of the cross product may be used in a similar way to expand $\mathbf{A} \times \mathbf{B}$, but care must be taken to keep the correct order, because the cross product is not commutative. Thus

$$\mathbf{A} \times \mathbf{B} = (A_1\hat{\mathbf{u}}_1 + A_2\hat{\mathbf{u}}_2 + A_3\hat{\mathbf{u}}_3) \times (B_1\hat{\mathbf{u}}_1 + B_2\hat{\mathbf{u}}_2 + B_3\hat{\mathbf{u}}_3)$$

With the cross-product relations of the base vectors, $\mathbf{A} \times \mathbf{B}$ reduces to

$$\mathbf{A} \times \mathbf{B} = (A_2B_3 - B_2A_3)\hat{\mathbf{u}}_1 + (A_3B_1 - B_3A_1)\hat{\mathbf{u}}_2 + (A_1B_2 - B_1A_2)\hat{\mathbf{u}}_3 \tag{1.17}$$

Equation (1.17) can be conveniently remembered as the expansion of the determinant

$$\mathbf{A} \times \mathbf{B} = \begin{vmatrix} \hat{\mathbf{u}}_1 & \hat{\mathbf{u}}_2 & \hat{\mathbf{u}}_3 \\ A_1 & A_2 & A_3 \\ B_1 & B_2 & B_3 \end{vmatrix} \tag{1.18}$$

It should be noted that, in general, the relations between $\hat{\mathbf{u}}_1$, $\hat{\mathbf{u}}_2$, and $\hat{\mathbf{u}}_3$ are true only at a given coordinate point, because the base vectors can be variable vectors. For example, in cylindrical coordinates, $\hat{\mathbf{r}}$ is a function of φ. It is obvious that

$$\hat{\mathbf{r}}(\varphi) \cdot \hat{\mathbf{r}}(\varphi) = 1$$

but

$$\hat{\mathbf{r}}(\varphi_1) \cdot \hat{\mathbf{r}}(\varphi_2) \neq 1 \tag{1.19}$$

as can clearly be seen from Fig. 1.21. This point is important with respect to the use of Eqs. (1.15), (1.16), and (1.18). For example, let us find the dot or cross product of the two vectors shown in Fig. 1.22 in a cylindrical coordinate system. We might be tempted to write

$$\mathbf{A} = A_r\hat{\mathbf{r}}$$

$$\mathbf{B} = B_r\hat{\mathbf{r}}$$

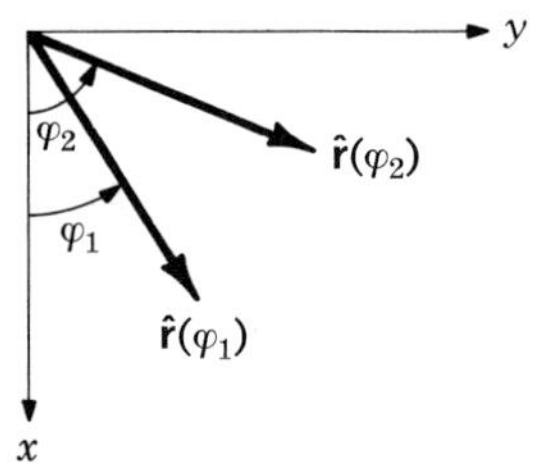

Fig. 1.21 Illustration of the vector of Eq. (1.19).

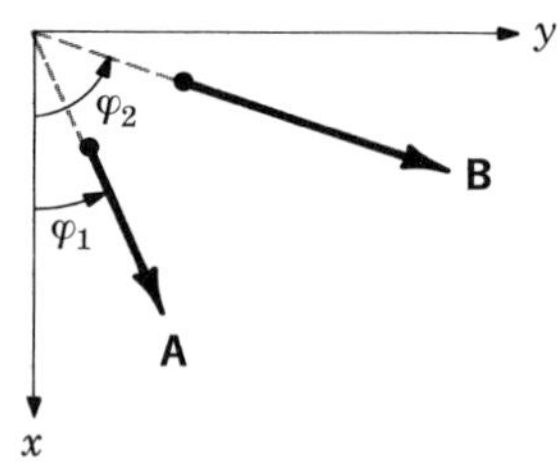

Fig. 1.22 Vectors used in example of dot and cross products in a cylindrical coordinate system.

and hastily and falsely conclude from Eq. (1.18) that $\mathbf{A} \times \mathbf{B} = 0$. It is obvious from the basic definition of the cross product given in Sec. 1.2 that $\mathbf{A} \times \mathbf{B}$ is not zero. To get the correct answer from Eq. (1.18), we must evaluate $\mathbf{A}$ and $\mathbf{B}$ *at the same coordinate point,* which means that one or the other of the vectors will have a φ component.

GENERALIZED ORTHOGONAL CURVILINEAR COORDINATES

Although the variables u_1, u_2, and u_3 and the base vectors $\hat{\mathbf{u}}_1$, $\hat{\mathbf{u}}_2$, and $\hat{\mathbf{u}}_3$ were used in the previous discussion only to represent the variables and base vectors of the rectangular, cylindrical, or spherical coordinate systems, the definitions may be applied to other coordinate systems. We may generalize by specifying that $\hat{\mathbf{u}}_1$, $\hat{\mathbf{u}}_2$, and $\hat{\mathbf{u}}_3$ are mutually orthogonal, but otherwise general, unit base vectors. This means that the surfaces $u_1 =$ constant, $u_2 =$ constant, and $u_3 =$ constant are mutually orthogonal surfaces. The resulting coordinate system is called a *generalized orthogonal curvilinear coordinate system.* All the results of the previous section apply to the generalized coordinate system. Although we shall be concerned in this book mainly with the three coordinate systems already discussed, there are some problems which are more easily solved in other coordinate systems. In addition, it is very convenient to be able to express vector relations independently of a particular coordinate system. For these reasons we have introduced the concept of the generalized orthogonal curvilinear coordinate system, which we make further use of throughout the book.

Nonorthogonal coordinate systems can be defined, but problems requiring such systems are usually difficult. Consequently, nonorthogonal systems will not be needed in this book and our attention will be restricted to orthogonal coordinate systems.

1.6 TRANSFORMATIONS BETWEEN COORDINATE SYSTEMS

It is often convenient to be able to obtain the representation of a vector in one coordinate system from its representation in another coordinate system. This is called *transforming* a vector from one coordinate system to another.

RECTANGULAR-TO-CYLINDRICAL TRANSFORMATION

Suppose we have the vector $\mathbf{A}$ represented in a rectangular coordinate system as

$$\mathbf{A} = A_x(x,y,z)\hat{\mathbf{x}} + A_y(x,y,z)\hat{\mathbf{y}} + A_z(x,y,z)\hat{\mathbf{z}} \tag{1.20}$$

and we wish to represent it in a cylindrical coordinate system as

$$\mathbf{A} = A_r(r,\varphi,z)\hat{\mathbf{r}} + A_\varphi(r,\varphi,z)\hat{\boldsymbol{\varphi}} + A_z(r,\varphi,z)\hat{\mathbf{z}} \tag{1.21}$$

This is called transforming **A** from a rectangular coordinate system to a cylindrical coordinate system.

There are two necessary steps: A_r, A_φ, and A_z must be obtained in terms of $A_x(x,y,z)$, $A_y(x,y,z)$, and $A_z(x,y,z)$, and then x, y, and z must be obtained in terms of r, φ, and z so that A_r, A_φ, and A_z will be functions of r, φ, and z rather than x, y, and z.

First A_r is obtained in terms of A_x, A_y, and A_z. From Eq. (1.21), we find by taking the dot product of $\hat{\mathbf{r}}$ with both sides of the equation that

$$\hat{\mathbf{r}} \cdot \mathbf{A} = A_r$$

From Eq. (1.20), we find similarly that

$$\hat{\mathbf{r}} \cdot \mathbf{A} = A_x \hat{\mathbf{r}} \cdot \hat{\mathbf{x}} + A_y \hat{\mathbf{r}} \cdot \hat{\mathbf{y}} + A_z \hat{\mathbf{r}} \cdot \hat{\mathbf{z}}$$

Therefore

$$A_r = A_x \hat{\mathbf{r}} \cdot \hat{\mathbf{x}} + A_y \hat{\mathbf{r}} \cdot \hat{\mathbf{y}} + A_z \hat{\mathbf{r}} \cdot \hat{\mathbf{z}} \tag{1.22}$$

Since $\hat{\mathbf{r}}$ and $\hat{\mathbf{x}}$, $\hat{\mathbf{y}}$, and $\hat{\mathbf{z}}$ are unit vectors, the dot products in Eq. (1.22) reduce to the cosines of the angles between the unit vectors. From the definitions of the coordinate systems it is apparent that $\hat{\mathbf{r}} \cdot \hat{\mathbf{z}} = 0$. The other dot products may be deduced by referring to Fig. 1.23. It is evident that

$$\hat{\mathbf{r}} \cdot \hat{\mathbf{x}} = \cos \varphi$$

$$\hat{\mathbf{r}} \cdot \hat{\mathbf{y}} = \cos \left(\frac{\pi}{2} - \varphi\right)$$

$$= \sin \varphi$$

Therefore

$$A_r = \cos \varphi \, A_x + \sin \varphi \, A_y$$

Similarly, it is found that

$$A_\varphi = - \sin \varphi \, A_x + \cos \varphi \, A_y$$

$$A_z = A_z$$

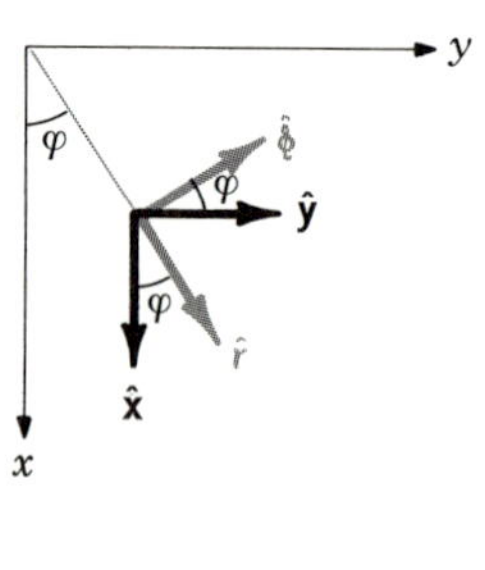

Fig. 1.23 The relations between unit vectors.

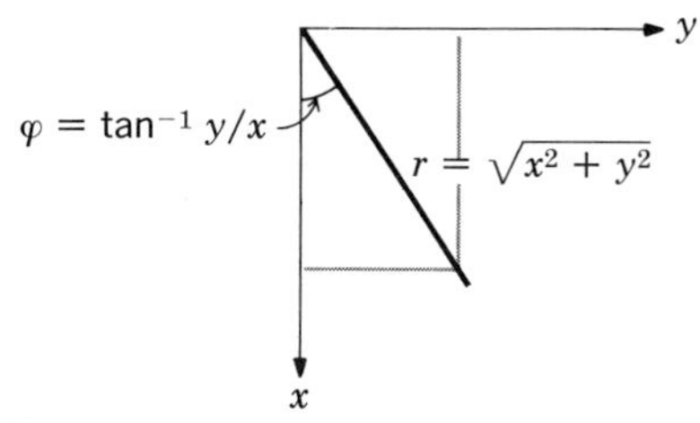

Fig. 1.24 Relations between the independent variables of the rectangular and cylindrical coordinate systems.

The relations between the independent variables of the two coordinate systems may be found by referring to Fig. 1.24. From simple trigonometry,

$$x = r \cos \varphi$$
$$y = r \sin \varphi$$

and z is the same in each coordinate system and need not be transformed. The inverse relations are

$$r = \sqrt{x^2 + y^2}$$
$$\varphi = \tan^{-1} \frac{y}{x}$$

The same procedure is followed in transforming vectors to or from any one of the three coordinate systems. In fact, this method can be used with any orthogonal coordinate system.

Example 1.2 Rectangular-to-cylindrical transformation As a simple illustration of the rectangular-to-cylindrical transformation, consider the vector $\mathbf{A} = \hat{\mathbf{x}} + \hat{\mathbf{y}}$. We need not consider the z components, because they transform directly; that is, the z component of the vector in rectangular coordinates equals the z component of the vector in cylindrical coordinates. In cylindrical coordinates, $\mathbf{A} = A_r\hat{\mathbf{r}} + A_\varphi\hat{\boldsymbol{\varphi}}$, where

$$A_r = \hat{\mathbf{r}} \cdot \mathbf{A}$$
$$A_\varphi = \hat{\boldsymbol{\varphi}} \cdot \mathbf{A}$$

From Eq. (1.22),

$$A_r = A_x\hat{\mathbf{r}} \cdot \hat{\mathbf{x}} + A_y\hat{\mathbf{r}} \cdot \hat{\mathbf{y}}$$

but since $A_x = A_y = 1$,

$$A_r = \hat{\mathbf{r}} \cdot \hat{\mathbf{x}} + \hat{\mathbf{r}} \cdot \hat{\mathbf{y}}$$

The corresponding expression for A_φ is

$$A_\varphi = \hat{\boldsymbol{\varphi}} \cdot \hat{\mathbf{x}} + \hat{\boldsymbol{\varphi}} \cdot \hat{\mathbf{y}}$$

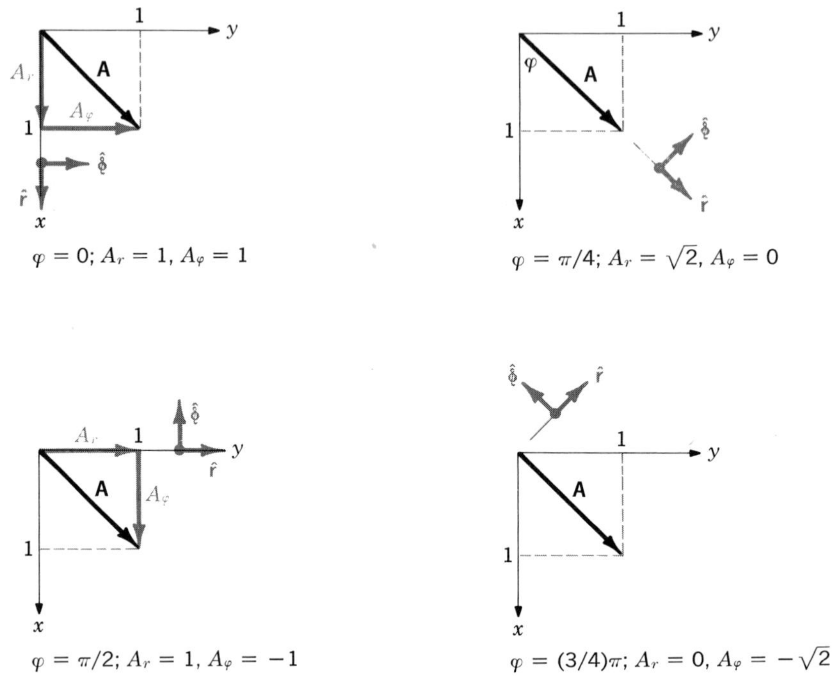

Fig. 1.25 Construction of a constant vector from the cylindrical form with varying φ.

The dot products of the unit vectors are simply the cosines of the angles between the unit vectors; thus from Fig. 1.23 we see that

$$A_r = \cos\varphi + \sin\varphi$$
$$A_\varphi = -\sin\varphi + \cos\varphi$$

There is no need to transform the independent variables, as none appear in the vector components; thus the vector may be written out directly in cylindrical form,

$$\begin{aligned}\mathbf{A} &= A_r\hat{\mathbf{r}} + A_\varphi\hat{\boldsymbol{\varphi}} \\ &= (\cos\varphi + \sin\varphi)\hat{\mathbf{r}} + (-\sin\varphi + \cos\varphi)\hat{\boldsymbol{\varphi}}\end{aligned}$$

It is interesting to compare the cylindrical form of the vector and the rectangular form

$$\mathbf{A} = \hat{\mathbf{x}} + \hat{\mathbf{y}}$$

The cylindrical form is much more complicated, and the components are variables, rather than constants, as in the rectangular form. This is necessary, of course, because $\hat{\mathbf{r}}$ and $\hat{\boldsymbol{\varphi}}$ are variables. Although we may be tempted to regard the vector as a variable because the components are variables, the base-vector variations in

φ combine with the component variations to give a constant vector. This may be easily verified by graphically constructing the vector at different φ values, as in Fig. 1.25. In each case the vector components add to the same vector, $\mathbf{A} = \hat{\mathbf{x}} + \hat{\mathbf{y}}$.

RECTANGULAR-TO-SPHERICAL TRANSFORMATION

The rectangular-to-spherical transformation is accomplished by the same method as the rectangular-to-cylindrical transformation. What is needed basically is an evaluation of the dot products of the unit vectors and a transformation of the independent variables. In finding the dot products of the rectangular and spherical base vectors, it is convenient first to resolve the spherical base vectors into components perpendicular and parallel to the xy plane. Superimposed rectangular and spherical coordinate systems are illustrated in Fig. 1.26, where the radial spherical unit base vector $\hat{\mathbf{r}}$ is shown. Remember that $\hat{\mathbf{r}}$ in spherical coordinates is different from $\hat{\mathbf{r}}$ in cylindrical coordinates. The components of $\hat{\mathbf{r}}$ are

$$\hat{\mathbf{r}} = \mathbf{r}_{\parallel} + \mathbf{r}_{\perp}$$

Therefore

$$\hat{\mathbf{x}} \cdot \hat{\mathbf{r}} = \hat{\mathbf{x}} \cdot \mathbf{r}_{\parallel} + \hat{\mathbf{x}} \cdot \mathbf{r}_{\perp}$$

Note that $\mathbf{r}_{\parallel}$ and $\mathbf{r}_{\perp}$ are not unit vectors, but components of a unit vector. Since $\mathbf{r}_{\perp}$ is perpendicular to the xy plane,

$$\hat{\mathbf{x}} \cdot \mathbf{r}_{\perp} = 0$$
$$\hat{\mathbf{y}} \cdot \mathbf{r}_{\perp} = 0$$

Figure 1.27 illustrates the relation between $\hat{\mathbf{x}}$, $\hat{\mathbf{y}}$, and $\mathbf{r}_{\parallel}$. Since the mag-

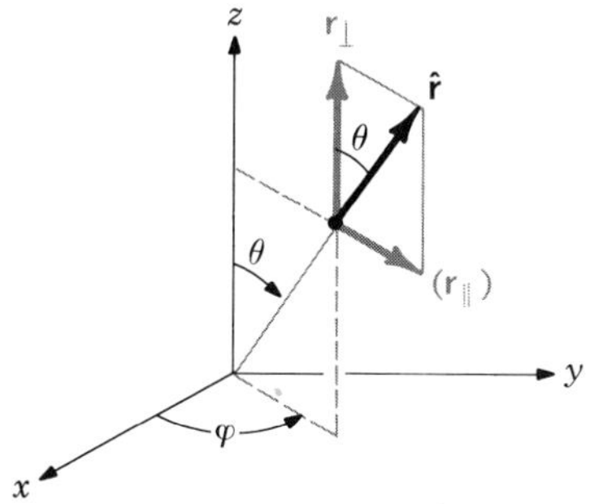

Fig. 1.26 The vector $\hat{\mathbf{r}}$ resolved into components perpendicular and parallel to the xy plane.

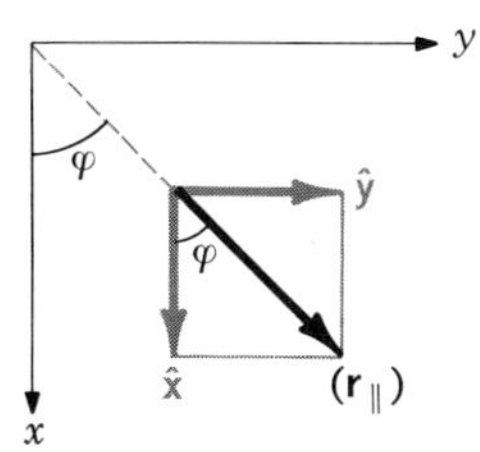

Fig. 1.27 The relations between $\hat{\mathbf{x}}$, $\hat{\mathbf{y}}$, and $\hat{\mathbf{r}}_{\parallel}$.

nitude of $\mathbf{r}_{\|}$ is $\sin\theta$, we find that

$$\hat{\mathbf{x}} \cdot \mathbf{r}_{\|} = \sin\theta \cos\varphi$$

$$\hat{\mathbf{y}} \cdot \mathbf{r}_{\|} = \sin\theta \sin\varphi$$

and therefore

$$\hat{\mathbf{x}} \cdot \hat{\mathbf{r}} = \sin\theta \cos\varphi$$

$$\hat{\mathbf{y}} \cdot \hat{\mathbf{r}} = \sin\theta \sin\varphi$$

The relations among the independent variables can be easily obtained by referring to Fig. 1.17 and using simple trigonometry. They are

$$x = r \sin\theta \cos\varphi$$

$$y = r \sin\theta \sin\varphi$$

$$z = r \cos\theta$$

The inverse relations are

$$r = \sqrt{x^2 + y^2 + z^2}$$

$$\varphi = \tan^{-1} \frac{y}{x}$$

$$\theta = \tan^{-1} \frac{\sqrt{x^2 + y^2}}{z}$$

TRANSFORMATIONS FROM ANOTHER POINT OF VIEW

An alternate procedure to the formal transformation technique just developed is to express the base vectors of one system in terms of the base vectors of the other system. For example, we could express

$$\mathbf{A} = A_r\hat{\mathbf{r}} + A_\varphi\hat{\boldsymbol{\varphi}} + A_z\hat{\mathbf{z}}$$

in rectangular coordinates by substitution of

$$\hat{\mathbf{r}} = \cos\varphi\, \hat{\mathbf{x}} + \sin\varphi\, \hat{\mathbf{y}}$$

$$\hat{\boldsymbol{\varphi}} = -\sin\varphi\, \hat{\mathbf{x}} + \cos\varphi\, \hat{\mathbf{y}}$$

$$\hat{\mathbf{z}} = \hat{\mathbf{z}}$$

and then make the same change of independent variables as in the formal method. The above relations among $\hat{\mathbf{r}}$, $\hat{\boldsymbol{\varphi}}$, $\hat{\mathbf{z}}$, $\hat{\mathbf{x}}$, $\hat{\mathbf{y}}$, and $\hat{\mathbf{z}}$ can be obtained by referring to Fig. 1.23 and writing $\hat{\mathbf{r}}$ as the sum of two vectors, one in the $\hat{\mathbf{x}}$ direction and one in the $\hat{\mathbf{y}}$ direction, etc.

The expressions for $\hat{\mathbf{r}}$ and $\hat{\boldsymbol{\varphi}}$, as well as for $\hat{\mathbf{r}}$, $\hat{\boldsymbol{\theta}}$, and $\hat{\boldsymbol{\varphi}}$ in terms of $\hat{\mathbf{x}}$, $\hat{\mathbf{y}}$, and $\hat{\mathbf{z}}$, show explicitly that these vectors are variable vectors (remember that $\hat{\mathbf{x}}$, $\hat{\mathbf{y}}$, and $\hat{\mathbf{z}}$ are constant vectors). It is often useful to have the variable base vectors expressed in terms of constant vectors, as we shall see in the next section. Obtaining the expressions for $\hat{\mathbf{r}}$, $\hat{\boldsymbol{\theta}}$, and $\hat{\boldsymbol{\varphi}}$ in terms of $\hat{\mathbf{x}}$, $\hat{\mathbf{y}}$, and $\hat{\mathbf{z}}$ is left as Prob. 1.6-8. The results are

$$\hat{\mathbf{r}} = \sin\theta\cos\varphi\,\hat{\mathbf{x}} + \sin\theta\sin\varphi\,\hat{\mathbf{y}} + \cos\theta\,\hat{\mathbf{z}} \tag{1.23}$$

$$\hat{\boldsymbol{\theta}} = \cos\theta\cos\varphi\,\hat{\mathbf{x}} + \cos\theta\sin\varphi\,\hat{\mathbf{y}} - \sin\theta\,\hat{\mathbf{z}} \tag{1.24}$$

$$\hat{\boldsymbol{\varphi}} = -\sin\varphi\,\hat{\mathbf{x}} + \cos\varphi\,\hat{\mathbf{y}} \tag{1.25}$$

1.7 DIFFERENTIATION OF VECTORS

A good understanding of differentiation of vectors is essential in electromagnetic field theory. We shall review the results of a rigorous mathematical development and strive for practical understanding, which then allows us to use vector calculus as a tool in our understanding of electromagnetic fields.

The fundamental definition of the derivative of a vector is the same as that of any other function. Recall that if f is a function of x, then the definition of df/dx is

$$\frac{df}{dx} = \lim_{\Delta x \to 0} \frac{f(x + \Delta x) - f(x)}{\Delta x} \tag{1.26}$$

Similarly, if $\mathbf{A}$ is a function of x, then

$$\frac{d\mathbf{A}}{dx} = \lim_{\Delta x \to 0} \frac{\mathbf{A}(x + \Delta x) - \mathbf{A}(x)}{\Delta x} \tag{1.27}$$

It should be apparent from this definition that the derivatives of sums and products of vectors can be found in the same way as for scalars, provided that the proper order is maintained in vector products, where this is important. Thus

$$\frac{d(\mathbf{A} + \mathbf{B})}{dx} = \frac{d\mathbf{A}}{dx} + \frac{d\mathbf{B}}{dx}$$

$$\frac{d(\Phi\mathbf{A})}{dx} = \mathbf{A}\frac{d\Phi}{dx} + \Phi\frac{d\mathbf{A}}{dx}$$

$$\frac{d(\mathbf{A}\cdot\mathbf{B})}{dx} = \frac{d\mathbf{A}}{dx}\cdot\mathbf{B} + \mathbf{A}\cdot\frac{d\mathbf{B}}{dx}$$

$$\frac{d(\mathbf{A}\times\mathbf{B})}{dx} = \frac{d\mathbf{A}}{dx}\times\mathbf{B} + \mathbf{A}\times\frac{d\mathbf{B}}{dx}$$

. . . .

Since any vector can be written in the form

$$\mathbf{A}(x) = A(x)\hat{\mathbf{A}}(x)$$

(see Sec. 1.2), we can write

$$\frac{d\mathbf{A}(x)}{dx} = \hat{\mathbf{A}}\frac{dA}{dx} + A\frac{d\hat{\mathbf{A}}}{dx} \tag{1.28}$$

which is sometimes a convenient way to evaluate a derivative. In rectangular coordinates, we have simply that

$$\frac{d\mathbf{A}}{dx} = \hat{\mathbf{x}}\frac{dA_x}{dx} + \hat{\mathbf{y}}\frac{dA_y}{dx} + \hat{\mathbf{z}}\frac{dA_z}{dx} \tag{1.29}$$

because $\hat{\mathbf{x}}$, $\hat{\mathbf{y}}$, and $\hat{\mathbf{z}}$ are constants, and their derivatives are thus zero. When a vector is expressed in rectangular coordinates, we can find its derivative simply by taking the derivatives of A_x, A_y, and A_z. A similar statement can be made about partial derivatives.

When a vector is expressed in cylindrical or spherical coordinates, however, some or all of the base vectors are functions of the coordinates, and the derivative is more complicated. But since the derivative can be written as the derivative of a product, the variable base vectors will cause no great problem if we can find their derivatives. One way to find derivatives of base vectors is to transform them to rectangular coordinates, take the derivative, and then transform them back. In general, the base vectors could be functions of all three variables; thus

$$\frac{\partial\mathbf{A}}{\partial u_1} = \hat{\mathbf{u}}_1\frac{\partial A_1}{\partial u_1} + A_1\frac{\partial\hat{\mathbf{u}}_1}{\partial u_1} + \hat{\mathbf{u}}_2\frac{\partial A_2}{\partial u_1} + A_2\frac{\partial\hat{\mathbf{u}}_2}{\partial u_1} + \hat{\mathbf{u}}_3\frac{\partial A_3}{\partial u_1} + A_3\frac{\partial\hat{\mathbf{u}}_3}{\partial u_1}$$

and it is necessary to find $\partial\hat{\mathbf{u}}_1/\partial u_1$, $\partial\hat{\mathbf{u}}_2/\partial u_1$, ... An easy way to find these partial derivatives is to write the base vectors in terms of $\hat{\mathbf{x}}$, $\hat{\mathbf{y}}$, and $\hat{\mathbf{z}}$, as in Sec. 1.6.

First let us consider the cylindrical coordinate system. It was found in Sec. 1.6 that

$$\hat{\mathbf{r}} = \cos\varphi\,\hat{\mathbf{x}} + \sin\varphi\,\hat{\mathbf{y}} \tag{1.30}$$

$$\hat{\boldsymbol{\varphi}} = -\sin\varphi\,\hat{\mathbf{x}} + \cos\varphi\,\hat{\mathbf{y}} \tag{1.31}$$

$$\hat{\mathbf{z}} = \hat{\mathbf{z}}$$

Since there is no dependence on r, we have

$$\frac{\partial\hat{\mathbf{r}}}{\partial r} = 0 \tag{1.32}$$

$$\frac{\partial\hat{\boldsymbol{\varphi}}}{\partial r} = 0 \tag{1.33}$$

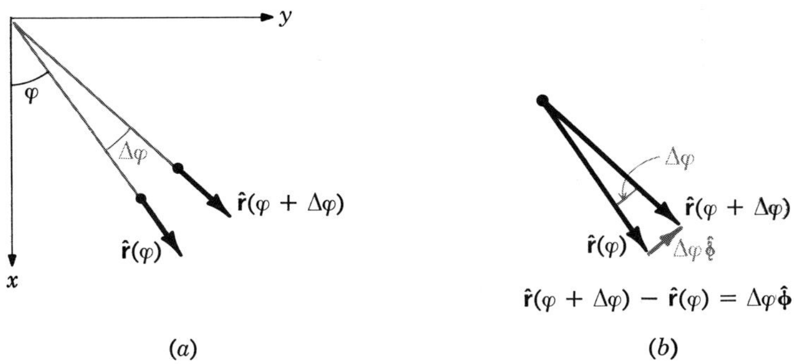

Fig. 1.28 (*a*) The vectors $\hat{\mathbf{r}}(\varphi)$ and $\hat{\mathbf{r}}(\varphi + \Delta\varphi)$; (*b*) the vectors $\hat{\mathbf{r}}(\varphi)$ and $\hat{\mathbf{r}}(\varphi + \Delta\varphi)$ transferred to the same point to show their difference.

The other partial derivatives are

$$\begin{aligned}\frac{\partial \hat{\mathbf{r}}}{\partial \varphi} &= -\sin\varphi\,\hat{\mathbf{x}} + \cos\varphi\,\hat{\mathbf{y}} \\ &= \hat{\boldsymbol{\varphi}}\end{aligned} \tag{1.34}$$

$$\begin{aligned}\frac{\partial \hat{\boldsymbol{\varphi}}}{\partial \varphi} &= -\cos\varphi\,\hat{\mathbf{x}} - \sin\varphi\,\hat{\mathbf{y}} \\ &= -\hat{\mathbf{r}}\end{aligned} \tag{1.35}$$

It is easy to see from Fig. 1.28 how $\partial\hat{\mathbf{r}}/\partial\varphi = \hat{\boldsymbol{\varphi}}$ is consistent with the definition

$$\frac{\partial \hat{\mathbf{r}}}{\partial \varphi} = \lim_{\Delta\varphi \to 0} \frac{\hat{\mathbf{r}}(\varphi + \Delta\varphi) - \hat{\mathbf{r}}(\varphi)}{\Delta\varphi}$$

As shown in Fig. 1.28,

$$\hat{\mathbf{r}}(\varphi + \Delta\varphi) - \hat{\mathbf{r}}(\varphi) = \Delta\varphi\,\hat{\boldsymbol{\varphi}}$$

and therefore

$$\begin{aligned}\frac{\partial \hat{\mathbf{r}}}{\partial \varphi} &= \lim_{\Delta\varphi \to 0} \frac{\Delta\varphi\,\hat{\boldsymbol{\varphi}}}{\Delta\varphi} \\ &= \hat{\boldsymbol{\varphi}}\end{aligned}$$

The derivation of the derivatives of the spherical unit vectors is given as Prob. 1.7-1. The results are

$$\frac{\partial \hat{\mathbf{r}}}{\partial \theta} = \hat{\boldsymbol{\theta}} \tag{1.36}$$

$$\frac{\partial \hat{\mathbf{r}}}{\partial \varphi} = \sin\theta\,\hat{\boldsymbol{\varphi}} \tag{1.37}$$

$$\frac{\partial \hat{\boldsymbol{\theta}}}{\partial \theta} = -\hat{\mathbf{r}} \tag{1.38}$$

$$\frac{\partial \hat{\boldsymbol{\theta}}}{\partial \varphi} = \cos\theta\,\hat{\boldsymbol{\varphi}} \tag{1.39}$$

$$\frac{\partial \hat{\boldsymbol{\varphi}}}{\partial \theta} = 0 \tag{1.40}$$

$$\frac{\partial \hat{\boldsymbol{\varphi}}}{\partial \varphi} = -\frac{\mathbf{r}_{\|}}{\sin\theta} \qquad \text{(see Sec. 1.6)} \tag{1.41}$$

Example 1.3 Velocity in cylindrical coordinates As a simple example of vector differentiation, let us find the velocity (expressed in cylindrical coordinates) of a point. A point in the xy plane is located by the vector

$$\mathbf{r} = r\hat{\mathbf{r}}$$

as shown in Fig. 1.29. The velocity of the point is given by

$$\mathbf{v} = \frac{d\mathbf{r}}{dt}$$

$$= \hat{\mathbf{r}}\frac{dr}{dt} + r\frac{d\hat{\mathbf{r}}}{dt}$$

Since

$$\frac{d\hat{\mathbf{r}}}{dt} = \frac{\partial \hat{\mathbf{r}}}{\partial r}\frac{dr}{dt} + \frac{\partial \hat{\mathbf{r}}}{\partial \varphi}\frac{d\varphi}{dt}$$

$$= 0 + \hat{\boldsymbol{\varphi}}\frac{d\varphi}{dt}$$

we have

$$\mathbf{v} = \hat{\mathbf{r}}\frac{dr}{dt} + \hat{\boldsymbol{\varphi}}r\frac{d\varphi}{dt} \tag{1.42}$$

which is the familiar expression for velocity as expressed in a cylindrical coordinate system.

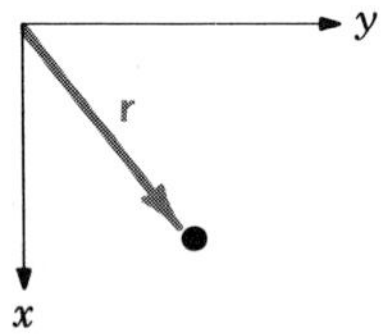

Fig. 1.29 A point in the xy plane located by the vector **r**.

1.8 INTEGRATION OF VECTORS

We shall be concerned with two kinds of integrals involving vectors. One kind contains an integrand involving dot products of vectors; this is simply a scalar integral which can be integrated in the usual way. The other kind involves vector integrands, and we shall be concerned with vector line integrals, vector surface integrals, and scalar volume integrals.

LINE INTEGRALS

Let us consider first the ordinary scalar line integral of the form

$$\int_a^b A(l)\,dl$$

where l is the arc length along some curve in space and a and b are two points on that curve, as shown in Fig. 1.30. The fundamental definition of the line integral is the limit of

$$\sum_{i=1}^{N} A(l_i)\,\Delta l_i$$

as $N \to \infty$ and the maximum of the $\Delta l_i \to 0$. As shown in Fig. 1.30, the Δl_i are segments of arc length along the path, and $A(l_i)$ is the value of $A(l)$ at the point l_i within the segment Δl_i. Although an understanding of the fundamental definition is important because it often provides much insight, our main concern here is the evaluation of this type of integral in terms of a coordinate system. We shall do this by expressing dl in terms of du_1, du_2, and du_3, as in Sec. 1.5, and writing $A(l)$ as $A(u_1,u_2,u_3)$. Then evaluation of the line integral can be reduced to the evaluation of ordinary integrals.

By definition, l and dl are always positive, and the line integral has the property that

$$\int_a^b A(l)\,dl = \int_b^a A(l)\,dl$$

The coordinate variables and differentials, however, are signed quantities. Hence we must be careful to choose proper signs in expressing dl in terms of du_1, du_2, and du_3.

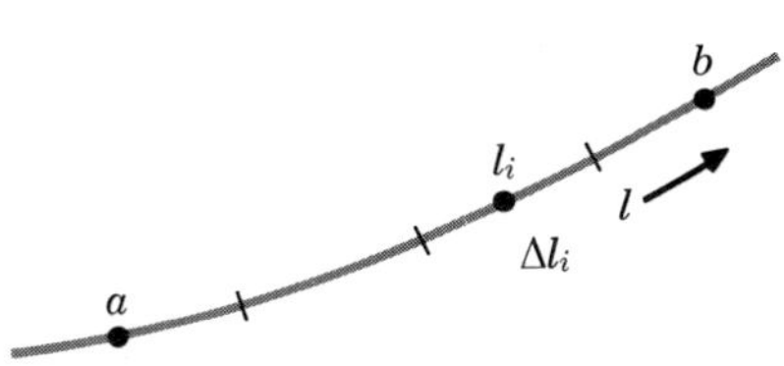

Fig. 1.30 The variables in the scalar line integral.

The relation

$$(dl)^2 = (h_1\,du_1)^2 + (h_2\,du_2)^2 + (h_3\,du_3)^2$$

can be rewritten in the three forms

$$dl = \pm\sqrt{1 + \left(\frac{h_2}{h_1}\right)^2\left(\frac{du_2}{du_1}\right)^2 + \left(\frac{h_3}{h_1}\right)^2\left(\frac{du_3}{du_1}\right)^2}\;h_1\,du_1 \tag{1.43}$$

$$dl = \pm\sqrt{1 + \left(\frac{h_1}{h_2}\right)^2\left(\frac{du_1}{du_2}\right)^2 + \left(\frac{h_3}{h_2}\right)^2\left(\frac{du_3}{du_2}\right)^2}\;h_2\,du_2 \tag{1.44}$$

$$dl = \pm\sqrt{1 + \left(\frac{h_1}{h_3}\right)^2\left(\frac{du_1}{du_3}\right)^2 + \left(\frac{h_2}{h_3}\right)^2\left(\frac{du_2}{du_3}\right)^3}\;h_3\,du_3 \tag{1.45}$$

The problem to be solved will dictate which of the three forms is the most convenient to use. The curve l along which the integration is to be carried out will be defined by a relation between u_1, u_2, and u_3. The expressions du_1/du_2, etc., can be evaluated from this relation. The $\pm$ sign is included to assure that dl is always positive. Thus, if the integration were to be carried out in a direction in which u_1 were decreasing, the minus sign would be used in the expression for dl in Eq. (1.43).

Example 1.4 Evaluation of a scalar line integral Consider the very simple line integral

$$\int_a^b dl$$

along the curve shown in Fig. 1.31. The path of integration is defined by $y = 1$ and $z = 0$. With $u_1 = x$, $u_2 = y$, and $u_3 = z$, Eq. (1.43) is the most convenient one to use, because

$$\frac{dy}{dx} = 0$$

$$\frac{dz}{dx} = 0$$

according to the definition of the path of integration. Since x is decreasing in the

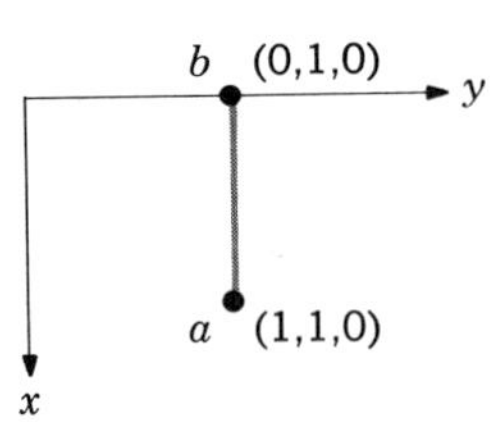

Fig. 1.31 The path of integration in Example 1.4.

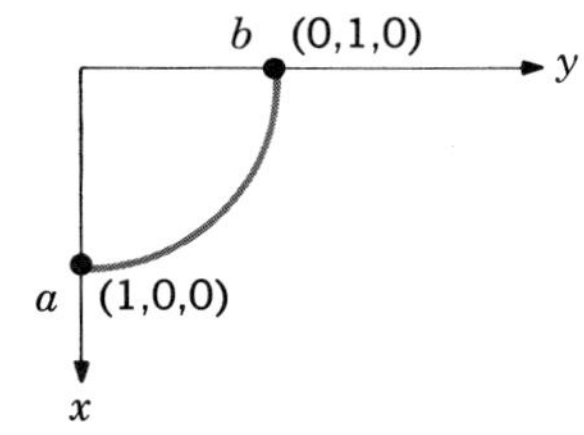

Fig. 1.32 The path of integration in Example 1.5.

direction of integration, the minus sign in Eq. (1.43) is used, and

$$dl = -dx$$

Therefore

$$\int_a^b dl = \int_1^0 - dx$$
$$= 1$$

which is simply the length of the path of integration, as we know it must be.

To evaluate $\int_b^a dl$ we would use the same procedure, except with

$$dl = dx$$

since x is increasing in the direction of integration. The result is the same, as it must be.

Example 1.5 Evaluation of a scalar line integral For further illustration, let us evaluate $\int_a^b dl$ along the path shown in Fig. 1.32. The path is defined by

$$x^2 + y^2 = 1$$
$$z = 0$$

Therefore

$$\frac{dy}{dx} = -\frac{x}{y}$$

$$\frac{dz}{dx} = 0$$

Using Eq. (1.43), we obtain

$$dl = \pm \sqrt{1 + \frac{x^2}{y^2}}\, dx$$

Since $x^2 + y^2 = 1$,

$$dl = \pm \sqrt{\frac{1}{1 - x^2}}\, dx$$

Since x is decreasing in the direction of integration, the minus sign is used. Hence

$$\int_a^b dl = -\int_1^0 \sqrt{\frac{1}{1-x^2}}\, dx$$
$$= -\sin^{-1} x \Big|_1^0$$
$$= \frac{\pi}{2}$$

which is one-fourth the circumference of a unit radius circle.

It is possible to integrate along y by using Eq. (1.44). Then we would use

$$\frac{dx}{dy} = -\frac{y}{x}$$
$$\frac{dz}{dy} = 0$$

Since y increases in the direction of integration, the plus sign is used, and

$$dl = +\sqrt{\frac{1}{1-y^2}}\, dy$$

Then

$$\int_a^b dl = \int_0^1 \sqrt{\frac{1}{1-y^2}}\, dy$$
$$= \frac{\pi}{2}$$

In this example there was no particular advantage in using either Eq. (1.43) or Eq. (1.44), but in some cases one form will be much easier to use than the other.

Another type of line integral which is often encountered is

$$\int_a^b \mathbf{A} \cdot d\mathbf{l}$$

where $d\mathbf{l}$ is a differential vector. The definition of $d\mathbf{l}$ is

$$d\mathbf{l} = dl\, \hat{\boldsymbol{\tau}} \tag{1.46}$$

where $\hat{\boldsymbol{\tau}}$ is a unit vector tangent to the curve and *pointing in the direction of integration,* as shown in Fig. 1.33. An example of this kind of integral

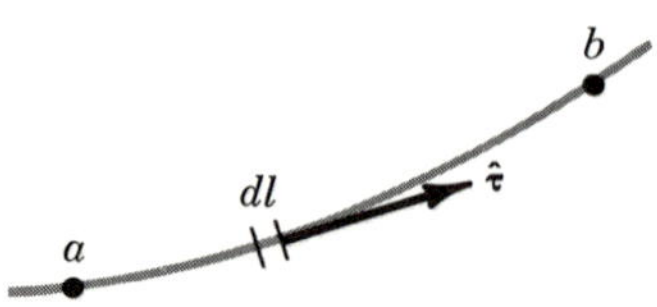

Fig. 1.33 An illustration of $d\mathbf{l}$. $\hat{\boldsymbol{\tau}}$ is defined as pointing in the direction of integration.

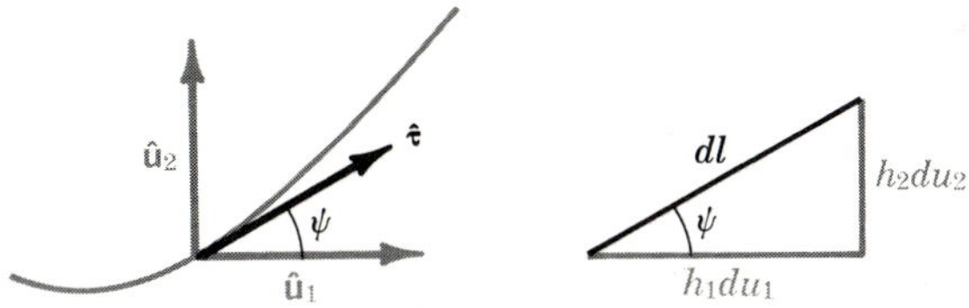

Fig. 1.34 The two-dimensional relation between $\hat{\boldsymbol{\tau}}$ and the base vectors.

is $W = \int \mathbf{F} \cdot d\mathbf{l}$, where $\mathbf{F}$ is the force applied and W is the work done on a mass.

In two dimensions, $\hat{\boldsymbol{\tau}}$ may be expressed in terms of $\hat{\mathbf{u}}_1$ and $\hat{\mathbf{u}}_2$ by referring to Fig. 1.34,

$$\hat{\boldsymbol{\tau}} = \cos\psi\, \hat{\mathbf{u}}_1 + \sin\psi\, \hat{\mathbf{u}}_2 \tag{1.47}$$

Since

$$\cos\psi = \frac{h_1\, du_1}{dl} \tag{1.48}$$

$$\sin\psi = \frac{h_2\, du_2}{dl} \tag{1.49}$$

we obtain

$$dl\, \hat{\boldsymbol{\tau}} = h_1\, du_1\, \hat{\mathbf{u}}_1 + h_2\, du_2\, \hat{\mathbf{u}}_2$$

Generalizing this to three dimensions gives

$$dl\, \hat{\boldsymbol{\tau}} = h_1\, du_1\, \hat{\mathbf{u}}_1 + h_2\, du_2\, \hat{\mathbf{u}}_2 + h_3\, du_3\, \hat{\mathbf{u}}_3 \tag{1.50}$$

Therefore

$$\int_a^b \mathbf{A} \cdot d\mathbf{l} = \int_{u_{1a}}^{u_{1b}} A_1 h_1\, du_1 + \int_{u_{2a}}^{u_{2b}} A_2 h_2\, du_2 + \int_{u_{3a}}^{u_{3b}} A_3 h_3\, du_3 \tag{1.51}$$

where u_{1a}, u_{2a}, and u_{3a} and u_{1b}, u_{2b}, and u_{3b} are the coordinates of the points a and b. In contrast to the scalar line integral, we see that

$$\int_a^b \mathbf{A} \cdot d\mathbf{l} = - \int_b^a \mathbf{A} \cdot d\mathbf{l}$$

The reason for this is that $\hat{\boldsymbol{\tau}}$ changes sign with the direction of integration, and hence $dl\, \hat{\boldsymbol{\tau}}$ changes sign, whereas in the scalar line integral only dl appears, which does not change sign. There are no plus-minus signs in Eq. (1.51) because expressing $\hat{\boldsymbol{\tau}}$ in terms of the base vectors automatically accounts for the fact that the integration might be in the direction of decreasing u_1, u_2, or u_3. As an illustration, consider $dl\, \hat{\boldsymbol{\tau}}$ for the path of

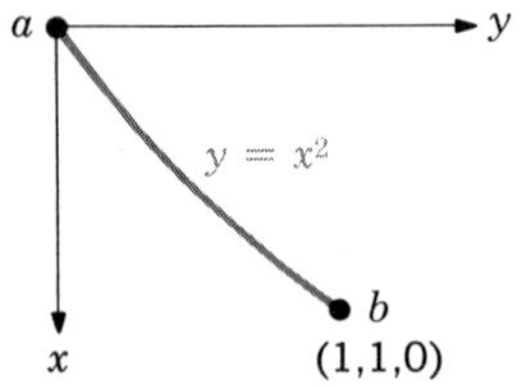

Fig. 1.35 The curve used in connection with Example 1.6.

integration from a to b shown in Fig. 1.31. In this case $dl = -dx$ and $\hat{\boldsymbol{\ell}} = -\hat{\mathbf{x}}$, so that $dl\,\hat{\boldsymbol{\ell}} = -dx\,(-\hat{\mathbf{x}}) = dx\,\hat{\mathbf{x}}$. If the path of integration is changed to be from b to a, $dl = dx$, $\hat{\boldsymbol{\ell}} = \hat{\mathbf{x}}$, and again $dl\,\hat{\boldsymbol{\ell}} = dx\,\hat{\mathbf{x}}$. Thus, as predicted by Eq. (1.50), the sign on $dl\,\hat{\boldsymbol{\ell}}$ is independent of the direction of integration.

Example 1.6 Evaluation of a line integral Suppose that $\mathbf{A} = y\hat{\mathbf{x}} + x\hat{\mathbf{y}}$, point a is the origin, point b is (1,1,0), and the curve over which the integration is to be carried out is $y = x^2$, as illustrated in Fig. 1.35. Then

$$\int_a^b \mathbf{A} \cdot d\mathbf{l} = \int_a^b (y\hat{\mathbf{x}} + x\hat{\mathbf{y}}) \cdot (dx\,\hat{\mathbf{x}} + dy\,\hat{\mathbf{y}})$$
$$= \int_0^1 y\,dx + \int_0^1 x\,dy$$

Note that the integral has been written down directly from Eq. (1.51). Since $y = x^2$ and $dy = 2x\,dx$ along the path of integration, the integral becomes

$$\int_a^b \mathbf{A} \cdot d\mathbf{l} = \int_0^1 x^2\,dx + \int_0^1 x2x\,dx$$
$$= 1$$

Other line integrals with which we shall be concerned are those of the type

$$\int_a^b \mathbf{A} \cdot \mathbf{B}\,dl$$

These are just scalar line integrals, because the integrand is a scalar.

Line integrals with vector integrands are handled in a similar way, but care must be taken to treat the unit vectors in the cylindrical and spherical coordinate systems as variables of integration when that is the case. As in the differentiation of vectors, a convenient way to handle variable unit vectors in integration is to write them in terms of $\hat{\mathbf{x}}$, $\hat{\mathbf{y}}$, and $\hat{\mathbf{z}}$.

Example 1.7 Evaluation of a vector line integral Consider the simple vector line integral $\int_a^b d\mathbf{l}$. Just as $\int_a^b dl$ is the total arc length between points a and b, $\int_a^b d\mathbf{l}$ is $\mathbf{P}_{ab}$, the vector between points a and b, pointing from a to b. For exam-

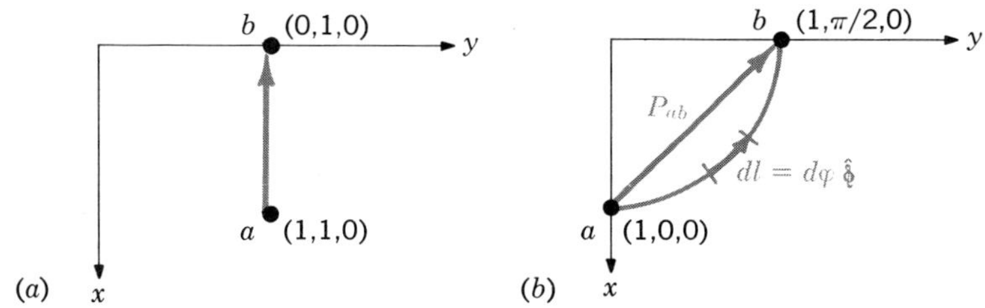

Fig. 1.36 Path of integration used in Example 1.7.

ple, for the path shown in Fig. 1.36*a*, $d\mathbf{l} = dl\,\hat{\boldsymbol{\tau}} = -dx\,(-\hat{\mathbf{x}}) = dx\,\hat{\mathbf{x}}$, and

$$\int_a^b d\mathbf{l} = \int_1^0 dx\,\hat{\mathbf{x}}$$
$$= -\hat{\mathbf{x}}$$

which is just $\mathbf{P}_{ab}$. A slightly more complicated example is illustrated in Fig. 1.36*b*. Here it is convenient to use a cylindrical coordinate system, in which case $d\mathbf{l} = d\varphi\,\hat{\boldsymbol{\varphi}}$. Thus

$$\int_a^b d\mathbf{l} = \int_0^{\pi/2} d\varphi\,\hat{\boldsymbol{\varphi}}$$
$$= \int_0^{\pi/2} (-\sin\varphi\,\hat{\mathbf{x}} + \cos\varphi\,\hat{\mathbf{y}})\,d\varphi$$
$$= -\hat{\mathbf{x}} + \hat{\mathbf{y}} = \mathbf{P}_{ab}$$

since $\hat{\boldsymbol{\varphi}} = -\sin\varphi\,\hat{\mathbf{x}} + \cos\varphi\,\hat{\mathbf{y}}$, and since $\hat{\mathbf{x}}$ and $\hat{\mathbf{y}}$ are constant vectors. It would have been obviously incorrect to write the equation

$$\int_a^b d\mathbf{l} = \int_0^{\pi/2} d\varphi\,\hat{\boldsymbol{\varphi}}$$
$$= \hat{\boldsymbol{\varphi}} \int_0^{\pi/2} d\varphi$$
$$= \frac{\pi}{2}\,\hat{\boldsymbol{\varphi}} \qquad \textit{incorrect}$$

Experience has shown that there is often much confusion about the proper expression of dl and $d\mathbf{l}$ in terms of coordinates, principally in the choice of sign. Figure 1.37 is an attempt to help recall the proper expressions for dl and $d\mathbf{l}$.

SURFACE INTEGRALS

There are scalar and vector surface integrals. A common scalar integral is $\int_S \mathbf{A} \cdot d\mathbf{S}$, where $d\mathbf{S}$ is the differential vector surface element and S is the surface over which the integral is carried out. $d\mathbf{S}$ is defined as

$$d\mathbf{S} = \hat{\mathbf{n}}\,dS$$

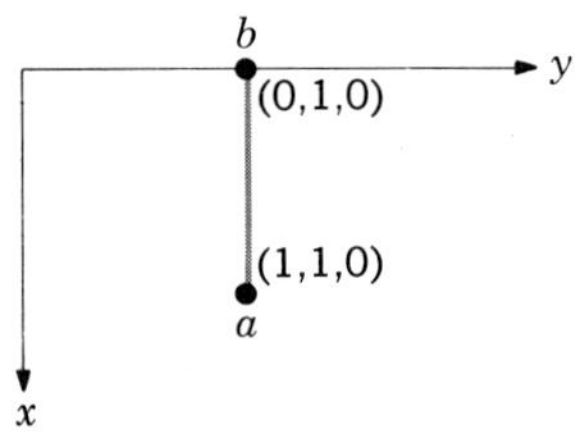

Fig. 1.37 A summary of the signs involved in line integrals. Since the signs involved in dl and $d\mathbf{l}$ are confusing, the following simple examples involving line integrals along the simple path shown are given to help summarize and recall the proper signs. (*a*) *Path of integration:* The equation for the path of integration shown is $y = 1$, $z = 0$. Therefore, $dy = 0$, $dz = 0$ everywhere along the path of integration. (*b*) *Scalar line integrals:* dl is defined as being positive in the direction of integration. Hence in the expression for dl in terms of coordinates [Eqs. (1.43) to (1.45)] choose a plus sign if the direction of integration is in the direction of increasing coordinate and a minus sign otherwise. For example:

$$\int_a^b dl = \int_1^0 (-dx) = 1 \qquad \int_b^a dl = \int_0^1 dx = 1$$

$dy = 0$, $dz = 0$ as noted in (*a*) above. (*c*) *Vector line integrals:* Since dl is positive in the direction of integration, and since $\hat{\mathbf{l}}$ points in the direction of integration (Fig. 1.33), the sign of $d\mathbf{l} = dl\,\hat{\mathbf{l}}$ when expressed in terms of a coordinate system is independent of the direction of integration. Thus $d\mathbf{l}$ is given by Eq. (1.50) with no change in signs needed. In rectangular coordinates $d\mathbf{l} = dx\,\hat{\mathbf{x}} + dy\,\hat{\mathbf{y}} + dz\,\hat{\mathbf{z}}$ *always*. However, dx, dy, and dz will depend on the path of integration as noted in (*a*) above. $d\mathbf{l}$ can also be found by choosing the signs of dl and $\hat{\mathbf{l}}$ to correspond to the direction of integration. For example:

$$\int_a^b d\mathbf{l} = \int_1^0 dx\,\hat{\mathbf{x}} = -\hat{\mathbf{x}} \qquad d\mathbf{l} = dx\,\hat{\mathbf{x}} \text{ from Eq. (1.50)}$$

and (*a*) above or $d\mathbf{l} = dl\,\hat{\mathbf{l}} = (-dx)(-\hat{\mathbf{x}}) = dx\,\hat{\mathbf{x}}$.

$$\int_b^a d\mathbf{l} = \int_0^1 dx\,\hat{\mathbf{x}} = \hat{\mathbf{x}} \qquad d\mathbf{l} = dx\,\hat{\mathbf{x}} \text{ from Eq. (1.50)}$$

and (*a*) above or $d\mathbf{l} = dl\,\hat{\mathbf{l}} = dx\,\hat{\mathbf{x}}$. (*d*) *Line integrals of the form* $\int \mathbf{A} \cdot d\mathbf{l}$: Line integrals involving $\mathbf{A} \cdot d\mathbf{l}$ can be easily handled by writing $d\mathbf{l}$ as in Eq. (1.50), taking the dot product and integrating. As explained in (*c*) above, the sign of $d\mathbf{l}$ does not depend on the direction of integration. For example, suppose $\mathbf{A} = x^2\,\hat{\mathbf{x}}$; then

$$\int_a^b \mathbf{A} \cdot d\mathbf{l} = \int_1^0 x^2\,\hat{\mathbf{x}} \cdot dx\,\hat{\mathbf{x}} = \int_1^0 x^2\,dx = -\tfrac{1}{3}$$

$$\int_b^a \mathbf{A} \cdot d\mathbf{l} = \int_0^1 x^2\,\hat{\mathbf{x}} \cdot dx\,\hat{\mathbf{x}} = \int_0^1 x^2\,dx = \tfrac{1}{3}$$

$dy = dz = 0$ as noted in (*a*) above.

where dS is the scalar differential surface and $\hat{\mathbf{n}}$ is a unit vector normal to the surface dS. When S is a closed surface, $\hat{\mathbf{n}}$ is the outward unit normal. When S is not a closed surface, it must be decided which of the two possible directions the unit normal $\hat{\mathbf{n}}$ is to take, normal to the top surface or bottom surface. This is done by defining the direction of $\hat{\mathbf{n}}$ with respect to the orientation of the surface boundary, the closed curve bounding the surface. Since $\hat{\mathbf{n}}$ will be continuous, we can define $\hat{\mathbf{n}}$ at a point on the boundary of S and then determine $\hat{\mathbf{n}}$ at other points by letting it vary continuously over S. First consider the planar surface shown in Fig. 1.38. The orientation of the boundary l is considered to be positive in the counterclockwise direction. $\hat{\mathbf{t}}$ is defined as a unit vector perpendicular to the boundary, directed inward from the boundary, and tangent to S. $\hat{\boldsymbol{\tau}}$ is defined as a unit vector tangent to the boundary l of S and directed in the positive direction along the boundary. Then, at that point, $\hat{\mathbf{n}}$ is defined as

$$\hat{\mathbf{n}} = \hat{\boldsymbol{\tau}} \times \hat{\mathbf{t}}$$

Note that $\hat{\mathbf{n}}$ changes sign if we change the orientation (direction of $\hat{\boldsymbol{\tau}}$) of the boundary l. The orientation of the surface with respect to its boundary follows the right-hand rule: if the fingers of the right hand curl in the direction of $\hat{\boldsymbol{\tau}}$, the thumb is in the direction of $\hat{\mathbf{n}}$. Figure 1.38*b* shows the definition of $\hat{\mathbf{n}}$ for a more general surface.

Before we consider the surface integral $\int_S \mathbf{A} \cdot d\mathbf{S}$, it is necessary to discuss vector surfaces. The differential vector surface for the surface element shown in Fig. 1.38*b* is $d\mathbf{S} = \hat{\mathbf{n}}\, dS$. The unit vector $\hat{\mathbf{n}}$ is normal to the top surface, in accordance with the definition of $\hat{\mathbf{n}}$. The total vector surface is defined as

$$\mathbf{S} = \int_S d\mathbf{S} \tag{1.52}$$

Note that $\mathbf{S}$ can represent an infinite number of surfaces (see Prob. 1.8-4); when S is closed, $\mathbf{S}$, of course, is zero. When S is a planar surface, then $\mathbf{S} = S\hat{\mathbf{n}}$, where S is the surface area and $\hat{\mathbf{n}}$ is perpendicular to the planar surface.

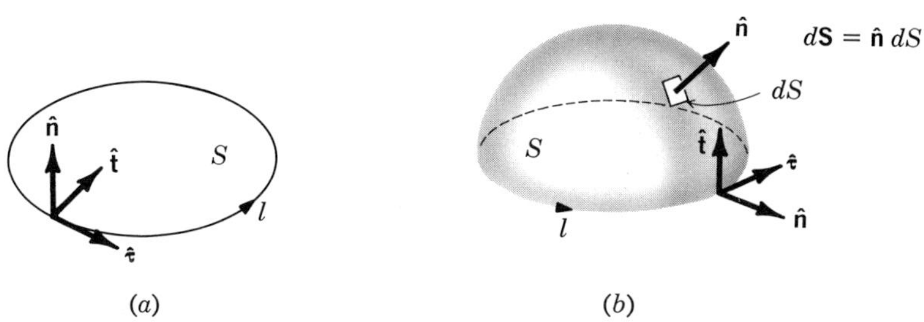

Fig. 1.38 Definition of $\hat{\mathbf{n}}$ and the differential vector surface $d\mathbf{S}$.

With the definition of $d\mathbf{S}$, the evaluation of $\int_S \mathbf{A} \cdot d\mathbf{S}$ is a straightforward surface integral. The notation $\oint_S \mathbf{A} \cdot d\mathbf{S}$ is used to denote that S is a closed surface.

Example 1.8 Evaluation of a surface integral Suppose $\mathbf{A} = (x - 1)\hat{\mathbf{x}} + xy\hat{\mathbf{z}}$, and we wish to evaluate $\int_S \mathbf{A} \cdot d\mathbf{S}$, where S is the surface consisting of the two surfaces in the $x = 1$ and $z = 1$ planes shown in Fig. 1.39. The integral can be written as the sum of two terms,

$$\int_S \mathbf{A} \cdot d\mathbf{S} = \int_{S_1} \mathbf{A} \cdot d\mathbf{S} + \int_{S_2} \mathbf{A} \cdot d\mathbf{S}$$

where S_1 is the surface in the $z = 1$ plane and S_2 is the surface in the $x = 1$ plane. On S_1, $z = 1$ and $d\mathbf{S} = dx\, dy\, \hat{\mathbf{z}}$. On S_2, $x = 1$ and $d\mathbf{S} = dy\, dz\, \hat{\mathbf{x}}$. Hence

$$\int_S \mathbf{A} \cdot d\mathbf{S} = \iint_0^1 [(x-1)\hat{\mathbf{x}} + xy\hat{\mathbf{z}}]_{z=1} \cdot dx\, dy\, \hat{\mathbf{z}} + \iint_0^1 [(x-1)\hat{\mathbf{x}} + xy\hat{\mathbf{z}}]_{x=1} \cdot dy\, dz\, \hat{\mathbf{x}}$$
$$= \tfrac{1}{4}$$

It is very important to remember to evaluate the integrand on the surface. Note that the second term on the right is zero, because the x component of $\mathbf{A}$ is zero on the surface S_2.

Example 1.9 Vector surface integration Consider the two adjoining surfaces occupying the $x = 1$ and $z = 1$ planes as shown in Fig. 1.39. The differential surface element on the $z = 1$ plane is $d\mathbf{S} = dx\, dy\, \hat{\mathbf{z}}$, and the total surface is obviously

$$\mathbf{S}_1 = \int_{S_1} d\mathbf{S} = \iint_0^1 dx\, dy\, \hat{\mathbf{z}} = 1\hat{\mathbf{z}}$$

Similarly, the surface occupying the xy plane may be shown to be

$$\mathbf{S}_2 = 1\hat{\mathbf{x}}$$

and the total surface is simply

$$\mathbf{S} = \hat{\mathbf{x}} + \hat{\mathbf{z}}$$

as shown in Fig. 1.39. The magnitude of the vector surface $\mathbf{S}$ is $\sqrt{2}$, not simply the sum of the magnitudes of the two component vector surfaces $\mathbf{S}_1$ and

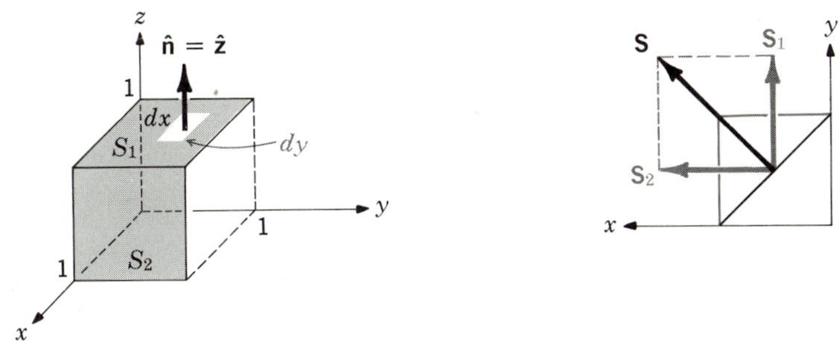

Fig. 1.39 Addition of vector surfaces.

$\mathbf{S}_2$ $(1 + 1 = 2)$. Vector surfaces must be added like any other vector, and not scalarly. The resultant total surface is the surface $\mathbf{S}$ shown in Fig. 1.39, which is the projection of $\mathbf{S}_1$ and $\mathbf{S}_2$ along the direction of $\mathbf{S}$.

VOLUME INTEGRALS

Since a vector differential volume is not defined, the volume integrals involving vectors are no different from scalar volume integrals, except that the variable unit vectors must be treated as variables of integration. Here again, expressing the variable base vectors in terms of $\hat{\mathbf{x}}$, $\hat{\mathbf{y}}$, and $\hat{\mathbf{z}}$ is a good way to take care of them.

1.9 GRADIENT

In addition to general vector differentiation, which was discussed in Sec. 1.7, there are some special vector operations involving differentiation which are very important. One of these is the gradient of a scalar point function.

By definition, the *gradient of a scalar point function* Φ is a vector (1) whose direction is the direction of maximum rate of change of the function Φ, and (2) whose magnitude is the magnitude of the maximum rate of change. An expression for the gradient can be obtained by starting with the directional derivative. The directional derivative of the scalar point function $\Phi(x,y,z)$ is

$$\frac{\partial \Phi}{\partial n} = \frac{\partial \Phi}{\partial x}\cos\alpha + \frac{\partial \Phi}{\partial y}\cos\beta + \frac{\partial \Phi}{\partial z}\cos\gamma \tag{1.53}$$

where $\cos\alpha$, $\cos\beta$, and $\cos\gamma$ are the direction cosines of the direction n; that is,

$$\cos\alpha = \hat{\mathbf{x}} \cdot \hat{\mathbf{n}} \tag{1.54}$$

$$\cos\beta = \hat{\mathbf{y}} \cdot \hat{\mathbf{n}} \tag{1.55}$$

$$\cos\gamma = \hat{\mathbf{z}} \cdot \hat{\mathbf{n}} \tag{1.56}$$

The vector $\hat{\mathbf{n}}$ is a unit vector in the direction the directional derivative is taken. Equation (1.53) may also be written as

$$\frac{\partial \Phi}{\partial n} = \left(\frac{\partial \Phi}{\partial x}\,\hat{\mathbf{x}} + \frac{\partial \Phi}{\partial y}\,\hat{\mathbf{y}} + \frac{\partial \Phi}{\partial z}\,\hat{\mathbf{z}} \right) \cdot \hat{\mathbf{n}} \tag{1.57}$$

For convenience, let us denote

$$\mathbf{G} = \frac{\partial \Phi}{\partial x}\,\hat{\mathbf{x}} + \frac{\partial \Phi}{\partial y}\,\hat{\mathbf{y}} + \frac{\partial \Phi}{\partial z}\,\hat{\mathbf{z}} \tag{1.58}$$

so that

$$\frac{\partial \Phi}{\partial n} = \mathbf{G} \cdot \hat{\mathbf{n}} = G \cos \theta \tag{1.59}$$

where θ is the angle between $\mathbf{G}$ and $\hat{\mathbf{n}}$. From Eq. (1.59) we see that $\partial\Phi/\partial n$ is a maximum when θ is zero, that is, where $\hat{\mathbf{n}}$ is in the direction of $\mathbf{G}$. Since $\hat{\mathbf{n}}$ is a unit vector, the maximum value of $\partial\Phi/\partial n$ is G. Thus the direction of $\mathbf{G}$ is the direction of maximum rate of change of Φ, and the magnitude of $\mathbf{G}$ is the maximum rate of change of Φ, and hence, by definition, $\mathbf{G}$ is the gradient of Φ. Therefore

$$\textbf{grad}\ \Phi = \frac{\partial \Phi}{\partial x}\,\hat{\mathbf{x}} + \frac{\partial \Phi}{\partial y}\,\hat{\mathbf{y}} + \frac{\partial \Phi}{\partial z}\,\hat{\mathbf{z}} \tag{1.60}$$

It has become standard practice to define an operator called *del* in rectangular coordinates by the expression

$$\boldsymbol{\nabla} = \hat{\mathbf{x}}\,\frac{\partial}{\partial x} + \hat{\mathbf{y}}\,\frac{\partial}{\partial y} + \hat{\mathbf{z}}\,\frac{\partial}{\partial z} \tag{1.61}$$

so that

$$\textbf{grad}\ \Phi = \boldsymbol{\nabla}\Phi \tag{1.62}$$

This operator and similar notation may conveniently be used to denote the divergence and curl, which are discussed in the next section.

The discussion thus far has been in terms of a rectangular coordinate system, although the definition of the gradient is independent of any coordinate system. If we had written the directional derivative in terms of a general orthogonal curvilinear coordinate system and followed through in the same way, we would have found that

$$\textbf{grad}\ \Phi = \frac{1}{h_1}\frac{\partial \Phi}{\partial u_1}\,\mathbf{u}_1 + \frac{1}{h_2}\frac{\partial \Phi}{\partial u_2}\,\mathbf{u}_2 + \frac{1}{h_3}\frac{\partial \Phi}{\partial u_3}\,\mathbf{u}_3 \tag{1.63}$$

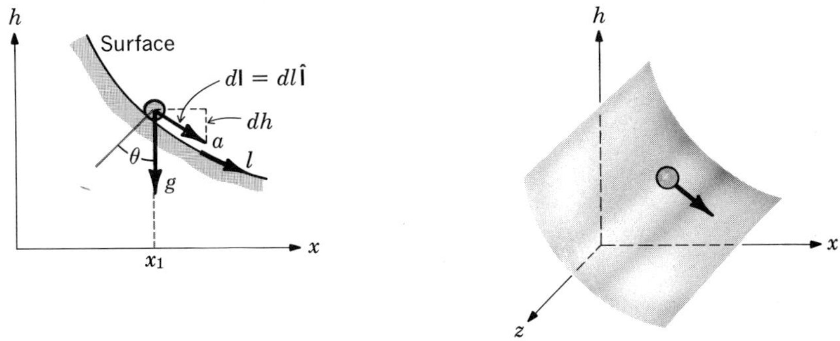

Fig. 1.40 A ball rolling down a sloping surface.

Equation (1.63) is a convenient way to remember the gradient in other coordinate systems because h_1, h_2, and h_3 are easily remembered or easily obtained from the expression for arc length in that coordinate system.

The definition of the $\boldsymbol{\nabla}$ operator given by Eq. (1.61) is strictly a formal one, useful only in the rectangular coordinate system, and *there is no corresponding definition in other coordinate systems.* It has become customary, however, to use $\boldsymbol{\nabla}\Phi$ to mean **grad** Φ in all coordinate systems, even though the operator $\boldsymbol{\nabla}$ may not be defined. In any case, $\boldsymbol{\nabla}\Phi$ means the expression given in Eq. (1.63).

Example 1.10 Use of the gradient in mechanics The gradient of the elevation of a sloping surface determines the acceleration of a ball down the sloping surface. Consider the surface shown in Fig. 1.40, which has no z variation. The scalar elevation function h changes most rapidly along the line l which lies in the xh plane; thus the gradient of h is, by definition, **grad** $h = (dh/dl)\hat{\mathbf{l}}$. The acceleration of the ball at the point x_1 is equal to the component of gravity g along the l, or $\mathbf{a} = g \sin \theta \hat{\mathbf{l}}$. But since $\sin \theta = dh/dl$, the acceleration is $\mathbf{a} = g$ **grad** h.

Example 1.11 The gradient in spherical coordinates If we use Eq. (1.63) as the defining equation for $\boldsymbol{\nabla}\Phi$ in spherical coordinates, together with the expressions $u_1 = r$, $u_2 = \theta$, and $u_3 = \varphi$ and the h values from Table 1.1, we obtain

$$\boldsymbol{\nabla}\Phi = \frac{\partial \Phi}{\partial r}\hat{\mathbf{r}} + \frac{1}{r}\frac{\partial \Phi}{\partial \theta}\hat{\boldsymbol{\theta}} + \frac{1}{r \sin \theta}\frac{\partial \Phi}{\partial \varphi}\hat{\boldsymbol{\varphi}}$$

1.10 DIVERGENCE

The concept of divergence of a vector field is very important with respect to understanding the sources of vector fields. If a closed surface S surrounds a source for the vector field $\mathbf{A}$, then field, or "flux," lines will pass

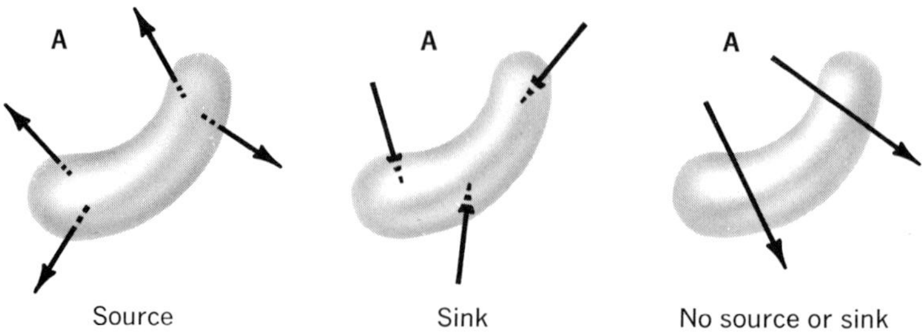

Fig. 1.41 Illustration of flux lines and sources and sinks.

out through the surface, as shown in Fig. 1.41. If the closed surface surrounds a sink, field lines will flow into the surface. It is useful to consider the fluid analog, where the vector field lines describe fluid flow.

The strength or magnitude of the source is given by the net flow through the surface S. The flow of $\mathbf{A}$ through a differential surface $d\mathbf{S}$ is illustrated in Fig. 1.42. If $\mathbf{A}$ represents a flux density, then the total flux passing through $d\mathbf{S}$ is $A_{\|}\, dS$, since $A_{\perp}$ denotes flow parallel to, and therefore not across, the surface. But $A_{\|}\, dS$ is simply $\mathbf{A} \cdot d\mathbf{S}$; thus the incremental flux is $\mathbf{A} \cdot d\mathbf{S}$, and the total flux through the closed surface S is $\oint_S \mathbf{A} \cdot d\mathbf{S}$. If $\oint_S \mathbf{A} \cdot d\mathbf{S}$ is positive, S encloses a source; if $\oint_S \mathbf{A} \cdot d\mathbf{S}$ is negative, S encloses a sink; if $\oint_S \mathbf{A} \cdot d\mathbf{S}$ is zero, S encloses no source or sink of $\mathbf{A}$. The total flux per unit volume is

$$\frac{\oint_S \mathbf{A} \cdot d\mathbf{S}}{V}$$

where V is the volume enclosed by the surface S. This quantity is a measure of the source density within V and is very useful when V is reduced to a differential volume. Then a point relation is obtained giving the source density per unit volume at that point. Since the source density will, in general, vary from point to point, a scalar field function is generated which gives the source density for $\mathbf{A}$ at any point. This scalar field function is called the *divergence of* $\mathbf{A}$.

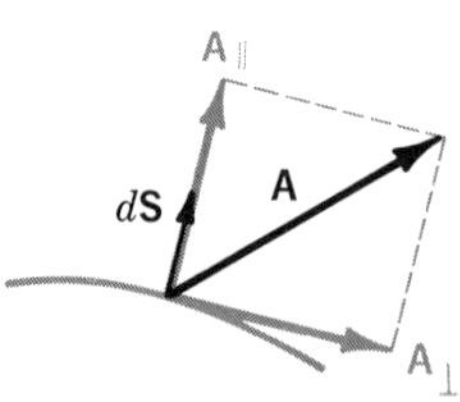

Fig. 1.42 Illustration of flow of $\mathbf{A}$ through a differential surface dS.

The fundamental definition of the divergence of a vector field **A** at a given point is

$$\operatorname{div} \mathbf{A} = \lim_{V \to 0} \frac{\oint_S \mathbf{A} \cdot d\mathbf{S}}{V} \tag{1.64}$$

where S is a closed surface surrounding the point and V is the volume enclosed by S. The divergence of **A** is a scalar, as is evident from the definition, which incidentally, is independent of any coordinate system. Although we could evaluate Eq. (1.64) in terms of general orthogonal curvilinear coordinates, for simplicity we shall derive the expression for div **A** in rectangular coordinates and simply state the expression in curvilinear coordinates.

The surface of the differential cube shown in Fig. 1.43 is S, and the point (x_0,y_0,z_0) in the center of the cube is the point at which the divergence is to be evaluated. The surface integral can be written as

$$\oint_S \mathbf{A} \cdot d\mathbf{S} = \int_{\text{front}} \mathbf{A} \cdot d\mathbf{S} + \int_{\text{back}} \mathbf{A} \cdot d\mathbf{S} + \int_{\text{left}} \mathbf{A} \cdot d\mathbf{S} + \int_{\text{right}} \mathbf{A} \cdot d\mathbf{S} + \int_{\text{top}} \mathbf{A} \cdot d\mathbf{S} + \int_{\text{bottom}} \mathbf{A} \cdot d\mathbf{S} \tag{1.65}$$

Since we intend to take the limit, it is convenient to expand **A** in a three-dimensional Taylor series about (x_0,y_0,z_0) in evaluating the terms in Eq. (1.65). The series expansion for **A** is

$$\mathbf{A}(x,y,z) = \mathbf{A}(x_0,y_0,z_0) + (x - x_0) \left.\frac{\partial \mathbf{A}}{\partial x}\right|_{(x_0,y_0,z_0)} + (y - y_0) \left.\frac{\partial \mathbf{A}}{\partial y}\right|_{(x_0,y_0,z_0)} + (z - z_0) \left.\frac{\partial \mathbf{A}}{\partial z}\right|_{(x_0,y_0,z_0)} + \text{higher-order terms}$$

Consider the first term $\int_{\text{front}} \mathbf{A} \cdot d\mathbf{S}$. Since $x = x_0 + \Delta x/2$ on the

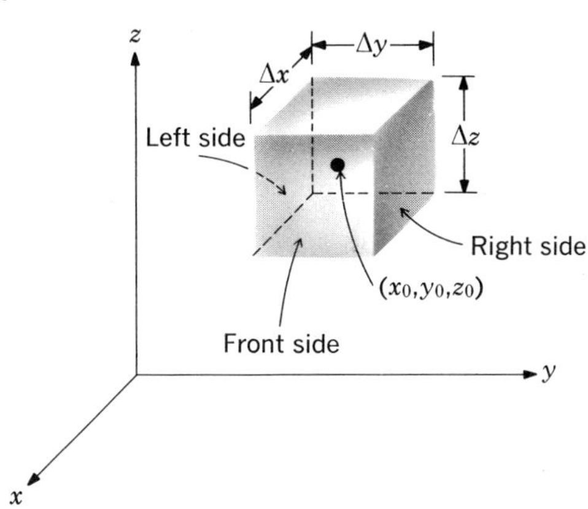

Fig. 1.43 Differential cube used in derivation of divergence.

front surface and $d\mathbf{S} = dy\,dz\,\hat{\mathbf{x}}$,

$$\int_{\text{front}} \mathbf{A} \cdot d\mathbf{S} = \Delta y\,\Delta z \left[A_x(x_0,y_0,z_0) + \frac{\Delta x}{2} \frac{\partial A_x}{\partial x}\bigg|_{(x_0,y_0,z_0)} \right]$$

$$+ \text{ higher-order terms in } \Delta x,\ \Delta y, \text{ and } \Delta z$$

On the back surface, $d\mathbf{S} = dy\,dz\,(-\hat{\mathbf{x}})$ and

$$\int_{\text{back}} \mathbf{A} \cdot d\mathbf{S} = \Delta y\,\Delta z \left[-A_x(x_0,y_0,z_0) - \frac{\Delta x}{2} \frac{-\partial A_x}{\partial x}\bigg|_{(x_0,y_0,z_0)} \right]$$

$$+ \text{ higher-order terms in } \Delta x,\ \Delta y, \text{ and } \Delta z$$

Therefore

$$\int_{\text{front}} \mathbf{A} \cdot d\mathbf{S} + \int_{\text{back}} \mathbf{A} \cdot d\mathbf{S} = \Delta x\,\Delta y\,\Delta z \frac{\partial A_x}{\partial x}\bigg|_{(x_0,y_0,z_0)}$$

$$+ \text{ higher-order terms in } \Delta x,\ \Delta y, \text{ and } \Delta z$$

Similarly, it is found that

$$\int_{\substack{\text{left}\\\text{side}}} \mathbf{A} \cdot d\mathbf{S} + \int_{\substack{\text{right}\\\text{side}}} \mathbf{A} \cdot d\mathbf{S} = \Delta x\,\Delta y\,\Delta z \frac{\partial A_y}{\partial y}\bigg|_{(x_0,y_0,z_0)}$$

$$+ \text{ higher-order terms in } \Delta x,\ \Delta y, \text{ and } \Delta z$$

and

$$\int_{\text{top}} \mathbf{A} \cdot d\mathbf{S} + \int_{\text{bottom}} \mathbf{A} \cdot d\mathbf{S} = \Delta x\,\Delta y\,\Delta z \frac{\partial A_z}{\partial z}\bigg|_{(x_0,y_0,z_0)}$$

$$+ \text{ higher-order terms in } \Delta x,\ \Delta y, \text{ and } \Delta z$$

Since $V = \Delta x\,\Delta y\,\Delta z$,

$$\lim_{V\to 0} \frac{\oint_S \mathbf{A} \cdot d\mathbf{S}}{V} = \left(\frac{\partial A_x}{\partial x} + \frac{\partial A_y}{\partial y} + \frac{\partial A_z}{\partial z} \right)_{(x_0,y_0,z_0)}$$

because

$$\lim_{\Delta x \Delta y \Delta z \to 0} \frac{\text{higher-order terms}}{\Delta x\,\Delta y\,\Delta z} = 0$$

Therefore div **A** at a given point is

$$\operatorname{div} \mathbf{A} = \frac{\partial A_x}{\partial x} + \frac{\partial A_y}{\partial y} + \frac{\partial A_z}{\partial z} \tag{1.66}$$

where the partial derivatives are evaluated at that point. It should be apparent that div **A** is a point relation; i.e., it is a scalar point function.

Although the expression in Eq. (1.66) provides a convenient method for finding div **A**, we should keep in mind the fundamental definition and the resulting physical significance of the divergence operation.

Evaluating Eq. (1.64) in terms of curvilinear coordinates results in

$$\operatorname{div} \mathbf{A} = \frac{1}{h_1 h_2 h_3}\left[\frac{\partial}{\partial u_1}(h_2 h_3 A_1) + \frac{\partial}{\partial u_2}(h_3 h_1 A_2) + \frac{\partial}{\partial u_3}(h_1 h_2 A_3)\right] \tag{1.67}$$

For the special case of rectangular coordinates,

$$\operatorname{div} \mathbf{A} = \nabla \cdot \mathbf{A} \tag{1.68}$$

where the ∇ operator is defined by Eq. (1.63) and the dot product is formed in the obvious way. Here again, a ∇ operator cannot be defined in the other coordinate systems where h_1, h_2, or h_3 are functions of u_1, u_2, or u_3, as is apparent from inspection of Eq. (1.63), but it is customary to let $\nabla \cdot \mathbf{A}$ mean div **A** in all coordinate systems.

1.11 CURL

In the previous section the differential field flux passing through a surface $d\mathbf{S}$ was defined as $d(\text{flux}) = \mathbf{A} \cdot d\mathbf{S}$. The divergence of the vector **A** was then developed as a measure of the source of flux density characteristic of the field. A second very important property of a field is its circulation. Anyone who has watched water drain out of a bathtub or sink has noticed the circulation of the water around the drain. Since circulation behavior of a field may be present where div $\mathbf{A} = 0$, we need another mechanism for describing the circulating properties of the field. For a perfectly symmetrical circulating fluid with angular velocity ω, a measure of the circulation may be defined as circulation = angular velocity $\times$ circumference. We can extend this concept of circulation to any vector field **A** which may not physically move by defining a differential circulation as

$$d(\text{circulation}) = \mathbf{A} \cdot d\mathbf{l}$$

Note that the differential circulation is the component of the vector **A** along **l** times dl. The total or net circulation about any arbitrary closed loop l is then

$$\text{Net circulation} = \oint_l \mathbf{A} \cdot d\mathbf{l}$$

Consider the general field **A** and closed loop l which bounds an open surface S. The net circulation per unit surface area is

$$\frac{\oint_l \mathbf{A} \cdot d\mathbf{l}}{S}$$

It is convenient to assign a direction to the net circulation per unit area. This direction is chosen to be that of the vector surface $\mathbf{S} = S\hat{\mathbf{S}}$, as shown in Fig. 1.38. S is the magnitude of the vector surface $\mathbf{S}$ and $\hat{\mathbf{S}}$ is a unit vector in the direction of $\mathbf{S}$ (see Sec. 1.8).

An important function called the *curl of a vector* is defined in terms of the limit as S approaches zero of the *maximum* net circulation of the vector. Suppose $\mathbf{S}$ is an *arbitrary surface* at a given point. The limit of the net circulation as S approaches zero is called $\mathbf{C}$,

$$\mathbf{C} = \lim_{S\to 0} \frac{\oint_l \mathbf{A} \cdot d\mathbf{l}}{S} \hat{\mathbf{S}} \tag{1.69}$$

Then **curl A** is a vector point function defined as the maximum of the vector $\mathbf{C}$ as $\hat{\mathbf{S}}$ is varied through all possible directions.

As with the divergence, the expression given in Eq. (1.69) can be evaluated at a general point in a given coordinate system to obtain a much more convenient expression in terms of partial derivatives. Then **curl A** can be found from this expression by finding its maximum value. This derivation is carried out in Sec. 1.12, where it is shown that

$$\textbf{curl A} = \left(\frac{\partial A_z}{\partial y} - \frac{\partial A_y}{\partial z}\right)\hat{\mathbf{x}} + \left(\frac{\partial A_x}{\partial z} - \frac{\partial A_z}{\partial x}\right)\hat{\mathbf{y}} + \left(\frac{\partial A_y}{\partial x} - \frac{\partial A_x}{\partial y}\right)\hat{\mathbf{z}} \tag{1.70}$$

in rectangular coordinates.

Although Eq. (1.70) is very convenient for calculating the curl of the vector $\mathbf{A}$, it is not convenient for physical interpretation of the curl. The physical interpretation of the curl is clear from the definition; the curl of a vector at a given point is the maximum net circulation per unit area of the vector at that point. This physical interpretation is illustrated in Example 1.12.

A convenient method for remembering Eq. (1.70) is the determinant form

$$\textbf{curl A} = \begin{vmatrix} \hat{\mathbf{x}} & \hat{\mathbf{y}} & \hat{\mathbf{z}} \\ \dfrac{\partial}{\partial x} & \dfrac{\partial}{\partial y} & \dfrac{\partial}{\partial z} \\ A_x & A_y & A_z \end{vmatrix} \tag{1.71}$$

where the partial-derivative operators operate only on the terms in the bottom row.

Comparison of Eq. (1.71) with Eq. (1.18) shows that in rectangular coordinates the curl can be written as

$$\textbf{curl A} = \nabla \times \mathbf{A} \tag{1.72}$$

Cylindrical:

$$\nabla \times A = \left(\frac{1}{r}\frac{\partial A_z}{\partial \phi} - \frac{\partial A_\phi}{\partial z}\right)\hat{r} + \left(\frac{\partial A_r}{\partial z} - \frac{\partial A_z}{\partial r}\right)\hat{\phi} + \frac{1}{r}\left(\frac{\partial}{\partial r}(r A_\phi) - \frac{\partial A_r}{\partial \phi}\right)\hat{z}$$

where ∇ is defined by Eq. (1.61) and the cross product is evaluated in the usual way.

In curvilinear coordinates, the curl is given by the expression

$$\text{curl } \mathbf{A} = \frac{1}{h_1 h_2 h_3} \begin{vmatrix} h_1\hat{\mathbf{u}}_1 & h_2\hat{\mathbf{u}}_2 & h_3\hat{\mathbf{u}}_3 \\ \dfrac{\partial}{\partial u_1} & \dfrac{\partial}{\partial u_2} & \dfrac{\partial}{\partial u_3} \\ h_1 A_1 & h_2 A_2 & h_3 A_3 \end{vmatrix} \tag{1.73}$$

and, as in the case of the divergence, a meaningful ∇ cannot be defined when h_1, h_2, and h_3 are functions of u_1, u_2, or u_3. However, once again, it is customary to interpret $\nabla \times \mathbf{A}$ in general as meaning the expression given in Eq. (1.73).

Example 1.12 Net circulation of a fluid in shear motion A simple example will help us see through the mathematics and arrive at a physical interpretation for the curl of a vector field. Consider the velocity field on the surface of water. Suppose the velocity on the surface is given by

$$\mathbf{v} = x\hat{\mathbf{y}} \tag{1.74}$$

which is graphically represented in Fig. 1.44. The density of the field lines indicates the relative magnitude of the field (see Sec. 1.3). We can easily see that there is a net circulation $\oint_l \mathbf{v} \cdot d\mathbf{l}$ around the path indicated in Fig. 1.44, because the field is stronger on side a than it is on side c, and there is no contribution to the line integral on sides b and d. In fact, Eq. (1.69) can quite easily be evaluated for this simple case. If side a is at $x + \Delta x/2$, side c at $x - \Delta x/2$, side d at $y - \Delta y/2$, and side b at $y + \Delta y/2$, then

$$\oint_l \mathbf{v} \cdot d\mathbf{l} = \left(x + \frac{\Delta x}{2}\right)\Delta y - \left(x - \frac{\Delta x}{2}\right)\Delta y$$
$$= \Delta x\, \Delta y$$

since $\mathbf{v}$ does not vary with y. Also, $S = \Delta x\, \Delta y$, and for the orientation of the boundary shown, $\hat{\mathbf{S}} = \hat{\mathbf{z}}$. Therefore, from the definition of Eq. (1.60), $\mathbf{C} = \hat{\mathbf{z}}$.

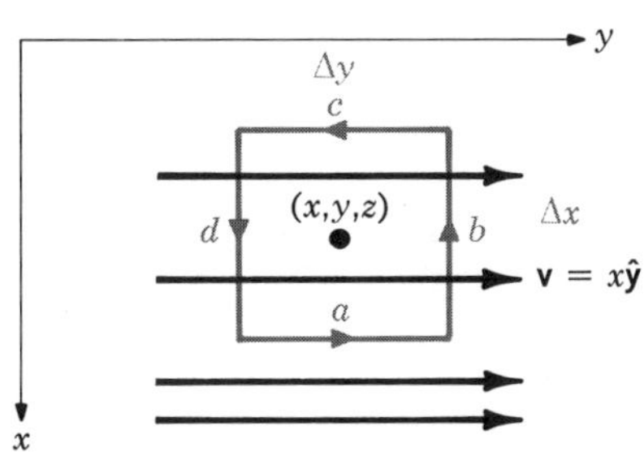

Fig. 1.44 Representation of the velocity field on a water surface.

Spherical:

$$\nabla \times \mathbf{A} = \frac{1}{r\sin\theta}\left[\frac{\partial}{\partial\theta}(A_\phi \sin\theta) - \frac{\partial A_\theta}{\partial\phi}\right]\hat{r} + \frac{1}{r}\left[\frac{1}{\sin\theta}\frac{\partial A_r}{\partial\phi} - \frac{\partial(rA_\phi)}{\partial r}\right]\hat{\theta} + \frac{1}{r}\left[\frac{\partial(rA_\theta)}{\partial r} - \frac{\partial A_r}{\partial\theta}\right]\hat{\phi}$$

It is not so easy to see that this is the maximum **C** that can be obtained by trying different values of $\hat{\mathbf{S}}$, but a little thought indicates this is so. Hence

$$\nabla \times \mathbf{v} = \hat{\mathbf{z}}$$

which, of course, is the same result as that obtained by using Eq. (1.70). Now, suppose we place an infinitesimal wood chip at the point on the surface of the water where we have just evaluated the curl. Since the velocity of the water is greater at a than it is at c, the chip would tend to rotate counterclockwise, indicating the *curl*, or net circulation of the velocity, at that point. Because of our definitions, the vector direction of the curl is perpendicular to the plane containing the net circulation.

★1.12 Derivation of an Expression for the Curl of a Vector

In this section we derive an expression for the curl of a vector, starting from the definition given with Eq. (1.69). For simplicity, the derivation is carried out in a rectangular coordinate system. The procedure is to evaluate the circulation at the point (x_0,y_0,z_0) in terms of the Taylor series expansion of **A** about that point, evaluate the net circulation, take the limit, and find the maximum value. The series expansion is used because it is convenient in the limit-taking process. The vector surface **S** is described in terms of two unit vectors $\hat{\mathbf{u}}$ and $\hat{\mathbf{v}}$ and variables u and v measured from the point (x_0,y_0,z_0) in the directions of $\hat{\mathbf{u}}$ and $\hat{\mathbf{v}}$, respectively. These unit vectors can be in any direction subject to the restriction that $\hat{\mathbf{u}} \cdot \hat{\mathbf{v}} = 0$; that is, they are perpendicular. The directions of $\hat{\mathbf{u}}$ and $\hat{\mathbf{v}}$ are unspecified, because **S** must be allowed to take on all possible directions if **curl A** is to be evaluated. Since the limit as S approaches zero is to be taken, the boundary of S is not critical. It could be rectangular, cylindrical, or arbitrary. For simplicity, it is chosen to be rectangular.

The coordinate system and one orientation of **S** are illustrated in Fig. 1.45. As indicated, the unit vector $\hat{\mathbf{S}}$ is $\hat{\mathbf{S}} = \hat{\mathbf{u}} \times \hat{\mathbf{v}}$, and $S = \Delta u \, \Delta v$. In preparation for writing **A** in a Taylor series expansion, a relation between x, y, and z and u and v is needed. This can be obtained by referring to Fig. 1.45*b*. Any point (x,y,z) which is on the surface S can be located by the vector $\mathbf{r}_0 + u\hat{\mathbf{u}} + v\hat{\mathbf{v}}$, where $\mathbf{r}_0 = x_0\hat{\mathbf{x}} + y_0\hat{\mathbf{y}} + z_0\hat{\mathbf{z}}$. In addition, the point can be located by $\mathbf{r} = x\hat{\mathbf{x}} + y\hat{\mathbf{y}} + z\hat{\mathbf{z}}$. Therefore, as indicated in Fig. 1.45*b*,

$$\mathbf{r} = \mathbf{r}_0 + u\hat{\mathbf{u}} + v\hat{\mathbf{v}}$$

$$\mathbf{r} - \mathbf{r}_0 = u\hat{\mathbf{u}} + v\hat{\mathbf{v}}$$

and

$$(x - x_0)\hat{\mathbf{x}} + (y - y_0)\hat{\mathbf{y}} + (z - z_0)\hat{\mathbf{z}} = u\hat{\mathbf{u}} + v\hat{\mathbf{v}} \tag{1.75}$$

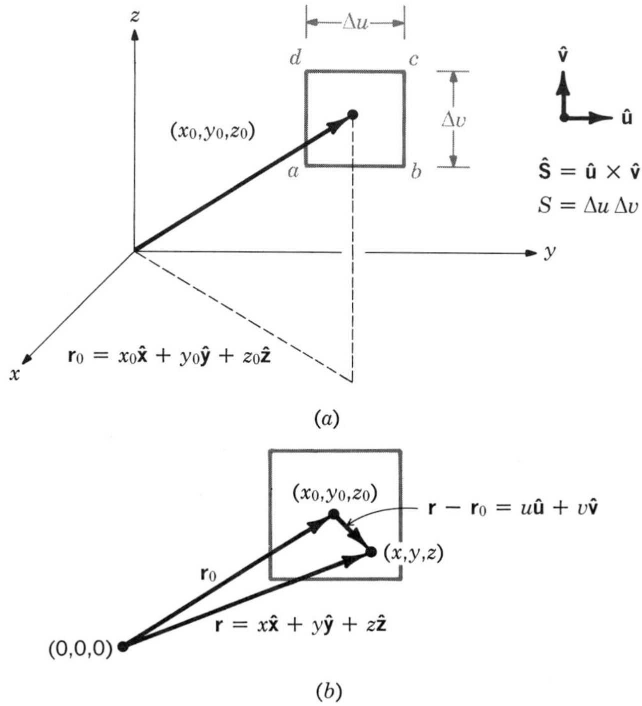

Fig. 1.45 (*a*) Illustration of the coordinate system and the surface used in the derivation of the curl; (*b*) illustration of the relation between x, y, z and u, v.

Furthermore, $\hat{\mathbf{u}}$ and $\hat{\mathbf{v}}$ can be expressed in terms of $\hat{\mathbf{x}}$, $\hat{\mathbf{y}}$, and $\hat{\mathbf{z}}$,

$$\hat{\mathbf{u}} = a_1\hat{\mathbf{x}} + a_2\hat{\mathbf{y}} + a_3\hat{\mathbf{z}} \tag{1.76}$$

$$\hat{\mathbf{v}} = b_1\hat{\mathbf{x}} + b_2\hat{\mathbf{y}} + b_3\hat{\mathbf{z}} \tag{1.77}$$

In rectangular coordinates, the a's and b's are constants (independent of x, y, and z) which depend on the directions of $\hat{\mathbf{u}}$ and $\hat{\mathbf{v}}$ (if $\hat{\mathbf{u}}$ and $\hat{\mathbf{v}}$ were written in terms of $\hat{\mathbf{r}}$, $\hat{\boldsymbol{\varphi}}$, and $\hat{\mathbf{z}}$, some of the a's and b's would depend on φ). From Eqs. (1.76) and (1.77) the following relations can be obtained:

$$a_1 = \hat{\mathbf{x}} \cdot \hat{\mathbf{u}} \tag{1.78}$$

$$a_2 = \hat{\mathbf{y}} \cdot \hat{\mathbf{u}} \tag{1.79}$$

$$a_3 = \hat{\mathbf{z}} \cdot \hat{\mathbf{u}} \tag{1.80}$$

$$b_1 = \hat{\mathbf{x}} \cdot \hat{\mathbf{v}} \tag{1.81}$$

$$b_2 = \hat{\mathbf{y}} \cdot \hat{\mathbf{v}} \tag{1.82}$$

$$b_3 = \hat{\mathbf{z}} \cdot \hat{\mathbf{v}} \tag{1.83}$$

Now the transformation from x, y, and z to u and v can be obtained by taking in turn the dot product of $\hat{\mathbf{x}}$, $\hat{\mathbf{y}}$, and $\hat{\mathbf{z}}$ with Eq. (1.75) and then using Eqs. (1.78) to (1.83). The results are

$$x = x_0 + a_1 u + b_1 v \tag{1.84}$$

$$y = y_0 + a_2 u + b_2 v \tag{1.85}$$

$$z = z_0 + a_3 u + b_3 v \tag{1.86}$$

With this transformation, it is clear that for any point (x,y,z) on S, $\mathbf{A}(x,y,z)$ can be written as a function of u and v, that is, $\mathbf{A}(u,v)$.

Thus on S, $\mathbf{A}(x,y,z)$ can be written as the Taylor series

$$\mathbf{A}(u,v) = \mathbf{A}(x_0,y_0,z_0) + u \left.\frac{\partial \mathbf{A}}{\partial u}\right|_{(x_0,y_0,z_0)} + v \left.\frac{\partial \mathbf{A}}{\partial v}\right|_{(x_0,y_0,z_0)} + \text{higher-order terms}$$

The circulation of $\mathbf{A}$ is

$$\oint_l \mathbf{A}\cdot d\mathbf{l} = \int_a^b A_u\,du + \int_b^c A_v\,dv + \int_c^d A_u\,du + \int_d^a A_v\,dv$$

since $d\mathbf{l} = du\,\hat{\mathbf{u}} + dv\,\hat{\mathbf{v}}$ [see Eq. (1.50)]. The series expansion results in

$$\begin{aligned}\int_a^b A_u\,du &= \int_{-\Delta u/2}^{\Delta u/2} A_u\,du + \frac{\partial A_u}{\partial u}\int_{-\Delta u/2}^{\Delta u/2} u\,du + \frac{\partial A_u}{\partial v}\int_{-\Delta u/2}^{\Delta u/2} \frac{-\Delta v}{2}\,du \\ &\qquad + \text{higher-order terms} \\ &= \Delta u\,A_u + 0 - \frac{\Delta v}{2}\frac{\partial A_u}{\partial u}\Delta u + \text{higher-order terms} \\ &= \left(A_u - \frac{\Delta v}{2}\frac{\partial A_u}{\partial v}\right)\Delta u + \text{higher-order terms}\end{aligned}$$

where it is understood that A_u and $\partial A_u/\partial v$ are evaluated at x_0, y_0, and z_0, even though this has not been written explicitly. Note that along the path ab, v has the constant value $-\Delta v/2$.

Similarly,

$$\int_b^c A_v\,dv = \left(A_v + \frac{\Delta u}{2}\frac{\partial A_v}{\partial u}\right)\Delta v + \text{higher-order terms}$$

$$\int_c^d A_u\,du = -\left(A_u + \frac{\Delta v}{2}\frac{\partial A_u}{\partial v}\right)\Delta u + \text{higher-order terms}$$

$$\int_d^a A_v\,dv = -\left(A_v - \frac{\Delta u}{2}\frac{\partial A_v}{\partial u}\right)\Delta v + \text{higher-order terms}$$

and

$$\oint_l \mathbf{A}\cdot d\mathbf{l} = \Delta u\,\Delta v\left(\frac{\partial A_v}{\partial u} - \frac{\partial A_u}{\partial v}\right) + \text{higher-order terms}$$

Since $S = \Delta u \, \Delta v$,

$$\mathbf{C} = \lim_{S\to 0} \oint_l \frac{\mathbf{A}\cdot d\mathbf{l}}{S}\,\hat{\mathbf{S}}$$

$$= \lim_{S\to 0}\left(\frac{\partial A_v}{\partial u} - \frac{\partial A_u}{\partial v} + \frac{\text{higher-order terms}}{\Delta u\,\Delta v}\right)\hat{\mathbf{S}}$$

$$= \left(\frac{\partial A_v}{\partial u} - \frac{\partial A_u}{\partial v}\right)\hat{\mathbf{S}} \tag{1.87}$$

because

$$\lim_{S\to 0}\frac{\text{higher-order terms}}{\Delta u\,\Delta v} = 0$$

The next step is to write **C** in Eq. (1.87) in terms of x, y, and z by making use of the transformation given in Eqs. (1.84) to (1.86). By the chain rule,

$$\frac{\partial}{\partial u} = \frac{\partial x}{\partial u}\frac{\partial}{\partial x} + \frac{\partial y}{\partial u}\frac{\partial}{\partial y} + \frac{\partial z}{\partial u}\frac{\partial}{\partial z}$$

$$\frac{\partial}{\partial v} = \frac{\partial x}{\partial v}\frac{\partial}{\partial x} + \frac{\partial y}{\partial v}\frac{\partial}{\partial y} + \frac{\partial z}{\partial v}\frac{\partial}{\partial z}$$

From Eqs. (1.84) to (1.86),

$$\frac{\partial x}{\partial u} = a_1$$

$$\frac{\partial y}{\partial u} = a_2$$

$$\frac{\partial z}{\partial u} = a_3$$

$$\frac{\partial x}{\partial v} = b_1$$

$$\frac{\partial y}{\partial v} = b_2$$

$$\frac{\partial z}{\partial v} = b_3$$

Therefore

$$\frac{\partial}{\partial u} = a_1\frac{\partial}{\partial x} + a_2\frac{\partial}{\partial y} + a_3\frac{\partial}{\partial z} \tag{1.88}$$

$$\frac{\partial}{\partial u} = b_1\frac{\partial}{\partial x} + b_2\frac{\partial}{\partial y} + b_3\frac{\partial}{\partial z} \tag{1.89}$$

Also,

$$A_v = \mathbf{A} \cdot \mathbf{v} = A_x\hat{\mathbf{x}} \cdot \mathbf{v} + A_y\hat{\mathbf{y}} \cdot \mathbf{v} + A_z\hat{\mathbf{z}} \cdot \mathbf{v}$$
$$= b_1A_x + b_2A_y + b_3A_z \tag{1.90}$$

and similarly,

$$A_u = a_1A_x + a_2A_y + A_3A_z \tag{1.91}$$

Using Eqs. (1.88) to (1.91) and collecting terms results in

$$\frac{\partial A_v}{\partial u} - \frac{\partial A_u}{\partial v} = (a_1b_2 - a_2b_1)\left(\frac{\partial A_y}{\partial x} - \frac{\partial A_x}{\partial y}\right) + (a_1b_3 - b_1a_3)$$
$$\left(\frac{\partial A_z}{\partial x} - \frac{\partial A_x}{\partial z}\right) + (a_2b_3 - b_2a_3)\left(\frac{\partial A_z}{\partial y} - \frac{\partial A_y}{\partial z}\right) \tag{1.92}$$

From Eqs. (1.76) and (1.77) we find that

$$\hat{\mathbf{u}} \times \hat{\mathbf{v}} = \hat{\mathbf{x}}(a_2b_3 - b_2a_3) + \hat{\mathbf{y}}(a_3b_1 - b_3a_1) + \hat{\mathbf{z}}(a_1b_2 - b_1a_2)$$

Now, by inspection, it can be seen that Eq. (1.92) can be written as

$$\frac{\partial A_v}{\partial u} - \frac{\partial A_u}{\partial v} = \left[\left(\frac{\partial A_z}{\partial y} - \frac{\partial A_y}{\partial z}\right)\hat{\mathbf{x}} + \left(\frac{\partial A_x}{\partial z} - \frac{\partial A_z}{\partial x}\right)\hat{\mathbf{y}}\right.$$
$$\left. + \left(\frac{\partial A_y}{\partial x} - \frac{\partial A_x}{\partial y}\right)\hat{\mathbf{z}}\right] \cdot \hat{\mathbf{u}} \times \hat{\mathbf{v}}$$

Since $\hat{\mathbf{S}} = \hat{\mathbf{u}} \times \hat{\mathbf{v}}$,

$$\frac{\partial A_v}{\partial u} - \frac{\partial A_u}{\partial v} = \mathbf{F} \cdot \hat{\mathbf{S}} \tag{1.93}$$

where $\mathbf{F}$ is defined as

$$\mathbf{F} = \left(\frac{\partial A_z}{\partial y} - \frac{\partial A_y}{\partial z}\right)\hat{\mathbf{x}} + \left(\frac{\partial A_x}{\partial z} - \frac{\partial A_z}{\partial x}\right)\hat{\mathbf{y}} + \left(\frac{\partial A_y}{\partial x} - \frac{\partial A_x}{\partial y}\right)\hat{\mathbf{z}} \tag{1.94}$$

Thus from Eqs. (1.87) and (1.93), $\mathbf{C}$ is

$$\mathbf{C} = \mathbf{F} \cdot \hat{\mathbf{S}}\hat{\mathbf{S}}$$

or

$$\mathbf{C} = F \cos \alpha\, \hat{\mathbf{S}} \tag{1.95}$$

where α is the angle between $\mathbf{F}$ and $\hat{\mathbf{S}}$.

Since the curl of $\mathbf{A}$ is defined as the maximum of $\mathbf{C}$ as the orientation of $\hat{\mathbf{S}}$ is varied through all possible directions, it now remains for us to find the direction of $\hat{\mathbf{S}}$, or equivalently, the angle α for which $\mathbf{C}$ is maximum. It is obvious from Eq. (1.95) that $\mathbf{C}$ is a maximum when $\alpha = 0$, which means that **S** is in the direction of **F**. Then $\hat{\mathbf{S}} = \hat{\mathbf{F}}$, and the maximum **C** is $\mathbf{C}_{\text{max}} = F\hat{\mathbf{F}} = \mathbf{F}$. Thus, by definition, **curl A** = **F**, or, writing out **F**,

$$\textbf{curl A} = \left(\frac{\partial A_z}{\partial y} - \frac{\partial A_y}{\partial z}\right)\hat{\mathbf{x}} + \left(\frac{\partial A_x}{\partial z} - \frac{\partial A_z}{\partial x}\right)\hat{\mathbf{y}} + \left(\frac{\partial A_y}{\partial x} - \frac{\partial A_x}{\partial y}\right)\hat{\mathbf{z}}$$

The expression for the curl in other coordinate systems can be obtained by appropriately transforming Eq. (1.87). Care must be taken, however, because in coordinate systems where the base vectors are not constant ($\hat{\mathbf{r}}$ and $\hat{\boldsymbol{\varphi}}$, for example, are functions of φ), the a's and b's corresponding to those in Eqs. (1.76) and (1.77) would be functions of the ★coordinates.

1.13 THE DIVERGENCE THEOREM (GAUSS'S THEOREM)

The divergence of a vector field is the outflow of flux per unit volume at a given point. It seems reasonable that integrating the divergence over a given volume would yield the total outflow of flux through the surface bounding the volume. This is indeed the case, as stated by the divergence theorem,

$$\int_V \nabla \cdot \mathbf{A}\, dV = \oint_S \mathbf{A} \cdot d\mathbf{S} \tag{1.96}$$

Here V is the volume enclosed by the closed surface S. As pointed out in Sec. 1.5, when S is closed, $d\mathbf{S}$ is defined as pointing away from the volume enclosed. Although we shall not rigorously prove the divergence theorem, it is easy to show how Eq. (1.96) follows from the definition of divergence given as Eq. (1.64). Consider the differential volume illustrated in Fig. 1.46*a*, with the differential surfaces enclosing the differential volume labeled as shown. From Eq. (1.64) we can write

$$\begin{aligned}\nabla \cdot \mathbf{A}\, dV &= \oint \mathbf{A} \cdot d\mathbf{S} \\ &= \mathbf{A} \cdot d\mathbf{S}_1 + \mathbf{A} \cdot d\mathbf{S}_2 + \mathbf{A} \cdot d\mathbf{S}_3 + \mathbf{A} \cdot d\mathbf{S}_4 + \mathbf{A} \cdot d\mathbf{S}_5 \\ &\qquad + \mathbf{A} \cdot d\mathbf{S}_6 \end{aligned} \tag{1.97}$$

assuming that dV is so small that **A** is essentially constant over the differential volume. Now consider two differential volumes, dV_1 and dV_2, as shown in Fig. 1.46*b*. Writing two equations like Eq. (1.97) and adding them results in

$$\begin{aligned}\nabla \cdot \mathbf{A}\, dV_1 + \nabla \cdot \mathbf{A}\, dV_2 &= \mathbf{A} \cdot d\mathbf{S}_{11} + \mathbf{A} \cdot d\mathbf{S}_{12} + \mathbf{A} \cdot d\mathbf{S}_{13} + \mathbf{A} \cdot d\mathbf{S}_{14} \\ &+ \mathbf{A} \cdot d\mathbf{S}_{15} + \mathbf{A} \cdot d\mathbf{S}_{16} + \mathbf{A} \cdot d\mathbf{S}_{21} + \mathbf{A} \cdot d\mathbf{S}_{22} + \mathbf{A} \cdot d\mathbf{S}_{23} \\ &+ \mathbf{A} \cdot d\mathbf{S}_{24} + \mathbf{A} \cdot d\mathbf{S}_{25} + \mathbf{A} \cdot d\mathbf{S}_{26}\end{aligned} \tag{1.98}$$

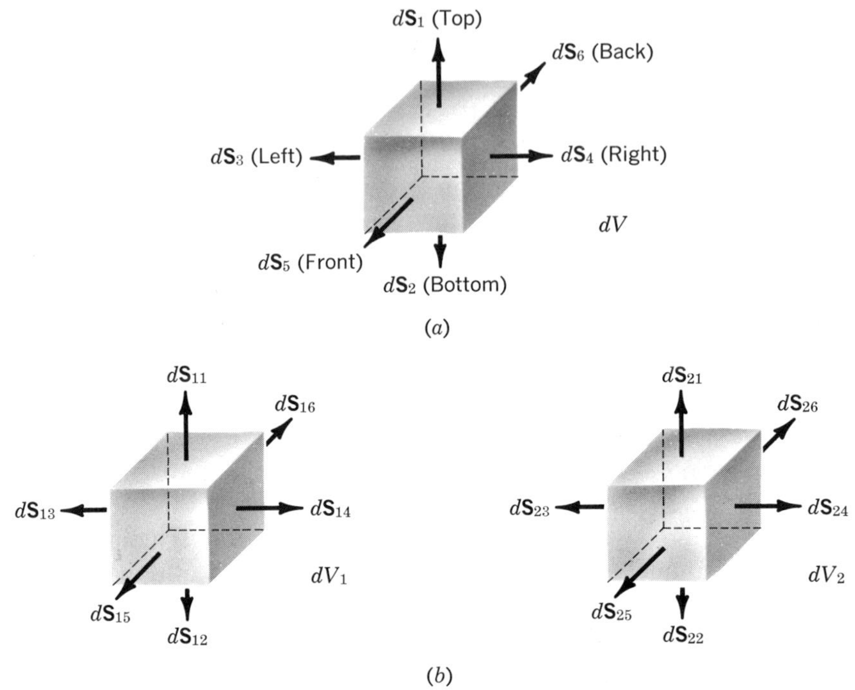

Fig. 1.46 (*a*) A differential volume with the enclosing differential surfaces labeled; (*b*) two differential volumes.

Now suppose that the two differential volumes are placed side by side, so that $d\mathbf{S}_{23} = -d\mathbf{S}_{14}$. Then the two terms on the right-hand side of Eq. (1.98) which contain $d\mathbf{S}_{23}$ and $d\mathbf{S}_{14}$ cancel. The only terms remaining on the right-hand side of Eq. (1.98) are those on the *outer* surfaces of the combined volume $dV_1 + dV_2$. Now suppose a volume V is constructed by placing many differential volumes together. Then an equation like Eq. (1.98) can be written,

$$\nabla \cdot \mathbf{A}\, dV_1 + \nabla \cdot \mathbf{A}\, dV_2 + \nabla \cdot \mathbf{A}\, dV_3 + \cdots = \mathbf{A} \cdot d\mathbf{S}_{11} + \mathbf{A} \cdot d\mathbf{S}_{12} + \cdots + \mathbf{A} \cdot d\mathbf{S}_{21} + \mathbf{A} \cdot d\mathbf{S}_{22} + \cdots + \cdots \tag{1.99}$$

All the terms on the right-hand side of Eq. (1.99) which are due to common surfaces will cancel, leaving only the terms due to the outer surfaces. In the limit as the differential volumes and surfaces approach zero and the number of them becomes infinite, Eq. (1.99) becomes a statement of the divergence theorem,

$$\int_V \nabla \cdot \mathbf{A}\, dV = \oint_S \mathbf{A} \cdot d\mathbf{S}$$

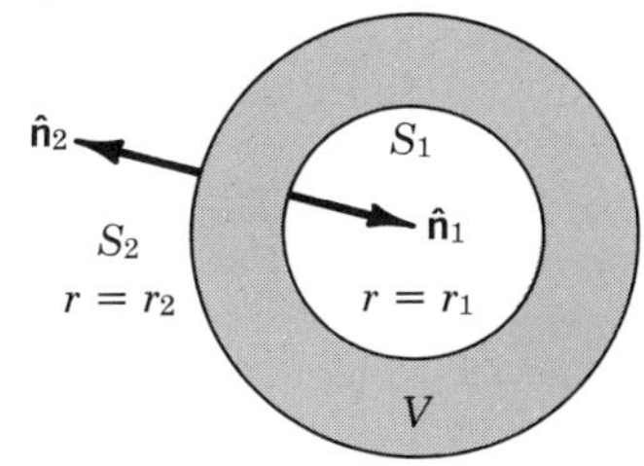

Fig. 1.47 Multiply-connected volume. S_1 and S_2 are spherical surfaces.

where the V on the left is the volume built up by adding the dV, and the S on the right is the surface enclosing V. This illustrates how the divergence theorem follows from the definition of divergence given in Eq. (1.64).

The divergence theorem also holds when V is multiply connected, i.e., when it has "holes" in it.† When V is multiply connected, the surface integral is taken over the sum of the component surfaces bounding V. For example, if V is the volume between the two concentric spheres shown in Fig. 1.47, the surface integration is taken over S_1 and S_2. Note that in each case $\hat{\mathbf{n}}$ points *away from* V.

1.14 STOKES'S THEOREM

The mathematical statement of Stokes's theorem is

$$\int_S \nabla \times \mathbf{A} \cdot d\mathbf{S} = \oint_l \mathbf{A} \cdot d\mathbf{l} \tag{1.100}$$

where S is any surface bounded by the oriented boundary l and $d\mathbf{S}$ is defined in relation to l as in Sec. 1.8. Since the curl is the net circulation per unit surface area, it would be expected that the total circulation around the boundary would be obtained by integrating the curl over the surface. This can be demonstrated by reference to Fig. 1.48, which shows a planar surface for simplicity. The surface is divided into infinitesimal surface

† See W. Kaplan, "Advanced Calculus," Addison-Wesley Publishing Company, Inc., Reading, Mass., 1952, p. 248.

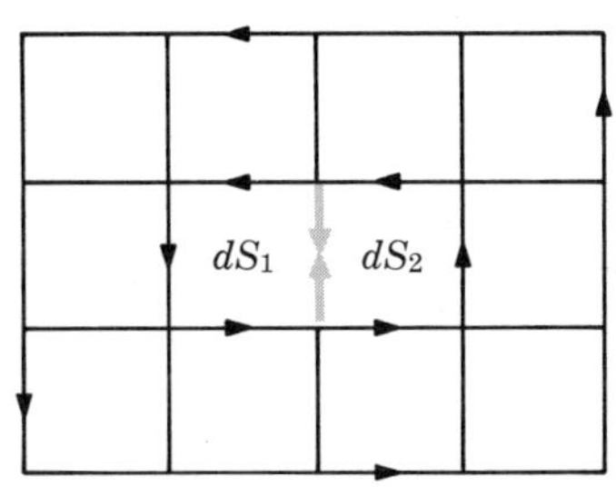

Fig. 1.48 Illustration of Stokes's theorem.

elements. Since the elements are infinitesimal, we get for element 1, from the definition of the curl,

$$\nabla \times \mathbf{A} = \frac{\oint_{l_1} \mathbf{A} \cdot d\mathbf{l}\ \hat{\mathbf{S}}_1}{dS_1}$$

and

$$\nabla \times \mathbf{A} \cdot d\mathbf{S}_1 = \oint_{l_1} \mathbf{A} \cdot d\mathbf{l}$$

Adding terms from all the surface elements gives

$$\nabla \times \mathbf{A} \cdot d\mathbf{S}_1 + \nabla \times \mathbf{A} \cdot d\mathbf{S}_2 + \cdots = \oint_{l_1} \mathbf{A} \cdot d\mathbf{l} + \oint_{l_2} \mathbf{A} \cdot d\mathbf{l} + \cdots$$

In the limit as the differential elements approach zero and their number becomes infinite, the left-hand side becomes $\int_S \nabla \times \mathbf{A} \cdot d\mathbf{S}$ and the right-hand side becomes $\oint_l \mathbf{A} \cdot d\mathbf{l}$, because the terms arising from the common boundary between any two elements cancel. The result is the statement of Stokes's theorem.

If the surface is closed, all the terms on the right-hand side cancel, because all the boundaries are common. Therefore

$$\oint_S \nabla \times \mathbf{A} \cdot d\mathbf{S} = 0 \tag{1.101}$$

for a closed surface.

When $\nabla \times \mathbf{A} = 0$, $\mathbf{A}$ is said to be a *conservative field*, regardless of what kind of vector field $\mathbf{A}$ is. The name stems from an analogy with force fields. If $\mathbf{A}$ is the force exerted on a particle at a given point, then $\int_1^2 -\mathbf{A} \cdot d\mathbf{l}$ is the energy which must be supplied to move the particle from point 1 to point 2, as discussed in Chap. 2. When $\oint_l \mathbf{A} \cdot d\mathbf{l} = 0$, no net energy is required to move the particle around a closed path; i.e., there is no friction or dissipation present, and energy is conserved. Stokes's theorem tells us that when $\nabla \times \mathbf{A} = 0$, $\oint_l \mathbf{A} \cdot d\mathbf{l} = 0$, and thus a field is said to be conservative when its curl is zero.

1.15 OTHER OPERATIONS INVOLVING ∇

In addition to the basic vector operations we have discussed, there are some often-used relations involving more than one application of the ∇ operator. One of these is the curl of the gradient. Since the gradient of a scalar point function is a vector, its curl may be obtained. In rectangular coordinates,

$$\begin{aligned}\boldsymbol{\nabla}\times\boldsymbol{\nabla}\Phi &= \boldsymbol{\nabla}\times\left(\hat{\mathbf{x}}\frac{\partial\Phi}{\partial x}+\hat{\mathbf{y}}\frac{\partial\Phi}{\partial y}+\hat{\mathbf{z}}\frac{\partial\Phi}{\partial z}\right)\\ &= \hat{\mathbf{x}}\left(\frac{\partial^2\Phi}{\partial y\,\partial z}-\frac{\partial^2\Phi}{\partial z\,\partial y}\right)+\hat{\mathbf{y}}\left(\frac{\partial^2\Phi}{\partial z\,\partial x}-\frac{\partial^2\Phi}{\partial x\,\partial z}\right)\\ &\qquad +\hat{\mathbf{z}}\left(\frac{\partial^2\Phi}{\partial z\,\partial y}-\frac{\partial^2\Phi}{\partial y\,\partial z}\right)\end{aligned}$$

and thus

$$\boldsymbol{\nabla}\times\boldsymbol{\nabla}\Phi = 0 \tag{1.102}$$

Since the gradient and curl are independent of coordinate systems, Eq. (1.102) is also independent of coordinate systems, even though it was shown to be true only in rectangular coordinates.

Another vector operation is the divergence of the curl,

$$\boldsymbol{\nabla}\cdot\boldsymbol{\nabla}\times\mathbf{A} = 0 \tag{1.103}$$

This expression can also be verified by direct expansion.

A third useful relation is obtained by taking the divergence of the gradient. The result, in rectangular coordinates, is

$$\begin{aligned}\boldsymbol{\nabla}\cdot\boldsymbol{\nabla}\Phi &= \left(\hat{\mathbf{x}}\frac{\partial}{\partial x}+\hat{\mathbf{y}}\frac{\partial}{\partial y}+\hat{\mathbf{z}}\frac{\partial}{\partial z}\right)\cdot\left(\hat{\mathbf{x}}\frac{\partial\Phi}{\partial x}+\hat{\mathbf{y}}\frac{\partial\Phi}{\partial y}+\hat{\mathbf{z}}\frac{\partial\Phi}{\partial z}\right)\\ &= \frac{\partial^2\Phi}{\partial x^2}+\frac{\partial^2\Phi}{\partial y^2}+\frac{\partial^2\Phi}{\partial z^2}\end{aligned} \tag{1.104}$$

Since Eq. (1.104) may also be obtained by defining the scalar operator

$$\begin{aligned}\boldsymbol{\nabla}\cdot\boldsymbol{\nabla} &= \left(\hat{\mathbf{x}}\frac{\partial}{\partial x}+\hat{\mathbf{y}}\frac{\partial}{\partial y}+\hat{\mathbf{z}}\frac{\partial}{\partial z}\right)\cdot\left(\hat{\mathbf{x}}\frac{\partial}{\partial x}+\hat{\mathbf{y}}\frac{\partial}{\partial y}+\hat{\mathbf{z}}\frac{\partial}{\partial z}\right)\\ &= \frac{\partial^2}{\partial x^2}+\frac{\partial^2}{\partial y^2}+\frac{\partial^2}{\partial z^2}\\ &= \nabla^2\end{aligned} \tag{1.105}$$

the divergence of the gradient is also called ∇^2, or the *laplacian*, so named because $\nabla^2\Phi = 0$ is called *Laplace's equation*. In general orthogonal curvilinear coordinates, ∇^2 is defined as the divergence of the gradient, which is

$$\nabla^2\Phi = \frac{1}{h_1h_2h_3}\left[\frac{\partial}{\partial u_1}\left(\frac{h_2h_3}{h_1}\frac{\partial\Phi}{\partial u_1}\right)+\frac{\partial}{\partial u_2}\left(\frac{h_3h_1}{h_2}\frac{\partial\Phi}{\partial u_2}\right)+\frac{\partial}{\partial u_3}\left(\frac{h_1h_2}{h_3}\frac{\partial\Phi}{\partial u_3}\right)\right] \tag{1.106}$$

There is a corresponding vector operation which is defined in connection with the curl of the curl in rectangular coordinates. This vector operation may be evaluated as follows:

$$\nabla \times \nabla \times \mathbf{A} = \nabla \times \left[\hat{\mathbf{x}} \left(\frac{\partial A_z}{\partial y} - \frac{\partial A_y}{\partial z} \right) + \hat{\mathbf{y}} \left(\frac{\partial A_x}{\partial z} - \frac{\partial A_z}{\partial x} \right) + \hat{\mathbf{z}} \left(\frac{\partial A_y}{\partial x} - \frac{\partial A_x}{\partial y} \right) \right]$$

$$= \hat{\mathbf{x}} \left[\frac{\partial}{\partial y} \left(\frac{\partial A_y}{\partial x} - \frac{\partial A_x}{\partial y} \right) - \frac{\partial}{\partial z} \left(\frac{\partial A_x}{\partial z} - \frac{\partial A_z}{\partial x} \right) \right] + \hat{\mathbf{y}} \left[\frac{\partial}{\partial z} \left(\frac{\partial A_z}{\partial y} - \frac{\partial A_y}{\partial z} \right) - \frac{\partial}{\partial x} \left(\frac{\partial A_y}{\partial x} - \frac{\partial A_x}{\partial y} \right) \right] + \hat{\mathbf{z}} \left[\frac{\partial}{\partial x} \left(\frac{\partial A_x}{\partial z} - \frac{\partial A_z}{\partial x} \right) - \frac{\partial}{\partial y} \left(\frac{\partial A_z}{\partial y} - \frac{\partial A_y}{\partial z} \right) \right]$$

Note that $\nabla(\nabla \cdot \mathbf{A})$ is

$$\nabla(\nabla \cdot \mathbf{A}) = \left(\frac{\partial}{\partial x} \hat{\mathbf{x}} + \frac{\partial}{\partial y} \hat{\mathbf{y}} + \frac{\partial}{\partial z} \hat{\mathbf{z}} \right) \left(\frac{\partial A_x}{\partial x} + \frac{\partial A_y}{\partial y} + \frac{\partial A_z}{\partial z} \right)$$

$$= \hat{\mathbf{x}} \left(\frac{\partial^2 A_x}{\partial x^2} + \frac{\partial^2 A_y}{\partial x\, \partial y} + \frac{\partial^2 A_z}{\partial x\, \partial z} \right) + \hat{\mathbf{y}} \left(\frac{\partial^2 A_x}{\partial y\, \partial x} + \frac{\partial^2 A_y}{\partial y^2} + \frac{\partial^2 A_z}{\partial y\, \partial z} \right) + \hat{\mathbf{z}} \left(\frac{\partial^2 A_x}{\partial z\, \partial x} + \frac{\partial^2 A_y}{\partial z\, \partial y} + \frac{\partial^2 A_z}{\partial z^2} \right)$$

and thus

$$\nabla \times \nabla \times \mathbf{A} = \nabla(\nabla \cdot \mathbf{A}) - \hat{\mathbf{x}} \left(\frac{\partial^2 A_x}{\partial x^2} + \frac{\partial^2 A_x}{\partial y^2} + \frac{\partial^2 A_x}{\partial z^2} \right) - \hat{\mathbf{y}} \left(\frac{\partial^2 A_y}{\partial x^2} + \frac{\partial^2 A_y}{\partial y^2} + \frac{\partial^2 A_y}{\partial z^2} \right) - \hat{\mathbf{z}} \left(\frac{\partial^2 A_z}{\partial x^2} + \frac{\partial^2 A_z}{\partial y^2} + \frac{\partial^2 A_z}{\partial z^2} \right)$$

From Eq. (1.102) we see that certain terms in the above equation may be written as $\nabla^2 A_x$, $\nabla^2 A_y$, and $\nabla^2 A_z$, and we obtain

$$\nabla \times \nabla \times \mathbf{A} = \nabla(\nabla \cdot \mathbf{A}) - (\hat{\mathbf{x}}\, \nabla^2 A_x + \hat{\mathbf{y}}\, \nabla^2 A_y + \hat{\mathbf{z}}\, \nabla^2 A_z)$$

This is written in shorthand notation as

$$\nabla \times \nabla \times \mathbf{A} = \nabla(\nabla \cdot \mathbf{A}) - \nabla^2 \mathbf{A} \tag{1.107}$$

where

$$\nabla^2 \mathbf{A} = \hat{\mathbf{x}}\, \nabla^2 A_x + \hat{\mathbf{y}}\, \nabla^2 A_y + \hat{\mathbf{z}}\, \nabla^2 A_z \tag{1.108}$$

This derivation is valid only in rectangular coordinates.

Equation (1.107) is used to define $\nabla^2\mathbf{A}$ in general, because in other coordinate systems no relation as convenient as Eq. (1.108) exists:

$$\nabla^2\mathbf{A} = \nabla(\nabla\cdot\mathbf{A}) - \nabla\times\nabla\times\mathbf{A} \tag{1.109}$$

Equation (1.109) is important in the discussion of the wave equation.
Other vector relations involving ∇ are found in the Appendix.

1.16 COMPLEX VECTOR NOTATION

The equations of field theory can be greatly simplified by assuming solutions that vary sinusoidally with time. Although sinusoidal time variation is admittedly a very special case, the technique is a powerful one because a general solution can be developed from the sinusoidal solution by Fourier transform methods. Furthermore, the sinusoidal case is often of considerable practical significance.

It is convenient in field theory, as it is in circuit theory, to use complex notation. The real vector field quantity $\mathbf{A}'$ is defined as

$$\mathbf{A}'(x,y,z,t) = \operatorname{Re}\,[\mathbf{A}(x,y,z)e^{j\omega t}] \tag{1.110}$$

where Re means real part† and ω is the radian frequency. For example, if a real physical vector is given by $\mathbf{A}' = \hat{\mathbf{x}}\sin\omega t$, we would write $\hat{\mathbf{x}}\sin\omega t = \operatorname{Re}\,(-j\hat{\mathbf{x}}e^{j\omega t})$, since, from Euler's equation,

$$e^{j\omega t} = \cos\omega t + j\sin\omega t$$

The quantity $\mathbf{A}(x,y,z)$ is called a *phasor* and is a complex vector quantity which is a function of space only. The phasor may be written as

$$\mathbf{A}(x,y,z) = \mathbf{A}_r(x,y,z) + j\mathbf{A}_i(x,y,z) \tag{1.111}$$

where $\mathbf{A}_r$ and $\mathbf{A}_i$ are real quantities. It has become common practice to abbreviate the notation in Eq. (1.110) by not writing Re and $e^{j\omega t}$, but denoting the vector field by the complex function $\mathbf{A}(x,y,z)$. Thus in the above example, $\mathbf{A} = -j\hat{\mathbf{x}}$ would be the abbreviated notation for

$$\mathbf{A}' = \hat{\mathbf{x}}\sin\omega t$$

It is assumed that the actual vector field is always obtained from $\mathbf{A}(x,y,z)$ by multiplying by $e^{j\omega t}$ and taking the real part.

One advantage of the notation is that

$$\begin{aligned}\frac{\partial}{\partial t}\mathbf{A}' &= \frac{\partial}{\partial t}\operatorname{Re}\,(\mathbf{A}e^{j\omega t})\\ &= \operatorname{Re}\,(j\omega\mathbf{A}e^{j\omega t})\end{aligned} \tag{1.112}$$

† We could just as well have defined $\mathbf{A}'(x,y,z,t) = \operatorname{Im}\,[\mathbf{A}(x,y,z)e^{j\omega t}]$, where Im means the imaginary part.

so that in our abbreviated notation, where Re and $e^{j\omega t}$ are not written, $\partial/\partial t$ can be replaced by $j\omega$.

As long as the equations and operations are linear, there is no problem. We can always work with $\mathbf{A}$ and, when the time comes, multiply by $e^{j\omega t}$ and take the real part to obtain the actual vector field. A problem arises, however, when the product of two quantities appears. This happens, for example, because

$$\text{Re}\,(\mathbf{A}e^{j\omega t}) \cdot \text{Re}\,(\mathbf{B}e^{j\omega t}) \neq \text{Re}\,(\mathbf{A} \cdot \mathbf{B}e^{j\omega t}) \tag{1.113}$$

The same thing is true of cross products and products of complex scalar functions. To avoid the problem, we must determine the correct form of Eq. (1.113). An easy way to do this is to note that

$$\text{Re}\,\mathbf{C} = \frac{\mathbf{C} + \mathbf{C}^*}{2} \tag{1.114}$$

where the asterisk denotes the *complex conjugate;* that is, $\mathbf{C}^*$ is the complex conjugate of $\mathbf{C}$. Thus

$$\begin{aligned}\text{Re}\,(\mathbf{A}e^{j\omega t}) \cdot \text{Re}\,(\mathbf{B}e^{j\omega t}) &= \frac{\mathbf{A}e^{j\omega t} + (\mathbf{A}e^{j\omega t})^*}{2} \cdot \frac{\mathbf{B}e^{j\omega t} + (\mathbf{B}e^{j\omega t})^*}{2} \\ &= \frac{\mathbf{A}e^{j\omega t} + \mathbf{A}^*e^{-j\omega t}}{2} \cdot \frac{\mathbf{B}e^{j\omega t} + \mathbf{B}^*e^{-j\omega t}}{2}\end{aligned}$$

Multiplying and collecting terms results in

$$\text{Re}\,(\mathbf{A}e^{j\omega t}) \cdot \text{Re}\,(\mathbf{B}e^{j\omega t}) = \frac{\mathbf{A} \cdot \mathbf{B}^* + \mathbf{A}^* \cdot \mathbf{B}}{4} + \frac{\mathbf{A} \cdot \mathbf{B}e^{2j\omega t} + (\mathbf{A} \cdot \mathbf{B}e^{2j\omega t})^*}{4}$$

Using Eq. (1.114) again on the right, we can write this as

$$\text{Re}\,(\mathbf{A}e^{j\omega t}) \cdot \text{Re}\,(\mathbf{B}e^{j\omega t}) = \tfrac{1}{2}\,\text{Re}\,(\mathbf{A} \cdot \mathbf{B}^* + \mathbf{A} \cdot \mathbf{B}e^{2j\omega t}) \tag{1.115}$$

The *time average* of a product is often desired; for example, we may want the time-average energy or power. The time average of any quantity F is defined by

$$\langle F \rangle = \frac{1}{T}\int_0^T F\,dt \tag{1.116}$$

where T is the time over which the average is taken. Usually the average of a sinusoidal quantity is taken over one period; then $T = 1/f = 2\pi/\omega$, where f is the frequency. Angular brackets $\langle\ \ \rangle$ are used to denote average. The time average of the product in Eq. (1.115) is frequently of interest. From Eq. (1.116) we find

$$\langle \text{Re}\,(\mathbf{A}e^{j\omega t}) \cdot \text{Re}\,(\mathbf{B}e^{j\omega t})\rangle = \tfrac{1}{2}\,\text{Re}\,(\mathbf{A}\cdot\mathbf{B}^*) \tag{1.117}$$

A similar relation holds for cross products and products of scalars.

1.17 SOURCE-POINT AND FIELD-POINT NOTATION

In the development of field theory it is often important to distinguish between two sets of coordinate points. One set of coordinate points is needed to designate the location of sources of fields, for example, point charges, which are sources of electric fields. These points are called *source points*. The other set of coordinate points is needed to designate *field points*, the points at which the field is to be found. The source points are designated by primed coordinates, (x',y',z'). The field points are designated by unprimed coordinates, (x,y,z). It is important to understand that the source points and field points are two general sets of points in the *same* coordinate system; since both points cannot be designated by (x,y,z) and still be distinguished, the source point is designated by (x',y',z') and the field point by (x,y,z). Sometimes the shorthand notation that $(\mathbf{r}')$ stands for (x',y',z') and $(\mathbf{r})$ stands for (x,y,z) is used.

The distance vector between the source points and field points, as illustrated in Fig. 1.49, is often used in field theory. The vector from the origin to the source point is called $\mathbf{r}'$. In rectangular coordinates,

$$\mathbf{r}' = x'\hat{\mathbf{x}}' + y'\hat{\mathbf{y}}' + z'\hat{\mathbf{z}}' \tag{1.118}$$

The vector from the origin to the field point is called $\mathbf{r}$,

$$\mathbf{r} = x\hat{\mathbf{x}} + y\hat{\mathbf{y}} + z\hat{\mathbf{z}} \tag{1.119}$$

The difference between these two vectors is designated as $\mathbf{R} = \mathbf{r} - \mathbf{r}'$. In rectangular coordinates,

$$\mathbf{R} = x\hat{\mathbf{x}} + y\hat{\mathbf{y}} + z\hat{\mathbf{z}} - (x'\hat{\mathbf{x}}' + y'\hat{\mathbf{y}}' + z'\hat{\mathbf{z}}')$$

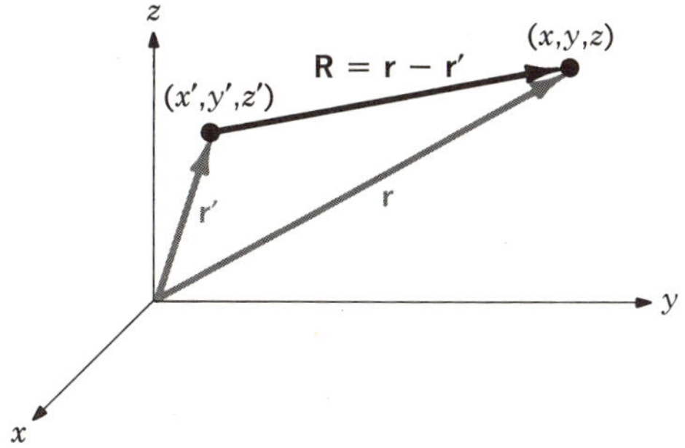

Fig. 1.49 The source-point and field-point vectors.

But since $\hat{\mathbf{x}}' = \hat{\mathbf{x}}$, etc.,

$$\begin{aligned}\mathbf{R} &= \mathbf{r} - \mathbf{r}' \\ &= (x - x')\hat{\mathbf{x}} + (y - y')\hat{\mathbf{y}} + (z - z')\hat{\mathbf{z}}\end{aligned} \tag{1.120}$$

In accordance with standard notation,

$$R = \sqrt{(x - x')^2 + (y - y')^2 + (z - z')^2} \tag{1.121}$$

and

$$\mathbf{R} = R\hat{\mathbf{R}} \tag{1.122}$$

where $\hat{\mathbf{R}}$ is the unit vector along $\mathbf{R}$. Sometimes it is convenient to express $\mathbf{R}$ in other coordinate systems. This can be done straightforwardly by writing $\mathbf{r}$ and $\mathbf{r}'$ in terms of the coordinate system and using the definition $\mathbf{R} = \mathbf{r} - \mathbf{r}'$, with care to perform the subtraction properly in coordinate systems where the base vectors are functions of the coordinates. For example, in cylindrical coordinates it is important to remember that $\hat{\mathbf{r}}'$ is not necessarily equal to $\hat{\mathbf{r}}$, and so on.

Example 1.13 Change in R due to a change in the source or field point It is often necessary to evaluate the way $\mathbf{R}$ changes as either (x,y,z) changes or (x',y',z') changes. Suppose the source point is $(0,0,z')$ and the field point is $(0,y,0)$. Then $\mathbf{R}$ is as shown in Fig. 1.50. Clearly, if z' remains constant and y changes, the $\hat{\mathbf{y}}$ component of $\mathbf{R}$ varies, and $\mathbf{R}$ changes accordingly. The rate of change is given by

$$\begin{aligned}\frac{\partial \mathbf{R}}{\partial y} &= \frac{\partial(y\hat{\mathbf{y}} - z'\hat{\mathbf{z}})}{\partial y} \\ &= \hat{\mathbf{y}}\end{aligned}$$

The rate of change of R (not $\mathbf{R}$) with y might also be of interest. Then

$$\begin{aligned}\frac{\partial R}{\partial y} &= \frac{\partial \sqrt{y^2 + z'^2}}{\partial y} \\ &= \frac{y}{\sqrt{y^2 + z'^2}}\end{aligned}$$

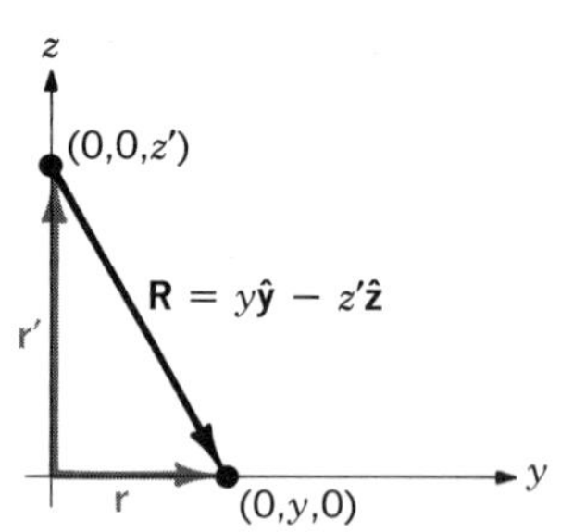

Fig. 1.50 The vector $\mathbf{R}$ used in Example 1.13.

The way **R** varies as y is fixed and z' varies might also be of interest. Then

$$\frac{\partial \mathbf{R}}{\partial z'} = \frac{\partial}{\partial z'}(y\hat{\mathbf{y}} - z'\hat{\mathbf{z}})$$

$$= -\hat{\mathbf{z}}$$

and

$$\frac{\partial R}{\partial z'} = \frac{-z'}{\sqrt{y^2 + z'^2}}$$

These ideas can be generalized by defining the gradient operator, as applied to the two coordinate designations, by the expressions

$$\nabla R = \hat{\mathbf{x}}\frac{\partial R}{\partial x} + \hat{\mathbf{y}}\frac{\partial R}{\partial y} + \hat{\mathbf{z}}\frac{\partial R}{\partial z} \tag{1.123}$$

and

$$\nabla' R = \hat{\mathbf{x}}\frac{\partial R}{\partial x'} + \hat{\mathbf{y}}\frac{\partial R}{\partial y'} + \hat{\mathbf{z}}\frac{\partial R}{\partial z'} \tag{1.124}$$

Note that the ∇' operator, which operates only on the primed coordinates, is defined by

$$\nabla' = \hat{\mathbf{x}}\frac{\partial}{\partial x'} + \hat{\mathbf{y}}\frac{\partial}{\partial y'} + \hat{\mathbf{z}}\frac{\partial}{\partial z'} \tag{1.125}$$

Some useful relations involving ∇ and R are indicated in Probs. 1.17-1 and 1.17-3. Some especially useful relations are

$$\nabla\left(\frac{1}{R}\right) = -\frac{\mathbf{R}}{R^3} \qquad \nabla'\left(\frac{1}{R}\right) = \frac{\mathbf{R}}{R^3} \tag{1.126}$$

In addition to differentiating with respect to either the primed or unprimed coordinates, it is sometimes necessary to integrate with respect to either the primed or unprimed coordinates. It will often be necessary to integrate over all the sources, in which case integration with respect to the primed coordinates only is carried out. For example, consider the integration of a source function f of the form

$$\int_V \frac{f(x',y',z')}{R^2}\,dV'$$

where $dV' = dx'\,dy'\,dz'$. In evaluating this integral, the unprimed coordinates in R are constants in the integration.

Another very useful mathematical relation is

$$\nabla^2\left(\frac{1}{R}\right) = -4\pi\,\delta(R) \tag{1.127}$$

where $\delta(R)$ is a *Dirac delta function,* defined by

$$\int_V \mathbf{A}(R)\,\delta(R)\,dV = \begin{cases} \mathbf{A}(0) & \text{if } V \text{ includes the point } R = 0 \\ 0 & \text{otherwise} \end{cases} \tag{1.128}$$

or, more appropriately for our purposes,

$$\int_V \mathbf{A}(x',y',z',x,y,z)\,\delta(R)\,dV' = \begin{cases} \mathbf{A}(x,y,z) & \text{if } V \text{ includes the point } R = 0 \\ 0 & \text{otherwise} \end{cases} \tag{1.129}$$

since $R = 0$ when $x' = x$, $y' = y$, and $z' = z$. Equation (1.127) is derived in the next section.

★1.18 The Delta Function

It is the purpose of this section to verify Eq. (1.127). This may be done by showing that

$$\int_V \mathbf{A}(x',y',z',x,y,z)\,\nabla^2\left(\frac{1}{R}\right) dV' = \begin{cases} -4\pi\mathbf{A}(x,y,z) & \text{if } V \text{ includes } R = 0 \\ 0 & \text{otherwise} \end{cases} \tag{1.130}$$

It can be shown by direct differentiation that

$$\nabla^2\left(\frac{1}{R}\right) = 0 \qquad \text{when } R \neq 0 \tag{1.131}$$

Because of Eq. (1.131), it is easy to see that the second part of Eq. (1.130) is true. The main task, then, is to evaluate the integral at the singular point $R = 0$.

Let V_0 be a small spherical volume of radius ϵ whose center is at the point (x,y,z), as shown in Fig. 1.51. Because of Eq. (1.131), we have

$$\int_V \mathbf{A}(x',y',z',x,y,z)\,\nabla^2\left(\frac{1}{R}\right) dV' = \int_{V_0} \mathbf{A}(x',y',z',x,y,z)\,\nabla^2\left(\frac{1}{R}\right) dV' + 0 \tag{1.132}$$

Now suppose that V_0 is small enough so that $\mathbf{A}$ has everywhere in V_0 approximately the same value it has at (x,y,z). Then

$$\int_V \mathbf{A}(x',y',z',x,y,z)\,\nabla^2\left(\frac{1}{R}\right) dV' = \mathbf{A}(x,y,z) \int_{V_0} \nabla^2\left(\frac{1}{R}\right) dV'$$

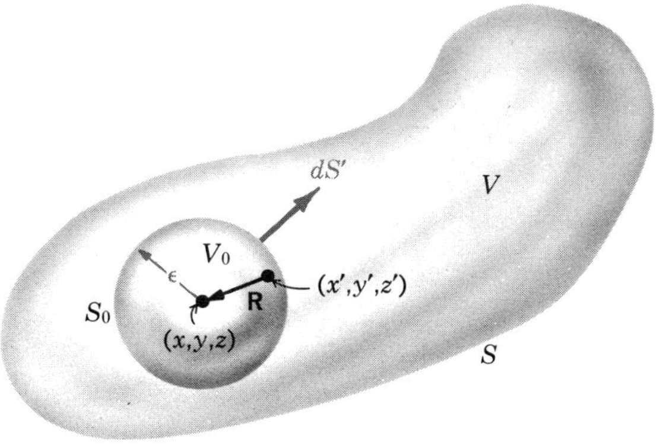

Fig. 1.51 Illustration of V_0.

Using the results of Prob. 1.17-3 and Eq. (1.126), we have

$$\int_{V_0} \nabla^2 \left(\frac{1}{R}\right) dV' = \int_{V_0} \boldsymbol{\nabla}' \cdot \boldsymbol{\nabla}' \left(\frac{1}{R}\right) dV' = \int_{V_0} \boldsymbol{\nabla}' \cdot \left(\frac{\mathbf{R}}{R^3}\right) dV'$$

Then the divergence theorem gives us

$$\int_{V_0} \nabla^2 \left(\frac{1}{R}\right) dV' = \oint_{S_0} \frac{\mathbf{R}}{R^3} \cdot d\mathbf{S}'$$

Note that it is necessary to get the integrand in terms of the source-point divergence in order to use the divergence theorem in a source-point integral. In evaluating the surface integral, the integrand $\mathbf{R}/R^3$ must be evaluated on the surface. From Fig. 1.51, it is clear that when (x',y',z') is on S_0 that

$$\mathbf{R} \cdot d\mathbf{S}' = -R\, dS'$$

Then

$$\int_{V_0} \nabla^2 \left(\frac{1}{R}\right) dV' = -\oint_{S_0} \frac{dS'}{R^2}$$

which may be evaluated by noting that $dS'/R^2 = d\Omega$, where $d\Omega$ is an element of solid angle, or by writing dS' in terms of a spherical coordinate system with origin at (x,y,z). The result is

$$-\oint_{S_0} \frac{dS'}{R^2} = -4\pi$$

from which we conclude that

$$\int_V \mathbf{A}(x',y',z',x,y,z)\, \nabla^2 \left(\frac{1}{R}\right) dV' = -4\pi \mathbf{A}(x,y,z)$$

when V includes $R = 0$

Thus, in accordance with Eq. (1.127),

$$\bigstar \quad \nabla^2\left(\frac{1}{R}\right) = -4\pi\,\delta(R)$$

PROBLEMS

1.2-1 Show by graphical construction that Eqs. (1.1) and (1.2) are true for any vectors **A**, **B**, and **C**.

1.2-2 Show that the dot product is commutative and distributive.

1.2-3 Show that $\mathbf{A}\cdot\mathbf{B}$ is equal to the projection of **A** on **B** times B as well as the projection of **B** on **A** times A.

1.2-4 Show that $\mathbf{A}\times\mathbf{B} = -\mathbf{B}\times\mathbf{A}$.

1.2-5 Prove that $|\mathbf{A}\times\mathbf{B}|$ is equal to the area of the parallelogram shown in Fig. P1.2-5. Note that $\mathbf{A}\times\mathbf{B}$ equals $\mathbf{A}\times\mathbf{B}_\perp$, where $\mathbf{B}_\perp$ is the component of **B** perpendicular to **A**.

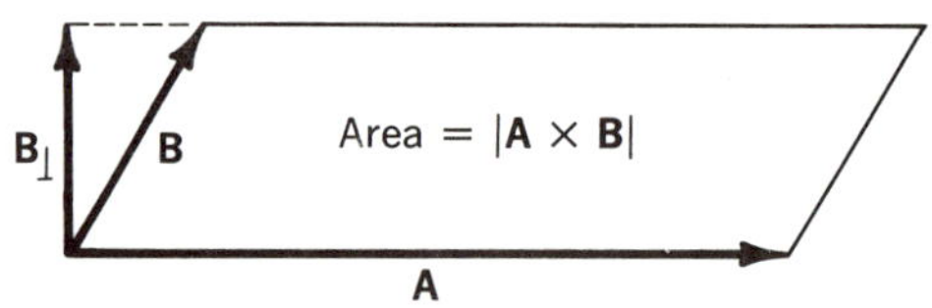

Fig. P1.2-5

1.2-6 Show that the cross product is distributive. *Hint:* You may want to use the fact that $\mathbf{A}\times\mathbf{B} = \mathbf{A}\times\mathbf{B}_\perp$.

1.2-7 Show that $\mathbf{A}\cdot\mathbf{B}\times\mathbf{C}$ is the volume of the parallelepiped defined by the vectors **A**, **B**, and **C**, when **A**, **B**, and **C** have a common-base point.

1.3-1 Two small orifices are located on an infinite flat plane. One orifice is a source of fluid flow and the other is a sink. Sketch roughly the expected vector field for fluid flow on the plane.

1.4-1 Express a known vector **A** in terms of three base vectors $\hat{\mathbf{a}}$, $\hat{\mathbf{b}}$, and $\hat{\mathbf{c}}$ which are *not* orthogonal. Write $\mathbf{A} = A_a\hat{\mathbf{a}} + A_b\hat{\mathbf{b}} + A_c\hat{\mathbf{c}}$, scalarly multiply in turn by each of the base vectors, and solve the resulting system of equations for A_a, A_b, and A_c. The expressions for A_a, A_b, and A_c will involve $\hat{\mathbf{a}}\cdot\hat{\mathbf{b}}$, etc. Note that much simpler expressions would be obtained if $\hat{\mathbf{a}}$, $\hat{\mathbf{b}}$, and $\hat{\mathbf{c}}$ were mutually orthogonal.

1.4-2 Express the vector from the origin to the point (x_1,y_1,z_1) in the form $\mathbf{A} = A_x\hat{\mathbf{x}} + A_y\hat{\mathbf{y}} + A_z\hat{\mathbf{z}}$. Express the vector from the point (x_1,y_1,z_1) to the point (x_2,y_2,z_2) in the same form.

1.4-3 Find two unit vectors which are orthogonal to the line from the origin to the point $(x_1,y_1,0)$ and which lie in the xy plane.

1.4-4 Find the r, φ, and z and r, θ, and φ coordinates (for a cylindrical and spherical, coordinate system, respectively) for the point $x = 3$, $y = 2$, $z = 4$ in rectangular coordinates.

1.4-5 Write the equation for a cylindrical surface of radius a which is infinitely long in rectangular and cylindrical coordinates. Which is easier?

1.4-6 Write out the vector from the point in cylindrical coordinates $r = 2$, $\varphi = \pi$, and $z = 0$ to the point $r = 3$, $\varphi = \frac{1}{2}\pi$, and $z = 1$ in terms of the rectangular base vectors. Then write the vector in terms of the cylindrical base vectors. Remember that $\hat{\mathbf{r}}$ and $\hat{\boldsymbol{\varphi}}$ vary with φ; decide which $\hat{\mathbf{r}}$ and $\hat{\boldsymbol{\varphi}}$ to use, and label them accordingly.

1.5-1 For the two vectors shown in Fig. 1.22, show that

$$\mathbf{A} \cdot \mathbf{B} \equiv AB \cos (\varphi_2 - \varphi_1) = A_x B_x + A_y B_y$$

by expanding $\cos (\varphi_2 - \varphi_1)$.

1.5-2 Show that

$$\psi \mathbf{A} \times \Phi \mathbf{B} = \psi \Phi \mathbf{A} \times \mathbf{B}$$

1.5-3 Starting with the definitions that $\hat{\mathbf{u}}_1 \times \hat{\mathbf{u}}_2 = \hat{\mathbf{u}}_3$ and $\hat{\mathbf{u}}_1$, $\hat{\mathbf{u}}_2$, and $\hat{\mathbf{u}}_3$ are mutually orthogonal, show that as a consequence of these definitions,

$$\hat{\mathbf{u}}_2 \times \hat{\mathbf{u}}_3 = \hat{\mathbf{u}}_1$$

$$\hat{\mathbf{u}}_3 \times \hat{\mathbf{u}}_1 = \hat{\mathbf{u}}_2$$

The other cross products may be obtained from these and the fact that $\mathbf{A} \times \mathbf{B} = -\mathbf{B} \times \mathbf{A}$. A convenient way to remember the cross products is to write $u_1u_2u_3u_1u_2u_3$ and remember that traveling to the right results in a plus sign and traveling to the left results in a minus sign. For example, $\hat{\mathbf{u}}_2 \times \hat{\mathbf{u}}_3 = \hat{\mathbf{u}}_1$ and $\hat{\mathbf{u}}_1 \times \hat{\mathbf{u}}_3 = -\hat{\mathbf{u}}_2$.

1.6-1 Find A_φ and A_z in the cylindrical coordinate system in terms of A_x, A_y, and A_z and the dot product of the rectangular and cylindrical unit vectors.

1.6-2 Find $\hat{\boldsymbol{\varphi}} \cdot \hat{\mathbf{x}}$ and $\hat{\boldsymbol{\varphi}} \cdot \hat{\mathbf{y}}$, where $\hat{\boldsymbol{\varphi}}$ is the unit vector in cylindrical coordinates.

1.6-3 Transform the vector $\mathbf{A} = x\hat{\mathbf{x}} + y\hat{\mathbf{y}}$ into cylindrical coordinates.

1.6-4 A vector located at the origin of a cylindrical coordinate system is given by $\mathbf{A} = \hat{\mathbf{r}}$, where $\hat{\mathbf{r}}$ is the unit vector defined at the origin with $\varphi = \pi/4$. The vector is moved a distance d along the x axis but is otherwise unchanged in magnitude and direction. Write out the expression for the vector in cylindrical coordinates, using the unit vectors defined at the point where the vector is located, $x = d$, $y = 0$.

1.6-5 Find $\hat{\mathbf{x}} \cdot \hat{\boldsymbol{\theta}}$ and $\hat{\mathbf{y}} \cdot \hat{\boldsymbol{\theta}}$.

1.6-6 Transform the vector $\mathbf{A} = A_x\hat{\mathbf{x}} + A_y\hat{\mathbf{y}} + A_z\hat{\mathbf{z}}$ from rectangular coordinates to spherical coordinates.

1.6-7 Let $\mathbf{r}$ be the vector from the origin to the point (r,θ,φ) and pointing away from the origin. Express $\mathbf{r}$ in spherical coordinates, and then transform $\mathbf{r}$ to rectangular coordinates and then to cylindrical coordinates.

1.6-8 Derive Eqs. (1.23), (1.24), and (1.25).

1.7-1 Derive Eqs. (1.36) to (1.41).

1.7-2 Find $d\mathbf{v}/dt$, where $\mathbf{v}$ is given by Eq. (1.42).

1.7-3 Derive the expression for the velocity of a point in spherical coordinates.

1.7-4 Let $\mathbf{r}$ be the vector from the origin to a point on the line, $y = -2x + 2$, $z = 0$. If the point moves along the line with a velocity of 3 m/sec, find $d\mathbf{r}/dt$.

1.8-1 Evaluate $\int_1^2 \mathbf{A} \cdot d\mathbf{l}$ when point 1 is (1,0,0), point 2 is (0,1,0), and the curve is that part of a unit circle in the xy plane between points 1 and 2. $\mathbf{A} = y\hat{\mathbf{x}} - x\hat{\mathbf{y}}$.

1.8-2 Evaluate $\int_a^b \hat{\mathbf{r}}\, d\varphi$ along the path shown in Fig. 1.32.

1.8-3 Evaluate $\int_a^b (\cos\varphi\,\hat{\mathbf{r}} + \sin\varphi\,\hat{\boldsymbol{\varphi}})\,d\varphi$ along the path shown in Fig. 1.32.

1.8-4 Find the vector surface $\mathbf{S}$ of the hemisphere shown in Fig. P1.8-4 by using Eq. (1.52). What planar surface is represented by the same $\mathbf{S}$?

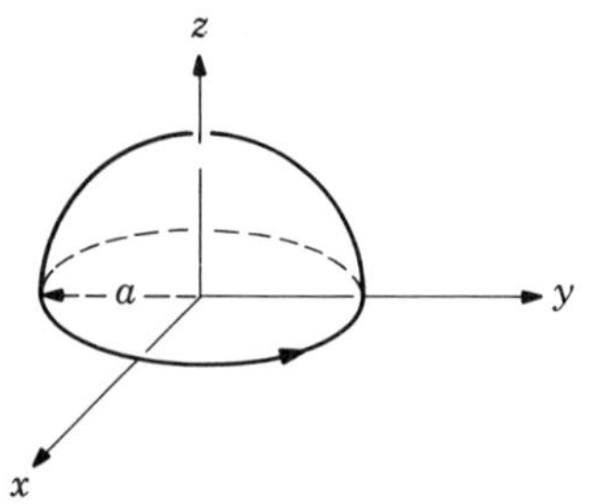

Fig. P1.8-4

1.8-5 Show that $\oint_S \cos\theta\,\hat{\mathbf{r}}\cdot d\mathbf{S} = 0$ if S is any sphere centered about the origin.

1.8-6 Evaluate $\int_V \sin\varphi\,\hat{\mathbf{r}}\,dV$, where V is the volume of a sphere of unit radius centered at the origin ($\hat{\mathbf{r}}$ in spherical coordinates).

1.8-7 Find $\oint_S x\hat{\mathbf{x}}\cdot d\mathbf{S}$, where S is the surface of the unit cube with a corner at the origin of a rectangular coordinate system and three legs along the coordinate axes.

1.8-8 A vector field function $\mathbf{A}$ is given by $\mathbf{A} = x^2\hat{\mathbf{x}} + 3y\hat{\mathbf{y}} + yz\hat{\mathbf{z}}$. Determine the line integral $\oint \mathbf{A}\cdot d\mathbf{l}$ taken around a square in the xy plane, with opposite corners at the origin and the point (1,1). The direction of integration is from (0,0) to (1,0), etc.

1.8-9 A circle of radius 2 is centered at the origin of a rectangular coordinate system and lies in the xy plane. Find $\oint_l \mathbf{A}\cdot d\mathbf{l}$ for the vector field $\mathbf{A} = 2y\hat{\mathbf{x}} + 3yz\hat{\mathbf{y}} + y\hat{\mathbf{z}}$, where l is along the circle in the $+\varphi$ direction.

1.8-10 A strand of spider web lies along the path $y = x^2$ and $z = 0$ from the point (1,1,0) to the point (4,16,0). The diameter of the strand is uniform, but the mass density of the strand is given by $\rho_l(x,y,z) = y/x$. ρ_l stands for line mass density; that is, a length dl of strand has a mass given by $\rho_l dl$. Find the total mass of the strand. ρ_l is in milligrams per meter and x and y are in meters.

1.8-11 Find the work required to move a particle from a to b along the path shown in Fig. P1.8-11. The force required to move the particle is given by $\mathbf{F} = x\hat{\mathbf{x}} + y\hat{\mathbf{y}} + z\hat{\mathbf{z}}$. $\mathbf{F}$ is in millinewtons and x, y, and z are in meters.

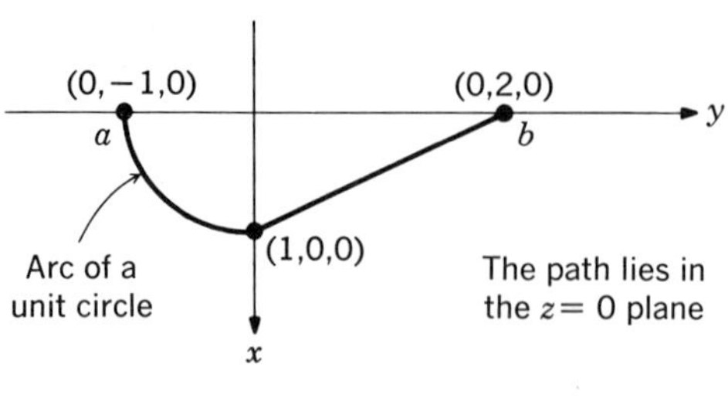

Fig. P1.8-11

1.8-12 A vector field **F** is given by $\mathbf{F} = \mathbf{A} \times \mathbf{B}$, where

$$\mathbf{A} = \frac{z\hat{\mathbf{x}}}{\sqrt{x^2 + y^2 + z^2}} + \frac{\sqrt{x^2 + y^2}\,\hat{\mathbf{y}}}{\sqrt{x^2 + y^2 + z^2}}$$

$$\mathbf{B} = \hat{\mathbf{x}} + \hat{\mathbf{y}}$$

Evaluate $\int_S \mathbf{F} \cdot d\mathbf{S}$, where S is the hemisphere shown in Fig. P1.8-12.

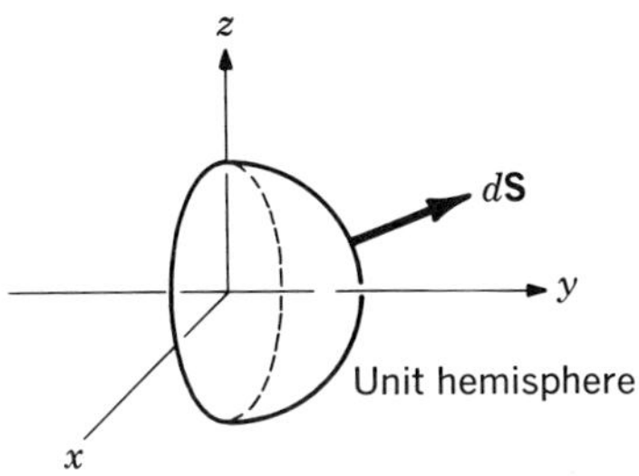

Fig. P1.8-12

1.9-1 Show that $\nabla\Phi$ is perpendicular to surfaces of constant Φ.

1.9-2 Solve for $\nabla\Phi$, where $\Phi = a^2 - x^2 - y^2$.

1.9-3 Find the maximum rate of change of the scalar-point function $\Phi = x^2 + y^2$ at any point (x,y,z). Find the direction of the maximum rate of change of Φ at the point (1,2,0).

1.9-4 Find the work required to move a particle from a to b along the path shown in Fig. 1.32. The force which must be overcome to move the particle is equal in magnitude to the maximum rate of change of L^2 and is in the direction of the maximum rate of change of L^2. L is the straight-line distance from the point a to the point at which the force is being evaluated. The work required to move the particle is given by $\int_a^b \mathbf{F} \cdot d\mathbf{l}$, where **F** is the force moving the particle.

1.10-1 Determine whether the vector field $\mathbf{A} = 3xy^2\hat{\mathbf{x}} + 5z\hat{\mathbf{y}} + xz\hat{\mathbf{z}}$ has a source or a sink at the point (1,3,2).

1.10-2 Evaluate div **A** in cylindrical and spherical coordinates from Eq. (1.67).

1.10-3 The position vector from the origin to the point (x,y,z) is $\mathbf{R} = x\hat{\mathbf{x}} + y\hat{\mathbf{y}} + z\hat{\mathbf{z}}$. Solve for $\nabla \cdot \mathbf{R}$ and show that $\oint_S \mathbf{R} \cdot d\mathbf{S}$ over any arbitrary closed surface is equal to three times the volume enclosed by that surface.

1.10-4 Find $\nabla \cdot \mathbf{A}$ by evaluating Eq. (1.64), where S and V in this case are the surface and volume, respectively, of a cube centered at the origin. $\mathbf{A} = x\hat{\mathbf{x}} + y\hat{\mathbf{y}} + z\hat{\mathbf{z}}$. Also find $\nabla \cdot \mathbf{A}$ by using Eq. (1.66), and compare results.

1.10-5 Repeat Prob. 1.10-4, but use a sphere centered about the origin instead of a cube. Find $\nabla \cdot \mathbf{A}$ by using Eq. (1.67), and compare the results.

1.11-1 A symmetrical circulating field $\mathbf{A} = r\hat{\boldsymbol{\varphi}}$ exists in the $r\varphi$ plane. Find **curl A** at $r = 0$ from Eq. (1.69) and the accompanying definition of curl by evaluating the line integral around a circular path of radius r and letting $r \to 0$. Then show that the same result is obtained from Eq. (1.73).

1.13-1 For $\mathbf{A} = r^2\hat{\mathbf{r}}$ in spherical coordinates, evaluate $\nabla \cdot \mathbf{A}$, and then show that $\int_V \nabla \cdot \mathbf{A}\, dV = \oint_S \mathbf{A} \cdot d\mathbf{S}$, where V is the multiply connected volume enclosed by the two spheres as shown in Fig. 1.47.

1.13-2 Evaluate $\nabla \cdot \mathbf{A}$ when $\mathbf{A} = x\hat{\mathbf{x}} + y\hat{\mathbf{y}} + z\hat{\mathbf{z}}$, and then show that $\int_V \nabla \cdot \mathbf{A}\, dV = \oint_S \mathbf{A} \cdot d\mathbf{S}$, where V is the volume of a unit cube centered at the origin and S is the surface of the unit cube.

1.14-1 Verify Stokes's theorem when $\mathbf{A} = \sin\theta\, \hat{\boldsymbol{\varphi}}$ in spherical coordinates and S is the surface of a hemisphere of unit radius located as in Fig. P1.8-4.

1.14-2 Verify Stokes's theorem when $\mathbf{A} = \sin\varphi\, \hat{\mathbf{r}} + \cos\varphi\, \hat{\boldsymbol{\theta}} + \hat{\boldsymbol{\varphi}}$ and the surface is a unit hemisphere. Orient the hemisphere to your advantage.

1.14-3 Integrate $\nabla \times \mathbf{A} \cdot d\mathbf{S}$ over the plane surface bounded by the square of Prob. 1.8-8 and show that Stokes's theorem holds for that case.

1.15-1 Verify Eq. (1.102) by expanding $\nabla \times \nabla\Phi$ in general orthogonal curvilinear coordinates.

1.15-2 Verify Eq. (1.103) by expansion in general orthogonal curvilinear coordinates.

1.15-3 Verify Eq. (1.106).

1.15-4 A vector field $\mathbf{A} = \sinh x \cos y\, \hat{\mathbf{x}} - \cosh x \sin y\, \hat{\mathbf{y}}$ exists in space. Find $\nabla^2\mathbf{A}$.

1.16-1 If $\mathbf{A}' = \cos\omega t\, \hat{\mathbf{x}}$, find $\langle \mathbf{A}' \cdot \mathbf{A}' \rangle$ directly from Eq. (1.116) and indirectly by writing $\mathbf{A}' = \mathrm{Re}\,(\hat{\mathbf{x}}e^{j\omega t})$ and using Eq. (1.117). Show that the two results are the same.

1.16-2 If $\mathbf{A}' = 4y\hat{\mathbf{x}} \sin\omega t + xz\hat{\mathbf{y}} \cos\omega t$, find $\mathbf{A}$.

1.16-3 If $\mathbf{A}' = A_0\hat{\mathbf{x}} \sin\omega t$ and $\mathbf{B}' = B_0\hat{\mathbf{x}} \sin(\omega t + \phi)$, find $\langle \mathbf{A}' \cdot \mathbf{B}' \rangle$.

1.17-1 Show that

$$\nabla R = \hat{\mathbf{R}}$$

$$\nabla' R = -\hat{\mathbf{R}}$$

1.17-2 Show that

$$\nabla f(R) = -\nabla' f(R)$$

where $f(R)$ is some function of R. Note that

$$\frac{\partial f}{\partial x} = \frac{df}{dR}\frac{\partial R}{\partial x}, \text{ etc.}$$

1.17-3 Show that $\nabla^2(1/R) = \nabla'^2(1/R)$.

1.17-4 Verify Eq. (1.126).

1.17-5 Evaluate $\int_V x' R^2\, dV'$, where V is a unit cube centered at the origin.

1.17-6 Verify Eq. (1.131) by direct differentiation.

CHAPTER

2

electromagnetic fields

2.1 INTRODUCTION

The purpose of Chap. 1 was to review and fully develop the mathematical techniques required for a course in field theory. Now that a familiarity with scalar and vector functions and the necessary associated mathematical techniques have been acquired, we may proceed with the development of electromagnetic field theory. An elegant approach to the subject postulates the final set of basic equations and Maxwell's equations and then derives all the electromagnetic laws, showing that they are consistent and agree with experimental findings. Another approach develops the electromagnetic laws from Coulomb's law and the Lorentz transformation. We choose here to formulate the simpler electromagnetic laws first and then develop the full set of electromagnetic field equations from these laws. In this manner the interrelations of electromagnetic fields, charges, and currents are developed gradually with the ability to use the necessary mathematical techniques. It is interesting, and perhaps not accidental, that the historical development of electromagnetics follows this sequence.

The main concern of this chapter is with electric and magnetic forces and fields. Electric and magnetic forces are observed at points removed from the electric and magnetic sources and are thus analogous to gravitational force. Gravitational force varies inversely as the square of the distance between two masses and along a straight line connecting the centers of mass. The gravitational force field is illustrated in Fig. 2.1. Electrical forces, like gravitational forces, are vector forces; thus a vector formulation of the electric field problem is needed (as discussed in Sec. 1.3).

In the eighteenth century Coulomb discovered that electrical forces are in many respects analogous to gravitational forces. Whereas the source of gravitational force was matter, the source of electrical force was electric charge. Coulomb experimentally determined that the force between two electric charges varies inversely as the square of the distance between the charges, and along a line connecting the two charges. Oersted discovered that electric current can produce magnetic effects, and that the force between two current elements varies as the inverse square of the distance between the elements. These early experimental laws were explained in terms of a mysterious "action at a distance." Faraday introduced the concept of field to aid in the understanding of the action-at-a-distance phenomenon. He stated that a force field is generated in association with electric charges and currents. The resulting action at a distance is the logical response of the test element to the force field.

These early experiments were static experiments involving stationary charges and constant current elements. However, the basic laws developed from these static experiments are generally true, even in the time-varying case, with certain modifications. As the time-varying laws are introduced, these modifications are fully discussed and justified.

Faraday discovered that electric fields may be generated in a system where magnetic flux is time varying. This was an important experiment which helped to show how electric and magnetic fields are interrelated. The subsequent development of Faraday's law fully supported the concept of electric field which he had introduced earlier.

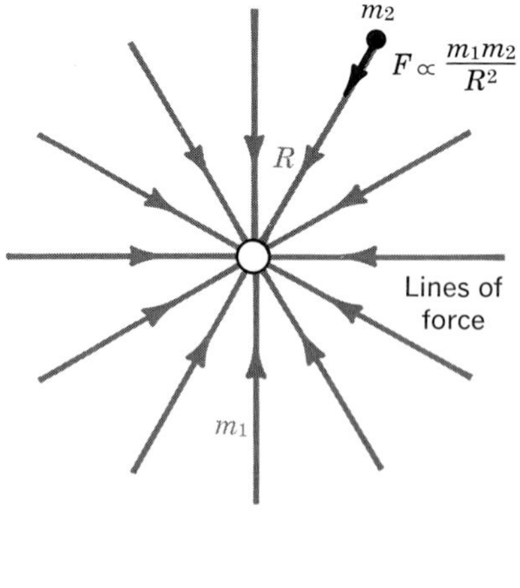

Fig. 2.1 The gravitational field associated with the mass m_1 is shown as inward-directed radial lines. The vector force exerted on a test mass m_2 is indicated.

In the nineteenth century Maxwell used the field concepts introduced by Faraday to develop a consistent set of electromagnetic field equations, including time variations. This set of equations correctly described all the previous experimentally obtained electromagnetic laws. Perhaps the most important impact of Maxwell's equations was the prediction of electromagnetic waves, the wave behavior of time-varying electric and magnetic fields and the propagation of electromagnetic energy in free space at the velocity of light. This startling prediction from Maxwell's equations immediately implied a connection between the basic electromagnetic laws and the wave theory of light. Hertz later provided the experimental verification of electromagnetic waves and was able to measure the wavelength of electromagnetic radiation. Thus a unified field theory was developed from the efforts of Maxwell and Hertz in which one system of equations describes both electrical and optical phenomena. It is interesting to quote Hertz in this new discovery:

> The details of the experiments further prove that the particular manner in which the electrical force is propagated exhibits the closest analogy with the propagation of light; indeed that it corresponds almost completely to it. The hypothesis that light is an electrical phenomenon is thus made highly probable . . . . Certainly it is a fascinating idea that the processes in air which we have been investigating represent to us on a millionfold larger scale [in wavelength] the same processes which go on in the neighborhood of a fresnel mirror or between the glass plates used for exhibiting Newton's rings.†

The great contributions which resulted from Maxwell's equations are:

1. The interconnection of electric and magnetic fields
2. The theory of electromagnetic waves
3. The unification of the electrical and optical sciences

Chapters 2 and 3 deal exclusively with electromagnetic fields in a vacuum. Matter responds to electromagnetic fields and creates new effects which only complicate the picture at this point. Electromagnetic fields and materials are described in Chap. 5, where induced field effects caused by the interaction of fields and matter are incorporated into the field equations.

2.2 THE ELECTRIC FIELD

Electric force is used in this section to define the *electric field-intensity vector* **E**, commonly called the *electric field*. The vector **E** is a vector point

† Heinrich Hertz, "Electric Waves," The Macmillan Company, New York, 1900.

function, as described and illustrated in Sec. 1.3. At any point in space there exist a magnitude and a direction for the vector field **E**. Electric charges are sources for the electric field, and the field associated with an isolated electric charge is similar to the gravitational force field shown in Fig. 2.1.

Charges are a fundamental property of matter and may not be created or destroyed. The elementary subatomic particles, the proton, neutron, and electron, are charged positive, zero, and negative, respectively. A material body is charged if a net charge exists, that is, if there is an excess of positive charge over negative charge, or vice versa. Electrical experiments by Coulomb, as described in the next section, describe the electric force generated by charges. The basic atomic unit of electric charge is the charge on an electron, which is denoted by the symbol e. It is customary to use the symbol Q or q to denote the total net charge on a body, and $Q = e$ for an electron. The practical unit of charge in the rationalized mks system of units is the coulomb. The charge on an electron is

$$e = -1.6008 \times 10^{-19} \text{ coul}$$

The electric field-intensity vector **E** is defined in terms of a very simple and idealized model experiment. A point test body charged to a very small net charge q is brought into a region of space where an electric force field exists. It is observed that the force **F** on the test charge is proportional to q (this is stated in Coulomb's law as described in the next section). The vector electric force is thus equal to q times a vector field function which describes the properties of the vector force field. This vector field function is the electric field intensity **E**, and thus **E** is defined as

$$\mathbf{E} = \frac{\mathbf{F}}{q} \qquad \text{volts/m} \tag{2.1}$$

Equation (2.1) is subject to a very important restriction: the test charge q must be small enough that it produces no interaction effects on the source charges which generate the field **E**. If the test charge q were as large or larger than the total source charge Q, the presence of the test charge would significantly alter the distribution of charge on the source test body and hence would change **E**. A more rigorous definition of the electric field is

$$\mathbf{E} = \lim_{q \to 0} \frac{\mathbf{F}}{q} \tag{2.2}$$

Example 2.1 Deflection of charged particles An electrostatic deflection system for a charged particle is shown in Fig. 2.2. Two metal plates of length l are

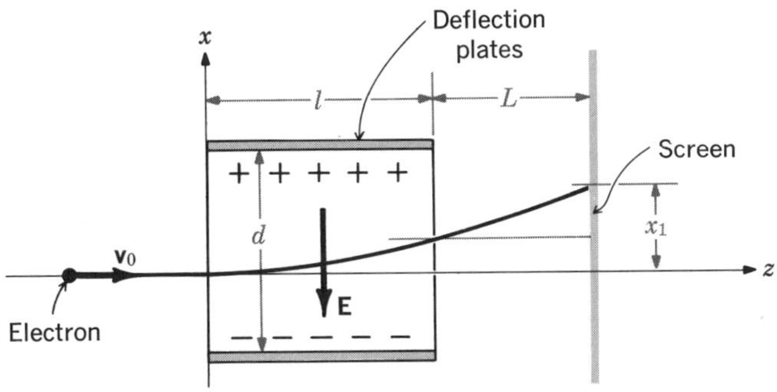

Fig. 2.2 Electrostatic deflection system for a moving charged particle.

separated by a gap d. Charges are induced on the plates such that a uniform electric field $\mathbf{E}$ is generated in the $-x$ direction, as shown. This electric field is assumed to exist only in the range $0 < z < l$. An electron is injected into this system with a z velocity v_0. The electron is deflected in the x direction by the electric field force and strikes the screen at $z = l + L$ at a position x_1.

The vector equation of motion for a body of mass m subjected to a force $\mathbf{F}$ is

$$\mathbf{F} = m \frac{d\mathbf{v}}{dt}$$

For this case there are x and z velocity components. Thus the component equations are

$$F_x = m \frac{dv_x}{dt} \qquad F_z = m \frac{dv_z}{dt}$$

From a knowledge of the electric field $\mathbf{E}$, the force $\mathbf{F}$ is known from Eq. (2.1) to be

$$\mathbf{F} = q\mathbf{E} = qE_x\hat{\mathbf{x}}$$

Since $F_z = 0$, $v_z = v_0$ and does not change. The electron position is $z = v_0 t$ for $t = 0$ when the electron is at $z = 0$.

The x-component equation becomes

$$qE_x = m \frac{dv_x}{dt}$$

and by integrating once we obtain

$$v_x = \frac{q}{m} E_x t + C_1$$

The constant C_1 is zero, since $v_x = 0$ at $t = 0$. The x displacement is found by integrating again,

$$x = \frac{1}{2}\frac{q}{m}E_x t^2 + C_2$$

and $C_2 = 0$, since $x = 0$ at $t = 0$. Since $t = z/v_0$,

$$x = \frac{1}{2}\frac{q}{m}E_x\left(\frac{z}{v_0}\right)^2$$

The additional deflection picked up in the range $l < z < l + L$ is

$$\begin{aligned} x(l+L) - x(l) &= v_x(l)\frac{L}{v_0} \\ &= \frac{q}{m}E_x\frac{l}{v_0}\frac{L}{v_0} \end{aligned}$$

The total deflection observed at the screen is

$$\begin{aligned} x_1 &= x(l+L) \\ &= \frac{q}{m}E_x\left(\frac{l}{v_0}\right)^2\left(\frac{1}{2}+\frac{L}{l}\right) \end{aligned}$$

Consider a practical case where

$$\begin{aligned} v_0 &= 10^7 \text{ m/sec} \\ l &= 5 \text{ cm} \\ L &= 30 \text{ cm} \\ E_x &= -10 \text{ volts/cm} \\ &= -10^3 \text{ volts/m} \\ \frac{q}{m} &= -1.7578 \times 10^{11} \text{ coul/kg (for an electron)} \end{aligned}$$

The x displacement at the screen becomes

$$\begin{aligned} x_1 &= (-1.7578 \times 10^{11} \text{ coul/kg})(-10^3 \text{ volts/m})\left(\frac{5 \times 10^{-2} \text{ m}}{10^7 \text{ m/sec}}\right)^2 (\tfrac{1}{2} + 6) \\ &= 2.86 \text{ cm} \end{aligned}$$

2.3 COULOMB'S LAW

The electric field defined by Eq. (2.1) may be obtained in terms of the force exerted on a test charge. It is inconvenient to measure force in order to determine **E**, and a method for calculating the electric field directly, given an arbitrary source charge distribution, is required. In order to find the force produced by the source charges, we need a basic

Fig. 2.3 Two static point charges Q and q, separated by a distance R, generate a mutual interaction force. The force on charge q is $\mathbf{F}$.

electric force law relating force to electric charge. Once we know the force in terms of the electric charge, the electric field is easily determined from Eq. (2.1).

Coulomb provided the needed force law by experimentally measuring the force between two static point charges, using a delicate balance. He measured the force on the test charge q as indicated in Fig. 2.3 and determined how that force varied with q, Q, and the separation vector $\mathbf{R}$. The force is proportional to the product qQ, inversely proportional to the square of the separation distance R, and in the direction of $\hat{\mathbf{R}}$:

$$\mathbf{F} \propto \frac{qQ\hat{\mathbf{R}}}{R^2} \tag{2.3}$$

There is also an identical force exerted on the source charge Q in the opposite direction. In Coulomb's experiment the separation distance R was much larger than the size of either charge, and only under these conditions is Eq. (2.3) valid. Note that Coulomb's law is an inverse-square law. Force is proportional to the product of the charges and is directed along a vector connecting the two charges. Note the close similarity with Newton's law of gravity.

In order to convert Eq. (2.3) into an explicit quantitative force equation, we must define a proportionality constant. In the rationalized mks system of units, the proportionality constant is $1/4\pi\epsilon_0$, and thus Coulomb's law becomes

$$\mathbf{F} = \frac{Qq\hat{\mathbf{R}}}{4\pi\epsilon_0 R^2} \qquad \text{newtons} \tag{2.4}$$

The constant ϵ_0 is called the *permittivity of free space*. From Eq. (2.4) we see that permittivity has the dimensions square coulombs per newton per square meter, which is called farads per meter. The numerical value for permittivity of free space is

$$\epsilon_0 = 8.854 \times 10^{-12} \text{ f/m}$$

Note that the force, and thus the electric field, is dependent upon the value of permittivity. In Chap. 5 expressions are derived for permittivity in dielectric materials, and we note now that $\mathbf{E}$ is dependent upon the permittivity of the medium. Since the quantities Q and q carry their own algebraic sign, we see from Eq. (2.4) that if the two charges have the same sign they are repelled, and if they have opposite signs they are attracted.

Since Coulomb has provided an explicit expression for the force between two point charges [Eq. (2.4)], we may revert to Eq. (2.1) and express this force in terms of the electric field-intensity vector **E**,

$$\mathbf{E} = \frac{Q\hat{\mathbf{R}}}{4\pi\epsilon_0 R^2} \tag{2.5}$$

Equation (2.5) gives the electric field **E** associated with a point source charge Q isolated in free space. Coulomb's law holds for any charged particle, including electrons, protons, positrons, and nuclei up to a point where the nuclear forces predominate. Equation (2.5) may be put in an alternate form by using Eq. (1.126) to obtain

$$\begin{aligned}\frac{\hat{\mathbf{R}}}{R^2} &= \frac{\mathbf{R}}{R^3}\\ &= -\nabla\left(\frac{1}{R}\right)\end{aligned} \tag{2.6}$$

and thus

$$\mathbf{E} = -\frac{Q}{4\pi\epsilon_0}\nabla\left(\frac{1}{R}\right) \tag{2.7}$$

Note that the operator ∇ used here is a field-point operator.

We may go one step further and write the electric field as

$$\mathbf{E} = -\nabla\Phi \tag{2.8}$$

where

$$\Phi = \frac{Q}{4\pi\epsilon_0 R} \tag{2.9}$$

The vector electric field may thus be determined in terms of a scalar field function Φ. The scalar field function Φ is introduced at this point because it is very important and widely used. The importance and physical meaning of the scalar function Φ is discussed in Sec. 2.4.

Equation (2.5), or Eqs. (2.8) and (2.9), are limited in application as they give the field from only a single point charge. It is of practical importance to find the field generated by arbitrary charge distributions; thus it is necessary to generalize Coulomb's law. The problem is to determine the electric field intensity **E** at the field point **r**, generated by many

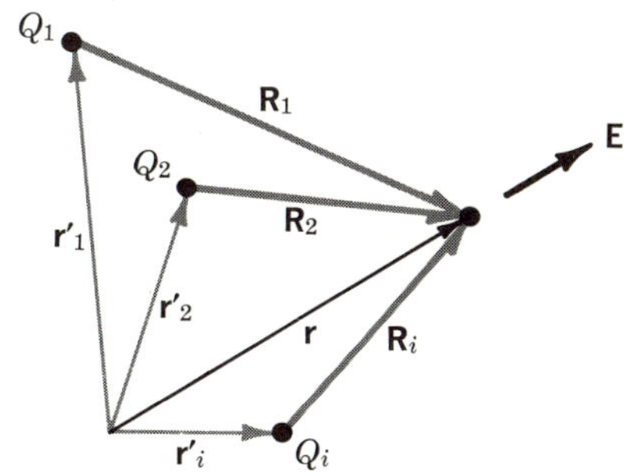

Fig. 2.4 The field at the field point **r** is the sum of the coulomb fields associated with the charges $Q_1, Q_2, \ldots, Q_i$.

point charges Q_i, as shown in Fig. 2.4, in terms of the charges $Q_1, Q_2, \ldots,$ Q_i, and their respective locations. The total field is simply the sum of the field from each source; this is the experimentally derived *superposition principle*, similar to the one used in circuit theory. Thus, from Eq. (2.5), the total field at the field point **r** is

$$\mathbf{E} = \frac{Q_1\hat{\mathbf{R}}_1}{4\pi\epsilon_0 R_1{}^2} + \frac{Q_2\hat{\mathbf{R}}_2}{4\pi\epsilon_0 R_2{}^2} + \cdots + \frac{Q_i\hat{\mathbf{R}}_i}{4\pi\epsilon_0 R_i{}^2} \tag{2.10}$$

and, from Eq. (2.6), this becomes

$$\mathbf{E} = -\frac{1}{4\pi\epsilon_0}\sum_i Q_i \nabla\left(\frac{1}{R_i}\right) \tag{2.11}$$

Equation (2.11) may be written in the form of Eq. (2.8) with

$$\Phi = \frac{1}{4\pi\epsilon_0}\sum_i \frac{Q_i}{R_i} \tag{2.12}$$

In many practical source-charge systems, the charges (electrons, for example) are so extremely small and close together that the fluctuation of the electric field between the particles, that is, the *microscopic* variation of the fields, cannot be measured. What can be measured is the average field, where the average is over a region large in comparison to the spacing of the particles, but still small enough to be considered a point by a human observer. These average fields, which are usually the ones of most interest, are called *macroscopic fields*. For the calculation of macroscopic fields, the distribution of discrete charges can be approximated by a continuous charge distribution. Thus it is convenient to rewrite Eq. (2.11) in a form appropriate for a continuous charge distribution. There are several charge distributions such as volume, surface, and line charge distributions. First let us consider a volume charge distribution, where charge is continuously distributed over a source volume V as shown in Fig. 2.5. The

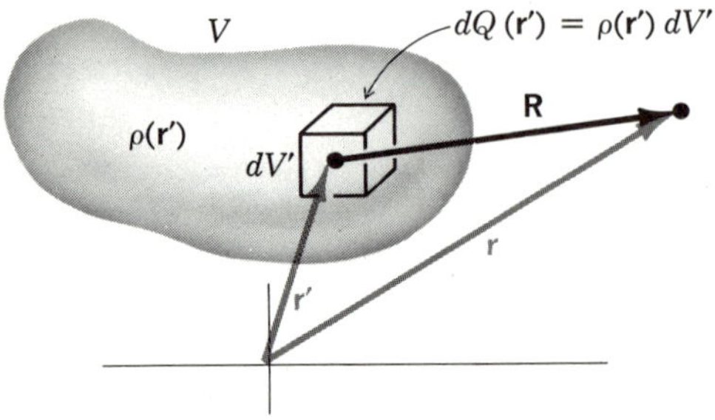

Fig. 2.5 The field generated at the field point **r**, as generated by the continuous-charge-distribution $\rho(\mathbf{r}')$ in the source volume V, is found by integrating Coulomb's law over V.

net charge in the elemental volume $\Delta V'$ located at $\mathbf{r}'$ is $\Delta Q(\mathbf{r}')$, and the volume charge density at that source point is defined as

$$\rho(\mathbf{r}') = \lim_{\Delta V' \to 0} \frac{\Delta Q(\mathbf{r}')}{\Delta V'}$$
$$= \frac{dQ(\mathbf{r}')}{dV'} \qquad \text{coul/m}^3$$

The notation $\rho(\mathbf{r}')$ means $\rho(x',y',z')$. A surface charge distribution exists when charges are continuously scattered over a surface, and a surface charge density $\rho_s(\mathbf{r}')$ may be defined as

$$\rho_s(\mathbf{r}') = \lim_{\Delta S' \to 0} \frac{\Delta Q(\mathbf{r}')}{\Delta S'}$$
$$= \frac{dQ(\mathbf{r}')}{dS'} \qquad \text{coul/m}^2$$

Similarly, a line charge distribution exists when charges are continuously distributed along a line, and

$$\rho_l(\mathbf{r}') = \lim_{\Delta l' \to 0} \frac{\Delta Q(\mathbf{r}')}{\Delta l'}$$
$$= \frac{dQ(\mathbf{r}')}{dl'} \qquad \text{coul/m}$$

The differential charges dQ associated with the volume, surface, and line charges are

$$dQ = \rho \, dV' \tag{2.13}$$
$$dQ = \rho_s \, dS' \tag{2.14}$$
$$dQ = \rho_l \, dl' \tag{2.15}$$

Obviously, the total charge in the source regions is

$$Q = \int_V \rho(\mathbf{r}')\, dV' = \int_S \rho_s(\mathbf{r}')\, dS' = \int_l \rho_l(\mathbf{r}')\, dl'$$

The appropriate form of Eqs. (2.10) and (2.11) for the case of a continuous charge distribution is

$$\mathbf{E} = \frac{1}{4\pi\epsilon_0} \sum_i \frac{\Delta Q_i \, \mathbf{R}_i}{R_i{}^3} = -\frac{1}{4\pi\epsilon_0} \sum \Delta Q_i \, \nabla \left(\frac{1}{R_i}\right) \tag{2.16}$$

In the limit as $\Delta V_i' \to 0$, $\Delta Q_i \to dQ$ and R_i becomes a continuous variable R. Equation (2.16) becomes an integral

$$\mathbf{E} = \frac{1}{4\pi\epsilon_0} \int \frac{dQ\, \mathbf{R}}{R^3} = -\frac{1}{4\pi\epsilon_0} \int dQ\, \nabla \left(\frac{1}{R}\right) \tag{2.17}$$

which is a volume, surface, or line integral, depending upon the charge distribution and use of Eq. (2.13), (2.14), or (2.15). Note in Eq. (2.17) that $R = |\mathbf{r} - \mathbf{r}'|$ and that the differential operation is a field-point-gradient operation. The source-point gradient operator may be used in Eq. (2.17) by reversing the sign of the equation. However, the field-point gradient operator is preferable, since in this case it may be removed from the source integral to give

$$\mathbf{E} = -\nabla \int \frac{dQ}{4\pi\epsilon_0 R}$$

This is permissible because the field-point gradient does not operate on the source variables. It is immediately obvious by analogy with Eqs. (2.8) and (2.9) that the electric field for the continuous-charge-distribution case may be written in terms of a scalar field function

$$\mathbf{E} = -\nabla\Phi \tag{2.8}$$

where

$$\Phi = \int \frac{dQ}{4\pi\epsilon_0 R} \tag{2.18}$$

For many applications it is easier to calculate the electric field from Eqs. (2.8) and (2.18) than from Eq. (2.17), because it is easier to integrate a scalar than a vector.

Example 2.2 Electric field from a line charge As an illustration of the use of Coulomb's law for a line charge distribution, the electric field associated with an infinite line charge in free space is calculated. An infinitely long, straight filamentary charge of uniform charge density ρ_l lies on the z axis in a cylindrical coordinate system, as shown in Fig. 2.6.

Equation (2.15) is used in Eq. (2.17) for the line-charge case to give

$$\mathbf{E} = \int_{-\infty}^{+\infty} \frac{\rho_l \, dl' \, \mathbf{R}}{4\pi\epsilon_0 R^3}$$

The vector $\mathbf{R}$ from the source point z' to the field point, as shown in Fig. 2.6, is $\mathbf{R} = r\hat{\mathbf{r}} + (z - z')\hat{\mathbf{z}}$; thus

$$\mathbf{E} = \frac{\rho_l}{4\pi\epsilon_0} \int_{-\infty}^{+\infty} \frac{[r\hat{\mathbf{r}} + (z - z')\hat{\mathbf{z}}] \, dz'}{[r^2 + (z - z')^2]^{3/2}}$$

The z component of this integral is zero; thus only an r component of $\mathbf{E}$ exists,

$$\mathbf{E} = \frac{\rho_l r\hat{\mathbf{r}}}{4\pi\epsilon_0} \int_{-\infty}^{+\infty} \frac{dz'}{[r^2 + (z - z')^2]^{3/2}}$$

$$E_r = \frac{\rho_l}{4\pi\epsilon_0 r} \left[\frac{-(z - z')}{\sqrt{r^2 + (z - z')^2}} \right]_{-\infty}^{+\infty}$$

$$= \frac{\rho_l}{2\pi\epsilon_0 r} \tag{2.19}$$

The radial electric field from an infinite uniform line charge varies as $1/r$ in a cylindrical system. Recall from Eq. (2.5) that the radial electric field from a point charge varies as $1/r^2$ in a spherical coordinate system.

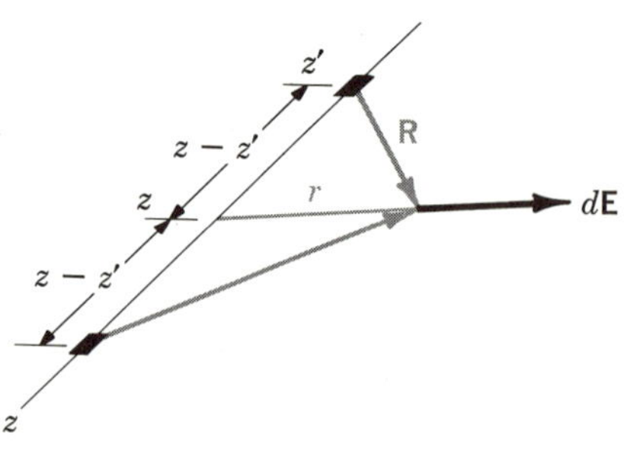

Fig. 2.6 The electric fields generated by an infinitely long uniform line charge in free space are calculated.

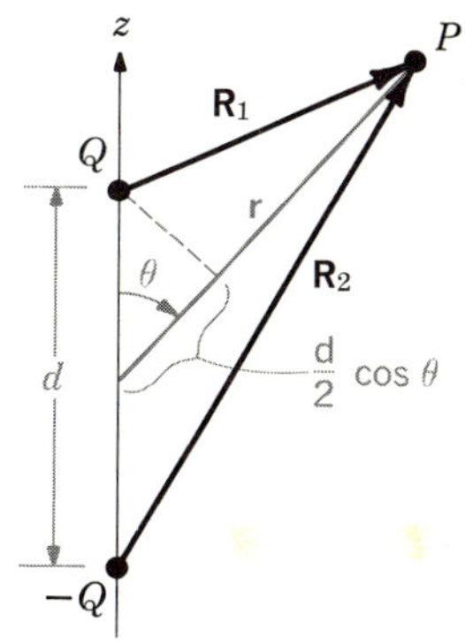

Fig. 2.7 The electrostatic dipole consists of two opposite charges in close proximity.

Example 2.3 The static electric dipole The electrostatic dipole, illustrated in Fig. 2.7, consists of two equal charges of opposite sign separated by a distance d. The dipole problem affords an excellent example of the convenience in using the scalar potential function for determining $\mathbf{E}$, in contrast to carrying out a vector field integration.

Using Eq. (2.12), the potential function for the dipole is obtained by superimposing the potential functions associated with each charge,

$$\begin{aligned}\Phi &= \frac{Q}{4\pi\epsilon_0 R_1} - \frac{Q}{4\pi\epsilon_0 R_2} \\ &= \frac{Q}{4\pi\epsilon_0}\frac{R_2 - R_1}{R_1 R_2}\end{aligned}$$

At distances far from the dipole, where $r \gg d$, the potential function may be written approximately as

$$\Phi \simeq \frac{Q}{4\pi\epsilon_0}\frac{d\cos\theta}{r^2}$$

Using $\hat{\mathbf{z}} \cdot \hat{\mathbf{r}} = \cos\theta$, it is convenient to define an electric-dipole moment $\mathbf{p} = Qd\,\hat{\mathbf{z}}$, and Φ becomes

$$\Phi = \frac{1}{4\pi\epsilon_0}\frac{\mathbf{p}\cdot\hat{\mathbf{r}}}{r^2} \tag{2.20}$$

Note how easily the scalar potential function has been obtained. The problem now is to solve for the electric field from Eqs. (2.8) and (2.20). Spherical coordinates are used; thus Eq. (2.8) is written out as

$$\begin{aligned}\mathbf{E} &= -\nabla\Phi \\ &= -\left(\frac{\partial\Phi}{\partial r}\hat{\mathbf{r}} + \frac{1}{r}\frac{\partial\Phi}{\partial\theta}\hat{\boldsymbol{\theta}} + \frac{1}{r\sin\theta}\frac{\partial\Phi}{\partial\varphi}\hat{\boldsymbol{\varphi}}\right)\end{aligned}$$

It is immediately seen that the φ component of **E** is zero. The final expression for the field is obtained by carrying out the indicated differential operations,

$$\mathbf{E} = -\left(-\frac{p\cos\theta}{2\pi\epsilon_0 r^3}\hat{\mathbf{r}} - \frac{p\sin\theta}{4\pi\epsilon_0 r^3}\hat{\boldsymbol{\theta}}\right)$$

$$= \frac{p}{4\pi\epsilon_0 r^3}(2\cos\theta\,\hat{\mathbf{r}} + \sin\theta\,\hat{\boldsymbol{\theta}}) \qquad r \gg d \tag{2.21}$$

The above result is valid only at distances far from the dipole, in accordance with the approximation $r \gg d$ used in obtaining Eq. (2.20). Note that far from the dipole the electric field intensity varies as $1/r^3$, in contrast with the point-charge variation $1/r^2$ and the line-charge variation $1/r$.

2.4 ELECTRIC POTENTIAL

The scalar potential function Φ was introduced in Sec. 2.3 as a convenience in solving for the electric field **E** generated by a charge distribution. In this section we examine the physical significance of the scalar field function Φ.

Consider the two-point-charge system shown in Fig. 2.8, where a test charge q is moved with respect to the source charge Q. If the charges Q and q have the same sign, the field force **F** from Coulomb's law is in the direction indicated. A mechanical force $\mathbf{F}_m$ which is equal and opposite in direction to the field force must be applied to the charge in order to overcome the field force **F**. When this is done, the total net force on the charge q is zero, and the charge may then be moved the incremental distance $d\mathbf{l}$. The incremental work dW done by the external mechanical force on the charge is equal to force times the incremental distance along **F**, or, in vector notation,

$$dW = \mathbf{F}_m \cdot d\mathbf{l} \tag{2.22}$$

Since the mechanical force is equal and opposite to the field force, the incremental work done on the charge may be expressed in terms of the

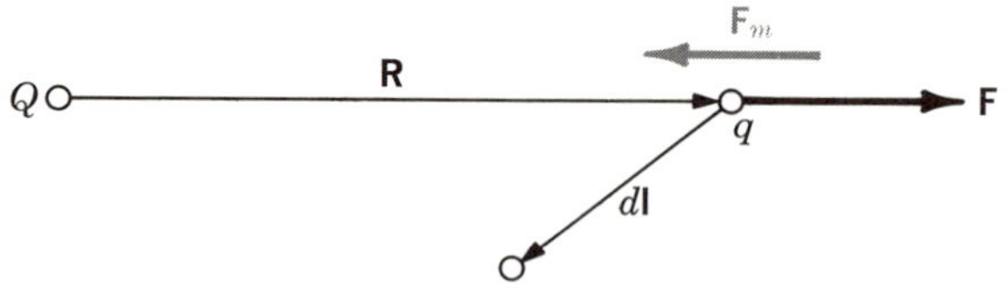

Fig. 2.8 Force diagram for a charge in an electric field. If Q and q are of the same sign, the field force **F** is directed as shown, and a mechanical force $\mathbf{F}_m$ is required in order to overcome the field force.

field force by the equation

$$dW = -\mathbf{F} \cdot d\mathbf{l} \tag{2.23}$$

The field force $\mathbf{F}$ in Eq. (2.23) is the force on the charge q from Q. Using Eq. (2.1), the total work done in moving the charge q from point 1 to point 2 becomes

$$W = -q \int_1^2 \mathbf{E} \cdot d\mathbf{l} \qquad \text{joules} \tag{2.24}$$

The unit of work in the mks system is joules.

If the external force exerted on the charge q has a component along the direction of motion, the work done on q is positive. From Eq. (2.24) we see that if the particle is moved in a direction opposite to the electric field $\mathbf{E}$, the work is positive. This is analogous to the mechanical problem of requiring positive work to push a ball uphill, against the gravitational force. On the other hand, if the charge is moved in the same direction as the electric field, the work done is negative. This is analogous to pushing a ball downhill, in the same direction as the gravitational force; the work done in this case is negative.

The concept of potential energy as developed in mechanics may be applied with equal rigor and usefulness in an electrical system. In mechanics the change in potential energy is equal to the work done in moving from point 1 to point 2. The analogous concept in the electrical case states that the difference in electric potential energy of a charge q between points 1 and 2 equals the work required to move the charge from point 1 to point 2; that is, $U_2 - U_1 = W$, where U denotes electric potential energy. Using Eq. (2.24), the potential difference may be written as

$$\begin{aligned} U_2 - U_1 &= W \\ &= -q \int_1^2 \mathbf{E} \cdot d\mathbf{l} \end{aligned} \tag{2.25}$$

Note that if the work done is positive in moving from point 1 to point 2, the potential energy at point 2 is greater than the potential energy at point 1. This is analogous to pushing a ball up to a higher elevation. The work done is positive; therefore the potential energy at the higher elevation is greater than the potential energy at the original elevation. It is useful to remove the quantity q from Eq. (2.25) and speak of an electric potential difference involving the field alone, and thus define an *electric field potential* as the potential energy per unit charge. The electric field potential is denoted by the symbol V. The electric potential difference, obtained from Eq. (2.25) by dividing by q, is

$$V_2 - V_1 = -\int_1^2 \mathbf{E} \cdot d\mathbf{l} \qquad \text{volts} \tag{2.26}$$

The electric field potential has the unit of joules per coulomb, which is defined as volts.

The scalar field function Φ is related to the electric potential. Recall that the electric field **E** is related to the scalar potential function by Eq. (2.8). Inserting this expression for **E** in Eq. (2.26) yields

$$\begin{aligned} V_2 - V_1 &= +\int_1^2 \nabla\Phi \cdot d\mathbf{l} \\ &= \int_1^2 d\Phi \\ &= \Phi_2 - \Phi_1 \end{aligned} \tag{2.27}$$

The complete derivation of this relation is left as a problem. Thus the scalar field function Φ is the electric potential, and Φ is called the *scalar potential field function*, or simply the potential. The electric potential function is derived from Coulomb's law, which is a static law; thus the identification of Φ as the electric potential is applicable only to static systems. In time-varying field problems it is incorrect to say that $\mathbf{E} = -\nabla\Phi$; thus in this case Φ is not the electric potential as defined in Eq. (2.26). A more general definition and use of Φ for time-varying systems is developed in Chap. 6.

Example 2.4 The coulomb potential The electric potential associated with a point charge may be obtained by calculating the work done in moving a test charge q from infinity to a distance R from the point charge Q. If Q is located at the origin of a spherical coordinate system, the electric field is given by Eq. (2.5) as

$$\mathbf{E} = \frac{Q}{4\pi\epsilon_0 r^2}\hat{\mathbf{r}} \tag{2.28}$$

where r is the radial variable in spherical coordinates. The work done in moving q in this field may be calculated from Eqs. (2.24) and (2.28). Since the electric field has only a radial component, $\mathbf{E} \cdot d\mathbf{l}$ becomes simply $E_r\, dr$, and Eq. (2.24) reduces to

$$\begin{aligned} W &= -q\int_\infty^R E_r\, dr \\ &= -\frac{qQ}{4\pi\epsilon_0}\int_\infty^R \frac{dr}{r^2} \end{aligned}$$

The integral may be readily evaluated to give

$$W = \frac{qQ}{4\pi\epsilon_0 R}$$

Since electric potential difference is defined as a potential energy change or work done per unit charge, the electric potential difference in moving from infinity to the point R along any arbitrary path is

$$\Phi(R) - \Phi(\infty) = \frac{Q}{4\pi\epsilon_0 R} \tag{2.29}$$

It is customary to assume the electric potential at infinity to be zero, $\Phi(\infty) = 0$. Equation (2.29) gives the electric potential field function associated with the point charge Q. This potential is called the *coulomb potential* and is the same potential as that given in Eq. (2.9), assuming $\Phi(\infty) = 0$.

The surfaces of constant potential are called *equipotentials* and are concentric spheres. The electric field lines are perpendicular to the equipotential surfaces and point in the direction of decreasing potential.

Equation (2.29) may be generalized to an assembly of charges by superimposing the potential at r due to i particles of charge Q_i at $\mathbf{r}_i$,

$$\Phi = \frac{1}{4\pi\epsilon_0} \sum_i \frac{Q_i}{R_i} \tag{2.30}$$

where $R_i = |\mathbf{r} - \mathbf{r}_i|$. The difference in potential between two arbitrary points $\mathbf{r}_2$ and $\mathbf{r}_1$ is

$$\Phi_2 - \Phi_1 = \frac{1}{4\pi\epsilon_0} \sum_i \left(\frac{Q_i}{R_{i2}} - \frac{Q_i}{R_{i1}}\right) \tag{2.31}$$

where $R_{i1} = |\mathbf{r}_1 - \mathbf{r}_i|$ and $R_{i2} = |\mathbf{r}_2 - \mathbf{r}_i|$. A relation analogous to Eq. (2.29) is obtained by letting $\mathbf{r}_1$ go to infinity. In this case $\Phi_1 = 0$, since $1/R_{i1} = 0$, and Eq. (2.30) is the potential referenced to zero potential at infinity.

The continuous-charge-distribution case is obtained from Eq. (2.30) by replacing R_i by the variable R, Q_i by $\rho(\mathbf{r}')\,dV'$, and the summation by an integral; thus

$$\Phi = \int_V \frac{\rho(\mathbf{r}')}{4\pi\epsilon_0 R}\,dV'$$

2.5 THE MAGNETIC FIELD

The discussion so far has been limited to forces generated by static electric charges. These forces have been used to define an electric field $\mathbf{E}$, which is parallel to the force. Another type of force, called *magnetic force,* is generated by electric current and by magnets which contain atomic circulating currents. Magnetic force is used in this section to define a *magnetic flux-density vector* $\mathbf{B}$, commonly called the *magnetic field.*

It has been recognized for many centuries that certain types of material, called magnets, attract iron and other metals. Magnetic force effects are observed in magnetic materials, and the earth was discovered to possess a magnetic force field. Early navigators realized the advantage of this phenomenon, and the compass has been used ever since. It was later discovered by Oersted that electric current could also exert force on a compass needle. Further experiments by Ampère showed that strong magnetic forces were exerted between adjacent current-carrying wires. Ampère observed that the magnetic force on a localized current element was perpendicular to the direction of current flow, and that no force was present if there was no current. These magnetic forces were thus obviously not related to electric forces.

The magnetic field is defined by an equation analogous to Eq. (2.1), but the formulation of such an equation is complicated by the fact that the test charge q must move, and that the force is perpendicular to the charge velocity. The test element is a charge q moving with a vector velocity $\mathbf{v}$, and magnetic field is now defined in terms of the force on a small test-current element $q\mathbf{v}$. Following the development of Eq. (2.1), we allowed the symbol $\mathbf{B}$ to represent the force per unit current element $q\mathbf{v}$. The magnetic force $\mathbf{F}$ has been found experimentally to be proportional to the product $q\mathbf{v}$ and perpendicular to the direction of current flow $\mathbf{v}$. vel. In Eq. (2.1) the defining equation for $\mathbf{E}$ could be written down immediately, since the force vector is parallel to the electric field vector. However, magnetic force is perpendicular to velocity, and so we must content ourselves for the moment with a scalar equation relating the magnitude of force and magnetic field,

$$B = \frac{F_{\text{max}}}{qv} \qquad \text{webers/m}^2 \tag{2.32}$$

The symbol F_{max} represents the peak magnetic force amplitude observed as the velocity vector is oriented in different directions. The units for magnetic field are newton seconds per coulomb per meter which are called webers per square meter in the mks system. The units are in terms of a flux density, with webers the unit of magnetic flux, consistent with calling $\mathbf{B}$ a flux-density vector. Equation (2.32) is accurate only when the current element $q\mathbf{v}$ is small enough not to influence the source of magnetic field. A more rigorous definition of the magnetic field, analogous to Eq. (2.2), would be

$$B = \lim_{qv \to 0} \frac{F_{\text{max}}}{qv}$$

Equation (2.32) is unsatisfactory for subsequent use, since the vector relationship is not given. We require an equation in vector form which expresses the fact that the magnetic force is perpendicular to the charge

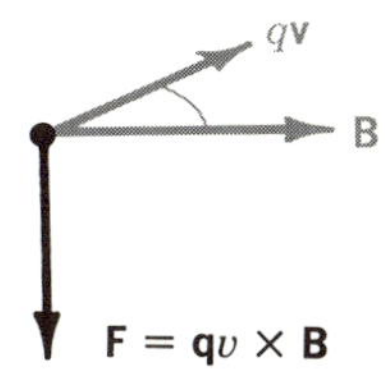

Fig. 2.9 The magnetic force exerted on a test current element $q\mathbf{v}$ is used to define a magnetic flux density vector $\mathbf{B}$.

velocity. Such an equation is obtained by rewriting Eq. (2.32) in vector form, consistent with the experimental results, as

$$\mathbf{F} = q\mathbf{v} \times \mathbf{B} \tag{2.33}$$

This equation serves as a defining equation for the vector magnetic field $\mathbf{B}$ and explicitly gives the force on a moving test charge in terms of a magnetic field vector $\mathbf{B}$. The relationship expressed in Eq. (2.33) is illustrated in Fig. 2.9. A small test-current element $q\mathbf{v}$ is located in a $\mathbf{B}$ field; the force exerted on the test element is perpendicular to the vectors $\mathbf{v}$ and $\mathbf{B}$, as indicated.

It is immediately obvious from Eq. (2.33) that the force, and hence the acceleration vector, for a moving test charge in a $\mathbf{B}$ field is always perpendicular to the velocity vector. Thus the energy delivered to the charged particle by the magnetic field must always be zero, since

$$\begin{aligned} dW &= \mathbf{F} \cdot d\mathbf{l} \\ &= q\mathbf{v} \times \mathbf{B} \cdot \mathbf{v}\, dt \equiv 0 \end{aligned}$$

The magnetic field may deflect, but not change, the total energy of charged particles. This is in contrast to the electric field, which exerts a force independent of the direction in which the particle is moving. The electric field generates a velocity component in the same direction as the electric field. The work and potential-energy calculations described in Sec. 2.4 hold when a $\mathbf{B}$ field is present in addition to an $\mathbf{E}$ field. When both $\mathbf{B}$ and $\mathbf{E}$ are present, the total force on q is given by the sum of Eqs. (2.1) and (2.33),

$$\mathbf{F} = q(\mathbf{E} + \mathbf{v} \times \mathbf{B}) \tag{2.34}$$

CURRENT RELATIONS

It is common to write Eq. (2.33) in a variety of forms, depending on the physical problem under consideration. Equation (2.33) is convenient for problems involving point charges q moving with a velocity $\mathbf{v}$. However, in many instances the force is exerted on a continuous volume distribution of moving charges, or on current-carrying wires. Thus it is necessary to relate the $q\mathbf{v}$ term in Eq. (2.33) to an equivalent term involving current

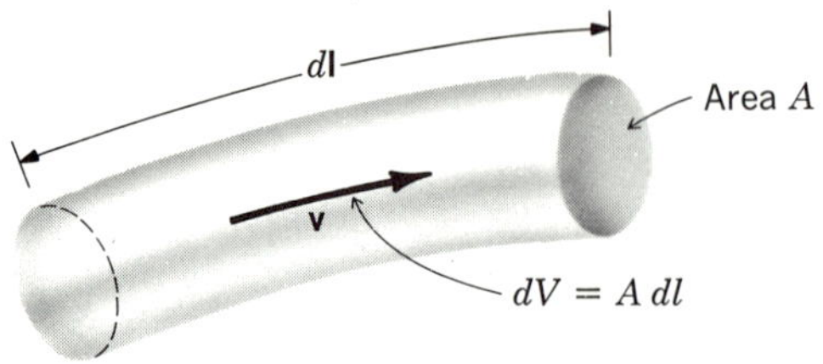

Fig. 2.10 A tube of moving charge containing a charge dQ moving at a velocity $\mathbf{v}$.

density or line current. In Fig. 2.10, a continuous tubular distribution of charge moving with velocity $\mathbf{v}$ is shown. The differential volume dV contains charge moving with a velocity vector $\mathbf{v}$. The total charge in the differential volume is dQ. We may relate dQ to the volume charge density ρ by the expression

$$dQ = \rho \, dV$$

and thus the term $q\mathbf{v}$ for this elemental tube of charge becomes

$$dQ \, \mathbf{v} = \rho \, dV \, \mathbf{v} \tag{2.35}$$

The current density J passing through the surface A may be related to the charge density and electron velocity. The current density J equals the coulombs per second per square meter passing through the surface A. The charge dQ passes the surface A in time $dt = dl/v$; thus

$$\begin{aligned} J &= \frac{dQ}{A\,dt} \\ &= \frac{dQ\,v}{A\,dl} \\ &= \frac{dQ}{dV}\,v \end{aligned}$$

Since dQ/dV is the volume charge density ρ, and since the vector direction of $\mathbf{J}$ is along $\mathbf{v}$, we write

$$\mathbf{J} = \rho \mathbf{v} \qquad \text{amp/m}^2 \tag{2.36}$$

The $dQ \, \mathbf{v}$ term in the force equation may be expressed in terms of the current-density vector by using Eq. (2.36) in Eq. (2.35),

$$\begin{aligned} dQ \, \mathbf{v} &= \rho \, dV \, \mathbf{v} \\ &= \mathbf{J} \, dV \end{aligned}$$

and the magnetic force equation assumes the alternate form

$$d\mathbf{F} = \mathbf{J} \times \mathbf{B} \, dV \tag{2.37}$$

The force $d\mathbf{F}$ is exerted on the current element $\mathbf{J}\,dV$ through the magnetic field $\mathbf{B}$. The corresponding equation for a system where both $\mathbf{B}$ and $\mathbf{E}$ are present is

$$d\mathbf{F} = (\rho\mathbf{E} + \mathbf{J} \times \mathbf{B})\,dV \tag{2.38}$$

The important practical case of current-carrying wires is described by Fig. 2.10 for a wire of cross-sectional area A, where J is constant over A. In this case it is convenient to use the total current I, which is related to the current density J by the expression $I = JA$. Note that

$$\begin{aligned} dQ\,\mathbf{v} &= \mathbf{J}\,dV \\ &= I\,d\mathbf{l} \end{aligned} \tag{2.39}$$

Thus Eq. (2.37) may be written in the alternate form

$$d\mathbf{F} = I\,d\mathbf{l} \times \mathbf{B} \tag{2.40}$$

The defining equation for the magnetic field $\mathbf{B}$ (written as a force equation) is given for the point-charge, current-density-element, and current-element cases, by Eqs. (2.33), (2.37), and (2.40), respectively.

Example 2.5 Magnetic deflection of a moving electron An electron moves into a uniform magnetic field region of length l as shown in Fig. 2.11. The electron experiences a transverse deflecting force in accordance with Eq. (2.33), as well as a decelerating force. The electron motion in the magnetic field may be determined from the equations of motion,

$$\begin{aligned} \frac{dv_x}{dt} &= \frac{q}{m}(-v_z)B_y \\ &= -\omega_c v_z \\ \frac{dv_z}{dt} &= \frac{q}{m}v_x B_y \\ &= \omega_c v_x \end{aligned}$$

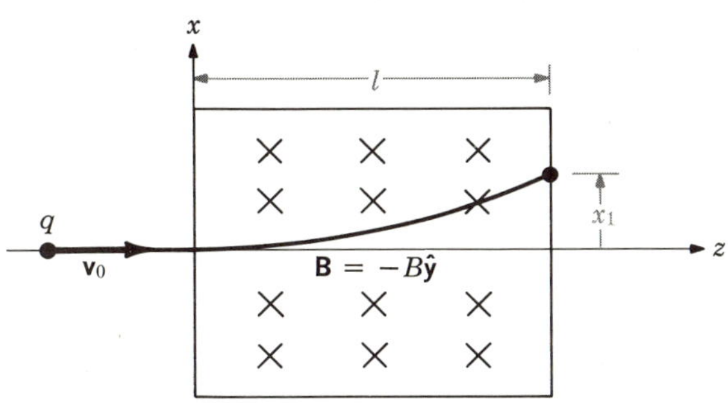

Fig. 2.11 Charged particle deflection by a uniform transverse magnetic field.

where $\omega_c = qB_y/m$. These two equations may be combined to obtain a differential equation for v_x,

$$\frac{d^2v_x}{dt^2} = -\omega_c{}^2 v_x$$

The well-known solution to this equation is

$$v_x = A \sin \omega_c t + B \cos \omega_c t$$

where A and B are constants to be determined by initial conditions. Setting $t = 0$ at $z = 0$, where $v_x = 0$, it is necessary to choose $B = 0$, and

$$v_x = A \sin \omega_c t$$

Then v_z is obtained from the first equation of motion,

$$\begin{aligned} v_z &= -\frac{1}{\omega_c}\frac{dv_x}{dt} \\ &= -A \cos \omega_c t \end{aligned}$$

But since $v_z = v_0$ at $t = 0$, $A = -v_0$, and

$$v_z = v_0 \cos \omega_c t$$

$$v_x = -v_0 \sin \omega_c t$$

These equations may be integrated and the initial conditions $x = z = 0$ at $t = 0$ applied to obtain

$$z = \frac{v_0}{\omega_c} \sin \omega_c t$$

$$x = -\frac{v_0}{\omega_c}(1 - \cos \omega_c t)$$

These equations describe a circular path of radius v_0/ω_c. The path of motion in the magnetic field is a semicircle, and the electron is reflected from the magnetic field region.

The magnetic deflection system illustrated in Fig. 2.11 requires $l \ll v_0/\omega_c$, or alternately, $\omega_c t \ll 1$. The displacement equations under these conditions are approximately

$$z = v_0 t$$

$$x = -\tfrac{1}{2} v_0 \omega_c t^2$$

and the net deflection x_1 is

$$x_1 = -\tfrac{1}{2} v_0 \omega_c \left(\frac{z}{v_0}\right)^2$$

The deflection shown in Fig. 2.11 is for q positive and B_y negative, so that ω_c is negative.

As an illustration of the magnitude of magnetic deflection, consider a typical set of data:

$$\frac{q}{m} \text{ for an electron} = -1.7578 \times 10^{11} \text{ coul/kg}$$
$$B = 10 \text{ gauss} = 0.001 \text{ webers/m}^2$$
$$l = 10 \text{ cm}$$
$$= 0.1 \text{ m}$$
$$v_0 = 3 \times 10^7 \text{ m/sec}$$

For these parameters $x_1 = -2.9$ cm, indicating that large deflection results from quite reasonable parameter values.

Example 2.6 The moving-coil galvanometer An important practical use of the magnetic force between a magnetic field and current-carrying wire is the moving-coil galvanometer. This device is used to measure current in a coil, and is thus a dc ammeter. The force on a current-carrying wire is obtained from Eq. (2.40), and a uniform magnetic field vector **B** is considered. The total net force on a current loop in a uniform field is obtained by integrating Eq. (2.40) around the loop,

$$\mathbf{F} = I \oint_l d\mathbf{l} \times \mathbf{B}$$
$$= -I\mathbf{B} \times \oint_l d\mathbf{l}$$

It is obvious that the line integral of $d\mathbf{l}$ around a closed loop is zero; thus the net force **F** on a closed current loop in a uniform magnetic field is zero. This is not true, however, for a nonuniform magnetic field.

We are more interested, in the case of the galvanometer, in the torque generated on the current loop shown in Fig. 2.12. The magnetic field is in the

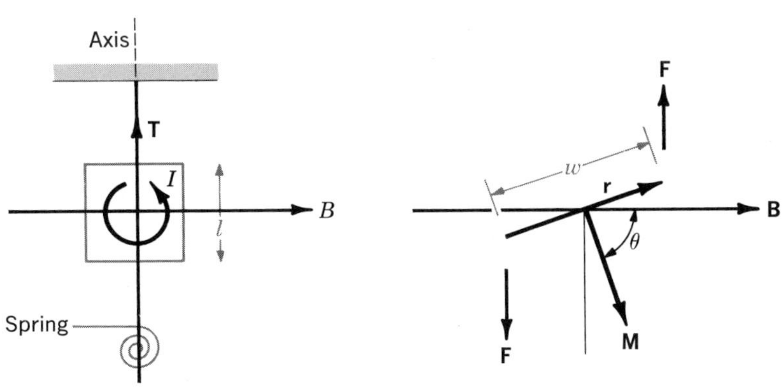

Fig. 2.12 The moving-coil galvanometer used in the measurement of direct current.

plane of the loop, and it is necessary to derive an expression for the torque generated about the loop axis by the interaction of the current and magnetic field. The torque will displace the loop with respect to the magnetic field plane by an angle $\pi/2 - \theta$. The induced torque is resisted by a mechanical spring arrangement, as indicated, and the loop comes to rest when the spring torque equals the induced electromagnetic torque. It is seen from Eq. (2.40) that the top and bottom sides of the loop generate no torque. The sides of the loop carry current perpendicular to the magnetic field, and the force on each side element is $F = IlB$, in the direction indicated in Fig. 2.12. Torque = force × the distance from a specified axis. The distance in this case is $\frac{1}{2}w \sin\theta$; thus the total torque on the loop is

$$\begin{aligned} T &= 2\frac{w}{2}\sin\theta\, IlB \\ &= IAB\sin\theta \end{aligned}$$

where $A = wl$ is the loop area. The general vector expression from mechanics relating torque $\mathbf{T}$ and force $\mathbf{F}$ is

$$\mathbf{T} = \mathbf{r} \times \mathbf{F} \tag{2.41}$$

where $\mathbf{r}$ is the distance vector perpendicular from a specified axis to the point where the force $\mathbf{F}$ is applied. Comparison of the previous two equations shows that the vector expression for torque on the loop may be written as

$$\mathbf{T} = \mathbf{M} \times \mathbf{B} \tag{2.42}$$

where

$$\mathbf{M} = I\mathbf{A} \tag{2.43}$$

Note that $\mathbf{M}$ is a vector oriented as shown in Fig. 2.12, and $\mathbf{A}$ is the vector surface enclosed by the loop. The vector $\mathbf{M}$ is called the *magnetic moment* of the coil and is oriented in a direction according to the right-hand rule in association with the direction of circulating current in the loop. Although Eqs. (2.42) and (2.43) were derived for a rectangular loop, these equations are also true for a current loop of arbitrary shape.

The magnitude of electromagnetic torque exerted on the spring for small deflection angles is $T = MB$. The coil moves in response to this torque until an equilibrium is established between the electromagnetic torque and the spring torque. The torque balance equation is

$$\begin{aligned} T &= MB \\ &= K\alpha \end{aligned}$$

where $\alpha = \pi/2 - \theta$ is the small deflection angle and K is a spring constant. The current may then be obtained in terms of the known constants K, A, B, and the observed small deflection angle α, in accordance with the equation

$$I = \frac{K}{AB}\alpha$$

The principle illustrated in the moving-coil galvanometer is the basic principle underlying electrical machinery. An electric motor is constructed such that a coil carries current in the presence of a magnetic field. A torque is generated on the coil structure, or "armature." In electric motors the coil rotates in response to the torque, and a constant torque is maintained on the coil by having the magnetic field rotate at the same rate as the coil. Some machinery is designed with a static magnetic field. The coil rotates to a position of zero torque and begins to enter a region of negative torque. The current in the coil is then reversed, and the torque again becomes positive such that a net torque is continuously exerted on the coil.

Now that the magnetic field has been defined in terms of magnetic force, an experimental magnetic force law analogous to Coulomb's law is needed in order to establish **B** in terms of the source current. Such a law is discussed in the next section, where an expression for **B** in terms of the source current is given.

2.6 AMPÈRE'S LAW OF FORCE

Now that the magnetic flux density **B** has been defined in terms of magnetic force by means of Eq. (2.33), (2.37), or (2.40), an experimental magnetic force law is required in order to determine **B** in terms of the source current. The situation is analogous to the electric-field case presented in Secs. 2.2 and 2.3. The electric field was defined in terms of electric force, and Coulomb's law was required in order to obtain an explicit expression for **E** in terms of the electric sources (charges). The magnetic force law which is analogous to Coulomb's electric force law is Ampère's law of force, which is an experimentally determined law for the force between two current loops. Ampère's law of force is a magnetostatic law; i.e., it applies only to steady currents. It will be necessary later to generalize the results obtained here for the time-varying case.

Equation (2.40) states that magnetic force is proportional to $I\, d\mathbf{l}$. Ampère's force law states that the force between two current elements $I_1\, d\mathbf{l}_1$ and $I_2\, d\mathbf{l}_2$ is proportional to the vector product $I_1\, d\mathbf{l}_1 \times I_2\, d\mathbf{l}_2$ and is inversely proportional to the square of the distance separating the two current elements. This law is obviously a direct analog of Coulomb's law, which states that the force between two point charges is proportional to the product of the two charges and inversely proportional to the square of the separation distance. Ampère's experimental law is complicated by the fact that isolated current elements may not exist in any physical system; thus complete current loops are required. In Fig. 2.13, two current loops are shown, a source loop (a) and a test loop (b). The test loop is brought into the vicinity of the source loop,

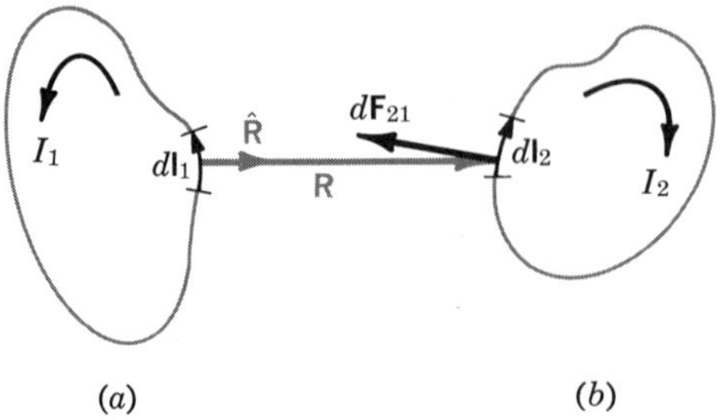

Fig. 2.13 Ampère's law of force gives the force between two current loops. (*a*) Source loop; (*b*) test loop.

and the force on a test loop is measured. The total force exerted on the test loop is denoted as $\mathbf{F}_{21}$, where the subscript 21 refers to the force on loop (*b*) due to the presence of loop (*a*). Ampère's experimentally determined force $\mathbf{F}_{21}$ is given by the equation

$$\mathbf{F}_{21} = \frac{\mu_0}{4\pi} \oint_{l_1} \oint_{l_2} \frac{I_2\, d\mathbf{l}_2 \times (I_1\, d\mathbf{l}_1 \times \hat{\mathbf{R}})}{R^2} \qquad \text{newtons} \tag{2.44}$$

The proportionality constant $\mu_0/4\pi$ is introduced in accordance with the rationalized mks system of units. The factor μ_0 is called the *permeability of free space* and has units of henrys per meter. The value of μ_0 is

$$\mu_0 = 4\pi \times 10^{-7}\ \text{h/m}$$

Note in Eq. (2.44) that the total force is obtained only after a complete line integration is carried out around each loop.

Equation (2.44) is not in a convenient form for the development of an expression for magnetic field in terms of the source current. We must relate the defining equation for **B**, Eq. (2.40), to the force law, where the $I\, d\mathbf{l}$ term in Eq. (2.40) is $I_2\, d\mathbf{l}_2$ in Eq. (2.44). A convenient form of Eq. (2.44) is obtained by examining the incremental force exerted on the test-loop element $d\mathbf{l}_2$ by the source-loop element $d\mathbf{l}_1$. This incremental force $d\mathbf{F}_{21}$ is inferred from Eq. (2.44),

$$d\mathbf{F}_{21} = \frac{\mu_0}{4\pi} \frac{I_2\, d\mathbf{l}_2 \times (I_1\, d\mathbf{l}_1 \times \hat{\mathbf{R}})}{R^2} \tag{2.45}$$

The rather complicated vector directions implicit in Eq. (2.45) are pictured graphically in Fig. 2.13. The vector $d\mathbf{l}_1 \times \hat{\mathbf{R}}$ is a vector pointing into the paper. The vector $d\mathbf{l}_2$ crossed into this vector gives an incremental force vector $d\mathbf{F}_{21}$ normal to $d\mathbf{l}_2$, as indicated. Thus for current flow as indicated in Fig. 2.13, the force on the two current elements is in the general direction of pulling the current elements together. Equation (2.40) may now be rewritten in the notation associated with Fig. 2.13. Since the force $d\mathbf{F}$ represents the force on the test-loop element, we write

$$d\mathbf{F}_{21} = I_2\, d\mathbf{l}_2 \times d\mathbf{B} \tag{2.46}$$

where $d\mathbf{B}$ is now the incremental magnetic flux-density vector generated by the source-current element $d\mathbf{l}_1$. From Eqs. (2.45) and (2.46), we may see immediately that the incremental magnetic flux-density vector due to the source loop increment $d\mathbf{l}_1$ is

$$d\mathbf{B} = \frac{\mu_0}{4\pi} \frac{I_1 \, d\mathbf{l}_1 \times \hat{\mathbf{R}}}{R^2} \tag{2.47}$$

The total magnetic field generated by the source loop is thus

$$\mathbf{B} = \frac{\mu_0}{4\pi} \oint_{l_1} \frac{I_1 \, d\mathbf{l}_1 \times \hat{\mathbf{R}}}{R^2} \tag{2.48}$$

Equation (2.47) [or (2.48)] is commonly called the *Biot-Savart law.*

The relationships between current density and current were discussed in Sec. 2.5. These relationships are now used to develop an equation analogous to Eq. (2.47) for a current-density element. Since $\mathbf{J}\,dV = I\,d\mathbf{l}$, Eq. (2.47) may be written in the alternate form

$$d\mathbf{B} = \frac{\mu_0}{4\pi} \frac{\mathbf{J} \times \hat{\mathbf{R}}}{R^2} \, dV \tag{2.49}$$

If the source current is contained in a source volume V, the total field generated is

$$\mathbf{B} = -\frac{\mu_0}{4\pi} \int_V \mathbf{J}(\mathbf{r}') \times \nabla \left(\frac{1}{R}\right) dV' \tag{2.50}$$

Comparing Eq. (2.50) with the corresponding equation for electric field obtained from Eqs. (2.17) and (2.13), we see a close analogy in the source relations for electric and magnetic fields,

$$\mathbf{E} = -\frac{1}{4\pi\epsilon_0} \int_V \rho(\mathbf{r}') \, \nabla \left(\frac{1}{R}\right) dV'$$

Since the source-current density $\mathbf{J}(\mathbf{r}')$ is a function of only the source coordinates $\mathbf{r}'$, the only variable in the integrand of Eq. (2.50) which contains a field variable is the term $1/R$. It is convenient at this point to use the vector identity

$$\mathbf{J} \times \nabla \left(\frac{1}{R}\right) = \frac{1}{R} \nabla \times \mathbf{J} - \nabla \times \left(\frac{\mathbf{J}}{R}\right) \tag{2.51}$$

and recognize that since ∇ is a field-point operator and $\mathbf{J}$ is a source variable, $\nabla \times \mathbf{J} = 0$. Equation (2.50) may then be written in the form

$$\mathbf{B} = \frac{\mu_0}{4\pi} \int_V \nabla \times \left(\frac{\mathbf{J}}{R}\right) \, dV' \tag{2.52}$$

We recognize that the field-point curl operator may be removed from the source integration, and Eq. (2.52) becomes

$$\mathbf{B} = \nabla \times \frac{\mu_0}{4\pi} \int_V \frac{\mathbf{J}}{R}\, dV' \tag{2.53}$$

The obvious implication from Eq. (2.53) is that **B** may be derived from a vector potential function **A** in accordance with the equations

$$\mathbf{B} = \nabla \times \mathbf{A} \tag{2.54}$$

$$\mathbf{A} = \frac{\mu_0}{4\pi} \int_V \frac{\mathbf{J}(\mathbf{r}')}{R}\, dV' \tag{2.55}$$

A vector potential function for the magnetic flux-density vector **B** is thus defined.

The vector potential **A** is not of great physical significance, as is the scalar potential Φ. **A** is a vector field function which depends on the field position, and its magnitude and direction are determined by the integrated source current [see Eq. (2.55)]. For a unidirectional current, **A** is in the same direction as **J** and is proportional to **J**.

It is immediately seen from Eq. (2.54) that $\nabla \cdot \mathbf{B}$ is identically equal to zero. This fact will be discussed more fully in Sec. 3.3.

Example 2.7 Force between two long parallel filamentary wires A magnetic force exists between two adjacent, parallel current-carrying wires. It is impractical to use Eq. (2.44) to find the force; it is easier to derive the magnetic flux-density vector from Eq. (2.48) associated with one of the wires and then calculate the force per unit length on the other wire from Eq. (2.46).

Consider the geometry shown in Fig. 2.14. From Eq. (2.48) we write

$$\mathbf{B} = \frac{\mu_0 I_1}{4\pi} \int_{-\infty}^{+\infty} \frac{dz'\, \hat{\mathbf{z}} \times \hat{\mathbf{R}}}{z'^2 + r^2}$$

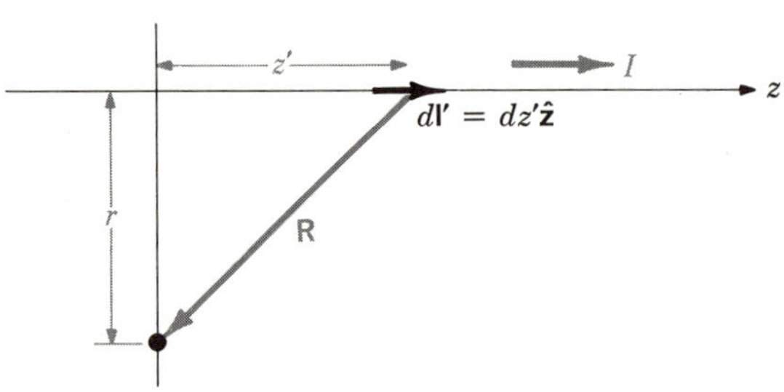

Fig. 2.14 Calculation of the magnetic field **B** associated with a long straight filamentary current-carrying wire.

The cross product $\hat{\mathbf{z}} \times \hat{\mathbf{R}}$ is $(r/R)\hat{\boldsymbol{\varphi}}$. The preceding equation then gives $\mathbf{B} = B_\varphi \hat{\boldsymbol{\varphi}}$, where

$$B_\varphi = \frac{\mu_0 I_1}{4\pi} \int_{-\infty}^{+\infty} \frac{r\,dz'}{(z'^2 + r^2)^{3/2}}$$

and the solution is immediately obtained from integral tables as

$$B_\varphi = \frac{\mu_0 I_1}{4\pi r} \frac{z'}{\sqrt{r^2 + z'^2}} \Bigg|_{-\infty}^{+\infty}$$

$$= \frac{\mu_0}{2\pi} \frac{I_1}{r}$$

Now that the magnetic field generated by one of the current-carrying wires is known, Eq. (2.40) may be used to calculate the force on the second wire,

$$d\mathbf{F}_{21} = I_2\,dz\,\hat{\mathbf{z}} \times \frac{\mu_0}{2\pi} \frac{I_1}{r} \hat{\boldsymbol{\varphi}}$$

The force per unit length along the wire is obtained immediately from this equation as

$$\mathbf{F}_{21} = -\frac{\mu_0}{2\pi} \frac{I_1 I_2}{r} \hat{\mathbf{r}} \qquad \text{newtons/m}$$

Note that when I_2 and I_1 are in the same direction, the force pulls the wires together. In the case where the wires carry current in opposite directions, the wires are repelled by the magnetic force.

When $I_1 = I_2 = 100$ amp and $r = 1$ cm, the force between the two wires is 0.2 newtons/m, or approximately 1 oz/m. In some solenoid configurations where the distance between wires is small with pulsed currents of the order of thousands of amperes, the force can be quite significant and an important design consideration.

2.7 MAGNETIC FIELD–GENERATING SYSTEMS

A very important practical configuration for the generation of magnetic fields is the single wire loop or coil shown in Fig. 2.15. From symmetry considerations, it is obvious that the transverse components of magnetic field on the z axis are zero. For example, the current element at φ' shown in Fig. 2.15 generates a radial as well as longitudinal magnetic field component at the point P. The radial component is exactly canceled by the opposite current element at the position $\varphi' + \pi$. For a current-carrying wire, Eq. (2.47) is used to calculate the generated magnetic field. Integrating around the loop yields the total field generated,

$$\mathbf{B} = \frac{\mu_0 I}{4\pi} \oint_l \frac{a\,d\varphi'\,\hat{\boldsymbol{\varphi}}' \times \hat{\mathbf{R}}}{a^2 + z^2}$$

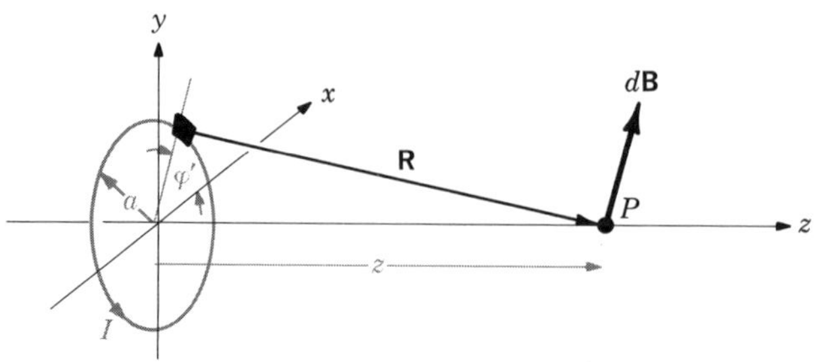

Fig. 2.15 Calculation of the magnetic field on the axis of a current loop.

The $\hat{\mathbf{r}}$ component of $\mathbf{B}$ may be shown to be zero. The z component of the unit-vector cross product $\hat{\boldsymbol{\varphi}}' \times \hat{\mathbf{R}}$ is a/R, and thus B_z is

$$B_z = \frac{\mu_0 I a^2}{4\pi} \int_0^{2\pi} \frac{d\varphi'}{(a^2 + z^2)^{3/2}}$$
$$= \frac{\mu_0 I}{2} \frac{a^2}{(a^2 + z^2)^{3/2}} \tag{2.56}$$

Equation (2.56) gives the longitudinal magnetic field on the axis associated with a single turn of wire. If the coil is a tight bundle of N loops, it is a good approximation to replace I by NI in Eq. (2.56).

It is often necessary in many practical applications to have a constant B_z field over a considerable distance along the axis. One disadvantage in using a single coil for this purpose is that the z variation in Eq. (2.56) is significant. A more uniform field is obtained by using two coils separated by a distance d, as illustrated in Fig. 2.16. If each coil contains N turns, the total magnetic field associated with the two-coil system may be inferred from Eq. (2.56),

$$B_z(z) = \frac{\mu_0 N I a^2}{2} \left[\frac{1}{(a^2 + z^2)^{3/2}} + \frac{1}{(a^2 + (z - d)^2)^{3/2}} \right] \tag{2.57}$$

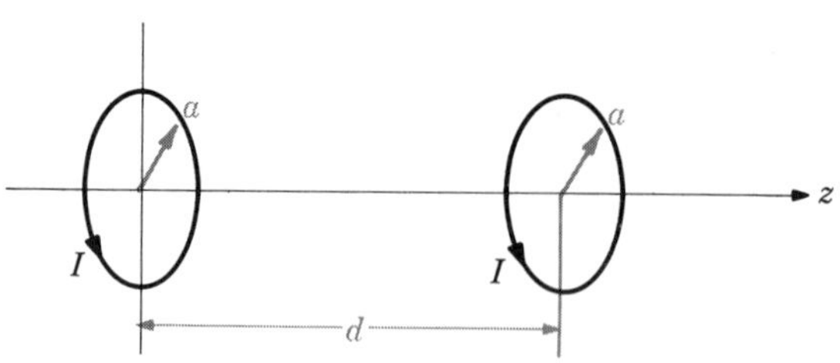

Fig. 2.16 The Helmholtz-coil configuration for generating a uniform B_z field.

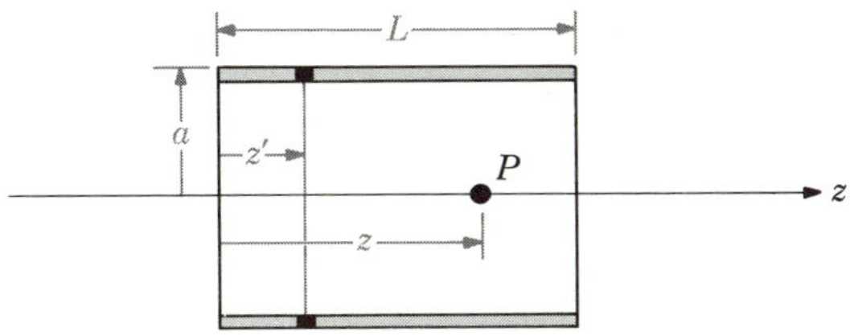

Fig. 2.17 The solenoid consists of an extended continuously wound coil.

From Eq. (2.57) it is easily shown that dB_z/dz at the midpoint ($z = d/2$) is zero. It is left as a problem to show that if $d = a$, the second derivative of the field vanishes at the midpoint.

A second very important application of Eq. (2.56) is in connection with the solenoid. A *solenoid* is a continuously wound cylinder of current-carrying coils, as shown in Fig. 2.17. For the purposes of this analysis it is assumed that the coil thickness is small. The B_z field on the axis is found by considering the magnetic field contribution from each element of the solenoid. If the solenoid has a total of N turns uniformly wound along its length L, the number of coils in each element of distance dz' is $N\,dz'/L$. From Eq. (2.56) in conjunction with the geometry depicted in Fig. 2.17, the total longitudinal magnetic field at the field point z on the axis is

$$B_z = \frac{\mu_0 N I a^2}{2L} \int_0^L \frac{dz'}{[a^2 + (z - z')^2]^{3/2}}$$

This integral may be carried out to yield the final result,

$$B_z = \frac{\mu_0 N I}{2L} \left[\frac{z}{\sqrt{z^2 + a^2}} + \frac{L - z}{\sqrt{(L - z)^2 + a^2}} \right] \tag{2.58}$$

For the long solenoid, where $a \ll L$ and $|z - L/2| \ll L$, Eq. (2.58) reduces to

$$B_z = \frac{\mu_0 N I}{L}$$

and the magnetic field is uniform.

★2.8 The Magnetic Dipole

In the previous section the relatively simple calculation of magnetic field along the axis of a current-carrying wire loop was carried out. The more

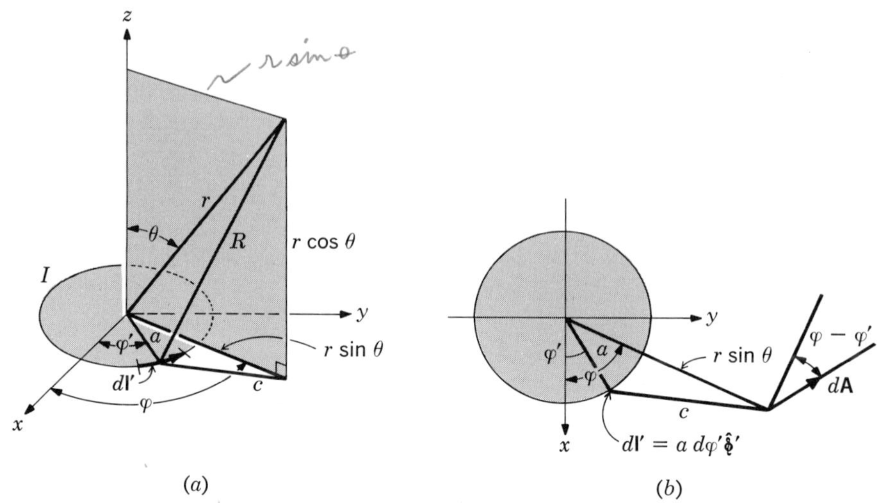

Fig. 2.18 The magnetic dipole in spherical field coordinates.

general case involves the calculation of magnetic field at an arbitrary field point. The coordinates used are illustrated in Fig. 2.18. The current-carrying wire loop is called a *magnetic dipole* because the magnetic fields generated are similar in form to the electric fields generated by the electric dipole.

It is more convenient to calculate the potential **A** associated with the loop than to calculate **B** directly. In order to simplify the calculation of **A**, it is first necessary to utilize all the symmetry properties of the source system. The system has φ symmetry, and thus **A** and **B** have no φ variation. We see from Eqs. (2.39) and (2.55) that the potential $d\mathbf{A}$ generated by $I\,d\mathbf{l}'$ is

$$d\mathbf{A} = \frac{\mu_0 I\, d\mathbf{l}'}{4\pi R} \tag{2.59}$$

Note from Eq. (2.59) that the vector $d\mathbf{A}$ is parallel to $d\mathbf{l}'$. As Fig. 2.19 shows, symmetrical current elements produce only a φ component of $d\mathbf{A}_1 + d\mathbf{A}_2$, since $R_1 = R_2$ and I is not φ dependent. The potential function is thus of the form $\mathbf{A} = A_\varphi(r,\theta)\hat{\boldsymbol{\varphi}}$. The vector problem is now reduced to an evaluation of the scalar function $A_\varphi(r,\theta)$. From Fig. 2.18 and Eq. (2.59), we obtain

$$d\mathbf{A} = \frac{\mu_0 I a\, d\varphi'\, \hat{\boldsymbol{\varphi}}'}{4\pi R} \tag{2.60}$$

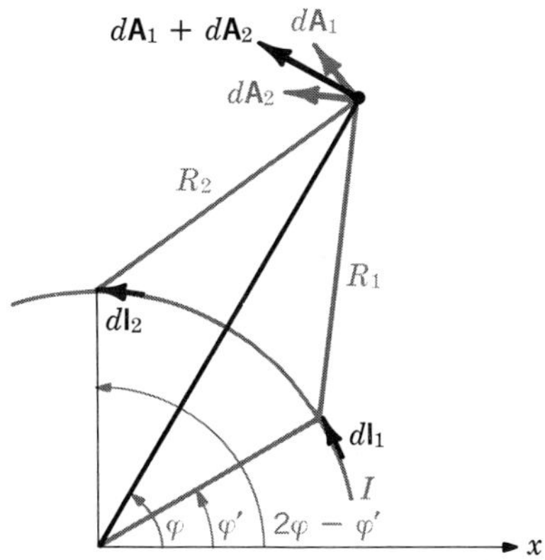

Fig. 2.19 Symmetry conditions indicate that **A** has only a φ component.

where $d\mathbf{A}$ is the increment of $\mathbf{A}$ at the field point (r,θ,φ) generated by the source element at $(a,\pi/2,\varphi')$. The component of $d\mathbf{A}$ in the $\hat{\boldsymbol{\varphi}}$ direction is of interest, and from Fig. 2.18 it is seen that

$$dA_\varphi = \frac{\mu_0 I a \, d\varphi' \cos(\varphi - \varphi')}{4\pi R} \tag{2.61}$$

The total A_φ is found by integrating around the loop,

$$A_\varphi = \frac{\mu_0 I a}{4\pi} \int_0^{2\pi} \frac{\cos(\varphi - \varphi') \, d\varphi'}{R} \tag{2.62}$$

It is now necessary to obtain R as a function of φ' and the field coordinates. From Fig. 2.18 we see that R is the hypotenuse of a right triangle with legs $r \cos\theta$ and c. The length c is found from the law of cosines for the triangle shown in Fig. 2.18,

$$c^2 = a^2 + r^2 \sin^2\theta - 2ar \sin\theta \cos(\varphi - \varphi')$$

and R is then obtained from the pythagorian theorem as

$$\begin{aligned} R^2 &= r^2 \cos^2\theta + r^2 \sin^2\theta + a^2 - 2ar \sin\theta \cos(\varphi - \varphi') \\ &= r^2 + a^2 - 2ar \sin\theta \cos(\varphi - \varphi') \end{aligned} \tag{2.63}$$

This is the desired relationship, and we may now use this R formally in Eq. (2.62).

It is of primary practical interest to know A_φ at large values of r where $r \gg a$. In this case Eq. (2.63) can be written in the approximate form

$$R \simeq r\left[1 - 2\frac{a}{r}\sin\theta\cos(\varphi - \varphi')\right]^{1/2}$$

$$\frac{1}{R} \simeq \frac{1}{r}\left[1 + \frac{a}{r}\sin\theta\cos(\varphi - \varphi')\right]$$

where only the first two terms in the binomial expansion of $1/R$ have been retained. This greatly simplifies the integration in Eq. (2.62),

$$A_\varphi \simeq \frac{\mu_0 I a}{4\pi r} \int_0^{2\pi} \cos(\varphi - \varphi') \left[1 + \frac{a}{r} \sin\theta \cos(\varphi - \varphi')\right] d\varphi'$$

$$\simeq \frac{\mu_0 I a}{4\pi r} \frac{a\pi \sin\theta}{r} = \frac{\mu_0}{4\pi} \frac{I\pi a^2 \sin\theta}{r^2}$$

This expression may be converted into the common vector form by remembering that $\nabla(1/r) = -\hat{\mathbf{r}}/r^2$ and that $\hat{\mathbf{z}} \times \hat{\mathbf{r}} = \hat{\boldsymbol{\varphi}} \sin\theta$. It is also convenient to define the magnetic-dipole moment $\mathbf{m}$ as $\mathbf{m} = I\pi a^2 \hat{\mathbf{z}}$; thus

$$\mathbf{A} = -\frac{\mu_0}{4\pi} \mathbf{m} \times \nabla\left(\frac{1}{r}\right) \tag{2.64}$$

The magnetic fields are now obtained from Eq. (2.64) as

$$\begin{aligned} \mathbf{B} &= \nabla \times \mathbf{A} \\ &= \nabla \times A_\varphi \hat{\boldsymbol{\varphi}} \\ &= \frac{\mu_0 m}{4\pi r^3} (2 \cos\theta\, \hat{\mathbf{r}} + \sin\theta\, \hat{\boldsymbol{\theta}}) \qquad r \gg a \end{aligned} \tag{2.65}$$

Notice the similarity in form of Eq. (2.65) for **B** and Eq. (2.21) for the **E** field generated by an electric dipole. Remember that Eqs. (2.21) and (2.65) are valid only at large distances away from the source, where $r \gg d$ or a.

2.9 REVIEW OF THE FORCE AND FIELD RELATIONS

It is useful to compile the important results of this chapter in one location so that the similarities between the magnetic and electric relations are easily seen. This is done in Table 2.1.

Although a relationship has not been established between the **E** and **B** fields, the close analogy seen in Table 2.1 indicates that the **E** and **B** fields are similar in form. The relationship between **E** and **B** is developed in Chap. 3.

PROBLEMS

2.2-1 A mass $m = 10^{-10}$ kg is charged to a net charge $q = 10^{-8}$ coul and placed in an electric field. The charge is observed to have an acceleration $\mathbf{a} = 10^2\hat{\mathbf{x}} + 10^3\hat{\mathbf{y}}$. Find the electric field **E**.

2.2-2 The electric field for an electric deflection system is $\mathbf{E} = -10 \sin(\pi z/l)\hat{\mathbf{x}}$ in the region $0 < z < l$. Work Example 2.1 for this deflection field.

2.3-1 Use the law of cosines to find the exact expression for Φ for the electric dipole. Find Φ and **E** for $r \gg d$.

Table 2.1 The basic electric and magnetic field equations

Description	*Electric*	*Magnetic*
Physical problem	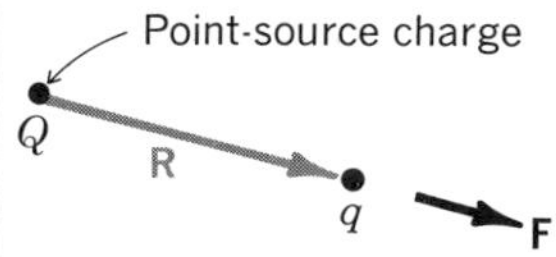	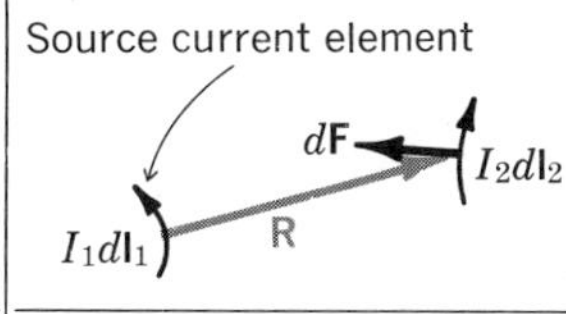
Basic experimental law	Coulomb's law: $\mathbf{F} = \dfrac{Qq\hat{\mathbf{R}}}{4\pi\epsilon_0 R^2}$	Ampère's law of force: $d\mathbf{F} = \dfrac{\mu_0}{4\pi} \dfrac{I_2\, d\mathbf{l}_2 \times (I_1\, d\mathbf{l}_1 \times \hat{\mathbf{R}})}{R^2}$
Definition of field	$\mathbf{F} = q\mathbf{E}$	$d\mathbf{F} = I_2\, d\mathbf{l}_2 \times d\mathbf{B}$
Field equation for a source element	$\mathbf{E} = \dfrac{Q\hat{\mathbf{R}}}{4\pi\epsilon_0 R^2}$	$d\mathbf{B} = \dfrac{\mu_0}{4\pi} \dfrac{I_1\, d\mathbf{l}_1 \times \hat{\mathbf{R}}}{R^2}$
Field equation for a continuous source distribution	$\mathbf{E} = -\dfrac{1}{4\pi\epsilon_0} \int_V \rho \nabla \left(\dfrac{1}{R}\right) dV'$	$\mathbf{B} = -\dfrac{\mu_0}{4\pi} \int_V \mathbf{J} \times \nabla \left(\dfrac{1}{R}\right) dV'$
Definition of the potential function	$\mathbf{E} = -\nabla\Phi$	$\mathbf{B} = \nabla \times \mathbf{A}$
Potential function	$\Phi = \dfrac{1}{4\pi\epsilon_0} \int_V \dfrac{\rho}{R}\, dV'$	$\mathbf{A} = \dfrac{\mu_0}{4\pi} \int_V \dfrac{\mathbf{J}}{R}\, dV'$
General force equations	$\mathbf{F} = q(\mathbf{E} + \mathbf{v} \times \mathbf{B})$ $d\mathbf{F} = (\rho\mathbf{E} + \mathbf{J} \times \mathbf{B})\, dV$	

2.3-2 A uniform line charge of charge density ρ_l exists on the axis of a cylindrical coordinate system in the range $-L/2 < z < L/2$. Solve for Φ. Find E_r as a function of r at $z = 0$ and compare with E_r for the infinite line charge.

2.3-3 There are 101 point charges located on the z axis at points $z = -50, -49, -48, \ldots, -1, 0, +1, +2, \ldots, 49, 50$. Each charge is 10^{-6} coul. Use a computer to solve for $\mathbf{E}$ at the point $(r,z) = (20,0)$. Compare this result with the field generated by an infinite uniform line charge on the z axis of 10^{-6} coul/unit length, and the finite line charge of length 100 m (see Prob. 2.3-2).

2.3-4 Use Eq. (2.10) to solve for $\mathbf{E}$ for the electric dipole. Assume that $r \gg d$.

2.3-5 Calculate the electric field intensity $\mathbf{E}$ at the field coordinate point $x = 2$ m, $y = 0$, $z = 1$ m generated by a line charge of 10^{-2} coul/m on the z axis plus a point charge of 10^{-1} coul at the coordinate point $x = 1$ m, $y = 0$, and $z = 0$.

2.3-6 An infinite, planar charged sheet is located in the $z = 0$ plane and is charged to a uniform surface charge density ρ_s. Solve for the electric field generated by the charged sheet. Calculate the $\mathbf{E}$ field by first finding the field produced by the ring of charge shown in Fig. P2.3-6 and then integrating from $\theta' = 0$ to $\theta' = \pi/2$.

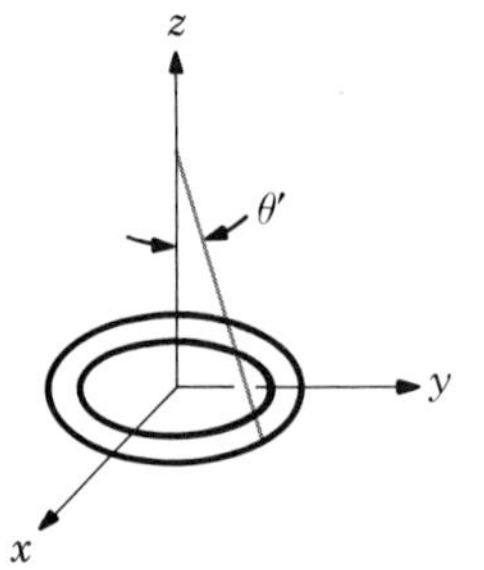

Fig. P2.3-6

2.3-7 Assume that two infinite, parallel charged sheets occupy the $z = 0$ and $z = +d$ planes, and carry a uniform charge density $+\rho_s$ and $-\rho_s$, respectively. Solve for the force per square meter existing on each charged sheet. First show that the net force on one sheet due to all the charges in that sheet is zero; then calculate the force due to the electric fields from the other sheet.

2.3-8 A point charge $+Q$ is located at the origin of a coordinate system and two point charges of magnitude $-Q/2$ are located at $z = +d/2$ and $z = -d/2$. Find Φ and $\mathbf{E}$ everywhere.

2.3-9 Two point charges, $Q_1 = 1$ coul and $Q_2 = 3$ coul, are located at the rectangular coordinate points (1,1,0) and (0,2,1), respectively. Solve for $\mathbf{E}$ at (3,5,5), first by vector addition of the coulomb fields and then by finding Φ and using Eq. (2.8).

2.3-10 A scalar potential function is given by $\Phi = x^2y$. Determine the electric field everywhere. Make a rough sketch of the electric field pattern generated by this potential function.

2.3-11 Calculate the $\mathbf{E}$ field along the axis of a hemispherical shell of radius a which carries a total charge Q uniformly distributed over its surface, as shown in Fig. P2.3-11. Check your answer by showing that $\mathbf{E} = Q\hat{\mathbf{z}}/4\pi\epsilon_0 z^2$ for $z \gg a$.

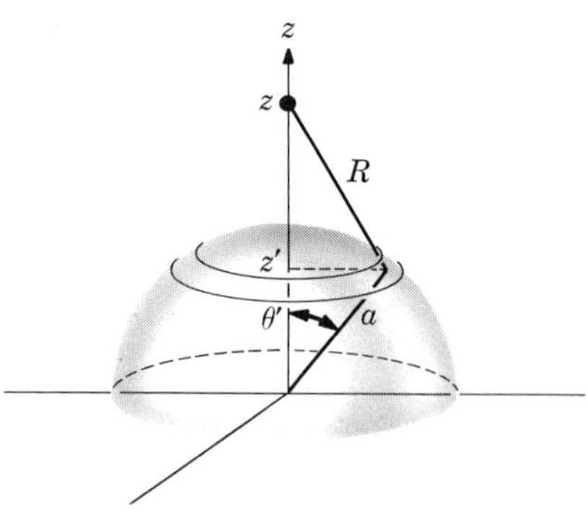

Fig. P2.3-11

2.4-1 Prove that $\nabla\Phi \cdot d\mathbf{l} = d\Phi$ as used in Eq. (2.27).

2.4-2 Find the electric-potential difference between two arbitrary points in the potential field associated with an infinite, straight, filamentary line charge of uniform charge density ρ_l coul/m.

2.4-3 Calculate the work required per square meter of surface area to separate two infinite, parallel charged sheets which are charged to a surface charge density $+\rho_s$ and $-\rho_s$ a distance d_1 to d_2, where $d_2 > d_1$. Use Eq. (2.26) to calculate the potential difference between the sheets at the separation distances d_1 and d_2. What is the relation between the change in potential difference and work for this case? If $\rho_s = 10^{-6}$ coul/m^2 and $d_2 - d_1 = 1$ cm, find the work required, in joules per square meter and in kilowatthours, and the voltage change between the plates when they are moved from d_1 to d_2.

2.4-4 An electron is at rest next to a positive point charge $+Q$ at $t = 0$. The electron is a distance d from the point charge. Solve for the velocity of the electron as a function of r for $t > 0$. Find the electric potential energy and kinetic energy of the electron versus r. Is the total energy conserved? *Hint:* Use $(d/dt)(\dot{r})^2 = 2\dot{r}\ddot{r}$, where $\dot{r} = dr/dt$ and $\ddot{r} = d^2r/dt^2$.

2.5-1 A proton in free space moving at a velocity v is directed toward a second stationary proton. Assume that the protons are spherical balls of diameter 6×10^{-16} m. How large must v be for the two protons to collide? Assume that only coulomb forces are present.

2.5-2 A particle of charge q, mass m, and velocity $v_0\hat{\mathbf{x}}$ at $t = 0$ is placed in a magnetic field $\mathbf{B}$ which has no x component. The acceleration observed on the particle at $t = 0$ is $a_z\hat{\mathbf{z}}$. Find $\mathbf{B}$.

2.5-3 A charge q of mass m is injected into a field region containing electric and magnetic fields. When the charge velocity is $\mathbf{v} = v_x\hat{\mathbf{x}}$, the observed acceleration is $\mathbf{a} = a_x\hat{\mathbf{x}} + a_y\hat{\mathbf{y}}$. Find an $\mathbf{E}$ and $\mathbf{B}$ combination which would generate this $\mathbf{a}$.

2.5-4 An electron is in a crossed electric and magnetic field system with a uniform electric field $\mathbf{E} = E_y\hat{\mathbf{y}}$ and a uniform magnetic field $\mathbf{B} = B_x\hat{\mathbf{x}}$. If the electron is at rest at the origin at $t = 0$, solve the equations of motion and describe the electron motion for $t > 0$.

2.5-5 Repeat Example 2.5 for a nonuniform magnetic field $\mathbf{B} = -B_0 \sin(\pi z/l)\ \hat{\mathbf{y}}$. Assume that $v_z \approx v_0$ and make an approximation.

2.7-1 The B_z field for the Helmholtz coil system is given by Eq. (2.57). It is desired to generate a B_z field which does not deviate by more than 20 percent from its peak value over the greatest possible longitudinal length $L_{\max}$ for a given a. Find the values of d/a and $L_{\max}/a$ which give the desired result, assuming that the peak B_z field equals $\mu_0 NI/2a$ at $z = 0$ and d.

2.7-2 Let $\mathcal{L}$ be the length over which the B_z field is within 10 percent of its peak value in a finite solenoid. Obtain from a computer program a plot of $\mathcal{L}/L$ versus a/L, over the range $0.1 < a/L < 2.0$.

2.8-1 Compare $\mathbf{B}$ generated by the magnetic dipole and $\mathbf{E}$ generated by the electric dipole in Example 2.3. Sketch the field patterns for the electric and magnetic dipoles, illustrating the differences for small r and the similarities for $r \gg a$ or d.

2.8-2 Calculate the magnetic vector potential $\mathbf{A}$ and the magnetic flux density $\mathbf{B}$ associated with a short, thin wire element of length d carrying a uniform current I at the origin of a spherical coordinate system. Assume $d \ll r$ such that $1/R \approx 1/r$. Solve for $\mathbf{B}$ in spherical coordinates when the wire is aligned with the polar axis.

2.8-3 Starting from Eq. (2.60), write $\hat{\boldsymbol{\phi}}'$ in terms of the constant base vectors $\hat{\mathbf{x}}$ and $\hat{\mathbf{y}}$. Integrate to obtain $\mathbf{A}$, thereby proving that $A_r = 0$.

CHAPTER

3

electromagnetic field laws

3.1 INTRODUCTION

The electric and magnetic fields were defined in terms of electric and magnetic forces in Chap. 2. The two basic force laws were introduced: Coulomb's law, describing the force between electric charges, and Ampère's law, describing the force between current elements.

A series of experiments with electric and magnetic phenomena conducted by Coulomb, Henry, Faraday, Ampère, Gauss, and Hertz led to the development of a number of powerful electromagnetic laws which were generally consistent, with some redundancy. Along with the discovery of the important experimental laws, theoretical work by Faraday, Gauss, and Maxwell helped shape the laws into the desired consistent set of descriptive equations. This theoretical development was completed about a century ago and has provided the basis for the growth and application of electrodynamic field theory ever since. The body of laws discussed in this chapter include the Coulomb and Ampère force laws, as discussed in the last chapter, relationships involving the electric and magnetic fields and their sources, and continuity equations.

3.2 GAUSS'S LAW

Gauss's law makes use of the concept of flux lines, as discussed in Sec. 1.3. The direction of the flux lines represents the direction of the vector field function, and the distance between the flux lines denotes the magnitude of the vector field function. The flux lines emanating from a point source of flux are shown in Fig. 3.1. This may represent, in a fluid model, a fluid source with spherical flow radially away from the source. For an electrical source, the flux lines represent electric field lines $\mathbf{E}$ emanating from a point charge Q. The electric field lines, or flux lines, decrease in intensity as r^{-2}, as the drawing indicates. The increment of flux $d\psi$ passing through the incremental surface $d\mathbf{S}$ shown in Fig. 3.1 equals the component of flux density normal to the surface times dS. The total flux emanating from the source is obtained by integrating the incremental flux over any surface which encloses the source.

Consider the general case of a point charge Q surrounded by an arbitrary closed surface S, as shown in Fig. 3.2. The electric field intensity $\mathbf{E}$ is known at any point on the surface from Coulomb's law. Since $\mathbf{E}$ is the electric field density vector, the electric field flux passing through the element of surface dS is

$$d\psi = \mathbf{E} \cdot d\mathbf{S}$$

The total flux is then obtained by integrating over the enclosed surface S,

$$\psi = \oint_S \mathbf{E} \cdot d\mathbf{S} \tag{3.1}$$

The projection of the vector surface element $d\mathbf{S}$ along the direction of the electric field vector $\mathbf{E}$ is denoted as dS_n, where

$$\begin{aligned} dS_n &= \hat{\mathbf{R}} \cdot d\mathbf{S} \\ &= \hat{\mathbf{R}} \cdot \hat{\mathbf{n}}\, dS \end{aligned}$$

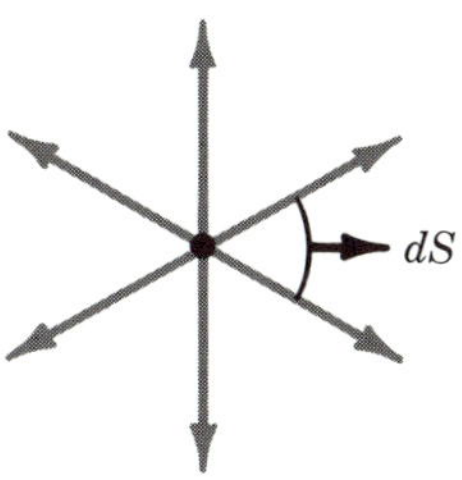

Fig. 3.1 Vector flux lines emanating from an isolated point source.

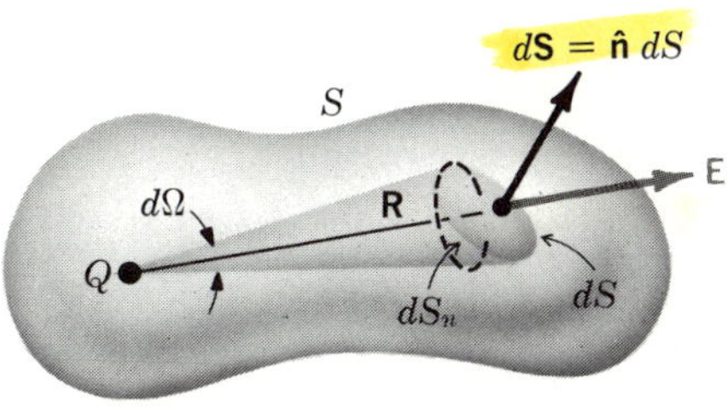

Fig. 3.2 A point charge Q enclosed by an arbitrary surface S. The unit vector normal to the surface is denoted as $\hat{\mathbf{n}}$.

Using Eq. (2.5) in Eq. (3.1), the flux in terms of an integral over the surface element dS_n is

$$\psi = \oint_S \frac{Q}{4\pi\epsilon_0 R^2} \hat{\mathbf{R}} \cdot \hat{\mathbf{n}}\, dS$$

$$= \oint_S \frac{Q}{4\pi\epsilon_0 R^2}\, dS_n$$

The integral is carried out over a sphere of radius R to obtain

$$\psi = \frac{Q}{\epsilon_0} \tag{3.2}$$

The total electric field flux is equal to Q divided by the permittivity of the medium. It is easily seen that the location of the point charge Q within the surface S is completely arbitrary. Thus, by superposition, the total electric field passing through any surface is proportional to the total charge enclosed, for any distribution of point charges or any continuous distribution of charge ρ within S.

Gauss's law is concerned with the source of **E** flux in terms of electric charge. The total flux per unit volume originating at a point in space is, by definition, the divergence of the flux-density vector (see Sec. 1.10). Thus a measure of the source density of **E** is $\nabla \cdot \mathbf{E}$. We now seek an expression for $\nabla \cdot \mathbf{E}$ which will be a basic source law for the **E** field.

In Sec. 2.3 an expression for **E** was derived using Coulomb's law in terms of an integral over the electric charge,

$$\mathbf{E} = -\int \frac{dQ}{4\pi\epsilon_0} \nabla \left(\frac{1}{R}\right) \tag{2.17}$$

Taking the field-point divergence (see Sec. 1.17) of this expression yields

$$\nabla \cdot \mathbf{E} = -\int \frac{dQ}{4\pi\epsilon_0} \nabla^2 \left(\frac{1}{R}\right)$$

When the integration is carried out over a source volume V containing a charge density ρ, $\nabla \cdot \mathbf{E}$ is written as

$$\nabla \cdot \mathbf{E} = -\int_V \frac{\rho(\mathbf{r}')}{4\pi\epsilon_0} \nabla^2 \left(\frac{1}{R}\right) dV'$$

and Eq. (1.127) is used to give

$$\nabla \cdot \mathbf{E} = \frac{\rho(\mathbf{r})}{\epsilon_0} \tag{3.3}$$

which is Gauss's law in point form. Gauss's law in integral form may be obtained by integrating Eq. (3.3) over a volume V,

$$\int_V \nabla \cdot \mathbf{E}\, dV = \int_V \frac{\rho}{\epsilon_0}\, dV$$
$$= \frac{Q}{\epsilon_0}$$

The divergence theorem gives

$$\oint_S \mathbf{E} \cdot d\mathbf{S} = \frac{Q}{\epsilon_0} \tag{3.4}$$

Three general points may be made with regard to Gauss's law. First, Gauss's law, expecially when written in the form of Eq. (3.4), clearly shows that electric charges are the source of electric field lines. It is also implicit in the derivation that Eq. (3.4) holds also for multiply connected volumes. Second, Gauss's law is good for the time-varying case as well as the static case discussed here. For the time-varying case, it has been shown experimentally that Gauss's law gives the correct field at the instant of time corresponding to the instantaneous charge density. Third, it is easier to obtain the electric fields from Gauss's law than from Coulomb's law for cases with certain symmetry.

3.3 APPLICATIONS OF GAUSS'S LAW

One of the most important uses of Gauss's law is for the solution for **E** in terms of source charges. There are now two techniques for calculating **E** in terms of the source charges. Equation (2.11) or (2.17) in Sec. 2.3 may be used to obtain the electric field by summing or integrating over the source charges. The alternate procedure using Gauss's law is much easier if symmetry allows us to carry out the surface integral in Eq. (3.4) in a very simple manner. Several examples are now considered which illustrate some of the methods and applications of Gauss's law.

Example 3.1 The electric field generated by an infinite planar charged sheet in free space An infinite plane is charged to a surface charge density ρ_s. The electric field generated by this charged plane may be found using either Coulomb's law (see Prob. 2.3-7) or Gauss's law. The solution for **E** from Coulomb's law requires a vector integration, whereas Gauss's law requires a trivial scalar integration.

Gauss's law as given by Eq. (3.4) provides a very simple solution for **E** when S is chosen such that $d\mathbf{S}$ is either perpendicular or parallel to **E** and **E** is a constant over S. **E** is then obtained at the surface in space where S is located. From symmetry considerations it is clear that only a normal component of **E** exists, as

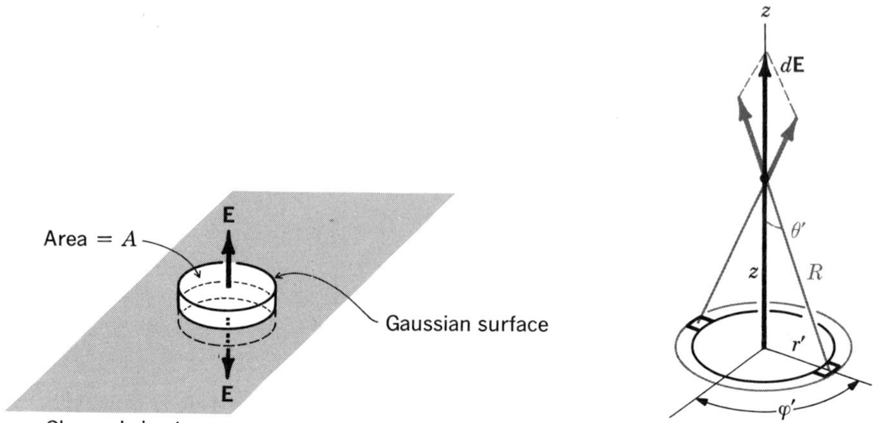

Fig. 3.3 Evaluation of the field **E** from an infinite charged sheet.

shown in Fig. 3.3. This was proved in Prob. 2.3-7, where the field from a charged sheet was calculated from Coulomb's law. Consider the ring of charge shown in Fig. 3.3. An element of charge at the angle φ' in the xy plane produces an incremental field $d\mathbf{E}$ with a component in the z direction and a component in the xy plane. The element of charge at $\varphi' + \pi$ produces an incremental field which adds to the z component and cancels the xy component of the element of charge at φ'. The same cancellation process occurs for all φ' values; thus the ring of charge produces only a z component of field. Similar arguments apply to all the elemental rings from $\theta' = 0$ to $\pi/2$, and thus only a normal electric field is generated by a charged plane. Furthermore, E_z is not dependent on x and y, since the charged plane is infinite.

It is desirable to choose a disk-shaped surface with flat sides parallel to the charged sheet, as shown in Fig. 3.3. Since the only component of electric field present is in the normal direction, the surface integral in Eq. (3.4) is trivial, and we obtain

$$2EA = \frac{\rho_s A}{\epsilon_0}$$

$$E = \frac{\rho_s}{2\epsilon_0} \tag{3.5}$$

The same result is obtained for E as was obtained from Coulomb's law in Prob. 2.3-7. In this case the solution may be written down immediately, since the electric field is uniform over the gaussian surface.

Example 3.2 The electric field between two infinite parallel charged sheets Two infinite parallel charged sheets are located as shown in Fig. 3.4. The fields are contained entirely between the two charged sheets, as is easily demonstrated by

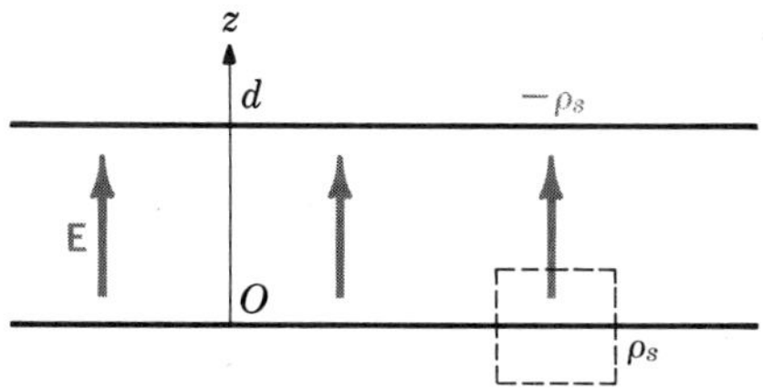

Fig. 3.4 Electric field generated by two oppositely charged planar sheets.

superimposing the fields of each charged sheet. They add in the region $0 < z < d$ to give

$$E_z = \frac{\rho_s}{\epsilon_0} \tag{3.6}$$

and they cancel everywhere else. The field is twice as large as in the previous example, because all the fields lines go in the $+z$ direction, instead of only half of them.

The result obtained in this example is also valid for the field associated with a charged conducting plane in free space. It will be shown in Chap. 5 that no **E** field may exist in a perfect conductor; thus all the **E** lines are forced to leave the surface in the same direction, and Eq. (3.6) is obtained by applying Gauss's law to a gaussian surface as shown in Fig. 3.3.

Example 3.3 The evaluation of charge density from E The source charge distribution which generates a known electric field **E** may be calculated. Consider first the simple case of a uniform field where $\mathbf{E}$ = constant. For this field distribution it is obvious that $\nabla \cdot \mathbf{E} = 0$, and thus, from Eq. (3.3), the charge density in the region is zero.

The more interesting case of a linearly increasing field vector $\mathbf{E} = E_0 x \hat{\mathbf{x}}$ gives $\nabla \cdot \mathbf{E} = E_0$, and from Eq. (3.3),

$$\rho = \epsilon_0 E_0$$

The charge density required for a linearly increasing electric field intensity is a uniform charge density.

Example 3.4 Poisson's equation and Laplace's equation The concept of a scalar potential function associated with a charge distribution was discussed and presented in Sec. 2.3. The equation for Φ is given by Eq. (2.18), and the electric field is derived from Φ by means of Eq. (2.8). Since Gauss's law provides a relationship between electric field and charge density, it is clear that we may use Gauss's law to obtain a relationship between the scalar potential function Φ and charge density. Equation (2.8) is used with Eq. (3.3) to obtain

$$\nabla \cdot (-\nabla \Phi) = \frac{\rho}{\epsilon_0}$$

$$\nabla^2 \Phi = -\frac{\rho}{\epsilon_0} \tag{3.7}$$

An alternate way of obtaining electric field by means of Gauss's law is to solve for the scalar potential function for a given charge distribution from Eq. (3.7) and then use Eq. (2.8). Equation (3.7), an important equation used in both electrostatics and electrodynamics, is called *Poisson's equation.*

In many instances the potential function is needed in a region where the charge density ρ is zero. In this case Eq. (3.7) reduces to

$$\nabla^2\Phi = 0 \tag{3.8}$$

a fundamental equation in electrostatics known as *Laplace's equation.* The techniques required for solving Poisson's equation and Laplace's equation are developed in Chap. 9.

3.4 THE MAGNETIC SOURCE LAW

The magnetic source law describes the source property of **B** and is analogous to Gauss's law. Magnetic flux may be defined analogous to electric flux, as given in the last section. The magnetic flux-density vector is **B**; thus the total magnetic flux is, by analogy with Eq. (3.1),

$$\psi = \int_S \mathbf{B} \cdot d\mathbf{S} \qquad \text{webers} \tag{3.9}$$

where ψ is now the total magnetic flux passing through the open surface S. In the mks system, the unit of **B** is webers/m^2; thus the unit of flux is webers.

It has been found experimentally that there are no magnetic charges analogous to the electric charges in Gauss's law. Thus there are no sources of magnetic flux, and by analogy with Eqs. (3.3) and (3.4),

$$\nabla \cdot \mathbf{B} = 0 \tag{3.10}$$

$$\oint_S \mathbf{B} \cdot d\mathbf{S} = 0 \tag{3.11}$$

These two equations are the basic magnetic source equation in point form and integral form and are widely used in the determination of magnetic field distributions.

Although there are no sources of magnetic field analogous to the sources of electric field in Gauss's law, we obviously may not conclude that there are no sources of magnetic field. It is known from Ampère's law of force that magnetic field is generated by current, not by magnetic charges. Since $\nabla \cdot \mathbf{B} = 0$, there are no magnetic charges which provide termination points for magnetic field lines. In Sec. 3.10 it will be seen that $\nabla \times \mathbf{B} \neq 0$, and circulation-type sources for **B** exist as described in Sec. 1.11. Magnetic field lines are always closed lines and are called solenoidal or source free, but source free only in the sense of Eq. (3.11), where the total flux emanating from a closed surface is zero.

Equations (3.10) and (3.11) are based on experimental evidence that no magnetic sources analogous to the electric sources in Gauss's law exist. However, just as Gauss's law is derived from Coulomb's law, the magnetic source law may be derived from Ampère's law of force. From Ampère's law of force, it was shown in Sec. 2.6 that

$$\mathbf{B} = \nabla \times \mathbf{A} \tag{2.54}$$

The divergence of B may be obtained by taking the divergence of Eq. (2.54),

$$\nabla \cdot \mathbf{B} = \nabla \cdot \nabla \times \mathbf{A} = 0$$

and we obtain Eq. (3.10)

It has been determined experimentally that Eqs. (3.10) and (3.11) hold in the time-varying case as well as in the static case.

Example 3.5 Determination of magnetic field components The longitudinal component of magnetic field B_z is measured over a limited region along the axis of a pole piece. It is determined that

$$B_z = \tfrac{1}{2}B_0\left(1 - \cos\frac{\pi z}{L}\right)$$

in the range $0 < z < L$. Because of pole-piece symmetry, it is easily seen that $B_\varphi = 0$; thus Eq. (3.10) becomes

$$\frac{1}{r}\frac{\partial}{\partial r}(rB_r) + \frac{\partial B_z}{\partial z} = 0$$

The preceding two equations may be combined to yield the differential equation

$$\frac{\partial}{\partial r}(rB_r) = -rB_0\frac{\pi}{2L}\sin\frac{\pi z}{L}$$

which may be integrated to give the radial component of magnetic field,

$$B_r = -r\frac{\pi B_0}{4L}\sin\frac{\pi z}{L}$$

3.5 FARADAY'S LAW

The divergence of electric and magnetic fields was obtained in Secs. 3.2 and 3.4, respectively. The divergence equations describe the generation and extinction source properties of **E** and **B**. We now turn our attention to the circulation source properties of electric and magnetic fields, i.e., the curl values for the fields (see Sec. 1.11). Taking the curl of Eq. (2.8) gives

$$\nabla \times \mathbf{E} = 0 \tag{3.12}$$

for the static case. Static electric fields therefore have no circulation. In this chapter we are endeavoring to develop a set of laws which are also valid in the time-varying case; thus the static relation $\nabla \times \mathbf{E} = 0$ is now reexamined for the time-varying case.

Some historic experiments conducted by Oersted showed that electric current generates a magnetic field. Faraday then set about to demonstrate the converse of this statement; that magnetic fields produce a current. He was finally able to show experimentally that an electric field (an electrical potential) is created by a *changing* magnetic field.

Faraday's experiment is illustrated in Fig. 3.5. Faraday attempted to measure the voltage induced in a detector loop placed close to a current-carrying source loop which generates a magnetic field. The results of the experiment showed that no voltage is induced when a steady current flows in the source loop, but that a voltage is induced when the source current changes. A time-varying magnetic field is required to induce a voltage. Faraday then showed that a voltage could also be induced by moving the detector loop while the current in the source loop was held constant. Thus a change in the magnetic flux linked by the detector loop, by either time or space changes, generates an electric potential.

These experimental results may be written mathematically in the form

$$\Delta V = \frac{d\psi}{dt}$$

where ΔV is the voltage difference measured around the detector loop and ψ is the magnetic flux enclosed by the detector loop. The total derivative is required, since ΔV is generated by a time-varying total flux. The proportionality constant in the above equation is unity in the rationalized

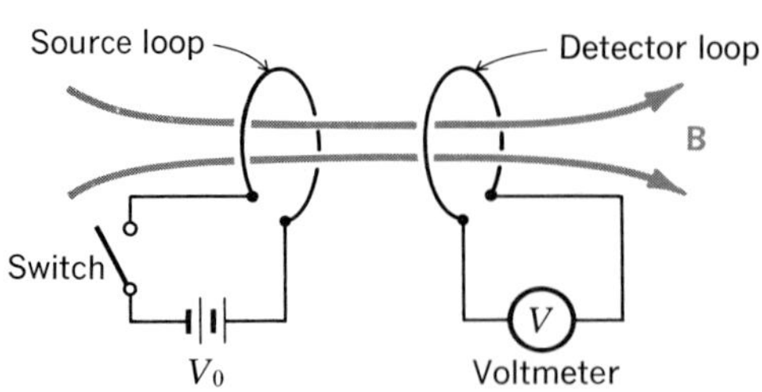

Fig. 3.5 Faraday's experiment which led to the development of Faraday's law.

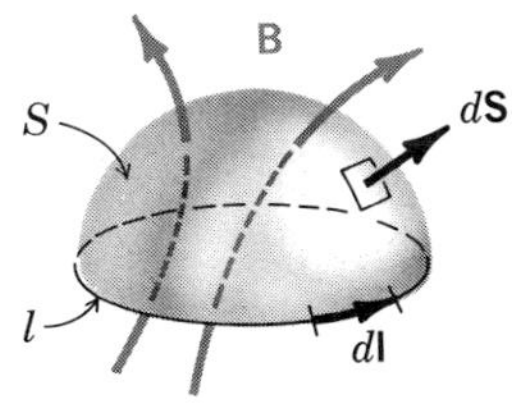

Fig. 3.6 Physical description of the geometry used in Faraday's law.

mks system. The voltage generated between two adjacent points on the loop is related to the electric field by means of Eq. (2.26),

$$\Delta V = -\int_1^2 \mathbf{E} \cdot d\mathbf{l}$$

The basic experimental law may be written in the convenient form

$$\oint_l \mathbf{E} \cdot d\mathbf{l} = -\frac{d}{dt}\int_S \mathbf{B} \cdot d\mathbf{S} \tag{3.13}$$

Equation (3.13) is Faraday's law in integral form, where the vectors $d\mathbf{l}$ and $d\mathbf{S}$ are defined in Fig. 3.6. Note that $d\mathbf{S}$ is oriented in relation to $d\mathbf{l}$ in accordance with the right-hand rule, as in the development of Stokes's theorem. A time rate of change of magnetic flux induces an electric field, according to Eq. (3.13), even in the absence of a physical detector loop.

Since the change in magnetic flux may be due to a change in the surface S or a change in the magnetic field $\mathbf{B}$, it is necessary to consider both cases. In the next two sections we consider each case with illustrations.

3.6 A STATIONARY LOOP IN A TIME-VARYING MAGNETIC FIELD

An important practical application of Faraday's law is a stationary loop in a time-varying magnetic field. In this case $d\mathbf{S}$ is time independent, $\mathbf{B}$ is time varying, and Eq. (3.13) becomes

$$\oint_l \mathbf{E} \cdot d\mathbf{l} = -\int_S \frac{\partial \mathbf{B}}{\partial t} \cdot d\mathbf{S} \tag{3.14}$$

Applying Stokes's theorem to the left-hand side of Eq. (3.14) gives

$$\int_S \nabla \times \mathbf{E} \cdot d\mathbf{S} = -\int_S \frac{\partial \mathbf{B}}{\partial t} \cdot d\mathbf{S}$$

If the surface S is allowed to shrink to an elemental surface at a field point, we obtain the point relation

$$\nabla \times \mathbf{E} = -\frac{\partial \mathbf{B}}{\partial t} \tag{3.15}$$

which is a fundamental equation in electromagnetic theory called the *differential* or *point form* of Faraday's law. This equation shows that $\nabla \times \mathbf{E}$ is not zero in the general time-varying case, and that the "source" for the circulation of $\mathbf{E}$ is a time-varying magnetic field. Equation (3.15) provides a fundamental interrelationship between the electric and magnetic field vectors. Note that if $\mathbf{B}$ = constant, Eq. (3.15) reduces to the static form, Eq. (3.12). Faraday's law thus reduces to $\nabla \times \mathbf{E} = 0$, as derived from Coulomb's law, for no time variations.

Although Eq. (3.15) was derived for a stationary loop in a time-varying magnetic field, the same result is obtained in the general case of a moving loop in a time-varying magnetic field, as shown in Sec. 3.8.

Example 3.6 The betatron The betatron is an electron accelerator which utilizes the circulating electric field induced by a time-varying magnetic field in space. An electron executes an approximately circular path in the betatron, as illustrated in Fig. 3.7. The magnetic field increases linearly with time $\mathbf{B} = B_0' t\hat{\mathbf{z}}$, and Eq. (3.13) gives

$$\oint_l \mathbf{E} \cdot d\mathbf{l} = -\int_S \frac{\partial \mathbf{B}}{\partial t} \cdot d\mathbf{S}$$

$$E_\varphi 2\pi r = -B_0' \pi r^2$$

for constant E_φ. It is seen immediately that there is a net circulation of the $\mathbf{E}$ field. E_φ is then obtained as

$$E_\varphi = -\frac{r}{2} B_0'$$

The electric potential ΔV received in one orbit is obtained from Eq. (2.26),

$$\Delta V = \pi r^2 B_0'$$

During each orbit the electron picks up an increment of energy

$$\Delta U = e\,\Delta V = e\pi r^2 B_0' \text{ ev}$$

If the magnetic field changes by 1 weber/m² in 1 msec,

$$B_0' = 10^3 \text{ webers} \cdot \text{m}^2 \cdot \text{sec}^{-1}$$

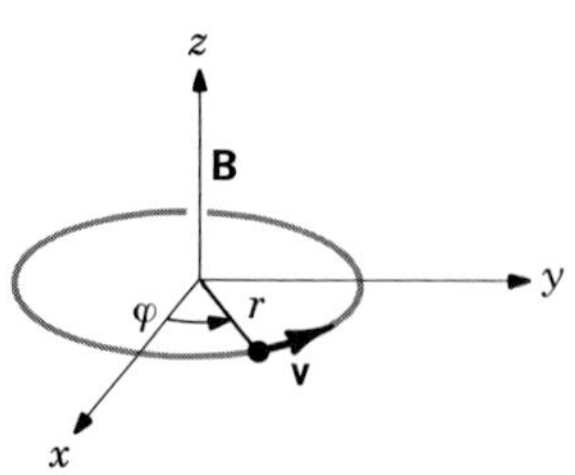

Fig. 3.7 The betatron electron accelerator.

For a 1-cm radius the potential increase per cycle is

$$\Delta V = \pi 10^{-4} \times 10^{3} = \frac{\pi}{10} \text{ volts/cycle}$$

If the electron orbital frequency is 10^9 Hz, the total energy picked up in 1 msec is approximately 10^6 ev, or 1 mev, assuming a constant orbital frequency and radius.

3.7 A MOVING LOOP IN A CONSTANT MAGNETIC FIELD

When a loop moves with a velocity **v** in a constant magnetic field, as pictured in Fig. 3.8, forces are generated on any conduction charges in the loop in accordance with Eq. (2.33),

$$\mathbf{F} = q\mathbf{v} \times \mathbf{B} \tag{2.33}$$

The force per unit charge exerted on each element of the loop is

$$\frac{\mathbf{F}}{q} = \mathbf{v} \times \mathbf{B}$$

To an observer moving with the loop there is no apparent motion; thus this force is interpreted as an electric field,

$$\frac{\mathbf{F}}{q} = \mathbf{E}$$
$$= \mathbf{v} \times \mathbf{B}$$

The moving observer calculates the voltage around the loop in accordance with the expression

$$\oint_l \mathbf{E} \cdot d\mathbf{l} = \oint_l (\mathbf{v} \times \mathbf{B}) \cdot d\mathbf{l} \tag{3.16}$$

Equation (3.16) is a companion equation to Eq. (3.14).

It is shown in the next section that the total net circulation of **E** in the general case of a moving loop in a time-varying magnetic field is obtained by simply summing the terms on the right-hand side of Eqs. (3.14) and (3.16).

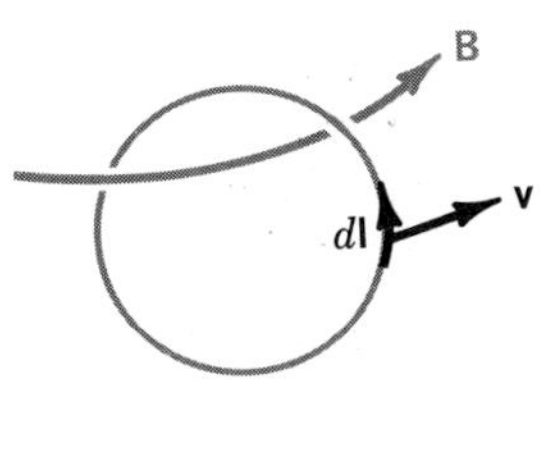

Fig. 3.8 A moving loop in a constant magnetic field.

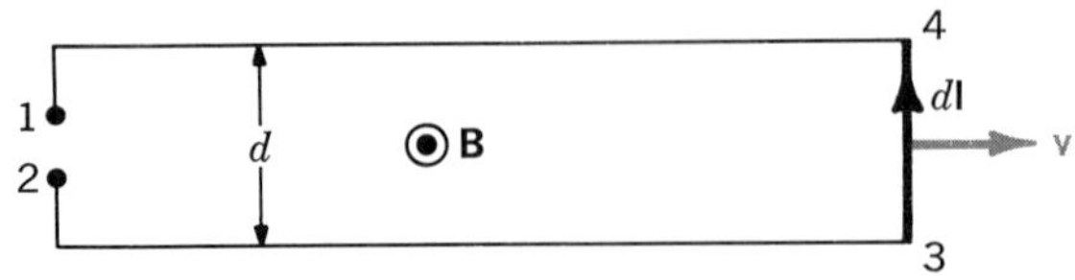

Fig. 3.9 An expanding loop in a constant magnetic field. The magnetic field points out of the paper.

Example 3.7 An expanding loop in a constant uniform magnetic field A conducting wire loop is oriented in a plane perpendicular to a uniform magnetic field, as illustrated in Fig. 3.9. The end of the loop moves with a constant velocity **v**, as indicated, thereby steadily increasing the size of the loop. The voltage generated between terminals 1 and 2 may be calculated by using the appropriate form of Faraday's law. Since the magnetic field is constant, the appropriate expression is Eq. (3.16). It is assumed that $\mathbf{E} \cdot d\mathbf{l}$ is zero along the wire loop. This is equivalent to assuming that the wire is a perfect conductor such that the **E** field is shorted out along $d\mathbf{l}$ (see Chap. 5). Thus

$$\oint_l \mathbf{E} \cdot d\mathbf{l} = \int_{\substack{1\\ \text{gap}}}^{2} \mathbf{E} \cdot d\mathbf{l}$$

$$= V_1 - V_2$$

When this expression is combined with Eq. (3.16), we obtain

$$V_1 - V_2 = \int_3^4 (\mathbf{v} \times \mathbf{B}) \cdot d\mathbf{l}$$

From the geometry pictured in Fig. 3.9, we see that the above integral reduces to

$$V_1 - V_2 = -vBd$$

and terminal 2 becomes positive with respect to terminal 1. If an electrical load is connected across the terminals, a current flows in a direction opposite to $d\mathbf{l}$. If a resistor R is connected across the terminals, a current $I = Bvd/R$ flows. The power dissipated in the resistor is

$$P = I^2R$$

$$= \frac{(Bvd)^2}{R}$$

From energy-conservation considerations the power required to move the end of the loop in the magnetic field must equal the power dissipated in the resistor. Energy is transferred from the mechanical source which moves the loop to the resistor. From the basic definition of force on a current element,

$$d\mathbf{F} = I\, d\mathbf{l} \times \mathbf{B}$$

the total magnetic field force exerted on the moving portion of the loop is

$$\begin{aligned}\mathbf{F} &= I\int_3^4 d\mathbf{l} \times \mathbf{B} \\ &= -IBd\,\hat{\mathbf{v}}\end{aligned}$$

where a minus sign has been inserted because current flows in the direction opposite to $d\mathbf{l}$. The induced field force opposes the direction of motion. In order to move the loop it is necessary to impress a mechanical force equal and opposite to the induced field force. The mechanical force and velocity are thus in the same direction, and positive energy is required to move the loop. The mechanical power is

$$\begin{aligned}P &= \mathbf{F} \cdot \mathbf{v} \\ &= IBvd\end{aligned}$$

Since $I = Bvd/R$,

$$P = \frac{(Bvd)^2}{R}$$

and it is thus shown that the mechanical power required to move the loop equals the electrical power dissipated in the resistor.

Example 3.8 A rotating coil in a uniform magnetic field Consider the rectangular coil illustrated in Fig. 3.10, where $\mathbf{B}$ is perpendicular to the coil axis. The voltage induced across the terminals 1 and 2 is to be determined. Since the magnetic field is not time varying, the appropriate form of Faraday's law is Eq. (3.16). It is simpler mathematically to revert back to the original equation, Eq. (3.13), and calculate the total time rate of change of magnetic flux passing through the rectangular loop. We will proceed with Eq. (3.13) and leave the derivation based on Eq. (3.16) as a problem.

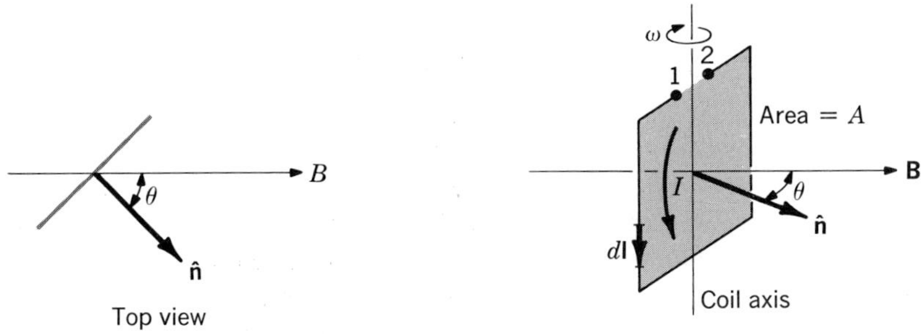

Fig. 3.10 A rotating coil in a uniform static magnetic field.

The net circulation of **E** around the loop consists of a term obtained from integrating along the wire (which is zero) plus a term obtained from integrating across the gap,

$$\oint_l \mathbf{E} \cdot d\mathbf{l} = \underset{\text{along wire}}{\int_1^2} \mathbf{E} \cdot d\mathbf{l} + \underset{\text{gap}}{\int_2^1} \mathbf{E} \cdot d\mathbf{l}$$

$$= 0 + \underset{\text{gap}}{\int_2^1} \mathbf{E} \cdot d\mathbf{l}$$

From the definition of the dot product, Eq. (3.13) becomes

$$\int_2^1 \mathbf{E} \cdot d\mathbf{l} = -\frac{d}{dt} \int_S \mathbf{B} \cdot d\mathbf{S}$$

$$= -\frac{d}{dt} BA \cos \theta$$

If $t = 0$ at $\theta = 0$, then $\theta = \omega t$, where ω is the coil rotation frequency in radians per second. The preceding equation reduces to

$$\int_2^1 \mathbf{E} \cdot d\mathbf{l} = BA\omega \sin \omega t$$

The voltage induced across the terminals is

$$V_2 - V_1 = BA\omega \sin \omega t$$

For an N-turn coil, the voltage is simply N times the single-turn coil voltage.

The above result indicates that by mechanically rotating a loop in a constant magnetic field, an alternating voltage may be generated. This is the principle of the electric generator, and if terminals 1 and 2 are attached to slip rings, an alternating-voltage generator is obtained. If the terminals are connected to a load, and current is allowed to flow through the loop, electromagnetic forces are induced which oppose the rotational motion. Mechanical power is then required to rotate the coil, and this power is converted into electrical power delivered at the load. This is the principle of the ac electric generator.

★3.8 A Moving Loop in a Time-varying Magnetic Field

The general case involves motion of the loop l in addition to a time variation of magnetic field. Consider the moving loop $l_1(t)$, shown in Fig. 3.11, at time t. The surface S_1 and surface element $d\mathbf{S}_1$ are indicated. The magnetic field at time t is $\mathbf{B}(t)$. At time $t + \Delta t$ the loop moves a distance $\mathbf{v}\,\Delta t$. The surface element and magnetic field at time $t + \Delta t$ are denoted as $d\mathbf{S}_2$ and $\mathbf{B}(t + \Delta t)$, respectively, and the loop is denoted as $l_2(t + \Delta t)$. During the time increment Δt the surface has swept out the volume indicated in Fig. 3.11.

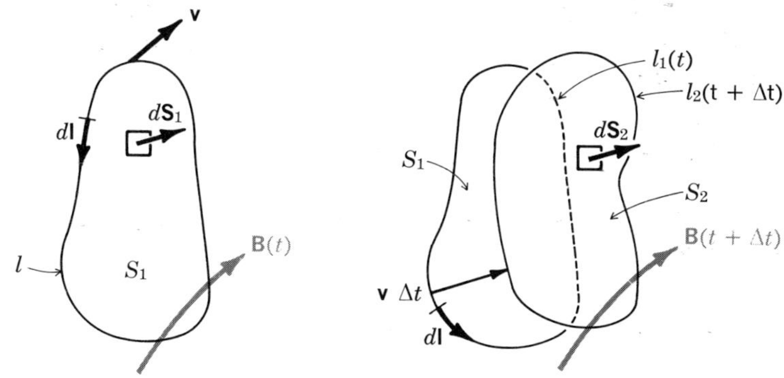

Fig. 3.11 A moving loop in a time-varying magnetic field.

Applying the basic rules of differentiation to the right-hand side of Eq. (3.13) gives

$$\frac{d}{dt}\int_S \mathbf{B}\cdot d\mathbf{S} = \lim_{\Delta t\to 0}\frac{1}{\Delta t}\left[\int_{S_2}\mathbf{B}(t+\Delta t)\cdot d\mathbf{S}_2 - \int_{S_1}\mathbf{B}(t)\cdot d\mathbf{S}_1\right]$$

It is desirable to convert this expression into a form with simultaneous values of magnetic field; thus the magnetic field is expanded at time t in accordance with a Taylor series expansion,

$$\mathbf{B}(t+\Delta t) = \mathbf{B}(t) + \frac{\partial \mathbf{B}(t)}{\partial t}\Delta t + \text{higher-order terms}$$

to obtain the first-order expression

$$\frac{d}{dt}\int_S \mathbf{B}\cdot d\mathbf{S} = \lim_{\Delta t\to 0}\frac{1}{\Delta t}\left[\int_{S_2}\left(\mathbf{B}\cdot d\mathbf{S}_2 + \frac{\partial \mathbf{B}}{\partial t}\Delta t\cdot d\mathbf{S}_2\right) - \int_{S_1}\mathbf{B}\cdot d\mathbf{S}_1\right] \tag{3.17}$$

where $\mathbf{B}(t)$ is denoted now simply as $\mathbf{B}$.

A useful relation may be developed for use in Eq. (3.17) by examining the divergence theorem for $\mathbf{B}$ at time t in association with the volume shown in Fig. 3.11,

$$\begin{aligned}\int_V \nabla\cdot\mathbf{B}\,dV &= \oint_S \mathbf{B}\cdot d\mathbf{S}\\ &= \int_{S_2}\mathbf{B}\cdot d\mathbf{S}_2 - \int_{S_1}\mathbf{B}\cdot d\mathbf{S}_1 + \oint_l \mathbf{B}\cdot(d\mathbf{l}\times\mathbf{v})\,\Delta t\end{aligned}$$

where the enclosing surface includes not only S_1 and S_2, but also the area swept out by the moving loop in the time Δt. Note that the peripheral incremental surface vector is $d\mathbf{l} \times \mathbf{v}\,\Delta t$ and the peripheral surface integral reduces to a line integral. Since $\nabla \cdot \mathbf{B} = 0$, the above expression may be written in the form

$$\int_{S_2} \mathbf{B} \cdot d\mathbf{S}_2 - \int_{S_1} \mathbf{B} \cdot d\mathbf{S}_1 = \oint_l \mathbf{B} \cdot (\mathbf{v} \times d\mathbf{l})\,\Delta t$$

When this equation is substituted into Eq. (3.17), the desired result is obtained,

$$\frac{d}{dt}\int_S \mathbf{B} \cdot d\mathbf{S} = \oint_l \mathbf{B} \cdot (\mathbf{v} \times d\mathbf{l}) + \int_S \frac{\partial \mathbf{B}}{\partial t} \cdot d\mathbf{S}$$

Using this result in Eq. (3.13) gives

$$\begin{aligned}\oint_l \mathbf{E}' \cdot d\mathbf{l} &= -\int_S \frac{\partial \mathbf{B}}{\partial t} \cdot d\mathbf{S} - \oint_l \mathbf{B} \cdot (\mathbf{v} \times d\mathbf{l}) \\ &= -\int_S \frac{\partial \mathbf{B}}{\partial t} \cdot d\mathbf{S} + \oint_l (\mathbf{v} \times \mathbf{B}) \cdot d\mathbf{l} \qquad (3.18)\end{aligned}$$

Equation (3.18) gives the general form of Faraday's law for a moving loop in a time-varying magnetic field. The line integral is evaluated around the periphery of the *moving* loop. The electric field thus measured is the electric field in the *moving frame of reference;* it is designated $\mathbf{E}'$ to distinguish it from the electric field $\mathbf{E}$ measured in a stationary frame of reference. As explained in Sec. 3.7, $\mathbf{E}'$ includes the term $\mathbf{v} \times \mathbf{B}$, which is not included in $\mathbf{E}$. Hence

$$\mathbf{E} = \mathbf{E}' - \mathbf{v} \times \mathbf{B}$$

Using this result in Eq. (3.18) gives

$$\oint_l \mathbf{E} \cdot d\mathbf{l} = -\int_S \frac{\partial \mathbf{B}}{\partial t} \cdot d\mathbf{S}$$

from which the point relation

$$\nabla \times \mathbf{E} = -\frac{\partial \mathbf{B}}{\partial t}$$

is obtained. This result, which is valid for a moving loop in a time-varying magnetic field, is the same as Eq. (3.15), which was obtained for a stationary loop in a time-varying magnetic field. Thus the point form of Faraday's law given in Eq. (3.15) is valid for the general case.

When the loop velocity v is zero, Eq. (3.18) reduces immediately to Eq. (3.14). Conversely, when $\partial\mathbf{B}/\partial t$ is zero, the expression for electric ★field as seen by an observer moving with the loop is Eq. (3.16).

3.9 THE CONTINUITY EQUATION

In this section we deviate from the systematic consideration of electromagnetic field divergence and curl to consider the source law for electric current. A fundamental law governing the relationship between current and charge in a time-varying situation is required. An expression for $\nabla \cdot \mathbf{J}$ is desired, to establish the source relation for electric current.

Electric charges may not be created or destroyed; therefore charges must be accounted for by means of either current flow or stored charge. Consider the source volume V pictured in Fig. 3.12, which contains a net charge Q. Electric current is allowed to flow through the enclosing surface S, and the current-density vector at any element of surface $d\mathbf{S}$ is denoted as $\mathbf{J}$. Thus the total net current leaving the volume V is

$$I = \oint_S \mathbf{J} \cdot d\mathbf{S}$$

The total current I leaving V must be accounted for by a decrease in the total stored charged within V,

$$\oint_S \mathbf{J} \cdot d\mathbf{S} = -\frac{dQ}{dt} \tag{3.19}$$

In the general case the total charge within V may be distributed according to a scalar volume charge-density function ρ, and

$$\oint_S \mathbf{J} \cdot d\mathbf{S} = -\frac{d}{dt}\int_V \rho\, dV \tag{3.20}$$

The divergence theorem gives

$$\int_V \nabla \cdot \mathbf{J}\, dV = -\int_V \frac{\partial \rho}{\partial t}\, dV \tag{3.21}$$

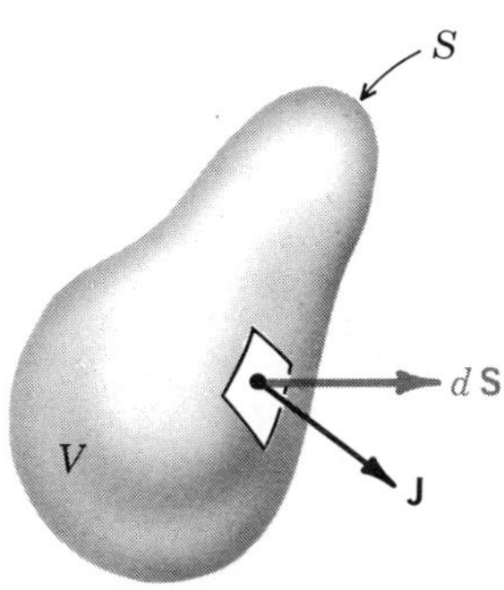

Fig. 3.12 Charge is stored in the volume V, and current flows through the surface S.

If V is allowed to shrink to an elemental volume at the field point, a point relation is obtained,

$$\nabla \cdot \mathbf{J} = -\frac{\partial \rho}{\partial t} \tag{3.22}$$

Equations (3.21) and (3.22) are called the *current-continuity equations* in integral and differential or point form, respectively.

The current-continuity equation for the case of steady current with no time variation is $\nabla \cdot \mathbf{J} = 0$, and there are thus no current sources for this case; Eq. (3.20) gives $\oint_S \mathbf{J} \cdot d\mathbf{S} = 0$, and for any enclosed surface the net outflow of current must be zero. $\mathbf{J}$ can have only a nonzero divergence at a point where charge density can change with time.

3.10 AMPÈRE'S CIRCUITAL LAW

Oersted showed experimentally that magnetic fields are generated by electric current. However, in Sec. 3.4 we saw that there are no magnetic sources which originate or terminate magnetic field lines; that is, $\nabla \cdot \mathbf{B} = 0$. The sources of magnetic field (except for permanent magnets) generate a net circulation of $\mathbf{B}$ at the source point. In this section we develop an equation for $\nabla \times \mathbf{B}$, thereby obtaining the magnetic analog of Faraday's law.

Experiments with magnetic fields associated with current-carrying wires led Ampère to an experimental law for *steady* currents, called *Ampère's circuital law,*

$$\oint_l \mathbf{B} \cdot d\mathbf{l} = \mu_0 I \tag{3.23}$$

where I is the total electric current enclosed by the closed loop l. Clearly, Eq. (3.23) must be related to Ampère's law of force and the Biot-Savart law. This relation is shown in the next section.

Equation (3.23) may be generalized to the case where a current density $\mathbf{J}$ exists, as depicted in Fig. 3.13. For the loop l and surface S shown, Eq. (3.23) assumes the form

$$\oint_l \mathbf{B} \cdot d\mathbf{l} = \mu_0 \int_S \mathbf{J} \cdot d\mathbf{S} \tag{3.24}$$

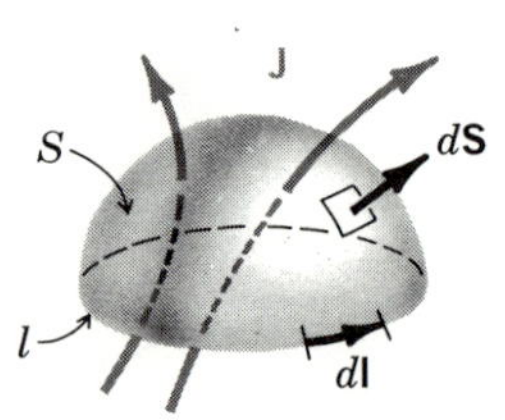

Fig. 3.13 Surface and loop geometry used in Ampère's circuital law.

Note a similarity in form between Eqs. (3.24) and (3.13). Equation (3.13) states that the net circulation of electric field comes from a varying magnetic field. Equation (3.24) states that the net circulation of magnetic field is electric current. Stokes's theorem is applied to Eq. (3.24) to give

$$\int_S \nabla \times \mathbf{B} \cdot d\mathbf{S} = \mu_0 \int_S \mathbf{J} \cdot d\mathbf{S}$$

If the surface S shrinks to an elemental surface, the point form of Ampère's circuital law is obtained,

$$\nabla \times \mathbf{B} = \mu_0 \mathbf{J} \qquad \text{(steady current)} \tag{3.25}$$

Example 3.9 The magnetic field generated by a line current The magnetic field associated with a long, straight current-carrying wire may be obtained from Ampère's circuital law. This problem was solved in Example 2.7 from the Biot-Savart law. Figure 3.14 shows the geometry considered. A filament of steady current I lies on the z axis and flows in the $+z$ direction. It is obvious that there are no variations in either z or φ; this is a useful symmetry property in the application of Ampère's circuital law. The vector $I\, d\mathbf{l}_1 \times \mathbf{R}$ in Eq. (2.47) is in the φ direction; thus the only component of magnetic field present is the φ component. Since there are no φ or z variations, the φ component of magnetic field may only be a function of r. A constant r loop is chosen in the evaluation of B_φ, as shown in Fig. 3.14. From Eq. (3.23) we obtain

$$\begin{aligned}\oint_l \mathbf{B} \cdot d\mathbf{l} &= \int_0^{2\pi} B_\varphi r\, d\varphi \\ &= 2\pi r B_\varphi \\ &= \mu_0 I\end{aligned}$$

The magnetic field component B_φ is thus immediately obtained in terms of the current I and the radius r, in agreement with the result of Example 2.7,

$$B_\varphi = \frac{\mu_0 I}{2\pi r}$$

Note that in this symmetrical example Ampère's circuital law is easier to apply than the Biot-Savart law. The situation is obviously analogous to the

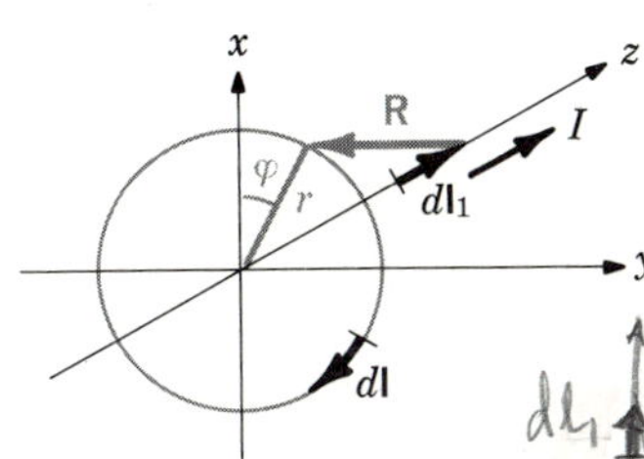

Fig. 3.14 Determination of **B** associated with an infinite filamentary current-carrying wire.

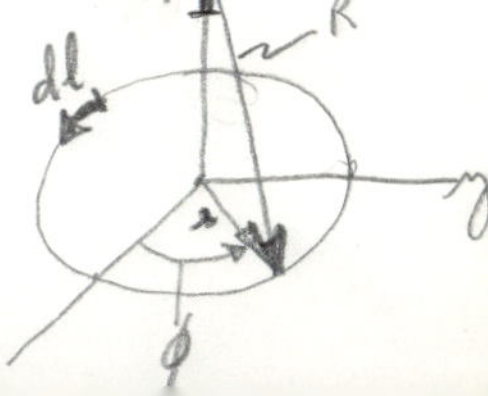

use of Gauss's law and Coulomb's law in the determination of electric fields, where for certain symmetrical cases Gauss's law is much easier to apply than Coulomb's law.

Example 3.10 The magnetic field generated by a current sheet A current-carrying sheet occupies the yz plane as shown in Fig. 3.15, with a uniform surface current in the $+z$ direction. The surface current density is denoted as

$$\mathbf{J}_s = J_{sz}\hat{\mathbf{z}} \text{ amp/m}$$

The total current flowing in the z direction in a width d is $I = J_{sz}d$.

It is easily seen from the Biot-Savart law and symmetry that there is no z component of $\mathbf{B}$. The magnetic field may be determined by considering the current sheet as an infinite layer of line currents and using the results of Example 2.7, $B_\varphi = \mu_0 I/2\pi R$. The current I is related to the surface current J_{sz} by the relation $I = J_{sz}\,dy'$; thus, from the geometry of Fig. 3.15,

$$\mathbf{B} = \frac{\mu_0}{2\pi}\int_{-\infty}^{\infty} \frac{J_{sz}\,dy'[-(y-y')\hat{\mathbf{x}} + x\hat{\mathbf{y}}]}{x^2 + (y-y')^2}$$

The two components of $\mathbf{B}$ are obtained by carrying out the indicated integration,

$$\begin{aligned} B_y &= \tfrac{1}{2}\mu_0 J_{sz} \\ B_x &= 0 \end{aligned} \qquad x > 0$$

If the equation is set up for negative x values, we obtain

$$\begin{aligned} B_y &= -\tfrac{1}{2}\mu_0 J_{sz} \\ B_x &= 0 \end{aligned} \qquad x < 0$$

A uniform magnetic field parallel to the current sheet is generated everywhere in space.

The calculation of magnetic field is simpler from the circuital law. The symmetry properties of the field must be recognized and used in this evaluation; this is not required in the calculation directly from the Biot-Savart law. Note

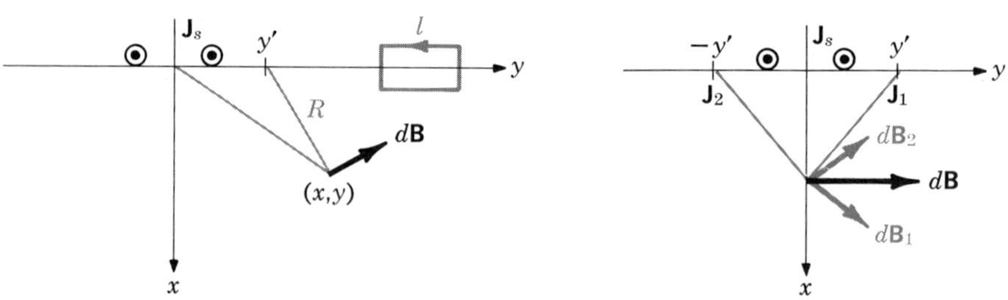

Fig. 3.15 A current-carrying sheet in the yz plane. The symmetrical surface-current elements $\mathbf{J}_1$ and $\mathbf{J}_2$ at $+y'$ and $-y'$, respectively, generate a magnetic field $d\mathbf{B}$ in the y direction only.

that the x component of magnetic field from a source element at $+y'$ is canceled by the magnetic field from the source element at $-y'$ for all x values at $y = 0$. For any value of y there will always be two symmetrically displaced source elements which will cause the x component of magnetic field to be zero. Thus from symmetry considerations the only component of magnetic field present is the y component, as demonstrated above. With this knowledge we can evaluate Eq. (3.23) for the loop l shown in Fig. 3.15. The only contribution to the line integral is along the y-directed portions of the loop; thus Eq. (3.23) gives

$$B_y = \tfrac{1}{2}\mu_0 J_{sz}$$

as before.

From this result we may generalize to the arbitrary vector relation

$$\mathbf{B} = \tfrac{1}{2}\mu_0 \mathbf{J}_s \times \hat{\mathbf{n}} \tag{3.26}$$

and $\hat{\mathbf{n}}$ is the surface normal pointing into the region where $\mathbf{B}$ is evaluated.

★3.11 Derivation of Ampère's Circuital Law from the Biot-Savart Law

In Sec. 2.6 Ampère's law of force was used to develop an expression for the magnetic field generated by an electric current. This law, known as the *Biot-Savart law*, is

$$\mathbf{B} = \frac{\mu_0}{4\pi} \int_V \nabla \times \left(\frac{\mathbf{J}}{R}\right) dV' \tag{2.52}$$

The curl of $\mathbf{B}$ is found by taking the curl of Eq. (2.52), from which it can be shown that the experimental Ampère circuital law is, in fact, a consequence of Ampère's law of force and the Biot-Savart law. The curl of Eq. (2.52) is

$$\nabla \times \mathbf{B} = \frac{\mu_0}{4\pi} \int_V \nabla \times \nabla \times \left(\frac{\mathbf{J}}{R}\right) dV'$$

where the field-point curl operator has been placed under the source integral. By using the appropriate vector identities, the integrand may be converted into a more convenient form,

$$\nabla \times \mathbf{B} = \frac{\mu_0}{4\pi} \int_V \left\{\nabla \left[\nabla \cdot \left(\frac{\mathbf{J}}{R}\right)\right] - \nabla^2 \left(\frac{\mathbf{J}}{R}\right)\right\} dV' \tag{3.27}$$

Recall that the integration is carried out over the source volume V, which includes all the source currents $\mathbf{J}(\mathbf{r}')$, as shown in Fig. 3.16. The curl operators are field-point operators involving derivatives with respect to the field point $\mathbf{r}$, with the source point $\mathbf{r}'$ held constant. The field point $\mathbf{r}$ is included in the volume of integration as indicated.

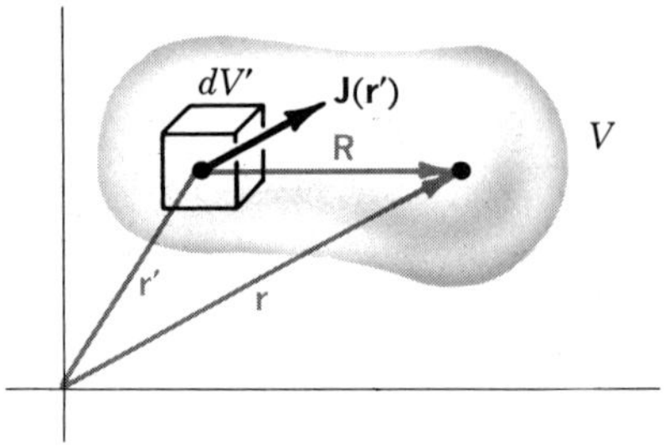

Fig. 3.16 Variables used in the source-point integration of the Biot-Savart law.

The contribution to $\nabla \times \mathbf{B}$ from the second term in the integrand of Eq. (3.27) is denoted as $\nabla \times \mathbf{B}\Big|_2$, and

$$\nabla \times \mathbf{B}\Big|_2 = -\frac{\mu_0}{4\pi}\int_V \mathbf{J}(\mathbf{r}')\ \nabla^2\left(\frac{1}{R}\right) dV'$$

Note that the current-density source variable $\mathbf{J}$ has been removed from the ∇^2 operation, since ∇^2 is a field-point operator. Equation (1.127) is used to obtain

$$\nabla \times \mathbf{B}\Big|_2 = \mu_0 \int_V \mathbf{J}(\mathbf{r}')\ \delta(R)\ dV'$$

From the basic properties of the δ function given in Eq. (1.129), this integral is immediately evaluated to yield

$$\nabla \times \mathbf{B}\Big|_2 = \mu_0\mathbf{J}(\mathbf{r})$$

which is identical with Eq. (3.25), Ampère's circuital law in point form.

Note that the correct result has been obtained without consideration of the first term in the integrand of Eq. (3.27). It remains to be shown that this term gives a zero contribution to $\nabla \times \mathbf{B}$. If the gradient operator is removed from the integral, the integral becomes

$$\nabla \times \mathbf{B}\Big|_1 = \frac{\mu_0}{4\pi}\nabla\int_V \nabla\cdot\left(\frac{\mathbf{J}}{R}\right) dV'$$

We may be tempted to apply the divergence theorem to the integrand and obtain the result

$$\nabla \times \mathbf{B}\Big|_1 = \frac{\mu_0}{4\pi}\nabla\int_V \nabla\cdot\left(\frac{\mathbf{J}}{R}\right) dV' \neq \frac{\mu_0}{4\pi}\nabla\oint_S \frac{\mathbf{J}\cdot d\mathbf{S}}{R}$$

from which we might deduce that since $\mathbf{J}$ does not exist on the bounding surface S, the surface integral is zero. The inequality sign has been used to indicate that this is an incorrect manipulation. The divergence theorem has been incorrectly applied to a source integral with a field-point divergence in the integrand.

The integrand in the volume integral is rewritten using the identity

$$\nabla \cdot \left(\frac{\mathbf{J}}{R}\right) = \mathbf{J} \cdot \nabla \left(\frac{1}{R}\right) + \frac{1}{R} \nabla \cdot \mathbf{J}$$

and since $\nabla \cdot \mathbf{J} = 0$, the second term on the right-hand side is zero. Replacing $\nabla(1/R)$ by $-\nabla'(1/R)$ [see Eq. (1.126)] gives

$$\nabla \cdot \left(\frac{\mathbf{J}}{R}\right) = -\mathbf{J} \cdot \nabla' \left(\frac{1}{R}\right)$$

Rewriting the identity in terms of the source-point coordinate gives

$$\nabla' \cdot \left(\frac{\mathbf{J}}{R}\right) = \mathbf{J} \cdot \nabla' \left(\frac{1}{R}\right) + \frac{1}{R} \nabla' \cdot \mathbf{J}$$

Since the Biot-Savart law applies only for steady currents with no time variation, the continuity equation, Eq. (3.22), gives $\nabla' \cdot \mathbf{J} = 0$, and the above two relations are combined to give

$$\nabla \cdot \left(\frac{\mathbf{J}}{R}\right) = -\nabla' \cdot \left(\frac{\mathbf{J}}{R}\right)$$

The volume integration becomes

$$\begin{aligned} \frac{\mu_0}{4\pi} \nabla \int_V \nabla \cdot \left(\frac{\mathbf{J}}{R}\right) dV' &= -\frac{\mu_0}{4\pi} \nabla \int_V \nabla' \cdot \left(\frac{\mathbf{J}}{R}\right) dV' \\ &= -\frac{\mu_0}{4\pi} \nabla \oint_S \frac{\mathbf{J} \cdot d\mathbf{S}}{R} \\ &= 0 \end{aligned}$$

The surface integral is zero because V includes all $\mathbf{J}$, and hence $\mathbf{J} = 0$ on S. The contribution from the first integral term is zero; thus Ampère's ★circuital law is derived from the Biot-Savart law.

3.12 DISPLACEMENT CURRENT AND THE GENERAL TIME–VARYING FORM OF AMPÈRE'S CIRCUITAL LAW

It has been consistently emphasized that Ampère's circuital law is a steady-current law and does not account for time variations. This was further clarified in Sec. 3.11, where we derived the circuital law from the static Biot-Savart law.

The relationship between the circuital law and the current-continuity equation may be obtained by taking the divergence of Eq. (3.25),

$$\nabla \cdot (\nabla \times \mathbf{B}) = \mu_0 \nabla \cdot \mathbf{J}$$

Since the divergence of the curl of any vector is identically zero, this expression gives

$$0 = \nabla \cdot \mathbf{J}$$

which is the static form of the current-continuity equation. We now have a consistent set of static laws relating current and magnetic field, but the main interest in this chapter is to develop a set of general laws which hold for the time-varying case. It is thus necessary to develop a general time-varying form of Ampère's circuital law which is consistent with the time-varying current-continuity equation.

Many of the laws discussed in this chapter have been developed from static or steady-current experiments, and it has been carefully stated which laws are also valid in the time-varying case. Gauss's law and the magnetic source law were developed from static experiments and have subsequently been found to hold for the time-varying case. Faraday's law and the current-continuity equation are obviously laws which hold in the time-varying case.

Maxwell developed the time-varying form of the circuital law by introducing an additional term. He noted that if an additional term were added to Eq. (3.25) such that

$$\nabla \times \mathbf{B} = \mu_0 \left(\mathbf{J} + \epsilon_0 \frac{\partial \mathbf{E}}{\partial t} \right) \tag{3.28}$$

then taking the divergence gives

$$0 = \nabla \cdot \mathbf{J} + \epsilon_0 \frac{\partial \nabla \cdot \mathbf{E}}{\partial t}$$

Gauss's law in point form, Eq. (3.3), may be used to obtain the current-continuity equation, Eq. (3.22),

$$0 = \nabla \cdot \mathbf{J} + \frac{\partial \rho}{\partial t}$$

Thus Eq. (3.28) is consistent with the time-varying current-continuity equation by the application of Gauss's law. It also reduces to the static circuital law for no time variation. Equation (3.28) has subsequently been demonstrated to be one of the most fundamental laws of electrodynamics.

The integral form of Eq. (3.28) is

$$\oint_l \mathbf{B} \cdot d\mathbf{l} = \mu_0 \int_S \left(\mathbf{J} + \epsilon_0 \frac{\partial \mathbf{E}}{\partial t} \right) \cdot d\mathbf{S} \tag{3.29}$$

Equations (3.28) and (3.29) are the general time-varying forms of Ampère's circuital law. Note that Eq. (3.29) states that the net circulation of **B** is due to the sum of real current plus $\epsilon_0 \, \partial\mathbf{E}/\partial t$, and thus $\nabla \times \mathbf{B}$ may be generated at a point in space (even in the absence of **J**) when a time-varying electric field is present. This is analogous to Faraday's law, which states that $\nabla \times \mathbf{E}$ may be generated at a point in space when a time-varying magnetic field is present.

DISPLACEMENT CURRENT

The additional term appearing in Eq. (3.28) is a current term called *displacement current*. It does not correspond to a physical current, but rather to a time rate of change of **E**. Since changing **E** implies charge buildup, which requires current flow, there is an indirect relation. This relation may be clarified by considering a large parallel-plate capacitor as shown in Fig. 3.17. A current I charges up the left plate to a surface charge density ρ_s, and current is generated from the right plate to create an opposing charge density $-\rho_s$. The intervening electric field is given by Eq. (3.6), $E = \rho_s/\epsilon_0$. If a continuous current flows into the capacitor, ρ_s increases with time, and thus **E** increases with time. Therefore current flow through the capacitor is associated with a time rate of change of **E** in the capacitor, and $\partial\mathbf{E}/\partial t$ in the capacitor may be associated with a fictitious current flow across the capacitor plates. The current I is read-

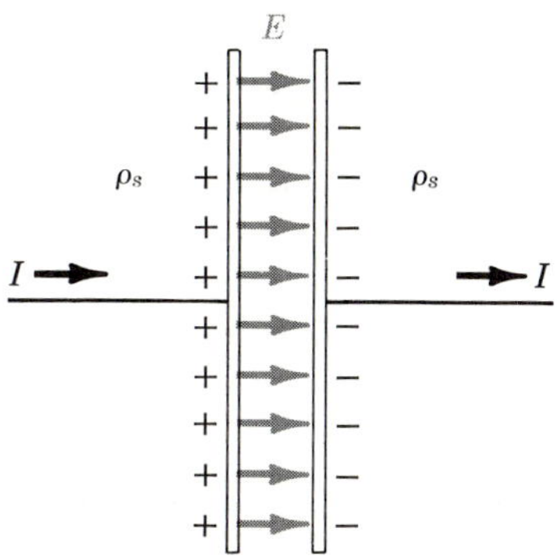

Fig. 3.17 The concept of displacement current.

ily evaluated from current-continuity considerations,

$$I = \frac{\partial Q}{\partial t} = \frac{\partial}{\partial t}(A\rho_s)$$

where A is the area of one capacitor plate. Since $\rho_s = \epsilon_0 E$,

$$I = A\epsilon_0 \frac{\partial E}{\partial t}$$

If this total current is considered to flow as a fictitious current (displacement current) across the plates, the displacement-current density J_d is

$$J_d = \frac{I}{A}$$

$$= \epsilon_0 \frac{\partial E}{\partial t}$$

or, in vector form,

$$\mathbf{J}_d = \epsilon_0 \frac{\partial \mathbf{E}}{\partial t}$$

Note that this is just the current term Maxwell inserted in Eq. (3.28).

Example 3.11 Conduction and displacement current at the interface between a semi-infinite conductor and free space A semi-infinite conductor occupies the $z < 0$ space and terminates the flow of conduction current as shown in Fig. 3.18. An alternating conduction current exists in the conductor, as indicated. It is

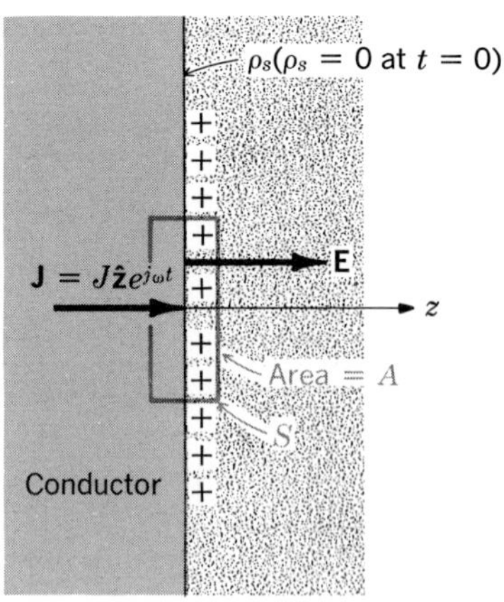

Fig. 3.18 The relationship between conduction and displacement current.

possible to calculate the electric field-intensity vector **E** for $z > 0$ by either of two methods: It is possible to solve for ρ_s and apply Gauss's law to obtain **E**, or equate the conduction current to the displacement current. Both these methods are applied in this example.

The surface charge density ρ_s is obtained from current-continuity considerations, assuming that $\rho_s = 0$ at $t = 0$. The continuity equation is

$$\frac{\partial Q}{\partial t} = -\oint_S \mathbf{J} \cdot d\mathbf{S}$$

where S is the surface indicated in Fig. 3.18. **J** only flows into the left surface; thus

$$\frac{\partial}{\partial t}(\rho_s A) = AJe^{j\omega t}$$

This equation is integrated to give

$$\rho_s = \int_0^t Je^{j\omega t}\,dt$$

$$= \frac{J}{j\omega}(e^{j\omega t} - 1)$$

The surface charge on a planar conductor generates a uniform field $\mathbf{E} = \rho_s \hat{\mathbf{z}}/\epsilon_0$. This result is obtained by applying Gauss's law to the surface S and stipulating that the **E** field is zero inside the conductor (see Chap. 5). The final result is then obtained,

$$\mathbf{E} = \frac{J}{j\omega\epsilon_0}(e^{j\omega t} - 1)\hat{\mathbf{z}}$$

This same result may be obtained by simply equating the current density **J** to the displacement-current density $\epsilon_0\, \partial\mathbf{E}/\partial t$,

$$Je^{j\omega t}\hat{\mathbf{z}} = \epsilon_0 \frac{\partial \mathbf{E}}{\partial t}$$

$$\mathbf{E} = \int_0^t \frac{J}{\epsilon_0} e^{j\omega t}\hat{\mathbf{z}}\,dt$$

$$= \frac{J}{j\omega\epsilon_0}(e^{j\omega t} - 1)\hat{\mathbf{z}}$$

3.13 MAXWELL'S EQUATIONS

A full set of equations relating the field vectors and the source parameters have now been developed. The important relations are summarized below in a set of equations called *Maxwell's equations.* The equations as written here apply only for fields in free space.

$$\nabla \times \mathbf{B} = \mu_0 \left(\mathbf{J} + \epsilon_0 \frac{\partial \mathbf{E}}{\partial t} \right) \tag{3.30}$$

$$\nabla \times \mathbf{E} = - \frac{\partial \mathbf{B}}{\partial t} \tag{3.31}$$

$$\nabla \cdot \mathbf{E} = \frac{\rho}{\epsilon_0} \tag{3.32}$$

$$\nabla \cdot \mathbf{B} = 0 \tag{3.33}$$

The above equations constitute Maxwell's equations in differential or point form. The corresponding equations in integral form are

$$\oint_l \mathbf{B} \cdot d\mathbf{l} = \mu_0 \int_S \left(\mathbf{J} + \epsilon_0 \frac{\partial \mathbf{E}}{\partial t} \right) \cdot d\mathbf{S} \tag{3.34}$$

$$\oint_l \mathbf{E} \cdot d\mathbf{l} = - \int_S \frac{\partial \mathbf{B}}{\partial t} \cdot d\mathbf{S} \tag{3.35}$$

$$\oint_S \mathbf{E} \cdot d\mathbf{S} = \int_V \frac{\rho}{\epsilon_0} \, dV \tag{3.36}$$

$$\oint_S \mathbf{B} \cdot d\mathbf{S} = 0 \tag{3.37}$$

Two other very important equations relating the current and charge parameters in a vacuum are

$$\nabla \cdot \mathbf{J} = - \frac{\partial \rho}{\partial t} \tag{3.38}$$

$$\mathbf{J} = \rho \mathbf{v} \tag{3.39}$$

Other important equations will be introduced in Chap. 5 when material effects are considered.

PROBLEMS

3.2-1 An electric field $\mathbf{E} = (\sin x \, \hat{\mathbf{x}} + \cos x \, \hat{\mathbf{y}})e^{-y}$ exists in free space. Find the electric charge density everywhere.

3.2-2 Find the electric charge density associated with the scalar potential:

(*a*) $\Phi = xyz$

(*b*) $\Phi = xy^2z$

3.3-1 An infinitely long filamentary line charge of charge density ρ_l coul/m generates an electric field **E**. Solve for **E** by making use of the symmetry properties of the configuration and Gauss's law. Compare this method of obtaining **E** with Example 2.2.

3.3-2 A cylindrical electron beam in a concentric conducting cylinder consists of a uniform net volume charge density moving at a constant axial velocity $v_0 = 10^7$ m/sec. The total current carried by a beam of radius $a = 1$ mm is $I_0 = 10^{-2}$ amp. Calculate the electric field intensity inside and outside the electron beam. Is **E** changed if the conducting-cylinder diameter is changed?

3.3-3 A spherical ball of charge in free space is characterized by a volume charge density

$$\rho = \begin{cases} \rho_0 \left(1 - \dfrac{r^2}{a^2}\right) & r < a \\ 0 & r > a \end{cases}$$

where a is the sphere radius and ρ_0 is a constant. Solve for the electric field intensity for all values of r.

3.3-4 Two square planar arrays of point charges exist in the planes $z = 0$ and $z = 1$ m, with point charges located at the points $(i,j,0)$ and $(i,j,1)$, where $i = 0, \pm 1, \pm 2, \ldots, \pm 5$ and $j = 0, \pm 1, \pm 2, \ldots, \pm 5$. The charges in the $z = 0$ plane are all $+1$ coul, and the charges in the $z = 1$ plane are all -1 coul. Solve for E_z/E_0 versus x at $y = 0$ and $z = 0.5$ and 0.25, using the computer, where E_0 is the field given by Eq. (3.6) for the equivalent uniform-distribution case of Example 3.2.

3.3-5 A loop of conducting wire of radius a is located in the xy plane with its center at the origin of a rectangular coordinate system. A total charge Q is placed on the loop and is evenly distributed over the wire. Solve for the electric field **E** generated by the charged loop on the axis at the field point $(0,0,z)$.

3.4-1 In Example 2.7 the magnetic flux density associated with an infinite current-carrying wire was calculated as

$$\mathbf{B} = \frac{\mu_0 I}{2\pi r} \hat{\boldsymbol{\varphi}}$$

where I is the total current carried by the wire. Verify by direct calculation that $\nabla \cdot \mathbf{B} = 0$. Show that Eq. (3.11) holds for the closed surface consisting of two radial planes, two $r =$ constant surfaces, and two $z =$ constant planes.

3.4-2 Under what conditions is it possible to define **B** in terms of the gradient of a scalar magnetic potential, $\mathbf{B} = -\nabla\Phi_m$? What is the differential equation for Φ_m in this case?

3.5-1 Solve for $\oint_l \mathbf{E} \cdot d\mathbf{l}$, when $\mathbf{E} = 2\hat{\mathbf{x}} + x\hat{\mathbf{y}}$, for the closed loop in the xy plane starting at the point (0,0,0) and moving to (1,0,0) to (1,1,0) to (0,1,0), and back to the origin. The electric field is generated by a time-varying uniform field **B** in the z direction. Solve for **B**.

3.6-1 A magnetic field is described in cylindrical coordinates by the two component equations

$$B_z = B_0 r^2 t \cos \frac{2\pi z}{L}$$

$$B_\varphi = 0$$

There are no φ variations in the electric or magnetic field. Find B_r and E_φ.

3.7-1 Calculate the voltage induced across the terminals of the rotating coil described in Example 3.8, starting from Eq. (3.16).

3.7-2 A resistor R is connected across terminals 1 and 2 in Fig. 3.10. Find the current flowing through the resistor. Prove that the instantaneous power dissipated in the resistor equals the instantaneous power required to keep the coil rotating at the frequency ω when the current is flowing.

3.9-1 Derive the fluid continuity equation for a flow of particles with velocity $\mathbf{v}$ and number density n,

$$\nabla \cdot n\mathbf{v} = -\frac{\partial n}{\partial t}$$

3.9-2 A short, thin wire carries a time-varying current along its axis $I = I_0 e^{j\omega t}$. Solve for the total charge Q accumulated at each end of the wire as a function of time. Note that the short wire generates an oscillating dipole-type charge, and the fields which are generated are time-varying dipole fields.

3.9-3 A current density $\mathbf{J} = J_x' x\,\hat{\mathbf{x}} + J_y \hat{\mathbf{y}}$ exists in free space, where J_x' and J_y are constants. Solve for $\oint_S \mathbf{J} \cdot d\mathbf{S}$, where S is the surface of a unit cube with one corner at the origin and the opposite corner at the point (1,1,1).

3.9-4 A current density $\mathbf{J} = J_0 \sin\theta \cos\varphi\,\hat{\mathbf{r}}$ exists in free space. Solve for $\oint_S \mathbf{J} \cdot d\mathbf{S}$, where S is the surface of a unit sphere with its center at the origin of a spherical coordinate system.

3.9-5 A current density of the form $\mathbf{J} = x^2\hat{\mathbf{x}} + yz\hat{\mathbf{y}} + xyz\hat{\mathbf{z}}$ exists in free space. Calculate the total current flowing out of a unit cube with its opposite corners at the origin and the point (1,1,1). Obtain the result first by a direct calculation of $\oint_S \mathbf{J} \cdot d\mathbf{S}$ and second by integrating $\nabla \cdot \mathbf{J}$ over the enclosed volume and using the divergence theorem.

3.10-1 A toroidal ring of magnetic field may be generated by wrapping a wire around a toroidal form or a magnetic ring, as shown in Fig. P3.10-1. Show that the magnetic field inside the ring is approximately

$$B = \frac{\mu_0 NI}{l}$$

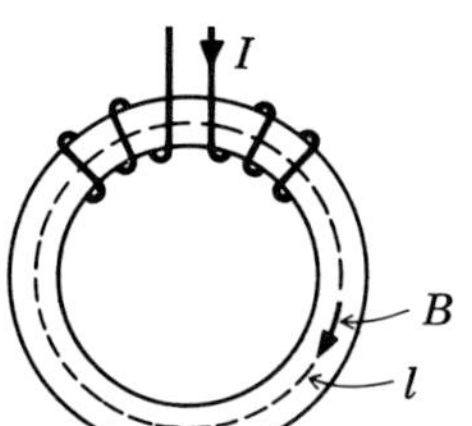

Fig. P3.10-1 An N-turn toroidal solenoid.

3.10-2 A metallic disk of radius a is located in the xy plane, with its center at the origin of a rectangular coordinate system. The disk is charged to a uniform surface charge density ρ_s and rotates about the z axis with a frequency ω. Find the B_z field along the z axis. *Hint:* Start from Eq. (2.56).

3.10-3 An electron beam of radius a, volume charge density ρ_0, and velocity v_0 is moving in the $+z$ direction of a cylindrical coordinate system and is concentric with the z axis. Solve for the magnetic field **B** generated by the beam both inside and outside the beam by first using the Biot-Savart law to determine the symmetry of the field and then applying the circuital law to the most advantageous loop.

3.10-4 Find **B** everywhere generated by the current sheet shown in Fig. 3.15 plus a current sheet at $x = d$ carrying a current density $\mathbf{J}_s = -J_{sz}\hat{\mathbf{z}}$.

3.10-5 What is the restriction on the current density **J** such that **B** may be derived from a scalar potential $\mathbf{B} = -\nabla\Phi_m$?

3.10-6 What is the differential equation for the magnetic vector potential **A** when **J** is nonzero and $\nabla \cdot \mathbf{A} = 0$?

3.13-1 Equations (3.30) to (3.33) are not independent, as the two divergence relationships may be obtained from the two curl equations. Prove that Eqs. (3.32) and (3.33) may be derived from Eqs. (3.30), (3.31), and (3.38).

CHAPTER

4

physical properties of fields

4.1 INTRODUCTION

In Chap. 2 the electric and magnetic fields were defined in terms of the electric and magnetic forces exerted on point charges and current elements, respectively. Experimental force laws were then used to obtain expressions for the electric and magnetic fields in terms of the source charges and currents. Then the force laws were written in terms of the charges and current, and the electric and magnetic fields, as in Eq. (2.34).

In this chapter we begin with a consideration of the basic force law for a particle and generalize to volume forces exerted on fluids or gases containing charges. From this force law it is possible to investigate the energy acquired by charged particles as they accelerate in response to the field force. The particles gain energy in this acceleration process, and it is logical to question where this energy and associated power come from. Since there are no mechanical forces applied, the only creditable answer is that energy must come from the fields. Thus the concept of field energy and field power is necessarily introduced in order to explain the fact that energy and power are given to charged particles in the presence of fields.

The field energy and power equations are developed in this chapter, and a power-energy conservation theorem is formulated for a system containing fields and particles. This chapter thus constitutes a description of the physical properties of fields quite analogous to the description of mechanical force, energy, and power in a physical mechanics course.

4.2 FIELD FORCE ON CHARGES

The force on a charge in an electric field and the force on a moving charge in a magnetic field are given by Eqs. (2.1) and (2.33), respectively. In a region of space where both electric and magnetic fields are present, the force on a charge q moving with a velocity $\mathbf{v}$ is

$$\mathbf{F} = q(\mathbf{E} + \mathbf{v} \times \mathbf{B}) \tag{2.34}$$

This expression is the fundamental force equation for point charges and is called the *Lorentz force equation.*

Equation (2.34) gives the total force on a point charge q moving with a velocity $\mathbf{v}$ in the presence of fields $\mathbf{E}$ and $\mathbf{B}$ and is the fundamental equation from which energy and power relationships are derived for point charges. However, before we proceed with the development of Eq. (2.34) for the case of point charges, it is of great practical interest to consider the analogous expression for a continuous distribution of moving charges. Consider an incremental volume in a moving continuous charge distribution, as shown in Fig. 4.1. The total electric charge in the incremental volume ΔV is ΔQ, and the velocity of the charges in the incremental volume is $\mathbf{v}$. From the relation given in Eq. (2.13), it is clear that the charge ΔQ in volume ΔV is $\Delta Q = \rho \, \Delta V$. By applying Eq. (2.34) to the incremental volume shown in Fig. 4.1, we obtain

$$\Delta\mathbf{F} = \rho \, \Delta V(\mathbf{E} + \mathbf{v} \times \mathbf{B}) \tag{4.1}$$

where $\Delta\mathbf{F}$ is the incremental vector force on the charges in ΔV. Using Eq. (2.36), we see that $\rho\mathbf{v} \, \Delta V = \mathbf{J} \, \Delta V$, and Eq. (4.1) becomes

$$\Delta\mathbf{F} = (\rho\mathbf{E} + \mathbf{J} \times \mathbf{B}) \, \Delta V \tag{4.2}$$

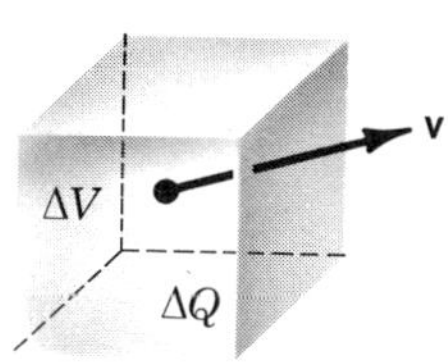

Fig. 4.1 An incremental volume ΔV containing a net charge ΔQ moving with a velocity $\mathbf{v}$.

It is now convenient to define a volume force density, or force per unit volume, $\mathfrak{F}_v$, in accordance with the equation

$$\mathfrak{F}_v = \lim_{\Delta V \to 0} \frac{\Delta \mathbf{F}}{\Delta V} \qquad \text{newtons/m}^3 \tag{4.3}$$

From Eqs. (4.2) and (4.3) it is clear that the volume force density on the continuous charge distribution is

$$\mathfrak{F}_v = \rho \mathbf{E} + \mathbf{J} \times \mathbf{B} \qquad \text{newtons/m}^3 \tag{4.4}$$

In this chapter we shall denote density functions by capital script letters.

Equation (4.4) gives the total volume force density due to **E** and **B** at the field point **r** where the parameters ρ, **J**, **E**, and **B** are defined. The total force on a macroscopic volume containing a charge density ρ and current density **J**, in the presence of fields **E** and **B**, is found by integrating Eq. (4.4) over the volume of interest,

$$\begin{aligned} \mathbf{F} &= \int_V \mathfrak{F}_v \, dV \\ &= \int_V (\rho \mathbf{E} + \mathbf{J} \times \mathbf{B}) \, dV \qquad \text{newtons} \end{aligned} \tag{4.5}$$

Example 4.1 Plasma-propulsion rocket motor using the J × B force A type of plasma-propulsion rocket motor operates on the principle of generating thrust by means of the **J** × **B** force term in Eq. (4.4). The current density **J** is created by an electron current which passes through an ionized gas containing a neutral mixture of ions and electrons. This ionized gas is called a *plasma*. The physical configuration is shown in Fig. 4.2. The region between the cathode and anode is filled with plasma, moving at an average velocity **v**. An electron current is induced across the gas by applying a positive voltage on the anode. The resulting current density **J** is generated as shown. A dc magnetic field **B** is oriented perpendicular to the current-density vector **J** such that a volume force density $\mathfrak{F}_v$ is exerted on the plasma in the direction shown. The plasma responds to the

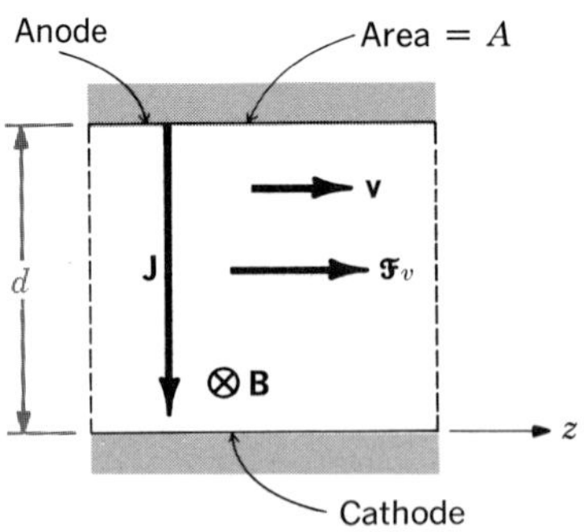

Fig. 4.2 A plasma-propulsion rocket motor; the cathode-anode spacing is d and the cathode area is A.

force and accelerates. Since the $\rho\mathbf{E}$ term in Eq. (4.4) is generally small and not in the direction of $\mathbf{J} \times \mathbf{B}$, it can be neglected.

The volume force density exerted at a point in the plasma medium is, from Eq. (4.4),

$$\begin{aligned} \mathfrak{F}_v &= \mathbf{J} \times \mathbf{B} \\ &= JB\hat{\mathbf{z}} \end{aligned}$$

The power transferred to the plasma by the fields is $P = \mathbf{F} \cdot \mathbf{v}$. The power delivered to the incremental volume dV at the velocity $\mathbf{v}$ is

$$\begin{aligned} dP &= \mathfrak{F}_v \cdot \mathbf{v}\, dV \\ &= \mathfrak{F}_v v\, dV \\ &= JBv\, dV \end{aligned}$$

If it is assumed that the current density, magnetic field, and velocity v are uniform over the plasma region, this equation may be integrated directly to give the total power transferred,

$$P = JBvV$$

where V is the volume of the plasma region. If we set $V = Ad$ and $I = JA$, the power is

$$P = IBvd \tag{4.6}$$

Equation (4.6) is an approximate expression for kinetic power delivered to the plasma by the electrical source which generates the current I. It may be shown that this power is quite significant for practical values of the parameters. For example, if $I = 1$ amp, $d = 10$ cm, $B = 1{,}000$ gauss $= 0.1$ webers/m^2, and $v = 10^6$ m/sec, the power delivered to the plasma, given by Eq. (4.6), is 10 kw.

4.3 ENERGY ASSOCIATED WITH AN ASSEMBLY OF ELECTRIC CHARGES

The electric energy associated with an assembly of electric charges may be found by calculating the work required to gather the charges together. For an assembly of point charges or a continuous charge distribution ρ, it is obvious that energy must be stored in a charge system. This is seen by considering the motion of the charges if they are released from fixed source points. The large coulomb forces which exist between the charges would cause the charge assembly to fly apart. The net kinetic energy gained by the charges after they have been separated equals the initial stored electric field energy.

We begin by considering a series of separated point charges at infinity, and then we calculate the energy required to bring these charges together, one by one. The physical situation is illustrated in Fig. 4.3. The energy required to bring the first charge q_1 from infinity to the region

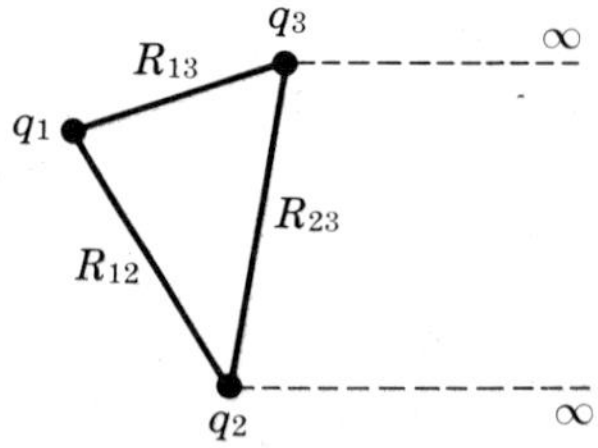

Fig. 4.3 Gathering of charges from infinity.

of interest is zero, because no other charges are present to generate an opposing coulomb field. The energy required to bring the second charge q_2 to a distance R_{12} from q_1 is

$$W_2 = q_2\Phi_2{}^1 \tag{4.7}$$

where $\Phi_2{}^1$ is the electric potential at the location of charge q_2 due to the presence of charge q_1,

$$\Phi_2{}^1 = \frac{q_1}{4\pi\epsilon_0 R_{12}}$$

The subscript denotes the location where the potential is measured, and the superscript denotes the source charge for the potential. If a third charge q_3 is brought from infinity to a distance R_{13} from q_1 and R_{23} from q_2, the energy required is

$$W_3 = q_3(\Phi_3{}^1 + \Phi_3{}^2)$$

The energy required to bring in a fourth charge is

$$W_4 = q_4(\Phi_4{}^1 + \Phi_4{}^2 + \Phi_4{}^3)$$

Thus the total energy required to gather together a series of charges is

$$W_e = q_2\Phi_2{}^1 + q_3(\Phi_3{}^1 + \Phi_3{}^2) + q_4(\Phi_4{}^1 + \Phi_4{}^2 + \Phi_4{}^3) + q_5(\Phi_5{}^1 + \Phi_5{}^2 + \Phi_5{}^3 + \Phi_5{}^4) + \cdots \tag{4.8}$$

It is possible to develop a convenient series representation for W_e by recognizing, from Eq. (4.7), that W_2 may be written in the alternate form

$$\begin{aligned} W_2 &= q_2\Phi_2{}^1 \\ &= \frac{q_2 q_1}{4\pi\epsilon_0 R_{12}} \\ &= q_1 \frac{q_2}{4\pi\epsilon_0 R_{21}} \\ &= q_1\Phi_1{}^2 \end{aligned}$$

The energy terms are related by the expression

$$q_i\Phi_i{}^k = q_k\Phi_k{}^i \tag{4.9}$$

Thus it is possible to rewrite Eq. (4.8) in the alternate form

$$W_e = q_1\Phi_1{}^2 + q_1\Phi_1{}^3 + q_2\Phi_2{}^3 + q_1\Phi_1{}^4 + q_2\Phi_2{}^4 + q_3\Phi_3{}^4 + q_1\Phi_1{}^5 + q_2\Phi_2{}^5 + q_3\Phi_3{}^5 + q_4\Phi_4{}^5 + \cdots \tag{4.10}$$

Equations (4.8) and (4.10) may be added to give

$$2W_e = q_1(\Phi_1{}^2 + \Phi_1{}^3 + \Phi_1{}^4 + \Phi_1{}^5 + \cdots) + q_2(\Phi_2{}^1 + \Phi_2{}^3 + \Phi_2{}^4 + \Phi_2{}^5 + \cdots) + q_3(\Phi_3{}^1 + \Phi_3{}^2 + \Phi_3{}^4 + \Phi_3{}^5 + \cdots) + \cdots$$

which may be written in the convenient form

$$W_e = \tfrac{1}{2} \sum_{i=1}^{N} q_i\Phi_i \tag{4.11}$$

where

$$\Phi_i = \Phi_i{}^1 + \Phi_i{}^2 + \Phi_i{}^3 + \cdots + \Phi_i^{i-1} + \Phi_i^{i+1} + \cdots + \Phi_i{}^N \tag{4.12}$$

is the total potential at the ith location due to all the other $N - 1$ total charges present. Equation (4.11) gives the total electric energy stored by an assembly of N charges in terms of a simple summation over the charges.

Equation (4.11) may be generalized to the case of a continuous charge distribution in a volume V by making the transformations

$$q_i \rightarrow \rho(r)\, dV$$
$$\Phi_i \rightarrow \Phi(r)$$

In the limit as $N \rightarrow \infty$, the summation becomes the definition of an integral,

$$\sum_{i=1}^{N} \rightarrow \int_V$$

Equation (4.11) then assumes the form

$$W_e = \tfrac{1}{2} \int_V \rho\Phi\, dV \tag{4.13}$$

Equation (4.13) may be interpreted as an integral over the volume V of an electric energy density $\mathcal{W}_e = \tfrac{1}{2}\rho\Phi$, which exists in regions where $\rho \neq 0$.

It is useful to convert Eq. (4.13) into an expression involving the **E** field alone. The electric field associated with Φ in Eq. (4.13) is that generated by ρ, given by Eq. (3.32). Thus ρ may be eliminated in Eq. (4.13) by using Eq. (3.32),

$$W_e = \tfrac{1}{2}\epsilon_0 \int_V (\nabla \cdot \mathbf{E})\Phi \, dV$$

By using the vector identity

$$\nabla \cdot \Phi\mathbf{E} = \Phi(\nabla \cdot \mathbf{E}) + \mathbf{E} \cdot \nabla\Phi$$

the energy expression becomes

$$W_e = \tfrac{1}{2}\epsilon_0 \int_V (\nabla \cdot \Phi\mathbf{E} - \mathbf{E} \cdot \nabla\Phi) \, dV$$

Since **E** in this static case is $\mathbf{E} = -\nabla\Phi$ from Eq. (2.8), W_e becomes

$$W_e = \tfrac{1}{2}\epsilon_0 \oint_S \Phi\mathbf{E} \cdot \hat{\mathbf{n}} \, dS + \tfrac{1}{2}\epsilon_0 \int_V \mathbf{E} \cdot \mathbf{E} \, dV \tag{4.14}$$

where S is the surface boundary of V. The surface and volume must be large enough to enclose all the charges in the region of interest. It is permissible to let the surface S extend to infinity, in which case the surface integration in Eq. (4.14) reduces to zero, since

$$\Phi \sim \frac{1}{R}$$

$$E \sim \frac{1}{R^2} \qquad dS \sim R^2$$

and thus

$$\lim_{R\to\infty} \Phi\mathbf{E} \cdot \hat{\mathbf{n}} \, dS \to \lim_{R\to\infty} \frac{1}{R}\frac{1}{R^2} R^2 \to 0$$

We are then left with the volume-integral term in Eq. (4.14),

$$W_e = \tfrac{1}{2}\epsilon_0 \int_V \mathbf{E} \cdot \mathbf{E} \, dV \qquad \text{joules} \tag{4.15}$$

Thus, by letting $V \to \infty$ the total electric energy becomes an integral of the square of the electric field intensity over all space. From this expression we see that a volume energy density may be defined as

$$\begin{aligned} \mathcal{W}_e &= \tfrac{1}{2}\epsilon_0 \mathbf{E} \cdot \mathbf{E} \\ &= \tfrac{1}{2}\epsilon_0 E^2 \qquad \text{joules/m}^3 \end{aligned} \tag{4.16}$$

and

$$W_e = \int_V \mathcal{W}_e \, dV$$

Thus the concept of electric energy density associated with **E** is introduced. As the charges are gathered together, the total electric field **E** builds up, and Eq. (4.15) gives the relation between total energy and a volume integral containing **E**.

The energy expression of Eq. (4.13) has been written in a much different but equivalent form in Eq. (4.15). Equation (4.13) defines energy density at a point as $\frac{1}{2}\rho\Phi$. According to this definition, energy exists where the charges exist, and where $\rho = 0$ there is no energy. However, Eq. (4.15) defines energy density at a point as $\frac{1}{2}\epsilon_0 E^2$. According to this second definition, wherever an **E** field exists, electric energy exists. These two equations may appear to be conflicting, as $\mathcal{W}_e$ can exist where $\rho = 0$ in one case but not in the other. There is no conflict, however, because the integrals give the same result for the total energy. The second definition was introduced because it was convenient to eliminate the surface integral in Eq. (4.14) by extending V to infinity. In doing so, the concept of electric energy density given in Eq. (4.16) was introduced. Both Eq. (4.13) and Eq. (4.15) must give the same results, based on two different definitions of electric energy density, as demonstrated in Example 4.3. However, the definition $\mathcal{W}_e = \frac{1}{2}\epsilon_0 E^2$ is used more often in subsequent work.

In connection with the two definitions of energy density given above, we might wonder where the energy is actually stored. Is it stored in the charges, as implied by Eq. (4.13), where the energy density is zero if $\rho = 0$? Or is it stored in the electric field, as implied by Eq. (4.16)? The question is like that of the potential energy of a flowerpot on a windowsill. The flowerpot possesses potential energy, because if it is pushed over the edge of the windowsill, it gains kinetic energy. Is the potential energy stored in the flowerpot, in the windowsill, or in the gravitational field? It is impossible to say. Similarly, it is impossible to say where electric energy is stored. It is convenient to think of it as being stored in the electric field in connection with Eq. (4.15), and this is the approach we shall take.

Example 4.2 Energy required to gather three point charges The energy required to gather three charges from infinity to a line at the points $x = -1$, 0, and $+1$ is calculated by adding the coulomb energies. Charge q_1 is brought to $x = 0$, charge q_2 to $x = -1$, and charge q_3 to $x = +1$. The coulomb energies are added in Eq. (4.8),

$$\begin{aligned} W_e &= q_2\Phi_2{}^1 + q_3\Phi_3{}^1 + q_3\Phi_3{}^2 \\ &= q_2 \frac{q_1}{4\pi\epsilon_0 R_{12}} + q_3 \frac{q_1}{4\pi\epsilon_0 R_{13}} + q_3 \frac{q_2}{4\pi\epsilon_0 R_{23}} \end{aligned}$$

where it is clear that $R_{12} = 1$, $R_{13} = 1$, and $R_{23} = 2$. If $q_1 = q_2 = q_3 = q$, then

$$W_e = \frac{5q^2}{8\pi\epsilon_0}$$

This same result may be obtained from Eq. (4.11), which is just a convenient way of writing Eq. (4.8):

$$W_e = \frac{1}{2}\left[q_1\left(\frac{q_2}{4\pi\epsilon_0 R_{12}} + \frac{q_3}{4\pi\epsilon_0 R_{13}}\right) + q_2\left(\frac{q_1}{4\pi\epsilon_0 R_{12}} + \frac{q_3}{4\pi\epsilon_0 R_{23}}\right) + q_3\left(\frac{q_1}{4\pi\epsilon_0 R_{13}} + \frac{q_2}{4\pi\epsilon_0 R_{23}}\right)\right]$$

We see immediately by adding terms that this gives the same result as Eq. (4.8).

Example 4.3 Electric energy in a spherical ball of charge The electric energy required to assemble a spherical ball of charge may be calculated from Eq. (4.13), (4.14), or (4.15), with V including all space where $\mathbf{E} \neq 0$. For a ball of radius a containing a uniform charge density ρ_0, Gauss's law may be applied to determine the radial electric field everywhere,

$$E_r = \begin{cases} \dfrac{\rho_0 r}{3\epsilon_0} & r < a \\[2ex] \dfrac{\rho_0 a^3}{3\epsilon_0 r^2} & r > a \end{cases}$$

There are no other electric field components. The electric potential Φ is required for use in Eq. (4.13). Since $\mathbf{E} = -\nabla\Phi$, Φ becomes [see Eq. (2.27)], in spherical coordinates,

$$\Phi = -\int_\infty^r E_r\, dr$$

with $\Phi = 0$ at $r = \infty$. Φ may be evaluated at any r value by evaluating the integral.

$$\Phi = \begin{cases} \dfrac{\rho_0 a^3}{3\epsilon_0 r} & r > a \\[2ex] \dfrac{\rho_0}{2\epsilon_0}\left(a^2 - \dfrac{r^2}{3}\right) & r < a \end{cases}$$

These potential relations may now be used in Eq. (4.13) to obtain W_e,

$$W_e = \frac{1}{2}\frac{\rho_0^2}{2\epsilon_0}\int_0^a \left(a^2 - \frac{r^2}{3}\right) 4\pi r^2\, dr$$

$$= \frac{4\pi}{15}\frac{\rho_0^2 a^5}{\epsilon_0}$$

The electric energy may be calculated from Eq. (4.15) without the necessity of calculating Φ:

$$W_e = \tfrac{1}{2}\epsilon_0 \left(\int_0^a \frac{\rho_0{}^2 r^2}{9\epsilon_0{}^2} 4\pi r^2\, dr + \int_a^\infty \frac{\rho_0{}^2 a^6}{9\epsilon_0{}^2 r^4} 4\pi r^2\, dr \right)$$

$$= \frac{2\pi}{9} \frac{\rho_0{}^2 a^5}{\epsilon_0} (\tfrac{1}{5} + 1)$$

$$= \frac{4\pi}{15} \frac{\rho_0{}^2 a^5}{\epsilon_0}$$

The same result is obtained as from Eq. (4.13). Note that with electric energy density as defined by Eq. (4.16), about 80 percent of the electric energy is stored outside the sphere of charge.

This result is also obtained from Eq. (4.14); this calculation is left as a problem.

4.4 POWER-ENERGY CONSERVATION THEOREM

This section is devoted to a description of the energy and power characteristics of electric and magnetic fields. The force equation, Eq. (2.34), $F = q(\bar{E} + \bar{v} \times \bar{B})$ describes the force transmitted by fields to charges. The charges respond to the force and gain energy; it is now necessary to determine where this energy comes from. Since fields exert the force from which particle energy is obtained, it is quite reasonable to suppose that the increased particle energy is obtained at the expense of field energy. It is thus suggested that fields store energy which is available to charged particles when the fields exert force on the particles. Since field energy is transferred to particles at a specific time rate, the fields may be said to transmit power. The general power and energy properties of electric and magnetic fields are now developed.

The power transmitted by means of the field force to charged particles is given by the simple particle equation from mechanics

$$P_c = \mathbf{F} \cdot \mathbf{v} \qquad \text{watts} \tag{4.17}$$

where P_c = power delivered to the charged particle
$\mathbf{v}$ = particle velocity
$\mathbf{F}$ = force exerted on the particle by the fields

The dimension of energy in the rationalized mks system of units is the joule, and 1 watt equals 1 joule/sec. The force equation for charged particles, Eq. (2.34), is used in Eq. (4.17) to derive the particle power relationship.

$$P_c = q(\mathbf{E} + \mathbf{v} \times \mathbf{B}) \cdot \mathbf{v}$$
$$= q\mathbf{E} \cdot \mathbf{v} \tag{4.18}$$

Note that the magnetic force term is not involved in the power-transfer mechanism to a moving charged particle. The reason for this is that the magnetic force $\mathbf{F}_m$ is always perpendicular to the particle velocity, and thus $\mathbf{F}_m \cdot \mathbf{v} = 0$ at all times. Power is defined as the time rate of change of energy,

$$P_c = \frac{d}{dt} W_c$$

This is easily seen by recognizing that since $\mathbf{F} = m\, d\mathbf{v}/dt$,

$$\begin{aligned} P_c &= \mathbf{F} \cdot \mathbf{v} \\ &= m\mathbf{v} \cdot \frac{d\mathbf{v}}{dt} \\ &= \frac{d}{dt} (\tfrac{1}{2} m v^2) \end{aligned}$$

where the particle energy W_c is $\frac{1}{2}mv^2$.

For a continuous charge distribution the volume force density exerted on an incremental volume of charge moving with a velocity $\mathbf{v}$ is considered. The expression for power analogous to Eq. (4.17) is

$$\mathcal{P}_c = \mathfrak{F}_v \cdot \mathbf{v} \tag{4.19}$$

where $\mathcal{P}_c$ is power density in watts/m³. Using Eq. (4.4) in Eq. (4.19), we obtain

$$\begin{aligned} \mathcal{P}_c &= \rho \mathbf{E} \cdot \mathbf{v} \\ &= \mathbf{J} \cdot \mathbf{E} \qquad \text{watts/m}^3 \end{aligned} \tag{4.20}$$

where $\mathbf{J} = \rho\mathbf{v}$. Equation (4.20) is a power-density relation describing the power delivered to a charged medium (characterized by a current-density vector $\mathbf{J}$) by the field $\mathbf{E}$ at the point where $\mathbf{J}$ is defined. The energy density of the charges is denoted as $\mathcal{W}_c$. The time rate of change of charge energy density is related to the charge power density by the simple equation $\mathcal{P}_c = \partial \mathcal{W}_c / \partial t$, and thus the following equation results:

$$\begin{aligned} \mathcal{P}_c &= \frac{\partial \mathcal{W}_c}{\partial t} \\ &= \mathbf{J} \cdot \mathbf{E} \qquad \text{watts/m}^3 \end{aligned} \tag{4.21}$$

The energy $\mathcal{W}_c$ delivered to the charges by the electric field $\mathbf{E}$ may be used for accelerating the charges, or, if collisions occur, for heating the medium by means of particle impact. Note that if the complex current $\mathbf{J}$ has a component in time phase with $\mathbf{E}$, the time rate of change of energy $\mathcal{W}_c$ is real and describes a real power loss, characteristic of joule heating through particle collisions. If the current $\mathbf{J}$ is out of time phase with $\mathbf{E}$, characteristic of a collisionless acceleration of charges, the time rate of change of medium energy density is imaginary, characteristic of an energy storage in the medium.

The current-density vector $\mathbf{J}$ in Eq. (4.21) is now replaced by its field equivalent, thereby giving an expression for charge power and energy density in terms of the fields alone. Equation (3.30) is used in Eq. (4.21) to give

$$\mu_0 \mathcal{P}_c = (\nabla \times \mathbf{B}) \cdot \mathbf{E} - \mu_0 \epsilon_0 \frac{\partial \mathbf{E}}{\partial t} \cdot \mathbf{E}$$

The vector identity

$$\nabla \cdot (\mathbf{E} \times \mathbf{B}) = \mathbf{B} \cdot (\nabla \times \mathbf{E}) - \mathbf{E} \cdot (\nabla \times \mathbf{B})$$

is used to obtain the expression

$$\mu_0 \mathcal{P}_c = \mathbf{B} \cdot (\nabla \times \mathbf{E}) - \nabla \cdot (\mathbf{E} \times \mathbf{B}) - \mu_0 \epsilon_0 \frac{\partial \mathbf{E}}{\partial t} \cdot \mathbf{E}$$

and by means of Eq. (3.31) we obtain

$$\mu_0 \mathcal{P}_c = -\nabla \cdot (\mathbf{E} \times \mathbf{B}) - \mathbf{B} \cdot \frac{\partial \mathbf{B}}{\partial t} - \mu_0 \epsilon_0 \mathbf{E} \cdot \frac{\partial \mathbf{E}}{\partial t}$$

The last two terms in this equation can be rewritten in a more useful form,

$$\mu_0 \mathcal{P}_c = -\nabla \cdot (\mathbf{E} \times \mathbf{B}) - \frac{\partial}{\partial t} \frac{1}{2} (\mathbf{B} \cdot \mathbf{B} + \mu_0 \epsilon_0 \mathbf{E} \cdot \mathbf{E})$$

The power density $\mathcal{P}_c$ represents a time rate of change of medium energy density $\mathcal{W}_c$ according to Eq. (4.21); thus the above equation may be written in the form of a conservation theorem,

$$\nabla \cdot \left(\mathbf{E} \times \frac{\mathbf{B}}{\mu_0} \right) + \frac{\partial}{\partial t} \left(\mathcal{W}_c + \frac{1}{2\mu_0} \mathbf{B} \cdot \mathbf{B} + \frac{\epsilon_0}{2} \mathbf{E} \cdot \mathbf{E} \right) = 0 \qquad (4.22)$$

This is the power-energy conservation theorem in point form for a charged medium where field effects are included. The integral form of the conservation theorem may be obtained by integrating Eq. (4.22) over a volume V and enclosing surface S. The divergence theorem is used to give

$$\oint_S \left(\mathbf{E} \times \frac{\mathbf{B}}{\mu_0} \right) \cdot \hat{\mathbf{n}}\, dS + \frac{\partial}{\partial t} \int_V \left(\mathcal{W}_c + \frac{1}{2\mu_0} \mathbf{B} \cdot \mathbf{B} + \frac{\epsilon_0}{2} \mathbf{E} \cdot \mathbf{E} \right) dV = 0 \qquad (4.23)$$

or

$$\oint_S \left(\mathbf{E} \times \frac{\mathbf{B}}{\mu_0} \right) \cdot \hat{\mathbf{n}}\, dS + \frac{\partial}{\partial t} \int_V \left(\mathcal{W}_c + \tfrac{1}{2} \epsilon_0 E^2 + \frac{1}{2\mu_0} B^2 \right) dV = 0 \qquad (4.24)$$

Equations (4.22) to (4.24) are forms of the power-energy conservation theorem for a medium containing charges and fields.

Equations (4.23) and (4.24) may be interpreted in terms of a simple physical picture. Suppose a volume V contains an energy density $\mathcal{W}$ which is changing in time. At the surface S enclosing the volume V a power-density vector $\boldsymbol{\mathcal{P}}$ exists such that $\boldsymbol{\mathcal{P}} \cdot \hat{\mathbf{n}}\, dS$ is the power *leaving* the volume V through the surface dS. The total power P leaving the volume V is

$$P = \oint_S \boldsymbol{\mathcal{P}} \cdot \hat{\mathbf{n}}\, dS$$

Since a net power P leaves V, the time rate of change of total energy W within V must equal $-P$; or, put another way, energy conservation requires that

$$P + \frac{\partial W}{\partial t} = 0$$

$$\oint_S \boldsymbol{\mathcal{P}} \cdot \hat{\mathbf{n}}\, dS + \frac{\partial}{\partial t} \int_V \mathcal{W}\, dV = 0 \tag{4.25}$$

It is immediately obvious that Eqs. (4.23) and (4.24) are of the form of Eq. (4.25), and thus they may be regarded as power-energy conservation theorems. More important, Eq. (4.25) provides a physical interpretation of the field quantities in Eqs. (4.23) and (4.24). For example, we see that the quantity $\mathbf{E} \times (\mathbf{B}/\mu_0)$ may be regarded as a field power density $\boldsymbol{\mathcal{P}}$ at the surface S of the form,

$$\boldsymbol{\mathcal{P}} = \mathbf{E} \times \frac{\mathbf{B}}{\mu_0} \qquad \text{watts/m}^2 \tag{4.26}$$

The terms in the volume integral of Eq. (4.23) or (4.24) are obviously energy-density terms, and the electric and magnetic field energy densities, $\mathcal{W}_e$ and $\mathcal{W}_m$, may be written as

$$\mathcal{W}_e = \frac{\epsilon_0}{2} \mathbf{E} \cdot \mathbf{E}$$

$$= \tfrac{1}{2}\epsilon_0 E^2 \qquad \text{joules/m}^3 \tag{4.27}$$

$$\mathcal{W}_m = \frac{1}{2\mu_0} \mathbf{B} \cdot \mathbf{B}$$

$$= \frac{1}{2\mu_0} B^2 \qquad \text{joules/m}^3 \tag{4.28}$$

The conservation theorem then states that the total field power leaving the volume V through S, plus the time rate of change of total energy within V (charged particle energy plus field energy), equals zero.

The field power-density vector $\boldsymbol{\mathcal{P}}$ is commonly called the *Poynting vector.* Note that an electric field alone may not possess a power density, nor may a magnetic field alone. A combination of electric and magnetic fields is required for a field power density to exist.

COMPLEX POWER AND ENERGY

The conservation theorem and the power and energy expressions derived above are instantaneous relations; they give power and energy at an instant of time. Since products of field quantities are involved, great care must be taken in evaluating these products when phasor notation is used (see Sec. 1.16) with $e^{j\omega t}$ time variations.

Time-average values of power and energy are of great practical interest. From Sec. 1.16, the time-average power and energy expressions are

$$\langle\mathcal{P}\rangle = \frac{1}{2\mu_0}\,\mathrm{Re}\,(\mathbf{E}\times\mathbf{B}^*)$$

$$\langle\mathcal{W}_e\rangle = \tfrac{1}{4}\epsilon_0\,\mathrm{Re}\,\mathbf{E}\cdot\mathbf{E}^* = \tfrac{1}{4}\epsilon_0 E^2$$

$$\langle\mathcal{W}_m\rangle = \frac{1}{4\mu_0}\,\mathrm{Re}\,\mathbf{B}\cdot\mathbf{B}^* = \frac{1}{4\mu_0}B^2$$

$$\langle\mathcal{P}_c\rangle = \tfrac{1}{2}\,\mathrm{Re}\,(\mathbf{E}\cdot\mathbf{J}^*)$$

It is now necessary to determine how these time-average quantities are related in a power-energy conservation theorem.

The power term desired is of the form $\nabla\cdot(\mathbf{E}\times\mathbf{B}^*)$. Starting with the two Maxwell curl equations for an $e^{j\omega t}$ time variation,

$$\nabla\times\mathbf{E} = -j\omega\mathbf{B}$$

$$\nabla\times\mathbf{B}^* = \mu_0\mathbf{J}^* - j\omega\mu_0\epsilon_0\mathbf{E}^*$$

and using the identity

$$\nabla\cdot(\mathbf{E}\times\mathbf{B}^*) = \mathbf{B}^*\cdot(\nabla\times\mathbf{E}) - \mathbf{E}\cdot(\nabla\times\mathbf{B}^*)$$

we have

$$\frac{1}{\mu_0}\nabla\cdot(\mathbf{E}\times\mathbf{B}^*) + \mathbf{E}\cdot\mathbf{J}^* + j\frac{\omega}{\mu_0}(\mathbf{B}\cdot\mathbf{B}^*) - j\omega\epsilon_0(\mathbf{E}\cdot\mathbf{E}^*) = 0 \tag{4.29}$$

This is the complex form of Eq. (4.22). The integral form of Eq. (4.29) is

$$\oint_S \left(\mathbf{E} \times \frac{\mathbf{B}^*}{\mu_0}\right) \cdot \hat{\mathbf{n}}\, dS + j\omega \int_V \left(\epsilon_0 \mathbf{E} \cdot \mathbf{E}^* - \frac{1}{\mu_0} \mathbf{B} \cdot \mathbf{B}^*\right) dV + \int_V \mathbf{E} \cdot \mathbf{J}^*\, dV = 0 \quad (4.30)$$

The terms in this equation are readily recognized as being related to the time-average power and energy densities defined above. One-half the real part of Eq. (4.30) is

$$\tfrac{1}{2}\,\mathrm{Re} \oint_S \left(\mathbf{E} \times \frac{\mathbf{B}^*}{\mu_0}\right) \cdot \hat{\mathbf{n}}\, dS + \tfrac{1}{2} \int_V \mathrm{Re}\, \mathbf{E} \cdot \mathbf{J}^*\, dV = 0$$

$$\oint_S \langle \boldsymbol{\mathcal{P}} \rangle \cdot \hat{\mathbf{n}}\, dS + \int_V \langle \mathcal{P}_c \rangle\, dV = 0 \quad (4.31)$$

and one-half the imaginary part is

$$\tfrac{1}{2}\,\mathrm{Im} \oint_S \left(\mathbf{E} \times \frac{\mathbf{B}^*}{\mu_0}\right) \cdot \hat{\mathbf{n}}\, dS + \frac{\omega}{2} \int_V \mathrm{Re}\left(\epsilon_0 \mathbf{E} \cdot \mathbf{E}^* - \frac{1}{\mu_0} \mathbf{B} \cdot \mathbf{B}^*\right) dV = 0$$

$$\tfrac{1}{2}\,\mathrm{Im} \oint_S \left(\mathbf{E} \times \frac{\mathbf{B}^*}{\mu_0}\right) \cdot \hat{\mathbf{n}}\, dS + 2\omega \int_V (\langle \mathcal{W}_e \rangle - \langle \mathcal{W}_m \rangle)\, dV = 0 \quad (4.32)$$

A complex Poynting vector is often defined as

$$\boldsymbol{\mathcal{P}} = \frac{1}{2\mu_0} \mathbf{E} \times \mathbf{B}^*$$

Equation (4.31) states that the time-average power transferred across the surface S is equal to the time-average power transferred to the charged particles inside S. If $\langle \mathcal{P}_c \rangle$ is positive, indicating that real time-average power is being transferred to particles in V, then the real time-average Poynting vector $\langle \boldsymbol{\mathcal{P}} \rangle$ must flow into V to supply the power. Equation (4.32) states that the imaginary time-average power transferred across S is related to the difference of the time-average electric and magnetic energy stored in V. This may seem like a strange result, but a similar result is obtained from circuit theory, as illustrated in a problem.

Example 4.4 Power dissipation in a resistor Every student knows how to calculate the power dissipated in a resistor if the resistance R and the dc current I or voltage V is given. In this example the power dissipated in a resistor is calculated from a knowledge of the **E** and **B** fields alone. This calculation is made possible by the development in this section of the field vector power density $\boldsymbol{\mathcal{P}}$.

Consider a cylindrical resistor of radius a and length L carrying a dc current I, as shown in Fig. 4.4. A dc voltage V across the resistor generates an electric field $E = V/L$. All the electric and magnetic fields in this example are static

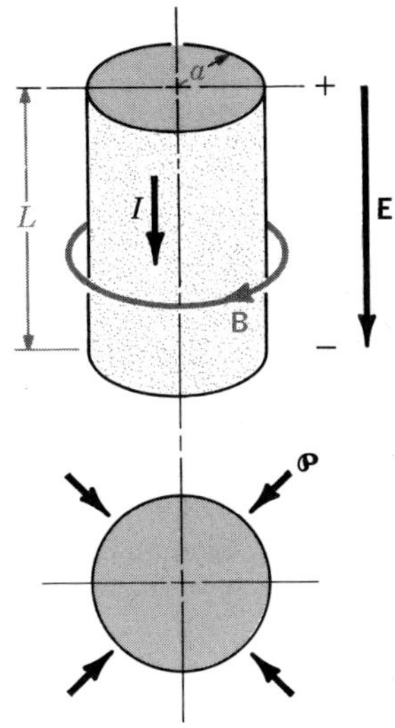

Fig. 4.4 A cylindrical resistor.

fields. The circuital law may be applied to obtain the magnetic field H_φ at the surface of the resistor $r = a$,

$$2\pi a B_\varphi = \mu_0 I$$

As the figure shows, the orientation of the electric and magnetic vectors is such that the Poynting vector $\mathcal{P}$ points radially into the resistor at the surface $r = a$, indicating that a continuous dc power flows into the resistor. The Poynting vector is

$$\mathcal{P} = \frac{1}{\mu_0} E_z B_\varphi$$

$$= \frac{1}{\mu_0} \frac{V}{L} \frac{\mu_0 I}{2\pi a}$$

The total power flowing into the resistor is equal to $\mathcal{P}$ times the surface area $2\pi a L$; thus the total power becomes

$$P = VI$$

which is the well-known result.

Example 4.5 Electric energy stored in a capacitor Equation (4.27) gives the electric field energy density in terms of the electric field $\mathbf{E}$ and the permittivity ϵ_0. It is obvious that in a parallel-plate capacitor, where an extended region of uniform electric field E exists, electric field energy is stored in the region between the plates. The energy stored in a 1-m² area of the capacitor is

$$W_e = \tfrac{1}{2}\epsilon_0 E^2 d$$

where d is the capacitor-plate separation distance.

The equation for capacitor energy from circuit theory is $W_e = \frac{1}{2}CV^2$, where $C = \epsilon_0/d$ for a 1 m² area and $V = Ed$. Thus $W_e = \frac{1}{2}\epsilon_0 E^2 d$, and the circuit energy relation agrees with the energy calculation based on the concept of field energy.

★4.5 The Electric Force Field

The force on a point charge given by Eq. (2.34) and the volume force density at a point in a continuous charge distribution given by Eq. (4.4) are expressions which give force in terms of the charge parameters q and $\mathbf{v}$ or ρ and $\mathbf{J}$ and the field parameters $\mathbf{E}$ and $\mathbf{B}$. It is possible to express these force relations in an entirely different form by eliminating the charge parameters in favor of their equivalent field expressions. Thus by writing the charge parameters ρ and $\mathbf{J}$ in terms of $\mathbf{E}$ and $\mathbf{B}$, expressions for force may be obtained in terms of the fields alone. This is often a convenient form of the force expressions for problems where the fields are known and the charges or currents are not specified. In addition, an expression for force in terms of the fields alone brings out the concept that force is transmitted by fields. The reader is cautioned not to forget in this formulation that forces cannot exist unless charges or currents are present for the field force to act upon. Writing $\mathbf{J}$ and ρ in terms of the fields tends to obscure the fact that $\mathbf{J}$ and ρ must be present for a force to exist.

In this section we restrict our attention to a calculation of the electric volume force density associated with a volume charge density ρ. Consider first the electric force term of Eq. (4.4), $\mathfrak{F}_e = \rho\mathbf{E}$. Equation (3.32) is used in Eq. (4.4) to obtain the electric volume force density,

$$\begin{aligned}\mathfrak{F}_{ve} &= \rho\mathbf{E}\\ &= \epsilon_0(\nabla\cdot\mathbf{E})\mathbf{E} \qquad \text{newtons/m}^3\end{aligned} \tag{4.33}$$

As this equation illustrates, an arbitrary electric field $\mathbf{E}$ may not necessarily generate a volume force density. The field must have a nonzero divergence, indicative of charges at the field point, for a volume force density to exist.

It is desired to calculate the total force exerted by an electric field on a volume containing charges. The total force is found by integrating the volume force density given by Eq. (4.33) over the volume under consideration,

$$\begin{aligned}\mathbf{F}_e &= \int_V \mathfrak{F}_{ve}\,dV\\ &= \int_V \epsilon_0\mathbf{E}(\nabla\cdot\mathbf{E})\,dV\end{aligned} \tag{4.34}$$

It is possible by an appropriate vector manipulation to convert Eq. (4.34) into a surface integral over the surface S enclosing the volume V. This procedure is quite analogous to the divergence theorem, where a volume integral is converted into a surface integral. However, Eq. (4.34) is not in the appropriate form for a direct application of the divergence theorem, and a more complicated mathematical development is required. This manipulation is carried out in Sec. 4.6. The only restriction on the process of converting the volume integral to an equivalent surface integral is that effects due to time-varying fields are neglected. This restriction is called the *quasi-static approximation* and is valid for a great number of problems involving static fields, fields with slow time variations, and localized regions of fields with rapid time variations. Thus, under the quasi-static approximation, Eq. (4.34) becomes

$$\begin{aligned}\mathbf{F}_e &= \epsilon_0 \int_V \mathbf{E}(\boldsymbol{\nabla} \cdot \mathbf{E})\, dV \\ &= \epsilon_0 \oint_S \left[\mathbf{E}(\mathbf{E} \cdot \hat{\mathbf{n}}) - \frac{E^2}{2} \hat{\mathbf{n}} \right] dS \end{aligned} \tag{4.35}$$

where $\hat{\mathbf{n}}$ is the outward-surface-normal unit vector.

It is obvious that the integrand in the surface integration may be interpreted as a surface force density, or stress, existing at the surface S enclosing the volume V. Equation (4.35) then assumes the form

$$\mathbf{F}_e = \oint_S \mathfrak{F}_{se}\, dS \tag{4.36}$$

where the electric surface force density $\mathfrak{F}_{se}$ is

$$\mathfrak{F}_{se} = \epsilon_0 \left[\mathbf{E}(\mathbf{E} \cdot \hat{\mathbf{n}}) - \frac{E^2}{2} \hat{\mathbf{n}} \right] \qquad \text{newtons/m}^2 \tag{4.37}$$

An illustration of the volume and surface force densities is given in Fig. 4.5.

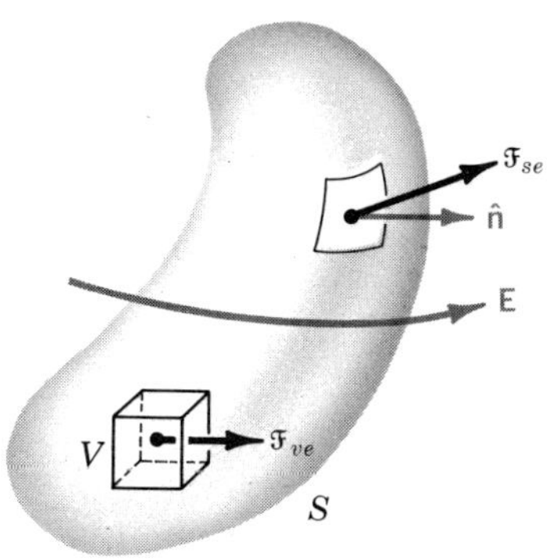

Fig. 4.5 The total force due to **E** on the charges ρ in V may be found by a volume integration of $\mathfrak{F}_{ve}$ over V, or an equivalent surface integration of $\mathfrak{F}_{se}$ over S.

We now consider the nature of the surface force density as given by Eq. (4.37). Note, first of all, that a surface force density apparently exists at a point on the surface even if there are no charges on the surface. This is in contrast to the volume force density, which must be zero at a point where there are no charges. Equation (4.36) correctly gives the total force $\mathbf{F}_e$ in terms of a surface integration involving $\mathfrak{F}_{se}$, and thus the mathematical concept of a surface force density is useful. However, it is incorrect to imply from this that a physically measurable surface density exists; there can be none when no surface charge density exists, and Eqs. (4.35) and (4.36) are concerned only with the total force, not with the force density. When the surface supports charges which are sources of field, then, of course, a physically measurable surface force density is present.

Consider the surface dS shown in Fig. 4.6. An arbitrary electric field $\mathbf{E}$ exists at the surface and may be resolved into components normal and tangential to the surface,

$$\mathbf{E} = E \cos \theta \, \hat{\mathbf{n}} + E \sin \theta \, \hat{\boldsymbol{\tau}} \tag{4.38}$$

The surface-force–density vector at the surface dS may be calculated by using Eq. (4.38) in Eq. (4.37); thus

$$\mathfrak{F}_{se} = \epsilon_0 \left[E(\cos \theta \, \hat{\mathbf{n}} + \sin \theta \, \hat{\boldsymbol{\tau}}) E \cos \theta - \frac{E^2}{2} \hat{\mathbf{n}} \right]$$

This equation is easily converted into the simplified form

$$\mathfrak{F}_{se} = \frac{\epsilon_0 E^2}{2} (\cos 2\theta \, \hat{\mathbf{n}} + \sin 2\theta \, \hat{\boldsymbol{\tau}}) \tag{4.39}$$

describing a surface force density as depicted in Fig. 4.7. Note the curious result that the vector $\mathfrak{F}_{se}$ is at an angle 2θ from $\hat{\mathbf{n}}$, whereas the electric

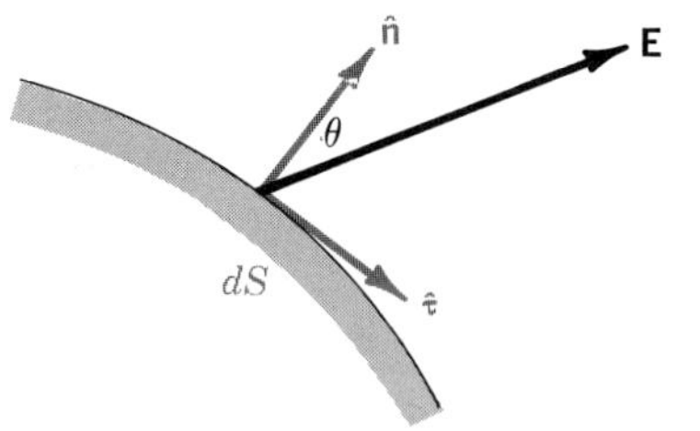

Fig. 4.6 The electric field at a surface element dS.

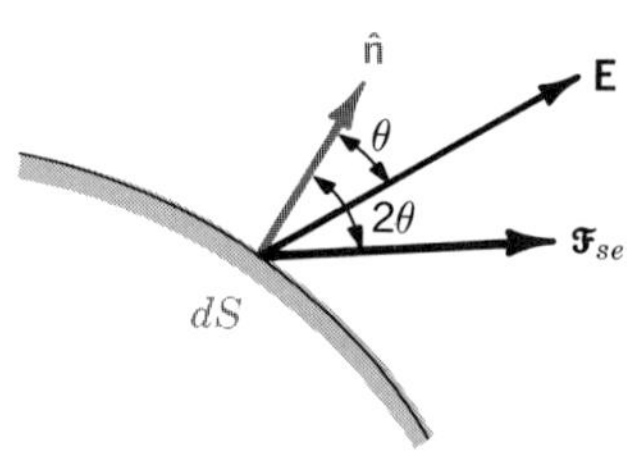

Fig. 4.7 The surface force density $\mathfrak{F}_{se}$ due to $\mathbf{E}$.

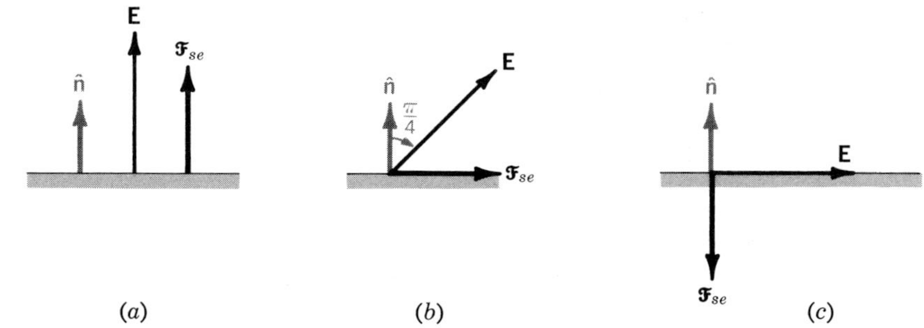

Fig. 4.8 The nature of the surface force density.

vector **E** is at an angle θ. The surface force-density vector is thus not parallel to **E**, and this result goes against our intuitive feeling that the electric force must always be parallel to the electric field. We must remember, however, that this is only a localized component force on a mathematical surface, and not a total force on a volume of charge. The total force, obtained by integrating $\mathfrak{F}_{se}$ around a surface which encloses a region of charge, must be, and indeed is, parallel to the electric field **E**.

Figure 4.8 illustrates the nature of the surface vector force density $\mathfrak{F}_{se}$ for several different orientations of the electric field vector at the surface. For a field perpendicular to the surface, the electric force-density vector pulls on the surface. When the electric field is tangential to the surface, the electric force pushes on the surface.

It is apparent from Eq. (4.39) that the electric force-density vector is independent of the sign of the vector **E**. Thus, whether an electric vector **E** points toward or away from the surface, the electric force-density vector $\mathfrak{F}_{se}$ pulls on the surface. It is also obvious from Eq. (4.39) that the magnitude of the electric surface force density is

$$\mathfrak{F}_{se} = \frac{\epsilon_0 E^2}{2} \qquad \text{newtons/m}^2 \tag{4.40}$$

Example 4.6 Electric force on a planar charged sheet The total force may be represented by either the volume integral or the surface integral in Eq. (4.35). Consider the symmetrical case of an electric field normal to a planar charged sheet, as shown in Fig. 4.9. The planar sheet is charged to a uniform surface charge density ρ_s, and it generates fields E_1 and E_2 perpendicular to the sheet and pointing away from the sheet on each side. In addition to the fields E_1 and E_2 generated by ρ_s, there is an external field E normal to the sheet, as shown. It is desired to evaluate the force per square meter on the sheet due to the presence of the external field E.

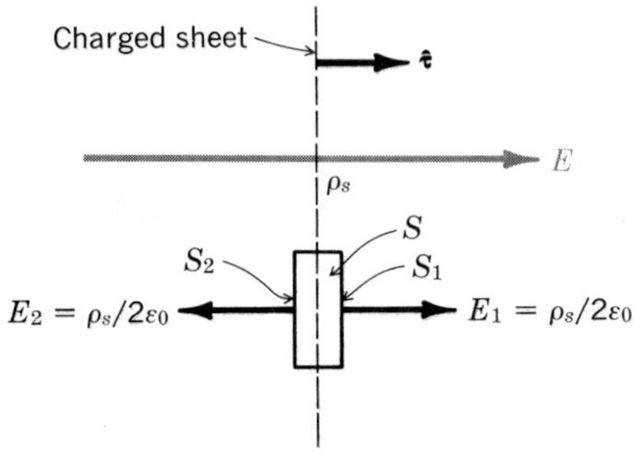

Fig. 4.9 Electric field and force exerted on a planar charged sheet.

The force on a sheet of area A is obtained from the basic volume integration in Eq. (4.5),

$$\mathbf{F} = \int_V \rho \mathbf{E}\, dV$$

$$= \int_A \rho_s \mathbf{E}\, dA$$

Since both ρ_s and E are uniform in this symmetrical case, the force becomes

$$\mathbf{F} = \rho_s \mathbf{E} A$$

and the surface force density exerted by the external field is simply

$$\mathfrak{F}_{se} = \rho_s \mathbf{E}$$

This result may also be obtained by integrating the surface force density over an enclosing surface S as illustrated in Fig. 4.9. A unit normal vector $\hat{\boldsymbol{\tau}}$ is defined in the direction of the external electric field $\mathbf{E}$. The surface integration is given by Eq. (4.35),

$$\mathbf{F} = \epsilon_0 \oint_S \left[\mathbf{E}(\mathbf{E} \cdot \hat{\mathbf{n}}) - \frac{E^2}{2} \hat{\mathbf{n}} \right] dS$$

where $\hat{\mathbf{n}}$ is the outward unit normal associated with the closed surface S. Thus

$$\mathbf{F} = \epsilon_0 \left[\left(E + \frac{\rho_s}{2\epsilon_0} \right)^2 \hat{\boldsymbol{\tau}} - \frac{1}{2} \left(E + \frac{\rho_s}{2\epsilon_0} \right)^2 \hat{\boldsymbol{\tau}} \right] S_1 + \epsilon_0 \left[- \left(E - \frac{\rho_s}{2\epsilon_0} \right)^2 \hat{\boldsymbol{\tau}} + \frac{1}{2} \left(E - \frac{\rho_s}{2\epsilon_0} \right)^2 \hat{\boldsymbol{\tau}} \right] S_2$$

If we set $S_1 = S_2 = A$ and evaluate the terms in the above expression, the force equation becomes

$$\mathbf{F} = \tfrac{1}{2} \epsilon_0 A \hat{\boldsymbol{\tau}} \left[\left(E + \frac{\rho_s}{2\epsilon_0} \right)^2 - \left(E - \frac{\rho_s}{2\epsilon_0} \right)^2 \right] \tag{4.41}$$

$$= \rho_s \mathbf{E} A$$

and the same result is obtained as from the volume integration.

This result may also be obtained by using Eq. (4.40) and recognizing that the electric force density pulls on the surfaces S_1 and S_2. The net force on the volume enclosed by the surface S is simply the force at surface S_1 minus the force at surface S_2, as written in Eq. (4.41), and the result is obtained immediately.

Example 4. 7 Electric force on a point charge It is well known that the force on a point charge is given by the expression $\mathbf{F} = q\mathbf{E}$. It is the purpose of this example to obtain this expression by means of integrating the electric surface force-density vector around a small spherical surface which encloses a point charge. Consider the geometry depicted in Fig. 4.10. A spherical coordinate system is used with the polar axis aligned with $\mathbf{E}_0$. The external field is $\mathbf{E}_0$, and the local field generated by the point charge q is $\mathbf{E}_q$. The total force exerted on the sphere of radius a surrounding the point charge q is given by Eq. (4.35),

$$\mathbf{F}_e = \epsilon_0 \oint_S \left[\mathbf{E}(\mathbf{E} \cdot \hat{\mathbf{n}}) - \frac{E^2}{2} \hat{\mathbf{n}} \right] dS$$

The electric field in this case is $\mathbf{E} = \mathbf{E}_q + \mathbf{E}_0$, where $\mathbf{E}_q = (q/4\pi\epsilon_0 a^2)\hat{\mathbf{n}}$. From the geometry of Fig. 4.10 it is obvious that there are no variations in the total field with the spherical azimuthal angle φ. The incremental surface dS is chosen, as shown. It is obvious that the components of force perpendicular to $\mathbf{E}_0$ will cancel, and the resultant force will be directed along the $\mathbf{E}_0$ direction,

$$F_{ez} = \epsilon_0 \oint_S \{(E_0 + E_q \cos\theta)(E_q + E_0 \cos\theta) - \tfrac{1}{2}[(E_0 + E_q \cos\theta)^2 + (E_q \sin\theta)^2] \cos\theta\} \, dS$$

The integrand in this equation may be expanded to yield the much simpler integral equation

$$F_{ez} = \epsilon_0 \int_0^\pi [E_0 E_q + \tfrac{1}{2}(E_q{}^2 + E_0{}^2) \cos\theta] 2\pi a^2 \sin\theta \, d\theta$$

The integral may be immediately carried out to give

$$F_{ez} = 2\pi a^2 \epsilon_0 E_0 E_q (-\cos\theta) \Big|_0^\pi$$

$$= qE_0$$

The result of the surface integration gives the well-known result

$$\bigstar \quad \mathbf{F}_e = q\mathbf{E}_0$$

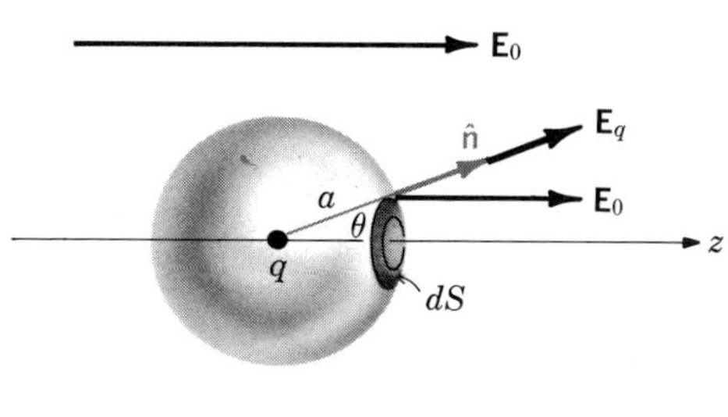

Fig. 4.10 Surface integration of $\mathfrak{F}_{se}$ to obtain the electric force on a point charge.

★4.6 Derivation of the Electric Surface-force–Density Relation

This section is devoted to an analytical derivation of the volume-to-surface integral transformation given in Eq. (4.35). Consider the volume integral

$$\int_V \mathbf{E}(\nabla \cdot \mathbf{E})\, dV \tag{4.42}$$

This volume integral is written out in component form as

$$\int_V [\hat{\mathbf{x}}E_x(\nabla \cdot \mathbf{E}) + \hat{\mathbf{y}}E_y(\nabla \cdot \mathbf{E}) + \hat{\mathbf{z}}E_z(\nabla \cdot \mathbf{E})]\, dV$$

and the vector identity

$$\nabla \cdot (E_i\mathbf{E}) = \mathbf{E} \cdot \nabla E_i + E_i \nabla \cdot \mathbf{E}$$

is used to convert each component of the volume integral into a more appropriate form. For the x component we have

$$\int_V \hat{\mathbf{x}}E_x(\nabla \cdot \mathbf{E})\, dV = \int_V \hat{\mathbf{x}}\,(\nabla \cdot E_x\mathbf{E} - \mathbf{E} \cdot \nabla E_x)\, dV$$

The divergence theorem is applied to obtain

$$\int_V \hat{\mathbf{x}}E_x(\nabla \cdot \mathbf{E})\, dV = \oint_S E_x\hat{\mathbf{x}}(\mathbf{E} \cdot \hat{\mathbf{n}})\, dS - \int_V \mathbf{E} \cdot \nabla E_x\, \hat{\mathbf{x}}\, dV$$

It is easily seen that by applying the same type of manipulation to the y and z components, the volume integration of Eq. (4.42) becomes

$$\int_V \mathbf{E}(\nabla \cdot \mathbf{E})\, dV = \oint_S \mathbf{E}(\mathbf{E} \cdot \hat{\mathbf{n}})\, dS - \int_V (\mathbf{E} \cdot \nabla)\mathbf{E}\, dV \tag{4.43}$$

The volume integral has now been partially reduced to the desired surface-integral form, but we are left with one further volume integral in Eq. (4.43). This integral may be reduced to a more convenient form by using the vector identity

$$\tfrac{1}{2}\nabla E^2 = (\mathbf{E} \cdot \nabla)\mathbf{E} + \mathbf{E} \times (\nabla \times \mathbf{E})$$

The volume integral on the right-hand side of Eq. (4.43) then becomes

$$-\int_V (\mathbf{E} \cdot \nabla)\mathbf{E}\, dV = -\int_V [\tfrac{1}{2}\nabla E^2 - \mathbf{E} \times (\nabla \times \mathbf{E})]\, dV$$

By using a well-known transformation from a volume integral to a surface integral (see the Appendix) and Eq. (3.31), this equation becomes

$$-\int_V (\mathbf{E} \cdot \nabla)\mathbf{E}\, dV = -\oint_S \tfrac{1}{2}E^2\hat{\mathbf{n}}\, dS - \int_V \mathbf{E} \times \frac{\partial \mathbf{B}}{\partial t}\, dV$$

This equation is now used in Eq. (4.43) to obtain the desired result,

$$\int_V \mathbf{E}(\nabla \cdot \mathbf{E})\, dV = \oint_S [\mathbf{E}(\mathbf{E} \cdot \hat{\mathbf{n}}) - \tfrac{1}{2}E^2\hat{\mathbf{n}}]\, dS - \int_V \mathbf{E} \times \frac{\partial \mathbf{B}}{\partial t}\, dV \tag{4.44}$$

Note that Eq. (4.44) is not in the same form as Eq. (4.35), as an additional volume-integral term appears with the integrand $\mathbf{E} \times (\partial\mathbf{B}/\partial t)$. The derivation thus makes very clear the statement appearing in conjunction with Eq. (4.35) that Eq. (4.35) is valid only in the quasi-static approximation. The meaning of this statement is obvious in Eq. (4.44). The quasi-static approximation involves neglecting time derivatives of fields. Certainly for static fields this term will be zero. It is also true that in many cases terms of this type are small and may be neglected. ★When this is done, we say we are applying the quasi-static approximation.

★4.7 The Magnetic Force Field

In addition to the electric force transmitted by electric fields, there are magnetic forces transmitted by magnetic fields. We now return to an examination of the second term in Eq. (4.4), the term which describes magnetic force effects on current elements. Obviously, there can be no magnetic forces present at a field point unless $\mathbf{J}$ is present at that field point. Just as in the electric case, the charge parameter $\mathbf{J}$ may be replaced by the equivalent field parameter from Maxwell's equations. Thus the magnetic force density may be written as

$$\begin{aligned} \mathfrak{F}_{vm} &= \mathbf{J} \times \mathbf{B} \\ &= \frac{1}{\mu_0}(\nabla \times \mathbf{B}) \times \mathbf{B} - \epsilon_0 \frac{\partial \mathbf{E}}{\partial t} \times \mathbf{B} \qquad \text{newtons/m}^3 \end{aligned} \tag{4.45}$$

which is obtained by combining Eqs. (3.30) and (4.4). The volume force density associated with the magnetic force on a current element is reduced to an expression involving the magnetic and electric fields alone.

The volume force exerted on a macroscopic volume V may be obtained by integrating Eq. (4.45) over the volume,

$$\mathbf{F}_m = \int_V \frac{1}{\mu_0}(\nabla \times \mathbf{B}) \times \mathbf{B}\, dV - \int_V \epsilon_0 \frac{\partial \mathbf{E}}{\partial t} \times \mathbf{B}\, dV$$

Notice that a volume integral involving the time derivative of a field vector appears, and it is consistent with the quasi-static approximation to neglect this term. The force equation thus reduces to

$$\mathbf{F}_m = \frac{1}{\mu_0}\int_V (\nabla \times \mathbf{B}) \times \mathbf{B}\, dV \tag{4.46}$$

By a very fortunate coincidence, this volume integral may be converted into an equivalent surface integral over the surface S which encloses the volume V, just as in the electric case:

$$\mathbf{F}_m = \frac{1}{\mu_0} \oint_S \left[\mathbf{B}(\mathbf{B} \cdot \hat{\mathbf{n}}) - \frac{B^2}{2} \hat{\mathbf{n}} \right] dS \tag{4.47}$$

Note that Eq. (4.47) is of the same form as Eq. (4.35), with $\mathbf{B}$ replacing $\mathbf{E}$ and $1/\mu_0$ replacing ϵ_0. As in the case of the derivation of electric force, it has been possible to use a divergencelike manipulation to convert a volume integral into a surface integral. A derivation of Eq. (4.47) from Eq. (4.46) is carried out in Sec. 4.8.

Since Eq. (4.47) describes the total force on a volume in terms of an integral of a vector force density over the enclosing surface, the integrand in Eq. (4.47) may be interpreted as a magnetic vector force density or stress,

$$\boldsymbol{\mathfrak{F}}_{sm} = \frac{1}{\mu_0} \left[\mathbf{B}(\mathbf{B} \cdot \hat{\mathbf{n}}) - \frac{B^2}{2} \hat{\mathbf{n}} \right] \qquad \text{newtons/m}^2 \tag{4.48}$$

Since Eq. (4.48) is directly analogous to Eq. (4.37), all electric field and force density relationships illustrated in Fig. 4.8 also hold for the magnetic case. The magnetic force density pulls on a surface as illustrated in Fig. 4.8*a* if $\mathbf{B}$ is normal to the surface, and it exerts a compressive force on the surface as shown in Fig. 4.8*c* if $\mathbf{B}$ is tangential to the surface. Furthermore, the magnitude of the magnetic force density is given by the analog of Eq. (4.40),

$$\mathfrak{F}_{sm} = \frac{1}{\mu_0} \frac{B^2}{2} \qquad \text{newtons/m}^2 \tag{4.49}$$

The characteristics of electric and magnetic forces are quite different, owing to the different source properties of the $\mathbf{E}$ and $\mathbf{B}$ fields. Electric fields terminate on charges which may reside on surfaces; thus the electric force is generally of such a nature as to pull on a charged surface. Magnetic fields are generated in entirely a different manner. Quasi-static magnetic field lines encircle current elements such that $\oint_l \mathbf{B} \cdot d\mathbf{l} = \mu_0 I$. The magnetic field generated by a current-carrying wire is tangential to the wire surface and will push on the surface. Thus, by the nature of the generation mechanism for electric and magnetic fields, electric forces and magnetic forces are generally opposed to each other at conducting surfaces. The boundary conditions on electric and magnetic fields at perfectly conducting surfaces require that $\mathbf{E}$ be normal and $\mathbf{B}$ be tangential, as will be shown in Chap. 5. Thus the electric force pulls on the surface and the magnetic force pushes on the surface.

Consider the important practical example of forces exerted on a conducting plane which stores charge and carries a surface current. Since the electric field must be normal to the conducting surface (because of the boundary condition of zero tangential field), the electric field lines associated with the surface charge pull on the surface with a force density

$$\mathfrak{F}_{se} = \frac{\epsilon_0 E^2}{2}\,\hat{\mathbf{n}}$$

The magnetic field at the surface of a conductor is tangential to the conducting surface; thus the magnetic force density pushes on the surface. The resultant total force at a conducting surface is thus given by

$$\mathfrak{F}_s = \left(\frac{\epsilon_0 E^2}{2} - \frac{1}{\mu_0}\frac{B^2}{2}\right)\hat{\mathbf{n}} \tag{4.50}$$

Since magnetic force usually predominates over electric force, conductors which carry current are either attracted or repelled in accordance with magnetic force effects.

Example 4.8 Magnetic forces associated with two current-carrying conducting planes Consider the case of two infinite conducting surfaces located in the $y = 0$ and $y = a$ planes, as shown in Fig. 4.11. A uniform surface current density J_s flows out of the paper on the upper conducting plane and into the paper in the $x = a$ plane. From an application of Ampère's circuital law, as carried out in detail in Example 3.10, it is easily shown that the magnetic field between the conductors is

$$\mathbf{B} = \mu_0 J_s \hat{\mathbf{y}}$$

The magnetic field is uniform and in the y direction between the conductors; thus magnetic forces are present which tend to repel the two conducting surfaces. The magnetic force density is obtained from Eq. (4.49) as

$$\mathfrak{F}_{sm} = \frac{\mu_0 J_s^2}{2} \qquad \text{newtons/m}^2$$

An order-of-magnitude estimate of the magnetic force density may be obtained by carrying out a typical example. For a surface current density of

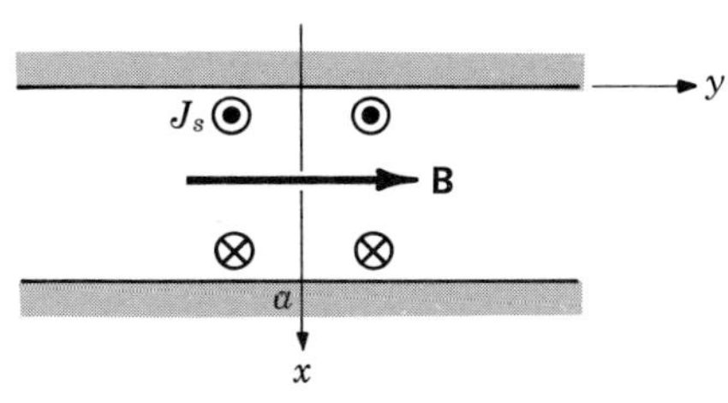

Fig. 4.11 Forces on current-carrying conductors.

100 amp/cm the magnetic force density is

$$\mathfrak{F}_{sm} = \frac{(4\pi \times 10^{-7})(10^4)^2}{2}$$
$$= 62.8 \text{ newtons/m}^2$$

Example 4.9 Plasma containment by a strong dc magnetic field An important practical application of the phenomenon of magnetic pressure is plasma containment for fusion purposes. If the plasma, consisting of a very hot mixture of ions, electrons, and molecules, can be contained effectively while it is heated to fusion temperature and pressure, a controlled thermonuclear power plant may be realized. Since it is impossible to contain a plasma at the required temperatures by mechanical means, other containment mechanisms, such as the magnetic field pressure system analyzed here, are needed.

The magnetic field required to balance a proposed fusion plasma pressure of 100 atm may be calculated from magnetic force density considerations. It is assumed that a planar interface exists between the plasma at 100 atm and free space containing a magnetic field B parallel to the interface. For a magnetic pressure to exist at the interface, it is necessary that the magnetic field in the plasma be discontinuously less than that in free space. Initially the B field in the plasma is zero. Since the magnetic field diffuses into the plasma with time, the results obtained are valid only for a short time period, where significant field diffusion does not occur. The plasma force density in mks units is

$$\mathfrak{F}_p = 100 \times 14.7 \times 6.895 \times 10^3 \text{ newtons/m}^2$$

and by using the force-balance expression $\mathfrak{F}_p = \mathfrak{F}_{sm} = (1/\mu_0)B^2/2$, the magnetic field B is obtained:

$$B = \sqrt{2 \times 100 \times 14.7 \times 6.895 \times 10^3 \times 4\pi \times 10^{-7}}$$
$$= 4.9 \text{ webers/m}^2$$

The magnetic field, in gauss, required to balance the 100-atm plasma pressure is

$$B = 49 \text{ kgauss}$$

This is a large field, but one that may be obtained in practice.

Unfortunately, in practice, magnetic field diffusion into the plasma is very rapid, and the magnetic pressure cannot be maintained. Furthermore, there are unstable time-varying interactions between the plasma and the magnetic field ★which hamper the containment process.

★4.8 Derivation of the Magnetic Surface-force–Density Relation

This section is devoted to the mathematical development of Eq. (4.47) from Eq. (4.46), under the quasi-static approximation. It is desired to convert the volume integration into an equivalent surface integration over the surface S which encloses the volume V. In this way surface force density is defined, and the important concept of magnetic surface force density is introduced.

We start with a consideration of Eq. (4.46), or more specifically the volume integral

$$\int_V (\nabla \times \mathbf{B}) \times \mathbf{B}\, dV$$

The vector identity

$$(\nabla \times \mathbf{B}) \times \mathbf{B} = (\mathbf{B} \cdot \nabla)\mathbf{B} - \tfrac{1}{2} \nabla B^2$$

may be used to convert this volume integral into a more convenient form,

$$\int_V (\nabla \times \mathbf{B}) \times \mathbf{B}\, dV = \int_V [(\mathbf{B} \cdot \nabla)\mathbf{B} - \tfrac{1}{2} \nabla B^2]\, dV$$

A volume integral involving the gradient of a scalar function may be converted to an equivalent surface integral over the boundary surface S, as given by an expression in the Appendix; thus

$$\int_V (\nabla \times \mathbf{B}) \times \mathbf{B}\, dV = \int_V (\mathbf{B} \cdot \nabla)\mathbf{B}\, dV - \oint_S \tfrac{1}{2}B^2\hat{\mathbf{n}}\, dS \qquad (4.51)$$

The volume integral becomes

$$\int_V (\mathbf{B} \cdot \nabla)\mathbf{B}\, dV = \int_V (\mathbf{B} \cdot \nabla)B_x\hat{\mathbf{x}}\, dV + \int_V (\mathbf{B} \cdot \nabla)B_y\hat{\mathbf{y}}\, dV + \int_V (\mathbf{B} \cdot \nabla)B_z\hat{\mathbf{z}}\, dV \qquad (4.52)$$

The identity

$$\nabla \cdot (B_i\mathbf{B}) = \mathbf{B} \cdot \nabla B_i + B_i \nabla \cdot \mathbf{B}$$

may be used. Note that $\nabla \cdot \mathbf{B}$ must be zero in this identity. The x component in Eq. (4.52) reduces to

$$\int_V (\mathbf{B} \cdot \nabla)B_x\hat{\mathbf{x}}\, dV = \int_V \nabla \cdot (B_x\mathbf{B})\hat{\mathbf{x}}\, dV = \oint_S \hat{\mathbf{x}}B_x\mathbf{B} \cdot \hat{\mathbf{n}}\, dS$$

The same type of expression is obtained for each component of Eq. (4.52); thus

$$\int_V (\mathbf{B} \cdot \nabla)\mathbf{B}\, dV = \oint_S \mathbf{B}(\mathbf{B} \cdot \hat{\mathbf{n}})\, dS$$

This relation is used in Eq. (4.45) to give the final result,

$$\mathbf{F}_m = \frac{1}{\mu_0} \oint_S [\mathbf{B}(\mathbf{B} \cdot \hat{\mathbf{n}}) - \tfrac{1}{2}B^2\hat{\mathbf{n}}]\, dS \qquad (4.53)$$

This completes the formulation of the equivalent surface-integral repre-★sentation for the magnetic force under the quasi-static approximation.

PROBLEMS

4.2-1 In addition to the kinetic power delivered to the plasma by the $\mathbf{J} \times \mathbf{B}$ force in accordance with Eq. (4.6), there is also power lost in the plasma because of joule heating losses, since there is a resistance R to the flow of current I through the plasma. Develop an expression for the ratio of the power lost to the kinetic power transferred to the plasma, and evaluate this ratio for the parameters given in Example 4.1 for $R = 10$ ohms.

4.2-2 A current $\mathbf{J} = (x^2 - 1)\hat{\mathbf{y}}$ exists in a uniform magnetic field $\mathbf{B} = \hat{\mathbf{z}}$. Solve for the total force on a unit cube centered at the origin in a rectangular coordinate system.

4.2-3 A medium consists of a volume charge density ρ moving at a velocity $v = 10^7$ m/sec. The charge moves in a medium containing an electric and a magnetic field. The magnetic field is perpendicular to the velocity vector for the moving charges. The static electric and magnetic field magnitudes are related by the expression $E/B = \sqrt{1/\mu_0\epsilon_0}$. Solve for the ratio of electric force to magnetic force per unit volume in the charged medium.

What charge velocity v is required for the magnetic force to equal the electric force?

4.2-4 A stationary electron is located at the origin in a rectangular coordinate system. An electric field $\mathbf{E} = E_0\hat{\mathbf{x}} \sin \omega t$ and a magnetic field $\mathbf{B} = B_0\hat{\mathbf{y}} \sin \omega t$ are present. Solve for the motion of the electron in response to the electric field, neglecting the $\mathbf{v} \times \mathbf{B}$ force.

Take the peak electron velocity v from the solution and determine the ratio of the peak $\mathbf{v} \times \mathbf{B}$ force to the electric force, assuming $E_0/B_0 = \sqrt{1/\mu_0\epsilon_0}$. Neglect the velocity in the x direction generated by the $\mathbf{v} \times \mathbf{B}$ effect. At $E_x = 1.0$ volt/m, what is the radian frequency ω at which the magnetic force is 10 percent of the electric force?

4.3-1 Find the total electric energy required to assemble a cubic array of point charges, five on a side, containing 125 charges. Assume that each point charge is $+10^{-6}$ coul and the charges are located at the rectangular coordinate points (x,y,z), where $x = 1, 2, 3, 4, 5$; $y = 1, 2, 3, 4, 5$; and $z = 1, 2, 3, 4, 5$. Use Eq. (4.11) to solve for the total energy by means of an appropriate computer program.

4.3-2 Assume that the total charge contained in the cube of Prob. 4.3-1 is now uniformly distributed over a sphere of diameter 5 m. Solve by means of Eq. (4.15) for the total electric energy associated with this spherical charged ball isolated in free space. Compare the result with the result of Prob. 4.3-1.

4.3-3 Solve for W_e in Example 4.3 by using Eq. (4.14). Does it matter what the size of the sphere S is in the calculation?

4.3-4 Two separate source-charge systems generate electric fields $\mathbf{E}_1$ and $\mathbf{E}_2$, respectively. These two charge systems are brought into the same region of space. Prove that the total electric energy is equal to the sum of the individual energies associated with each charge system, plus an interaction energy term

$$W_{\text{int}} = \epsilon_0 \int_V \mathbf{E}_1 \cdot \mathbf{E}_2 \, dV$$

4.3-5 Calculate the total electric energy per meter associated with an infinitely long line charge of 10^{-5} coul/m and diameter 1 cm concentric with a grounded conducting cylinder of diameter 10 cm. Calculate the energy only in the free-space region between the line charge and cylinder.

4.4-1 Derive the expression for complex power $P = \frac{1}{2}VI^*$ flowing into a series RLC circuit. Prove that $\text{Im } P = 2\omega(W_L - W_C)$, where W_L and W_C are the time-average energies stored in L and C.

4.4-2 A sinusoidal time-varying electric field is applied to a medium containing a charge density ρ. A current $\mathbf{J}_c$ is generated which consists of moving charges which undergo collisions with neutral particles. The equation of motion for this system is $\mathbf{F} = m[(d\mathbf{v}/dt) + \nu_c\mathbf{v}]$, where ν_c is a constant collision frequency. Solve for the power density $\mathbf{E} \cdot \mathbf{J}^*$ in this medium.

Calculate the ratio of imaginary time-average power density to the real or dissipated power density for copper, where $\nu_c = 4.1 \times 10^{13}$ collisions/sec at a frequency $f = 10^{10}$ Hz.

4.4-3 An RC circuit is connected as shown in Fig. P4.4-3. The switch is closed at $t = 0$, and current flows momentarily through the resistor R. Find (*a*) the power dissipated in R, (*b*) the power delivered by the battery, and (*c*) the power delivered to C. Is power conserved?

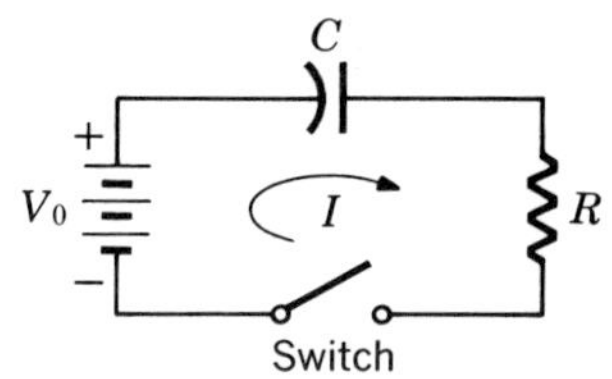

Fig. P4.4-3

4.4-4 Calculate the total magnetic energy per meter between a wire 1 mm in diameter and a concentric hollow conductor of diameter 1 cm. The wire carries a current of 1 amp.

4.4-5 A coaxial line consists of an inner rod of radius a and an outer concentric conducting cylinder of radius b. A perfectly conducting coaxial line carries dc power by means of dc surface current flowing in opposite directions on the rod and cylinder. A voltage V exists between the two conductors, and the total current is I. Show that the power carried by the coaxial line is IV by integrating Poynting's vector over a cross-sectional plane.

4.5-1 A parallel-plate capacitor of separation d is used in an ac circuit where a voltage $V = V_0 \cos \omega t$ is applied across the plates. Solve for the instantaneous and time-average force density exerted on the capacitor plates, neglecting fringing fields at the edges of the plates. What is the time-average force density for $d = 1$ cm and $V_0 = 100$ volts?

4.5-2 One plate of a parallel-plate capacitor is fixed and the other is driven by an externally applied mechanical force such that the separation between the plates is $x = d + x_0 \sin (2\omega t + \varphi)$. An alternating field exists between the plates of the form $E = E_0 \cos \omega t$. Solve for the time-average power density delivered by the field to the moving plate as a function of the phase angle φ. Describe the power transfer properties of this system when $\varphi = 0$ and $\varphi = \pi$. Explain physically the results which are obtained from the solution.

Explain how power is transferred from an external mechanical source into the fields of a capacitor when the capacitor plate is driven at twice the frequency ω, whereas no power is transferred to the fields when the plates are driven at ω.

The energy-exchange mechanism illustrated by this problem is the basic interaction process in diode parametric amplifiers, which are widely used in low-noise preamplifier systems.

Answer: $P = \dfrac{-\epsilon_0}{4} E_0{}^2 x_0 \omega \cos \varphi \qquad \text{watts/m}^2$

CHAPTER

5

electromagnetic fields and materials

5.1 INTRODUCTION

In previous chapters attention has been focused on electromagnetic fields produced by point charges, either singly or in a continuous distribution. In this chapter the main consideration is the interaction of electromagnetic fields and charges in materials. Because of the complexity of materials, an exact field analysis in terms of the fundamental particles and their charges would be extremely difficult, if not impossible. Fortunately, it is possible to obtain a great deal of understanding about some important characteristics of materials from very simple models.

The model used for nonmagnetic materials consists of immobile lattice ions surrounded by conduction electrons, which are so loosely bound that they can be considered "free," and bound electrons, which are bound to the lattice ions by a Hooke's law force. The number of conduction charges determines whether the material is a metal, a semiconductor, or an insulator. This model is equivalent to a combination of the Drude model of metals and the Lorentz model of insulators.

In the treatment of magnetic materials, it is assumed that the magnetic effects are produced by a distribution of magnetic dipoles which are associated with orbiting and spinning electrons.

The discussion in this chapter is limited to the macroscopic fields in materials, that is, the average field over an infinitesimal volume which is large enough to contain many molecules. The microscopic variation in field as the field point moves from atom to atom or molecule to molecule is not considered.

In the previous chapters it has been assumed that the charge density ρ and the current density $\mathbf{J}$ were known, and the resulting electromagnetic fields were calculated. However, in some cases the charges can move, and the force $q\mathbf{E}$ produced by the electric field can cause charge movement, and hence a change in ρ. This change in ρ produces a change in $\mathbf{E}$, which produces more change in ρ, and so on. These two effects, the effect of ρ on $\mathbf{E}$ and $\mathbf{E}$ on ρ, must be accounted for simultaneously. This leads, as one might expect, to the solution of simultaneous equations. More generally, the effects of $\mathbf{E}$ and $\mathbf{B}$ on ρ and $\mathbf{J}$ and the effects of ρ and $\mathbf{J}$ on $\mathbf{E}$ and $\mathbf{B}$ must be accounted for simultaneously. The effects of $\mathbf{E}$ and $\mathbf{B}$ on ρ and $\mathbf{J}$ are described by Eq. (2.34), which is the Lorentz force equation. The effects of ρ and $\mathbf{J}$ on $\mathbf{E}$ and $\mathbf{B}$ are described in Maxwell's equations, where ρ and $\mathbf{J}$ are sources of $\mathbf{E}$ and $\mathbf{B}$. Both these effects are taken into account in this chapter.

The principal results of this chapter are the electromagnetic field equations, which are valid when materials are present. These equations have the same form as those developed in Chap. 3, but they differ in that the free-space dielectric constant ϵ_0 and permeability μ_0 in the previous equations are replaced by ϵ and μ which depend on the materials present. These results are used extensively in Chap. 6 in developing wave-propagation characteristics.

5.2 INTERACTION OF CHARGES AND FIELDS

In this section, two hypothetical cases which illustrate the interaction between charges and fields are considered. These illustrations do not necessarily have direct significance with respect to charges in materials, but they do illustrate how the interaction between charges and fields occurs.

Example 5.1 Interaction between a mobile charge and an applied field Figure 5.1 illustrates a system of three charges and an externally applied constant field $\mathbf{E}_0$. First, suppose that all the charges are fixed and cannot move. Then the total field at the field point x is

$$\mathbf{E}_f = \frac{Q\hat{\mathbf{x}}}{4\pi\epsilon_0(x+d)^2} + \frac{Q\hat{\mathbf{x}}}{4\pi\epsilon_0(x-d)^2} + \frac{q\hat{\mathbf{x}}}{4\pi\epsilon_0 x^2} + \mathbf{E}_0 \tag{5.1}$$

where $\mathbf{E}_f$ stands for the total field present when the charges are fixed. There is no interaction in this case, and the total field is the superposition of the applied field $\mathbf{E}_0$ and the field produced by the three charges.

Fig. 5.1 A system of three charges and an externally applied constant field $\mathbf{E}_0$.

Now suppose that the Q's are fixed but q can move. Note that when $\mathbf{E}_0 = 0$, q remains at $x = 0$ because of the balance of forces due to the Q's on the left and right. When $\mathbf{E}_0$ is not zero, q moves to the position indicated by the unshaded circle in Fig. 5.1. This is the position where the total force on q, that produced by $\mathbf{E}_0$ and the two Q's, is zero; that is, x' is such that

$$\frac{qQ\hat{\mathbf{x}}}{4\pi\epsilon_0(d + x')^2} + \frac{-qQ\hat{\mathbf{x}}}{4\pi\epsilon_0(d - x')^2} + q\mathbf{E}_0 = 0$$

The first term is due to the Q on the left, the second to the Q on the right, and the third to $\mathbf{E}_0$. For convenience, suppose now that $x' \ll d$. Then

$$\frac{qQ}{4\pi\epsilon_0(d + x')^2} + \frac{-qQ}{4\pi\epsilon_0(d - x')^2} = \frac{-qQ4x'd}{4\pi\epsilon_0(d + x')^2(d - x')^2}$$
$$\approx \frac{-qQ4x'}{4\pi\epsilon_0 d^3}$$

and x' may be determined,

$$x' \approx \frac{\pi\epsilon_0 d^3}{Q} E_0 \tag{5.2}$$

The total field at the field point x is now

$$\mathbf{E}_m = \frac{Q\hat{\mathbf{x}}}{4\pi\epsilon_0(x + d)^2} + \frac{Q\hat{\mathbf{x}}}{4\pi\epsilon_0(x - d)^2} + \frac{q\hat{\mathbf{x}}}{4\pi\epsilon_0(x - x')^2} + \mathbf{E}_0$$

where $\mathbf{E}_m$ stands for the total field when q is mobile. Assuming that $x' \ll x$, and keeping only the first term in the binomial expansion for $1/(x - x')^2$, results in

$$\mathbf{E}_m \approx \frac{Q\hat{\mathbf{x}}}{4\pi\epsilon_0(x + d)^2} + \frac{Q\hat{\mathbf{x}}}{4\pi\epsilon_0(x - d)^2} + \frac{q\hat{\mathbf{x}}}{4\pi\epsilon_0 x^2} + \frac{qx'\hat{\mathbf{x}}}{2\pi\epsilon_0 x^3} + \mathbf{E}_0$$

With Eqs. (5.1) and (5.2), this becomes

$$\mathbf{E}_m = \mathbf{E}_f + \frac{qd^3}{2Qx^3}\mathbf{E}_0$$

Thus the total field is larger when q is mobile than when q is fixed, by a term proportional to the applied field $\mathbf{E}_0$. It is easy to see why; q has moved closer to the field point x because of the force $q\mathbf{E}_0$. This means that the field at x produced by q will be stronger. This illustrates a very simple interaction between charges and fields and shows how both the net field and the charge can be affected when the charge can move. The system is unstable if q and Q have opposite signs.

Example 5.2 Interaction between a continuous charge distribution and an applied field The situation considered here is illustrated in Fig. 5.2. There is a continuous neutralized charge density which is free to move within the region $-d \leq z \leq d$ but cannot move outside that region. The charge density is neutral, because in any differential volume dV there are equal numbers of positive and negative charges. Because of the neutralization, no net electric field is produced by the charge density when there is no external applied field.

When $\mathbf{E}_0$ is applied, however, the positive charges move up and the negative charges move down because of the resulting $q\mathbf{E}_0$ forces they experience. Since the charges are constrained to the region (by some method not explained), they collect on the surfaces and form equal and opposite surface charge densities on the top and bottom surfaces. These surface charge densities produce fields, as explained in Example 3.2. These fields are

$$\mathbf{E}_i = \begin{cases} \dfrac{-|\rho_s|\hat{\mathbf{z}}}{\epsilon_0} & -d < z < d \\ 0 & d < z,\ z < -d \end{cases}$$

where $|\rho_s|$ is the magnitude of the surface charge densities and $\mathbf{E}_i$ stands for induced fields. They are induced fields because they are induced by the application of $\mathbf{E}_0$ and the resulting movement of the charge.

The total field is the sum of the applied field $\mathbf{E}_0$ and the induced fields $\mathbf{E}_i$; that is,

$$\mathbf{E}_t = \begin{cases} \mathbf{E}_0 - \dfrac{|\rho_s|\hat{\mathbf{z}}}{\epsilon_0} & -d < z < d \\ \mathbf{E}_0 + 0 = \mathbf{E}_0 & d < z,\ z < -d \end{cases}$$

It is important to remember that $\mathbf{E}_0$ is produced by an external system of charges which is unaffected by the charges in the region $-d < z < d$. Hence $\mathbf{E}_0$ is

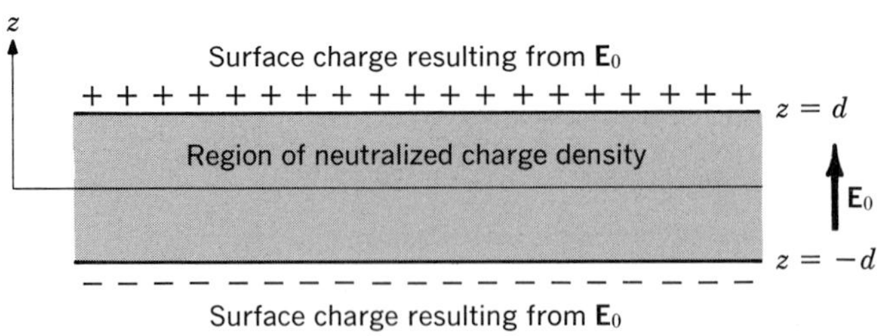

Fig. 5.2 Neutralized charge density is constrained to the region $-d \leq z \leq d$. When $\mathbf{E}_0$ is applied, charges move to the boundaries.

always constant. The remaining step is to find a value for $|\rho_s|$ so that $\mathbf{E}_t$ can be evaluated. Since the charges in the region $-d < z < d$ move according to the force exerted by the total field $\mathbf{E}_t$, $|\rho_s|$ will increase as long as $\mathbf{E}_t$ is not zero. What happens, then, is that charges move to the surfaces until $\mathbf{E}_i = -\mathbf{E}_0$ and $\mathbf{E}_t = 0$ in the region $-d < z < d$. Then equilibrium is maintained. Consequently,

$$|\rho_s| = \epsilon_0 E_0$$

$$\mathbf{E}_t = \begin{cases} 0 & -d < z < d \\ \mathbf{E}_0 & d < z,\ z < -d \end{cases}$$

If the charges had been fixed and could not have moved to the surfaces when $\mathbf{E}_0$ was applied, the net charge density would have remained zero, and the total field everywhere would have been $\mathbf{E}_0$. The interaction between the mobile charges and $\mathbf{E}_0$, however, caused surface charge densities and resulting induced fields which made the total field zero in the region $-d < z < d$.

The interaction described in this example is the kind that makes the electric field zero inside a conductor.

5.3 EFFECTS OF FIELDS ON NONMAGNETIC MATERIALS

The two examples in the previous section illustrate the interaction between charges and fields. These simple examples, however, are not necessarily related to real materials. In this section the effects of fields on materials are discussed in terms of simplified models of physical materials.

POLARIZATION OF BOUND CHARGES

The commonly used simple classical model of an atom can be used to show how electric fields affect the bound charges. This model consists of a nucleus with a total charge q, surrounded by an electron cloud. It is assumed that the electron cloud can be approximated by a sphere of charge having a uniform continuous charge density ρ and radius r_o. The value of $|\rho|$ is such that the total charge is q; that is, $\frac{4}{3}\pi r_0^3 |\rho| = q$. The model is illustrated in Fig. 5.3.

When an electric field is applied, the nucleus and the electron cloud move in opposite directions, as shown in Fig. 5.3. In this simple model it is assumed that the sphere of charge moves as a sphere. The nucleus and the sphere of charge separate, until the restoring force is equal to the force exerted by $\mathbf{E}_0$. The restoring force is perhaps best thought of in terms of the force on q produced by the electric field of the sphere of charge. This force tends to move q toward the center of the sphere.

The electric field produced by the sphere of charge can be found easily from Gauss's law as explained in Chap. 3. For convenience, the origin of the coordinate system shown in Fig. 5.3 is placed at the center

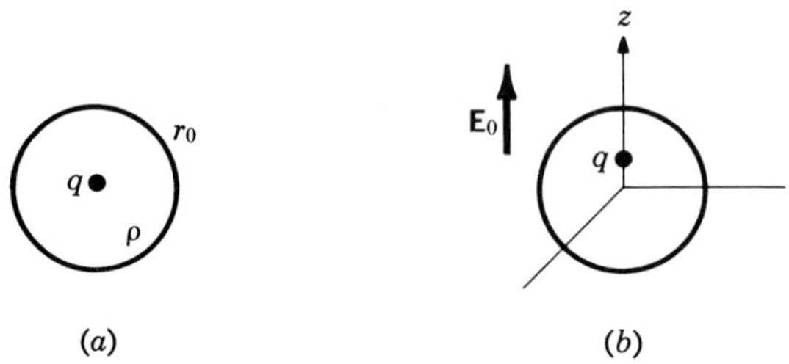

Fig. 5.3 Simple classical model of an atom: (*a*) no applied field; (*b*) with applied field $\mathbf{E}_0$.

of the sphere. From Gauss's law, Eq. (3.4), we have

$$\oint_S \epsilon_0 \mathbf{E} \cdot d\mathbf{S} = \int_V \rho \, dV$$

where S is taken to be a sphere of radius r centered at the origin. Because of symmetry, $\mathbf{E}$ has only an r component which varies only with r. Hence, since ρ is constant, the integrals can be evaluated to give

$$\epsilon_0 4\pi r^2 E_r = \frac{4\pi r^3 \rho}{3}$$

Since ρ is negative for electrons,

$$E_r = \frac{\rho r}{3\epsilon_0} = -\frac{|\rho| r}{3\epsilon_0}$$

If $\mathbf{E}_0$ is along the z axis, q will be displaced along the z axis. On the z axis the field of the sphere of charge is

$$E_z = -\frac{|\rho| z}{3\epsilon_0}$$

Hence the restoring force is

$$F = -\frac{|\rho| z q}{3\epsilon_0}$$

and the equilibrium position z is the point where

$$\frac{|\rho| z q}{3\epsilon_0} = qE_0$$

The separation between q and the sphere of charge is then

$$z = \frac{3\epsilon_0 E_0}{|\rho|} = \frac{4\pi\epsilon_0 r_0{}^3 E_0}{q} \tag{5.3}$$

It is interesting to estimate the ratio z/r_0,

$$\frac{z}{r_0} = \frac{4\pi\epsilon_0 r_0{}^2 E_0}{q}$$

Since r_0 is of the order of 10^{-10} m, we have

$$\frac{z}{r_0} = \frac{4\pi \times 8.854 \times 10^{-12} \times 10^{-20}}{Z1.6 \times 10^{-19}} E_0 \approx \frac{7 \times 10^{-12}}{Z} E_0$$

where Z is the number of electrons in an atom. Even for a one-electron atom with a relatively high E_0 of 10^6 volts/m, z/r_0 is only

$$\frac{z}{r_0} \approx 7 \times 10^{-6} \tag{5.4}$$

which shows that the separation z is typically very small compared to the atomic radius.

The separation of charge just described is called *polarization*. It is convenient to describe this polarization in terms of the dipole moment, which in the case just considered is defined as qz. The more general definition of dipole moment is

$$\mathbf{P} = q\boldsymbol{\xi} \text{ coul/m} \tag{5.5}$$

where $\boldsymbol{\xi}$ is the vector separation distance of the charge. This is the same definition as given in Example 2.3. Since the separation is usually quite small, as indicated by Eq. (5.4), the approximate field expressions given in Example 2.3 are also usually valid for the dipole moments resulting from the separation of charge in an atom.

The kind of charge separation just discussed and illustrated in Fig. 5.3 is called the *electronic polarization* and is designated by $\mathbf{p}_e$. Since, as indicated by Eq. (5.3), $\mathbf{p}_e$ is proportional to the applied field, it is often written as

$$\mathbf{p}_e = \alpha_e \mathbf{E}_{\text{mol}} \tag{5.6}$$

where α_e is called the *electronic polarizability* and $\mathbf{E}_{\text{mol}}$ is the actual microscopic field at the atom or molecule (see Sec. 2.3 for a discussion of "microscopic field").

In addition to electronic polarization, there are other kinds of charge separation. Electric fields may displace atoms or ions in a molecule, thus causing polarization. This kind of polarization is called *atomic* or *ionic polarization*, $\mathbf{p}_a$. Like $\mathbf{p}_e$, $\mathbf{p}_a$ can be written as

$$\mathbf{p}_a = \alpha_a \mathbf{E}_{\text{mol}}$$

where α_a is the atomic or ionic polarizability.

A third kind of polarization results when molecules have permanent dipole moments. Without an applied electric field, these permanent dipoles are randomly oriented, and the effects cancel out on the average. However, when an electric field is applied, the dipoles tend to line up with the electric field, as indicated in Fig. 5.4. As one would expect, the extent of alignment depends on the strength of $\mathbf{E}_0$. This kind of polarization is called *orientational polarization*.

Since further consideration of the molecular fields and polarization becomes very complex, it is desirable at this point to consider macroscopic fields, using the above discussion of polarizability as a basis for understanding the macroscopic field behavior (microscopic and macroscopic fields are discussed in Sec. 2.3).

In each of the three cases of polarization discussed, the polarization is proportional to the microscopic electric field at the molecule. This microscopic field is the sum of any applied field and the fields produced by all the other molecules. It is *not* the same as the average macroscopic field, because the average macroscopic field at the position of a molecule includes the field produced by that molecule, while the microscopic field at the position of the molecule includes fields produced by all the other molecules and external fields, but not fields produced by that molecule itself. Consequently, $\mathbf{E}_{\text{mol}}$ in the above expressions cannot be replaced by the average macroscopic fields.

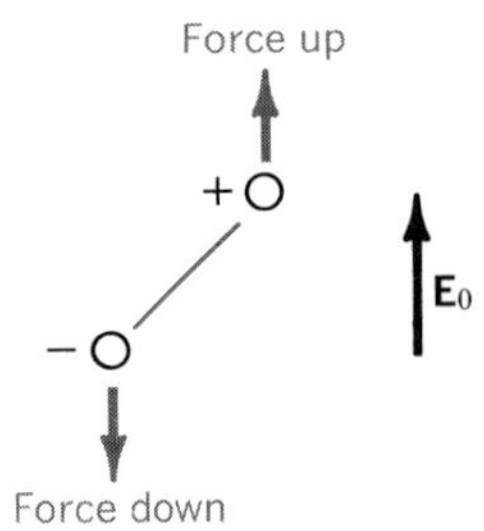

Fig. 5.4 An applied field $\mathbf{E}_0$ tends to align a permanent dipole.

The macroscopic approach can be taken, however, by approximating the microscopic distribution of dipole moments by a continuous macroscopic distribution of dipole moments, just as a distribution of point charges was approximated by a continuous distribution called ρ in Chap. 2. Thus $\mathbf{P}$ is defined as the average dipole moment per unit volume,

$$\mathbf{P} = \lim_{\Delta V \to 0} \frac{\sum_{i=1}^{N} \mathbf{p}_i}{\Delta V}$$

where the $\mathbf{p}_i$ are the microscopic dipole moments. $\mathbf{P}$ is called the *polarization.*

Although we shall not attempt a proof here, there is a corresponding proportionality between $\mathbf{P}$ and the average macroscopic field $\mathbf{E}$ which results from the proportionality between $\mathbf{p}$ and $\mathbf{E}_{\text{mol}}$. Therefore

$$\mathbf{P}_e = \chi_E \epsilon_0 \mathbf{E} \tag{5.7}$$

$$\mathbf{P}_a = \chi_A \epsilon_0 \mathbf{E} \tag{5.8}$$

$$\mathbf{P}_d = \chi_D \epsilon_0 \mathbf{E} \tag{5.9}$$

where $\mathbf{P}_e$, $\mathbf{P}_a$, and $\mathbf{P}_d$ are the polarizations resulting from electronic polarization, ionic polarization, and alignment of permanent dipoles, respectively, and the χ's are proportionality constants. Note that $\chi_E\epsilon_0$ is *not* equal to α_e, etc. Corresponding macroscopic definitions are

$$\mathbf{P}_e = N_e q \xi_e \tag{5.10}$$

$$\mathbf{P}_a = N_a q \xi_a \tag{5.11}$$

where N_e is the *average* number of electronic dipole moments per unit volume and ξ_e is the *average* separation, etc. The total polarization is the sum of the various kinds of polarizations,

$$\begin{aligned} \mathbf{P} &= \mathbf{P}_e + \mathbf{P}_a + \mathbf{P}_d \\ &= (\chi_E + \chi_A + \chi_D)\epsilon_0 \mathbf{E} \\ &= \chi_e \epsilon_0 \mathbf{E} \end{aligned} \tag{5.12}$$

where χ_e is called the *electric susceptibility.* ϵ_0 was included in the proportionality constant to make χ_e dimensionless. Equation (5.12) holds only for a class of materials called *linear materials.* For other materials χ_e is a tensor; that is, the x component of $\mathbf{P}$ may depend on the x, y, and z components of $\mathbf{E}$. Only linear materials are considered here.

In the time-varying case, $\mathbf{P}$ may be out of time phase with $\mathbf{E}$, and hence the χ's in general are not constant with respect to ω. Since ξ_e is proportional to **E** and may differ in time phase, the relation between $\boldsymbol{\xi}_e$ and **E** is like that of a driven harmonic oscillator with damping due to viscous friction. The differential equation describing such an oscillator is

$$m\frac{d^2\mathbf{r}}{dt^2} = \mathbf{F}_d - m\omega_0{}^2\mathbf{r} - m\nu\frac{d\mathbf{r}}{dt}$$

which is in the form $m\mathbf{a} = \Sigma\mathbf{F}$, where m is the mass, **a** the acceleration, and **F** the forces acting on the particle. $\mathbf{F}_d$ is the driving force, $-m\omega_0{}^2\mathbf{r}$ is the Hooke's law restoring force, which might be due to a spring, and $-m\nu(d\mathbf{r}/dt)$ is the retarding force due to viscous friction. ω_0 is the natural oscillation frequency, and ν is the damping factor. This differential equation would describe the motion of a mass on a spring in a fluid and driven by a force $\mathbf{F}_d$.

Writing the same kind of equation to describe the motion of the bound charges results in

$$m_e\frac{d^2\boldsymbol{\xi}_e}{dt^2} = q\mathbf{E} - m_e\omega_{se}{}^2\boldsymbol{\xi}_e - m_e\nu_e\frac{d\boldsymbol{\xi}_e}{dt} \tag{5.13}$$

where

$q\mathbf{E}$ = driving force
ω_{se} = natural frequency of oscillation
ν_e = damping factor
m_e = mass of the particle which is moving

In the case of electronic polarization, m_e may be taken as the effective mass of an electron, because the nucleus is so much heavier that its movement is very slight in comparison to the motion of the electron. Hence $\boldsymbol{\xi}_e$ results mostly from the movement of the electron. In the dc case, Eq. (5.13) reduces to

$$\boldsymbol{\xi}_e = \frac{q}{m_e\omega_s{}^2}\mathbf{E} \tag{5.14}$$

which, when combined with Eqs. (5.7) and (5.10), leads to

$$\omega_s{}^2 = \frac{q^2n_e}{m_e\chi_E\epsilon_0}$$

Hence the term in Eq. (5.13) containing $\omega_s{}^2$ corresponds to the displacement $\boldsymbol{\xi}_e$ being proportional to the force $q\mathbf{E}$, which is characteristic of a harmonic oscillator.

The damping term $m\nu_b\, d\boldsymbol{\xi}_e/dt$ in Eq. (5.13) corresponds to energy loss from radiation due to the acceleration of the charge.

In the sinusoidal case $d/dt \to j\omega$, and Eq. (5.13) may be solved for $\boldsymbol{\xi}_e$,

$$\boldsymbol{\xi}_e = \frac{(q/m_e)\mathbf{E}}{-\omega^2 + \omega_{se}{}^2 + j\omega\nu_e} \tag{5.15}$$

A corresponding relation can be obtained for $\boldsymbol{\xi}_a$,

$$\boldsymbol{\xi}_a = \frac{(q/m_a)\mathbf{E}}{-\omega^2 + \omega_{sa}{}^2 + j\omega\nu_a} \tag{5.16}$$

The relation between $\mathbf{P}_d$ and $\mathbf{E}$, which is not derived here, is of the form

$$\mathbf{P}_d = \frac{\chi_{d0}\epsilon_0\mathbf{E}}{1 + j\omega\tau} \tag{5.17}$$

where χ_{d0} is the dc value of χ_d and τ is the *relaxation time.*

By combining Eqs. (5.15) and (5.16) with Eqs. (5.10) to (5.12), we can write $\mathbf{P}$ as

$$\mathbf{P} = \left(\frac{N_e q^2/m_e}{-\omega^2 + \omega_{se}{}^2 + j\omega\nu_e} + \frac{N_a q^2/m_a}{-\omega^2 + \omega_{sa}{}^2 + j\omega\nu_a} + \frac{\chi_{d0}\epsilon_0}{1 + j\omega\tau}\right)\mathbf{E} \tag{5.18}$$

In general, there may be several species of electronic polarization, each with a different ω_{se}. The same is true of the two other kinds of polarization. Hence Eq. (5.18) may be generalized to

$$\mathbf{P} = \left(\sum_i \frac{N_{ei} q_i{}^2/m_{ei}}{-\omega^2 + \omega_{sei}^2 + j\omega\nu_{ei}} + \sum_i \frac{N_{ai} q_i{}^2/m_{ai}}{-\omega^2 + \omega_{sai}^2 + j\omega\nu_{ai}} + \sum_i \frac{\chi_{d0i}\epsilon_0}{1 + j\omega\tau_i}\right)\mathbf{E}$$

which can be conveniently shortened to

$$\mathbf{P} = \chi_e(\omega)\epsilon_0\mathbf{E} \tag{5.19}$$

where

$$\chi_e(\omega) = \sum_i \frac{N_{ei} q_i{}^2/\epsilon_0 m_{ei}}{-\omega^2 + \omega_{sei}^2 + j\omega\nu_{ei}} + \sum_i \frac{N_{ai} q_i{}^2/\epsilon_0 m_{ai}}{-\omega^2 + \omega_{sai}^2 + j\omega\nu_{ai}} + \sum_i \frac{\chi_{d0i}}{1 + j\omega\tau_i} \tag{5.20}$$

Because the average macroscopic field is not the same as $\mathbf{E}_{\text{mol}}$, ω_{se} in $\chi(\omega)$ may depend on N_e, and ω_{sa} may depend on N_a.

Equations (5.19) and (5.20) describe the effect of the fields on bound charges. According to Eq. (5.19), the fields cause a polarization which is a rather complicated function of frequency, as well as the characteristics of the material, N_{ei}, m_{ei}, ω_{sei}, ν_{ei}, N_{ai}, etc. A discussion of the effects of the frequency and the material parameters on electric fields is postponed until the sections on permittivity (Sec. 5.5) and planewaves (Sec. 6.15), where much more meaningful discussions are possible.

Polarization, then, is the effect of electric fields on bound charges. The effects of the electric field on conduction charges is discussed next.

DRIFT OF CONDUCTION CHARGES

The effect of electric fields on conduction charges is to cause them to drift. Conduction charges can drift through a material, because they are not tightly bound to any one atom and hence are relatively free to move. As pointed out in Sec. 5.2, a surface charge density results when charges are free to move within a region but not past a given surface boundary. The situation in a good conductor with an applied electric field is much like that of Fig. 5.2, the difference being that the conduction charges in a good conductor are electrons only, and hence no movement of positive charge occurs. Consequently, for a conductor, the surface charge on the bottom in Fig. 5.2 would be due to excess electrons which moved there because of the applied field. The positive surface charge on the top surface would be due to unneutralized positive ions which became unneutralized when the mobile electrons moved away because of the force exerted by $\mathbf{E}_0$.

The surface charge in Fig. 5.2 results because the charges are constrained to the indicated region by an unspecified method. In a conductor, of course, the constraint results from the charges not being able to leave the conductor (except in cases of thermionic emission, field emission, etc.). If the circuit were completed, that is, if the surface barrier in Fig. 5.2 were removed, a dc flow of current would result.

The motion of the conduction charges is described by an equation like Eq. (5.13), except that the Hooke's law restoring force is zero. Hence

$$m\frac{d\mathbf{v}}{dt} = -\nu_c m\mathbf{v} + q\mathbf{E} \tag{5.21}$$

where $\mathbf{v}$ is the average macroscopic velocity and the $\nu_c m\mathbf{v}$ term is a damping term. The magnetic force term which should appear on the right of Eq. (5.21) has been neglected because it is very small when $\mathbf{v}$ is small compared to the velocity of light, as it is here. The damping results primarily from collisions of the conduction charges with lattice ions. In the absence of an applied field, the motion of the conduction charges is random, and the average velocity is zero. The conduction charges may be thought of as bouncing from one lattice ion to another in a random fashion, never getting anywhere. When an electric field is applied, the conduction charges are accelerated by the electric field during the time between collisions. This superimposes an average drift velocity on the random motion. In the absence of collisions, the acceleration of the charges caused by the electric field would result in velocities increasing with time toward infinity. The collisions, however, limit the average drift velocity to a finite value. This can be seen from Eq. (5.21) in the sinusoidal case in the following way.

For sinusoidal time variation, Eq. (5.21) can be solved for $\mathbf{v}$,

$$\mathbf{v} = \frac{q\mathbf{E}}{m(j\omega + \nu_c)} \tag{5.22}$$

When $\omega = 0$, $\mathbf{v}$ has the steady-state value

$$\mathbf{v} = \frac{q\mathbf{E}}{m\nu_c}$$

which is inversely proportional to ν_c, the average frequency of collisions. If no collisions occurred, ν_c would be zero and $\mathbf{v}$ would be infinite, as stated above.

In summary, the effect of electric fields on the conduction electrons is to cause the conduction charges to "drift." The average drift velocity is given by Eq. (5.22).

5.4 EFFECTS OF NONMAGNETIC MATERIALS ON FIELDS

In the previous section the effects of fields on nonmagnetic materials were described in terms of polarization of bound charges and drift of conduction charges. In this section the effects that the polarization and drift have on the fields are discussed. The effect of polarization is to produce a charge density and current which are sources of fields. The effect of the drift of conduction charges is to produce a current which is a source of fields.

POLARIZATION CHARGE DENSITY AND CURRENT

Before polarization occurs, a material is macroscopically neutral, because the positive charges and negative charges are equal, on the average, and their effects cancel. However, when polarization occurs, there is a separation of positive and negative charge, as explained in Sec. 5.3. In fact, polarization means a separation of charge. This separation of charge can mean that the positive and negative charges no longer cancel, on the average, resulting in a nonzero macroscopic average charge density. This can be shown by consideration of Fig. 5.5.

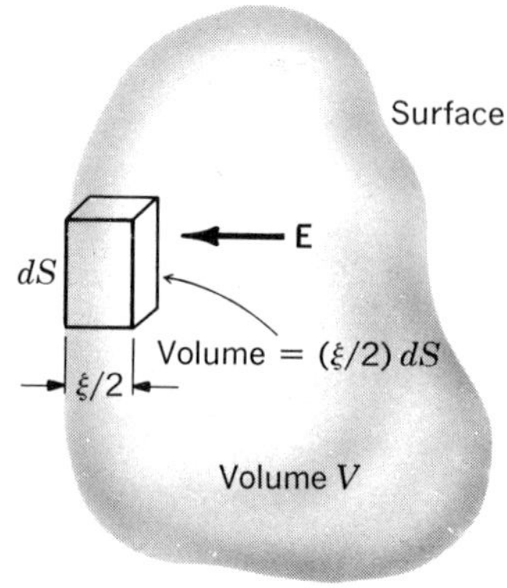

Fig. 5.5 A mathematical surface inside a material and the charge which passes through it when polarization occurs.

Figure 5.5 shows a mathematical surface inside a material. The objective is to find the net charge inside the surface S which results from polarization. Since there will be no net charge inside S when there is no polarization, the net charge inside S due to polarization can be found by finding the net charge passing in through S which results from the movement of the charges when polarization occurs. Consider first a differential surface dS at a point where the polarization is normal to S; that is, the charge separates in a direction normal to the surface. With $\mathbf{E}$ in the direction shown, positive charge moves left and negative charge moves right. From the definition of $\mathbf{P}$, the total charge separation is $\boldsymbol{\xi}$, so each charge moves a distance $\boldsymbol{\xi}/2$. Hence all charges in a volume $(\xi/2)\,dS$ on each side of dS will move through dS. The total positive charge passing through dS to the left is then $Nq(\xi/2)\,dS$, where N is the number of charges per unit volume and q is the magnitude of each charge. Similarly, the negative charge passing through dS to the right is $-Nq(\xi/2)\,dS$. Since positive charge passing through dS to the left is equivalent to negative charge passing through dS to the right, the net charge passing through dS to the *right* is

$$-Nq\frac{\xi}{2}\,dS - Nq\frac{\xi}{2}\,dS = -Nq\xi\,dS$$

Since $\mathbf{P} = Nq\boldsymbol{\xi}$, this is just $-P\,dS$.

When the polarization is not normal to the surface dS, the charges a distance $\hat{\mathbf{n}} \cdot \boldsymbol{\xi}/2$ on each side of dS will pass through dS, as illustrated in Fig. 5.6. Hence the total positive charge passing through dS to the left is $Nq(\hat{\mathbf{n}} \cdot \boldsymbol{\xi}/2)\,dS$, and the negative charge passing through dS to the right is then $-Nq(\hat{\mathbf{n}} \cdot \boldsymbol{\xi}/2)\,dS$. The total net charge passing through dS to the right is $-Nq\hat{\mathbf{n}} \cdot \boldsymbol{\xi}\,dS$. But since $\mathbf{P} = Nq\boldsymbol{\xi}$ and $d\mathbf{S} = \hat{\mathbf{n}}\,dS$, this can be written as $-\mathbf{P} \cdot d\mathbf{S}$.

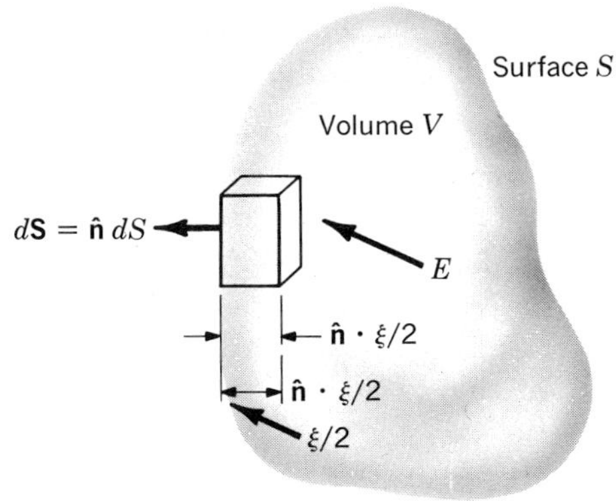

Fig. 5.6 The situation in Fig. 5.5 when **E** is not normal to $d\mathbf{S}$.

Since $-\mathbf{P} \cdot d\mathbf{S}$ is the charge passing through dS, the total charge passing in through S is found by integrating; thus

$$Q_p = \oint_S - \mathbf{P} \cdot d\mathbf{S} \tag{5.23}$$

where Q_p is the total charge passing into the volume V through S. It is clear from the derivation that Q_p is an actual physical charge present in the volume enclosed by S and resulting from the polarization $\mathbf{P}$. Note that $Q_p = 0$ if $\mathbf{P} = 0$. This fits with the statement made previously that in the absence of polarization the material is neutral and the average macroscopic charge density is zero.

A polarization charge density can be defined in the same way the charge density ρ was defined in Sec. 2.3. The definition is made by using Eq. (5.23) in connection with a differential volume ΔV. Let S be the surface enclosing ΔV and let ΔQ_p be the polarization charge in ΔV. Then

$$\Delta Q_p = \oint_S - \mathbf{P} \cdot d\mathbf{S} \tag{5.24}$$

The polarization volume charge density is defined as

$$\begin{aligned} \rho_p &= \lim_{\Delta V \to 0} \frac{\Delta Q_p}{\Delta V} \\ &= \frac{dQ_p}{dV} \end{aligned} \tag{5.25}$$

Using Eq. (5.24) and Eq. (1.64), we have

$$\begin{aligned} \rho_p &= \lim_{\Delta V \to 0} \frac{\oint_S - \mathbf{P} \cdot d\mathbf{S}}{\Delta V} \\ &= -\nabla \cdot \mathbf{P} \end{aligned} \tag{5.26}$$

Equation (5.26) states that there is a polarization volume charge density which results from the divergence of the polarization **P**. If **P** is uniform, $\nabla \cdot \mathbf{P} = 0$ and $\rho_p = 0$. This corresponds to $\oint_S \mathbf{P} \cdot d\mathbf{S}$ being zero when **P** is uniform, because as much charge leaves S as enters S. At this point it should be clear from the derivation that in a neutral material separation of charge can create an actual physical volume charge density ρ_p, which has been shown to be equal to $-\nabla \cdot \mathbf{P}$.

Since ρ_p is a polarization volume charge density, the total polarization charge Q_p in a volume V can be found by integrating

$$\begin{aligned} Q_p &= \int_V \rho_p \, dV \\ &= \int_V -\nabla \cdot \mathbf{P} \, dV \end{aligned} \tag{5.27}$$

This same result can also be obtained from Eq. (5.23) and the divergence theorem.

There is another point which needs to be made in connection with polarization charge density. At the surface of a material **P** is discontinuous, because outside the material there are no charges to polarize. This results in a surface charge density, as illustrated in Fig. 5.7. The positive charges move left and the negative charges move right. But the positive charges cannot move past the surface of the material, and there are no negative charges present to the left of the surface which can move to the surface to cancel the positive charges there. Hence there is a net surface charge density.

The magnitude of the surface charge density in terms of **P** can be found from Eq. (5.23). The surface of integration is taken to be a surface which encloses the surface of the material, as shown in Fig. 5.7. Since **P** is zero outside the material, the surface integral can be written as the sum of two terms,

$$\begin{aligned} Q_p &= \oint_S -\mathbf{P} \cdot d\mathbf{S} \\ &= -\int_{S_2} \mathbf{P} \cdot d\mathbf{S}_2 - \int_{S_3} \mathbf{P} \cdot d\mathbf{S}_3 \end{aligned}$$

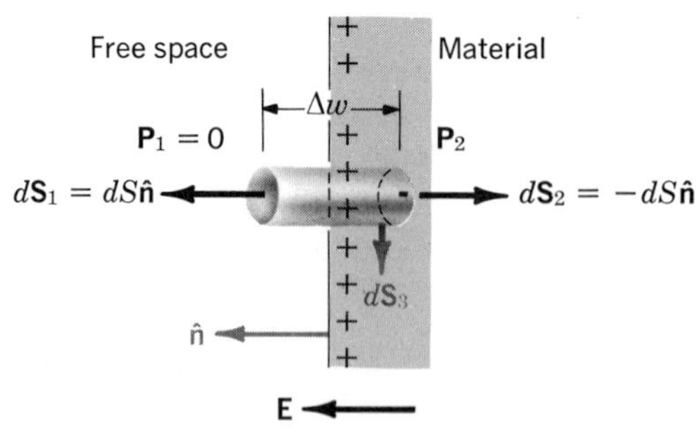

Fig. 5.7 Surface charge density produced by polarization.

Assuming that the area of the surface is ΔS, which is so small that **P** is constant over S_2, the equation can be written as

$$Q_p = -\mathbf{P}\cdot\hat{\mathbf{n}}\,\Delta S - \int_{S_3} \mathbf{P}\cdot d\mathbf{S}_3$$

Now letting $\Delta w \to 0$ results in $\int_{S_3} \mathbf{P}\cdot d\mathbf{S}_3 \to 0$, and

$$Q_p = \mathbf{P}\cdot\hat{\mathbf{n}}\,\Delta S \tag{5.28}$$

The Q_p in Eq. (5.28) is now the total charge at the surface in the area ΔS. The polarization surface charge density is defined as

$$\rho_{ps} = \lim_{\Delta S\to 0} \frac{Q_p}{\Delta S} \tag{5.29}$$

Hence

$$\rho_{ps} = \mathbf{P}\cdot\hat{\mathbf{n}} \tag{5.30}$$

where $\mathbf{P}\cdot\hat{\mathbf{n}}$ is the normal component of **P** *at the surface* of the material. If there are conduction charges present, an additional surface charge density can be present, as illustrated in Fig. 5.2.

Note that in the case where **P** does not vary spatially, ρ_p can be zero while ρ_{ps} is not zero. This is important to a good understanding of Eq. (5.27). Consider the evaluation of

$$Q_p = -\int_V \nabla\cdot\mathbf{P}\,dV \tag{5.27}$$

where V is the volume shown in Fig. 5.8. Since **P** is discontinuous at the surface of the material, $\nabla\cdot\mathbf{P}$, which contains derivatives of **P**, becomes infinite. This must be taken into account in evaluating $\int_V \nabla\cdot\mathbf{P}\,dV$.

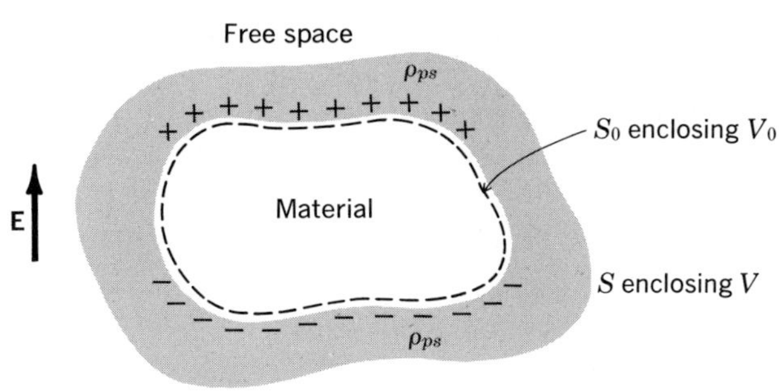

Fig. 5.8 The surface polarization-charge density produced by discontinuities in **P**.

Since it has been shown that the discontinuity in **P** causes ρ_{ps}, Q_p can be found by

$$Q_p = \int_{V_0} \rho_p \, dV + \oint_{S_0} \rho_{ps} \, dS$$
$$= - \int_{V_0} \nabla \cdot \mathbf{P} \, dV + \oint_{S_0} \mathbf{P} \cdot d\mathbf{S} \tag{5.31}$$

where S_0 is the surface infinitesimally smaller than the material surface, as shown in Fig. 5.8. Equation (5.31) is equivalent to evaluating Eq. (5.27) and taking into account the discontinuity in **P** which causes $\nabla \cdot \mathbf{P}$ to become infinite. It is important to note that the polarization of the material does not affect the net charge of the material, and hence the Q_p in Eq. (5.27), where V is the volume in Fig. 5.8, must be zero if the material was initially uncharged. Hence Q_p as obtained from Eq. (5.31) must also be zero. It is, because by the divergence theorem,

$$\int_{V_0} \nabla \cdot \mathbf{P} = \oint_{S_0} \mathbf{P} \cdot d\mathbf{S}$$

Thus polarization can produce both a volume charge density and a surface charge density. Now, how does this affect the fields? Since ρ_p is a physical charge density, Gauss's law, as given in Eq. (3.4), must include ρ_p; that is, Gauss's law is written

$$\oint_S \epsilon_0 \mathbf{E} \cdot d\mathbf{S} = \int_V (\rho + \rho_p) \, dV \tag{5.32}$$

when V includes polarizable charges. Hence one effect of the polarization on fields is that the polarization produces a charge density ρ_p which is a source of electric field. In connection with Eq. (5.32), it is important to note that ρ is all the charge density not resulting from polarization, and any discontinuities in ρ_p must be taken into account in some way, such as by using Eq. (5.31). Equation (5.32) is valid in both the static and the time-varying case, since the derivation of ρ_p is valid at any instant of time.

In the time-varying case there is an additional effect, because the change of ρ_p with time produces a current, which is also a source of fields. Since it has been shown how polarization can cause net charge to move into a surface, the ideas of Sec. 3.9 can be used to find what the corresponding current is. From the conservation of charge,

$$\oint_S \mathbf{J}_p \cdot d\mathbf{S} = - \frac{d}{dt} \int_V \rho_p \, dV$$

as explained in Sec. 3.9. Here $\mathbf{J}_p$ is the polarization current, that is, the current produced by the variation of ρ_p with time, and S and V are arbitrary. Assuming no ρ_{ps} in the volume, then

$$\int_V \rho_p \, dV = -\int_V \nabla \cdot \mathbf{P} \, dV$$
$$= -\oint_S \mathbf{P} \cdot d\mathbf{S}$$

Hence

$$\oint_S \mathbf{J}_p \cdot d\mathbf{S} = -\frac{d}{dt}\int_V \rho_p \, dV$$
$$= \frac{d}{dt}\oint_S \mathbf{P} \cdot d\mathbf{S}$$

Assuming that S does not change with time, then

$$\oint_S \mathbf{J}_p \cdot d\mathbf{S} = \oint_S \frac{\partial \mathbf{P}}{\partial t} \cdot d\mathbf{S}$$

Since S is arbitrary,

$$\mathbf{J}_p = \frac{\partial \mathbf{P}}{\partial t} \tag{5.33}$$

Note that $\mathbf{J}_p$ is zero for dc polarization. This makes sense, because for dc polarization the charge separates, and there is no further motion of charge, and hence no current. The point form of the continuity relation for $\mathbf{J}_p$ and ρ_p can easily be obtained by taking the divergence of Eq. (5.33) and using Eq. (5.26) to give

$$\nabla \cdot \mathbf{J}_p = \nabla \cdot \frac{\partial \mathbf{P}}{\partial t} = \frac{\partial}{\partial t} \nabla \cdot \mathbf{P}$$
$$= -\frac{\partial}{\partial t} \rho_p \tag{5.34}$$

which is just what we would expect on the basis of Eq. (3.22).

For the sinusoidal time-varying case, $\mathbf{J}_p = j\omega \, \mathbf{P}$. Using Eq. (5.19), we have

$$\mathbf{J}_p = j\omega\epsilon_0\chi_e(\omega)\mathbf{E} \tag{5.35}$$

In summary, the effect of polarization on the field is that polarization produces a volume charge density given by Eq. (5.26) and a current density given by Eq. (5.33), both of which act as sources of fields. The effect of ρ_p is shown in Eq. (5.32). The effect of $\mathbf{J}_p$ on the fields can be taken into account by including $\mathbf{J}_p$ in the $\mathbf{J}$ term in

$$\nabla \times \frac{\mathbf{B}}{\mu_0} = \mathbf{J} + \epsilon_0 \frac{\partial \mathbf{E}}{\partial t}$$

This is done in Sec. 5.5.

CONDUCTION CURRENT

The current due to the movement of conduction charges in the material is called *conduction current.* Unlike polarization current, conduction current can be produced by the application of dc fields because the conduction charges are "free" to move throughout the material. As pointed out in Eq. (2.36), the current resulting from the movement of conduction charges is

$$\mathbf{J}_c = \rho_c \mathbf{v} \tag{5.36}$$

where $\mathbf{J}_c$ stands for macroscopic conduction current and ρ_c for macroscopic conduction charge density.

The velocity $\mathbf{v}$ can be found from Eq. (5.21). For the case of sinusoidal time variation, $\mathbf{v}$ is given by Eq. (5.22). Then $\mathbf{J}_c$ is

$$\mathbf{J}_c = \frac{\rho_c q \mathbf{E}}{m(j\omega + \nu_c)} \tag{5.37}$$

The drift of the conduction charges affects the fields by producing a current $\mathbf{J}_c$, which is a source of new fields which add to the fields producing the drift. Like $\mathbf{J}_p$, $\mathbf{J}_c$ can be taken into account as a field source in the $\mathbf{J}$ term in the $\nabla \times \mathbf{B}$ equation. This is done in the next section.

5.5 THE DISPLACEMENT VECTOR D AND PERMITTIVITY ϵ

At this point we have found that fields produce polarization and conduction-charge drift in materials, which in turn produces the currents $\mathbf{J}_p$ and $\mathbf{J}_c$ given by

$$\mathbf{J}_p = \frac{\partial \mathbf{P}}{\partial t} \tag{5.33}$$

$$\mathbf{J}_c = \rho_c \mathbf{v} \tag{5.36}$$

where $\mathbf{P}$ and $\mathbf{v}$ each depend on $\mathbf{E}$, as described by Eqs. (5.12) and (5.21). In addition, the currents $\mathbf{J}_p$ and $\mathbf{J}_c$ affect the fields through Maxwell's equations

$$\nabla \times \frac{\mathbf{B}}{\mu_0} = \mathbf{J}_T + \epsilon_0 \frac{\partial \mathbf{E}}{\partial t} \tag{3.30}$$

$$\nabla \times \mathbf{E} = -\frac{\partial \mathbf{B}}{\partial t} \tag{3.31}$$

where the current in Eq. (3.30) has been written as $\mathbf{J}_T$ to emphasize that *all* currents must be included.

Since the currents depend on the fields and the fields depend on the currents, it is necessary to solve the two sets of equations simultaneously. One good way to do this is to include the currents $\mathbf{J}_p$ and $\mathbf{J}_c$ in $\mathbf{J}_T$ in Eq. (3.30). First, however, it is helpful to discuss some of the various kinds of current that might be included in $\mathbf{J}_T$.

Although current is fundamentally the time rate of change of charge, it is convenient to categorize currents according to the nature of the charge. *Conduction current* results from the movement of conduction charges in materials. *Convection current* results from the movement of charge not in materials, e.g., an electron beam in a vacuum tube. *Polarization current* results from the movement of polarizing charges, as explained previously. *Magnetic current* results from magnetic effects in materials, as explained in Sec. 5.10.

Although other kinds of current might be defined, the ones listed above are sufficient for our purposes. Hence the total current is written as

$$\mathbf{J}_T = \mathbf{J} + \mathbf{J}_p + \mathbf{J}_m \tag{5.38}$$

where $\mathbf{J}_m$ is magnetic current and $\mathbf{J}$ includes both convection and conduction current. Since current produced by movement of conduction charges in materials and by free charge in a vacuum is of the same nature within the limits of the simple macroscopic model for materials used here, it is convenient to let $\mathbf{J}$ stand for both. The four kinds of current are included in Eq. (5.38) for generality, although, obviously, all four kinds will not usually exist at the same point.

Now Eq. (3.30) may be rewritten

$$\nabla \times \frac{\mathbf{B}}{\mu_0} = \mathbf{J} + \mathbf{J}_p + \mathbf{J}_m + \epsilon_0 \frac{\partial \mathbf{E}}{\partial t}$$

For the present, $\mathbf{J}_m$ is assumed to be zero; it will be included in Sec. 5.10. Hence

$$\nabla \times \frac{\mathbf{B}}{\mu_0} = \mathbf{J} + \mathbf{J}_p + \epsilon_0 \frac{\partial \mathbf{E}}{\partial t} \tag{5.39}$$

Now, as mentioned above, Eqs. (5.33), (5.36), and (5.39) are to be solved simultaneously. The first step is to substitute Eq. (5.33) into Eq. (5.39),

$$\begin{aligned} \nabla \times \frac{\mathbf{B}}{\mu_0} &= \mathbf{J} + \frac{\partial \mathbf{P}}{\partial t} + \epsilon_0 \frac{\partial \mathbf{E}}{\partial t} \\ &= \mathbf{J} + \frac{\partial}{\partial t} (\mathbf{P} + \epsilon_0 \mathbf{E}) \end{aligned} \tag{5.40}$$

It is obvious from Eq. (5.40) that it would be convenient to make the definition

$$\mathbf{D} = \epsilon_0\mathbf{E} + \mathbf{P} \tag{5.41}$$

so that Eq. (5.40) could be written in the compact form

$$\nabla \times \frac{\mathbf{B}}{\mu_0} = \mathbf{J} + \frac{\partial \mathbf{D}}{\partial t} \tag{5.42}$$

It is not obvious, however, that the definition in Eq. (5.41) is also important as well as convenient, because **D** has special physical significance. This physical significance is discussed below and in Example 5.5. **D** is called the *displacement-flux density* for reasons explained in Example 5.5.

Another convenient definition can be made by using Eq. (5.12) in Eq. (5.41) to give

$$\mathbf{D} = \epsilon_0(1 + \chi_e)\mathbf{E} \tag{5.43}$$

The definition is

$$\epsilon = \epsilon_0(1 + \chi_e) \tag{5.44}$$

where ϵ is called the *permittivity*. Then

$$\mathbf{D} = \epsilon\mathbf{E} \tag{5.45}$$

As pointed out in connection with Eq. (5.12), $\mathbf{D} = \varepsilon_0\chi_e\mathbf{E}$ is true only for certain materials called *linear materials*. The same restrictions apply to the definition of ϵ, which depends on Eq. (5.12). Note also that in the time-varying case χ is a function of frequency, as shown explicitly in Eq. (5.19); in this case ϵ is also a function of frequency. This frequency dependence is discussed in Sec. 5.9. Some typical values for the relative dielectric constant ϵ/ϵ_0 are shown in Table 5.1.

Table 5.1 Some low-frequency relative dielectric constants ϵ/ϵ_0

Material	ϵ/ϵ_0	Material	ϵ/ϵ_0
Styrofoam (25% filler)	1.03	Low-loss glass (Corning 7770)	4.1
Firwood	1.8–2.0	Nonex glass (Corning 7720)	4.7
Paper	2.0–3.0	Pyrex glass (Corning 7740)	5.1
Petroleum	2.1	Muscovite (mica)	5.4
Paraffin	2.1	Mica	5.6–6.0
Teflon	2.1	Magnesium silicate	5.7–6.4
Rubber	2.3–4.0	Porcelain	5.7
Polystyrene	2.55	Aluminum oxide	8.8
Plexiglass	2.6–3.5	Diamond	16.5
Fused quartz	3.78	Distilled water	81.1
Vycor glass (Corning 7900, 7913)	3.8	Titanium dioxide	100.0

The importance of the permittivity ϵ and the displacement-flux density $\mathbf{D}$ lies in Eqs. (5.45) and (5.42). For linear materials, and from the macroscopic point of view, the polarization of a material need not be considered at all if ϵ is known. This has far-reaching practical implications. In practice the permittivity of a material is measured, and then all the polarization effects are taken into account through the permittivity simply by replacing ϵ_0 by ϵ and solving Maxwell's equations in the standard way. This is illustrated extensively in Chap. 6 in connection with reflection, refraction, and propagation of plane waves.

Now, for some interpretation of what $\mathbf{D}$ is, consider Gauss's law, Eq. (5.32):

$$\oint_S \epsilon_0 \mathbf{E} \cdot d\mathbf{S} = \int_V (\rho + \rho_p)\, dV \tag{5.32}$$

where now ρ is understood to include both excess-conduction-charge density and free-charge density. Excess-conduction-charge density means the conduction charges whose effect is not canceled by the lattice-ion charges. Macroscopically, the situation in a conductor is like that of Fig. 5.2. In the absence of unbalancing forces, the macroscopic net charge density is zero because of the equal number of positive and negative charges. This is shown more clearly in Sec. 5.7.

Substituting Eq. (5.26) into Eq. (5.32) results in

$$\oint_S \epsilon_0 \mathbf{E} \cdot d\mathbf{S} = \int_V (\rho - \nabla \cdot \mathbf{P})\, dV$$

Then rearranging and using the divergence theorem gives

$$\oint_S (\epsilon_0 \mathbf{E} + \mathbf{P}) \cdot d\mathbf{S} = \int_V \rho\, dV$$

$$\oint_S \mathbf{D} \cdot d\mathbf{S} = \int_V \rho\, dV \tag{5.46}$$

which is Gauss's law in terms of $\mathbf{D}$. Equation (5.46) is significant because it states that the integral of $\mathbf{D} \cdot d\mathbf{S}$ over *any* closed surface is equal to the total conduction and free charge enclosed, regardless of any polarization which may be present. How this is related to the displacement-flux density is shown in Example 5.5.

The point relation corresponding to Eq. (5.46) is

$$\nabla \cdot \mathbf{D} = \rho \tag{5.47}$$

As explained in Sec. 1.10, this equation means that ρ is a source of $\mathbf{D}$. Hence one characteristic of $\mathbf{D}$ is that it is a vector field whose divergence is independent of the polarization-charge density. The next three examples illustrate the nature of $\mathbf{D}$.

5.6 DIELECTRICS

When there are essentially no conduction charges present, a material is a good insulator and is called a *dielectric.* In this case $\mathbf{J} \approx 0$, and polarization is the principal effect. Some of these effects are illustrated in the dc case by the following two examples. Examples for the ac case are given in Chap. 6.

Example 5.3 Fields produced by a point charge inside a spherical dielectric shell Figure 5.9 shows a point charge Q inside a spherical dielectric shell having permittivity ϵ. The point of this example is to find the **D** and **E** produced by Q in the presence of the dielectric. Because of the spherical symmetry, Gauss's law can be used to find **D**. From Eq. (5.46),

$$\oint_S \mathbf{D} \cdot d\mathbf{S} = \int_V \rho \, dV \tag{5.46}$$

which states that total flux passing through any closed surface S is equal to the charge enclosed. In terms of a spherical coordinate system with Q at the origin, **D** will have only an r component, which varies only with R because of symmetry. Hence, if the S in Eq. (5.46) is chosen as a spherical surface of radius r centered about the origin, **D** will be constant on S and

$$\begin{aligned}\oint_S \mathbf{D} \cdot d\mathbf{S} &= 4\pi r^2 D_r \\ &= \int_V \rho \, dV \\ &= Q\end{aligned}$$

Hence the value of D_r at a distance r from Q is

$$D_r = \frac{Q}{4\pi r^2}$$

This value holds in regions I, II, and III, that is, both inside and outside the dielectric. This is true because Eq. (5.46) does not depend on ϵ and because the dielectric is symmetrical, so that the symmetry argument is valid. Thus, in this case, **D** is completely unaffected by polarization. If symmetry were removed by moving Q from the center of the spherical shell, however, **D** would be affected by polarization.

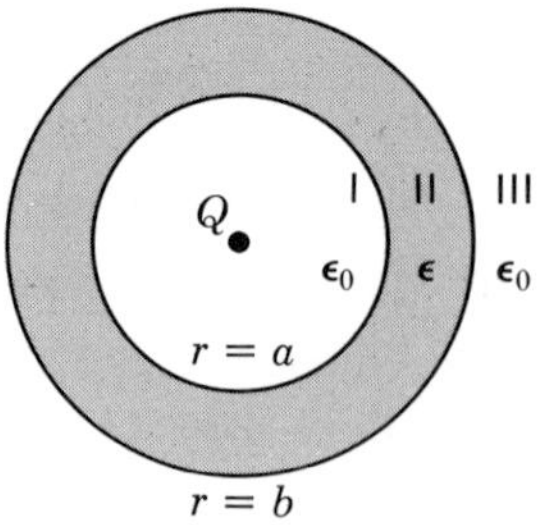

Fig. 5.9 A point charge Q inside a spherical dielectric shell having permittivity ϵ.

The value of **E** can now be found from Eq. (5.45),

$$E_r = \begin{cases} \dfrac{D_r}{\epsilon_0} = \dfrac{Q}{4\pi\epsilon_0 r^2} & r < a,\ b < r \\ \dfrac{D_r}{\epsilon} = \dfrac{Q}{4\pi\epsilon r^2} & a < r < b \end{cases}$$

Note that in region II, E_r is less than it would have been if no dielectric were present. This is because the polarization of the dielectric has reduced **E** in the dielectric, as explained in the next example. Also note that E_r is discontinuous at $r = a$ and $r = b$. This results from the surface charge density produced by the polarization and is also explained in the next example.

Example 5.4 Polarization resulting from a point charge inside a spherical dielectric shell The polarization in the dielectric shell in Fig. 5.9 resulting from the **E** produced by Q can be calculated from Eq. (5.41) and the values of **E** found in Example 5.3. From Eq. (5.41), **P** is given by

$$\mathbf{P} = \mathbf{D} - \epsilon_0\mathbf{E} \tag{5.48}$$

Putting the values of **D** and **E** found in Example 5.3 in Eq. (5.48) results in

$$\begin{aligned} P_r &= \frac{Q}{4\pi r^2} - \frac{\epsilon_0 Q}{4\pi\epsilon r^2} \\ &= \frac{Q}{4\pi r^2}\left(1 - \frac{\epsilon_0}{\epsilon}\right) \qquad a < r < b \end{aligned} \tag{5.49}$$

Of course, **P** is zero in regions I and III, where there is no dielectric.

The value of ρ_p can now be calculated from Eq. (5.26),

$$\begin{aligned} \rho_p &= -\nabla \cdot \mathbf{P} \\ &= -\frac{1}{r^2}\frac{\partial}{\partial r}(r^2 P_r) \\ &= -\frac{1}{r^2}\frac{\partial}{\partial r}\left[\frac{r^2 Q}{4\pi r^2}\left(1 - \frac{\epsilon_0}{\epsilon}\right)\right] \\ &= 0 \end{aligned}$$

Thus there is no polarization volume charge density. However, **P** is discontinuous at $r = a$ and $r = b$, the surfaces of the material. Hence, according to Eq. (5.30), the polarization surface charge density is

$$\begin{aligned} \rho_{ps1} &= \mathbf{P} \cdot (-\hat{\mathbf{r}}) \\ &= -\frac{Q}{4\pi a^2}\left(1 - \frac{\epsilon_0}{\epsilon}\right) \qquad r = a \end{aligned} \tag{5.50}$$

$$\begin{aligned} \rho_{ps2} &= \mathbf{P} \cdot \hat{\mathbf{r}} \\ &= \frac{Q}{4\pi b^2}\left(1 - \frac{\epsilon_0}{\epsilon}\right) \qquad r = b \end{aligned} \tag{5.51}$$

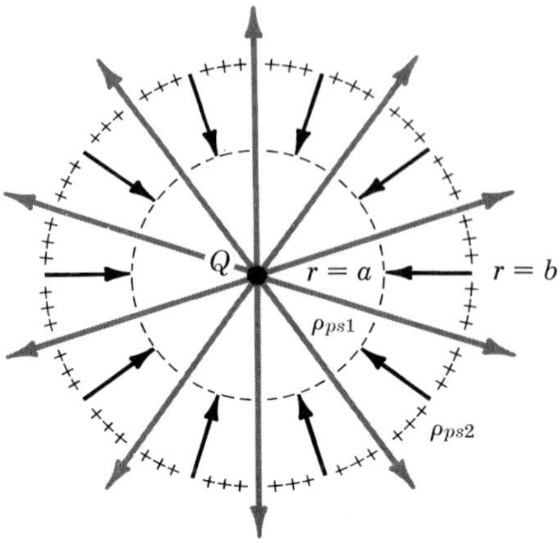

Fig. 5.10 The fields produced by the Q and ρ_{ps1} and ρ_{ps2} of Example 5.4.

Now the results of Example 5.3 can be explained in terms of polarization of the dielectric. The electric field produced by the charge Q caused the dielectric to polarize according to Eq. (5.49). This polarization results in zero polarization volume charge density and polarization surface charge density given by Eqs. (5.50) and (5.51). The net resultant field is that produced by Q and ρ_{ps1} and ρ_{ps2}. It is easy now to see why the **E** field inside the dielectric is reduced. As illustrated in Fig. 5.10, in the dielectric the **E** field produced by the combination of ρ_{ps1} and ρ_{ps2} opposes the **E** field produced by Q, and therefore **E** is reduced inside the dielectric, as noted in Example 5.3.

It is left to Prob. 5.6-1 to show that the same net **E** field as obtained in Example 5.3 is obtained by finding the total field produced by Q, ρ_{ps1}, and ρ_{ps2}.

Examples 5.3 and 5.4 illustrate how dielectrics affect electric fields and how this effect can be fully accounted for by the permittivity ϵ.

5.7 CONDUCTORS

When a great number of conduction charges are present in a material, so that the conduction current and charge density overshadow the polarization effects, the material is called a *conductor*.

In the static case, the **E** field inside a perfect conductor is zero, for the same reasons given in Example 5.2. Since the conduction charges are mobile, they move if an **E** field is present. But since they cannot pass out through the surface (except in cases of thermionic emission, etc.), they collect on the surfaces of the conductor. This surface charge density builds up until the field it produces just cancels the applied field, and then no further movement of the charges occurs. This is like the situation in Example 5.2, except that the positive charges in a conductor are immobile. Thus, in a conductor, the positive surface charge is produced by the immobile positive charges left unneutralized when the negative charges move.

When equilibrium is reached, and the fields are zero inside the conductor, the net charge density is also zero. This can be shown from Gauss's law, Eq. (5.32). Assuming ρ_p is negligible, we have

$$\oint_S \epsilon_0 \mathbf{E} \cdot d\mathbf{S} = \int_V \rho \, dV$$

If S is taken entirely inside the conductor, $\oint_S \epsilon_0 \mathbf{E} \cdot d\mathbf{S} = 0$ because $\mathbf{E} = 0$, and hence $\int_V \rho \, dV = 0$. Since this is true for any arbitrary V inside the conductor, ρ must be zero. Hence it can be said that in the static case the *net* charge density is zero everywhere except on the surface. Therefore, if a conductor is given an excess charge, that charge will be found as surface charge. This is an important and often-used result.

When a circuit is completed, so that the charges are not limited by a surface barrier, there is nothing to keep the charges from moving continuously, and they drift through the material, as explained in Sec. 5.3. The motion of the charges reaches a steady-state value which is determined by the collisions with the lattice. This results in a conduction current, which is given by Eq. (5.37) for the sinusoidal case,

$$\mathbf{J}_c = \frac{\rho_c q \mathbf{E}}{m(j\omega + \nu_c)} \tag{5.37}$$

The *conductivity* is defined by the relation

$$\mathbf{J}_c = \sigma \mathbf{E} \tag{5.52}$$

Hence

$$\sigma = \frac{\rho_c q}{m(j\omega + \nu_c)} \tag{5.53}$$

The collision frequency ν_c is discussed in Sec. 5.3 in connection with the drift of conduction charges. Equation (5.52) is called the *point form of Ohm's law*. When $\omega = 0$, σ as given by Eq. (5.53) is the ordinary dc conductivity. Some typical values for the dc conductivity are given in Table 5.2. Note that σ is defined by Eq. (5.53) even for materials which are not good conductors. Table 5.2 shows the extremely wide variation in the value of σ from good conductors to poor conductors.

Since a typical value of ν_c for a good conductor is about 10^{13} Hz, $\omega \ll \nu_c$ until ω gets up into the hundreds of gigahertzes, and σ changes very little with ω in this range. Hence σ can be approximated by its dc value up through the microwave range, i.e., up through the hundreds of gigahertzes range. Also, in this frequency range, conduction current is the dominant effect. This is because $\chi_e \approx 0$ for good conductors, and

PP179

Table 5.2 Some values of dc conductivity in mhos/m

Silver	6.14×10^7	Monel	0.24×10^7
Copper	5.80×10^7	Mercury	0.10×10^7
Gold	4.10×10^7	Sea water	3–5
Aluminum	3.54×10^7	Distilled water	2×10^{-4}
Tungsten	1.81×10^7	Bakelite	10^{-8}–10^{-10}
Brass	1.57×10^7	Glass	10^{-12}
Nickel	1.28×10^7	Mica	10^{-11}–10^{-15}
Iron (pure)	1.0×10^7	Petroleum	10^{-14}
Steel	0.5–1.0×10^7	Fused quartz	$< 2 \times 10^{-17}$
Lead	0.48×10^7		

therefore $\epsilon \approx \epsilon_0$ according to Eq. (5.44). In addition, $\sigma \gg j\omega\epsilon_0$ for good conductors, and hence $\sigma\mathbf{E} \gg j\omega\epsilon_0\mathbf{E}$. Thus conduction current is the main effect in good conductors at microwave frequencies and below.

At frequencies up to about 1 GHz, the point form of Ohm's law and circuit theory are used to describe conduction-current effects, as discussed in Chap. 7. At microwave frequencies, conduction-current effects are discussed in terms of propagating waves in Chap. 6, with the dc value of σ. At optical frequencies, both $\mathbf{J}_c$ and $\mathbf{J}_p$ are important, and the dc value of σ is no longer a good approximation. It is shown in Chap. 6 how the effects of $\mathbf{J}_p$ and $\mathbf{J}_c$ combine to produce the frequency-dependent reflection which results in the color of some metals.

Example 5.5 Explanation of the name "displacement flux" Now that the characteristics of dielectrics and metals have both been discussed, the meaning of displacement flux can be explained by considering the configuration shown in Fig. 5.11. Consider first the case where the sphere is ungrounded. Since the same symmetry is present here as in Fig. 5.9, the same procedure used for finding **D** and **E** in Example 5.3 can be used here. From this procedure, it is found that **D** and **E** are the same in regions I, II, and III in both Figs. 5.9 and 5.11:

$$D_r = \frac{Q}{4\pi r^2} \qquad 0 < r < c$$

$$E_r = \begin{cases} \dfrac{Q}{4\pi\epsilon_0 r^2} & r < a,\ b < r < c \\[2ex] \dfrac{Q}{4\pi\epsilon r^2} & a < r < b \end{cases}$$

In region IV, **D** and **E** are zero, as explained just before this example. Hence $\oint_S \mathbf{D} \cdot d\mathbf{S} = 0$ if S is a spherical surface in region IV. But according to Gauss's law, Eq. (5.46),

$$\oint_S \mathbf{D} \cdot d\mathbf{S} = \int_V \rho\, dV \tag{5.46}$$

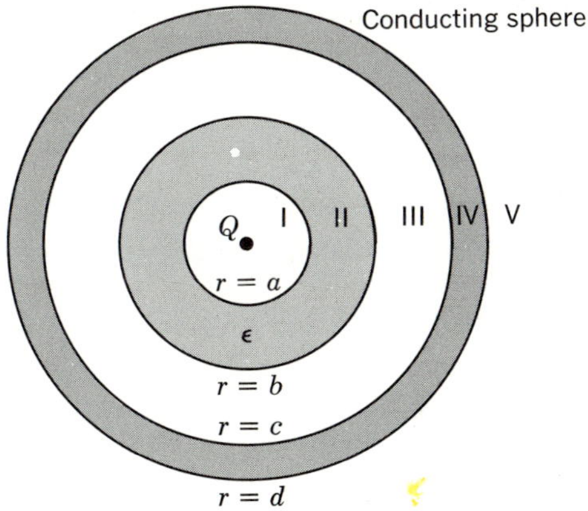

Fig. 5.11 A point charge enclosed in a dielectric spherical shell inside a hollow spherical conductor.

Hence $\int_V \rho \, dV = 0$, and Q must not be the total charge enclosed in the volume, or $\int_V \rho \, dV$ would be equal to Q. What happens is that a surface charge density is induced on the inner surface of the conductor. Since ρ includes conduction charge, as explained in connection with Eq. (5.46),

$$\int_V \rho \, dV = Q + \oint_{S_c} \rho_{sc} \, dS$$

where S_c is the inner surface of the conductor and ρ_{sc} is the surface charge density on S_c. Since $\int_V \rho \, dV = 0$,

$$\oint_{S_c} \rho_{sc} \, dS = -Q$$

Because of the symmetry involved, ρ_{sc} is constant on S_c and

$$-Q = \oint_{S_c} \rho_{sc} \, dS$$
$$= 4\pi c^2 \rho_{sc}$$

Then

$$\rho_{sc} = \frac{-Q}{4\pi c^2}$$

If Eq. (5.46) is evaluated for S outside the conductor, the result is

$$\oint_S \mathbf{D} \cdot d\mathbf{S} = \int_V \rho \, dV$$
$$= Q$$

because the total *net* charge enclosed is Q, since the conductor was initially neutral. However, since we found that ρ_{sc} existed on the inner surface of the conductor, we must now conclude that a surface charge density also exists on the outer surface of the conductor, so that

$$\begin{aligned}\int_V \rho\, dV &= Q + \oint_{S_c} \rho_{sc}\, dS + \oint_{S_d} \rho_{sd}\, dS \\ &= Q\end{aligned}$$

Since we found that $\oint_{S_c} \rho_{sc}\, dS = -Q$, we must conclude that

$$\oint_{S_d} \rho_{sd}\, dS = Q$$

Thus the fields produced by Q induced a total surface charge of $-Q$ on the inner surface of the conductor and a total surface charge of $+Q$ on the outer surface of the conductor, but the *total net* charge on the conductor remains zero. This result could also have been obtained by the same reasoning used in Example 5.2.

Suppose now that the conducting sphere is grounded for a short time and then ungrounded again. This will produce a net charge on the conductor, because the electrons supplied by the ground will rush in to neutralize the surface charge on the outer surface of the conductor. However, the inner-surface charge density of $-Q$ must remain, because it is still true that $\oint_S \mathbf{D} \cdot d\mathbf{S} = 0$ if S is inside the conductor. But this inner-surface charge density is now excess charge, and the conductor is no longer neutral.

One important point is that now $\mathbf{D} = \mathbf{E} = 0$ outside the conductor, because

$$\begin{aligned}\oint_S \mathbf{D} \cdot d\mathbf{S} &= \int_V \rho\, dV \\ &= Q - Q \\ &= 0\end{aligned}$$

if S is outside the conductor, because the charge on the conductor is $-Q$. This is called *shielding* because the (grounded) conductor shields the fields of the point charge Q.

Another very important point is that $\mathbf{D}$ is independent of the permittivity of the dielectric shell, as is apparent from Eq. (5.46) and the symmetry involved. Also, since

$$\rho_{sc} = \frac{-Q}{4\pi c^2}$$

and the value of D_r at $r = c$ is

$$D_r = \frac{Q}{4\pi c^2}$$

then

$$\rho_{sc} = -D_r \Big|_{r=c}$$

independently of the permittivity of the dielectric (this relation is derived more generally in Sec. 5.13 on boundary conditions).

It was from this property that the name "displacement-flux density" for **D** was derived. The configuration shown in Fig. 5.11 is an idealization of an experiment performed by Faraday. He found that a charge of Q was always induced on the conducting sphere, no matter what dielectric was placed inside the sphere. Thus he concluded there was a *displacement flux* equal to Q which induced this charge. Hence **D** is called the *displacement-flux density*, since $\oint_S \mathbf{D} \cdot d\mathbf{S} = Q$ and **D** is obviously a density. This is the physical meaning of **D**.

5.8 SEMICONDUCTORS

In a semiconductor, as the name implies, both the conduction current $\mathbf{J}_c$ and the polarization current $\mathbf{J}_p$ are important. A simplified model of a semiconductor is obtained by including both $\mathbf{J}_c$ and $\mathbf{J}_p$, which results in using both the conductivity σ and the permittivity ϵ. Also, $\mathbf{J}_c$ must include both electron current and hole current. The characteristics of wave propagation in semiconductors can be found from the results of Chap. 6 with the proper σ and ϵ.

However, many interesting situations involve the presence of applied dc electric and/or magnetic fields. When a dc magnetic field is present, Eq. (5.21) must be modified to include the magnetic field force on the right-hand side. When this is done, σ will be a function of the magnetic field. This effect is called *magnetoresistance*. A related effect is the *Hall effect*, which involves crossed dc electric and magnetic fields. These kinds of effects are not pursued in this book.

5.9 COMPLEX PERMITTIVITY FOR SINUSOIDAL TIME VARIATION

In the sinusoidal time-varying case, it is convenient to extend the definition of permittivity to include the effects of conduction current $\mathbf{J}_c$. This can easily be done by using Eq. (5.52) in Eq. (5.42). Since **J** in Eq. (5.42) includes both conduction current and convection current, Eq. (5.42) can be written as

$$\nabla \times \frac{\mathbf{B}}{\mu_0} = \mathbf{J} + \sigma\mathbf{E} + j\omega\epsilon\mathbf{E}$$

where $\mathbf{D} = \epsilon\mathbf{E}$ has also been used, and now **J** is only convection current. This equation may be written in the form

$$\nabla \times \frac{\mathbf{B}}{\mu_0} = \mathbf{J} + j\omega\left(\frac{\sigma}{j\omega} + \epsilon\right)\mathbf{E} \tag{5.54}$$

It is convenient now to define a complex permittivity ϵ_c by

$$\epsilon_c = \frac{\sigma}{j\omega} + \epsilon \tag{5.55}$$

so that

$$\nabla \times \frac{\mathbf{B}}{\mu_0} = \mathbf{J} + j\omega\epsilon_c\mathbf{E} \tag{5.56}$$

The definition

$$\mathbf{D}_c = \epsilon_c\mathbf{E} \tag{5.57}$$

can also be made to denote that $\mathbf{D}_c$ is $\mathbf{D}$ with the effects of conduction current included. However, this is not a common definition because many authors make no distinction between $\mathbf{D}$ and $\mathbf{D}_c$.

A useful expression for ϵ_c can be obtained by using Eqs. (5.20), (5.44), and (5.53),

$$\begin{aligned}\epsilon_c &= \epsilon_0 \left\{1 + \frac{\rho_c q/m}{\epsilon_0\omega(-\omega + j\nu_c)} + \sum_k \left[\frac{N_{bk}q_k^2/m_k}{\epsilon_0(-\omega^2 + \omega_{sk}^2 + j\omega\nu_{bk})} + \frac{\chi_{d0k}}{1 + j\omega\tau_k}\right]\right\} \\ &= \epsilon_0 \left[1 + \frac{\rho_c q/m}{\epsilon_0\omega(-\omega + j\nu_c)} + \chi_e(\omega)\right]\end{aligned} \tag{5.58}$$

where the summation over k now includes all the terms in Eq. (5.20), that is, all different species of all three kinds of polarization. For example, one material might exhibit two kinds of electronic polarization, one kind of atomic polarization, and orientational polarization. The subscript b in N_{bk} and ν_{bk} stands for "bound," since N_{bk} and ν_{bk} are bound-charge quantities.

It is clear from Eq. (5.58) that ϵ_c is complex. Note that in each case, the complex term involves a damping factor ν or τ, and that if all the ν and τ were zero, ϵ_c would be real. This is significant because, as will be shown in Sec. 5.14, the imaginary part of ϵ_c corresponds to dissipation. This makes sense, because, for example, ν_c specifies the frequency of collisions of the charges with the lattice ions. These collisions result in dissipation through heating of the material. The ν_k associated with polarization also represents heating of the material caused by the movement of the bound charge.

The behavior of ϵ_c with respect to frequency is also important. The characteristics of ϵ_c/ϵ_0 for an insulator are shown in Fig. 5.12. For low frequencies, Re ϵ_c/ϵ_0 is approximately constant. Then, typically, in the

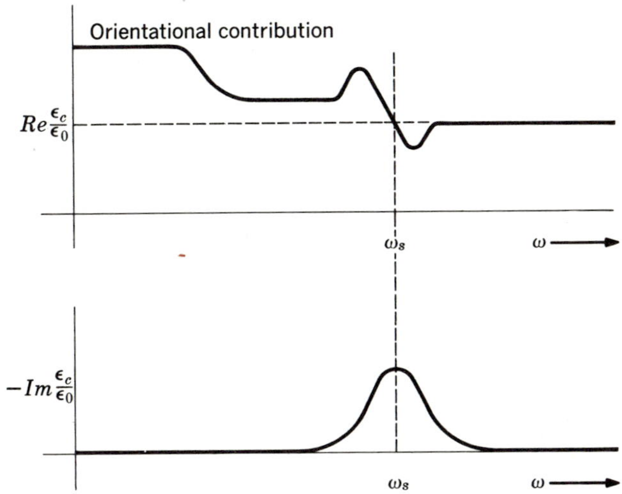

Fig. 5.12 Frequency characteristics of ϵ_c for an insulator (not to scale).

microwave range the contribution of the orientational part goes to zero, as indicated by the gradual decrease. The peak and dip at higher frequencies are characteristic of an ionic or electronic resonance, which occurs when ω approaches one of the ω_s. Typically, ionic resonances might occur in the infrared and electronic resonances in the ultraviolet range. Im ϵ_c/ϵ_0, which indicates absorption, is very small except in the region of ω_s.

Figure 5.13 shows the quite different behavior of ϵ_c/ϵ_0 for a good conductor. Re ϵ_c/ϵ_0 goes through zero somewhere in the ultraviolet range or beyond for a good conductor. The interpretation of the characteristics of materials in terms of ϵ_c is discussed in Chap. 6. Generally speaking, the imaginary part of ϵ_c means absorption of a wave inside the material and reflection of a wave at the surface of the material. Thus Fig. 5.13 indicates that good conductors are good reflectors and high absorbers at frequencies below the ultraviolet.

5.10 MAGNETIC MATERIALS

In all materials there are microscopic currents due to electron spin and the motion of electrons around the nucleus. Although these microscopic currents do not produce macroscopic charge transport, they do act as sources of macroscopic magnetic fields. The electrons or atoms are characterized by magnetic-dipole moments. Since the microscopic currents

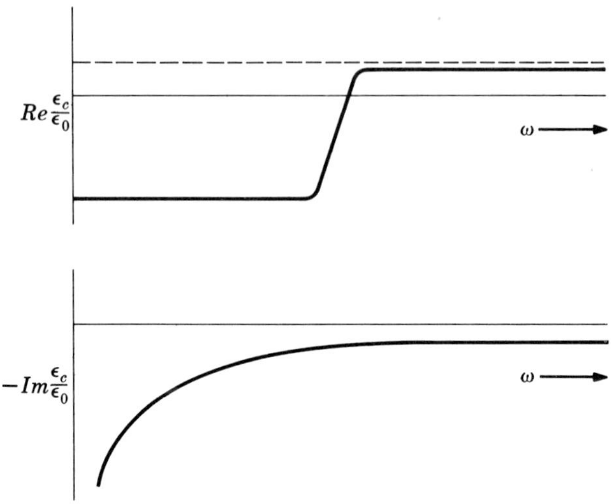

Fig. 5.13 Frequency characteristics of ϵ_c for a conductor (not to scale).

cause a magnetic-dipole moment, it is convenient to describe the currents by a single magnetic-dipole moment called **m**. The average of these magnetic-dipole moments may be described in terms of the macroscopic magnetic-dipole moment per unit volume, **M**, in much the same way as the average of the electric-dipole moment **p** was described in terms of **P** in Sec. 5.3. When a magnetic field **B** is applied to a material, the resulting force on the circulating currents affects **M** in a way that parallels the way **E** affects **P**. It will be shown that a spatially varying **M** is equivalent to a macroscopic current $\mathbf{J}_m$, which is the magnetic analog to $\mathbf{J}_p$. This current $\mathbf{J}_m$ is the source of magnetic fields, and thus there is a parallel between polarization and magnetization. The same interaction occurs—an applied **B** produces **M**, and $\nabla \times \mathbf{M} = \mathbf{J}_m$ acts as a source of **B**. The term $\mathbf{J}_m$ is used in Maxwell's equation to define a permeability μ in a way which parallels the definition of permittivity from $\mathbf{J}_p$.

MAGNETIZATION-CURRENT DENSITY

Let $\mathbf{m}_i$ be the ith microscopic magnetic-dipole moment; then the definition is made that

$$\mathbf{M} = \lim_{\Delta V \to 0} \frac{\sum_{i=1}^{N} \mathbf{m}_i}{\Delta V} \tag{5.59}$$

where **M** is the macroscopic average magnetic-dipole moment per unit volume and N is the number of magnetic dipoles in ΔV. Note that **M** is a

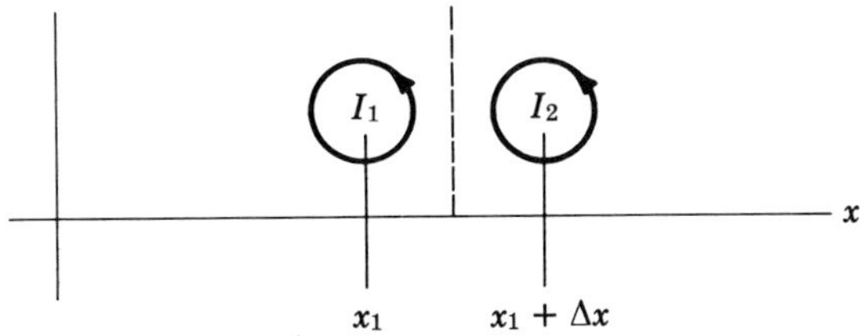

Fig. 5.14 Current produced by spatially varying **M**.

vector point function. The ΔV in Eq. (5.59) is a very small volume which, although very small, still contains a large number of atoms.

As defined in Eq. (2.43), a circulating current produces a magnetic-dipole moment [observe the change in notation: **M** is used from this point on as defined in Eq. (5.59)]. Therefore it is possible to define macroscopic circulating currents which would produce the same **M** as that produced by the atomic currents. From Fig. 5.14 we can see that if **M** is spatially varying in x, so that I_1 at x_1 does not equal I_2 at $x_1 + \Delta x$, there will be a net current upward along the dotted line. The net current density at the point x is called $\mathbf{J}_m$. It now remains to find the relation between $\mathbf{J}_m$ and **M**. Since $\mathbf{J}_m$ depends upon the variation of **M**, we would expect to find that $\mathbf{J}_m$ is related to derivatives of **M**. It is assumed that **M** varies with x, y, and z, and $\mathbf{M}(x,y,z)$ is expanded about the point (x_0,y_0,z_0) by means of the Taylor series

$$\mathbf{M}(x,y,z) = \mathbf{M}_0 + (x - x_0)\frac{\partial \mathbf{M}}{\partial x} + (y - y_0)\frac{\partial \mathbf{M}}{\partial y} + (z - z_0)\frac{\partial \mathbf{M}}{\partial z} + \text{higher-order terms} \qquad (5.60)$$

Here

$$\mathbf{M}_0 = \mathbf{M}(x_0,y_0,z_0)$$

and the partial derivatives are all evaluated at (x_0,y_0,z_0). From the idea of Eq. (2.43), **M** is defined as

$$\Delta V\,\mathbf{M} = I\mathbf{S} \qquad (5.61)$$

(ΔV is necessary because **M** is the dipole moment per unit volume). I in this definition is an equivalent macroscopic current which would produce the same **M** as that produced by the atomic currents. Figure 5.15 illustrates four components of **M** at the four points labeled a, b, c, and d whose corresponding macroscopic currents would pass through the point (x_0,y_0,z_0) in the $\pm z$ direction. Since any **M** can be written as the sum of three components, M_x, M_y, and M_z, only these three components need

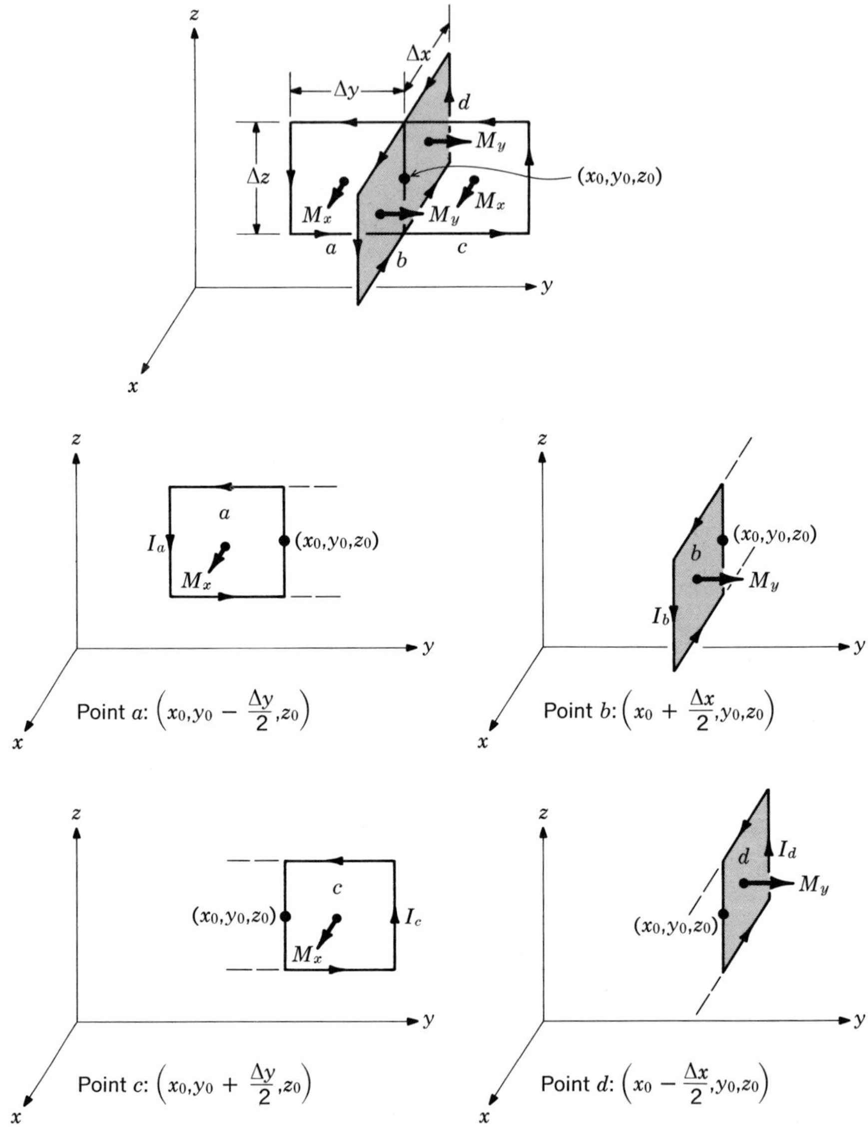

Fig. 5.15 The relation between M and I.

be considered. Since there is no current in the $\pm z$ direction associated with M_z, only the x and y components of $\mathbf{M}$ need be considered. Evaluating Eq. (5.61) at point a in Fig. 5.15 gives

$$\Delta x\,\Delta y\,\Delta z\,M_x = I_a\,\Delta y\,\Delta z$$
$$I_a = \Delta x\,M_x$$

Putting $x = x_0$, $y = y_0 - \Delta y/2$, and $z = z_0$ in Eq. (5.60) results in

$$M_x = M_{x0} - \frac{\Delta y}{2}\frac{\partial M_x}{\partial y} + \text{higher-order terms}$$

at point a. Thus

$$I_a = \Delta x\,M_x$$
$$= \Delta x\left(M_{x0} - \frac{\Delta y}{2}\frac{\partial M_x}{\partial y} + \text{higher-order terms}\right) \tag{5.62}$$

Similarly, at point b,

$$\Delta x\,\Delta y\,\Delta z\,M_y = I_b\,\Delta x\,\Delta z$$
$$I_b = \Delta y\left(M_{y0} + \frac{\Delta x}{2}\frac{\partial M_y}{\partial x} + \text{higher-order terms}\right) \tag{5.63}$$

and in the same way,

$$I_c = \Delta x\left(M_{x0} + \frac{\Delta y}{2}\frac{\partial M_x}{\partial y} + \text{higher-order terms}\right) \tag{5.64}$$

$$I_d = \Delta y\left(M_{y0} - \frac{\Delta x}{2}\frac{\partial M_y}{\partial x} + \text{higher-order terms}\right) \tag{5.65}$$

It is clear from Fig. 5.15 that at (x_0,y_0,z_0)

$$I_z = I_a + I_b - I_c - I_d \tag{5.66}$$

where I_z is the net current in the z direction. Combining Eqs. (5.62) to (5.66) results in

$$I_z = \Delta x\,\Delta y\left(\frac{\partial M_y}{\partial x} - \frac{\partial M_x}{\partial y}\right) + \Delta x\,\Delta y\,(\text{higher-order terms})$$

Since, by definition,

$$J_{mz} = \lim_{\Delta x,\Delta y \to 0} \frac{I_z}{\Delta x\,\Delta y}$$

then

$$J_{mz} = \frac{\partial M_y}{\partial x} - \frac{\partial M_x}{\partial y} \tag{5.67}$$

because

$$\lim_{\Delta x, \Delta y \to 0} \text{(higher-order terms)} = 0$$

We see immediately from Eq. (5.67) that

$$J_{mz} = (\nabla \times \mathbf{M})_z$$

Carrying out the derivations for J_{mx} and J_{my} in a similar way gives

$$\mathbf{J}_m = \nabla \times \mathbf{M} \tag{5.68}$$

which is the desired relation between $\mathbf{J}_m$ and $\mathbf{M}$. Thus $\mathbf{J}_m$ is an equivalent macroscopic current density within the magnetic material which would generate the same macroscopic average magnetic field as that generated by the microscopic dipole moments. Thus the microscopic dipole moments which act as sources of magnetic field may be accounted for by $\mathbf{J}_m$ in Maxwell's equations. Note that $\mathbf{J}_m$ is not a "true" current density denoting macroscopic charge transport, but instead represents a bound-charge magnetic current density. Equation (5.68) is valid for both time-varying and steady currents.

MAGNETIC FIELD INTENSITY H AND PERMEABILITY

The effect of $\mathbf{M}$, and therefore the effect of the atomic currents, may be taken into account by including $\mathbf{J}_m$ in $\mathbf{J}_T$ in Eq. (5.38). Then the $\nabla \times \mathbf{B}$ equation is Eq. (5.42) with $\mathbf{J}_m$ included,

$$\nabla \times \frac{\mathbf{B}}{\mu_0} = \mathbf{J}_m + \mathbf{J} + \frac{\partial \mathbf{D}}{\partial t} \tag{5.69}$$

Putting Eq. (5.68) into Eq. (5.69) and rearranging gives

$$\nabla \times \left(\frac{\mathbf{B}}{\mu_0} - \mathbf{M}\right) = \mathbf{J} + \frac{\partial \mathbf{D}}{\partial t} \tag{5.70}$$

It is obviously convenient to define a new field quantity by

$$\mathbf{H} = \frac{\mathbf{B}}{\mu_0} - \mathbf{M} \tag{5.71}$$

so that

$$\nabla \times \mathbf{H} = \mathbf{J} + \frac{\partial \mathbf{D}}{\partial t} \tag{5.72}$$

The new magnetic vector field function so defined, $\mathbf{H}$, is called the *magnetic field intensity*. From Eq. (5.72) it is clear that $\nabla \times \mathbf{H}$ is independent of $\mathbf{M}$ and $\mathbf{J}_m$. This is like $\nabla \cdot \mathbf{D}$ being independent of $\mathbf{P}$ and $\mathbf{J}_p$.

The same interaction between applied fields and induced fields described in connection with electric fields occurs in connection with magnetic fields. An applied field results in some magnetization **M**, which in turn induces a field. In many materials the magnetization **M** is proportional to the applied external field **H**. These materials are called *linear isotropic materials,* and are characterized by the equation

$$\mathbf{M} = \chi_m \mathbf{H} \tag{5.73}$$

where χ_m is called the *magnetic susceptibility.* From Eqs. (5.71) and (5.73) we have

$$\mathbf{B} = \mu_0(1 + \chi_m)\mathbf{H} = \mu\mathbf{H} \tag{5.74}$$

where the *permeability* μ is defined as

$$\mu = \mu_0(1 + \chi_m) \tag{5.75}$$

The *relative permeability* is

$$\frac{\mu}{\mu_0} = (1 + \chi_m) \tag{5.76}$$

Like the permittivity, the permeability is usually obtained from experimental measurement.

When χ_m is negative, the material is called *diamagnetic.* Diamagnetic materials produce magnetic fields which oppose the applied field. When χ_m is positive, the material is called *paramagnetic.* Paramagnetism is caused by another phenomenon, the alignment of permanent magnetic-dipole moments within the material by the applied **H** field. For both paramagnetic and diamagnetic materials, the magnitude of χ_m is very small compared to unity, and the magnetic effects are small.

Another class of magnetic materials are the *ferromagnetic* materials. In ferromagnetic materials Eq. (5.73) does not hold because the material is nonlinear. It is customary, however, to use $\mathbf{B} = \mu\mathbf{H}$ and treat μ as a function of **H**. In this case, μ can range in value from $-\infty$ to $+\infty$, and the problem must be solved by nonlinear techniques. A typical **BH** curve is shown in Fig. 5.16. **B** depends not only on the magnitude of **H**, but also on the past history of the material. This phenomenon is called *hysteresis.* The arrows indicate the **BH** relationship as **H** is increased from zero to a, then decreased to $-a$, and then increased again to a. In ferromagnetic materials, **M** can be present even in the absence of external applied fields. In this case the material is said to be a *permanent magnet.* In this respect magnetic materials are different from common dielectrics, in which a permanent **P** does not exist. There are some

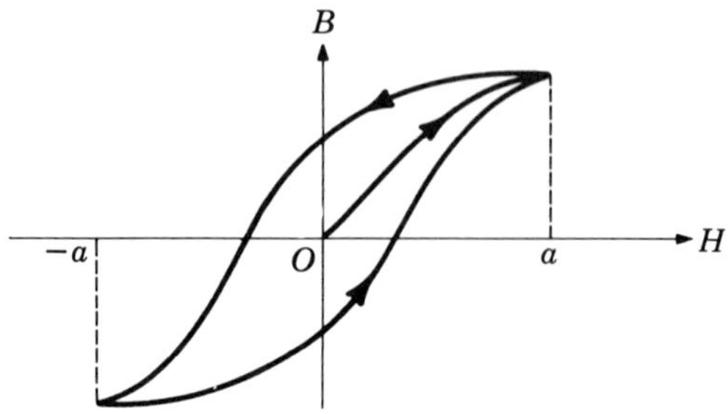

Fig. 5.16 A typical BH curve showing hysteresis.

materials called *ferroelectrics* in which **P** is permanent, but these materials are not very common. Thus **M** is used more often than is **P**.

5.11 MAGNETIC SCALAR POTENTIAL

In the special static case where $\mathbf{J} = 0$,

$$\nabla \times \mathbf{H} = 0$$

and **H** can be written as the gradient of a scalar field function Φ_m,

$$\mathbf{H} = -\nabla\Phi_m \tag{5.77}$$

This parallels the similar relations for the static **E** field. Taking the divergence of Eq. (5.71), we have

$$\nabla \cdot \mathbf{H} = \frac{1}{\mu_0}\nabla \cdot \mathbf{B} - \nabla \cdot \mathbf{M}$$

Since $\nabla \cdot \mathbf{B} = 0$ from Eq. (3.33),

$$\nabla \cdot \mathbf{H} = -\nabla \cdot \mathbf{M} \tag{5.78}$$

The magnetic analog of Poisson's equation may be obtained by taking the divergence of Eq. (5.77) and using Eq. (5.78),

$$\nabla^2\Phi_m = \nabla \cdot \mathbf{M}$$

For the sake of symmetry, a fictitious magnetic charge density is defined as

$$\nabla \cdot \mathbf{M} = -\rho_m \tag{5.79}$$

so that

$$\nabla^2\Phi_m = -\rho_m \tag{5.80}$$

Since Eq. (5.80) is formally the same as Poisson's equation, all the mathematical techniques that apply to the solution of Poisson's equation also apply to Eq. (5.80). These techniques will be treated extensively in Chap. 9.

It must be emphasized that ρ_m is purely a mathematical function and does not imply the existence of a physical magnetic charge density. However, ρ_m is very useful. Because of the similarity between ρ_m and ρ_p, as indicated by comparing Eqs. (5.79) and (5.26), it is obvious that following the derivation leading to Eq. (5.30) would lead to

$$\rho_{ms} = \mathbf{M} \cdot \hat{\mathbf{n}} \tag{5.81}$$

where ρ_{ms} is a fictitious magnetic surface charge density resulting from a discontinuity in $\mathbf{M}$. Because of the similarities between Eq. (2.8),

$$\mathbf{E} = -\nabla\Phi \tag{2.8}$$

and Eq. (5.77) and between Eq. (3.7),

$$\nabla^2\Phi = -\frac{\rho}{\epsilon_0} \tag{3.7}$$

and Eq. (5.80), it is possible to solve some magnetic problems by using the known solutions to analogous electrical problems and replacing

$$\mathbf{E} \quad \text{by} \quad \mathbf{H} \tag{5.82}$$

$$\frac{\rho}{\epsilon_0} \quad \text{by} \quad \rho_m \tag{5.83}$$

$$\Phi \quad \text{by} \quad \Phi_m \tag{5.84}$$

It is important to note that solving Eqs. (3.7) and (2.8) is equivalent to finding $\mathbf{E}$ and Φ from a known ρ by using the integral expressions given in Chap. 2. Thus, if the solution to the right electrical problem is found by any correct technique, the corresponding magnetic field problem can be found by making the above substitutions. This method works when ρ can be made to correspond to $\rho_m\epsilon_0$ (and, remember, when $\mathbf{J} = 0$ and $\partial\mathbf{D}/\partial t = 0$). One such problem is illustrated in Example 5.6.

Example 5.6 Slab permanent magnet The region of space given by $0 < x < d$ is occupied by a magnetized medium in which $\mathbf{M} = M\hat{\mathbf{x}}$, as shown in Fig. 5.17. The magnetic field relationships may be found from the expression

$$\nabla \cdot \mathbf{H} = -\nabla \cdot \mathbf{M}$$

Since $\mathbf{M} = M\hat{\mathbf{x}}$, $\nabla \cdot \mathbf{M} = 0$, and therefore $\rho_m = 0$. However, $\mathbf{M}$ is discontinuous at $x = 0$ and $x = d$, and hence, from Eq. (5.81),

$$\rho_{ms} = \begin{cases} M & x = d \\ -M & x = 0 \end{cases}$$

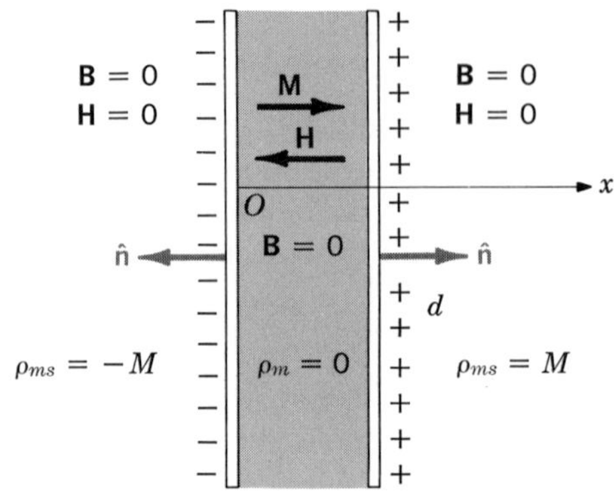

Fig. 5.17 The slab permanent magnet of Example 5.6.

Thus this magnetic problem is like the problem of finding the electric field produced by two planar sheets of charge. This problem was solved in Example 3.2. Changing that answer to fit the coordinate system in Fig. 5.17 results in

$$\mathbf{E} = \begin{cases} -\dfrac{\rho_s}{\epsilon_0}\hat{\mathbf{x}} & 0 < x < d \\ 0 & \text{elsewhere} \end{cases}$$

where a positive surface charge density ρ_s is on the plate at $x = d$ and a negative surface charge density $-\rho_s$ is on the plate at $x = 0$. Making the substitutions indicated in Eqs. (5.82) and (5.83),

$$\frac{\rho_s}{\epsilon_0} \rightarrow \rho_{ms}$$

$$E_x \rightarrow H_x$$

we find that

$$\mathbf{H} = \begin{cases} -\rho_{ms}\hat{\mathbf{x}} = -M\hat{\mathbf{x}} & 0 < x < d \\ 0 & \text{elsewhere} \end{cases}$$

Now that **H** is known, **B** can be found from Eq. (5.71),

$$\mathbf{B} = \mu_0(\mathbf{H} + \mathbf{M})$$

$$\mathbf{B} = \begin{cases} \mu_0(-M\hat{\mathbf{x}} + M\hat{\mathbf{x}}) = 0 & 0 < x < d \\ \mu_0(0 + 0) = 0 & \text{elsewhere} \end{cases}$$

Hence **B** is zero everywhere and is also continuous, as it must be according to Sec. 5.13.

In this example both **B** and **H** are zero outside the magnetic material because of the symmetry due to the infinite extent of the material in the y and z

directions. In the more physical case of a finite magnet, **B** and **H** will not generally be zero outside the material.

5.12 MATERIALS AND MAXWELL'S EQUATIONS

For convenience, the fundamental electromagnetic equations which include the effects of materials by means of the permittivity and permeability are summarized in this section. The equations are Maxwell's equations in point form,

$$\nabla \times \mathbf{E} = -\frac{\partial \mathbf{B}}{\partial t} \tag{5.85}$$

$$\nabla \times \mathbf{H} = \mathbf{J} + \frac{\partial \mathbf{D}}{\partial t} \tag{5.86}$$

and the auxiliary relations

$$\mathbf{D} = \epsilon \mathbf{E} \tag{5.87}$$

$$\mathbf{B} = \mu \mathbf{H} \tag{5.88}$$

where, in practice, ϵ and μ for specific materials are obtained by measurement. In general, ϵ and μ may both be functions of frequency.

The divergence relations, which are often listed separately, can be obtained from Eqs. (5.85) and (5.86) and the continuity equation. They are

$$\nabla \cdot \mathbf{D} = \rho \tag{5.89}$$

$$\nabla \cdot \mathbf{B} = 0 \tag{5.90}$$

Although the equations involving ϵ and μ are usually of greater practical value, the relations involving **P** and **M** are often useful. Therefore we list

$$\mathbf{D} = \epsilon_0 \mathbf{E} + \mathbf{P} \tag{5.91}$$

$$\mathbf{B} = \mu_0(\mathbf{H} + \mathbf{M}) \tag{5.92}$$

Equations (5.85) to (5.92) are the basis of all electromagnetic theory (nonrelativistic and unquantized) in point form. Although the fundamental equations are concise and perhaps simple in appearance, the solution of a practical problem is generally difficult to obtain. Consequently, the above equations are often supplemented by additional definitions and manipulated into other forms to fit certain types of problems. For example, sometimes it is easier to use the integral form; sometimes it is easier to use the potential Φ and Poisson's equation; etc. The remainder of the text is devoted to methods of solution and interpretation and application.

5.13 BOUNDARY CONDITIONS

When more than one kind of material is present, the electromagnetic equations in point form must be solved separately in the region of each material and the resulting solutions related by the *boundary conditions*, the relations between the fields in each region at the boundary between the regions. In this section these boundary conditions are developed.

NORMAL COMPONENTS

The boundary conditions on the normal components of **D** are obtained from the integral form of Eq. (5.89). This is obtained by integrating Eq. (5.89) over a volume V,

$$\int_V \nabla \cdot \mathbf{D}\, dV = \int_V \rho\, dV$$

Using the divergence theorem,

$$\oint_S \mathbf{D} \cdot d\mathbf{S} = \int_V \rho\, dV \tag{5.93}$$

where S is the closed surface surrounding the volume V. If we evaluate this expression over a small volume which includes the boundary, the boundary conditions for the normal component of **D** can be obtained (by taking the limit).

For the volume V, the small "pillbox" shown in Fig. 5.18 is chosen. The intent is to let $\Delta w \to 0$ so that a relation between $\mathbf{D}_1$ and $\mathbf{D}_2$ at the boundary can be obtained. The surface integral in Eq. (5.93) can be written as the sum of three terms,

$$\oint_S \mathbf{D} \cdot d\mathbf{S} = \int_{S_1} \mathbf{D}_1 \cdot d\mathbf{S}_1 + \int_{S_2} \mathbf{D}_2 \cdot d\mathbf{S}_2 + \int_{S_3} \mathbf{D} \cdot d\mathbf{S}_3$$

If **D** is finite, the third term approaches zero as $\Delta w \to 0$. When the radius of the pillbox is very small, so that **D** is nearly constant over ΔS,

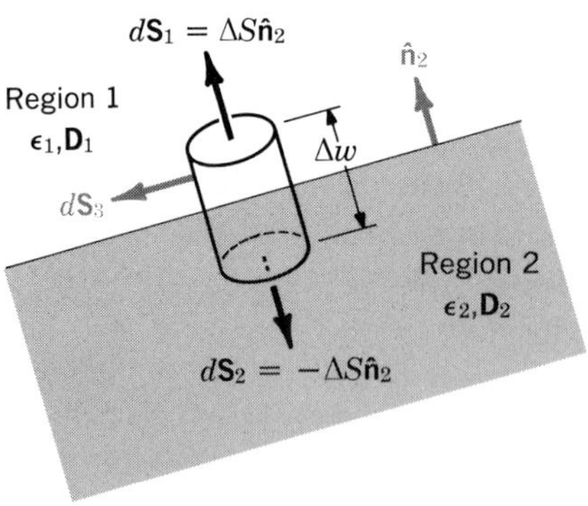

Fig. 5.18 The boundary between two dielectrics.

the integrals can be written as

$$\int_{S_1} \mathbf{D}_1 \cdot d\mathbf{S}_1 = \mathbf{D}_1 \cdot \hat{\mathbf{n}}_2 \, \Delta S$$

$$\int_{S_2} \mathbf{D}_2 \cdot d\mathbf{S}_2 = \mathbf{D}_2 \cdot (-\hat{\mathbf{n}}_2 \, \Delta S)$$

where $\hat{\mathbf{n}}_2$ is the unit vector pointing away from region 2. Thus

$$\oint_S \mathbf{D} \cdot d\mathbf{S} = \hat{\mathbf{n}}_2 \cdot (\mathbf{D}_1 - \mathbf{D}_2) \, \Delta S + \text{third term} \tag{5.94}$$

The volume integral in Eq. (5.93) is

$$\int_V \rho \, dV = Q \tag{5.95}$$

where Q is the total charge enclosed. Therefore, from Eqs. (5.93) to (5.95),

$$\hat{\mathbf{n}}_2 \cdot (\mathbf{D}_1 - \mathbf{D}_2) \, \Delta S + \text{third term} = Q$$

$$\hat{\mathbf{n}}_2 \cdot (\mathbf{D}_1 - \mathbf{D}_2) = \frac{Q}{\Delta S} + \frac{\text{third term}}{\Delta S}$$

$$\lim_{\Delta w \to 0} \hat{\mathbf{n}}_2 \cdot (\mathbf{D}_1 - \mathbf{D}_2) = \lim_{\Delta w \to 0} \frac{Q}{\Delta S} + 0 \tag{5.96}$$

Now, if the limit as $\Delta S \to 0$ is taken, the left-hand side of Eq. (5.96) becomes the value of $\hat{\mathbf{n}}_2 \cdot (\mathbf{D}_1 - \mathbf{D}_2)$ at a point on the boundary. The right-hand side becomes

$$\lim_{\substack{\Delta w \to 0 \\ \Delta S \to 0}} \frac{Q}{\Delta S} = \rho_s \tag{5.97}$$

where ρ_s is called the *surface charge density* because the charge is in an infinitely thin layer at the boundary. The boundary condition is then

$$\hat{\mathbf{n}}_2 \cdot (\mathbf{D}_1 - \mathbf{D}_2) = \rho_s \tag{5.98}$$

The boundary conditions on the normal component of $\mathbf{E}$ can be found by using $\mathbf{D} = \epsilon \mathbf{E}$ in Eq. (5.98). Thus

$$\hat{\mathbf{n}}_2 \cdot (\epsilon_1 \mathbf{E}_1 - \epsilon_2 \mathbf{E}_2) = \rho_s \tag{5.99}$$

The discontinuity in the normal components of $\mathbf{E}$ can be attributed to $\mathbf{P}$.

A similar derivation starting with Eq. (5.90) may be carried out to obtain the boundary conditions on $\mathbf{B}$ and $\mathbf{H}$ at the boundary between two magnetic media. They are

$$\hat{\mathbf{n}}_2 \cdot (\mathbf{B}_1 - \mathbf{B}_2) = 0 \tag{5.100}$$

and

$$\hat{\mathbf{n}}_2 \cdot (\mu_1\mathbf{H}_1 - \mu_2\mathbf{H}_2) = 0 \tag{5.101}$$

The discontinuity in the normal components of **H** can be attributed to **M**.

TANGENTIAL COMPONENTS

The boundary conditions on the tangential components are obtained from the curl equations. First consider Eq. (5.86). Integrating over a surface (not closed) results in

$$\int_S \nabla \times \mathbf{H} \cdot d\mathbf{S} = \int_S \mathbf{J} \cdot d\mathbf{S} + \int_S \frac{\partial \mathbf{D}}{\partial t} \cdot d\mathbf{S}$$

Using Stokes's theorem gives

$$\oint_l \mathbf{H} \cdot d\mathbf{l} = \int_S \mathbf{J} \cdot d\mathbf{S} + \int_S \frac{\partial \mathbf{D}}{\partial t} \cdot d\mathbf{S} \tag{5.102}$$

where l is the line boundary of the open surface S. The next step is to evaluate Eq. (5.102) under the conditions shown in Fig. 5.19. Let $\hat{\boldsymbol{\tau}}$ be any unit vector tangential to the boundary; it is shown pointing out of the paper in Fig. 5.19. The line integral is

$$\oint_l \mathbf{H} \cdot d\mathbf{l} = \int_a^b \mathbf{H}_2 \cdot d\mathbf{l}_2 + \int_b^c \mathbf{H} \cdot d\mathbf{l} + \int_c^d \mathbf{H}_1 \cdot d\mathbf{l}_1 + \int_d^a \mathbf{H} \cdot d\mathbf{l}$$

Since we intend to reduce Δw to zero, the second and fourth terms will not be evaluated because they approach zero as Δw does when **H** is finite. Now

$$d\mathbf{l}_1 = -dl\,\hat{\mathbf{n}}_2 \times \hat{\boldsymbol{\tau}}$$

$$d\mathbf{l}_2 = dl\,\hat{\mathbf{n}}_2 \times \hat{\boldsymbol{\tau}}$$

Then for small L the line integral may be written

$$\oint_l \mathbf{H} \cdot d\mathbf{l} = -\mathbf{H}_1 \cdot \hat{\mathbf{n}}_2 \times \hat{\boldsymbol{\tau}}L + \mathbf{H}_2 \cdot \hat{\mathbf{n}}_2 \times \hat{\boldsymbol{\tau}}L + \text{other terms}$$

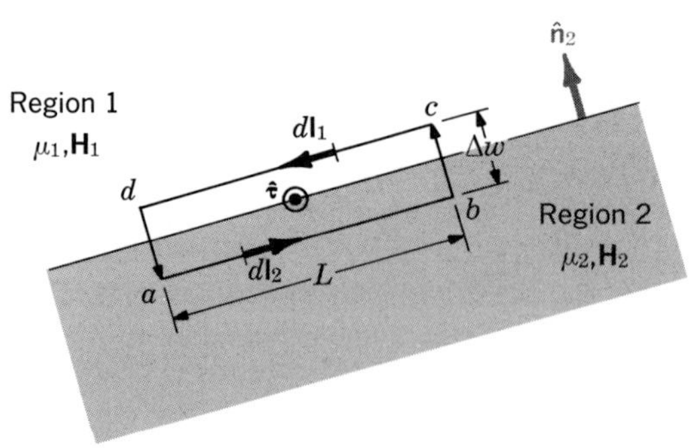

Fig. 5.19 The boundary between two magnetic materials.

The surface integrals in Eq. (5.102) may be written as

$$\int_S \mathbf{J} \cdot d\mathbf{S} + \int_S \frac{\partial \mathbf{D}}{\partial t} \cdot d\mathbf{S} = \mathbf{J} \cdot \hat{\mathbf{n}}\, \Delta S + \frac{\partial \mathbf{D}}{\partial t} \cdot \hat{\mathbf{n}}\, \Delta S$$

and Eq. (5.102) becomes

$$-\mathbf{H}_1 \cdot \hat{\mathbf{n}}_2 \times \hat{\boldsymbol{\tau}} + \mathbf{H}_2 \cdot \hat{\mathbf{n}}_2 \times \hat{\boldsymbol{\tau}} + \frac{\text{other terms}}{L} = \frac{\mathbf{J}\, \Delta S \cdot \hat{\boldsymbol{\tau}}}{L} + \frac{\partial \mathbf{D}}{\partial t} \cdot \hat{\boldsymbol{\tau}}\, \frac{\Delta S}{L}$$

where $\mathbf{J} \cdot \hat{\boldsymbol{\tau}}\, \Delta S$ is the total current passing through the surface. Taking the limit as $\Delta w \to 0$ and then as $L \to 0$ results in

$$-\mathbf{H}_1 \cdot \hat{\mathbf{n}}_2 \times \hat{\boldsymbol{\tau}} + \mathbf{H}_2 \cdot \hat{\mathbf{n}}_2 \times \hat{\boldsymbol{\tau}} + 0 = \mathbf{J}_s \cdot \hat{\boldsymbol{\tau}} - 0$$

where $\mathbf{J}_s$ is the surface current density per meter, $\mathbf{J}_s = \lim\limits_{\substack{\Delta w \to 0 \\ L \to 0}} \mathbf{J}\, \Delta S/L$, which is assumed to exist in an infinitely thin layer at the boundary. Rearranging the dot-cross product results in

$$\hat{\boldsymbol{\tau}} \cdot (\hat{\mathbf{n}}_2 \times \mathbf{H}_1 - \hat{\mathbf{n}}_2 \times \mathbf{H}_2 - \mathbf{J}_s) = 0$$

Since $\hat{\boldsymbol{\tau}}$ is any arbitrary unit vector parallel to the boundary, the above equation in general reduces to

$$\hat{\mathbf{n}}_2 \times (\mathbf{H}_1 - \mathbf{H}_2) = \mathbf{J}_s \tag{5.103}$$

The boundary conditions on the tangential components of **E** are easily obtained by starting with Eq. (5.85) and following the procedure just outlined for **H**. The result is

$$\hat{\mathbf{n}}_2 \times (\mathbf{E}_1 - \mathbf{E}_2) = 0 \tag{5.104}$$

which states that the component of $\mathbf{E}_1$ tangential to the boundary is equal to the component of $\mathbf{E}_2$ tangential to the boundary. The boundary conditions on the tangential components of **D** can be found by using $\mathbf{D} = \epsilon\mathbf{E}$ in Eq. (5.104).

INTERDEPENDENCE OF BOUNDARY CONDITIONS OF NORMAL AND TANGENTIAL COMPONENTS

As pointed out in Sec. 5.12, the divergence relation, Eq. (5.89), can be obtained by taking the divergence of Eq. (5.86) and using the continuity relation. Similarly, Eq. (5.90) can be obtained by taking the divergence of Eq. (5.85). Hence Eqs. (5.89) and (5.86) are not independent and Eqs. (5.90) and (5.85) are not independent. This means that the boundary conditions on the normal components of **D**, which were obtained from Eq. (5.89), and the boundary conditions on tangential **H**, which were obtained from Eq. (5.86), are not independent in the time-varying case. It turns out that they are equivalent. The same is true of the boundary conditions on normal **B**, obtained from Eq. (5.90), and the boundary conditions on tangential **E**, obtained from Eq. (5.85).

The result is, then, that in the time-varying case the boundary conditions in Eqs. (5.98) and (5.103) are equivalent, as are those in Eqs. (5.100) and (5.104).

BOUNDARY CONDITIONS FOR GOOD DIELECTRICS

At the boundaries of good dielectrics, ρ_s and $\mathbf{J}_s$ are usually zero. Hence the boundary conditions are

$$\hat{\mathbf{n}}_2 \cdot \mathbf{D}_1 = \hat{\mathbf{n}}_2 \cdot \mathbf{D}_2 \tag{5.105}$$

$$\hat{\mathbf{n}}_2 \cdot \mathbf{B}_1 = \hat{\mathbf{n}}_2 \cdot \mathbf{B}_2 \tag{5.106}$$

$$\hat{\mathbf{n}}_2 \times \mathbf{H}_1 = \hat{\mathbf{n}}_2 \times \mathbf{H}_2 \tag{5.107}$$

$$\hat{\mathbf{n}}_2 \times \mathbf{E}_1 = \hat{\mathbf{n}}_2 \times \mathbf{E}_2 \tag{5.108}$$

The other boundary conditions can be obtained by using $\mathbf{D} = \epsilon\mathbf{E}$ and $\mathbf{B} = \mu\mathbf{H}$. The normal components of **D** and **B** are continuous and the tangential components of **H** and **E** are continuous. The other components are discontinuous. It is left as Prob. 5.13-2 to show that the discontinuities in **E** can be attributed to the polarization.

As mentioned in the previous section, Eq. (5.105) is equivalent to Eq. (5.107) and Eq. (5.106) is equivalent to Eq. (5.108) *in the time-varying case.*

BOUNDARY CONDITIONS FOR PERFECT CONDUCTORS

In the static case, as explained in Sec. 5.7, the electric field is zero inside a good conductor, and any nonzero charge density is found only on the surface. As will be shown in Chap. 6, the same is true for perfect conductors in the time-varying case, and in addition, **B** and **H** are also zero inside the conductor. This results because **H** and **E** are related through Maxwell's equations in the time-varying case, and when **E** goes to zero because of the effects on conduction charges, **H** does too. However, in the static case, **H** is not necessarily related to **E**, and hence the conductor has no effect on **H**, and **H** does not go to zero. The conduction charges do not affect **H** directly, as they do **E**, because according to the Lorentz force equation, **H** does not exert a force on the charges unless they are moving. Thus **H** does not make the charge move around and induce new **H** fields to make the total **H** field zero. This explanation neglects the random thermal velocities, but the velocities are so low that the force exerted by **H** is negligible.

Thus the boundary conditions in the static case for a good conductor are

$$\left.\begin{aligned} \hat{\mathbf{n}}_2 \cdot \mathbf{D}_1 &= \rho_s \\ \hat{\mathbf{n}}_2 \times \mathbf{E}_1 &= 0 \\ \hat{\mathbf{n}}_2 \cdot \mathbf{B}_1 &= \hat{\mathbf{n}}_2 \cdot \mathbf{B}_2 \\ \hat{\mathbf{n}}_2 \times \mathbf{H}_1 &= \hat{\mathbf{n}}_2 \times \mathbf{H}_2 \end{aligned}\right\} \text{Static fields} \qquad \begin{aligned} &(5.109) \\ &(5.110) \\ &(5.111) \\ &(5.112) \end{aligned}$$

where medium 2 is the conductor.

The boundary conditions in the time-varying case for a good conductor are

$$\left.\begin{aligned} \hat{\mathbf{n}}_2 \cdot \mathbf{D}_1 &= \rho_s \\ \hat{\mathbf{n}}_2 \times \mathbf{E}_1 &= 0 \\ \hat{\mathbf{n}}_2 \cdot \mathbf{B}_1 &= 0 \\ \hat{\mathbf{n}}_2 \times \mathbf{H}_1 &= \mathbf{J}_s \end{aligned}\right\} \text{Time-varying fields} \qquad \begin{aligned} &(5.113) \\ &(5.114) \\ &(5.115) \\ &(5.116) \end{aligned}$$

where medium 2 is the perfect conductor.

The surface charge density ρ_s is known if the normal component of $\mathbf{D}$ at the conductor surface is known, and $\mathbf{J}_s$ is known if the tangential component of $\mathbf{H}$ at the conductor surface is known. As mentioned previously, Eq. (5.113) is equivalent to Eq. (5.116) and Eq. (5.114) is equivalent to Eq. (5.115). In the case of a perfect conductor, where all the fields are zero inside the conductor, it turns out that all four boundary conditions are satisfied if Eq. (5.114) is satisfied. Hence if Eq. (5.114) is satisfied, and the other field components are known, Eqs. (5.116) and (5.113) can be used to find $\mathbf{J}_s$ and ρ_s.

BOUNDARY CONDITIONS FOR MAGNETIC MATERIALS

The boundary conditions for magnetic materials are the same as those for dielectric materials, Eqs. (5.105) to (5.108). The discontinuities in the tangential components of $\mathbf{B}$ can be attributed to $\mathbf{M}$, as indicated in Prob. 5.13-3.

SUMMARY OF BOUNDARY CONDITIONS

For convenience, a summary of the results of this section are presented in Table 5.3.

Example 5.7 The boundary between two dielectrics Suppose region 1 ($y < 0$) is free space and region 2 ($y > 0$) is a dielectric with no surface charge, as shown in Fig. 5.20. Suppose that $\mathbf{D}_1$ has been found from a solution of Maxwell's equations in region 1 and is given by

$$\mathbf{D}_1 = D_0\hat{\mathbf{y}}$$

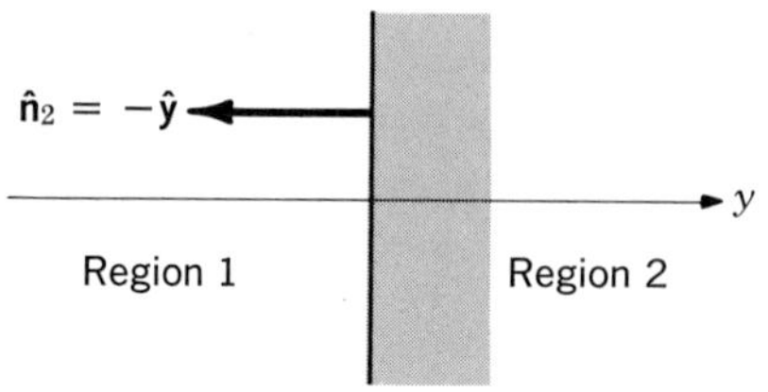

Fig. 5.20 The regions used in Example 5.7.

where D_0 = constant. If we know $\mathbf{D}_1$, it is possible to find $\mathbf{D}_2$ and $\mathbf{E}_2$ at the boundary. Since $\mathbf{E}_1 = \mathbf{D}_1/\epsilon_0 = (\mathbf{D}_0/\epsilon_0)\hat{\mathbf{y}}$, $\mathbf{E}_1$ has only a component normal to the boundary; the tangential component is zero. From Table 5.3, the normal components of $\mathbf{D}$ must be continuous and the tangential components of $\mathbf{E}$ must be continuous. Since the tangential component of $\mathbf{E}_1$ is zero, the tangential component of $\mathbf{E}_2$ must be zero, and $\mathbf{E}_2$ can have only a normal component. Then, since $\mathbf{D}_2 = \epsilon\mathbf{E}_2$, $\mathbf{D}_2$ will have only a normal component. Since the normal component of $\mathbf{D}$ is continuous,

$$\mathbf{D}_2 = \mathbf{D}_1$$
$$= D_0\hat{\mathbf{y}} \qquad \text{(at the boundary)}$$

Table 5.3 A summary of boundary conditions

Components at the boundary	*General*	*Dielectrics*	*Medium 2 is a perfect conductor*
Normal	$\hat{\mathbf{n}}_2 \cdot (\mathbf{D}_1 - \mathbf{D}_2) = \rho_s$ (normal components of $\mathbf{D}$ discontinuous by ρ_s)	$\hat{\mathbf{n}}_2 \cdot \mathbf{D}_1 = \hat{\mathbf{n}}_2 \cdot \mathbf{D}_2$	$\hat{\mathbf{n}}_2 \cdot \mathbf{D}_1 = \rho_s$
	$\hat{\mathbf{n}}_2 \cdot \mathbf{B}_1 = \hat{\mathbf{n}}_2 \cdot \mathbf{B}_2$ (normal components of $\mathbf{B}$ continuous)	$\hat{\mathbf{n}}_2 \cdot \mathbf{B}_1 = \hat{\mathbf{n}}_2 \cdot \mathbf{B}_2$	$\hat{\mathbf{n}}_2 \cdot \mathbf{B}_1 = 0$
Tangential	$\hat{\mathbf{n}}_2 \times (\mathbf{H}_1 - \mathbf{H}_2) = \mathbf{J}_s$ (tangential components of $\mathbf{H}$ discontinuous by $\mathbf{J}_s$)	$\hat{\mathbf{n}}_2 \times \mathbf{H}_1 = \hat{\mathbf{n}}_2 \times \mathbf{H}_2$	$\hat{\mathbf{n}}_2 \times \mathbf{H}_1 = \mathbf{J}_s$ (time-varying) $\hat{\mathbf{n}}_2 \times \mathbf{H}_1 = \hat{\mathbf{n}}_2 \times \mathbf{H}_2$ (static)
	$\hat{\mathbf{n}}_2 \times \mathbf{E}_1 = \hat{\mathbf{n}}_2 \times \mathbf{E}_2$ (tangential components of $\mathbf{E}$ continuous)	$\hat{\mathbf{n}}_2 \times \mathbf{E}_1 = \hat{\mathbf{n}}_2 \times \mathbf{E}_2$	$\hat{\mathbf{n}}_2 \times \mathbf{E}_1 = 0$

Other boundary conditions can be found by using $\mathbf{D} = \epsilon\mathbf{E}$ and $\mathbf{B} = \mu\mathbf{H}$.

$\hat{\mathbf{n}}_2$ is a normal unit vector pointing away from medium 2.

Except as noted, the boundary conditions given are valid for both the static and the time-varying case. As explained in the text, all the boundary conditions are not independent in the time-varying case.

Consequently,

$$\mathbf{E}_2 = \frac{\mathbf{D}_2}{\epsilon}$$

$$= \frac{D_0}{\epsilon}\,\hat{\mathbf{y}} \qquad \text{(at the boundary)}$$

We could have proceeded more formally by noting that $\hat{\mathbf{n}}_2 = -\hat{\mathbf{y}}$ and using Eq. (5.105) to obtain the same result.

Example 5.8 Boundary between two dielectrics Now let us consider a more complicated situation at the same boundary in Fig. 5.20. Suppose that $\mathbf{D}_1$ in region 1 is known, $\mathbf{D}_1 = 5x^2\hat{\mathbf{x}} + (3 + y)\hat{\mathbf{y}} + 5z\hat{\mathbf{z}}$, and there is no surface charge at $y = 0$. If we know $\mathbf{D}_1$, it is possible to find $\mathbf{D}_2$ and $\mathbf{E}_2$ at the boundary. In this case, the normal components are the y components. Hence, since the normal components of $\mathbf{D}$ are continuous at $y = 0$,

$$D_{2y} = D_{1y}\Big|_{y=0}$$

$$= 3$$

Since $\mathbf{D} = \epsilon\mathbf{E}$,

$$\mathbf{E}_1 = \frac{\mathbf{D}_1}{\epsilon_1}$$

$$= \frac{5x^2}{\epsilon_1}\,\hat{\mathbf{x}} + \frac{3 + y}{\epsilon_1}\,\hat{\mathbf{y}} + \frac{5z}{\epsilon_1}\,\hat{\mathbf{z}}$$

Since the tangential components of $\mathbf{E}$ are continuous at $y = 0$,

$$E_{2x} = E_{1x}\Big|_{y=0} = \frac{5x^2}{\epsilon_1}$$

$$E_{2z} = E_{1z}\Big|_{y=0} = \frac{5z}{\epsilon_1} \qquad \text{(at the boundary)}$$

It is left as Prob. 5.13-9 to show that if the tangential components of $\mathbf{E}$ are equal, it is necessary that $E_{2x} = E_{1x}$ and $E_{2z} = E_{1z}$.

At this point the normal component of $\mathbf{D}_2$ and the tangential components of $\mathbf{E}_2$ at the boundary are known. The other components can be found by using $\mathbf{D}_2 = \epsilon_2\mathbf{E}_2$. The results are

$$\mathbf{E}_2 = \frac{5x^2}{\epsilon_1}\,\hat{\mathbf{x}} + \frac{3}{\epsilon_2}\,\hat{\mathbf{y}} + \frac{5z}{\epsilon_1}\,\hat{\mathbf{z}}$$

$$\mathbf{D}_2 = \frac{5\epsilon^2 x^2}{\epsilon_1}\,\hat{\mathbf{x}} + 3\hat{\mathbf{y}} + \frac{5\epsilon_2 z}{\epsilon_1}\,\hat{\mathbf{z}} \qquad \text{(at the boundary)}$$

From the boundary conditions, we know (since $\mathbf{D}_1$ is given) what $\mathbf{E}_2$ and $\mathbf{D}_2$ must be *at the boundary*. We do not know anything about $\mathbf{E}_2$ and $\mathbf{D}_2$ elsewhere, even though $\mathbf{D}_1$ was given generally. Further information about $\mathbf{E}_2$ and $\mathbf{D}_2$ would be found by solving Maxwell's equations in region 2. The discussions of boundary-value problems in Chap. 9 will further illustrate this point.

5.14 MATERIALS AND POWER AND ENERGY

The concepts of power and energy developed in Chap. 4 are extended in this section to include the presence of materials. The polarization of a material involves stored energy in much the same way that the collection of charges described in Sec. 4.3 involves stored energy. When the forces causing polarization are removed, the polarized charges will return to their unpolarized position, just as the free charges described in Sec. 4.3 would fly apart. Stored energy is involved in the magnetization of a material in a similar way.

One way to extend the results of Chap. 4 to materials is to follow the same methods used there, but to replace $\mathbf{J}$ in Eq. (4.21) by the $\mathbf{J}_T$ in Eq. (5.38). This approach will be followed for dielectrics a little later. Another way is to start with Eqs. (5.85) to (5.88), in which $\mathbf{J}_T$ has been included, and follow the methods of Chap. 4, starting with Eq. (4.21). This will amount to letting $\mathcal{P}_c$ represent the power transferred to the conduction charges only and including the effects of the polarization current and magnetization current through $\mathbf{D}$ and $\mathbf{H}$.

Solving for $\mathbf{J}$ from Eq. (5.86), substituting this into Eq. (4.21), and following the same pattern as in Sec. 4.4 leads to

$$\oint_S \mathbf{E} \times \mathbf{H} \cdot \hat{\mathbf{n}}\, dS + \frac{\partial}{\partial t} \int_V (\mathcal{W}_c + \tfrac{1}{2}\mathbf{D} \cdot \mathbf{E} + \tfrac{1}{2}\mathbf{B} \cdot \mathbf{H})\, dV = 0 \tag{5.117}$$

where it has been assumed that μ and ϵ are not functions of time. This can be a valid assumption in the low-frequency case. The detailed derivation of Eq. (5.117) is given as a problem.

Comparison of Eqs. (4.23) and (5.117) shows that the volume energy densities are

$$\begin{aligned} \mathcal{W}_e &= \tfrac{1}{2}\mathbf{D} \cdot \mathbf{E} \\ &= \tfrac{1}{2}\epsilon\mathbf{E} \cdot \mathbf{E} \end{aligned} \tag{5.118}$$

$$\begin{aligned} \mathcal{W}_m &= \tfrac{1}{2}\mathbf{B} \cdot \mathbf{H} \\ &= \tfrac{1}{2}\mu\mathbf{H} \cdot \mathbf{H} \end{aligned} \tag{5.119}$$

Equation (5.118) can also be derived by starting with Eq. (4.13) and using $\nabla \cdot \mathbf{D} = \rho$ and $\mathbf{E} = -\nabla\Phi$ (see Prob. 5.14-2). Equations (5.118) and (5.119) are the same as Eqs. (4.27) and (4.28) with ϵ_0 replaced by ϵ and μ_0

replaced by μ. This is just what we would expect, since this is just the change in the field relations produced by the presence of materials.

From Eq. (5.117), the Poynting vector is

$$\mathcal{P} = \mathbf{E} \times \mathbf{H} \tag{5.120}$$

which is the same as Eq. (4.26) if μ_0 is replaced by μ and $\mathbf{B} = \mu\mathbf{H}$ is used. Equations (5.118) to (5.120) are the commonly used energy densities and Poynting vector. Note that the effects of the polarization and magnetization are included through ϵ and μ, but the effects of conduction current are not. Conduction-current effects are in the $\mathcal{W}_c = \mathbf{J} \cdot \mathbf{E}$ term in Eq. (5.117). These effects could also be included by using $\mathbf{J} = \sigma\mathbf{E}$.

A power-energy conservation theorem which is valid when the frequency variation of μ and ϵ is important can be obtained by using the sinusoidal-time form of Maxwell's equations in terms of ϵ_c and a corresponding complex μ, μ_c. With sinusoidal time variation, and with $\mathbf{J}$ included in ϵ_c, Eqs. (5.85) and (5.86) can be written as

$$\nabla \times \mathbf{E} = -j\omega\mu_c\mathbf{H} \tag{5.121}$$

$$\nabla \times \mathbf{H} = j\omega\epsilon_c\mathbf{E} \tag{5.122}$$

Here μ_c is a complex permeability which is analogous to ϵ_c. Now the procedure used in Sec. 4.4 to obtain the complex power-energy conservation theorem can be followed. From a vector identity,

$$\nabla \cdot (\mathbf{E} \times \mathbf{H}^*) = \mathbf{H}^* \cdot \nabla \times \mathbf{E} - \mathbf{E} \cdot \nabla \times \mathbf{H}^*$$

Substituting from Eqs. (5.121) and (5.122) results in

$$\nabla \cdot (\mathbf{E} \times \mathbf{H}^*) = -j\omega(\mu_c\mathbf{H} \cdot \mathbf{H}^* - \epsilon_c^*\mathbf{E} \cdot \mathbf{E}^*)$$

Integrating over a volume and using the divergence theorem now gives

$$\oint_S \mathbf{E} \times \mathbf{H}^* \cdot \hat{\mathbf{n}}\, dS = -j\omega \int_V (\mu_c\mathbf{H} \cdot \mathbf{H}^* - \epsilon_c^*\mathbf{E} \cdot \mathbf{E}^*)\, dV \tag{5.123}$$

It is convenient now to define real and imaginary parts of μ_c and ϵ_c as

$$\frac{\mu_c}{\mu_0} = \mu_1 - j\mu_2 \tag{5.124}$$

$$\frac{\epsilon_c}{\epsilon_0} = \epsilon_1 - j\epsilon_2 \tag{5.125}$$

Then taking one-half the real part of Eq. (5.123) results in

$$\oint_S \tfrac{1}{2} \operatorname{Re} (\mathbf{E} \times \mathbf{H}^*) \cdot \hat{\mathbf{n}}\, dS = \oint_S \langle \mathcal{P} \rangle \cdot \hat{\mathbf{n}}\, dS = \omega \int_V (\mu_2\mathbf{H} \cdot \mathbf{H}^* + \epsilon_2\mathbf{E} \cdot \mathbf{E}^*)\, dV \tag{5.126}$$

In the next section it will be shown that ϵ_2, the imaginary part of ϵ_c, corresponds to dissipation in the material. Similarly, μ_2 corresponds to dissipation. Hence the interpretation of Eq. (5.126) is that the average power through S, $\oint_S \langle \mathcal{P} \rangle \cdot \hat{\mathbf{n}}\, dS$, is equal to the expression on the right, which is the average energy loss. If $\mu_2 = 0$ and $\epsilon_2 = 0$, there is no loss, and $\oint_S \langle \mathcal{P} \rangle \cdot \hat{\mathbf{n}}\, dS = 0$ because the average rate of change of the stored energy is zero.

Equation (5.126) has been derived from the complex Maxwell's equations by the same technique used in Sec. 4.4 for the complex case. Another approach is used in the next section to find the dissipation in a dielectric.

5.15 POWER DISSIPATION IN A DIELECTRIC WITH LOSSES

Power loss is associated with the damping term for bound electrons, ν_{bk}, and the damping term associated with conduction electrons, ν_c in Eq. (5.58). Expressed another way, power loss is associated with components of $\mathbf{J}$ which are in phase with the electric field $\mathbf{E}$.

In Sec. 4.4 the power associated with a current density $\mathbf{J}$ and an electric field intensity $\mathbf{E}$ was given by Eq. (4.20). The quantity $\mathbf{J}_T \cdot \mathbf{E}$, where $\mathbf{J}_T$ is the total current in the medium, yields the power-density dissipation in the material. For sinusoidal time-varying fields, the time-average power-density dissipation is

$$\langle \mathcal{P}_c \rangle = \tfrac{1}{2} \operatorname{Re} (\mathbf{J}_T \cdot \mathbf{E}^*) \qquad \text{watts/m}^3 \tag{5.127}$$

The total current density $\mathbf{J}_T$ in a nonmagnetic material is composed of conduction and polarization current. The polarization current $\mathbf{J}_p$ and conduction current $\mathbf{J}_c$ are related to $\mathbf{E}$ by Eqs. (5.35) and (5.37),

$$\mathbf{J}_p = j\omega\epsilon_0\chi_e(\omega)\mathbf{E} \tag{5.35}$$

$$\mathbf{J}_c = \frac{\rho_c q \mathbf{E}}{m(j\omega + \nu_c)} \tag{5.37}$$

Thus

$$\begin{aligned} \mathbf{J}_T &= \mathbf{J}_p + \mathbf{J}_c \\ &= j\omega\epsilon_0 \left[\chi_e + \frac{\rho_c q/m}{j\omega\epsilon_0(j\omega + \nu_c)} \right] \mathbf{E} \end{aligned} \tag{5.128}$$

Comparison of Eqs. (5.128) and (5.58) shows that $\mathbf{J}_T$ can be written in the form

$$\mathbf{J}_T = j\omega(\epsilon_c - \epsilon_0)\mathbf{E} \tag{5.129}$$

The permittivity ϵ_c associated with the dielectric material is expressed in terms of its real and imaginary parts by Eq. (5.125). The term ϵ_1 is the real component of permittivity, and the term ϵ_2 is the imaginary component which represents loss due to the collision terms for polarization and conduction electrons. Introducing Eqs. (5.129) and (5.125) into Eq. (5.127) gives

$$\langle \mathcal{P}_c \rangle = \tfrac{1}{2} \operatorname{Re} (-j\omega + j\omega\epsilon_1 + \omega\epsilon_2)\epsilon_0 \mathbf{E} \cdot \mathbf{E}^*$$

which reduces to

$$\langle \mathcal{P}_c \rangle = \tfrac{1}{2}\omega\epsilon_2\epsilon_0|E|^2 \tag{5.130}$$

Consider now a simple case in which a dielectric is assumed to have only one kind of polarization and no orientational contribution. For frequencies below the optical spectrum, where $\omega \ll \nu_c$ and $\omega \ll \omega_s$, ϵ_c may be written approximately as

$$\epsilon_c \approx \epsilon_0 \left[1 + \frac{\rho_c q/m}{j\omega\epsilon_0\nu_c} + \frac{N_b q^2/m}{\epsilon_0(\omega_s^2 + j\omega\nu_b)} \right]$$

or

$$\epsilon_c \approx \epsilon_0 \left[1 + \frac{\omega_s^2 N_b q^2/m}{\epsilon_0(\omega_s^4 + \omega^2\nu_b^2)} - \frac{j\omega\nu_b N_b q^2/m}{\epsilon_0(\omega_s^4 + \omega^2\nu_b^2)} - \frac{j\rho_c q/m}{\omega\epsilon_0\nu_c} \right] \tag{5.131}$$

From the definition of Eq. (5.125) it can be seen that ϵ_2 can be written as

$$\epsilon_2 = \epsilon_{2m} + \epsilon_{2b}$$

$$\epsilon_{2m} = \frac{\rho_c q/m}{\epsilon_0\omega\nu_c} = \frac{\sigma}{\omega\epsilon_0}$$

$$\epsilon_{2b} = \frac{\omega\nu_b N_b q^2/m}{\epsilon_0(\omega_s^4 + \omega^2\nu_b^2)}$$

where ϵ_{2m} is the imaginary part of ϵ_c due to conduction-charge effects and ϵ_{2b} is the imaginary part of ϵ_c due to bound-charge effects. Equation (5.130) may thus be written in an alternate form which clearly identifies the conduction and polarization contributions to the time-average power-density dissipation,

$$\langle \mathcal{P}_c \rangle = \tfrac{1}{2}\omega(\epsilon_{2b} + \epsilon_{2m})\epsilon_0|E|^2 \tag{5.132}$$

It is clear from Eq. (5.132) that it is the imaginary part of ϵ_c that describes the loss, or power dissipation, and as mentioned in Sec. 5.9, the loss is related to the ν, which are damping factors. If ν_c and ν_b are both zero, then ϵ_2 is zero and there is no power dissipation. Note that if $\nu_c = 0$, the condition $\omega \ll \nu_c$ does not hold, and the approximation used to get ϵ_{2m} is not valid. If $\nu_c = 0$, it is clear from Eq. (5.58) that $\epsilon_{2m} = 0$.

It is clear from an expression such as Eq. (5.118) that the time-average electric energy density stored in a dielectric material is $\langle \mathcal{W}_e \rangle = \frac{1}{4}\epsilon_1\epsilon_0|E|^2$. Thus a term of great interest, the time-average power density dissipated per unit volume divided by the time-average stored electric energy density per unit volume, may be obtained,

$$\frac{\langle \mathcal{P}_c \rangle}{\langle \mathcal{W}_e \rangle} = 2\omega \frac{\epsilon_2}{\epsilon_1} \tag{5.133}$$

Note that Eq. (5.133) does not represent the ratio of power dissipated to *total* electromagnetic energy stored per unit volume, because magnetic energy may also be present.

Since Eq. (5.133) gives a measure of the efficiency by which electric energy may be stored in a material medium, this ratio must be kept low for efficient storage or transmission of energy. The ratio ϵ_2/ϵ_1 is called the *loss factor*. In free space the loss factor is zero. In good dielectric materials, where ϵ_2/ϵ_1 is very low, the loss factor is small. It is interesting to note that the conduction-loss term is

$$\epsilon_{2m}/\epsilon_1 = \frac{\sigma}{\omega\epsilon_0\epsilon_1}$$

The smaller σ is, the lower the conduction loss in the dielectric is. This is the opposite of a conductor, in which low σ means high loss. The reason is that the energy transfer in the conductor is mainly due to movement of conduction electrons, and therefore high σ means more energy transfer. The loss occurs through collisions. In a dielectric, however, the main energy transfer is through polarization current, which is relatively lossless compared to conduction current. In this case the conduction charges contribute very little to energy transport but quite a lot to the loss. Consequently, lower σ in a dielectric means lower loss.

It is useful to define a quality factor Q for a time-varying system as

$$Q = \frac{\text{time-average total energy density stored}}{\text{time-average energy-density loss per radian}} \tag{5.134}$$

This is a point relation defining the energy-storage properties of the medium at a point. In many applications involving resonant cavities and wave propagation, the total time-average energy equals the peak electric energy (e.g., see Sec. 6.11 for planewaves), and we now restrict our attention to this case. The peak electric energy density stored in the medium is $\frac{1}{2}\epsilon_1\epsilon_0|E_0|^2$, where E_0 is the peak E field. The average energy-density loss per radian equals the power dissipated per second, given by Eq.

(5.130), divided by the radian frequency ω in radians per second. Since the time-average total energy density is taken to be equal to the peak electric energy density stored, the quality factor Q becomes

$$Q = \frac{\frac{1}{2}\epsilon_1\epsilon_0|E_0|^2}{\frac{1}{2}\epsilon_2\epsilon_0|E_0|^2} = \frac{\epsilon_1}{\epsilon_2} \tag{5.135}$$

This expression may be written in the alternate form

$$Q = \frac{1}{\sigma/\omega\epsilon_1\epsilon_0 + \epsilon_{2b}/\epsilon_0}$$

which identifies the conduction and polarization contributions to the Q factor. It is readily seen from this expression that the quality factor is frequency dependent. In the case where ϵ_{2b} is small, the quality factor becomes $Q = \epsilon_0\epsilon_1\omega/\sigma$ and increases with frequency. When σ is small, $Q = \epsilon_1/\epsilon_{2b}$, and it is easily seen that Q decreases with frequency.

The quality factor for a dielectric material is of critical importance in making a design decision concerning its use in an energy-storage or power-transmission application. As a result, extensive experimental investigations have been conducted into the quality factor for several useful dielectric materials. An excellent compilation of such data has been made by Von Hippel.† Some of the dielectric constant and loss factor data at 25 GHz are shown in Table 5.4. For the materials shown, the loss due to conduction electrons is negligible; thus the ratio ϵ_2/ϵ_1 is approximately the reciprocal of the quality factor. When $\sigma = 0$, the quality factor is $Q = \epsilon_1/\epsilon_{2b}$. The quality factor for these materials is of the order of 1,000 or greater, which indicates that the material stores electric energy efficiently.

† A. R. Von Hippel (ed.), "Dielectric Materials and Applications," John Wiley & Sons, Inc., New York, 1954.

Table 5.4 Dielectric-constant and loss-factor data at 25 GHz

Material	ϵ_1	ϵ_{2b}/ϵ_1
Fused quartz	3.78	0.00025
Teflon	2.10	0.00060
Polystyrene	2.55	0.00100
Lucite	2.57	0.00300
Lead glass	6.80	0.00900

Example 5.9 The quality factor for a parallel-plate-capacitor tuned circuit A common and well-known example for the need of dielectric material with a high quality factor is the capacitor. It is often necessary to utilize dielectric material between capacitor plates. Because of loss in the material, the capacitor is lossy, and it is useful to consider the gross quality factor for the capacitor. In circuit theory it is common to define the gross circuit quality factor Q_c as

$$Q_c = \frac{\omega_0 U}{\langle P_c \rangle} \tag{5.136}$$

where

U = peak energy stored
ω_0 = radian frequency
$\langle P_c \rangle$ = time-average dissipated power

Assume that the circuit under consideration consists of a perfect inductance connected across a parallel-plate capacitor of area A and gap d, filled with a material with uniform dielectric constant $\epsilon_1 - j\epsilon_2$. The natural resonant frequency of the parallel LC circuit is ω_0. The time-average power dissipation per unit volume in the material is given by Eq. (5.130); thus the total time-average power dissipation is

$$\langle P_c \rangle = \tfrac{1}{2}\omega_0 \epsilon_2 \epsilon_0 |E_0|^2 A d$$

The total time-average electric energy stored is

$$\langle W_e \rangle = \tfrac{1}{4}\epsilon_1 \epsilon_0 |E_0|^2 A d$$

which is half the total energy U stored in the resonant circuit, and thus Eq. (5.136) gives

$$Q_c = \frac{\epsilon_1}{\epsilon_2} \tag{5.137}$$

Note that the circuit quality factor Q_c is identical to the medium quality-factor point relation given by Eq. (5.135).

The common circuit representation for the parallel LC circuit with finite capacitor losses is a parallel combination of a perfect inductor, a perfect capacitor, and conductance G. Elementary circuit theory shows that the quality factor for such an equivalent circuit is $Q_c = \omega_0 C/G$. This expression may easily be derived from the field equations for the imperfect dielectric material. It may be shown that the loss current, or current in phase with E, is

$$J = \omega_0 \epsilon_2 \epsilon_0 E \tag{5.138}$$

The total loss current flowing across capacitor plates of area A, in terms of the voltage across the plates V and gap d, is

$$\begin{aligned} I &= JA \\ &= \omega_0 \epsilon_2 \epsilon_0 A \frac{V}{d} \end{aligned} \tag{5.139}$$

The conductance G is defined as I/V, or

$$G = \frac{I}{V}$$

$$= \omega_0 \epsilon_2 \epsilon_0 \frac{A}{d} \tag{5.140}$$

Since $C = \epsilon_0 \epsilon_1 (A/d)$, it is seen from Eqs. (5.140) and (5.137) that

$$Q_c = \omega_0 \frac{C}{G} \tag{5.141}$$

and thus the quality factor for a parallel LC circuit with imperfect dielectric is derived.

PROBLEMS

5.2-1 Show that

$$\frac{q}{4\pi\epsilon_0 (x - x')^2} \approx \frac{q}{4\pi\epsilon_0 x^2} + \frac{qx'}{2\pi\epsilon_0 x^3} \qquad x \ll x'$$

as stated in Example 5.1.

5.2-2 A point charge q is constrained to the vicinity of the origin of a coordinate system by a force $\mathbf{F} = -k\mathbf{r}$, where $\mathbf{r}$ is the vector from the origin to the point where q is located and k is a constant. If a constant external field $\mathbf{E}_0 = E_0\hat{\mathbf{x}}$ is applied, find the resultant total field at the point $(x,0,0)$. Find the difference between this field and the resultant total field which would exist if q were fixed at the origin and could not move. Explain why the total resultant field is different when q can move than when it cannot.

5.3-1 Show that the total field produced by the point charge q and the sphere of charge is zero at any point $r > r_0$ when q is at the center of the sphere of charge, as shown in Fig. 5.3*a*. Recall that $\rho = -3q/4\pi r_0^3$.

5.4-1 Since polarization is a movement of charge, one would expect a current to result from the rate of change of polarization, as stated in Eq. (5.33). Show from the definition of $\mathbf{P}$ that $\mathbf{J}_p = \partial\mathbf{P}/\partial t$ is consistent with the expression $\mathbf{J}_p = \rho\mathbf{v}$, where ρ and $\mathbf{v}$ are an appropriate charge density and velocity, respectively.

5.4-2 Show that $\partial\mathbf{P}/\partial t$ has the dimensions of current density.

5.6-1 Show that the $\mathbf{E}$ produced by Q, ρ_{ps1}, and ρ_{ps2} of Example 5.4 is the same as that obtained in Example 5.3.

5.6-2 Show that the $\mathbf{E}$ produced by ρ_{ps1} and ρ_{ps2} is zero for $r < a$ and $r > b$ and is as pictured in Fig. 5.10.

5.6-3 Find the $\mathbf{E}$ and $\mathbf{D}$ produced by the two infinite, parallel charged sheets shown in Fig. 3.4 when there is a dielectric having permittivity ϵ between the sheets. Find the polarization $\mathbf{P}$ of the dielectric and the resulting ρ_{ps} at the surfaces of the dielectric. Explain in terms of ρ_{ps} why the $\mathbf{E}$ field between the sheets is less when the dielectric is present than when it is not.

5.6-4 Assume that a volume free-charge density given by $\rho = \rho_0(r/r_0)^2$ extending from $r = 0$ to $r = r_0$, with $r_0 < a$, replaces Q in Fig. 5.9. Assume that this free charge is fixed in position and is therefore unaffected by **E**. Find **D** and **E** everywhere.

5.6-5 From the **E** of Prob. 5.6-4 find the potential difference between a point at $r = a$ and a point at $r = b$. If $\epsilon > \epsilon_0$, is this potential difference greater or smaller than it would be if $\epsilon = \epsilon_0$?

5.6-6 When **E** is high enough, air will ionize and break down. How does the presence of the dielectric in Prob. 5.6-5 affect breakdown in the region $r_0 < r < a$? At breakdown, would the potential difference between points r_0 and b be greater or smaller when the dielectric is present than when it is not present?

5.7-1 A thin spherical conducting shell is given a net charge Q. Where is this Q found in the shell? Show that the **E** and **D** fields are zero in the region $r < a$, where a is the radius of the inner wall of the shell.

5.7-2 Assuming that there are 8.5×10^{22} electrons/cm^3 contributing to the ρ_c in Eq. (5.53), calculate ν_c based on the dc value of σ for copper from Table 5.2.

5.10-1 Write out the second-order terms in the expression for I_z in Eq. (5.66) and show that $\lim_{\substack{\Delta x \to 0 \\ \Delta y \to 0}}$ (second-order terms)$/\Delta x\, \Delta y = 0$.

5.10-2 In a certain infinitely long cylindrical rod of magnetic material, $\mathbf{M} = M_0(r/a)\hat{\boldsymbol{\varphi}}$. The rod radius is a. Solve for $\mathbf{J}_m$. Find B_φ everywhere.

5.10-3 Show explicitly that $J_{mx} = (\nabla \times \mathbf{M})_x$.

5.10-4 The **BH** curve for a ferromagnetic material is given by the analytic equation $\mathbf{B} = \mu_0 H^2 \mathbf{H}$. What are **M**, μ, and χ_m?

5.11-1 A spherical ball of magnetic material is magnetized such that $\mathbf{M} = M_0 r\hat{\mathbf{r}}$. The ball radius is a, and the ball is isolated in free space. Solve for ρ_m. Find a suitable scalar magnetic function Φ_m in the ball, and then solve for **H** and **B**.

5.12-1 Polarization and magnetization effects are accounted for in Eqs. (5.85) and (5.86) by means of ϵ and μ in Eqs. (5.87) and (5.88). Write out the two curl equations, Eqs. (5.85) and (5.86), in terms of the field vectors **E** and **B**, the polarization vector **P**, and the magnetization vector **M**.

5.13-1 Derive the boundary conditions on the normal components of **B** by starting with Eq. (5.90).

5.13-2 Assume that region 1 in Fig. 5.20 is free space. Show that $\hat{\mathbf{n}}_2 \cdot (\mathbf{E}_1 - \mathbf{E}_2) = \hat{\mathbf{n}}_2 \cdot (\mathbf{P}_2/\epsilon_0)$ at the boundary. This shows that the discontinuity in **E** is caused by **P**.

5.13-3 Assume that region 1 in Fig. 5.20 is free space. Show that $\hat{\mathbf{n}}_2 \cdot (\mathbf{H}_1 - \mathbf{H}_2) = \hat{\mathbf{n}}_2 \cdot \mathbf{M}_2$ at the boundary. This shows that the discontinuity in **H** is caused by **M**.

5.13-4 Starting with Eq. (5.85), derive the boundary conditions on the tangential components of **E**.

5.13-5 Let region 1 be free space, where $z > 0$, and region 2 be dielectric with $\epsilon_2 = 2\epsilon_0$, where $z < 0$. At $z = 0$, $\rho_s = 0.2$ coul/m^2. If $D_1 = 3x\hat{\mathbf{x}} + 4y^2\hat{\mathbf{y}} + 3\hat{\mathbf{z}}$ and $H_2 = 2\hat{\mathbf{x}} + 5y^3\hat{\mathbf{y}} + 5\hat{\mathbf{z}}$, find $\mathbf{E}_2$, $\mathbf{D}_2$, $\mathbf{B}_2$, $\mathbf{E}_1$, $\mathbf{B}_1$, and $\mathbf{H}_1$ at the boundary.

5.13-6 Explain why Eq. (5.104) does not require that $\mathbf{E}_1 = \mathbf{E}_2$.

5.13-7 A surface current density $\mathbf{J} = J_0\hat{\mathbf{x}}$ amp/m exists in the $z = 0$ plane. Region 1, with μ_1, is located in the space $z > 0$, and region 2, with μ_2, is located in the space

$z < 0$. The **H** field in region 1 is $\mathbf{H}_1 = H_{1x}\hat{\mathbf{x}} + H_{1y}\hat{\mathbf{y}} + H_{1z}\hat{\mathbf{z}}$. Solve for $\mathbf{H}_2$ at the boundary $z = 0$.

5.13-8 Show that the **E** and **D** fields obtained in Example 5.3 satisfy the proper boundary conditions at the boundaries of the dielectric shell.

5.13-9 Show for the boundary of Example 5.8 that if the tangential components of **E** are continuous, it is necessary that $E_{2x} = E_{1x}$ and $E_{2z} = E_{1z}$. *Hint:* The tangential $\mathbf{E}_2$ is $E_{2x}\hat{\mathbf{x}} + E_{2z}\hat{\mathbf{z}}$, and $\hat{\mathbf{x}}$ and $\hat{\mathbf{z}}$ are orthogonal.

5.14-1 Derive Eq. (5.117) by following the method suggested in Sec. 5.14.

5.14-2 Derive Eq. (5.118) by starting with Eq. (4.13) and using $\nabla \cdot \mathbf{D} = \rho$ and $\mathbf{E} = -\nabla\Phi$, and follow the same general procedure used to derive Eq. (4.15).

5.14-3 A cube of dielectric material 10 cm on a side is used to store 10^{-7} joule of time-average electric energy. The electric fields in the material are time varying at 10 GHz. The dielectric constant for the material is $\epsilon_1 = 4.0$ and $\epsilon_{2b}/\epsilon_1 = 0.002$, and the conductivity is $\sigma = 10^{-5}$ mhos/m. Determine the power consumed by the material and determine Q.

CHAPTER

6

the wave equation and planewave propagation

6.1 INTRODUCTION

The complete set of Maxwell's equations presented in Sec. 5.12 forms the basis for an analysis of the nature of electric and magnetic fields under time-varying conditions. Historically, it was immediately seen that waves of electric and magnetic field were possible solutions to Maxwell's equations, and Maxwell's equations were used to predict the existence of electromagnetic radiation at all frequencies. Hertz then conducted a series of dramatic experiments which proved that electromagnetic waves exist in the radio-frequency spectrum. Hertz's experiments were associated with the observation of radiation, reflection, and standing-wave effects leading to a measurement of wavelength. Since it was already realized that light was a wave phenomenon, light waves were recognized as being electromagnetic waves of very short wavelength. The concepts of electromagnetic fields and waves were thus shown to hold at all frequencies, and Maxwell's equations were destined to become one of the most important sets of physical laws.

In this chapter we start with an introduction to electromagnetic wave propagation and proceed to a formal development of the wave equations.

Planewaves are then described in a series of applications. Later chapters explore a wide variety of electromagnetic field and wave phenomena.

6.2 ONE-DIMENSIONAL ELECTROMAGNETIC PLANEWAVES

Before considering the wave equation in general, we introduce in this section the simple one-dimensional wave solution for an electromagnetic wave in a source-free medium with constant μ and ϵ. The basic wave-type solution is introduced, and the important wave parameters are discussed.

The two curl equations for a source-free medium are

$$\nabla \times \mathbf{H} = \epsilon \frac{\partial \mathbf{E}}{\partial t}$$

$$\nabla \times \mathbf{E} = -\mu \frac{\partial \mathbf{H}}{\partial t}$$

A differential equation for the electric field $\mathbf{E}$ may be obtained by combining these two equations. The curl of the second equation is taken, and the first equation is then used to obtain

$$\nabla \times (\nabla \times \mathbf{E}) = -\frac{\partial}{\partial t}\left(\mu\epsilon \frac{\partial \mathbf{E}}{\partial t}\right) = -\mu\epsilon \frac{\partial^2 \mathbf{E}}{\partial t^2}$$

$$\left(\nabla \times \nabla \times + \mu\epsilon \frac{\partial^2}{\partial t^2}\right) \mathbf{E} = 0 \tag{6.1}$$

The first term in Eq. (6.1) may be expanded as

$$\nabla \times (\nabla \times \mathbf{E}) = \nabla(\nabla \cdot \mathbf{E}) - \nabla^2 \mathbf{E}$$

Since $\nabla \cdot \mathbf{E} = 0$ in a source-free medium where $\rho = 0$, Eq. (6.1) may be written as

$$\left(\nabla^2 - \mu\epsilon \frac{\partial^2}{\partial t^2}\right) \mathbf{E} = 0 \tag{6.2}$$

Equation (6.1) or (6.2) is called the *homogeneous electromagnetic wave equation* for $\mathbf{E}$.

The solution of this equation is greatly simplified for the one-dimensional case, where only variations in z are present. The operator ∇^2 then reduces to $\partial^2/\partial z^2$, and Eq. (6.2) becomes

$$\left(\frac{\partial^2}{\partial z^2} - \mu\epsilon\,\frac{\partial^2}{\partial t^2}\right)\mathbf{E}(z,t) = 0$$

If we further restrict our attention to sinusoidal variations of $\mathbf{E}$, then

$$\mathbf{E}(z,t) \Rightarrow \operatorname{Re}\,[\mathbf{E}(z)e^{j\omega t}]$$

where the spatial vector $\mathbf{E}(z)$ is a complex phasor quantity. The $e^{j\omega t}$ time factor will apply to all electric and magnetic field vectors and will not be written. For the exponential time dependence, $\partial/\partial t$ is replaced by $j\omega$, and the wave equation becomes

$$\left(\frac{\partial^2}{\partial z^2} + \omega^2\mu\epsilon\right)\mathbf{E}(z) = 0$$

Inspection of this equation shows two possible solutions to be

$$\mathbf{E}(z) = \mathbf{E}_0 e^{\pm jkz}$$

where $\mathbf{E}_0$ is a constant vector and k is a constant called the *propagation constant.* The wave equation reduces to

$$(-k^2 + \omega^2\mu\epsilon)\mathbf{E}_0 = 0 \tag{6.3}$$

and Eq. (6.2) has been reduced to the simple algebraic equation (6.3). For a nonzero electric field vector $\mathbf{E}_0$, the only nontrivial solution for Eq. (6.3) is

$$k^2 = \omega^2\mu\epsilon$$

The final solution for $\mathbf{E}(z,t)$ is

$$\mathbf{E}(z,t) = \operatorname{Re}\,(\mathbf{E}_0 e^{j(\omega t \pm kz)}) \tag{6.4}$$

with $k = \omega\sqrt{\mu\epsilon}$. If $\mathbf{E}_0 = |\mathbf{E}_0|e^{j\phi}$, where $|\mathbf{E}_0|$ is the magnitude of $\mathbf{E}_0$ and a real vector, then

$$\mathbf{E}(z,t) = |\mathbf{E}_0| \cos\,(\omega t \pm kz + \phi) \tag{6.5}$$

The solutions expressed in Eqs. (6.4) and (6.5) are called *wave solutions* and describe an electric field vector which propagates in free space as a traveling wave in the $-z$ or $+z$ direction. It is seen from Eq. (6.5) that at the $z = 0$ plane the electric field vector oscillates at a frequency ω. At $t = 0$ the electric field vector variation with z, given in Eq. (6.5), is the cosine wave shown in Fig. 6.1 for $\phi = 0$. The only way the electric field vector can oscillate in the $z = 0$ plane at frequency ω and at the same

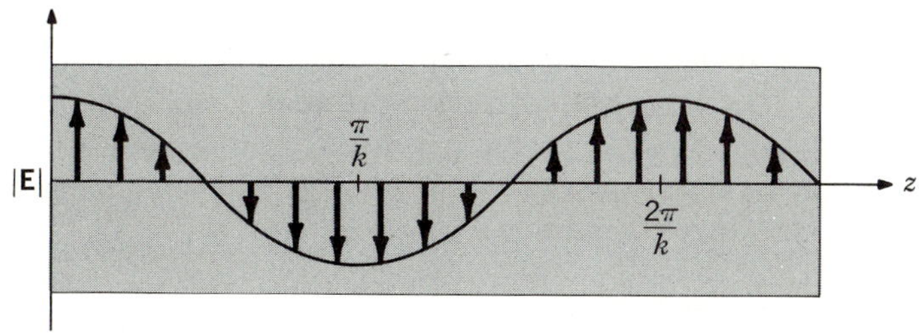

Fig. 6.1 A photograph of $|\mathbf{E}|$ at $t = 0$ in a traveling electromagnetic wave.

time maintain a sinusoidal z variation is to move in the $-z$ or $+z$ direction such that one cycle of the sine wave passes the $z = 0$ plane in one cycle of the time variation. The time it takes the wave to move 1 wavelength is $t = \lambda/v_p$, where v_p is the wave velocity and λ is the wavelength. The period of one cycle is $t = 1/f = 2\pi/\omega$. These two times are set equal in order to find the required wave velocity,

$$v_p = \pm\omega\frac{\lambda}{2\pi}$$

The wavelength is unknown, but it may be related to the known propagation constant k by reference to Fig. 6.1, where it is seen that the distance from crest to crest (defined as λ) is $2\pi/k$. The wave velocity may thus be written in terms of k as

$$v_p = \pm\frac{\omega}{k} \tag{6.6}$$

From Eq. (6.6) and the solution for k obtained from the wave equations, the velocity v_p may be evaluated in terms of the constants μ and ϵ,

$$|v_p| = \frac{1}{\sqrt{\mu\epsilon}}$$

In free space,

$$|v_p| = 3 \times 10^8 \text{ m/sec}$$

The wave velocity v_p is equal to the velocity of light, and thus Maxwell's equations predict waves of electric field which travel at the velocity of light.

Equation (6.6) may be obtained in a more direct way by defining the wave velocity v_p as the velocity of a point of constant phase on the **E** vector. We thus seek a relation between z and t which defines a point of constant phase on the wave. From Eq. (6.4), the phase θ of the electric field vector is $\theta = \omega t \pm kz + \phi$, and for θ to remain constant, $d\theta$ must be zero for changes in t and z,

$$\begin{aligned} d\theta &= \omega\, dt \pm k\, dz \\ &= 0 \end{aligned}$$

This expression is satisfied for

$$\frac{dz}{dt} = \pm \frac{\omega}{k}$$

which is Eq. (6.6) for $v_p \equiv dz/dt$. Note that for a phase $\omega t + kz$ the wave travels in the $-z$ direction; for $\omega t - kz$ the wave travels in the $+z$ direction. Since the surface of constant phase is a constant z plane, the wave described in this section is called a *planewave.* The direction of propagation is perpendicular to the surface of constant phase.

A magnetic field is present and is associated with the electric field through Maxwell's equations. For simplicity, $\mathbf{E}_0$ is aligned with $\hat{\mathbf{x}}$, and the $\nabla \times \mathbf{H}$ equation reduces to

$$-\frac{\partial H_y}{\partial z} = \epsilon j \omega E_x$$

Replacing $\partial/\partial z$ by $\pm jk$ in accordance with Eq. (6.4) gives

$$\begin{aligned} H_y &= \mp \epsilon \frac{\omega}{k} E_x \\ &= \mp \sqrt{\frac{\epsilon}{\mu}}\, E_x \end{aligned} \tag{6.7}$$

The associated magnetic field is perpendicular to the electric field and is in phase, as illustrated in Fig. 6.2. Note the interesting result that the magnetic field is a constant times the electric field everywhere in space and time. The magnetic fields differ in sign for the $+z$ and $-z$ traveling waves.

Several important consequences relating to circuit theory and electronics result from the wave nature of electric and magnetic fields. For example, we are accustomed to assuming that the current in a circuit is

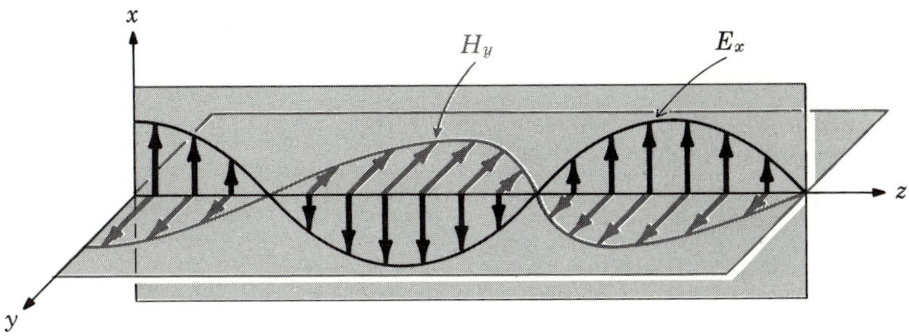

Fig. 6.2 **E** and **H** vectors in an electromagnetic wave traveling in the $+z$ direction.

in time phase everywhere in the circuit. The results just presented concerning the finite propagation velocity of electric and magnetic fields indicate that there is a phase retardation from one point to another in any circuit. In practical-sized circuits at radio frequencies the phase retardation is small compared with the *RF* phase. This phase-retardation process is responsible for the breakdown of conventional circuit techniques at frequencies of television carrier frequencies and above.

Example 6.1 Planewave relations If the electric field of a planewave is known, much may be learned about the wave and the medium in which it is propagating. When the electric field is

$$\mathbf{E}(z,t) = 10\hat{\mathbf{y}} \cos (10^9 t + 30z)$$

the electric field amplitude is 10 volts/m, $\omega = 10^9$, and $k = 30$. Since the phase is of the form $\omega t + kz$, the wave travels in the $-z$ direction. $\mathbf{H}(z,t)$ may be found from the $\nabla \times \mathbf{H}$ equation,

$$\nabla \times \mathbf{H} = \epsilon \frac{\partial \mathbf{E}(z,t)}{\partial t}$$

$$\frac{\partial H_x}{\partial z} = -\epsilon 10^{10} \sin (10^9 t + 30z)$$

$$\mathbf{H}(z,t) = \epsilon \frac{10^9}{3} \hat{\mathbf{x}} \cos (10^9 t + 30z)$$

The phase velocity is obtained from Eq. (6.6), where the minus sign goes with the positive kz term; thus

$$v_p = -\frac{10^9}{30}$$

$$= -\tfrac{1}{3} \times 10^8$$

Once the phase velocity is known, $\mu\epsilon$ may be determined using

$$
\begin{aligned}
|v_p| &= \frac{1}{\sqrt{\mu\epsilon}} \\
\mu\epsilon &= \frac{1}{|v_p|^2} \\
&= 9 \times 10^{-16}
\end{aligned}
$$

For a medium with $\mu = \mu_0$,

$$
\begin{aligned}
\epsilon &= \frac{9}{4\pi} \times 10^{-9} \\
\frac{\epsilon}{\epsilon_0} &= 81
\end{aligned}
$$

6.3 INHOMOGENEOUS WAVE EQUATIONS FOR THE FIELDS

Starting with Maxwell's equations in material media with ρ and $\mathbf{J}$ present, general equations may be derived which describe the wave-propagation properties of the electric and magnetic fields. These equations are called the inhomogeneous wave equations for the fields. The electric and magnetic field vectors are generated and interrelated by the following basic field equations from Chap. 5:

$$\nabla \times \mathbf{E} = -\frac{\partial \mathbf{B}}{\partial t} \tag{5.85}$$

$$\nabla \times \mathbf{H} = \mathbf{J} + \frac{\partial \mathbf{D}}{\partial t} \tag{5.86}$$

$$\mathbf{D} = \epsilon \mathbf{E} \tag{5.87}$$

$$\mathbf{B} = \mu \mathbf{H} \tag{5.88}$$

$$\nabla \cdot \mathbf{D} = \rho \tag{5.89}$$

$$\nabla \cdot \mathbf{B} = 0 \tag{5.90}$$

There are four field vectors and two source variables in this set of six equations. The six equations are usually reduced to four by replacing the $\mathbf{B}$ and $\mathbf{D}$ vectors by $\mu\mathbf{H}$ and $\epsilon\mathbf{E}$. The two curl equations then may be used to solve for $\mathbf{E}$ or $\mathbf{H}$ in terms of $\mathbf{J}$. Remember that the magnetization current is included in the $\mathbf{H}$ vector, and the polarization current is included in the $\mathbf{D}$ vector; thus the current-density vector $\mathbf{J}$ in Eq. (5.86) is the free-charge and conduction current in the medium. The polarization charge density ρ_p is included in the **D** vector in Eq. (5.89); thus the charge density ρ in Eq. (5.89) is the free-charge and conduction-charge density in the medium.

The **B** and **D** vectors are eliminated in Eqs. (5.85) and (5.86) by means of Eqs. (5.87) and (5.88). The field equations then become

$$\nabla \times \mathbf{E} = -\mu \frac{\partial \mathbf{H}}{\partial t} \tag{6.8}$$

$$\nabla \times \mathbf{H} = \mathbf{J} + \epsilon \frac{\partial \mathbf{E}}{\partial t} \tag{6.9}$$

$$\nabla \cdot \mathbf{E} = \frac{\rho}{\epsilon} \tag{6.10}$$

$$\nabla \cdot \mathbf{H} = 0 \tag{6.11}$$

The two unknowns **E** and **H** may be obtained from a simultaneous solution of Eqs. (6.8) and (6.9). It is easily seen that an equation involving **E** alone may be obtained by taking the curl of Eq. (6.8) and substituting Eq. (6.9),

$$\nabla \times \nabla \times \mathbf{E} = -\mu \frac{\partial}{\partial t}\left(\mathbf{J} + \epsilon \frac{\partial \mathbf{E}}{\partial t}\right)$$

The double curl operation on the left-hand side of this equation may be written in a more convenient form by reference to the appropriate identity; thus

$$\nabla(\nabla \cdot \mathbf{E}) - \nabla^2 \mathbf{E} = -\mu \frac{\partial \mathbf{J}}{\partial t} - \mu\epsilon \frac{\partial^2 \mathbf{E}}{\partial t^2}$$

Equation (6.10) is used to eliminate $\nabla \cdot \mathbf{E}$, and by regrouping terms we obtain

$$\left(\nabla^2 - \mu\epsilon \frac{\partial^2}{\partial t^2}\right) \mathbf{E} = \mu \frac{\partial \mathbf{J}}{\partial t} + \nabla \frac{\rho}{\epsilon} \tag{6.12}$$

Equation (6.12) is called the *inhomogeneous wave equation* for the electric field vector **E**. Note that in a source-free medium where $\rho = \mathbf{J} = 0$, the equation becomes homogeneous; i.e., the right-hand side is zero [see Eq. (6.2)]. Once the coordinate system is chosen for any specific problem, the gradient and laplacian operators may be written in terms of partial derivatives, and a partial-differential equation results. The solution of this partial-differential equation gives the electric field vector **E** in terms of the sources **J** and ρ.

Once **E** has been established from the solution of Eq. (6.12), the corresponding **H** vector may be obtained from either Eq. (6.8) or Eq. (6.9). Alternately, a wave equation for **H** may be obtained from the two equations and solved independently. Taking the curl of Eq. (6.9) and substituting in Eq. (6.8) gives

$$\nabla \times \nabla \times \mathbf{H} = \nabla \times \mathbf{J} - \mu\epsilon \frac{\partial^2 \mathbf{H}}{\partial t^2}$$

The left-hand side of this equation may be expanded to yield

$$\nabla(\nabla \cdot \mathbf{H}) - \nabla^2 \mathbf{H} = \nabla \times \mathbf{J} - \mu\epsilon \frac{\partial^2 \mathbf{H}}{\partial t^2}$$

but since $\nabla \cdot \mathbf{H} = 0$, from Eq. (6.11), we obtain

$$\left(\nabla^2 - \mu\epsilon \frac{\partial^2}{\partial t^2}\right) \mathbf{H} = -\nabla \times \mathbf{J} \qquad (6.13)$$

which is the inhomogeneous wave equation for **H**. Notice that the homogeneous wave equation for **H** is identical to the homogeneous wave equation for **E**, and thus the solutions are of the same form. This was seen in Sec. 6.2, where the **E** and **H** vectors were related by a constant.

Equations (6.12) and (6.13) are basic to the solution of electromagnetic wave problems. Several types of problems are encountered. First, it is often necessary to find the **E** and **H** vectors in free space where **J** and ρ are zero. These solutions are found from the homogeneous wave equations. Second, a class of problems arises where **J** and ρ are given source functions, and the electric and magnetic fields are to be determined in terms of these known source functions. Solutions are found from the inhomogeneous wave equations. A third class of problems involves the interaction effects between the sources of field, **J** and ρ, and the electric and magnetic fields themselves. Auxiliary equations are required which give **J** and ρ induced by the electric and magnetic fields. These equations are combined with the inhomogeneous wave equations, and a simultaneous solution is required.

6.4 POTENTIAL FUNCTIONS

In Sec. 6.3 the wave equations for the fields **E** and **H** were developed in terms of the sources ρ and **J**. It is often easier in practice to solve for the potential functions Φ and **A** first and then determine the fields **E** and **H** by the appropriate differentiation process.

In Sec. 2.3 it was demonstrated that the electric field is easily obtained from the scalar potential function Φ, as given by Eqs. (2.8) and (2.18) (with ϵ_0 replaced by ϵ),

$$\mathbf{E} = -\nabla\Phi \tag{2.8}$$

$$\Phi = \int \frac{dQ}{4\pi\epsilon R}$$

$$= \int_V \frac{\rho(\mathbf{r}')}{4\pi\epsilon R}\, dV' \tag{2.18}$$

The scalar function Φ is determined from an integral involving the source charges directly. The magnetic analog of these relations was considered in Sec. 2.6. Equations (2.54) and (2.55) illustrated how the magnetic field is obtained from a magnetic vector potential **A** (with μ_0 replaced by μ),

$$\mathbf{B} = \nabla \times \mathbf{A} \tag{2.54}$$

$$\mathbf{A} = \int_V \frac{\mu \mathbf{J}(\mathbf{r}')}{4\pi R}\, dV' \tag{2.55}$$

The magnetic and scalar potentials as defined in Chap. 2 apply only for the static case. It is now necessary in the time-varying case to consider a time-varying form of the scalar and magnetic vector potentials. The solutions for **E** and Φ, or **B** and **A**, were obtained for the static case by integrating Coulomb's law or the Biot-Savart law. In the time-varying case it is not possible to obtain Φ and **A** by this integration technique, since Coulomb's law and the Biot-Savart law are only static laws. It is necessary to obtain the potential functions from Maxwell's equations. The first step in such a solution is a determination of the wave equations for Φ and **A**.

It is first necessary to reexamine Eqs. (2.8) and (2.54) to see if they are appropriate for the time-varying case. Inserting Eq. (2.54) into Eq. (5.90) gives

$$\begin{aligned}\nabla \cdot \mathbf{B} &= \nabla \cdot (\nabla \times \mathbf{A})\\ &\equiv 0\end{aligned}$$

and thus Eq. (2.54) is consistent with Eq. (5.90). Equation (2.8), however, is a consequence of the relation $\nabla \times \mathbf{E} = 0$ and is thus not valid in the time-varying case:

$$\nabla \times \mathbf{E} = -\frac{\partial \mathbf{B}}{\partial t}$$

$$\begin{aligned}\nabla \times (-\nabla\Phi) &\equiv 0\\ &\neq -\frac{\partial \mathbf{B}}{\partial t}\end{aligned}$$

Since the curl of the gradient of a function is identically zero, we see that Eq. (2.8) requires that $\partial\mathbf{B}/\partial t$ be zero, which is true only in the static case. We are thus confronted with the problem of constructing a new relationship between **E** and the potential functions. Since Eq. (2.54) is valid, we may use it in Eq. (5.85) to obtain

$$\nabla \times \mathbf{E} = -\frac{\partial}{\partial t}(\nabla \times \mathbf{A})$$

The terms may be regrouped into an equation very similar to the equation used in obtaining Eq. (2.8),

$$\nabla \times \left(\mathbf{E} + \frac{\partial \mathbf{A}}{\partial t}\right) = 0$$

This equation states that the curl of a vector is zero; thus the vector may be derived from the gradient of a scalar,

$$\mathbf{E} + \frac{\partial \mathbf{A}}{\partial t} = -\nabla\Phi$$

where Φ is now a new scalar potential function. The electric field is thus seen to be related to both the magnetic potential and the new scalar potential,

$$\mathbf{E} = -\nabla\Phi - \frac{\partial \mathbf{A}}{\partial t} \tag{6.14}$$

★6.5 Potential-function Wave Equations

Equations (5.90) and (5.85) have been used in deriving Eqs. (2.54) and (6.14) from the four basic field equations, Eqs. (5.85) to (5.90). It is now necessary to solve independently for Φ and **A**, and we do so by using Eqs. (5.86) and (5.89). From these equations two explicit differential equations are developed from which solutions for Φ and **A** may be obtained. These equations are called the *wave equations for the potential functions.*

The differential equation for **A** is obtained from Eq. (6.9), written in the form

$$\nabla \times \mathbf{B} = \mu\mathbf{J} + \mu\epsilon\frac{\partial \mathbf{E}}{\partial t} \tag{6.15}$$

Equations (2.54) and (6.14) are now employed in Eq. (6.15) to yield an expression containing the potential functions and sources only,

$$\nabla \times \nabla \times \mathbf{A} = \mu\mathbf{J} + \mu\epsilon\frac{\partial}{\partial t}\left(-\nabla\Phi - \frac{\partial \mathbf{A}}{\partial t}\right)$$

The left-hand side of this equation may be expanded with a vector identity to yield

$$\nabla(\nabla \cdot \mathbf{A}) - \nabla^2\mathbf{A} = \mu\mathbf{J} - \nabla\left(\mu\epsilon \frac{\partial \Phi}{\partial t}\right) - \mu\epsilon \frac{\partial^2 \mathbf{A}}{\partial t^2}$$

This equation may now be grouped into a form reminiscent of the field wave equations,

$$\left(\nabla^2 - \mu\epsilon \frac{\partial^2}{\partial t^2}\right)\mathbf{A} = -\mu\mathbf{J} + \nabla\left(\nabla \cdot \mathbf{A} + \mu\epsilon \frac{\partial \Phi}{\partial t}\right) \tag{6.16}$$

We see that a wave equation has been obtained for **A** in which the current density **J** appears directly in undifferentiated form as a source term. The difficulty with Eq. (6.16) is the second term on the right-hand side. Fortunately, in many cases of practical interest, this term is zero, in which case the wave equation for **A** becomes

$$\left(\nabla^2 - \mu\epsilon \frac{\partial^2}{\partial t^2}\right)\mathbf{A} = -\mu\mathbf{J} \tag{6.17}$$

The consequences of dropping the last term in Eq. (6.16) to obtain Eq. (6.17) are discussed later in this section.

The corresponding inhomogeneous wave equation for the scalar potential function Φ is found from Eq. (6.10). Equation (6.10) is combined with Eq. (6.14) to obtain

$$\nabla \cdot \left(-\nabla\Phi - \frac{\partial \mathbf{A}}{\partial t}\right) = \frac{\rho}{\epsilon}$$

$$\nabla^2\Phi = -\frac{\rho}{\epsilon} - \frac{\partial}{\partial t}(\nabla \cdot \mathbf{A})$$

Note that this equation can be put in the same form as Eq. (6.16) by merely adding the term $-\mu\epsilon\, \partial^2\Phi/\partial t^2$ to both sides,

$$\nabla^2\Phi - \mu\epsilon \frac{\partial^2 \Phi}{\partial t^2} = -\frac{\rho}{\epsilon} - \frac{\partial}{\partial t}(\nabla \cdot \mathbf{A}) - \mu\epsilon \frac{\partial^2 \Phi}{\partial t^2}$$

The terms may be appropriately grouped to yield a wave equation for Φ,

$$\left(\nabla^2 - \mu\epsilon \frac{\partial^2}{\partial t^2}\right)\Phi = -\frac{\rho}{\epsilon} - \frac{\partial}{\partial t}\left(\nabla \cdot \mathbf{A} + \mu\epsilon \frac{\partial \Phi}{\partial t}\right) \tag{6.18}$$

Under circumstances where the second term on the right-hand side of Eq. (6.18) is zero, the wave equation for Φ assumes the simple form

$$\left(\nabla^2 - \mu\epsilon \frac{\partial^2}{\partial t^2}\right)\Phi = -\frac{\rho}{\epsilon} \tag{6.19}$$

The Lorentz Condition

The simplified potential-function wave equations, Eqs. (6.17) and (6.19), may be obtained by stipulating that

$$\nabla \cdot \mathbf{A} + \mu\epsilon \frac{\partial \Phi}{\partial t} = \text{constant} \tag{6.20}$$

This equation may be regarded as the defining equation for $\nabla \cdot \mathbf{A}$. The divergence and curl of a vector are independent; thus **A** is not uniquely defined until both $\nabla \times \mathbf{A}$ and $\nabla \cdot \mathbf{A}$ have been defined. This is accomplished by Eqs. (2.54) and (6.20). Other defining equations for $\nabla \cdot \mathbf{A}$ are possible, and are better for certain types of problems. Equation (6.20) is called the *Lorentz condition* when the constant is zero. One might well ask what the consequences are of imposing the Lorentz condition. **A** is related to the current density **J**, and Φ is related to the charge density ρ, as in the static case. Thus Eq. (6.20) gives a relationship between **J** and ρ, and it may be shown that the Lorentz condition is a statement of the time-varying current-continuity equation, Eq. (3.22).

The Lorentz condition is used for problems where the time-varying continuity equation applies. In static problems and in regions where $\rho = 0$, the current is not described by Eq. (3.22), but rather by the expression $\nabla \cdot \mathbf{J} = 0$. In this case the Lorentz condition would not be appropriate; the condition $\nabla \cdot \mathbf{A} = 0$ is appropriate. The differential equation for Φ, Eq. (6.18), reduces to Poisson's equation, Eq. (3.7), for a dielectric medium,

$$\bigstar \quad \nabla^2\Phi = -\frac{\rho}{\epsilon}$$

6.6 RETARDED POTENTIALS

Before the fields may be determined from the potential functions by means of Eqs. (2.54) and (6.14), it is necessary to construct integral expressions for the potential functions analogous to those of Eqs. (2.18) and (2.55). Equations (2.18) and (2.55) were obtained from an integration of the static Coulomb law and Biot-Savart law, respectively.

The correct time-varying solutions for **A** and Φ may be constructed by reexamining Coulomb's law and the Biot-Savart law, taking into account the fact that fields travel at a finite velocity v_p. If a source-current density $\mathbf{J}(\mathbf{r}',t')$ exists at time t', it takes a time $\tau = R/v_p$ for the fields generated by $\mathbf{J}(\mathbf{r}',t')$ to reach the field point **r** at the field-point time t. This time lapse is called the *time-retardation phenomenon* and is an obvious consequence of the finite wave-propagation velocity v_p. In the derivation of the static potential **A** from the Biot-Savart law, it was assumed that the field $\mathbf{B}(\mathbf{r},t)$ appeared instantaneously at the field point when $\mathbf{J}(\mathbf{r}',t')$ was present at the source point; that is, it was assumed that $t = t'$. An integral equation for $\mathbf{A}$ in the time-varying case may be constructed from the Biot-Savart law if we take into account the time-retardation effect. The static Biot-Savart law for a time-varying source current $\mathbf{J}(\mathbf{r}')e^{j\omega t'}$ is

$$d\mathbf{B}(\mathbf{r},t) = \frac{\mu}{4\pi}\frac{\mathbf{J}(\mathbf{r}')e^{j\omega t'} \times \hat{\mathbf{R}}}{R^2}\,dV' \tag{6.21}$$

The source time t' must precede the field-point time t at which the field $d\mathbf{B}$ is observed by an amount $\tau = R/v_p$ for Eq. (6.21) to give the field $d\mathbf{B}$ at the time t. Thus we set $t' = t - R/v_p$, and Eq. (6.21) becomes

$$\begin{aligned} d\mathbf{B}(\mathbf{r},t) &= \frac{\mu}{4\pi}\frac{\mathbf{J}(\mathbf{r}') \times \hat{\mathbf{R}}}{R^2}\,dV'\,e^{j\omega(t-R/v_p)} \\ &= \frac{\mu}{4\pi}\frac{\mathbf{J}(\mathbf{r}') \times \hat{\mathbf{R}}}{R^2}\,dV'\,e^{j(\omega t-kR)} \end{aligned} \tag{6.22}$$

where $k = \omega/v_p$, as defined previously. For a time-varying vector with time dependence $e^{j\omega t}$, the additional e^{-jkR} factor takes into account the finite propagation velocity of the field vector from the source point to the field point over the distance R. Equation (6.22) may be integrated, and by following the procedure of Sec. 2.6, we obtain the final vector potential equation,

$$\mathbf{A} = \frac{\mu}{4\pi}\int_V \frac{\mathbf{J}(\mathbf{r}')e^{j(\omega t-kR)}}{R}\,dV' \tag{6.23}$$

An exactly analogous procedure may be carried out, starting with Coulomb's law, to obtain the scalar potential function for a time-varying charge density,

$$\Phi = \frac{1}{4\pi\epsilon}\int_V \frac{\rho(\mathbf{r}')e^{j(\omega t-kR)}}{R}\,dV' \tag{6.24}$$

These two expressions give the general time-varying vector and scalar potential functions. Given any sinusoidal time-varying current or charge density, the vector and scalar potential functions are found from Eqs. (6.23) and (6.24), and the electric and magnetic fields are then found from Eqs. (2.54) and (6.14).

★Retarded Potentials as Solutions to the Potential Wave Equations

Now that solutions for the retarded-potential functions have been constructed by inserting the time-retardation factor into the static formulation, it is quite easy to verify the solutions by inserting them into the potential-function wave equations. If they satisfy the wave equations, then they are indeed valid solutions. Consider the scalar retarded-potential function given by Eq. (6.24), with the time factor not written,

$$\Phi = \frac{1}{4\pi\epsilon}\int_V \rho(\mathbf{r}')\,\frac{e^{-jkR}}{R}\,dV'$$

together with the inhomogeneous wave equation for Φ,

$$\left(\nabla^2 - \mu\epsilon\frac{\partial^2}{\partial t^2}\right)\Phi = -\frac{\rho(\mathbf{r})}{\epsilon} \tag{6.19}$$

Equation (6.19) takes the form

$$(\nabla^2 + k^2)\Phi = -\frac{\rho(\mathbf{r})}{\epsilon}$$

for an $e^{j\omega t}$ time variation, since $\partial^2/\partial t^2 = -\omega^2$ and $\omega^2\mu\epsilon = k^2$. The retarded-potential function is inserted into the wave equation in order to determine if it is a solution,

$$\frac{1}{4\pi\epsilon}\int_V \rho(\mathbf{r}')(\nabla^2 + k^2)\left(\frac{e^{-jkR}}{R}\right)dV' = -\frac{\rho(\mathbf{r})}{\epsilon} \tag{6.25}$$

Note that we must carefully keep track of the coordinates for ρ. In the source-volume integral the coordinates of ρ are obviously the primed source coordinates. The wave equation is a point relation which applies at the field point; thus $\rho(\mathbf{r})$ appears on the right-hand side of Eq. (6.25). The laplacian operator ∇^2 indicated in the integrand of Eq. (6.25) may be evaluated by direct expansion to yield

$$\nabla^2\left(\frac{e^{-jkR}}{R}\right) = e^{-jkR}\,\nabla^2\left(\frac{1}{R}\right) - k^2\,\frac{e^{-jkR}}{R} \tag{6.26}$$

and this evaluation is left as a problem. By using Eqs. (6.26) and (1.127) in Eq. (6.25), we obtain

$$\frac{1}{4\pi\epsilon}\int_V \rho(\mathbf{r}')e^{-jkR}\,[-4\pi\delta(R)]\,dV' = -\frac{\rho(\mathbf{r})}{\epsilon}$$

The volume integral here is in the form of Eq. (1.129); thus the integral is evaluated at $R = 0$ (or $\mathbf{r}' = \mathbf{r}$) to give

$$\frac{1}{4\pi\epsilon}\,[-4\pi\rho(\mathbf{r})] = -\frac{\rho(\mathbf{r})}{\epsilon}$$

$$-\frac{\rho(\mathbf{r})}{\epsilon} = -\frac{\rho(\mathbf{r})}{\epsilon}$$

and it is thus proved that Eq. (6.24) is a solution of Eq. (6.19). A similar ★procedure may be used to show that Eq. (6.23) is a solution of Eq. (6.17).

6.7 THE ELECTRIC DIPOLE ANTENNA

An important application of the retarded-potential function is for the analysis of electromagnetic wave generation. Current elements generate electromagnetic waves, and a straight filament of ac current is called the *electric dipole antenna.* Charges accumulate on the ends of the wire, and a dipole is thus formed. If the wire diameter and length are small compared to a wavelength, the current density is uniform everywhere in the wire. The physical configuration is shown in Fig. 6.3, where a superimposed spherical and rectangular coordinate system is shown. For a short wire element with $d \ll r$, spherical waves which travel in the $+r$ direction are expected. The current is assumed to be known; thus it is possible to refer directly to Eq. (6.23) and determine **A**. For a line-current element, we recall from Chap. 2 that $\mathbf{J}\,dV'$ may be replaced by $I\,d\mathbf{l}'$, and Eq. (6.23) becomes

$$\mathbf{A} = \frac{\mu}{4\pi}\int_l \frac{I_0 e^{j(\omega t - kR)}\,dz'}{R}\,\hat{\mathbf{z}} \tag{6.27}$$

The solution to Eq. (6.27) is especially simple in regions far from the wire element, where $r \gg r'$. In this case $1/R \simeq 1/r$. In Sec. 6.2 it was shown that $k = 2\pi/\lambda$, and thus $kR = 2\pi R/\lambda = 2\pi|\mathbf{r} - \mathbf{r}'|/\lambda$. If $r' \ll \lambda$, which is the case when $d \ll \lambda$, then $kR \approx kr$. Under this restriction Eq. (6.27) becomes

$$\mathbf{A} = \frac{\mu d I_0 e^{j(\omega t - kr)}}{4\pi r}\,\hat{\mathbf{z}} \tag{6.28}$$

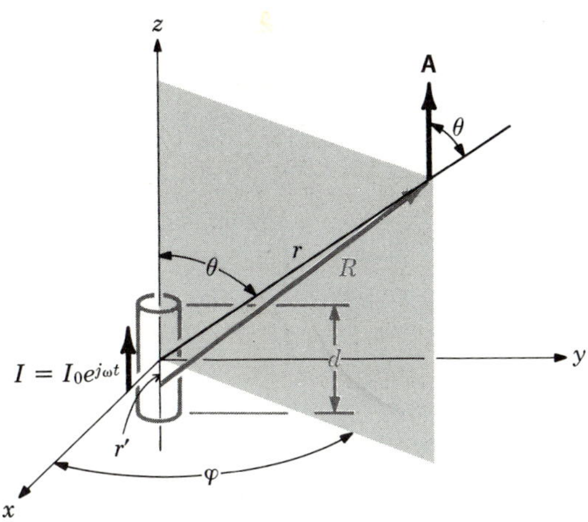

Fig. 6.3 The electric dipole antenna.

As expected, the vector potential is in the $\hat{\mathbf{z}}$ direction, the direction of current flow in a source element.

The electric and magnetic fields are now obtained from Eq. (2.54) and the curl equations. It is desirable to solve for the fields in the spherical coordinate system, since spherical waves are expected. Hence it is necessary to transform the vector potential in Eq. (6.28) into spherical components. From Fig. 6.3 it is easily seen that the components of **A** along the spherical coordinate directions are

$$A_r = A_z \cos\theta = \frac{\mu d I_0 \cos\theta\, e^{j(\omega t - kr)}}{4\pi r} \tag{6.29}$$

Amp-Henry / meter

$$A_\theta = -A_z \sin\theta = -\frac{\mu d I_0 \sin\theta\, e^{j(\omega t - kr)}}{4\pi r} \tag{6.30}$$

Since there is no φ variation in either component of **A**, the only component of $\nabla \times \mathbf{A}$ is in the φ direction, and thus the only component of **B** is B_φ. Equation (2.54) gives

$$B_\varphi = \frac{1}{r}\left[\frac{\partial}{\partial r}(rA_\theta) - \frac{\partial A_r}{\partial \theta}\right]$$

Equations (6.29) and (6.30) are then employed to obtain

$$B_\varphi = \frac{1}{r}\left[-\frac{\mu d I_0 \sin\theta}{4\pi}(-jk) + \frac{\mu d I_0 \sin\theta}{4\pi r}\right] e^{j(\omega t - kr)}$$

and the final expression for B_φ is

$$B_\varphi = \frac{\mu d I_0}{4\pi} \sin\theta \left(\frac{jk}{r} + \frac{1}{r^2}\right) e^{j(\omega t - kr)} \tag{6.31}$$

The corresponding expression for **E** may be obtained from the appropriate field equation relating **E** and **B**

$$E_r = \frac{d I_0}{4\pi} \cos\theta \left(\frac{2}{r^2}\sqrt{\frac{\mu}{\epsilon}} + \frac{2}{j\omega\epsilon r^3}\right) e^{j(\omega t - kr)} \tag{6.32}$$

$$E_\theta = \frac{d I_0}{4\pi} \sin\theta \left(\frac{j\omega\mu}{r} + \frac{1}{j\omega\epsilon r^3} + \frac{1}{r^2}\sqrt{\frac{\mu}{\epsilon}}\right) e^{j(\omega t - kr)} \tag{6.33}$$

Since the derivation has been limited to regions far from the source element, where $r \gg d$, it is appropriate in Eqs. (6.31) to (6.33) to neglect terms containing $1/r^2$ and $1/r^3$ in comparison to terms which vary as $1/r$.

Thus the only field components of importance far from the current element are

$$B_\varphi = \frac{jk\mu dI_0}{4\pi r} \sin\theta \, e^{j(\omega t - kr)} \tag{6.34}$$

$$E_\theta = \frac{j\omega\mu dI_0}{4\pi r} \sin\theta \, e^{j(\omega t - kr)} \tag{6.35}$$

These fields are called *radiation fields,* and they are the fields which transport energy away from the dipole antenna. Since the radiation fields vary as $\sin\theta$, the fields are strongest in a direction perpendicular to the antenna axis. This means that the energy is radiated maximally in the xy plane. Broadcast stations located in metropolitan areas with many receivers in all directions from the antenna are well suited to a vertical dipole-antenna radiation pattern. This pattern limits wasted radiation into the sky and distributes the field energy evenly over the horizon with no φ variation.

In Prob. 3.9-2 it was pointed out that a short, thin wire carrying a time-varying current along its axis is equivalent to an oscillating electric dipole. In Example 2.3 the case of the static electric dipole was considered in detail, and it was shown that the static electric fields vary as $1/r^3$. The results of this example show that if the dipole is time varying, additional fields are generated which vary as $1/r^2$ and $1/r$.

The radiation fields given in Eqs. (6.34) and (6.35) are in phase, have the same θ variation, and thus differ only by a constant. This is the same result we obtained for planewaves in Eq. (6.7). The constant is often written in terms of the ratio E/H, and from Eq. (6.7) we obtain

$$\frac{E_x}{H_y} = \sqrt{\frac{\mu}{\epsilon}}$$

for planewaves. The constant so defined has the dimensions of impedance and is called the *intrinsic impedance* of the medium, or the *wave impedance.* The wave impedance for spherical waves emanating from a dipole antenna is obtained from Eqs. (6.34) and (6.35) as

$$\frac{E_\theta}{H_\varphi} = \frac{\omega\mu}{k}$$

$$= \sqrt{\frac{\mu}{\epsilon}}$$

Example 6.2 A dipole antenna A dipole antenna is 10 cm long and carries a current of 1 amp, with $\omega = 10^8$. The antenna radiates into free space. It is desired to calculate the electric field intensity at a distance of 10 km from the antenna, and the distance where the $1/r^2$ and $1/r^3$ fields are negligible.

The radiation field E_θ at $\theta = \pi/2$, obtained from Eq. (6.35), is

$$|E_\theta| = \frac{10^8 \times 4\pi \times 10^{-7} \times 10^{-1} \times 1}{4\pi \times 10^4}$$
$$= 100\ \mu\text{volts/m}$$

The $1/r^2$ and $1/r^3$ field components are calculated from Eq. (6.33). The ratio of the $1/r^2$ component to the $1/r$ component is called A_2,

$$A_2 = \frac{1}{kr}$$
$$= \frac{v_p}{\omega r}$$
$$= \frac{3 \times 10^8}{10^8 r}$$
$$= \frac{3}{r}$$

At $r = 10$ km $A_2 = 3 \times 10^{-4}$ and is indeed negligible. The $1/r^2$ field component is 1 percent of the $1/r$ field component at $r = 300$ m. The ratio of the $1/r^3$ component to the $1/r$ component is called A_3,

$$A_3 = \frac{1}{(kr)^2}$$
$$= \frac{9}{r^2}$$

At $r = 10$ km $A_3 = 9 \times 10^{-8}$, and $A_3 = 0.01$ at 30 m.

★6.8 The Two-dipole Array

It is often desirable to concentrate the radiation fields in a certain direction, especially if there is a single remote receiving station. In order to do this it is necessary to introduce a φ variation with the peak radiation-field amplitude in the direction of the receiver. The more effectively this is done, the greater the field strength at the receiver for a given current amplitude in the antenna. Ideally, we would like a pencil beam consisting of a finite-width wave with no spread. As we shall see, this is not possible and may be approached only at frequencies in the optical spectrum and above.

Radiation fields may be directed by the use of several dipoles arranged in a geometric pattern or array. Consider two dipoles sepa-

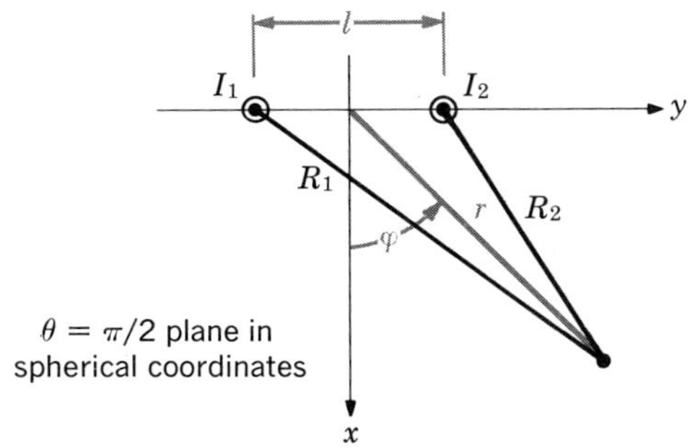

Fig. 6.4 A two-dipole array.

rated by a distance l and located in the xy plane on the y axis as shown in Fig. 6.4. It is desired to calculate the radiation fields generated by this two-dipole array in the $\theta = \pi/2$ plane by first superimposing the **A** vectors generated by each dipole to get the total **A** vector and then solving for **B** and **E** from **A**. The dipole **A** vector is given by Eq. (6.28); thus the sum of the two dipole **A** vectors is

$$\mathbf{A} = \frac{\mu d e^{j\omega t}}{4\pi}\,\hat{\mathbf{z}}\left(I_1 \frac{e^{-jkR_1}}{R_1} + I_2 \frac{e^{-jkR_2}}{R_2}\right) \tag{6.36}$$

It is now necessary to find R_1 and R_2 in terms of the field-point coordinates. Recall that in the derivation of Eq. (6.28) it was assumed that $d/r \ll 1$. The additional restriction $l/R \ll 1$ is now applied.

From the law of cosines we may write

$$R_1{}^2 = r^2 + \left(\frac{l}{2}\right)^2 - 2r\frac{l}{2}\cos\left(\frac{\pi}{2} + \varphi\right)$$

Using $\cos(\pi/2 + \varphi) = -\sin\varphi$ and $(l/2)^2 \ll r^2$ gives

$$R_1{}^2 = r^2\left(1 + \frac{l}{r}\sin\varphi\right)$$

The expansion $(1 + x)^{1/2} \simeq 1 + x/2$ for $x \ll 1$ is applied to yield the final approximate expression for R_1,

$$R_1 = r + \frac{l}{2}\sin\varphi$$

A similar derivation gives

$$R_2 = r - \frac{l}{2}\sin\varphi$$

Note that R_1 and R_2 appear in Eq. (6.36) in two ways, as $1/R$ factors describing the field amplitude reduction with R and in the phase factor e^{-jkR}. It is a good approximation for $r \gg l$ to neglect the amplitude difference caused by the fact that one dipole is slightly farther away from the field point than the other. We thus set $1/R = 1/r$. The phase factor must be examined more closely:

$$e^{-jkR_1} = e^{-jkr}e^{-j(kl/2)\sin\varphi}$$

Since the term R_1 appears as an exponent, a separate term is generated involving l and φ. The term e^{-jkr} is the phase factor describing propagation from the origin to the field point. The term $e^{-j(kl/2)\sin\varphi}$ accounts for the phase difference due to the displacement of element 1 from the origin, and it is negligible only if $(kl/2)\sin\varphi$ is small. Since $k = 2\pi/\lambda$,

$$\frac{kl}{2}\sin\varphi = \frac{\pi l}{\lambda}\sin\varphi$$

which is small only when $l \ll \lambda$. This is a restriction we do not wish to make, and thus this phase factor must be kept. This allows the analysis to describe effects which occur at wavelengths of the order of l. It is implicit in the derivation of Eq. (6.28) that $d \ll \lambda$.

We now return to Eq. (6.36) and write

$$\mathbf{A} = \frac{\mu d}{4\pi r}e^{j(\omega t - kr)}\hat{\mathbf{z}}(I_1e^{-j(kl/2)\sin\varphi} + I_2e^{+j(kl/2)\sin\varphi}) \tag{6.37}$$

The fields may now be calculated from Eq. (6.37). The **A** vector is the same as that for dipole 1 located at the origin, multiplied by a directivity function $F(\varphi)$ given by

$$F(\varphi) = e^{-j(kl/2)\sin\varphi} + \frac{I_2}{I_1}e^{+j(kl/2)\sin\varphi}$$

When the two currents are equal and in phase,

$$F(\varphi) = 2\cos\left(\frac{kl}{2}\sin\varphi\right) \tag{6.38}$$

and Eq. (6.38) is plotted in Fig. 6.5 for $\lambda = l$ and $\lambda = l/2$. Observe that some directivity of the **A** vector (and hence the **B** and **E** fields) has been obtained by the array, resulting in a doubling of the field intensity. The peaks in a plot of $F(\varphi)$ in directions other than $\varphi = 0$ are called *side lobes*. The side lobes may be greatly reduced in amplitude by utilizing an array ★with many dipole elements, rather than just two.

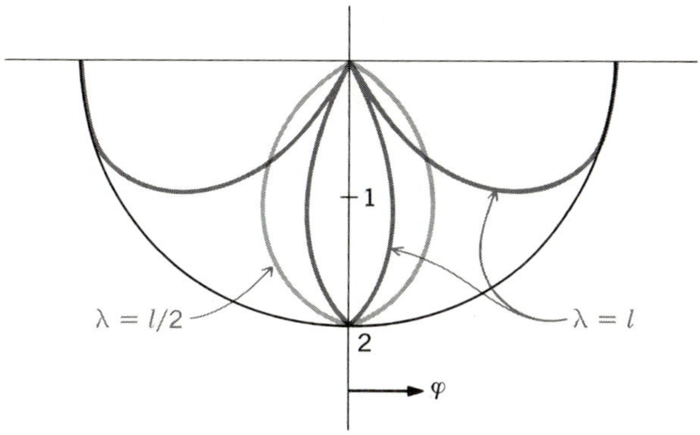

Fig. 6.5 Polar plot of the magnitude of the directivity function $F(\varphi)$ versus φ for the two-dipole array. The distance from the origin to the curve at each φ value is $|F(\varphi)|$.

6.9 POWER RADIATION FROM THE ELECTRIC DIPOLE ANTENNA

At distances far from the dipole antenna only the radiation fields are present, and it may be shown that only the radiation fields carry power away from the antenna. The power density may be calculated by means of the Poynting vector discussed in Sec. 4.4. Of particular interest is the real time-average power density.

The instantaneous Poynting vector is $\mathcal{P} = \mathbf{E} \times \mathbf{H}$, and the time-average Poynting vector is

$$\begin{aligned}\langle \mathcal{P} \rangle &= \tfrac{1}{2} \operatorname{Re} (\mathbf{E} \times \mathbf{H}^*) \\ &= \tfrac{1}{2} \operatorname{Re} (E_\theta H_\varphi^*)\hat{\mathbf{r}} \end{aligned} \tag{6.39}$$

The power radiated by the electric-dipole antenna is in the $+\hat{\mathbf{r}}$ direction in the spherical coordinate system. The time-average electromagnetic power density is obtained by combining Eqs. (6.34) and (6.35) with Eq. (6.39),

$$\langle \mathcal{P} \rangle = \frac{1}{2} \sqrt{\frac{\mu}{\epsilon}} \left(\frac{kdI_0}{4\pi r} \right)^2 \sin^2 \theta \, \hat{\mathbf{r}} \tag{6.40}$$

It is easily seen from Eq. (6.40) that no power is radiated along the polar axis of the antenna in the direction of current flow. Maximum power flows in the equatorial plane, where $\theta = \pi/2$, in all directions.

Of particular interest is the total power radiated by the electric-dipole antenna. The total power is obtained by integrating the Poynting vector over a large spherical surface. The only variable in the power-

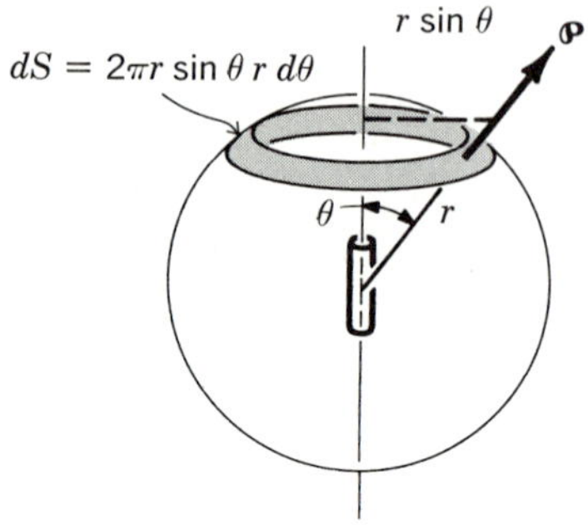

Fig. 6.6 Calculation of the total power radiated by the electric dipole antenna.

density expression of Eq. (6.40) is the angle θ; thus the incremental surface $dS = 2\pi r^2 \sin\theta \, d\theta$ is used, as shown in Fig. 6.6. The total power is obtained by integrating Eq. (6.40) over the entire spherical surface,

$$\langle P \rangle = \oint_S \langle \mathcal{P} \rangle \cdot \hat{\mathbf{r}} \, dS = \frac{1}{2}\sqrt{\frac{\mu}{\epsilon}}\left(\frac{kdI_0}{4\pi}\right)^2 \int_0^\pi \frac{\sin^2\theta}{r^2}\, 2\pi r^2 \sin\theta \, d\theta$$

The r^2 terms cancel in the integrand, and the integral is evaluated from $\theta = 0$ to $\theta = \pi$ to give

$$\langle P \rangle = \frac{\pi}{3}\sqrt{\frac{\mu}{\epsilon}}\, I_0{}^2 \left(\frac{d}{\lambda}\right)^2 \tag{6.41}$$

where λ is the wavelength in the medium.

It is customary to drive the electric dipole antenna by a transmission line which carries a current I_0 and delivers power to the antenna element. The transmission line senses that a total power $\langle P \rangle$ is lost, and thus responds as if it were terminated by a resistance

$$R = \frac{2\langle P \rangle}{I_0{}^2}$$

$$= \frac{2\pi}{3}\sqrt{\frac{\mu}{\epsilon}}\left(\frac{d}{\lambda}\right)^2 \tag{6.42}$$

This resistance is called the *radiation resistance* of the electric dipole antenna.

It is important to recognize the significance of radiated electromagnetic power as described in this section. Up to this point the only electric power-dissipation process discussed has been the power-loss mechanism through particle collisions in material media. A new power-loss mechanism associated with radiated electromagnetic energy is presented in this section. The field equations describe radiated power loss in very simple terms, but little physical understanding of the energy-loss mechanism is obtained. The power-radiation concept is a manifestation of the action-at-a-distance phenomenon associated with electric and magnetic fields. Greater physical insight into the mechanism of electromagnetic power radiation will be obtained in later chapters, where circuit concepts are developed from the field equations and transmission systems are discussed in detail.

Example 6.3 Electric dipole power The total time-average power radiated from the electric dipole discussed in Example 6.2 may be determined from Eq. (6.41). The wavelength λ is related to frequency and v_p by the relation

$$\begin{aligned}\lambda &= v_p/f \\ &= 2\pi \times 3 \times 10^8/\omega \\ &= 6\pi \text{ m}\end{aligned}$$

Thus

$$\begin{aligned}\langle P\rangle &= \frac{\pi}{3} \times 377 \times 1 \times \left(\frac{0.1}{6\pi}\right)^2 \\ &= 0.0111 \text{ watts}\end{aligned}$$

This is a small amount of power, and certainly not enough for many applications.

In circuit terminology, we say that the radiated power is low because the radiation resistance is low. The radiation resistance is obtained from Eq. (6.42), or simply from $R = 2\langle P\rangle/I_0^2$. Thus

$$\begin{aligned}R &= \frac{2 \times 0.0111}{1} \\ &= 0.0222\end{aligned}$$

Little power can be dissipated in a resistor this small unless very large currents are used. Therein lies the practical difficulty of the dipole antenna; the radiation resistance is too small to radiate much power for practical driving-current levels.

The power density at $\theta = \pi/2$ with $r = 10$ km may be obtained from Eq. (6.40), or more simply by recognizing that the wave impedance $E_\theta/H_\varphi = \sqrt{\mu/\epsilon}$, as stated in Sec. 6.7. Then, from Eq. (6.39), we have

$$\begin{aligned}\langle P_r\rangle &= \tfrac{1}{2} \text{ Re } E_\theta H_\varphi^* \\ &= \frac{1}{2} \frac{E_\theta^2}{\sqrt{\mu/\epsilon}}\end{aligned}$$

From Example 6.2 it was determined that $E_\theta = 100$ μvolts/m; thus

$$\begin{aligned}\langle P_r\rangle &= \frac{1}{2} \times \frac{10^{-8}}{377} \\ &= 13.3 \times 10^{-12} \text{ watts/m}^2\end{aligned}$$

6.10 GENERAL PLANEWAVE SOLUTION TO THE FIELD HOMOGENEOUS WAVE EQUATIONS

In many applications the electric and magnetic fields are to be determined in a region where no current or charges exist, for example, in free space, in transmission lines, and in cavities. The homogeneous wave equations for **E** and **H** are applicable and may be used to find the fields. The treatment given in this section serves as an introduction to the more general treatment in Chaps. 8 and 9.

The homogeneous wave equations for the fields apply for a region where $\rho = \mathbf{J} = 0$ and are obtained directly from Eqs. (6.12) and (6.13); thus

$$\left(\nabla^2 - \mu\epsilon \frac{\partial^2}{\partial t^2}\right) \mathbf{E} = 0 \tag{6.43}$$

$$\left(\nabla^2 - \mu\epsilon \frac{\partial^2}{\partial t^2}\right) \mathbf{H} = 0 \tag{6.44}$$

It is necessary to solve only Eq. (6.43), and the associated magnetic field **H** may always be obtained from the field equations. The one-dimensional solution for Eq. (6.43) was carried out in Sec. 6.2.

A general solution may be constructed from solutions of the form of Eq. (6.4), where k is the propagation constant for waves traveling in the $\pm z$ directions only. Propagation constants associated with the x, y, and z directions are introduced and labeled k_x, k_y, and k_z, respectively. We thus consider a solution to Eq. (6.43) for sinusoidal time variation,

$$\mathbf{E} = \mathbf{E}_0 e^{\pm j(k_x x + k_y y + k_z z)} \tag{6.45}$$

where Re and $e^{j\omega t}$ are not written and $\mathbf{E}_0$ is a constant vector. Equation (6.45) may be considered a trial solution and used with Eq. (6.43) to obtain

$$\left(\frac{\partial^2}{\partial x^2} + \frac{\partial^2}{\partial y^2} + \frac{\partial^2}{\partial z^2} - \mu\epsilon \frac{\partial^2}{\partial t^2}\right) \mathbf{E}_0 e^{\pm j(k_x x + k_y y + k_z z)} = 0$$

$$(-k_x{}^2 - k_y{}^2 - k_z{}^2 + \omega^2\mu\epsilon)\mathbf{E}_0 e^{\pm j(k_x x + k_y y + k_z z)} = 0$$

We see that Eq. (6.45) is an appropriate solution for Eq. (6.43) if

$$\begin{aligned} k_x{}^2 + k_y{}^2 + k_z{}^2 &= \omega^2\mu\epsilon \\ &\equiv k^2 \end{aligned} \tag{6.46}$$

A **k** vector is defined as

$$\mathbf{k} = k_x\hat{\mathbf{x}} + k_y\hat{\mathbf{y}} + k_z\hat{\mathbf{z}} \tag{6.47}$$

and by using the coordinate vector **r**,

$$\mathbf{r} = x\hat{\mathbf{x}} + y\hat{\mathbf{y}} + z\hat{\mathbf{z}}$$

we see that

$$\mathbf{k} \cdot \mathbf{r} = k_x x + k_y y + k_z z$$

Equation (6.45) may then be written in the shorthand notation

$$\mathbf{E} = \mathbf{E}_0 e^{\pm j\mathbf{k}\cdot\mathbf{r}} \tag{6.48}$$

If the unit vector $\hat{\mathbf{n}}$ is defined as a unit vector in the **k** direction, then $\mathbf{k} = \hat{\mathbf{n}}k$, and for a wave propagating in the $+\hat{\mathbf{n}}$ direction, Eq. (6.45) may be written in the form

$$\mathbf{E} = \mathbf{E}_0 e^{-jk\hat{\mathbf{n}}\cdot\mathbf{r}} \tag{6.49}$$

Equation (6.49) is a general three-dimensional solution to the homogeneous wave equation for **E**, describing a planewave traveling in the $\pm\hat{\mathbf{n}}$ directions with a propagation constant k. We saw in Sec. 6.2 that the direction of propagation of a planewave is perpendicular to the plane of constant phase. The surfaces of constant phase may be found by setting t = constant in Eq. (6.49) and requiring that the phase $\theta = \omega t - k\hat{\mathbf{n}}\cdot\mathbf{r}$ be constant. The constant-phase condition is thus

$$\begin{aligned}\hat{\mathbf{n}}\cdot\mathbf{r} &= r\cos\psi \\ &= \text{constant}\end{aligned}$$

which is the equation for a plane, as illustrated in Fig. 6.7. Setting the constant equal to r_0, the value of r at $\psi = 0$, gives

$$r = \frac{r_0}{\cos\psi}$$

The surface of constant phase is a plane, hence the term "planewave."

The phase velocity v_p along the $\hat{\mathbf{n}}$ direction may be found from Eq. (6.49) by setting the change in phase equal to zero for variation in r and t; thus

$$\begin{aligned}d\theta &= \omega\,dt - k\,dr\cos\psi \\ &= 0\end{aligned}$$

$$\frac{dr}{dt} = \frac{\omega}{k\cos\psi} \tag{6.50}$$

The direction of minimum phase velocity occurs at $\psi = 0$, and this is the direction of propagation, since it is the direction perpendicular to the

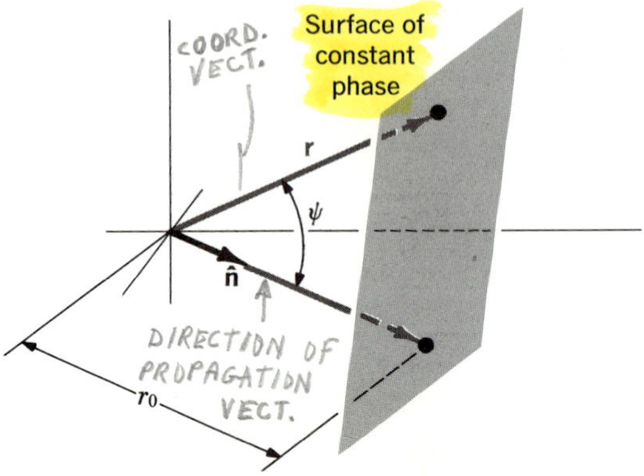

Fig. 6.7 The planar surface of constant phase which is characteristic of a planewave.

plane of constant phase. The wave propagates along $\hat{\mathbf{n}}$, normal to the plane of constant phase, at a phase velocity $v_p = 1/\sqrt{\mu\epsilon}$. The phase velocity along a direction other than $\hat{\mathbf{n}}$ is always larger than $1/\sqrt{\mu\epsilon}$.

FIELD RELATIONS IN A PLANEWAVE

A relation between $\mathbf{E}$ and $\hat{\mathbf{n}}$ is obtained by remembering that $\nabla \cdot \mathbf{E} = 0$ in a charge-free region. The divergence equation yields

$$\nabla \cdot (\mathbf{E}_0 e^{-jk\hat{\mathbf{n}}\cdot\mathbf{r}}) = 0$$

By using the vector identity $\nabla \cdot \mathbf{A}\Phi = \mathbf{A} \cdot \nabla\Phi + \Phi\, \nabla \cdot \mathbf{A}$, where $\mathbf{A}$ is a vector and Φ is a scalar, and remembering that $\mathbf{E}_0$ is a constant vector, the above equation reduces to

$$\mathbf{E}_0 \cdot (\nabla e^{-jk\hat{\mathbf{n}}\cdot\mathbf{r}}) = 0$$

The gradient operation is performed,

$$\begin{aligned}\nabla e^{-jk\hat{\mathbf{n}}\cdot\mathbf{r}} &= \left(\frac{\partial}{\partial x}\,\hat{\mathbf{x}} + \frac{\partial}{\partial y}\,\hat{\mathbf{y}} + \frac{\partial}{\partial z}\,\hat{\mathbf{z}}\right) e^{-j(k_x x + k_y y + k_z z)} \\ &= (-jk_x\hat{\mathbf{x}} - jk_y\hat{\mathbf{y}} - jk_z\hat{\mathbf{z}})e^{-jk\hat{\mathbf{n}}\cdot\mathbf{r}} \\ &= -jk\hat{\mathbf{n}}e^{-jk\hat{\mathbf{n}}\cdot\mathbf{r}}\end{aligned}$$

and thus

$$(\mathbf{E}_0 \cdot \hat{\mathbf{n}})jke^{-jk(\hat{\mathbf{n}}\cdot\mathbf{r})} = 0$$

The nontrivial solution to this equation is

$$\mathbf{E}_0 \cdot \hat{\mathbf{n}} = 0 \tag{6.51}$$

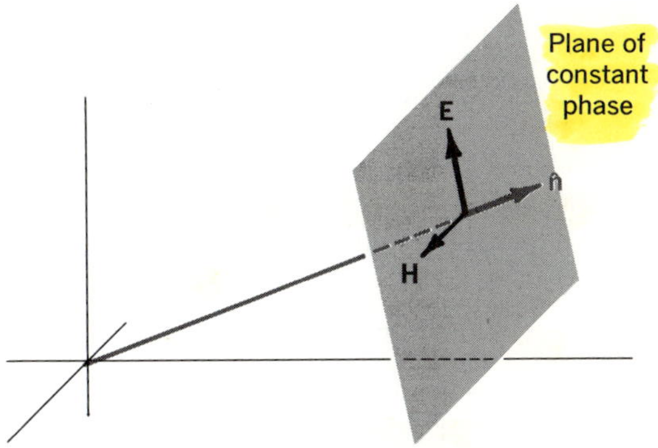

Fig. 6.8 Orientation of the field vectors in a planewave propagating along $\hat{\mathbf{n}}$.

The electric field vector in a planewave is therefore perpendicular to the direction of propagation $\hat{\mathbf{n}}$ and thus lies in the constant phase plane.

The magnetic field vector may be found from the field equations. Since $\mathbf{B} = \mu\mathbf{H}$, Eqs. (5.85) and (6.49) may be combined to yield

$$\nabla \times (\mathbf{E}_0 e^{-jk\hat{\mathbf{n}}\cdot\mathbf{r}}) = -j\omega\mu\mathbf{H}$$

The curl operation may be evaluated by using the appropriate identities, and an equation for $\mathbf{H}$ is obtained,

$$\mathbf{H} = \sqrt{\frac{\epsilon}{\mu}}\,\hat{\mathbf{n}} \times \mathbf{E} \tag{6.52}$$

The magnetic field-intensity vector $\mathbf{H}$ is therefore perpendicular to both $\hat{\mathbf{n}}$ and $\mathbf{E}_0$ and oriented as shown in Fig. 6.8.

Note that the vector $\mathbf{E} \times \mathbf{H}$ is in the direction of propagation $\hat{\mathbf{n}}$. The Poynting vector points in the direction of propagation, as expected. The wave impedance E/H is a constant which has the value $\sqrt{\mu/\epsilon}$.

6.11 POWER AND ENERGY IN A PLANEWAVE

This section is concerned with the application of field power and energy concepts to planewaves. The fields associated with planewaves are given by Eqs. (6.49) and (6.52). The instantaneous power density associated with planewave propagation may be immediately determined,

$$\mathcal{P} = \tfrac{1}{2}\,\mathrm{Re}\,(\mathbf{E} \times \mathbf{H}^* + \mathbf{E} \times \mathbf{H}e^{2j\omega t})$$

where phasor notation is used and the cross product is evaluated according to the cross-product form of Eq. (1.115). The time-average power density is

$$\langle\mathcal{P}\rangle = \tfrac{1}{2}\,\mathrm{Re}\left[\mathbf{E}_0 \times \sqrt{\frac{\epsilon}{\mu}}\,(\hat{\mathbf{n}} \times \mathbf{E}_0^*)\right]$$

The triple cross product is readily evaluated to give

$$\langle \mathcal{P} \rangle = \frac{1}{2}\sqrt{\frac{\epsilon}{\mu}}\, E_0{}^2\hat{\mathbf{n}} \tag{6.53}$$

The Poynting vector is in the direction of propagation $\hat{\mathbf{n}}$.

The electric energy density stored in a planewave may be calculated from Eq. (5.118). Thus the time-average electric energy density is

$$\begin{aligned}\langle \mathcal{W}_e \rangle &= \langle \tfrac{1}{2}\epsilon \mathbf{E} \cdot \mathbf{E} \rangle \\ &= \tfrac{1}{2}\,\mathrm{Re}\,(\tfrac{1}{2}\epsilon \mathbf{E} \cdot \mathbf{E}^*) \\ &= \tfrac{1}{4}\epsilon E_0{}^2\end{aligned} \tag{6.54}$$

Similarly, the time-average magnetic energy density is

$$\langle \mathcal{W}_m \rangle = \tfrac{1}{4}\mu H_0{}^2 \tag{6.55}$$

where H_0 is the peak H field. From the relationship between E_0 and H_0 for a planewave, it is easily seen that $\langle \mathcal{W}_e \rangle = \langle \mathcal{W}_m \rangle$. Thus the total time-average energy density associated with the electric and magnetic field in a planewave is

$$\begin{aligned}\langle \mathcal{W} \rangle &= 2\langle \mathcal{W}_e \rangle \\ &= \tfrac{1}{2}\epsilon E_0{}^2\end{aligned} \tag{6.56}$$

A comparison of Eqs. (6.53) and (6.56) readily verifies that the time-average power density and the time-average volume energy density are related by the expression

$$\langle \mathcal{P} \rangle = v_p \langle \mathcal{W} \rangle \tag{6.57}$$

where $v_p = 1/\sqrt{\mu\epsilon}$ is the phase velocity of planewave propagation. Thus the power associated with a planewave may be understood in terms of the transport of electric and magnetic energy at the propagation velocity.

Example 6.4 The laser discharge phenomenon in air If air is subjected to an electric field of sufficient intensity, an arc discharge is formed by an electron-impact ionization mechanism. Residual electrons are accelerated by the electric field to velocities large enough that electron impact with nitrogen or oxygen molecules causes ionization, releasing new electrons. The new electrons are then accelerated, and the resulting avalanche process produces an arc discharge. This is a common phenomenon which is seen in lightning, spark plugs, gas tubes, and in laboratory tesla-coil experiments.

It is possible to cause an arc discharge in air by means of a planewave if enough power density can be generated to develop the required electric field intensity. Assume that the electric field intensity required for discharge in air is 40,000 volts/cm. It is desired to calculate the spot diameter of a 1-kw laser beam in order to observe a discharge phenomenon in air. The electric field intensity is related to the power density by means of Eq. (6.53); thus the electric field generated by focusing the planewave to an area A is obtained from the relation $\langle P \rangle = \langle \mathcal{P} \rangle A$, which gives

$$\frac{1}{2}\sqrt{\frac{\epsilon_0}{\mu_0}}\,E_0{}^2 A = 10^3 \text{ watts}$$

By setting the electric field E_0 equal to the value required for discharge,

$$E_0 = 40{,}000 \text{ volts/cm}$$

an area A may be determined,

$$A = \frac{2 \times 10^3 \times 377}{16 \times 10^{12}} = 4.7 \times 10^{-8} \text{ m}^2$$

The area $A = 4.7 \times 10^{-8}$ m^2 corresponds to a round spot of approximately ¼ mm diameter, which is easily obtained by an appropriate lens. The phenomenon of arc discharge in air by means of laser excitation is an observable laboratory phenomenon.

6.12 PLANEWAVE REFLECTION AT A PERFECT CONDUCTOR: NORMAL INCIDENCE

Planewaves incident upon a perfectly conducting surface are totally reflected. As shown in Sec. 6.16, no **E** or **B** fields may penetrate a perfect conductor; thus no **J** may exist to generate power dissipation and no $\boldsymbol{\mathcal{P}}$ may exist to transmit power into the conductor. The incident wave induces surface current on the perfectly conducting surface with no I^2R losses, and the induced current in turn excites a reflected wave.

A planewave with sinusoidal time variation is written in complex notation as

$$\mathbf{E} = \mathbf{E}_0 e^{-jk\hat{\mathbf{n}}\cdot\mathbf{r}} \tag{6.49}$$

where Re and the $e^{j\omega t}$ factor are not written. The corresponding magnetic field is

$$\mathbf{H} = \sqrt{\frac{\epsilon}{\mu}}\,\hat{\mathbf{n}} \times \mathbf{E} \tag{6.52}$$

A rectangular coordinate system is oriented such that $\mathbf{E}_0$ lies along the x axis and $\hat{\mathbf{n}}$ lies along the $+z$ axis. For the incident planewave,

$$\mathbf{E}_i = E_0\hat{\mathbf{x}}e^{-jkz} \tag{6.58}$$

$$\mathbf{H}_i = \sqrt{\frac{\epsilon}{\mu}}\,E_0\hat{\mathbf{y}}e^{-jkz} \tag{6.59}$$

where subscript i denotes field components of the incident wave. For normal incidence a perfectly conducting plane may be conveniently located in the $z = 0$ plane. Obviously, a reflected wave is generated of the form of Eqs. (6.49) and (6.52), with positive exponent to describe a wave traveling in the $-z$ direction.

The total field consists of incident- and reflected-wave components, $\mathbf{E} = \mathbf{E}_i + \mathbf{E}_r$, and must be zero at the perfectly conducting surface $z = 0$,

$$\mathbf{E}_i + \mathbf{E}_r = 0 \qquad \text{at } z = 0$$

Therefore $\mathbf{E}_r$ must be

$$\mathbf{E}_r = -E_0\hat{\mathbf{x}}e^{+jkz}$$

in order to satisfy the boundary condition at $z = 0$ and describe a wave traveling in the $-z$ direction. **H** is found from Eq. (6.52) to be

$$\mathbf{H}_r = \sqrt{\frac{\epsilon}{\mu}}\, E_0\hat{\mathbf{y}}e^{+jkz}$$

It is seen that the E fields cancel at the conducting plane, but the H fields add. From Eq. (5.116), this means that a surface current exists on the perfectly conducting plane.

The total electric field is

$$\begin{aligned}\mathbf{E} &= E_0\hat{\mathbf{x}}e^{-jkz} - E_0\hat{\mathbf{x}}e^{+jkz} \\ &= -2jE_0\hat{\mathbf{x}} \sin kz \qquad (6.60)\end{aligned}$$

A sinusoidal time-varying electric field exists which varies as sin kz in the z direction. This is called a *standing wave,* as there is apparently no travel of the wave in the z direction. Clearly, a standing wave consists of two equal traveling waves propagating in opposite directions. Zeros or nulls of the standing wave occur at constant z planes parallel to the conducting $z = 0$ plane, at $k|z| = m\pi$, $m = 1, 2, 3, \ldots$. Since $k = \omega/v_p = 2\pi/\lambda$,

$$|z| = \frac{m}{2}\lambda \qquad (6.61)$$

and nulls occur every half-wavelength.

The standing-wave solution of Eq. (6.60) also applies to a region between two parallel perfectly conducting planes if the second plane is located at $z = -m\lambda/2$. The insertion of another conducting plane at a null does not violate either the field equations or the boundary conditions. The standing wave is composed of a planewave which bounces back and forth between the two planes. Electromagnetic energy is stored in the reflected waves, and the structure is called a *resonant circuit* or *cavity.*

The term "cavity" is used to denote a region completely or partially bounded by an enclosing surface.

Example 6.5 The Fabry-Perot parallel-mirror resonant cavity An important application of the resonant-cavity mode of operation of the parallel-plate structure at optical frequencies is the Fabry-Perot resonator. Optical energy may be stored between the plates (mirrors) by exciting waves which travel in the $\pm z$ directions. Only light at certain wavelengths may exist in a structure of plate separation a in accordance with Eq. (6.61),

$$\lambda_m = \frac{2a}{m} \qquad m = 1, 2, 3, \ldots \tag{6.62}$$

The Fabry-Perot parallel-plate structure will resonate, or store energy, at an infinite number of wavelengths λ_m. From Eq. (6.60) it is seen that the **E** field for each wavelength condition is

$$\mathbf{E}_m = -2jE_0\hat{\mathbf{x}} \sin \frac{m\pi z}{a} \qquad 0 > z > -a$$

Note that m denotes the number of half-cycle variations of field in the structure.

The Fabry-Perot cavity is often used as the resonant structure for lasers. A laser is an optical oscillator which generates discrete wavelengths in accordance with the properties of the resonant structure in which the optically active material is located. At optical wavelengths where the mirror separation may be tens of centimeters with wavelengths less than 1 μ, the "mode number" m is a very large number, of the order of 100,000. The percentage of separation between resonant wavelengths, $(\lambda_m - \lambda_{m+1})/\lambda_m$, is only of the order 10^{-5}, as seen from Eq. (6.62); thus oscillations may occur at several of the resonant wavelengths given by Eq. (6.62). The optically active material in the laser cavity generates waves over a narrow frequency range as shown in Fig. 6.9. When the active material is excited, energy over a narrow frequency range builds up at a rate according to the

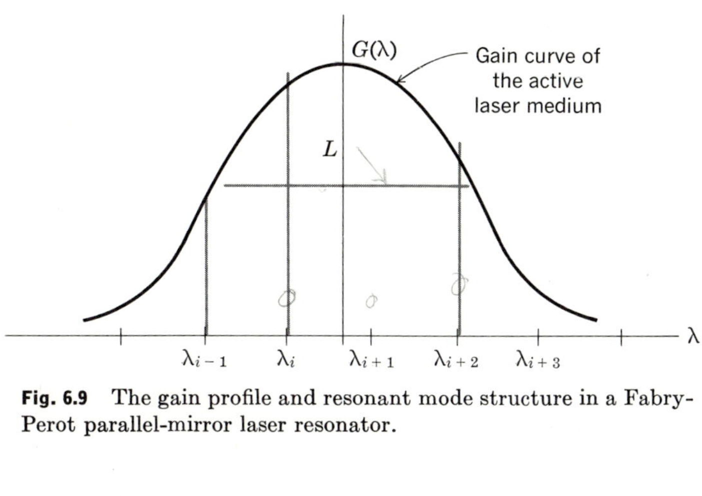

Fig. 6.9 The gain profile and resonant mode structure in a Fabry-Perot parallel-mirror laser resonator.

gain curve $G(\lambda)$ shown. There are losses due to radiation leakage and dissipation in the conducting plates. The rate of energy loss L is denoted on the figure. When the gain of the active laser material exceeds the losses, oscillation occurs, and the three modes λ_i, λ_{i+1}, and λ_{i+2} oscillate because $G > L$. The other modes will not be present in the system because for them $G < L$.

6.13 PLANEWAVE REFLECTION AT A PERFECT CONDUCTOR: OBLIQUE INCIDENCE

Planewave reflection from a perfectly conducting plane is described in this section for the case of oblique incidence. The restriction of normal incidence in Sec. 6.12 is released.

Consider the case where the electric vector lies in the plane of the conductor, as shown in Fig. 6.10. The coordinates are chosen such that

$$\hat{\mathbf{n}} = n_y\hat{\mathbf{y}} + n_z\hat{\mathbf{z}}$$

where $n_y = \cos\theta_i$ and $n_z = \sin\theta_i$. The vector $\mathbf{E}_i$ for the incident planewave traveling in the $+y$ and $+z$ directions is

$$\mathbf{E}_i = E_0\hat{\mathbf{x}}e^{-jk(n_yy+n_zz)}$$

where, for simplicity, Re and the $e^{j\omega t}$ factor are not written. The total field is composed of incident- and reflected-wave components,

$$\mathbf{E} = \mathbf{E}_i + \mathbf{E}_r$$

It is desired to find $\mathbf{E}_r$ and $\mathbf{E}$, given $\mathbf{E}_i$ and the conditions imposed by the boundary conditions at the conducting surface ($y = 0$).

The reflected-wave vector is found by applying the boundary condition $\mathbf{E} = 0$ at $y = 0$, which gives

$$\mathbf{E}_{r|y=0} = -E_0\hat{\mathbf{x}}e^{-jkn_zz}$$

Note that the phase factor describing propagation along z is the same for the reflected and incident waves. This is required for the electric field

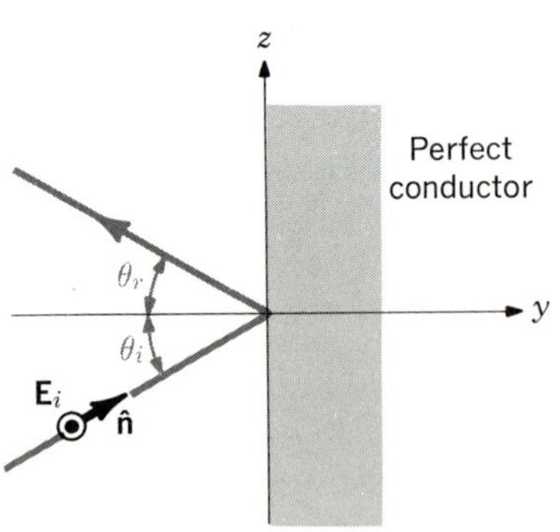

Fig. 6.10 A planewave impinging upon a perfect conductor with the electric vector parallel to the plane of the conductor.

to be continuous for all values of z. Since the magnitude of $\mathbf{k}$ is the same for the incident and reflected waves, and since the z components of $\mathbf{k}$ (or $\hat{\mathbf{n}}$) are the same, it is obvious that the reflected angle θ_r must equal the incident angle θ_i. Therefore the reflected-wave vector is

$$\mathbf{E}_r = -E_0 \hat{\mathbf{x}} e^{-jk(-n_y y + n_z z)}$$

The sign of n_y is reversed for the reflected wave because the reflected wave travels in the $-y$ direction. The total electric field vector is found by adding the incident and reflected components,

$$\begin{aligned} \mathbf{E} &= E_0 \hat{\mathbf{x}} (e^{-jk(n_y y + n_z z)} - e^{-jk(-n_y y + n_z z)}) \\ &= -2jE_0 \hat{\mathbf{x}} \sin (kn_y y)\, e^{-jkn_z z} \end{aligned} \tag{6.63}$$

Repeated zero $\mathbf{E}$ values occur in constant y planes given by

$$kn_y y = m\pi$$

The zeros occur at

$$|y| = \frac{m\lambda}{2n_y} \qquad m = 1, 2, 3, \ldots \tag{6.64}$$

Recall that for the case of normal incidence ($\theta_i = 0$ and $n_y = 1$), repeated zeros occurred at multiples of $\lambda/2$. Since $n_y < 1$, the zeros, or nulls, of electric field occur at planes separated by a distance greater than $\lambda/2$.

The magnetic field vector which accompanies the electric vector may be found from Eq. (6.63) and the curl equations,

$$\mathbf{H} = -2E_0 \sqrt{\frac{\epsilon}{\mu}} (n_y \cos kn_y y \, \hat{\mathbf{z}} + jn_z \sin kn_y y \, \hat{\mathbf{y}}) e^{-jkn_z z} \tag{6.65}$$

Example 6.6 The parallel-plate wave guide Since the electric field in Eq. (6.63) is zero at certain constant y planes, it is possible to place a perfectly conducting plate at any zero position without affecting the field pattern in the intervening space. Physically, the planewave is reflected at this second surface, and multiple reflections occur between the two plates. The wave bounces back and forth as it slowly works its way down between the plates in the $+z$ direction. The wave is thus "guided" in the z direction, even though its $\mathbf{k}$ vector is not in the z direction.

The field expressions in the region between the two plates are given by Eqs. (6.63) and (6.65). If we denote the plane separation by a, the n_y values required to satisfy the boundary conditions at the two plates are obtained from Eq. (6.64),

$$n_y = \frac{m\lambda}{2a} \qquad m = 1, 2, 3, \ldots \tag{6.66}$$

$\lambda = \frac{2a\, n_y}{m}$ $\qquad n_y = \cos\theta_i$

$\lambda = \frac{2a \cos\theta_i}{m}$ $\qquad n_z = \sin\theta_i$

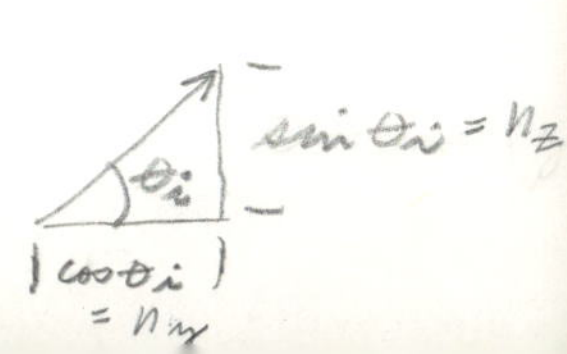

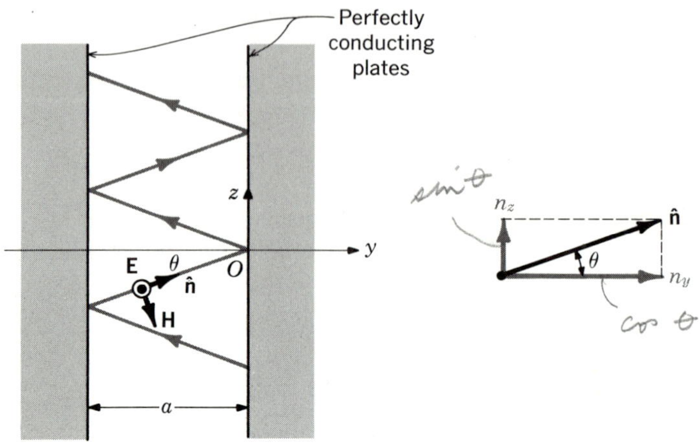

Fig. 6.11 A parallel-plate wave guide is characterized by multiple reflections of a planewave. The wave guide transports energy in the z direction at a velocity less than the velocity of light.

and this equation describes the allowed directions of planewave propagation between the plates. Observe that only discrete values of n_y are allowed.

The parallel-plate wave guide is illustrated in Fig. 6.11. Since complete reflection occurs at each conducting surface, the wave bounces back and forth with no loss between the two conducting plates. For a fixed value of a Eq. (6.66) states that n_y varies with λ. Since the direction of planewave propagation is denoted by the unit vector $\hat{\mathbf{n}}$, n_y is the cosine of the angle of incidence. When n_y equals zero, the direction of planewave propagation is in the z direction parallel to the conducting plates. This condition is approached only for very small values of λ/a, corresponding to very high frequencies. Thus planewaves travel predominantly in the z direction only when the wavelength λ is very much smaller than the plate separation a. As λ increases and approaches the plate-separation distance a, n_y increases, and the direction of propagation swings around in the transverse y direction. For the case where $m = 1$, corresponding to a half-cycle field variation between the plates, Eq. (6.66) gives $n_y = \lambda/2a$.

6.14 PLANEWAVE INCIDENCE UPON A DIELECTRIC INTERFACE

When a planewave impinges upon a plane dielectric interface, there is a reflected wave and a transmitted wave. Consider the case where the electric field vector lies in the plane of the dielectric interface, as shown in Fig. 6.12. The planewave-propagation constants in the two regions are $k_1 = \omega\sqrt{\mu_0\epsilon_{\mathrm{I}}}$ and $k_2 = \omega\sqrt{\mu_0\epsilon_{\mathrm{II}}}$. For continuity in the incident and reflected fields along the $y = 0$ interface, as seen in Sec. 6.13, the reflected

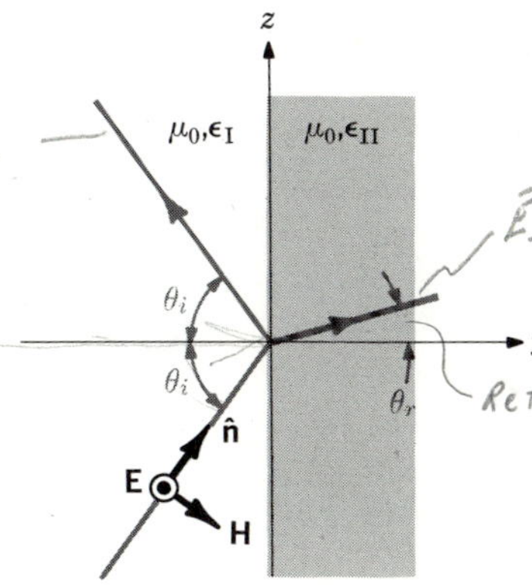

Fig. 6.12 A planewave impinging on a dielectric interface.

angle must equal the incident angle. The fields of the incident, reflected, and transmitted waves may then be written as

$$\mathbf{E}_i = E_i\hat{\mathbf{x}}e^{-jk_1(\sin\theta_i z + \cos\theta_i y)} \tag{6.67}$$

$$\mathbf{E}_r = E_r\hat{\mathbf{x}}e^{-jk_1(\sin\theta_i z - \cos\theta_i y)} \tag{6.68}$$

$$\mathbf{E}_t = E_t\hat{\mathbf{x}}e^{-jk_2(\sin\theta_i z + \cos\theta_r y)} \tag{6.69}$$

Since the tangential **E** fields must be continuous across the boundary plane $y = 0$ for all values of z, their variation along z must be the same. It is thus necessary that the transmitted wave have the same phase constant along z as the incident and reflected waves. Matching the phase constants along z in Eqs. (6.67) to (6.69) gives

$$k_1 \sin\theta_i = k_2 \sin\theta_r$$

which may be written in the form of Snell's law of refraction,

$$\frac{\sin\theta_i}{\sin\theta_r} = \sqrt{\frac{\epsilon_{II}}{\epsilon_I}} \tag{6.70}$$

Snell's law relates the incident and the refracted angles, θ_i and θ_r, in terms of ϵ_I and ϵ_{II}, and is a consequence of the requirement of field continuity at the interface.

It is interesting to consider Eq. (6.70) for the case where the wave passes into a region of lower dielectric constant, for example, from a dielectric into free space. Note that in this case $\epsilon_{II} < \epsilon_I$, and thus $\theta_r > \theta_i$. No transmission into free space can occur when $\theta_r \geq \pi/2$. The critical incident angle θ_c for which this occurs is found from Eq. (6.70) to be

$$\sin\theta_c = \sqrt{\frac{\epsilon_{II}}{\epsilon_I}} \tag{6.71}$$

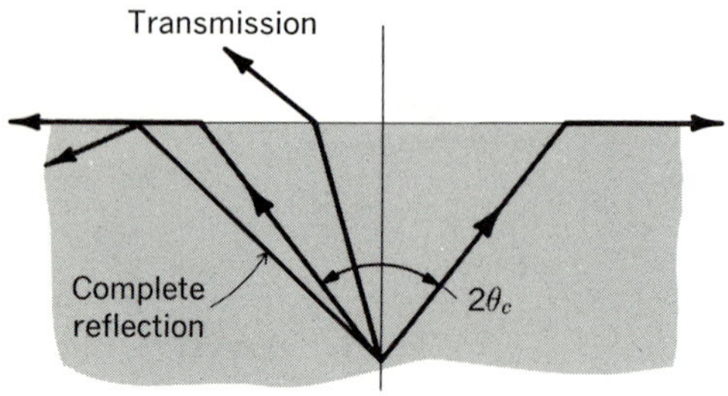

Fig. 6.13 Refraction and reflection characteristics of a plane-wave passing from a dielectric medium into free space.

An observer in the dielectric medium is able to receive waves only over a cone of angle $2\theta_c$, as shown in Fig. 6.13. This phenomenon is well known to skin divers and fish.

The complete solution for the fields is obtained by matching the **E** and **H** fields at $y = 0$. Equations (6.67) to (6.69) are used with $y = 0$. The exponential factors for all the field components are identical, and are thus not written, for simplicity. Matching the tangential **E** fields at $y = 0$ in accordance with Eq. (5.104) gives

$$E_i + E_r = E_t \tag{6.72}$$

Another expression is needed, from matching the **H** fields, as there are two unknowns, E_r and E_t, for a known E_i. The **H** fields may be obtained from the **E** fields for each wave from Eq. (6.52); thus

$$\mathbf{H} = \sqrt{\frac{\epsilon}{\mu}}\,\hat{\mathbf{n}} \times \mathbf{E} \tag{6.52}$$

For the incident wave

$$\begin{aligned}\mathbf{H}_i &= \sqrt{\frac{\epsilon_{\mathrm{I}}}{\mu_0}}(\sin\theta_i\,\hat{\mathbf{z}} + \cos\theta_i\,\hat{\mathbf{y}}) \times E_i\hat{\mathbf{x}} \\ &= \sqrt{\frac{\epsilon_{\mathrm{I}}}{\mu_0}}E_i(\sin\theta_i\,\hat{\mathbf{y}} - \cos\theta_i\,\hat{\mathbf{z}})\end{aligned} \tag{6.73}$$

For the reflected and transmitted waves

$$\mathbf{H}_r = \sqrt{\frac{\epsilon_{\mathrm{I}}}{\mu_0}}E_r(\sin\theta_i\,\hat{\mathbf{y}} + \cos\theta_i\,\hat{\mathbf{z}}) \tag{6.74}$$

$$\mathbf{H}_t = \sqrt{\frac{\epsilon_{\mathrm{II}}}{\mu_0}}E_t(\sin\theta_r\,\hat{\mathbf{y}} - \cos\theta_r\,\hat{\mathbf{z}}) \tag{6.75}$$

The boundary conditions at a dielectric interface for tangential H fields are given by Eq. (5.103), with $J_s = 0$, and thus the H_z fields must be matched:

$$\sqrt{\frac{\epsilon_{\rm I}}{\mu_0}} \cos\theta_i\,(-E_i + E_r) = -\sqrt{\frac{\epsilon_{\rm II}}{\mu_0}}\, E_t \cos\theta_r$$

Snell's law, Eq. (6.70), is used to eliminate the $\cos\theta_r$ term,

$$\sqrt{\frac{\epsilon_{\rm I}}{\epsilon_{\rm II}}} \cos\theta_i\,(E_i - E_r) = E_t\sqrt{1 - \frac{\epsilon_{\rm I}}{\epsilon_{\rm II}}\sin^2\theta_i}$$

$$E_i - E_r = E_t\sqrt{\frac{\epsilon_{\rm II}}{\epsilon_{\rm I}} - \sin^2\theta_i}\,\frac{1}{\cos\theta_i} \qquad (6.76)$$

Equations (6.72) and (6.76) may be combined to obtain the ratio of the reflected and incident E fields, or the ratio of the transmitted and incident E fields. The solution is usually expressed in terms of a reflection coefficient ρ and a transmission coefficient τ,

$$\rho \equiv \frac{E_r}{E_i} = \frac{\cos\theta_i - \sqrt{\epsilon_{\rm II}/\epsilon_{\rm I} - \sin^2\theta_i}}{\cos\theta_i + \sqrt{\epsilon_{\rm II}/\epsilon_{\rm I} - \sin^2\theta_i}} \qquad (6.77)$$

$$\tau \equiv \frac{E_t}{E_i} = 1 + \rho \qquad (6.78)$$

The reflection and transmission coefficients are, in general, complex quantities, indicating that the wave vectors are not in phase. The magnitude of the reflection coefficient for $\epsilon_{\rm II} > \epsilon_{\rm I}$ is plotted against the angle of incidence θ_i in Fig. 6.14. The reflection steadily increases to complete reflection as θ_i increases from normal to tangential incidence.

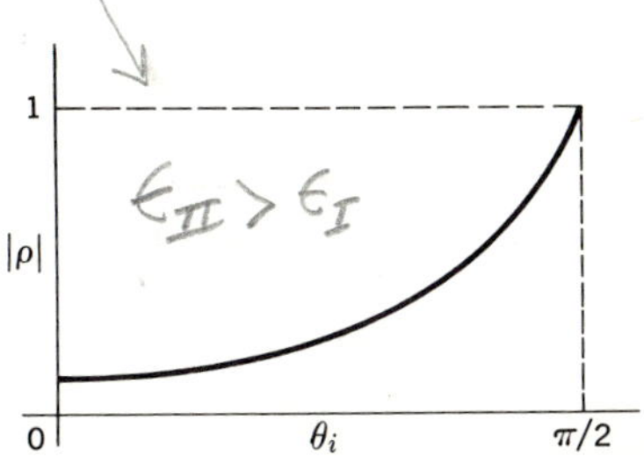

Fig. 6.14 Planewave reflection from a dielectric interface versus the angle of incidence θ_i for a wave with the electric vector parallel to the dielectric surface.

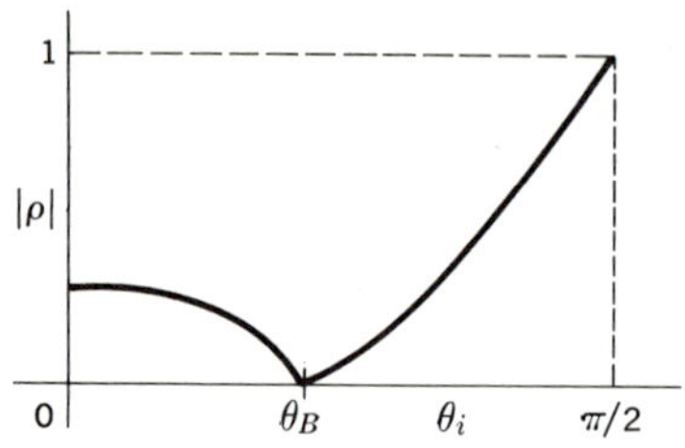

Fig. 6.15 Planewave reflection from a dielectric surface versus the angle of incidence θ_i for a wave with the electric vector in the plane of incidence. The reflection is zero at the *Brewster angle* θ_B.

Some interesting new phenomena are found to exist in the case where the electric vector is in the plane of incidence; i.e., the plane formed by the incident and reflected propagation vectors $\mathbf{k}_i$ and $\mathbf{k}_r$. Snell's law still holds for this case, but the reflection coefficient is different,

$$\rho = \frac{\sqrt{\epsilon_{II}/\epsilon_I - \sin^2\theta_i} - (\epsilon_{II}/\epsilon_I)\cos\theta_i}{\sqrt{\epsilon_{II}/\epsilon_I - \sin^2\theta_i} + (\epsilon_{II}/\epsilon_I)\cos\theta_i} \tag{6.79}$$

Note that at a particular angle of incidence called the Brewster angle θ_B the reflection coefficient is zero. The Brewster angle is found from Eq. (6.79) by setting the numerator equal to zero,

$$\sin\theta_B = \sqrt{\frac{\epsilon_{II}}{\epsilon_{II} + \epsilon_I}} \tag{6.80}$$

The reflection coefficient of Eq. (6.79) is plotted in Fig. 6.15. The zero-reflection property just described is used in the gas laser so that light with its **E** vector in the plane of incidence may pass through the glass walls of the tube with no reflection, as shown in Fig. 6.16.

Example 6.7 Transmission and reflection from a dielectric sheet A plane wave is normally incident upon a dielectric sheet of thickness d, permittivity ϵ, and permeability μ_0, as shown in Fig. 6.17. The reflection and transmission are not given by Eqs. (6.77) and (6.78), because additional reflection occurs at the second surface.

Incident and reflected waves exist in regions 1 and 2. Fields in regions 1, 2, and 3 are denoted by subscripts 1, 2, and 3, respectively. For the electric field

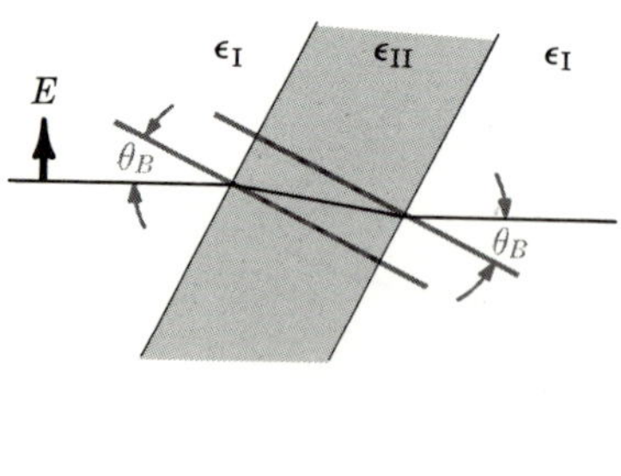

Fig. 6.16 The linearly polarized planewave shown passes through the dielectric slab with no reflection.

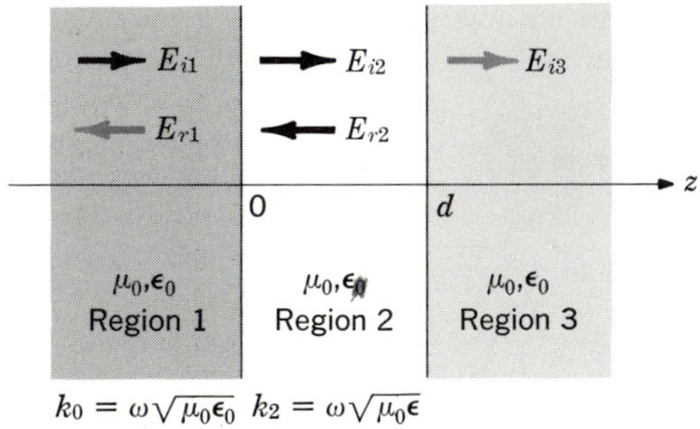

Fig. 6.17 Planewave propagation through a dielectric sheet.

vectors in the x direction, the field components in the three regions are

$$\mathbf{E}_{i1} = E_{i1}\hat{\mathbf{x}}e^{-jk_0z} \qquad \mathbf{E}_{r1} = E_{r1}\hat{\mathbf{x}}e^{+jk_0z}$$

$$\mathbf{H}_{i1} = \sqrt{\frac{\epsilon_0}{\mu_0}}\,E_{i1}\hat{\mathbf{y}}e^{-jk_0z} \qquad \mathbf{H}_{r1} = -\sqrt{\frac{\epsilon_0}{\mu_0}}\,E_{r1}\hat{\mathbf{y}}e^{+jk_0z}$$

$$\mathbf{E}_{i2} = E_{i2}\hat{\mathbf{x}}e^{-jk_2z} \qquad \mathbf{E}_{r2} = E_{r2}\hat{\mathbf{x}}e^{+jk_2z}$$

$$\mathbf{H}_{i2} = \sqrt{\frac{\epsilon}{\mu_0}}\,E_{i2}\hat{\mathbf{y}}e^{-jk_2z} \qquad \mathbf{H}_{r2} = -\sqrt{\frac{\epsilon}{\mu_0}}\,E_{r2}\hat{\mathbf{y}}e^{+jk_2z}$$

$$\mathbf{E}_{i3} = E_{i3}\hat{\mathbf{x}}e^{-jk_0z}$$

$$\mathbf{H}_{i3} = \sqrt{\frac{\epsilon_0}{\mu_0}}\,E_{i3}\hat{\mathbf{y}}e^{-jk_0z}$$

The equations for **E** are obtained from Eq. (6.49), as in Eq. (6.58). The equations for **H** are then obtained from Eq. (6.52). For a given input field amplitude E_{i1}, the unknowns are E_{r1}, E_{i2}, E_{r2}, and E_{i3}. Four equations are needed to solve for the four unknowns. Four equations are available from matching the boundary conditions on tangential **E** and **H** at $z = 0$ and d.

At the $z = 0$ plane the tangential electric fields in region 1 are matched to those in region 2,

$$E_{i1} + E_{r1} = E_{i2} + E_{r2} \tag{6.81}$$

Since there are no surface currents at a dielectric interface, the tangential **H** fields are matched at $z = 0$,

$$\sqrt{\frac{\epsilon_0}{\mu_0}}\,(E_{i1} - E_{r1}) = \sqrt{\frac{\epsilon}{\mu_0}}\,(E_{i2} - E_{r2}) \tag{6.82}$$

The fields are similarly matched at $z = d$ to give

$$E_{i2}e^{-jk_2d} + E_{r2}e^{+jk_2d} = E_{i3}e^{-jk_0d} \tag{6.83}$$

$$\sqrt{\frac{\epsilon}{\mu_0}}\,(E_{i2}e^{-jk_2d} - E_{r2}e^{+jk_2d}) = \sqrt{\frac{\epsilon_0}{\mu_0}}\,E_{i3}e^{-jk_0d} \tag{6.84}$$

Equations (6.81) to (6.84) may be algebraically manipulated to give the transmission and reflection coefficients,

$$\tau = \frac{E_{i3}}{E_{i1}} = \frac{e^{jk_0d}}{\cos k_2d + \frac{1}{2}j(\sqrt{\epsilon/\epsilon_0} + \sqrt{\epsilon_0/\epsilon})\sin k_2d} \tag{6.85}$$

$$\rho \equiv \frac{E_{r1}}{E_{i1}} = -\frac{\tau}{2}j\sin k_2d\left(\sqrt{\frac{\epsilon}{\epsilon_0}} - \sqrt{\frac{\epsilon_0}{\epsilon}}\right)e^{-jk_0d} \tag{6.86}$$

The reflection coefficient is a periodic function of k_2d and is zero when $k_2d = m\pi$. Thus when d is a multiple of a half-wavelength, there is no reflection from the dielectric sheet. It is clear from Eqs. (6.85) and (6.86) that for $\rho = 0$, $|\tau| = 1$, and all the power carried by the planewave is transmitted through the sheet. In practical applications where reflection from a dielectric sheet is to be minimized, the sheet is made an integral number of half-wavelengths thick, preferably one half-wavelength. This principle is used to determine the thickness of radomes (dielectric covering for airborne radar).

6.15 WAVE PROPAGATION IN HOMOGENEOUS DIELECTRICS

This chapter has been concerned with wave propagation in free space and homogeneous media with real constant permittivity and permeability. The nature of wave propagation in dielectric materials, considered in this section, is based on the electrical properties of dielectrics developed in Sec. 5. If we assume for simplicity that there is no orientational polarization and only one kind of electronic or atomic polarization, the total permittivity including the effects of both bound and conduction charges is found from Eq. (5.58) to be

$$\frac{\epsilon_c}{\epsilon_0} = 1 + \frac{\omega_{pb}^2}{\omega_s^2 - \omega^2 + j\omega\nu_b} + \frac{\omega_{pc}^2}{j\omega(j\omega + \nu_c)} \tag{6.87}$$

In this expression the definitions

$$\omega_{pc}^2 = \frac{\rho_c q}{\epsilon_0 m}$$

$$\omega_{pb}^2 = \frac{N_b q^2}{\epsilon_0 m}$$

have been made. ω_{pc} is called the *plasma frequency* for the conduction electrons. The reason for the name is found in the next section, where it is shown that ω_{pc} is a resonant frequency of a gaseous plasma. ω_{pb} is

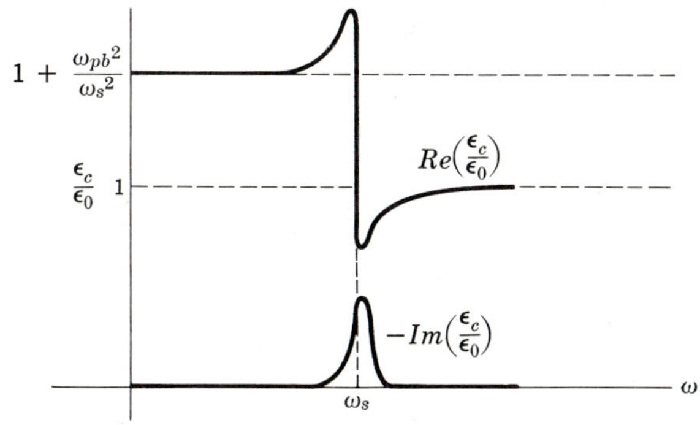

Fig. 6.18 Permittivity variation in a simple dielectric with no conduction charges.

defined in analogy to ω_{pc}. The real and imaginary parts of ϵ_c/ϵ_0 are sketched in Fig. 6.18 against ω for $\omega_{pc}^2 = 0$. At frequencies well below the bound-charge resonance frequency ω_s, the dielectric material has a constant permittivity $\epsilon_c/\epsilon_0 = 1 + \omega_{pb}^2/\omega_s^2$. Conversely, at frequencies well above ω_s, the dielectric material has a permittivity equal to the permittivity of free space. Only at frequencies near ω_s does ϵ_c/ϵ_0 deviate from these two limiting values. Thus it is a good approximation over a very wide frequency range to consider ϵ_c/ϵ_0 to be constant. Note that an imaginary component of ϵ_c arises near the resonance frequency ω_s. The actual permittivity characteristics in practical dielectrics deviate somewhat from this simple model, and other resonant frequencies may be present. For practical dielectric materials the permittivity is obtained experimentally, since ω_s, ν_b, and ω_{pb}^2 are not known.

The presence of conduction and bound-charge current is accounted for in the expression for permittivity; thus all the solutions to the wave equation in terms of ϵ may be used with Eq. (6.87). It is merely necessary to substitute the appropriate expression for permittivity into the propagation constant k, and the propagation characteristics for the material may be determined. Since the form of the solutions is the same for ϵ and ϵ_c, the subscript c can be dropped without ambiguity because it will be obvious from the expressions when the complex permittivity is being used. Hence, for convenience, ϵ will be used to mean the real or complex permittivity. For planewave propagation in a dielectric, the propagation factor is $k = \omega\sqrt{\mu\epsilon}$. If ϵ/ϵ_0 is written in the simpler general form of Eq. (5.125),

$$\frac{\epsilon}{\epsilon_0} = \epsilon_1 - j\epsilon_2 \tag{5.125}$$

the equation for k may be simplified. The real and imaginary parts of ϵ/ϵ_0 are, respectively, ϵ_1 and ϵ_2; thus k becomes

$$k = \omega\sqrt{\mu\epsilon_1}\sqrt{1 - j\frac{\epsilon_2}{\epsilon_1}} \tag{6.88}$$

and for $\epsilon_2 \ll \epsilon_1$

$$k = \omega\sqrt{\mu\epsilon_1}\left(1 - j\frac{\epsilon_2}{2\epsilon_1}\right) \tag{6.89}$$

It is customary to identify the imaginary and real parts of k as the attenuation and phase constants, α and β, in accordance with the definition

$$k = \beta - j\alpha \tag{6.90}$$

and Eqs. (6.90) and (6.89) give

$$\alpha = \omega\sqrt{\mu\epsilon_1}\frac{\epsilon_2}{2\epsilon_1} \tag{6.91}$$

$$\epsilon_2 \ll \epsilon_1$$

$$\beta = \omega\sqrt{\mu\epsilon_1} \tag{6.92}$$

For planewave propagation in the $+z$ direction, the final solution is obtained by substituting Eq. (6.90) into Eq. (6.49), with $\hat{\mathbf{n}}\cdot\mathbf{r} = z$, to give

$$\mathbf{E} = \mathbf{E}_0 e^{-j\beta z}e^{-\alpha z} \tag{6.93}$$

For the dielectric characterized by Eq. (6.87) with $\omega_{pc}{}^2 = 0$, Eqs. (6.91) and (6.92) become

$$\alpha = \omega\sqrt{\mu\epsilon_0}\sqrt{1 + \frac{\omega_{pb}{}^2}{\omega_s{}^2 - \omega^2}}\frac{\omega\nu_b\omega_{pb}{}^2}{2(\omega_s{}^2 - \omega^2)(\omega_s{}^2 - \omega^2 + \omega_{pb}{}^2)}$$

$$\beta = \omega\sqrt{\mu\epsilon_0}\sqrt{1 + \frac{\omega_{pb}{}^2}{\omega_s{}^2 - \omega^2}}$$

under the assumption that $\omega\nu_b \ll \omega_s{}^2 - \omega^2$. This result applies only when ω is not close to ω_s.

EFFECTS OF CONDUCTION CURRENT IN DIELECTRICS

Wave propagation in dielectrics where conduction current is present is now considered. Equation (6.87) is used for permittivity. It is useful to consider propagation in specific frequency ranges in order to simplify the equations. Below the optical spectrum, ω is usually well below the resonant frequency for bound electrons, ω_s, and the permittivity effects due to bound electrons are frequency independent. Typically, ν_b is small. If we further assume that $\omega \ll \nu_c$, Eq. (6.87) reduces to

$$\frac{\epsilon}{\epsilon_0} = 1 + \frac{{\omega_{pb}}^2}{{\omega_s}^2} - j\frac{{\omega_{pc}}^2}{\omega\nu_c} \tag{6.94}$$

If we insert Eq. (5.53) into Eq. (6.94), the permittivity is obtained in terms of the conductivity σ,

$$\frac{\epsilon}{\epsilon_0} = 1 + \frac{{\omega_{pb}}^2}{{\omega_s}^2} - j\frac{\sigma}{\omega\epsilon_0} \tag{6.95}$$

where $\sigma = {\omega_{pc}}^2\epsilon_0/\nu_c$. This formulation for permittivity is usually valid at low frequencies and up through the microwave spectrum $f = 10^{11}$. From Eq. (6.95), ϵ_1 and ϵ_2 are obtained, and the planewave propagation characteristics are found from Eqs. (6.88) and (6.90),

$$\beta = \omega\sqrt{\frac{\mu_0\epsilon_d}{2}}\sqrt{\sqrt{1 + \left(\frac{\sigma}{\omega\epsilon_d}\right)^2} + 1} \tag{6.96}$$

$$\alpha = \omega\sqrt{\frac{\mu_0\epsilon_d}{2}}\sqrt{\sqrt{1 + \left(\frac{\sigma}{\omega\epsilon_d}\right)^2} - 1} \tag{6.97}$$

with

$$\epsilon_d = \epsilon_0\left(1 + \frac{{\omega_{pb}}^2}{{\omega_s}^2}\right)$$

For good dielectric materials the effect of conduction electrons [as represented by the conductivity term in Eqs. (6.96) and (6.97)] is very small, and the equations become approximately

$$\beta \simeq \omega\sqrt{\mu_0\epsilon_d} \tag{6.98}$$

$$\alpha \simeq \omega\sqrt{\mu_0\epsilon_d}\,\frac{\sigma}{2\omega\epsilon_d} \tag{6.99}$$

The propagation characteristics in most practical dielectrics are described by Eqs. (6.98) and (6.99). The attentuation factor due to conduction electrons, given by Eq. (6.99), usually predominates over the damping factor associated with the bound electrons.

6.16 WAVE PROPAGATION IN CONDUCTORS

The basic equation for permittivity in a conducting medium is given by Eq. (6.87) with ${\omega_{pb}}^2 = 0$. Conductors are characterized by the effects of conduction charges, as described in Sec. 5.7. For good conductors the

ω_{pc} term is much larger than the ω_{pb} term in Eq. (6.87), and thus

$$\frac{\epsilon}{\epsilon_0} = 1 + \frac{\omega_{pc}{}^2}{j\omega(j\omega + \nu_c)} \tag{6.100}$$

TENUOUS GASEOUS CONDUCTORS

Many important practical problems involve a conducting material in which the collision frequency ν_c is very low. In this case Eq. (6.100) reduces to

$$\frac{\epsilon}{\epsilon_0} = 1 - \frac{\omega_{pc}{}^2}{\omega^2} \tag{6.101}$$

Equation (6.101) is appropriate for thin ionized conducting gases such as the ionosphere and certain gaseous plasmas. With respect to the model for materials discussed in Chap. 5, these gases may be considered as metals with very low charge density.

The propagation factor for planewave propagation in such media is

$$k = \omega \sqrt{\mu_0 \epsilon_0} \sqrt{1 - \left(\frac{\omega_{pc}}{\omega}\right)^2} \tag{6.102}$$

At radian frequencies well above ω_{pc}, planewaves propagate as in free space. As the operating radian frequency is reduced to a value near ω_{pc}, the propagation constant decreases with a corresponding increase in phase velocity. At $\omega = \omega_{pc}$ the propagation constant is zero, and planewaves cease to propagate, or are cut off. Because of this resonance at $\omega = \omega_{pc}$, ω_{pc} is called the *plasma frequency*. Below ω_{pc}, k is imaginary, and planewaves do not propagate. This result explains the observed phenomenon of long-range terrestrial radio communication by the reflection of low-frequency radio waves off the conducting ionospheric layer. Reflection occurs when ω is less than ω_{pc}. For the ionosphere the peak f_{pc} is approximately 10 MHz; thus radio-broadcast frequencies (which are typically in the order of 1 MHz) are reflected from the ionospheric conducting layer. Microwave and television planewaves, which are above 40 MHz, are easily transmitted through the conducting ionospheric layer with no reflection.

SOLID-STATE CONDUCTORS

In solid conducting materials the charge densities and collision rates are very much higher than in gaseous conductors. For many solid conducting materials ν_c is in the ultraviolet spectrum. Thus at frequencies well below the ultraviolet spectrum, Eq. (6.100) reduces to

$$\frac{\epsilon}{\epsilon_0} = 1 + \frac{\omega_{pc}^2}{j\omega\nu_c} \tag{6.103}$$

In addition, the free-electron density is often so high that ω_{pc}^2 is much larger than $\omega\nu_c$, in which case Eq. (6.103) becomes

$$\frac{\epsilon}{\epsilon_0} = \frac{\omega_{pc}^2}{j\omega\nu_c} = \frac{\sigma}{j\omega\epsilon_0} \tag{6.104}$$

The phase constant β and the attenuation constant α may now be obtained. Equation (6.88) becomes for this case

$$\begin{aligned} k &= \omega\sqrt{\mu\epsilon} \\ &= \omega\sqrt{\mu\epsilon_0}\sqrt{-j\sigma/\omega\epsilon_0} \\ &= \sqrt{\frac{\omega\mu\sigma}{2}}\,(1-j) \end{aligned}$$

and from Eq. (6.90)

$$\begin{aligned} \alpha &= \beta \\ &= \sqrt{\frac{\omega\mu\sigma}{2}} \qquad = \frac{1}{\delta \text{ meters}} \end{aligned} \tag{6.105}$$

Note that the attenuation constant equals the phase constant, and thus planewaves are severely attenuated in solid-state conductors. When the conductor is perfect ($\sigma \to \infty$), the attenuation constant becomes infinite. Thus **E** and **B** must be zero inside a perfect conductor. As the wave penetrates the material a distance δ,

$$\delta = \sqrt{\frac{2}{\omega\mu\sigma}} \quad \text{meters} \tag{6.106}$$

the wave is space shifted by 1 rad and is attenuated by the factor $1/e$. The factor δ is called the *skin depth*, and the skin depth is usually a very small distance in a good conductor; for copper at 10 GHz the skin depth is less than 1 μ.

Example 6.8 The wave equation in a conducting medium The wave analysis in this section has been based on a determination of k from the expression $k = \omega\sqrt{\mu\epsilon}$. An alternate approach would be to take the general wave equation for **E** in a medium where a conduction current exists and express the conduction-current density in terms of the electric field by means of Eq. (5.52). In a good conductor it is recognized that the net charge density ρ must be zero, since for every conduction electron in the material there is a positive lattice ion. For a good conductor it is also true that the conduction current is much larger than the displacement current; thus the wave equation of **E**, Eq. (6.12), reduces to

$$\nabla^2\mathbf{E} = \mu\sigma\frac{\partial\mathbf{E}}{\partial t}$$

For the $e^{j\omega t}$ time dependence this equation becomes

$$\nabla^2\mathbf{E} = j\omega\mu\sigma\mathbf{E}$$

For the one-dimensional case we obtain

$$\frac{\partial^2}{\partial z^2}\mathbf{E} = j\omega\mu\sigma\mathbf{E}$$

By assuming a solution for **E** of the form e^{-jkz}, we determine k,

$$k^2 = -j\omega\mu\sigma$$

$$k = \sqrt{\frac{\omega\mu\sigma}{2}}\,(1 - j)$$

This is the same result obtained from the permittivity analysis given above. It is thus demonstrated that propagation in conductors is characterized by the presence of conduction current, with negligible displacement current and zero net charge density.

Example 6.9 Frequency dependence of the reflectivity of metals In previous examples it has been assumed that $\omega \ll \omega_s$, and hence that the polarization terms in the permittivity of a good conductor are nearly independent of frequency. In the optical range, however, this is no longer true, and the frequency variation of the polarization terms in the permittivity produce some very interesting effects. The nature of these effects can be illustrated by considering the simplified case of reflection by a conductor with permittivity given by Eq. (6.87), where it has been assumed that only one kind of electronic polarization is present.

It is convenient to normalize the parameters in Eq. (6.87) by dividing by ω_s. Then ϵ/ϵ_0 can be written in terms of real and imaginary parts, according to the definition in Eq. (5.125), as

$$\frac{\epsilon}{\epsilon_0} = \epsilon_1 - j\epsilon_2$$

$$\epsilon_1 = 1 - \frac{\omega'^2_{pc}}{\omega'^2 + \nu'^2_c} + \frac{(1 - \omega'^2)\omega'^2_{pb}}{(1 - \omega'^2)^2 + \omega'^2\nu'^2_b}$$

$$\epsilon_2 = \frac{\omega'^2_{pc}\nu'_c}{\omega'(\omega'^2 + \nu'^2_c)} + \frac{\omega'\nu'_b\omega'^2_{pb}}{(1 - \omega'^2)^2 + \omega'^2\nu'^2_b}$$

where the primes mean normalized quantities, that is, $\omega' = \omega/\omega_s$, etc. In addition, it is convenient to define

$$\epsilon_{1m} = 1 - \frac{\omega'^2_{pc}}{\omega'^2 + \nu'^2_c}$$

$$\epsilon_{1b} = \frac{(1 - \omega'^2)\omega'^2_{pb}}{(1 - \omega'^2)^2 + \omega'^2\nu'^2_b}$$

$$\epsilon_{2m} = \frac{\omega'^2_{pc}\nu'_c}{\omega'(\omega'^2 + \nu'^2_c)}$$

$$\epsilon_{2b} = \frac{\omega'\nu'_b\omega'^2_{pb}}{(1 - \omega'^2)^2 + \omega'^2\nu'^2_b}$$

Putting in some typical numbers for charge density and conductivity and making some assumptions about ω_s and ν_b results in $\omega'^2_{pc} = 27.4$, $\omega'^2_{pb} = 27.4$, $\nu'_c = .0159$, and $\nu'_b = .05$.

Now the reflection coefficient can be found as a function of ω'. From Eq. (6.77), the reflection coefficient for normal incidence is

$$\rho = \frac{1 - \sqrt{\epsilon_{II}/\epsilon_I}}{1 + \sqrt{\epsilon_{II}/\epsilon_I}}$$

For our case, ϵ_{II} is the permittivity of the metal and ϵ_I is the permittivity of free space. Thus ρ can be written as

$$\rho = \frac{1 - \sqrt{\epsilon_1 - j\epsilon_2}}{1 + \sqrt{\epsilon_1 + j\epsilon_2}} \tag{6.107}$$

The ratio of the average reflected power to the average incident power, $\rho\rho^*$, is shown plotted against ω' in Fig. 6.19. Almost all the power is reflected at lower frequencies, as we know it is for a good conductor, but near $\omega' = 0.7$ the reflected

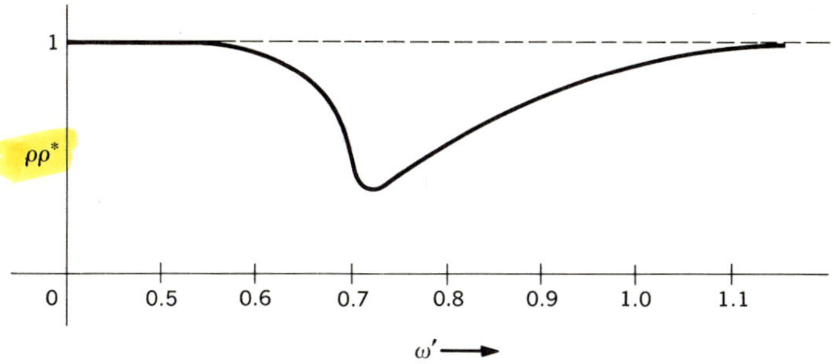

Fig. 6.19 The ratio of reflected power to incident power as a function of normalized frequency as calculated in Example 6.9.

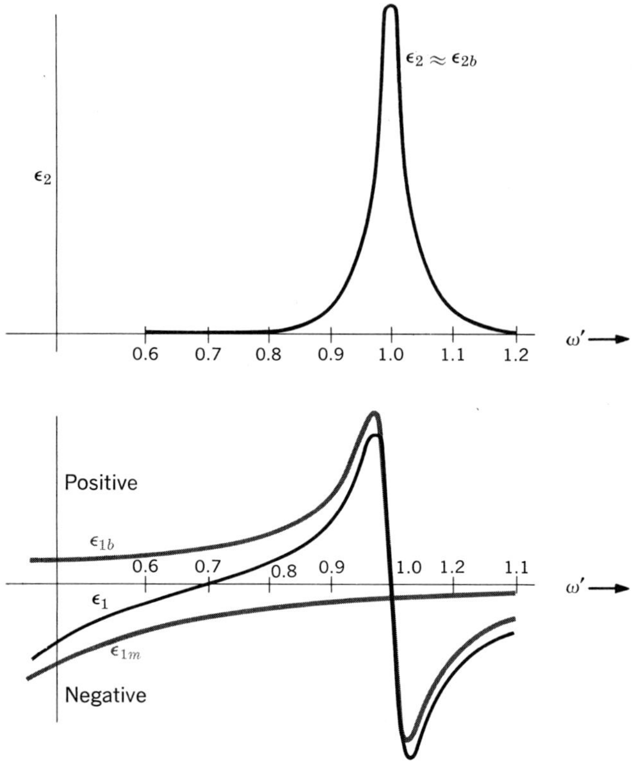

Fig. 6.20 The real and imaginary parts, ϵ_1 and ϵ_2, of the complex permittivity as a function of normalized frequency as used in Example 6.9.

power decreases markedly. Since the reflected power is a strong function of frequency, the metal has color, and in a simplified way, this explains what causes the color of some metals.†

The reason for the dip near $\omega' = 0.7$ can be seen from the behavior of ϵ with frequency. Figure 6.20 shows ϵ_{1b}, ϵ_{1m}, and $\epsilon_1 = \epsilon_{1b} + \epsilon_{1m}$. Also shown is ϵ_{2b}, which is approximately the same as ϵ_2, since ϵ_{2m} is negligible in this frequency range. Near $\omega' = 0.7$, ϵ_2 is very small and ϵ_1 is unity. From Eq. (6.107) it can be seen that this results in a very low value for ρ. If ϵ_2 were actually zero, ρ would be zero when $\epsilon_1 = 1$. Thus the decrease in reflected power results from the combination of low ϵ_2 and $\epsilon_1 = 1$. The latter condition, $\epsilon_1 = 1$, occurs because ϵ_{1b} gets large as ω approaches ω_s, and hence ϵ_{1b} can be large enough to cancel the effects of the large negative ϵ_{1m}. This cannot occur at frequencies low compared to ω_s,

† Henry Ehrenreich, The Optical Properties of Metals, *IEEE Spectrum*, March, 1965, pp. 162–170.

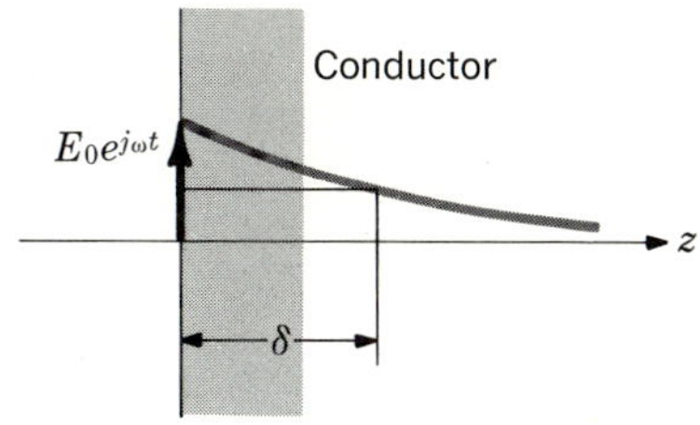

Fig. 6.21 Field penetration into a conductor.

because in that range ϵ_{1m} is very large and negative and ϵ_{1b} is much smaller and positive. This results in high reflection. Thus it is the combination of the bound-electron and conduction-electron effects which causes the characteristic color of some metals.

6.17 THE SKIN EFFECT

It was shown in Sec. 6.16 that planewaves are severely attenuated when they propagate in conducting material. If a wave is incident upon a conductor with finite conductivity, it will attenuate as it penetrates. For infinite conductivity no penetration occurs, because $\mathbf{E} = \mathbf{B} = 0$ in the material. For good conductors the penetration depth is very small.

Consider the case where a sinusoidal time-varying electric field of amplitude E_0 is impressed on the surface of a semi-infinite conductor, as shown in Fig. 6.21. The field penetration into the conductor is known, since k is known in the conductor. The attenuation constant is

$$\alpha = \sqrt{\frac{\omega\mu\sigma}{2}}$$

$$= \frac{1}{\delta}$$

Note in Eq. (6.93) that when $z = 1/\alpha = \delta$, the electric field amplitude has decayed from E_0 to a value E_0/e. The rapid decrease in field intensity into a conductor is known as the *skin effect*. The fields and associated currents are confined to a very thin layer close to the surface of a conductor in a skinlike fashion. For a perfect conductor, $\delta = 0$; the fields do not penetrate, and the current flows entirely on the surface.

PROBLEMS

6.2-1 A circuit is constructed which is 1 m across. An alternating voltage is imposed at one end of the circuit and is carried directly to the opposite side. What is the phase difference between the voltages at each end of the circuit as a function of frequency? At what frequency is the phase difference π rad?

6.2-2 Solve for the wavelength of a 1-MHz and a 1,000-MHz electromagnetic wave in free space and in teflon.

6.2-3 An electromagnetic wave is characterized by an **E** vector $\mathbf{E} = (E_x\hat{\mathbf{x}} + E_y\hat{\mathbf{y}}) e^{j(\omega t - kz)}$, where E_x and E_y are constants. Solve for **H**.

6.3-1 Derive the homogeneous wave equation for **E** for the case where ϵ is time varying.

6.3-2 Derive an equation analogous to Eq. (6.13) for the case where $\nabla \cdot \mathbf{H} = -\nabla \cdot \mathbf{M}$. Obtain the final equation in terms of a magnetic charge density ρ_m.

6.3-3 Starting from Eqs. (6.8) and (6.9), derive the wave equation for **E** for the case where the displacement current in the medium is very small compared to **J**, and **J** is the current resulting from the acceleration of free charges, $\mathbf{J} = \rho_0\mathbf{v}$. Assume that **E**, **J**, and **v** vary as $e^{j\omega t}$, and that $\nabla \cdot \mathbf{E} = 0$ and $\mathbf{B} = 0$.

6.4-1 An **E** and a **B** field exist in a region where $\mathbf{A} = y^2zt^2\hat{\mathbf{x}}$. Given that $\nabla\Phi = 0$, find **E** and **B**.

6.6-1 Assume that a steady current given by

$$\mathbf{J} = J_0 \sin \alpha x \, \hat{\mathbf{x}}$$

exists in free space. Solve for vector potential **A** generated by this steady-current density, assuming no y or z variation. Then find the magnetic field **B**.

6.6-2 Two infinite, parallel conducting planes occupy the $z = 0$ and $z = a$ planes. An alternating electric field is present between the planes of the form

$$\mathbf{E} = E_0 \sin \pi z/a \, \hat{\mathbf{x}} e^{j\omega t}$$

Find $\nabla \cdot \mathbf{E}$ and $\nabla \times \mathbf{E}$ at all points between the planes. Can **E** be expressed as $\mathbf{E} = -\nabla\Phi$, where Φ is a scalar potential function? Obtain an expression for the magnetic field associated with this electric field. Determine the surface charge and surface current density on the two conducting planes.

6.7-1 An electric-dipole antenna broadcasts at 1 MHz. The antenna height is 10 m, and $I_0 = 10$ amp. Calculate the electric field intensity E at a receiver 20 km away, neglecting the effect of the surface of the earth.

6.8-1 Solve for the vector potential **A** generated by two short electric dipole antennas as shown in Fig. 6.4 with currents $I_1 = e^{j\alpha}$ and $I_2 = e^{j\beta}$. Consider two cases, the currents in phase and out of phase. Assume that the $1/r$ amplitude variation at the field point may be neglected, but that l is large enough that the phase difference between the two dipoles is important. Plot $|\mathbf{A}|$ versus φ for $l = \lambda$ and 2λ.

6.8-2 Solve for the directivity function of a five-element dipole array with dipoles located at $y = 0, \pm l, \pm 2l$. All the currents are in phase and flow in the z direction. Plot $|F(\varphi)|$ as in Fig. 6.5 for $l = 2\lambda$.

6.9-1 A very small cylindrical resistor R dissipates power due to I^2R losses but also radiates power by electric dipole radiation. The resistor is in free space and is driven by an ac current at $f = 10^8$ Hz. The resistor length is 1 cm with area 1 mm². Solve for the ratio of radiated to dissipated power if the resistor is composed of (a) metal with $\sigma = 10^7$ mhos/m and (b) resistive material with $\sigma = 10^{-3}$ mhos/m. Neglect end effects.

6.9-2 An electric dipole antenna is driven at a frequency $f = 500$ MHz. The dipole is 1 cm in length and carries a current of 10 amp. A receiving antenna of area 1 m^2 is moved on a surface of a sphere with its origin at the dipole of radius 10 m. At what angle θ will the receiving antenna receive 2 mw of average power?

6.10-1 Derive Eq. (6.52).

6.10-2 If $k_x = 50$, $k_y = 40$, and $k_z = 0$ for a planewave at $f = 10^9$, what is the phase velocity v_p and the direction of propagation?

6.10-3 Equation (6.52) gives the **H** field for a planewave propagating in the $+\hat{\mathbf{n}}$ direction. Derive the corresponding equation for **H** for a planewave propagating in the $-\hat{\mathbf{n}}$ direction.

6.11-1 Calculate the time-average electric energy density in a planewave [Eq. (6.54)] by calculating the total electric energy at an instant contained in a volume 1 wavelength long in the direction of propagation with cross-sectional area 1 m^2 and dividing this total energy by the volume.

6.11-2 A directional transmitter generates a planewave in free space in a beam of area 1 m^2 which carries a total time-average power of 100 watts. Solve for the peak amplitude of the electric field E_0 and the peak amplitude of the magnetic field H_0. Solve for the total time-average energy density in joules per cubic meter.

6.12-1 A planewave in free space is normally incident upon a perfectly conducting planar surface. The amplitude of the electric field vector in the planewave is E_0. Calculate the time-average force density exerted on the conducting surface. What is the force density when the power carried in the planewave is 100 watts/m^2?

6.12-2 A laser cavity is constructed of two parallel mirrors. The gap between the planes is $a = 1$ cm. The laser cavity is filled with an active medium, with $\epsilon = \epsilon_0$, which generates energy in the wavelength range $0.69200 < \lambda < 0.69220\ \mu$. Assume that all the resonant modes of the structure which lie in this range are excited into oscillation. Solve for the mode numbers, m, and the oscillation wavelengths of the laser.

6.12-3 The mirrors in a parallel-mirror laser are supported on aluminum rods. The laser is 20 cm long and operates at 0.6328 μ. How much temperature change is allowed in the aluminum rods if it is specified that the modes may not shift by more than 10 percent of their spacing?

6.12-4 Find the magnetic field H in the standing wave associated with the electric field in Eq. (6.60).

6.13-1 A planewave is obliquely incident on a perfectly conducting plane. Explain why the constant y planes where $\mathbf{E} = 0$ are more widely separated when $n_y < 1$.

6.13-2 Derive the **H** vectors associated with the incident and reflected planewaves for oblique incidence at a conducting plane, and obtain Eq. (6.65).

6.13-3 Solve for θ, the direction of planewave propagation in the parallel-plate transmission line, as a function of λ, for a given m and a. Solve for θ if $m = 1$ and $\lambda/a = 1.0$.

6.13-4 A parallel-plate wave guide consists of plates 1 cm wide with $a = 1$ mm, separated by a teflon dielectric medium. What are the lowest frequencies for waveguide propagation for $m = 1, 2, 3$?

6.14-1 Derive Eq. (6.79).

6.14-2 A planewave is incident upon a dielectric-air interface as shown in Fig. 6.12 for $\epsilon_{II}/\epsilon_I = 5$. If $\theta_i = 30°$, what is θ_r? Construct a wave-front diagram to show that for these values of θ_i and θ_r the incident and refracted waves are phase matched along z.

6.14-3 Obtain from a computer program a plot of $|\rho|$ versus θ_i in Eq. (6.79) for $\epsilon_{II}/\epsilon_I = 2, 5, 25$.

6.14-4 Derive Eqs. (6.85) and (6.86).

6.14-5 Assume that region 3 in Example 6.7 has a permittivity ϵ_3 instead of ϵ_0. Solve for the reflection coefficient ρ. Zero reflection occurs for $k_2 d = \pi/2$ if ϵ is adjusted properly. What is the required ϵ value in terms of ϵ_0 and ϵ_3? The principle illustrated in this problem is used in antireflection coatings of dielectric film on lenses.

6.15-1 What is the phase velocity and attenuation constant for glass where $\epsilon_d/\epsilon_0 = 5$ and $\sigma = 10^{-12}$ mhos/m?

6.15-2 A planewave propagates in a dielectric material with finite conductivity and finite loss factor. Prove that the ratio of the time-average power lost in the medium to the time-average power transmitted through the medium is

$$\frac{\langle \mathcal{P}_c \rangle}{\langle \mathcal{P} \rangle} = \frac{\omega}{v_p Q}$$

A planewave propagates at a frequency 1 GHz in teflon and carries a total power of 100 watts. The planewave is confined to a cross-sectional area of 1 m². Assuming that the conductivity of teflon is negligible, calculate the total power lost in a 10-m path length in the material.

6.16-1 Derive the differential equations for **H** and **J** in a good conductor,

$$\nabla^2 \mathbf{H} = j\omega\mu\sigma\mathbf{H}$$
$$\nabla^2 \mathbf{J} = j\omega\mu\sigma\mathbf{J}$$

6.16-2 A planewave propagates in a medium of free charges characterized by $\epsilon_b = 0$ and $\nu_c/\omega_{pc} = 0.2$. Obtain from a computer program enough points to establish a plot of ω/ω_{pc} versus

$$\text{Re}\,\frac{k}{\omega_{pc}\sqrt{\mu_0\epsilon_0}} \qquad \text{Im}\,\frac{k}{\omega_{pc}\sqrt{\mu_0\epsilon_0}}$$

over the range $0 < \omega/\omega_{pc} < 3$. Plot the solution for $\nu_c = 0$ and compare. Explain the difference between planewave propagation in free space, in a medium of free charges with no collisions, and in a medium of free charges with collisions.

6.16-3 A rocket is fired vertically from the surface of the earth for the purpose of making ionospheric electron-density measurements. The rocket contains an antenna which is driven by a swept-frequency oscillator. The frequency is swept over the frequency range 1 to 10 MHz. It is possible to detect when radiation into the ionosphere takes place by the sudden change in the impedance of the antenna at a cutoff frequency. At frequencies above the cutoff frequency the antenna radiates into the ionosphere, whereas at frequencies below the cutoff frequency no radiation takes place. When the projectile reaches the peak of its trajectory, which is 500 km, we set $t = 0$. As the projectile descends, cutoff-frequency information is telemetered to a ground station every 20 sec. The following set of data is recorded:

Time t, sec	f_{cutoff}, *MHz*
0	0
20	0
40	1
60	1.5
80	2
100	2.5
120	3.5
140	6
160	10
180	5
200	2
220	1
240	0

Construct from these data a profile of the electron density versus altitude, assuming that air drag is negligible.

6.17-1 Look up in a suitable reference the conductivity for silver, copper, and brass, and calculate the skin depth for these materials at 1 MHz and 10 GHz.

6.17-2 From the circuital law it is known that $B_\varphi = \mu I r / 2\pi a^2$ inside a dc current-carrying wire of radius a, where the current density is uniform over the wire cross section. If the current is alternating at a frequency such that the wire diameter is about equal to the skin depth, discuss qualitatively how the radial current variation and B_φ are altered from the dc state.

6.17-3 If 1 kw of microwave power at $f = 100$ MHz is normally incident upon a 1 m^2 sheet of aluminum foil 0.001 in. thick, how much power penetrates the foil, neglecting reflection losses?

CHAPTER

7

circuit theory from field theory

7.1 INTRODUCTION

Because of the complexity of Maxwell's equations, many special techniques have been developed for solving the equations in special situations. There are three ranges in the frequency spectrum for which extensive special techniques have been developed. In terms of λ, the wavelength, and l, the approximate dimension of the apparatus, these ranges are

$$\lambda \gg l$$

$$\lambda \approx l$$

$$\lambda \ll l$$

In the first case, the special analysis techniques are known as *circuit theory;* in the second, as *microwave theory;* and in the third, as *optics*. It is our purpose here to show how the fundamental laws of circuit theory are obtained from Maxwell's equations by applying an approximation, called the *quasi-static field approximation* (as discussed in Chap. 4), which is valid when $\lambda \gg l$. It is fortunate indeed that such an approximation is valid and that it leads to simplified, but very powerful, methods of solving electromagnetic field problems. Imagine how little we would know about the nature of electric circuits if we had to analyze them by solving Maxwell's equations in the form given in Chap. 3.

Circuit theory was not developed by approximating Maxwell's equations, but rather was developed independently from experimentally obtained laws. The connection between circuit theory and Maxwell's equations is an important one, however, because it adds to the comprehension of the fundamentals of electromagnetics. Furthermore, an understanding of the relation of circuit theory to field theory is important in the analysis of transmission lines and antennas, which lie in the interface between field theory and circuit theory.

It is assumed that the reader is familiar with circuit theory, and therefore no attempt is made here to treat circuit theory in detail. For convenience, sinusoidal time variation is assumed throughout the chapter, but the extension to arbitrary time variation is not difficult.

7.2 QUASI-STATIC FIELDS

The underlying fundamental approximation that leads to circuit theory from field theory is that of quasi-static fields. Suppose that $l \ll \lambda$, where l is the largest dimension of a "circuit" and λ is the wavelength. Then the expressions for Φ and $\mathbf{A}$, Eqs. (6.24) and (6.23),

$$\Phi = \frac{e^{j\omega t}}{4\pi\epsilon} \int_V \frac{\rho e^{-jkR}}{R}\, dV' \tag{6.24}$$

$$\mathbf{A} = \frac{\mu e^{j\omega t}}{4\pi} \int_V \frac{\mathbf{J} e^{-jkR}}{R}\, dV' \tag{6.23}$$

can be simplified. The simplification results because $kR \ll 1$ when $l \ll \lambda$ (see Prob. 7.2-1). From the series expression

$$e^{-jkR} = 1 - jkR - \frac{k^2R^2}{2} + \cdots$$

we may set

$$e^{-jkR} \approx 1$$

when kR is small enough. In this case, Φ and $\mathbf{A}$ become

$$\Phi \approx \frac{e^{j\omega t}}{4\pi\epsilon} \int_V \frac{\rho}{R}\, dV' \tag{7.1}$$

and

$$\mathbf{A} \approx \frac{\mu e^{j\omega t}}{4\pi} \int_V \frac{\mathbf{J}}{R}\, dV' \tag{7.2}$$

These are called *quasi-static fields* because they have the same spatial variation as static fields, yet they vary as $e^{j\omega t}$.

The quasi-static approximation results because retardation is negligible; i.e., the circuit is small enough that the time required for the fields to propagate from one part of the circuit to another is negligible compared to a period, $2\pi/\omega$. Mathematically, this corresponds to $e^{-jkR} \approx 1$.

There are many important and practical applications of the quasi-static approximation. In addition to being the underlying approximation leading from field theory to circuit theory, this approximation is also very useful in solving some microwave field problems.

7.3 FUNDAMENTAL CIRCUIT RELATIONS

In this section the basic circuit relations are developed from field theory by starting with a very simple *RL* circuit and then proceeding to a general *RLC* circuit. The main purpose is to show the connection between circuit theory and field theory, rather than to develop circuit theory rigorously. For simplicity, only sinusoidal time variation is considered.

THE *RL* CIRCUIT

Suppose that a time-varying magnetic field is applied to the loop of filamentary conductor as illustrated in Fig. 7.1. As explained in Chap. 3, a time-varying applied **B** field, which is labeled $\mathbf{B}_a$ here, exerts forces on electrons in the conductor and thus causes current to flow. This current then produces another magnetic field, which is called the induced field $\mathbf{B}_i$. It is assumed that:

1. The induced current does not affect $\mathbf{B}_a$.
2. The quasi-static approximation is valid.
3. The conductors are filamentary.

Then

$$\mathbf{B}_i = \nabla \times \mathbf{A}_i \tag{7.3}$$

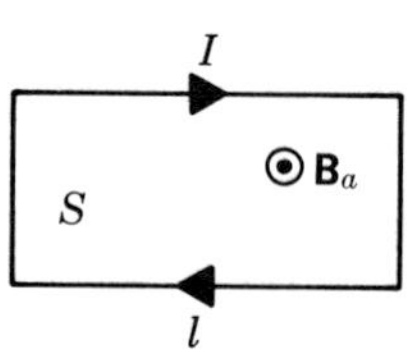

Fig. 7.1 A loop of filamentary conductor in an applied magnetic field. $\mathbf{B}_a$ is out of the paper.

and

$$\mathbf{A}_i = \frac{\mu e^{j\omega t}}{4\pi} \int_V \frac{\mathbf{J}}{R}\, dV'$$

$$= \frac{\mu I e^{j\omega t}}{4\pi} \int_l \frac{d\mathbf{l}'}{R} \tag{7.4}$$

In terms of the potential functions, **E** is

$$\mathbf{E} = -\nabla\Phi - j\omega\mathbf{A}$$

$$= -\nabla\Phi - j\omega\mathbf{A}_a - j\omega\mathbf{A}_i \tag{7.5}$$

since, by superposition, the total magnetic field is the sum of the applied and induced fields. Integrating along the filamentary conductor shown in Fig. 7.1 gives

$$\oint_l \mathbf{E} \cdot d\mathbf{l} = -\oint_l \nabla\Phi \cdot d\mathbf{l} - j\omega \oint_l \mathbf{A}_a \cdot d\mathbf{l} - j\omega \oint_l \mathbf{A}_i \cdot d\mathbf{l}$$

As noted in Sec. 1.14, when $\nabla \times \mathbf{F} = 0, \oint_l \mathbf{F} \cdot d\mathbf{l} = 0$. Since $\nabla \times \nabla\Phi = 0$,

$$\oint_l \nabla\Phi \cdot d\mathbf{l} = 0 \tag{7.6}$$

and therefore

$$\oint_l \mathbf{E} \cdot d\mathbf{l} = -j\omega \oint_l \mathbf{A}_a \cdot d\mathbf{l} - j\omega \oint_l \mathbf{A}_i \cdot d\mathbf{l} \tag{7.7}$$

This equation is equivalent to Kirchhoff's voltage law, as consideration of the individual terms will show. From Chap. 5 we know that in conductors at low frequencies, where the quasi-static approximation holds for ordinary circuits,

$$\mathbf{J} = \sigma\mathbf{E}$$

Therefore

$$\oint_l \mathbf{E} \cdot d\mathbf{l} = \oint_l \frac{\mathbf{J} \cdot d\mathbf{l}}{\sigma}$$

In the filamentary conductors the current density is uniform. Hence

$$\oint_l \frac{\mathbf{J} \cdot d\mathbf{l}}{\sigma} = I \oint_l \frac{dl}{C\sigma}$$

where C is the cross-sectional area of the conductor and I is the total current in the direction of $d\mathbf{l}$. For a uniform conductor, C is constant and

$$\oint_l \frac{dl}{C\sigma} = \frac{l}{C\sigma}$$

$$= R$$

where l is the total length of the conductor and R is the familiar dc resistance of the conductor. Then

$$\oint_l \mathbf{E} \cdot d\mathbf{l} = \oint_l \frac{\mathbf{J} \cdot d\mathbf{l}}{\sigma}$$
$$= IR \tag{7.8}$$

For thicker conductors (or higher frequencies) $\mathbf{J}$ is not uniform and the resistance is not the dc value. This is discussed in Sec. 7.5.

From Eq. (7.4) it can be seen that $\mathbf{A}_i$ is proportional to I for the filamentary case discussed here. The proportionality constant is called L, the inductance. Thus, by definition,

$$-j\omega \oint_l \mathbf{A}_i \cdot d\mathbf{l} = -j\omega LI \tag{7.9}$$

The familiar relation $L = \psi/I$ is obtained by using Stokes's theorem to get

$$\oint_l \mathbf{A}_i \cdot d\mathbf{l} = \int_S \mathbf{B}_i \cdot d\mathbf{S}$$
$$= \psi$$

Then $L = \psi/I$ follows from Eq. (7.9). Methods of calculating L are discussed in Sec. 7.4. Finally, a convenient definition is

$$-j\omega \oint_l \mathbf{A}_a \cdot d\mathbf{l} = \mathcal{E} \tag{7.10}$$

where $\mathcal{E}$ is called *electromotive force* or *emf*.

With these definitions, Eq. (7.7) becomes

$$IR + j\omega LI = \mathcal{E}$$

which is Kirchhoff's voltage law for the simple RL circuit. The simple circuit just discussed might represent the armature of a generator; in this case, the impedance terms would be the internal impedance of the generator.

THE *RLC* CIRCUIT

Figure 7.2 shows the circuit of Fig. 7.1 with the addition of a gap in the conductor. Since no conduction current can flow through the gap, charge

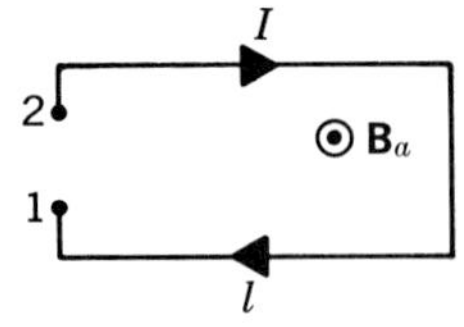

Fig. 7.2 An unclosed loop of filamentary conductor in an applied magnetic field.

builds up on the ends of the conductors and displacement current flows across the gap. The gap is called *capacitance*, and plates are often used to increase the charge storage on the ends of the conductors and thus increase the displacement current through the gap.

Kirchhoff's voltage law for this circuit can be obtained by integrating Eq. (7.5) from point 2 clockwise along the conductor around to point 1,

$$\int_{\substack{2\\ \text{wire}}}^{1} \mathbf{E} \cdot d\mathbf{l} = -\int_{\substack{2\\ \text{wire}}}^{1} \nabla\Phi \cdot d\mathbf{l} - j\omega \int_{\substack{2\\ \text{wire}}}^{1} \mathbf{A}_a \cdot d\mathbf{l} - j\omega \int_{\substack{2\\ \text{wire}}}^{1} \mathbf{A}_i \cdot d\mathbf{l} \tag{7.11}$$

Following the procedure of the previous section, we set

$$\int_{\substack{2\\ \text{wire}}}^{1} \mathbf{E} \cdot d\mathbf{l} = IR$$

$$-j\omega \int_{\substack{2\\ \text{wire}}}^{1} \mathbf{A}_a \cdot d\mathbf{l} = \mathcal{E}$$

$$-j\omega \int_{\substack{2\\ \text{wire}}}^{1} \mathbf{A}_i \cdot d\mathbf{l} = -j\omega LI$$

The remaining term (see Prob. 2.4-1) is

$$-\int_{\substack{2\\ \text{wire}}}^{1} \nabla\Phi \cdot d\mathbf{l} = -(\Phi_1 - \Phi_2)$$

where Φ_1 and Φ_2 are the values of the potential at points 1 and 2, respectively. Remember that the value of the integral does not depend on the path of integration, since $\nabla\Phi$ is a conservative field (see Sec. 1.14).

The values of Φ_1 and Φ_2 are a result of all the charges in the system, but principally of the charges on the capacitor plates. The charges in the conductors have negligible effect, because the conductors are essentially electrically neutral. It is assumed that any charges stored in the source of emf produce negligible values of Φ in the capacitor because the source charges are much farther removed than the capacitor charge. In addition, it is assumed that there are no other nearby capacitors whose charge would affect Φ in the capacitor. If there were other capacitors near enough to cause coupling, this could be taken into account by mutual capacitance.

The charge on the capacitor plates is directly proportional to the potential difference between the plates, $\Phi_1 - \Phi_2$. This proportionality constant is called capacitance. Thus

$$Q = C(\Phi_1 - \Phi_2) \tag{7.12}$$

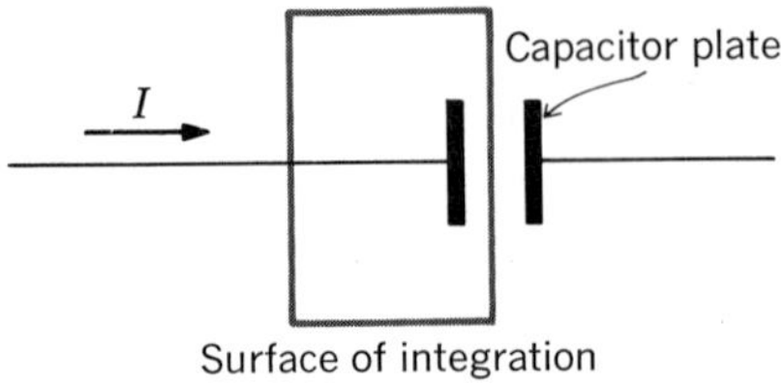

Fig. 7.3 Surface of integration between capacitor plates.

where Q is the magnitude of charge on one plate and C is defined as the capacitance. The nature and calculation of capacitance are discussed in Sec. 7.6. The capacitance is always positive and depends only on the geometry. Hence, in Eq. (7.12), Q is the charge on plate 1. If plate 1 is at a higher potential than plate 2, Q is positive, and vice versa.

The charge Q can be related to I through the continuity equation

$$\nabla \cdot \mathbf{J} = -j\omega\rho$$

Integrating over a volume and using the divergence theorem gives

$$\oint_S \mathbf{J} \cdot d\mathbf{S} = -j\omega \int_V \rho \, dV \tag{7.13}$$

If S is a surface which passes through the capacitor plates as shown in Fig. 7.3, then

$$-I = -j\omega Q$$

so

$$Q = \frac{I}{j\omega} \tag{7.14}$$

Combining Eqs. (7.14) and (7.12) results in

$$\Phi_1 - \Phi_2 = \frac{I}{j\omega C} \tag{7.15}$$

which is the familiar relation for the voltage drop across a capacitor.

Then Eq. (7.11) may be written as

$$IR + j\omega LI + \frac{I}{j\omega C} = \mathcal{E} \tag{7.16}$$

which is Kirchhoff's voltage law for an RLC circuit.

A GENERATOR AND AN EXTERNAL RL CIRCUIT

Suppose that $\mathbf{B}_a$ exits only in loop 1, which is shown as the shaded area in Fig. 7.4. Loops 1 and 2 are shielded, so that the $\mathbf{B}_i$ induced by the current in one loop does not extend to the other loop. Integrating Eq. (7.5) along l_1 results in

$$\begin{aligned}\oint_{l_1} \mathbf{E} \cdot d\mathbf{l} &= -\oint_{l_1} \nabla\Phi \cdot d\mathbf{l} - j\omega \oint_{l_1} \mathbf{A}_a \cdot d\mathbf{l} - j\omega \oint_{l_1} \mathbf{A}_i \cdot d\mathbf{l} \\ &= 0 + \mathcal{E} - j\omega \oint_{l_1} \mathbf{A}_i \cdot d\mathbf{l}\end{aligned}$$

Breaking up the integral on the left and using Eq. (7.9) gives

$$\underset{\text{wire}}{\int_1^2} \mathbf{E} \cdot d\mathbf{l} + \underset{\text{gap}}{\int_2^1} \mathbf{E} \cdot d\mathbf{l} = \mathcal{E} - j\omega L_1 I$$

Now using Eq. (7.8) results in

$$\begin{aligned}-\underset{\text{gap}}{\int_1^2} \mathbf{E} \cdot d\mathbf{l} &= \mathcal{E} - j\omega L_1 I - R_1 I \\ &\equiv \mathcal{E}_0 \end{aligned} \tag{7.17}$$

where the sign and the limits have been changed in the term on the left. The term on the left is the voltage difference between the points 2 and 1, $V_2 - V_1$. As shown in Sec. 2.4, this voltage difference is equal to the difference in potential, $\Phi_2 - \Phi_1$, in the static case. This is not true in the time-varying case, because $\mathbf{E} = -\nabla\Phi - j\omega\mathbf{A}$, and the $-j\omega\mathbf{A}$ term must be included. However, in the quasi-static case, $-j\omega\int \mathbf{A} \cdot d\mathbf{l}$ across a short gap is often negligible compared to $\Phi_2 - \Phi_1$, and the voltage difference between two points is considered to be the same as the potential difference between two points. How good this approximation is depends on the circuit size and the frequency.

Equation (7.17) states that the voltage across the terminals of the generator is the generated emf minus the internal-impedance voltage drops. This net emf is designated $\mathcal{E}_0$. In general, generators can be characterized by $\mathcal{E}_0$ whether the emf is produced by magnetic induction or by some other method, such as chemical or thermal means. The internal impedance of the generator accounts for the change in $\mathcal{E}_0$ with current.

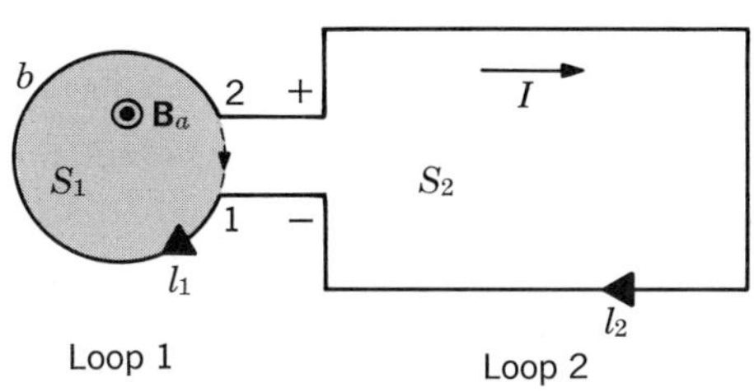

Fig. 7.4 A generator and an RL circuit. $\mathbf{B}_a$ exists only over the shaded portion. Loops 1 and 2 are shielded so no coupling occurs.

Integrating Eq. (7.5) along l_2 results in Kirchhoff's voltage law for the external circuit,

$$\oint_{l_2} \mathbf{E} \cdot d\mathbf{l} = -j\omega \oint_{l_2} \mathbf{A}_i \cdot d\mathbf{l}$$
$$= -j\omega L_2 I$$

Also, the left-hand side can be written as

$$\oint_{l_2} \mathbf{E} \cdot d\mathbf{l} = \int_{\substack{1 \\ \text{gap}}}^{2} \mathbf{E} \cdot d\mathbf{l} + \int_{\substack{2 \\ \text{wire}}}^{1} \mathbf{E} \cdot d\mathbf{l}$$
$$= \int_{\substack{1 \\ \text{gap}}}^{2} \mathbf{E} \cdot d\mathbf{l} + R_2 I$$

Hence

$$-\int_{\substack{1 \\ \text{gap}}}^{2} \mathbf{E} \cdot d\mathbf{l} = j\omega L_2 I + R_2 I \tag{7.18}$$

Equation (7.18) shows the relation between an inductance and the voltage drop across its terminals. In the practical case, inductors usually consist of many turns of wire, rather than the single turn considered here, but Eq. (7.18) still describes the inductance in terms of the voltage drop across its terminals. Combining Eqs. (7.17) and (7.18) results in the familiar form of Kirchhoff's voltage law for a generator connected to an RL circuit,

$$\mathcal{E} - j\omega L_1 I - R_1 I = j\omega L_2 I + R_2 I \tag{7.19}$$

A comment on a sign convention for voltage drops and emf's is in order. In Eq. (7.4) the current I was taken to be positive in the direction of $d\mathbf{l}'$. In Eq. (7.9) L is a positive quantity which depends only on geometry. Hence I is positive if $d\mathbf{l}' \cdot d\mathbf{l}$ is positive, that is, if $d\mathbf{l}$ is in the direction of $d\mathbf{l}'$. Therefore I is assumed to be positive in the direction of integration in integrating Eq. (7.5) to obtain Kirchhoff's voltage law. This is the same sign convention used in Eq. (7.8). From Eq. (7.18), it is clear that when

$$V_2 - V_1 = -\int_{\substack{1 \\ \text{gap}}}^{2} \mathbf{E} \cdot d\mathbf{l}$$

is positive, I is positive, that is, in the direction of integration. The sign convention is illustrated in Fig. 7.4. The plus sign at terminal 2 and the minus sign at terminal 1 indicate that $V_2 > V_1$, and hence $V_2 - V_1$ is positive. Then I is in the direction shown. Thus the current flows from a point of higher voltage to a point of lower voltage. The $\mathcal{E}$

produced by the generator causes terminal 2 to be a point of higher voltage than terminal 1 so that current will flow.

LUMPED-CIRCUIT THEORY

Up to this point the resistance and inductance of a single loop of wire and the capacitance of a gap in the wire have been considered. In practical circuits, however, inductance is obtained by using coils of wire, where the term $j\omega L$ predominates. Resistance is obtained by using a conductor with a low value of σ where the IR term predominates. The leads connecting the inductance and resistance elements often have negligible resistance and inductance, although this depends on the frequency and the size of the circuit.

Figure 7.5 shows a circuit which contains lumped inductance, capacitance, and resistance, with the connecting leads assumed to have negligible resistance and inductance. Assuming that the connecting leads have negligible inductance is equivalent to assuming that the effect of the magnetic field induced by the current in the leads is small compared to that of the inductor, and the $\mathbf{A}_i$ produced by the current in the inductor is localized in the inductor. The terms

$$\int_{\text{leads}} \mathbf{E} \cdot d\mathbf{l}$$

and

$$j\omega \int_{\text{leads}} \mathbf{A}_i \cdot d\mathbf{l}$$

are therefore neglected. In addition, the inductance term obtained by integrating through the resistor and across the capacitor are neglected; that is,

$$-j\omega \int_{\text{resistor}} \mathbf{A}_i \cdot d\mathbf{l} \qquad -j\omega \int_{\substack{\text{capacitor}\\ \text{gap}}} \mathbf{A}_i \cdot d\mathbf{l}$$

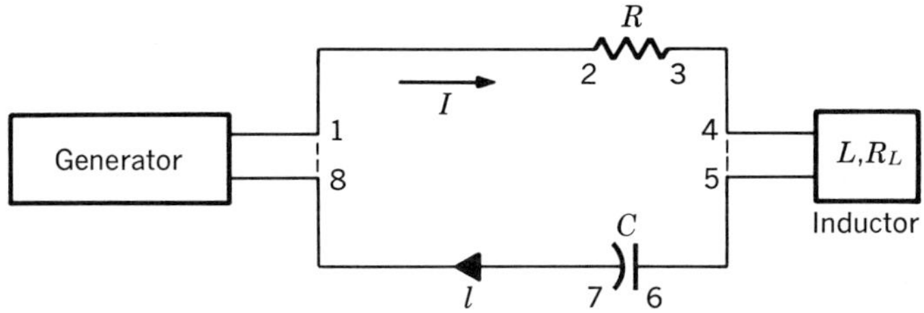

Fig. 7.5 A general RLC circuit.

are neglected. Integrating Eq. (7.5) along the path l shown in Fig. 7.5 results in

$$\oint_l \mathbf{E} \cdot d\mathbf{l} = -\oint_l \nabla\Phi \cdot d\mathbf{l} - j\omega \int_{\text{leads}} \mathbf{A}_i \cdot d\mathbf{l} - j\omega \int_{\text{cap}} \mathbf{A}_i \cdot d\mathbf{l}$$

Using Eq. (7.6) and neglecting the inductance in the leads, the resistor, and the capacitor results in

$$\oint_l \mathbf{E} \cdot d\mathbf{l} \approx 0 \tag{7.20}$$

The path l is along the conductor, with the exceptions that it follows the dotted lines from 4 to 5 and from 8 to 1. The integral in Eq. (7.20) can be written as the sum

$$\oint_l \mathbf{E} \cdot d\mathbf{l} = \int_2^3 \mathbf{E} \cdot d\mathbf{l} + \int_4^5 \mathbf{E} \cdot d\mathbf{l} + \int_6^7 \mathbf{E} \cdot d\mathbf{l} + \int_8^1 \mathbf{E} \cdot d\mathbf{l}$$

because $\int \mathbf{E} \cdot d\mathbf{l} = 0$ in the perfectly conducting leads. According to our previous results,

$$\int_2^3 \mathbf{E} \cdot d\mathbf{l} = IR$$

$$\int_4^5 \mathbf{E} \cdot d\mathbf{l} = j\omega LI + RLI \qquad \text{[see Eq. (7.18)]}$$

$$\int_6^7 \mathbf{E} \cdot d\mathbf{l} = \frac{I}{j\omega C} \qquad \text{[see Eq. (7.15)]}$$

$$\int_8^1 \mathbf{E} \cdot d\mathbf{l} = -\mathcal{E}_0 \qquad \text{[see Eq. (7.17)]}$$

Therefore

$$\mathcal{E}_0 = RI + j\omega LI + R_L I + \frac{I}{j\omega C}$$

which is Kirchhoff's voltage law for a general RLC circuit.

Thus it has been shown that Kirchhoff's voltage law can be obtained from a quasi-static approximation of Maxwell's equations. Next, another fundamental circuit law, Kirchhoff's current law, is shown to result from the continuity equation.

KIRCHHOFF'S CURRENT LAW

Consider the junction of current-carrying conductors shown in Fig. 7.6. Applying Eq. (7.13) and letting S be a very small surface at the junction yields

$$-(I_1 + I_2 + I_3) = -j\omega Q$$

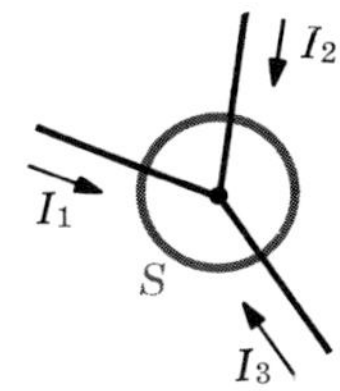

Fig. 7.6 A junction of current-carrying conductors.

where Q is the total charge stored at the junction. When no charge is stored, $Q = 0$, and the usual form of Kirchhoff's current law results,

$$I_1 + I_2 + I_3 = 0$$

If charge is stored at the junction, it is attributed to capacitance. In this case, from Eq. (7.14),

$$j\omega Q = I_{\text{cap}}$$

where I_{cap} is the current flowing in the capacitance. Stray capacitance between the junction and a ground plane could cause some charge storage at the junction and result in I_{cap}.

7.4 INDUCTANCE

Combining Eqs. (7.9) and (7.4) results in an expression for inductance called *Neumann's formula*,

$$L = \frac{\mu}{4\pi} \oint_l \oint_{l'} \frac{d\mathbf{l}' \cdot d\mathbf{l}}{R} \tag{7.21}$$

Although this expression looks simple, it is usually difficult to evaluate and hence is limited in practical value.

Probably a more familiar expression for inductance is the one mentioned in Sec. 7.3,

$$\begin{aligned} L &= \frac{\psi}{I} \\ &= \frac{1}{I} \int_S \mathbf{B} \cdot d\mathbf{S} \end{aligned} \tag{7.22}$$

where ψ is defined as

$$\psi = \int_S \mathbf{B} \cdot d\mathbf{S}$$

(the subscripts i and a are dropped henceforth because applied fields are not being considered). ψ is said to be the flux which *links*, or is enclosed by, the current loop. For closed loops, the definition of L in Eq. (7.22) is equivalent to the one given in Sec. 7.3 in terms of **A**. This can be shown by setting $\mathbf{B} = \nabla \times \mathbf{A}$ in Eq. (7.22) and using Stokes's theorem; thus

$$\begin{aligned} L &= \frac{1}{I}\int_S \mathbf{B} \cdot d\mathbf{S} \\ &= \frac{1}{I}\int_S \nabla \times \mathbf{A} \cdot d\mathbf{S} \\ &= \frac{1}{I}\oint_l \mathbf{A} \cdot d\mathbf{l} \end{aligned}$$

which coincides with Eq. (7.9). In Eq. (7.16) the L for a loop with a gap was defined as $L = (1/I)\int_l \mathbf{A} \cdot d\mathbf{l}$, where the integral was not over a closed loop. For this case Stokes's theorem could not be used to obtain a definition equivalent to Eq. (7.22). However, for small gaps the two definitions are approximately equivalent. If the coil is increased to N turns of fine wire very closely spaced, a good approximation is

$$L = \frac{N\psi}{I} \tag{7.23}$$

The inductance for a single loop is called *self-inductance* because the flux ψ which links the conductor is produced by the current in the conductor. When other loops are present, the flux produced by current in one loop may link another loop, thus inducing a current in that loop. This is called *mutual inductance* and is the topic of the next subsection.

When the radius of the conductors is assumed to be zero, the self-inductance becomes infinite. It is therefore necessary to assume a small, but finite, radius. In many cases the self-inductance is determined most easily from energy considerations. This method is discussed after mutual inductance.

MUTUAL INDUCTANCE

Figure 7.7 shows two loops with currents I_1 and I_2. Let B_{12} be the field produced at loop 1 by I_2 and B_{11} be the field produced at loop 1 by I_1. Then we define

$$\begin{aligned} \psi_{12} &= \int_{S_1} \mathbf{B}_{12} \cdot d\mathbf{S} \\ &= \oint_{l_1} \mathbf{A}_{12} \cdot d\mathbf{l} \\ \psi_{11} &= \int_{S_1} \mathbf{B}_{11} \cdot d\mathbf{S} \\ &= \oint_{l_1} \mathbf{A}_{11} \cdot d\mathbf{l} \end{aligned}$$

Fig. 7.7 Two loops having mutual inductance.

and the mutual inductance L_{12} is defined as

$$L_{12} = \frac{\psi_{12}}{I_2} \tag{7.24}$$

where ψ_{12} is the magnetic flux produced by the current I_2 which links the current loop I_1. L_{12} is said to be positive if the flux ψ_{12} links loop 1 in the same direction as the flux ψ_{11}, that is, if $\mathbf{B}_{12} \cdot d\mathbf{S}$ has the same sign as $\mathbf{B}_{11} \cdot d\mathbf{S}$. The sign of the mutual inductance can be changed by changing the direction of either I_1 or I_2.

Integrating

$$\mathbf{E} = -\nabla\Phi - j\omega\mathbf{A}_{11} - j\omega\mathbf{A}_{12}$$

over the surface of loop 1 results in

$$I_1R_1 + j\omega L_{11}I_1 + j\omega L_{12}I_2 = 0$$

which is Kirchhoff's voltage law when mutual inductance is present (and no emf is present in loop 1).

It can easily be shown that $L_{12} = L_{21}$ (see Prob. 7.4-2).

Example 7.1 Mutual inductance between a long, straight wire and a loop A long wire and rectangular loop are shown in Fig. 7.8. It is easiest to find L_{12} by finding

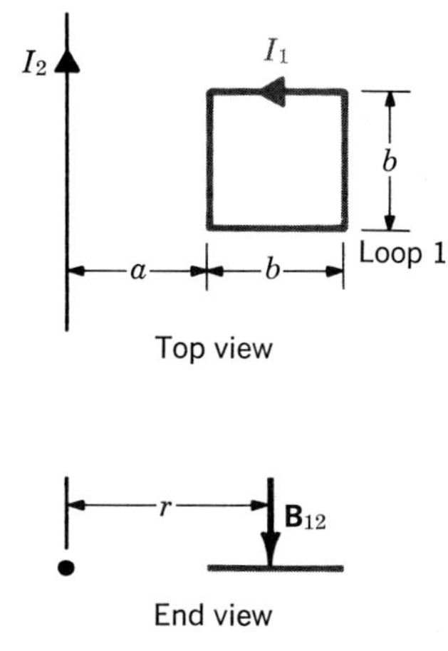

Fig. 7.8 A long, straight wire and loop.

ψ_{12}. The field at loop 1 due to I_2 is

$$B_{12} = \frac{\mu I_2}{2\pi r}$$

where r is the distance from the wire (see Example 2.7). Since $\mathbf{B}_{12}$ is perpendicular to the loop, as shown in Fig. 7.8,

$$\psi_{12} = \int_{S_1} \mathbf{B}_{12} \cdot d\mathbf{S}$$

$$= b \int_a^{a+b} \frac{\mu I_2}{2\pi r}\, dr$$

$$= \frac{\mu b I_2}{2\pi} \ln \frac{a+b}{a}$$

and

$$L_{12} = -\frac{\mu b}{2\pi} \ln \frac{a+b}{a} \tag{7.25}$$

INDUCTANCE AND ENERGY

Since inductance is directly related to the magnetic field, an expression for the energy stored in the magnetic field may be obtained in terms of inductance. The time-average energy stored in the magnetic field for sinusoidal time variation, obtained from Eq. (5.119), is

$$\langle W_m \rangle = \tfrac{1}{4} \int_V \mathbf{B} \cdot \mathbf{H}^*\, dV$$

$$= \tfrac{1}{4} \int_V \mathbf{H}^* \cdot \nabla \times \mathbf{A}\, dV \tag{7.26}$$

By a vector identity,

$$\nabla \cdot (\mathbf{A} \times \mathbf{H}^*) = \mathbf{H}^* \cdot \nabla \times \mathbf{A} - \mathbf{A} \cdot \nabla \times \mathbf{H}^*$$

Therefore

$$\mathbf{H}^* \cdot \nabla \times \mathbf{A} = \nabla \cdot (\mathbf{A} \times \mathbf{H}^*) + \mathbf{A} \cdot \nabla \times \mathbf{H}^*$$

Since

$$\nabla \times \mathbf{H}^* = \mathbf{J}^* - j\omega\epsilon \mathbf{E}^*$$

we have

$$\mathbf{H}^* \cdot \nabla \times \mathbf{A} = \nabla \cdot (\mathbf{A} \times \mathbf{H}^*) + \mathbf{A} \cdot (\mathbf{J}^* - j\omega\epsilon \mathbf{E}^*) \tag{7.27}$$

Combining Eqs. (7.27) and (7.26) gives

$$\langle W_m \rangle = \tfrac{1}{4} \int_V \nabla \cdot (\mathbf{A} \times \mathbf{H}^*)\, dV + \tfrac{1}{4} \int_V \mathbf{A} \cdot (\mathbf{J}^* - j\omega\epsilon \mathbf{E}^*)\, dV$$

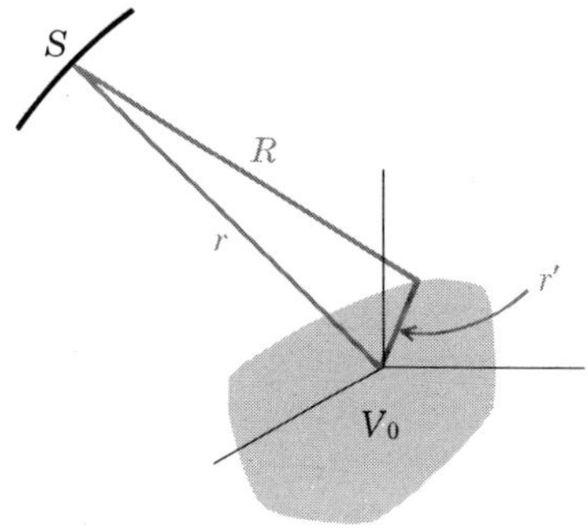

Fig. 7.9 The surface of integration of Eq. (7.28).

Using the divergence theorem on the first term results in

$$\frac{1}{4}\int_V \nabla \cdot (\mathbf{A} \times \mathbf{H}^*)\,dV = \frac{1}{4}\oint_S \mathbf{A} \times \mathbf{H}^* \cdot d\mathbf{S} \tag{7.28}$$

In order to obtain the total energy stored in the magnetic field of the inductor, the volume integral in the equation for $\langle W_m \rangle$ must include all space where there is magnetic field. Hence we must let $V \to \infty$ and hence $S \to \infty$. For convenience, S is chosen to be a sphere centered at the origin, and it is assumed that all the currents are contained in a finite volume, V_0. Figure 7.9 illustrates the situation. It is easy to see that as $S \to \infty$, and hence $r \to \infty$, that $R \to r$. The quasi-static $\mathbf{H}$ field is given by

$$\mathbf{H}^* = \frac{e^{-j\omega t}}{4\pi}\int_{V_0} \frac{\mathbf{J}^* \times \hat{\mathbf{R}}}{R^2}\,dV'$$

because, as explained in Sec. 7.2, the quasi-static fields are the same as static fields with $e^{j\omega t}$ time variation [see Eq. (2.49) for the static field]. Similarly, from Eq. (7.2),

$$\mathbf{A} = \frac{\mu e^{j\omega t}}{4\pi}\int_{V_0} \frac{\mathbf{J}}{R}\,dV'$$

As $R \to r$,

$$\mathbf{H}^* \to \frac{1}{4\pi}\frac{e^{-j\omega t}}{r^2}\int_{V_0} \mathbf{J}^* \times \hat{\mathbf{r}}\,dV'$$

$$\mathbf{A} \to \frac{\mu}{4\pi}\frac{e^{j\omega t}}{r}\int_{V_0} \mathbf{J}\,dV'$$

Hence

$$\mathbf{A} \times \mathbf{H}^* \propto \frac{1}{r^3}$$

Since

$$d\mathbf{S} = \hat{\mathbf{r}}r^2 \sin\theta \, d\theta \, d\varphi$$

$$\oint_S \mathbf{A} \times \mathbf{H}^* \cdot d\mathbf{S} = \frac{1}{r} \int_0^{2\pi} \int_0^{\pi} F(\theta,\varphi) \sin\theta \, d\theta \, d\varphi$$

and as $r \longrightarrow \infty$,

$$\oint_S \mathbf{A} \times \mathbf{H}^* \cdot d\mathbf{S} \rightarrow 0 \tag{7.29}$$

Therefore

$$\langle W_m \rangle = \tfrac{1}{4} \int_V \mathbf{A} \cdot \mathbf{J}^* \, dV - \tfrac{1}{4} j\omega\epsilon \int_V \mathbf{A} \cdot \mathbf{E}^* \, dV$$

For quasi-static fields associated with inductors, the second term on the right is small compared to the first. Hence

$$\langle W_m \rangle \approx \tfrac{1}{4} \int_V \mathbf{A} \cdot \mathbf{J}^* \, dV$$

Now consider the case where $\mathbf{J}$ exists only in conducting loops. From Fig. 7.10 we see that

$$\mathbf{J}^* \, dV = J^* \, dS \, d\mathbf{l} \tag{7.30}$$

and therefore

$$\langle W_m \rangle = \tfrac{1}{4} \int_{S_c} J^* \left(\oint_l \mathbf{A} \cdot d\mathbf{l} \right) dS \tag{7.31}$$

where S_c is the cross section of the conductor and l is a path through the conductor. For filamentary conductors where J is uniform, Eq. (7.31) reduces to

$$\begin{aligned} \langle W_m \rangle &= \tfrac{1}{4} I^* \oint_l \mathbf{A} \cdot d\mathbf{l} \\ &= \tfrac{1}{4} I^* \int_S \mathbf{B} \cdot d\mathbf{S} \end{aligned} \tag{7.32}$$

where S is any surface bounded by l. The definition of inductance in Eq. (7.22) gives

$$\langle W_m \rangle = \tfrac{1}{4} L I I^* \tag{7.33}$$

which is another familiar result from circuit theory. It is shown later in the section that with the definition of L for thick inductors given in Eq. (7.37), Eq. (7.33) is valid even when J is not uniform.

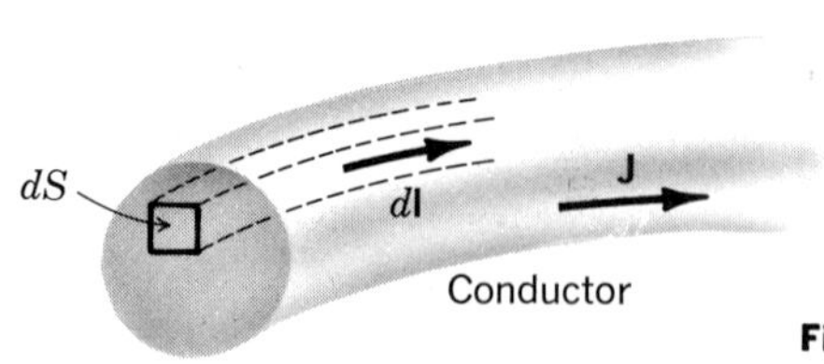

Fig. 7.10 A current-carrying conductor.

It is often easier to calculate L by first calculating $\langle W_m \rangle$ and then finding L from Eq. (7.33). In fact, many writers use Eq. (7.33) as the fundamental definition of L. The two definitions are consistent, as indicated by the derivation of Eq. (7.33). The example which follows illustrates one case where L is more meaningful as defined by Eq. (7.33) than by Eq. (7.22).

Example 7.2 Inductance of a coaxial cable The inductance per unit length of the thin-walled coaxial cable illustrated in Fig. 7.11 is to be determined. Although this circuit appears to be analogous to a filamentary loop, it is not easy to see how to apply Eq. (7.22). However, Eq. (7.33) can be used easily.

The magnetic field is zero inside the inner conductor and outside the outer conductor. Between the conductors,

$$\mathbf{B} = \frac{\mu I}{2\pi r} \hat{\boldsymbol{\phi}}$$

Therefore

$$\langle W_m \rangle = \tfrac{1}{4} 2\pi \int_a^b \frac{\mu I I^* r \, dr}{(2\pi r)^2}$$

$$= \frac{\mu I I^*}{8\pi} \ln \frac{b}{a}$$

and the inductance per unit length is

$$L = \frac{\mu}{2\pi} \ln \frac{b}{a} \qquad \text{henrys/m}$$

It is possible to use Eq. (7.22) and get the same answer, but the connection between coax and a filamentary loop is ambiguous (see Prob. 7.4-4).

FINITE CONDUCTORS

The calculation of inductance becomes more complicated for thick conductors. If the inductance is calculated from

$$L = \frac{4\langle W_m \rangle}{I I^*}$$

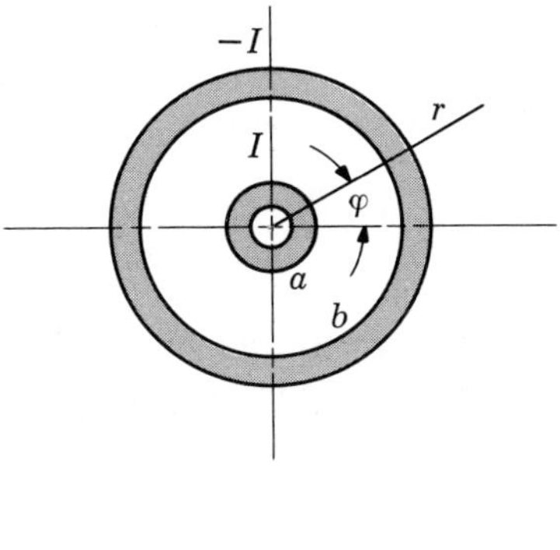

Fig. 7.11 A thin-walled coaxial cable.

there will be two terms. One term is due to the energy stored in the fields inside the conductor; the other is due to the energy in the external fields. The first term is labeled L_i and called *internal inductance*. The second is labeled L_e and called *external inductance*. The internal inductance is usually important only for low frequencies, where the current is nearly uniformly distributed in the conductor. At high frequencies the current is concentrated near the surface of the conductor (see Sec. 7.5), and there is relatively little energy stored in the internal fields.

Example 7.3 Internal and external inductance of a coaxial cable Suppose that the inner conductor of Fig. 7.11 is now solid and the current is approximately uniform over the cross section. Then

$$H_\varphi = \frac{Ir}{2\pi a^2} \qquad r < a \tag{7.34}$$

and the internal energy is

$$\langle W_i \rangle = \frac{\mu I I^*}{32\pi} \tag{7.35}$$

Hence

$$L_i = \frac{4\langle W_i \rangle}{II^*}$$

$$= \frac{\mu}{8\pi}$$

The external energy is the same as that obtained in Example 7.2. Thus

$$L_e = \frac{\mu}{2\pi} \ln \frac{b}{a}$$

Therefore

$$L = L_i + L_e$$

$$= \frac{\mu}{8\pi} + \frac{\mu}{2\pi} \ln \frac{b}{a}$$

An expression for the inductance of thick conductors which is like Eq. (7.9) for filamentary conductors can be obtained by returning to Eq. (7.7) and writing

$$\oint_l \frac{\mathbf{J} \cdot d\mathbf{l}}{\sigma} + j\omega \oint_l \mathbf{A} \cdot d\mathbf{l} = \mathcal{E}$$

For thick conductors l is some path inside the conductor (see Fig. 7.10). The next step is to multiply by J^*/I^* and integrate over the cross section of the conductor,

$$\int_{S_c} \frac{J^*}{I^*} \oint_l \frac{\mathbf{J} \cdot d\mathbf{l}}{\sigma}\, dS + j\omega \int_{S_c} \frac{J^*}{I^*} \oint_l \mathbf{A} \cdot d\mathbf{l}\, dS = \int_{S_c} \frac{J^*\, dS}{I^*}\, \mathcal{E} = \mathcal{E} \tag{7.36}$$

Note that

$$\int_{S_c} J\, dS = I$$

The first term in Eq. (7.36), which is discussed in the next section, is called the *internal-impedance term* for thick conductors. For filamentary conductors this term reduces to IR. Since the second term reduces to $j\omega LI$ for filamentary conductors, we would expect that the definition of inductance of a thick conductor would be given by

$$\int_{S_c} \frac{J^*}{I^*} \oint_l \mathbf{A} \cdot d\mathbf{l}\, dS = LI \tag{7.37}$$

We see that this definition is consistent because combining Eqs. (7.37) and (7.31) gives

$$\langle W_m \rangle = \tfrac{1}{4} LII^*$$

which is the same as Eq. (7.33), which was derived for uniform J. Thus Eq. (7.33) is valid even for nonuniform J, and Eq. (7.37) defines L for thick conductors. The L in Eq. (7.37) includes both internal and external inductance.

7.5 INTERNAL IMPEDANCE

The term $\int \mathbf{J} \cdot d\mathbf{l}/\sigma$ which occurred in the integration of Eq. (7.5) is the internal-impedance term. In previous discussions the internal impedance of a generating loop was reduced to IR (R is the dc resistance) when the current was assumed to be uniformly distributed over the cross section. However, the current is not uniform except at very low frequencies. It is the main purpose of this section to discuss the distribution of current in a semi-infinite conductor and to evaluate the internal impedance for that special case.

The first task is to determine $\mathbf{J}$ in the conductor. Starting with

$$\nabla \times \mathbf{H} = \mathbf{J} + j\omega\epsilon\mathbf{E}$$

and using

$$\mathbf{J} = \sigma\mathbf{E}$$

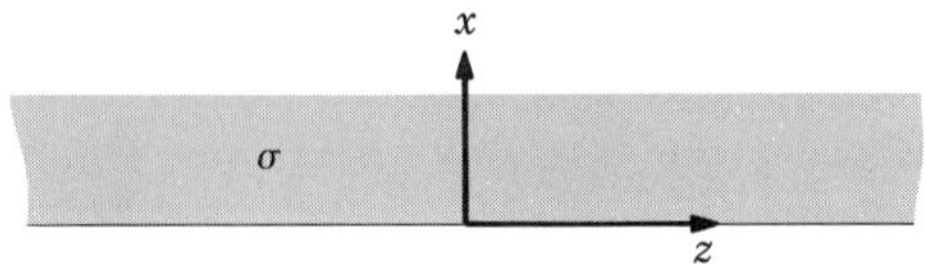

Fig. 7.12 A semi-infinite conductor.

in the conductor results in

$$\nabla \times \mathbf{H} = (\sigma + j\omega\epsilon)\mathbf{E}$$
$$= j\omega\left(\epsilon + \frac{\sigma}{j\omega}\right)\mathbf{E}$$

For good conductors at radio frequencies,

$$\epsilon \ll \frac{\sigma}{j\omega}$$

In the conductor, then,

$$\nabla \times \mathbf{H} \approx \sigma\mathbf{E}$$
$$= \mathbf{J} \tag{7.38}$$

This equation can be solved simultaneously with

$$\nabla \times \mathbf{E} = -j\omega\mu\mathbf{H} \tag{7.39}$$

and $\mathbf{J} = \sigma\mathbf{E}$ to find the current in the conductor.

Solving for $\mathbf{H}$ from Eq. (7.39) and substituting into Eq. (7.38) results in

$$\nabla \times \nabla \times \mathbf{J} = -j\omega\mu\sigma\mathbf{J}$$

With a vector identity from the Appendix, this can be written as

$$\nabla(\nabla \cdot \mathbf{J}) - \nabla^2\mathbf{J} = -j\omega\mu\sigma\mathbf{J} \tag{7.40}$$

which describes the current density in a conductor when $\epsilon \ll \sigma/j\omega$.

The semi-infinite conductor to be considered here is shown in Fig. 7.12, with the current taken to be in the z direction. The quasi-static mode of interest is the one in which there is no z variation. Since the conductor is infinite in the y direction, it is assumed that there is no variation with y. Then Eq. (7.40) reduces to

$$\frac{\partial^2 J_z}{\partial x^2} - j\omega\mu\sigma J_z = 0 \tag{7.41}$$

The solution to this equation is

$$J_z = Ae^{\tau x} + Be^{-\tau x}$$

where

$$\tau = \sqrt{j\omega\mu\sigma}$$
$$= (1 + j)\sqrt{\frac{\omega\mu\sigma}{2}} \tag{7.42}$$

and A and B are arbitrary constants yet to be evaluated. Since J_z must remain finite as $x \rightarrow \infty$, $A = 0$ and

$$J_z = Be^{-x/\delta}e^{-jx/\delta} \tag{7.43}$$

where, by definition,

$$\delta = \frac{1}{\sqrt{\omega\mu\sigma/2}} \tag{7.44}$$

From Eq. (7.43), the current decays exponentially away from the surface of the conductor. The factor δ is called the skin depth because δ represents the distance from the surface at which the current has decayed to e^{-1} of its value at the surface. This is the same result as obtained in Sec. 6.16. The total current per unit width in the y direction is

$$I = \int_0^\infty J_z\,dx$$
$$= \int_0^\infty Be^{-(1+j)x/\delta}\,dx$$
$$= \frac{B\delta}{1 + j} \tag{7.45}$$

The internal-impedance term in Eq. (7.36) can now be evaluated for the semi-infinite conductor,

$$\int_{S_c} \frac{J^*}{I^*} \oint_l \frac{\mathbf{J} \cdot d\mathbf{l}}{\sigma}\,dS$$

This can be rewritten slightly by noting from Fig. 7.10 that

$$J^*\,d\mathbf{l} = \mathbf{J}^*\,dl$$

and using Eq. (7.30); the result is

$$\int_{S_c} \frac{J^*}{I^*} \oint_l \frac{\mathbf{J} \cdot d\mathbf{l}}{\sigma}\,dS = \int_V \frac{\mathbf{J} \cdot \mathbf{J}^*}{\sigma I^*}\,dV$$

This expression can be used to define a resistance. The power dissipated in a conductor may be obtained by substituting $\mathbf{E} = \mathbf{J}/\sigma$ in Eq. (4.20) and integrating over the volume of the conductor. For sinusoidal time variation, this results in $\frac{1}{2}\int_V (\mathbf{J}\cdot\mathbf{J}^*/\sigma)\,dV$. Thus the resistance is defined as

$$\tfrac{1}{2}\int_V \frac{\mathbf{J}\cdot\mathbf{J}^*}{\sigma}\,dV = \frac{II^*R}{2}$$

or

$$R = \frac{\int_V (\mathbf{J}\cdot\mathbf{J}^*/\sigma)\,dV}{II^*} \tag{7.46}$$

and the internal-impedance term is

$$\int_{S_c} \frac{J^*}{I^*} \oint_l \frac{\mathbf{J}\cdot d\mathbf{l}}{\sigma}\,dS = IR$$

Using Eqs. (7.43) and (7.45) in Eq. (7.46), we find that for the semi-infinite conductor the resistance of a length l and unit width is

$$R = \frac{l}{\sigma\delta} \tag{7.47}$$

It is interesting to note that this is the same resistance as would be obtained if the current were uniform over a depth δ.

On the basis of the semi-infinite-conductor analysis, we would expect that when the thickness of a finite conductor is less than a skin depth, the current would be approximately uniform. However, when the thickness is much larger than a skin depth, we would expect that the current would be concentrated near the surface. This is the familiar skin effect.

7.6 CAPACITANCE

Consider two arbitrary conductors separated by a dielectric medium, as illustrated in Fig. 7.13. For quasi-static or static fields, it has been found experimentally that if the conductors have equal and opposite charges, the charge is proportional to the potential difference between the conductors, regardless of the shape or size of the conductors. The proportionality constant is defined as capacitance [see Eq. (7.12)],

$$C = \frac{Q}{V} \tag{7.48}$$

where Q is the charge on one conductor and V is the potential difference of that same conductor with respect to the other. If Q is positive, then that conductor is at a higher potential than the other, and V is positive. If Q is negative, the reverse is true. Hence C is always positive. Of course, C depends on the size and shape of the conductors.

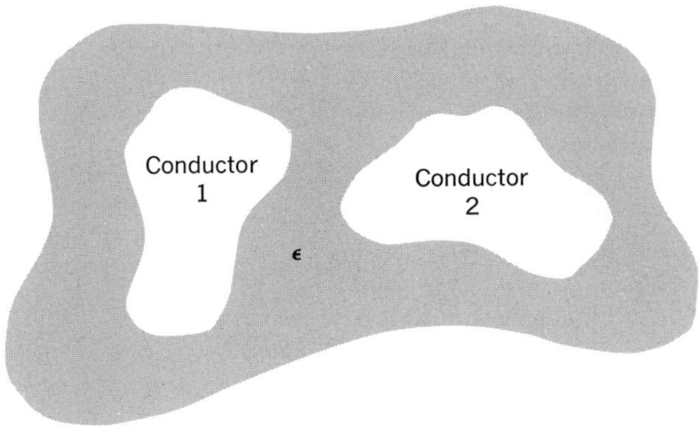

Fig. 7.13 Two arbitrary conductors in a dielectric medium.

There are two general ways to calculate C:

1. Assume a potential difference between the conductors and solve Laplace's equation to find Φ. Then find $\mathbf{E}$ from $\mathbf{E} = -\nabla\Phi$ and the surface charge density from $\rho_s = \epsilon E_n$. Then $Q = \int_S \rho_s \, dS$ yields Q in terms of V, and C can be found.
2. Assume a charge Q on the conductors. Then find $\mathbf{E}$ by using Gauss's law or some other means. The potential difference is then found using $V = -\int_l \mathbf{E} \cdot d\mathbf{l}$, resulting in V in terms of Q, and C can be found.

These two methods are illustrated in the following examples.

Example 7.4 A parallel-plate capacitor Two infinite parallel plates are located in a coordinate system as shown in Fig. 7.14. We wish to find the capacitance of an area S of these plates. Infinite plates have been chosen because of the

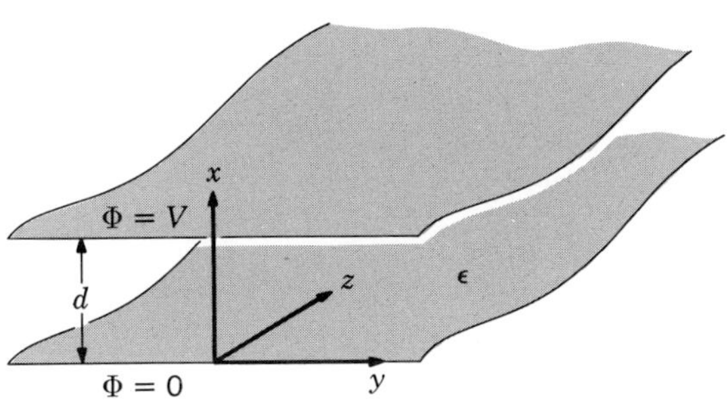

Fig. 7.14 A parallel-plate capacitor.

simplicity of the resulting uniform field. The capacitance of finite parallel plates will be slightly modified from the result here by the fringing of the fields near the edges.

Since the plates are infinite, it is assumed that

$$\frac{\partial\Phi}{\partial y} = \frac{\partial\Phi}{\partial z} = 0$$

Then Laplace's equation reduces to

$$\frac{\partial^2\Phi}{\partial x^2} = 0$$

The solution is

$$\Phi = Ax + B$$

Evaluating A and B from the boundary conditions

$$\Phi = \begin{cases} 0 & \text{at } x = 0 \\ V & \text{at } x = d \end{cases}$$

results in

$$\Phi = \frac{Vx}{d}$$

Then

$$\mathbf{E} = -\nabla\Phi = -\frac{V}{d}\hat{\mathbf{x}}$$

For the top plate, the boundary conditions in Chap. 5 indicate that

$$\rho_s = \epsilon E_n = -\epsilon E_x = \frac{\epsilon V}{d}$$

Therefore

$$Q = \int_S \rho_s \, dS = \frac{S\epsilon V}{d}$$

Thus

$$C = \frac{Q}{V} = \frac{\epsilon S}{d}$$

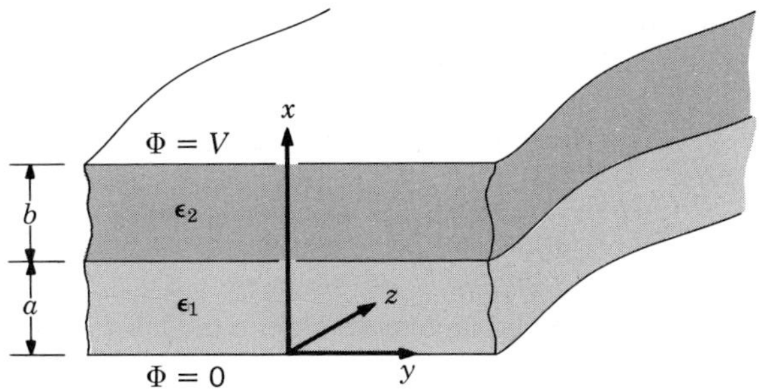

Fig. 7.15 An infinite parallel-plate capacitor with two dielectrics.

Example 7.5 The capacitance of a multiple-dielectric parallel-plate capacitor Figure 7.15 shows an infinite parallel-plate capacitor with two dielectrics. Following the procedure used in Example 7.4, Laplace's equation reduces to

$$\frac{\partial^2 \Phi}{\partial x^2} = 0$$

Hence the solutions for Φ are

$$\Phi_1 = Ax + B \qquad \text{(in the } \epsilon_1 \text{ dielectric)}$$
$$\Phi_2 = Cx + D \qquad \text{(in the } \epsilon_2 \text{ dielectric)}$$

Since $\mathbf{E} = -\nabla\Phi$,

$$\mathbf{E}_1 = -A\hat{\mathbf{x}}$$
$$\mathbf{E}_2 = -C\hat{\mathbf{x}}$$

According to the boundary conditions given in Chap. 5,

$$\epsilon_1 E_{1x} = \epsilon_2 E_{2x}$$
$$\epsilon_1 A = \epsilon_2 C$$

Thus

$$\mathbf{E}_1 = -A\hat{\mathbf{x}}$$
$$\mathbf{E}_2 = -\frac{\epsilon_1}{\epsilon_2} A\hat{\mathbf{x}}$$

The potential difference V can be found in terms of E,

$$\begin{aligned} V &= -\int_l \mathbf{E} \cdot d\mathbf{l} \\ &= -\int_0^a E_1\,dx - \int_a^{a+b} E_2\,dx \\ &= Aa + \frac{\epsilon_1}{\epsilon_2} Ab \end{aligned}$$

Therefore

$$A = \frac{V}{a + (\epsilon_1/\epsilon_2)b}$$

and

$$\mathbf{E}_2 = \frac{-(\epsilon_1/\epsilon_2)V}{a + (\epsilon_1/\epsilon_2)b}\hat{\mathbf{x}}$$

From the boundary conditions in Chap. 5, ρ_2 on the top plate is given by

$$\begin{aligned}\rho_s &= \epsilon_2 E_n \\ &= -\epsilon_2 E_{2x} \\ &= \frac{\epsilon_1 V}{a + (\epsilon_1/\epsilon_2)b}\end{aligned}$$

The charge on an area S of the top plate is given by

$$\begin{aligned}Q &= \int_S \rho_s \, dS \\ &= \frac{\epsilon_1 VS}{a + (\epsilon_1/\epsilon_2)b}\end{aligned}$$

Hence the capacitance is

$$\begin{aligned}C &= \frac{Q}{V} \\ &= \frac{\epsilon_1 S}{a + (\epsilon_1/\epsilon_2)b}\end{aligned}$$

As one would expect, this capacitance is equivalent to two capacitances, $\epsilon_1 S/a$ and $\epsilon_2 S/b$, in series.

Example 7.6 A spherical capacitor Figure 7.16 shows a concentric spherical capacitor. It is assumed that a charge Q is evenly distributed on the inner sphere. An even distribution can be assumed because of the symmetry of the spheres.

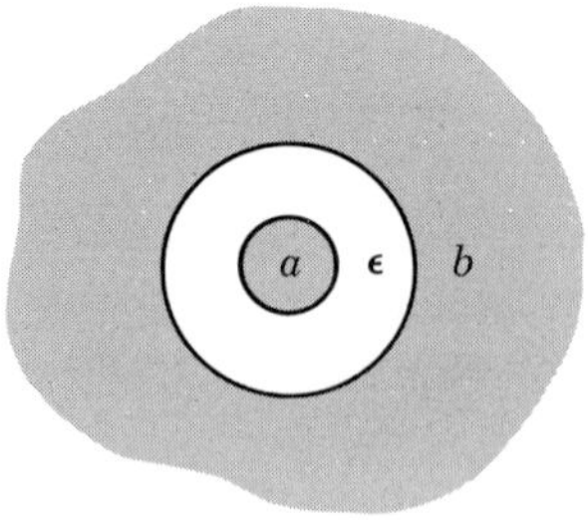

Fig. 7.16 A concentric spherical capacitor.

From Gauss's law (see Chap. 3),

$$\oint_S \mathbf{D} \cdot d\mathbf{S} = Q$$

Because of the symmetry, Gauss's law reduces to

$$4\pi r^2 D_r = Q$$

$$D_r = \frac{Q}{4\pi r^2}$$

$$E_r = \frac{D_r}{\epsilon}$$

$$= \frac{Q}{4\pi\epsilon r^2}$$

The potential difference is easily obtained,

$$V = -\int_b^a E_r \, dr$$

$$= \frac{Q}{4\pi\epsilon}\left(\frac{1}{a} - \frac{1}{b}\right)$$

and thus

$$\frac{1}{C} = \frac{1}{4\pi\epsilon}\left(\frac{1}{a} - \frac{1}{b}\right)$$

CAPACITANCE AND ENERGY

We can find the energy stored in the electric field between the conductors of a capacitor in terms of capacitance in a manner similar to that used in finding the energy stored in a magnetic field in terms of inductance.

The time-average energy stored in the electric field is

$$\langle W_e \rangle = \tfrac{1}{4} \int_V \mathbf{D} \cdot \mathbf{E}^* \, dV \tag{7.49}$$

where V is over all space where $\mathbf{E}$ exists. Using $\mathbf{E}^* = -\nabla\Phi^*$, we have

$$\langle W_e \rangle = -\tfrac{1}{4} \int_V \mathbf{D} \cdot \nabla\Phi^* \, dV$$

Since

$$\nabla \cdot \mathbf{D}\Phi^* = \mathbf{D} \cdot \nabla\Phi^* + \Phi^* \nabla \cdot \mathbf{D}$$

$$= \mathbf{D} \cdot \nabla\Phi^* + \Phi^* \rho$$

then

$$\mathbf{D} \cdot \nabla\Phi^* = \nabla \cdot \mathbf{D}\Phi^* - \rho\Phi^*$$

and

$$\langle W_e \rangle = -\tfrac{1}{4} \oint_S \Phi^* \mathbf{D} \cdot d\mathbf{S} + \tfrac{1}{4} \int_V \rho\Phi^* \, dV \tag{7.50}$$

An argument similar to that used with Eq. (7.28) can be employed to show that the first term approaches zero as S approaches infinity. Since ρ is zero everywhere except at the surface of the conductors, where it is ρ_s, and since Φ^* is constant on the surface of the conductor, we have

$$\langle W_e \rangle = \tfrac{1}{4}\Phi_1^* \int_{\text{cond. 1}} \rho_s \, dS + \tfrac{1}{4}\Phi_2^* \int_{\text{cond. 2}} \rho_s \, dS$$

$$\langle W_e \rangle = \tfrac{1}{4}\Phi_1^* Q_1 + \tfrac{1}{4}\Phi_2^* Q_2$$

Since $Q_2 = -Q_1$ and $\Phi_1 - \Phi_2 = V$,

$$\begin{aligned} \langle W_e \rangle &= \tfrac{1}{4} Q V^* \\ &= \tfrac{1}{4} C V V^* \end{aligned} \tag{7.51}$$

which is another familiar circuit-theory result. This same result was obtained in Chap. 4 from a slightly different point of view.

PROBLEMS

7.2-1 Show that $kR \ll 1$ when $l \ll \lambda/2\pi$. Assume that $R \leq l$, because l is the largest dimension of the circuit and therefore the longest distance between field point and source point.

7.2-2 Explore the validity of the quasi-static approximation in some practical cases by finding the value of kR in the following cases:

(*a*) Power application, where $f = 60$ Hz and $R = 1$ m
(*b*) Radio, where $f = 1$ MHz and $R = 1$ m
(*c*) Microcircuitry, where $R = 10^{-3}$ m and $f = 1$ MHz
(*d*) Microwaves, where $R = 2 \times 10^{-2}$ m and $f = 10$ GHz
(*e*) Optics, where $R = 10^{-2}$ m and $f = 10^{15}$ Hz

7.3-1 Show how Eq. (7.5) can be integrated to obtain the loop-voltage equations for a lumped-element circuit having two loops.

7.3-2 Show that the signs are correct in Eq. (7.14). Describe in physical terms why positive charge would result on the left plate with the direction of current shown in Fig. 7.3.

7.3-3 The loop shown in Fig. 7.1 is one turn in a generator coil. How much emf $\mathcal{E}$ is generated by this loop if $B_a = 1{,}000$ gauss, $S = 0.1$ m^2, and the loop rotates at 60 cps? Solve for the total current flow I in the loop if $B_i = 10$ gauss peak and is uniform over the loop, and the total resistance R is 1 ohm.

7.4-1 Show that **A** can be written as

$$\mathbf{A} = \frac{\mu I}{4\pi} \int_l \frac{d\mathbf{l}'}{R}$$

as given in Eq. (7.4) for a filamentary conductor, where **J** is assumed uniform over the conductor. Note that $dV' = dS'\,dl'$, where dS' is a cross-sectional differential surface area. Also note that since the directions of **J** and $d\mathbf{l}'$ coincide, the vector sense can be given to $d\mathbf{l}'$.

7.4-2 Write Neumann's equation for L_{12} by starting with Eq. (7.24) and using $\mathbf{B}_{12} = \nabla \times \mathbf{A}_{12}$. Show that $L_{12} = L_{21}$.

7.4-3 Verify the sign of the mutual inductance in Eq. (7.25).

7.4-4 Use Eq. (7.22) to find the inductance per unit length of the coaxial cable of Fig. 7.11 by considering S to be the planar surface $\varphi = 0$ between $r = a$ and $r = b$ and $z = 0$ and $z = 1$.

7.4-5 Solve for the external inductance per unit length of two long parallel wires of radius a carrying current in opposite directions. The wires are separated by a center-to-center distance d. Assume $d \gg a$.

7.4-6 Verify Eq. (7.34).

7.4-7 Verify Eq. (7.35).

7.5-1 Show that $\sqrt{j\omega\mu\sigma} = (1 + j)\sqrt{\omega\mu\sigma/2}$.

7.5-2 The conductivity of copper is about $\sigma = 5.8 \times 10^7$ mhos/m. Calculate the skin depth δ when the frequency is 10 KHz.

7.5-3 Show from the definition, Eq. (7.44), that δ has the dimensions of meters.

7.5-4 Show that Eq. (7.47) is the same resistance as would be obtained if the current were uniform over a depth δ.

7.5-5 Verify Eq. (7.47).

7.6-1 Find the capacitance per unit length of a coaxial cable.

7.6-2 Calculate the energy stored in the parallel-plate capacitor from Eq. (7.49), and show that it agrees with Eq. (7.51).

7.6-3 Repeat Prob. 7.6-2 for the spherical capacitor.

7.6-4 Show that the first term in Eq. (7.50) approaches zero as S approaches infinity.

7.6-5 Find the capacitance per unit length of two long, straight wires of radius a separated by a center-to-center distance d. Assume $d \gg a$.

7.6-6 Find the capacitance of a spherical capacitor which has two dielectrics. The boundary between the two dielectrics is $r = c$, where $a < c < b$ in Fig. 7.16.

7.6-7 Find the capacitance of a parallel-plate capacitor which has two dielectrics. The boundary between the dielectrics is perpendicular to the parallel plates.

CHAPTER

8

transmission of electromagnetic energy

8.1 INTRODUCTION

One of the most common needs in a system utilizing electromagnetic energy is to transport the energy from one point to another. For example, one application is the efficient transportation of 60-Hz electric power from the generating plant to the home. Another application involves the transmission of electromagnetic energy from the radio transmitting antenna to the radio receiver. Radio transmitting antennas may distribute electromagnetic energy in accordance with the electric-dipole antenna, as described in Sec. 6.9. In this case energy is transmitted uniformly over the horizon, with little power lost by radiation into the sky. The dipole array illustrates how energy may be directed by means of two or more antenna elements. Another application uses the familiar microwave towers, which are seen near cities and across the continent. Electromagnetic energy is directed by means of large antennas from one station to the next, which may be many miles away. Since significant energy is lost over the transmitting path length, each station amplifies the received signal for transmission.

The efficient transmission of electromagnetic energy is complicated by the fact that it is very difficult to obtain a wave which travels in a precise direction. Most antenna systems generate waves with considerable spread in the direction of their **k** vectors. Although it is possible to design antennas with some directivity, efficient transmission of power at frequencies below the optical spectrum is impossible. It is thus necessary to devise transmission systems which assist in guiding electromagnetic waves from the source to the destination. There are many familiar electrical transmission systems—the 60-Hz power-transmission lines that almost completely blanket cities and suburban areas, the two-wire transmission line from the television antenna to the receiver, and the common wave guide and coaxial transmission line for microwave frequencies.

Before we consider various types of transmission lines, it is important to understand under what circumstances transmission lines are required. It is extremely difficult in practice to direct electromagnetic waves at frequencies up through millimeter waves, and transmission lines are necessary. Conversely, it is known that at optical frequencies electromagnetic energy is readily directed by means of a lens; or, if a laser source is used, the beam is already highly directive owing to the nature of light generation in the laser cavity. Thus, from our superficial practical knowledge, we conclude that the directional characteristics of planewave propagation are frequency dependent. In Sec. 8.2 we investigate the spreading properties of a collimated planewave as a function of frequency.

The simplest way to guide microwave radiation is to radiate into a hollow conducting pipe. Multiple reflections occur at the walls, and the fields are efficiently confined to the interior of the pipe. Most of the power at the input end of the pipe, or *wave guide*, as it is called, is received at the output end, except for a small amount of I^2R losses at the walls. Since wave-guide dimensions are of the order of a wavelength, quasi-static techniques are inappropriate, and the general wave equation must be solved subject to the boundary conditions at the wave-guide wall. Solutions are sought which describe propagation along the wave-guide axis. The wave guide is an important and widely used guiding system at microwave frequencies, and is discussed in Chap. 9.

At lower frequencies, where the quasi-static approximation is valid, it is convenient to relate the fields to electric potential and current and use circuit concepts. Furthermore, one high-frequency mode which can propagate along transmission lines can also be analyzed in terms of voltage and current. This mode is called a *transverse electromagnetic (TEM) mode*, because it has electric and magnetic fields only in the directions transverse to the direction of propagation. A portion of this chapter is concerned with the application of circuit theory, involving both lumped and distributed circuit elements, for energy transmission at lower frequencies, and also at higher frequencies in TEM modes. In the latter portion of the chapter transmission-line discontinuities are considered, and matching and excitation techniques which are applicable to any transmission system are developed.

8.2 DIFFRACTION OF PLANEWAVES

The purpose of this section is to show, in a simplified manner, in what frequency ranges energy can be efficiently transmitted by collimated planewaves, and in what ranges a guiding structure is required. If a unidirectional planewave of limited transverse dimensions is generated by a source, the wave inevitably spreads as it propagates away from the source. This spreading phenomenon is called *diffraction* and is the basic limiting factor in establishing a highly directive beam of electromagnetic radiation.

Consider a planewave propagating in the $+z$ direction which has a finite width $2a$ at the $z = 0$ plane, as shown in Fig. 8.1. If the beam maintained its shape perfectly in the region $z > 0$, the power density would be uniform in the region $-a < x < +a$ for any z value. A calculation shows, however, that the power spreads in the x direction. The field pattern in the region $z > 0$ may be calculated by assuming that a uniform wavefront of width $2a$ exists at the $z = 0$ plane in the aperture $-a < x < +a$, and the fields are zero for $|x| > a$. The field radiation pattern in the region $z > 0$ may be calculated using Huygens' principle,

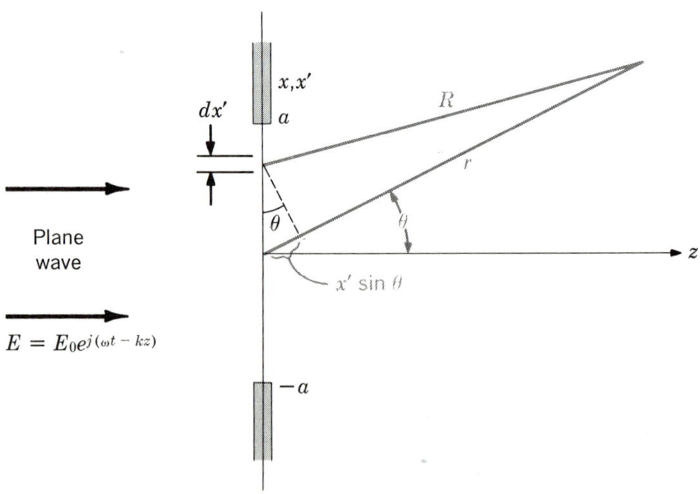

Fig. 8.1 A planewave of width $2a$ at the $z = 0$ plane propagates into the $z > 0$ region.

which states that each element of field in the aperture acts as an independent source of radiation. The elemental source at x' generates a wave which travels along the path labeled R to the field point at r. The element of electric field dE generated at a field point r is given by a relation similar to Eq. (6.27),

$$dE \propto \frac{dx' \, e^{j(\omega t - kR)}}{R} \tag{8.1}$$

As indicated by Eq. (8.1), the field dE is proportional to dx' and propagates in accordance with the well-known wave exponential t and R dependence. The resultant field may be referenced to the $r\theta$ coordinate system by rewriting R in terms of the independent coordinates,

$$R = r - x' \sin \theta \tag{8.2}$$

where it is assumed that $r \gg a$. Thus, with the assumption that $1/R \approx 1/r$, Eq. (8.1) becomes

$$dE \propto dx' \frac{e^{j(\omega t - kr)}}{r} e^{+jkx' \sin \theta} \tag{8.3}$$

This may readily be integrated to give

$$E \propto \frac{e^{j(\omega t - kr)}}{r} \int_{-a}^{+a} e^{jkx' \sin \theta} \, dx' \tag{8.4}$$

$$\propto \frac{e^{j(\omega t - kr)}}{r} \frac{\sin (ka \sin \theta)}{ka \sin \theta} \tag{8.5}$$

The θ dependence of the field far from the aperture is given by the last term. It is of great interest to investigate the θ dependence of the field intensity, as this determines the spreading properties of the beam. Since the last term in Eq. (8.5) is unity at $\theta = 0$, we may write a power-density equation

$$\frac{\mathcal{P}}{\mathcal{P}_0} = \frac{\sin^2 (ka \sin \theta)}{(ka \sin \theta)^2} \tag{8.6}$$

where $\mathcal{P}$ is the time-average electromagnetic power density (proportional to E^2) and $\mathcal{P}_0$ is the time-average power density at $\theta = 0$.

Equation (8.6), which is plotted in Fig. 8.2, is restricted to values of r much greater than a, as indicated in Eq. (8.2). The power-density ratio is replotted against x/a for fixed z/a and a/λ values in Fig. 8.3. The resulting power-distribution plots show that considerable spreading occurs for the smaller a/λ values. Ideally, for no spreading of the beam, a rectangular plot of width $2a$ is desired for any z/a or a/λ value. The

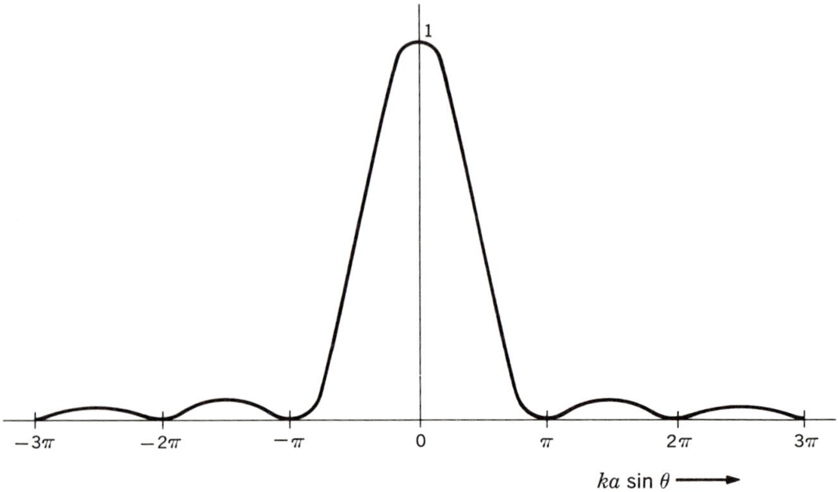

Fig. 8.2 A plot of $\dfrac{\sin^2 (ka \sin \theta)}{(ka \sin \theta)^2}$.

curves show that the beam is held to a width $2a$ only for $\lambda/a < 2a/z$; thus the wavelength must be much smaller than a for long-distance propagation.

The angle θ_n at which the first zero appears in Eq. (8.6) is given by the expression

$$ka \sin \theta_n = \pi$$

$$\sin \theta_n = \frac{\pi}{ka}$$

$$= \frac{\lambda}{2a} \tag{8.7}$$

When θ_n is a small angle, this equation reduces to

$$\theta_n = \frac{\lambda}{2a}$$

The total beam angle from null to null is thus

$$2\theta_n = \frac{\lambda}{a} \qquad \lambda \ll a \tag{8.8}$$

and is seen to vary linearly with wavelength. If we consider a typical aperture of 1 cm, we see that high directivity is possible only when λ is of the order of 1 μ or less. The criteria for good directivity at practical

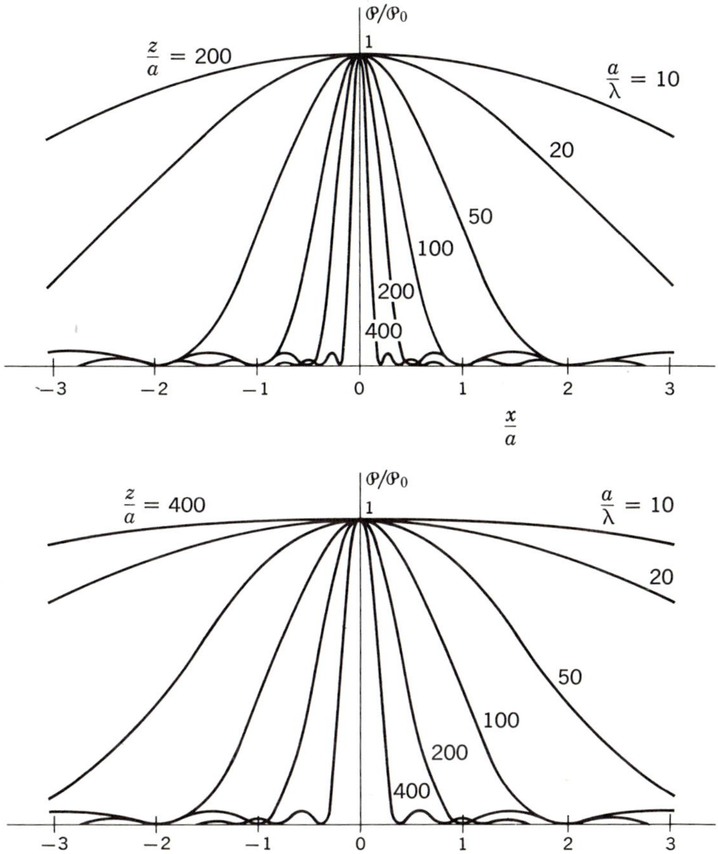

Fig. 8.3 Power-density patterns far from a unidirectional finite-width source.

laboratory aperture sizes is thus satisfied only for wavelengths in the infrared range and below.

The principal conclusion to be reached from the above discussion is that all radiation from low frequencies up through millimeter wavelengths cannot be directed efficiently. Arrays of antenna elements may be used to greatly improve the directivity compared to a single antenna, but the fundamental frequency-dependent diffraction problem remains. Efficient transfer of energy at these wavelengths requires a guiding structure. However, short-wavelength radiation may be beamed very efficiently over great distances. For example, at optical and infrared laser wavelengths, where $\lambda \leq 1\ \mu$, the beam-spread angle for practical aperture sizes is 10^{-3} to 10^{-4} rad. This angle is sufficient to direct energy very precisely over many miles, and a spot only 2 miles in diameter has been illuminated by optical laser radiation on the moon. At wavelengths approaching the aperture size, Eq. (8.7) gives beam-spread angles of the order of 1 rad.

8.3 THE DISTRIBUTED-CIRCUIT-ELEMENT TRANSMISSION LINE

At low frequencies, where electric potential and current are perhaps more meaningful concepts than electric and magnetic fields, it is well known that electrical energy may be transported from one point to another by current-carrying wires. We begin our consideration of transmission lines by examining transmission systems in the low-frequency or quasi-static frequency spectrum, where two wires support a potential difference and carry current.

The common two-conductor transmission system consists of two parallel conductors, such as two wires, two parallel plates, or a wire and plate. For simplicity, we represent the general two-conductor system by the two lines shown in Fig. 8.4. One conductor is at zero potential (ground), and the other conductor supports a potential $V(z,t)$ and carries a current $I(z,t)$. The current is returned to the source by means of the grounded conductor. The direction of the electric field is from the upper conductor to the lower conductor when the voltage V is positive, as indicated, and magnetic fields surround the two wires in accordance with

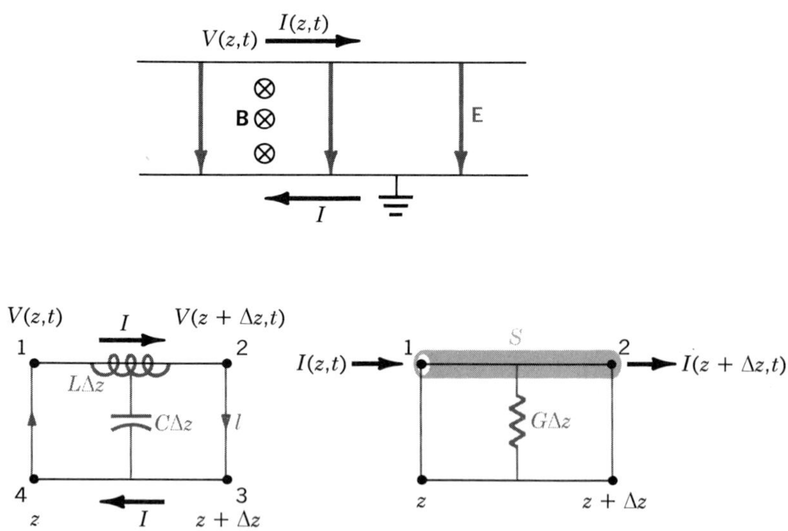

Fig. 8.4 A two-conductor transmission line.

Ampère's circuital law, as indicated. Note that since an electric field exists between the two conductors, a distributed charge density must be present, and thus a distributed capacitance exists between the two conductors. This distributed capacitance is denoted as C f/m. Since there are magnetic fields associated with the current flow, and magnetic fields link the surface bounded by the two wires, there is a distributed inductance associated with the two-conductor transmission line of L h/m.

In Fig. 8.4 an incremental length Δz of the transmission line is considered. The quasi-static approximation is assumed to be valid, and Faraday's law is applied to the loop l shown. The circuit properties of this loop will include an inductance and shunting capacitance, as indicated by the dotted elements in Fig. 8.4. Note that the magnetic and electric fields are transverse to the direction of current flow. This is characteristic of low-frequency transmission lines described by the quasi-static approximation, and these lines are said to propagate transverse electromagnetic (TEM) waves; this means that the electric and magnetic fields are transverse to the direction of propagation (see Sec. 3.8). Our objective is to determine the distributed circuit properties of the transmission line and a differential equation describing the voltage V and current I. The solution to the differential equation will describe a voltage and a current wave which is propagated along the transmission line.

The basic equation used to evolve the circuit equations for the two-conductor transmission line illustrated in Fig. 8.4 is Faraday's law. Faraday's law was applied to a current loop in Chap. 7. The loop shown in Fig. 7.1 is described in Eq. (7.7) when an impressed magnetic field is present. When no impressed field is present, as in the situation here, Eq. (7.7) becomes

$$\oint_l \mathbf{E} \cdot d\mathbf{l} + \frac{\partial}{\partial t} \int_S \mathbf{B}_i \cdot d\mathbf{S} = 0 \tag{8.9}$$

The line integral is carried out around the loop 1-2-3-4-1 illustrated in Fig. 8.4, to give

$$IR\,\Delta z + \int_2^3 \mathbf{E} \cdot d\mathbf{l} + \int_4^1 \mathbf{E} \cdot d\mathbf{l} + \frac{\partial}{\partial t} LI\,\Delta z = 0 \tag{8.10}$$

where the two resistive voltage drops associated with the path 1-2 and 3-4 are combined to form the term $IR\,\Delta z$ in Eq. (8.10). The inductance term is obtained from the defining equation, Eq. (7.22), where L is the total inductance associated with the surface bounded by the loop. The inductance per meter is defined as L; thus the inductance in a length Δz is $L\,\Delta z$, and similarly, the resistance in a length Δz is $R\,\Delta z$. On the basis of the quasi-static approximation, the electric field in Eq. (8.10) can be written in terms of a potential function, and the two integral terms are related to the voltage $V(z,t)$,

$$-\int_3^2 \mathbf{E} \cdot d\mathbf{l} = V(z + \Delta z,\ t)$$

$$-\int_4^1 \mathbf{E} \cdot d\mathbf{l} = V(z,t)$$

Then Eq. (8.10) becomes

$$V(z + \Delta z,\ t) - V(z,t) + IR\,\Delta z + \frac{\partial}{\partial t} LI\,\Delta z = 0 \tag{8.11}$$

Equation (8.11) gives the voltage change along the transmission line in terms of the transmission-line circuit parameters, R and L, and the current I.

We now need a similar expression for the change in current along the transmission system. In order to obtain this we use another of the field equations, the current-continuity equation. The current-continuity equation is applied to the surface S illustrated in Fig. 8.4. This surface encloses the upper wire of length Δz; the current-continuity equation becomes

$$\oint_S \mathbf{J} \cdot \hat{\mathbf{n}}\,dS = -\frac{\partial Q}{\partial t}$$

$$= -\frac{\partial}{\partial t} CV\,\Delta z \tag{8.12}$$

where the total charge Q within the enclosing surface S is written in terms of the capacitance between the wires, $C\,\Delta z$, and the voltage difference V. The left-hand side of Eq. (8.12) is written in terms of the current in the transmission line to obtain

$$I(z + \Delta z,\ t) - I(z,t) + GV\,\Delta z + \frac{\partial}{\partial t} CV\,\Delta z = 0 \tag{8.13}$$

where a leakage-current term is included which describes current flow through the material between the two wires. If the leakage current is described by a leakage conductance G mhos/m, the total leakage current flowing out of the surface S is $G\,\Delta z\,V$, as included in Eq. (8.13).

The next step is to divide Eqs. (8.11) and (8.13) by Δz and take the limit as $\Delta z \to 0$. The result is

$$\lim_{\Delta z \to 0} \frac{V(z + \Delta z,\ t) - V(z,t)}{\Delta z} + IR + \frac{\partial}{\partial t} LI = 0 \tag{8.14}$$

$$\lim_{\Delta z \to 0} \frac{I(z + \Delta z,\ t) - I(z,t)}{\Delta z} + GV + \frac{\partial}{\partial t} CV = 0 \tag{8.15}$$

According to elementary calculus,

$$\lim_{\Delta z \to 0} \frac{V(z + \Delta z, t) - V(z,t)}{\Delta z} = \frac{\partial V}{\partial z}$$

$$\lim_{\Delta z \to 0} \frac{I(z + \Delta z, t) - I(z,t)}{\Delta z} = \frac{\partial I}{\partial z}$$

Therefore Eqs. (8.14) and (8.15) become

$$\frac{\partial V}{\partial z} + RI + L\frac{\partial I}{\partial t} = 0 \tag{8.16}$$

$$\frac{\partial I}{\partial z} + GV + C\frac{\partial V}{\partial t} = 0 \tag{8.17}$$

where it is assumed that both L and C are not functions of time. Equations (8.16) and (8.17), called the *transmission-line equations,* are the basic equations sought; they describe voltage and current propagation on the transmission line.

For an $e^{j\omega t}$ time dependence for the variables V and I, Eqs. (8.16) and (8.17) may be put in the simplified form

$$\frac{\partial V}{\partial z} + ZI = 0 \tag{8.18}$$

$$\frac{\partial I}{\partial z} + YV = 0 \tag{8.19}$$

where Z and Y are the distributed series impedance and shunt admittance per meter associated with the transmission line,

$$Z = R + j\omega L \tag{8.20}$$

$$Y = G + j\omega C \tag{8.21}$$

The circuit properties of the specific transmission line under consideration are contained in the terms Z and Y. A general transmission-line theory may be developed from Eqs. (8.18) and (8.19) in terms of the parameters Z and Y; specific solutions require a determination of these parameters for the transmission line under consideration. Previous chapters have dealt with the circuit parameters associated with various circuit geometries and materials. For example, in Chap. 5 we considered the resistance and conductance associated with conductors and dielectric material, from which values of R and G for a specific two-conductor system may be obtained. The circuit properties of several two-conductor systems were analyzed in Chap. 7, where the distributed inductance L and the distributed capacitance C were obtained. These results now may be applied directly in Eqs. (8.20) and (8.21).

Equations (8.18) and (8.19) are also valid for TEM waves even at higher frequencies where the quasi-static approximations are not valid. This results from the fact that $E_z = H_z = 0$ for TEM waves (assuming propagation is in the z direction). This can be shown as follows. The **curl E** equation is

$$\nabla \times \mathbf{E} = -\frac{\partial \mathbf{B}}{\partial t}$$

When $E_z = H_z = 0$, the z component of this equation becomes, in rectangular coordinates,

$$\left(\frac{\partial E_y}{\partial x} - \frac{\partial E_x}{\partial y}\right)\hat{\mathbf{z}} = 0$$

This corresponds to a more general vector relation, which may be written as

$$\nabla_t \times \mathbf{E}_t = 0 \tag{8.22}$$

where $\nabla_t \times$ is understood to mean the part of the curl operator that contains derivatives other than z derivatives and $\mathbf{E}_t$ means the components of $\mathbf{E}$ transverse to z.

Just as $\nabla \times \mathbf{E} = 0$ means that $\mathbf{E}$ can be written as $\mathbf{E} = -\nabla\Phi$, where Φ is some scalar function (see Chap. 6), Eq. (8.22) means that $\mathbf{E}_t$ can be written as

$$\mathbf{E}_t = -\nabla_t\Phi \tag{8.23}$$

where ∇_t is the transverse part of the gradient. It is easy to show by direct substitution in rectangular coordinates that Eq. (8.23) satisfies Eq. (8.22) for any Φ (see Prob. 8.3-2).

Since Eq. (8.23) is the same as Eq. (2.8) when $E_z = 0$, the TEM fields have the same spatial distribution as static and quasi-static fields, even though they are not static or quasi-static. It follows, then, that capacitance and inductance, which are quasi-static parameters, can also be legitimately defined for high-frequency TEM modes on guiding structures. Consequently, the TEM modes are equivalent to quasi-static transmission-line modes, and the same transmission-line equations can be obtained either from the quasi-static approach, as shown in this section, or directly from Maxwell's equations, as will be shown in Chap. 9. An important difference between quasi-static TEM modes and high-frequency TEM modes is that when high-frequency TEM modes can exist on a transmission line, there are usually other modes that can also exist and must be taken into account. This will be clarified in Chap. 9.

We shall also see in Chap. 9 that the solution of Maxwell's equations for wave guides can be written in the same form as Eqs. (8.18) and (8.19).

Thus these transmission-line equations have wide application, and their characteristic solutions can be applied to many systems, including microwave systems.

8.4 THE LUMPED-CIRCUIT-ELEMENT TRANSMISSION LINE

It is a relatively trivial extension from the analysis of the distributed-circuit-element transmission line in Sec. 8.3 to the analysis of a lumped-circuit-element transmission line consisting of a chain of series inductance and resistance elements and shunt capacitance and conductance elements as shown in Fig. 8.5. Note that the model for the lumped-parameter transmission line is identical to the model for the distributed-parameter transmission line, except that the circuit elements are discrete, spaced by a periodic distance Δz, rather than continuous. The voltage and current vary along the transmission line with z and t. The voltage drop across the series elements in one section is

$$V(z) - V(z + \Delta z) = \frac{\partial}{\partial t} LI + RI \tag{8.24}$$

The current loss per section is simply the current shunted through the capacitor and conductance elements,

$$I(z) = I(z + \Delta z) + \frac{\partial}{\partial t} CV + GV \tag{8.25}$$

These two equations may be written in the form

$$\Delta V + \frac{\partial}{\partial t} LI + RI = 0 \tag{8.26}$$

$$\Delta I + \frac{\partial}{\partial t} CV + GV = 0 \tag{8.27}$$

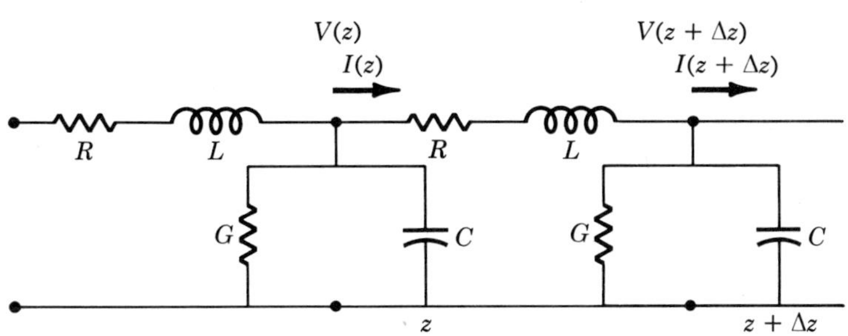

Fig. 8.5 A lumped-circuit-element transmission line.

These equations are difference equations analogous to the differential equations, Eqs. (8.11) and (8.13), for the distributed-parameter transmission line. Thus, if the period Δz is small, or conversely, if the transmission line consists of many sections, the transmission-line equations for the distributed-parameter system are a close approximation to those for the lumped-parameter system.

The incremental form of the distributed-parameter transmission-line differential equations is obtained by dividing Eqs. (8.26) and (8.27) by Δz,

$$\frac{\Delta V}{\Delta z} + \frac{RI}{\Delta z} + \frac{L}{\Delta z}\frac{\partial}{\partial t} I = 0 \tag{8.28}$$

$$\frac{\Delta I}{\Delta z} + \frac{GV}{\Delta z} + \frac{C}{\Delta z}\frac{\partial}{\partial t} V = 0 \tag{8.29}$$

For small Δz, Eqs. (8.28) and (8.29) reduce to the distributed form, Eqs. (8.16) and (8.17), where the L, C, R, and G per-unit-length parameters are simply $L/\Delta z$, $C/\Delta z$, $R/\Delta z$, and $G/\Delta z$, the circuit-element values per section divided by the length of a section in the lumped system.

The principal difference between the lumped-circuit-element system and the distributed-circuit-element system is that the lumped L and C values may be set at any value, according to the inductors and capacitors used. In the distributed system it will be found that the per-meter values obtained for inductance and capacitance are such that the phase velocity is the same as that for a planewave in the medium. Thus the lumped-circuit-element transmission line may be constructed to give phase velocities which differ appreciably from the planewave value. The ability to adjust the phase velocity (and thus the wavelength) in the lumped-circuit-element transmission line is important in some practical applications.

8.5 NORMAL-MODE ANALYSIS OF THE TRANSMISSION-LINE EQUATIONS

The previous sections have indicated that the electrical properties of two-conductor lines are described in terms of the two transmission-line equations

$$\frac{\partial V}{\partial z} + ZI = 0 \tag{8.18}$$

$$\frac{\partial I}{\partial z} + YV = 0 \tag{8.19}$$

Table 8.1 Transmission-line parameters

Transmission line	*Z, ohms/m*	*Y, mhos/m*	Z_0*, ohms*	$\Gamma = \alpha + j\beta,\ m^{-1}$
Distributed-circuit-element line	$R + j\omega L$	$G + j\omega C$	$\sqrt{\dfrac{R + j\omega L}{G + j\omega C}}$	$\sqrt{(R + j\omega L)(G + j\omega C)}$
Lumped-circuit-element line	$\dfrac{R}{\Delta z} + j\omega \dfrac{L}{\Delta z}$	$\dfrac{G}{\Delta z} + j\omega \dfrac{C}{\Delta z}$	$\sqrt{\dfrac{R + j\omega L}{G + j\omega C}}$	$\dfrac{\sqrt{(R + j\omega L)(G + j\omega C)}}{\Delta z}$

where V and I denote transverse voltage and longitudinal current, respectively. The Z and Y parameters are summarized in Table 8.1 for the distributed-element and lumped-element lines. The analysis here is restricted to an $e^{j\omega t}$ time dependence; transients on transmission lines are considered later in the chapter.

The transmission-line equations, Eqs. (8.18) and (8.19), are coupled; the voltage equation, Eq. (8.18), contains a current term, and the current equation, Eq. (8.19), contains a voltage term. This coupling may be inconvenient mathematically, as the two equations must be solved simultaneously in order to obtain the solution for V or I. The equations may be solved by taking the partial derivative with respect to z of either equation and then combining the two equations to form a second-order differential equation involving only one of the variables. By this means, two solutions for the second-order equation are obtained, which describe the voltage (or current) on the transmission line as a function of z and t. However, the wave nature of the voltage or current is somewhat obscured by the form of the solution obtained from the second-order differential equation.

With this introduction, we proceed with a modification of Eqs. (8.18) and (8.19) into a more convenient form and carry out what is called a *normal-mode analysis* of transmission lines. New dependent variables are formed which are linear combinations of V and I, such that the differential equations for the new variables are uncoupled. Since the appropriate linear combination of voltage and current is unknown, an arbitrary linear combination is defined,

$$a = V + AI \tag{8.30}$$

where a is the new dependent variable (a function of z and t) and A is an arbitrary constant. Equations (8.18) and (8.19) may be rewritten in terms of the new dependent variable a by simply multiplying Eq. (8.19) by A and adding it to Eq. (8.18). The result is

$$\frac{\partial}{\partial z}(V + AI) + AY\left(V + \frac{Z}{AY}I\right) = 0$$

Observe that if the two quantities in the parentheses are equal, an uncoupled first-order differential equation is obtained,

$$\frac{\partial}{\partial z} a + \lambda a = 0 \tag{8.31}$$

where $\lambda = AY$ is a constant. The two quantities are equal if

$$A = \frac{Z}{AY} \qquad \text{or} \qquad A^2 = \frac{Z}{Y}$$

This requires that the arbitrary constant be

$$A = \pm \sqrt{\frac{Z}{Y}} \tag{8.32}$$

The new variable a has two forms, one for each value of A (positive or negative). The two variables are denoted as $a^{\pm}$, the $+$ superscript for the positive value of A and the $-$ superscript for the negative value of A. Two first-order differential equations involving one new dependent variable each are obtained, because we started with two first-order equations and two dependent variables. Fortunately, the two equations are now independent, or uncoupled.

For the plus sign in Eq. (8.31), Eq. (8.32) becomes

$$\frac{\partial}{\partial z} a^+ + \sqrt{ZY}\, a^+ = 0 \tag{8.33}$$

and for the minus sign,

$$\frac{\partial}{\partial z} a^- - \sqrt{ZY}\, a^- = 0 \tag{8.34}$$

where the new dependent variables are obtained from Eqs. (8.30) and (8.32) as

$$a^+ = V + \sqrt{\frac{Z}{Y}}\, I \tag{8.35}$$

$$a^- = V - \sqrt{\frac{Z}{Y}}\, I \tag{8.36}$$

Equations (8.33) and (8.34) are first-order differential equations, obtained from Eqs. (8.18) and (8.19), which involve a single dependent variable instead of two. As we shall see, solutions to Eqs. (8.33) and (8.34) are easily obtained. Remember that the new dependent variables a^+ and a^- are simply linear combinations of V and I. The constant A has the dimensions of impedance. The impedance $A = \sqrt{Z/Y}$ is called the *characteristic impedance* of the transmission line and is denoted as Z_0 (see Table 8.1). The ratio of V to I for a transmission line is determined by the characteristic impedance of the transmission line.

The solutions to Eqs. (8.33) and (8.34) are the two "normal modes," or waves, which may exist on the transmission line. We leave for the moment a consideration of the V and I parameters but recognize that they may always be determined from Eqs. (8.35) and (8.36) once a^+ and a^- have been determined. It may easily be demonstrated that V and I, in terms of the normal-mode amplitudes a^+ and a^-, are

$$V = \frac{a^+ + a^-}{2} \tag{8.37}$$

$$I = \sqrt{\frac{Y}{Z}}\,\frac{a^+ - a^-}{2} \tag{8.38}$$

For the a^+ mode we see that $V/I = Z_0$, and the characteristic impedance Z_0 is the "impedance" of the line.

It is immediately obvious from an inspection of Eqs. (8.33) and (8.34) that exponential solutions are appropriate. Assuming an exponential z dependence of the form e^{bz}, Eqs. (8.33) and (8.34) become

$$(b + \Gamma)a^+ = 0$$

$$(b - \Gamma)a^- = 0$$

where Γ is defined as

$$\Gamma = \sqrt{ZY} \tag{8.39}$$

If the mode amplitudes a^+ and a^- are to be nonzero, the values of b must be

$$b = -\Gamma \qquad (a^+ \text{ mode})$$

$$b = \Gamma \qquad (a^- \text{ mode})$$

If we reinsert the exponential time dependence, the complete normal-mode solutions are

$$a^+(z,t) = a^+(0)e^{(j\omega t - \Gamma z)} \tag{8.40}$$

$$a^-(z,t) = a^-(0)e^{(j\omega t + \Gamma z)} \tag{8.41}$$

where $a^+(0)$ and $a^-(0)$ are the mode amplitudes at $z = 0$. These equations could also have been obtained by integrating Eqs. (8.33) and (8.34). It is seen from Table 8.1 that Γ is complex for a lossy line. A convenient definition is

$$\Gamma = \alpha + j\beta \tag{8.42}$$

where α and β are real quantities; α is called the *attenuation constant* and β the *propagation constant*. For a lossless line, Z and Y are purely imaginary, and hence Γ is purely imaginary. Thus $\alpha = 0$ for a lossless line. Equation (8.40) describes a wave traveling and being attenuated in the $+z$ direction, and Eq. (8.41) describes a wave traveling and being attenuated in the $-z$ direction. Since the mode amplitudes are merely linear combinations of V and I [see Eqs. (8.35) and (8.36)], Eq. (8.40) describes a voltage-current wave traveling in the $+z$ direction, and Eq. (8.41) describes a voltage-current wave traveling in the $-z$ direction. The transmission line allows two waves to be propagated, one in each direction, with propagation constant β.

Example 8.1 Current and field patterns on a transmission line Now that the solutions for wave propagation on a transmission line are available, it is possible to look at the I and V waveforms on the transmission line. The solution for a $+z$ traveling wave on a lossless line is given by Eq. (8.40), with $\Gamma = j\beta$. Since complex notation is used, the actual mode amplitude variation along the transmission line at the instant $t = 0$ is

$$a^+(z,0) = a^+(0) \cos \beta z$$

The V and I values along the transmission line, obtained from Eqs. (8.37) and (8.38), are

$$\begin{aligned} V^+(z,t) &= \tfrac{1}{2}a^+(0) \cos \beta z \\ &= V^+(0) \cos \beta z \\ I^+(z,t) &= \frac{a^+(0)}{2Z_0} \cos \beta z \\ &= I^+(0) \cos \beta z \end{aligned}$$

where

$$\frac{V^+(0)}{I^+(0)} = Z_0$$

Note that the V and I parameters are in phase; the current, voltage, and corresponding E field pattern are illustrated in Fig. 8.6. This figure describes conditions at one instant of time. As time progresses the patterns travel in the $+z$ direction.

8.6 TRANSMISSION-LINE PROPAGATION CHARACTERISTICS

The normal-mode analysis performed in Sec. 8.5 applies to any transmission system described by Eqs. (8.18) and (8.19). The results are thus valid for a wide variety of transmission lines. The results of the

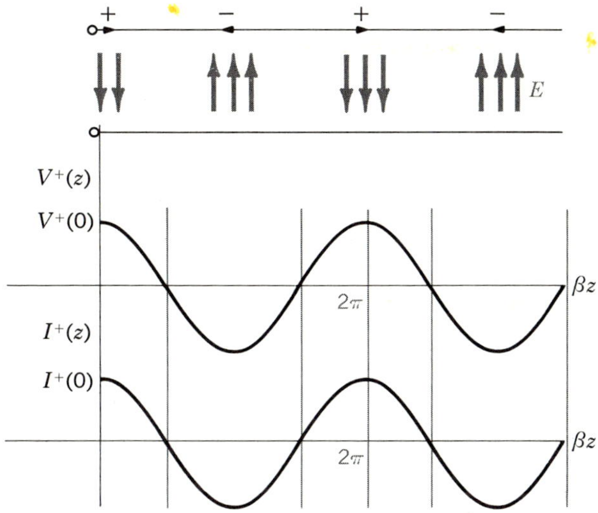

Fig. 8.6 Voltage, current, and field patterns associated with wave propagation on a transmission line. The plots are shown at the instant $t = 0$ for real $V^+(0)$ and $I^+(0)$.

normal-mode analysis are now examined in order to determine the general propagation characteristics of transmission lines.

Two independent propagating modes may exist on a transmission line. The only difference in these two modes is the direction of propagation; the magnitude of the propagation constant and characteristic impedance are the same. It is thus convenient to consider one wave, and we restrict our attention to the $+z$ traveling wave given by Eq. (8.40) and the corresponding V and I parameters obtained from Eqs. (8.37) and (8.38),

$$V^+ = \frac{a^+}{2} \tag{8.43}$$

$$I^+ = \sqrt{\frac{Y}{Z}}\, V^+ \tag{8.44}$$

The superscript plus on the V and I parameters denotes that these parameters describe the V and I associated with the $+z$ traveling wave.

CHARACTERISTIC IMPEDANCE

Note that the V and I parameters of the wave are related in Eq. (8.44) by the characteristic impedance of the transmission line, which is denoted as Z_0, where $V^+/I^+ = Z_0$,

$$Z_0 = \sqrt{\frac{Z}{Y}} \tag{8.45}$$

The characteristic impedance gives the ratio of voltage to current in one mode on a distributed- or lumped-circuit-element transmission line. For a lossless distributed-circuit-element transmission line the characteristic impedance is

$$Z_0 = \sqrt{\frac{j\omega L}{j\omega C}} = \sqrt{\frac{L}{C}}$$

and Z_0 is a real quantity.

Let us consider the important practical case where the resistance and conductance elements in the transmission line are small but not negligible. The equations for the distributed-circuit-element transmission line are used here, but the results are general if R and G are defined correctly. In this case Z_0 becomes

$$Z_0 = \sqrt{\frac{R + j\omega L}{G + j\omega C}} = \sqrt{\frac{L}{C}}\sqrt{\frac{1 + R/j\omega L}{1 + G/j\omega C}} \tag{8.46}$$

If we assume that the loss terms in Eq. (8.46) are small, Eq. (8.46) may be expanded to give

$$Z_0 = \sqrt{\frac{L}{C}}\,\frac{1 + R/2j\omega L + \cdots}{1 + G/2j\omega C + \cdots}$$

The series include first-order terms involving $R/\omega L$ and $G/\omega C$ and higher-order terms which may be neglected if $R/\omega L$ and $G/\omega C$ are small. This equation may be written in the approximate form

$$Z_0 = \sqrt{\frac{L}{C}}\left(1 + \frac{R}{2j\omega L}\right)\left(1 - \frac{G}{2j\omega C}\right)$$

where the denominator has been expanded and only the first-order term has been kept. This expression may be multiplied out to obtain the final result,

$$Z_0 = \sqrt{\frac{L}{C}}\left[\left(1 + \frac{RG}{4\omega^2 LC}\right) + j\left(\frac{G}{2\omega C} - \frac{R}{2\omega L}\right)\right] \tag{8.47}$$

Generally, the loss term in the real part of Eq. (8.47) is negligible, since it involves the product of two small loss terms; thus the principal effect of losses on the transmission line is to introduce a small imaginary component to the characteristic impedance. Note that for the case $G/C = R/L$ the imaginary component is zero, and the characteristic impedance is unchanged, to first order, by the presence of series and shunt loss elements.

PROPAGATION CONSTANT

The parameter which describes the propagation characteristics of a transmission line is the propagation constant β. The principal information given by the propagation constant is the phase velocity of propagation, which was defined in Sec. 6.2 as the velocity of a point of constant phase on the wave. From the results of that section, the phase velocity is found to be

$$v_p = \frac{\omega}{\beta} \tag{8.48}$$

We now examine the phase-velocity characteristics of the transmission lines discussed. The β values for these transmission lines are shown in Table 8.1. The circuit-element lines with no loss have an especially simple relationship for β,

$$\beta = \omega\sqrt{LC}$$

In these cases v_p is a constant,

$$v_p = \frac{1}{\sqrt{LC}} \tag{8.49}$$

Loss introduces first-order terms in the attenuation constant α, but to first order, the phase constant β is not changed.

Example 8.2 Propagation characteristics of the two-wire transmission line An important practical transmission line is the lossless two-wire transmission line. The inductance and capacitance per unit length for two round wires of radius a, separated by a center-to-center distance d, were calculated in Probs. 7.4-5 and 7.6-5 as

$$L = \frac{\mu_0}{\pi} \ln \frac{d - a}{a} \tag{8.50}$$

$$C = \frac{\pi\epsilon_0}{\ln [(d - a)/a]} \tag{8.51}$$

These two equations are valid only when $d \gg a$.

Equations (8.50) and (8.51) may be used to obtain the lossless characteristic impedance,

$$Z_0 = 120 \ln \frac{d-a}{a} \tag{8.52}$$

The inductance and capacitance equations may be inserted in Eq. (8.49) to obtain the phase velocity of wave propagation on a two-wire line,

$$\begin{aligned} v_p &= \frac{1}{\sqrt{\dfrac{\mu_0}{\pi} \ln \dfrac{d-a}{a} \dfrac{\pi \epsilon_0}{\ln [(d-a)/a]}}} \\ &= \frac{1}{\sqrt{\mu_0 \epsilon_0}} \\ &= 3 \times 10^8 \text{ m/sec} \end{aligned} \tag{8.53}$$

for lossless lines

Note that the phase velocity of voltage and current transmission on a two-wire transmission line is identical with the phase velocity of planewave propagation in the medium surrounding the transmission line. The presence of conducting surfaces confines and guides the fields but does not change the velocity of wave propagation.

The wavelength $\lambda = v_p/f$ is very large for low-frequency transmission lines. For example, the wavelength for a 60-Hz transmission line is

$$\begin{aligned} \lambda_{60} &= \frac{3 \times 10^8 \text{ m/sec}}{60} \\ &= 5 \times 10^6 \text{ m} \end{aligned}$$

The wavelength is so large that the voltage is nearly independent of z, even over transmission-line lengths of hundreds of miles. The nature of voltage transmission on 60-Hz power lines is more conveniently described in terms of circuit voltage and current, because the transmission lines are much shorter than a wavelength. In another practical case, that of television-signal transmission along a two-wire transmission line from the antenna to the television receiver, the wavelength at 100 MHz

$$\begin{aligned} \lambda_{100 \text{ MHz}} &= \frac{3 \times 10^8 \text{ m/sec}}{10^8} \\ &= 3 \text{ m} \end{aligned}$$

neglecting the dielectric effects of the supporting structure. Here the concept of voltage and current wave transmission is useful, as the transmission line may be several wavelengths long in a practical application.

Example 8.3 A laboratory lumped-parameter transmission line It is desired to construct, by means of a lossless chain of series inductance and shunt capacitor elements, a transmission line for laboratory experiments with a characteristic impedance 50 ohms, to operate at a frequency of 1 MHz. It is desired that the wavelength be 10 sections long, that is, $\lambda/\Delta z = 10$. The characteristic impedance is given in Table 8.1 as

$$Z_0 = \sqrt{\frac{L}{C}}$$

$$= 50 \text{ ohms} \tag{8.54}$$

and the phase velocity is

$$v_p = \frac{\omega}{\beta}$$

$$= \frac{\Delta z}{\sqrt{LC}}$$

Since wavelength is given by the expression $\lambda = v_p/f$, the wavelength–section-length ratio is

$$\frac{\lambda}{\Delta z} = \frac{1}{f\sqrt{LC}}$$

Since $\lambda/\Delta z = 10$, this becomes

$$10^7 = \frac{1}{\sqrt{LC}} \tag{8.55}$$

Equations (8.54) and (8.55) may be solved simultaneously to obtain the required inductance and capacitance values,

$$L = 5\ \mu\text{h}$$

$$C = 0.002\ \mu\text{f}$$

Example 8.4 The stripline One form of the stripline is shown in Fig. 8.7. Although modes other than TEM can exist, the stripline is used primarily for frequencies where these other modes do not propagate. That case is considered here.

When d/w is small, the fringing of the fields can be neglected to a good approximation. The electric field is assumed to be in the x direction and to exist only over the width w. In this case the capacitance is given by

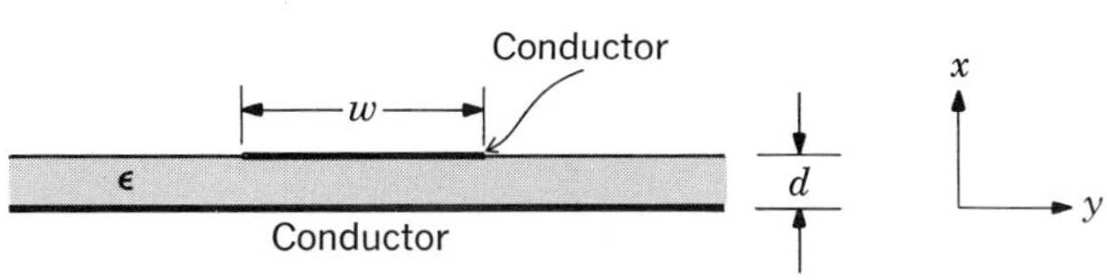

Fig. 8.7 Cross section of a stripline.

$$C = \frac{w\epsilon}{d} \tag{8.56}$$

The inductance per unit length is approximately equal to the inductance per unit length between two plates of width w. Calculating this inductance by the methods of Chap. 7 gives

$$L = \frac{\mu d}{w} \tag{8.57}$$

Then Z_0 is

$$\begin{aligned} Z_0 &= \sqrt{\frac{L}{C}} \\ &= \sqrt{\frac{\mu\epsilon}{C^2}} \\ &= \sqrt{\frac{\mu}{\epsilon}}\frac{\epsilon}{C} \end{aligned} \tag{8.58}$$

As explained in Sec. 6.7, $\sqrt{\mu/\epsilon}$ is the wave impedance of a planewave. Thus the characteristic impedance of the stripline is proportional to the planewave impedance. Combining Eqs. (8.56) to (8.58) results in

$$Z_0 = \sqrt{\frac{\mu}{\epsilon}}\frac{d}{w} \tag{8.59}$$

The propagation constant is

$$\begin{aligned} \beta &= \omega\sqrt{LC} \\ &= \omega\sqrt{\mu\epsilon} \\ &= \omega\sqrt{\mu_0\epsilon_0\,\epsilon_r} \\ &= k_0\sqrt{\epsilon_r} \end{aligned} \tag{8.60}$$

where ϵ_r is the relative dielectric constant.

Example 8.5 The coaxial-cable TEM mode The external inductance is given in Example 7.2 for the cable shown in Fig. 8.8 as

$$L = \frac{\mu}{2\pi}\ln\frac{b}{a} \tag{8.61}$$

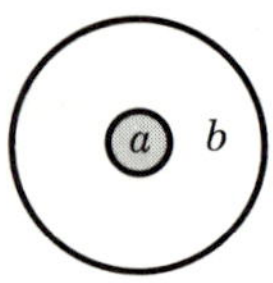

Fig. 8.8 Cross section of the coaxial cable.

Internal inductance is neglected. From the results of Prob. 7.6-1, the capacitance per unit length is

$$C = \frac{2\pi\epsilon}{\ln (b/a)} \tag{8.62}$$

The characteristic impedance is, then,

$$\begin{aligned} Z_0 &= \sqrt{\frac{L}{C}} \\ &= \sqrt{\frac{\mu}{\epsilon}} \frac{\ln (b/a)}{2\pi} \end{aligned} \tag{8.63}$$

The propagation constant is

$$\begin{aligned} \beta &= \omega \sqrt{LC} \\ &= \omega \sqrt{\mu\epsilon} \\ &= k_0 \sqrt{\epsilon_r} \end{aligned}$$

8.7 LOSSLESS–TRANSMISSION–LINE DISCONTINUITIES AND IMPEDANCES

In general, the discontinuities in transmission systems can be classed as discontinuities in the characteristic impedance Z_0 or discontinuities due to lumped elements. Abrupt changes in conductor spacing, permittivity ϵ, or permeability μ cause both a discontinuity in Z_0 and an equivalent lumped-element impedance at the discontinuity. In the quasi-static transmission system, lumped-element discontinuities are also produced by placing lumped-element impedances across the line. Both kinds of discontinuities produce reflections. As shown in this section, these reflections can be described in terms of the characteristic impedances of the transmission system and the lumped elements.

From a circuit point of view, the boundary conditions on V and I at a discontinuity are obtained from Kirchhoff's laws. At a discontinuity in Z_0, V and I must be continuous. When a lumped impedance is present, V and I may be discontinuous, depending on whether the impedance is in series or shunt with the transmission-line conductors. The lumped-impedance discontinuity is usually treated by finding the combined impedance of the lumped element and the rest of the line, as described later in this section.

From Eqs. (8.37), (8.38), (8.40), and (8.41), the solutions to the transmission-line equations for the lossless case are

$$V = \frac{a^+(0)}{2} e^{-j\beta z} + \frac{a^-(0)}{2} e^{j\beta z} \tag{8.64}$$

$$I = \frac{1}{Z_0}\left[\frac{a^+(0)}{2} e^{-j\beta z} - \frac{a^-(0)}{2} e^{j\beta z}\right] \tag{8.65}$$

A useful parameter in connection with a transmission-line discontinuity is the reflection coefficient. The reflection coefficient is defined as the ratio of the reflected wave to the transmitted wave; that is,

$$\begin{aligned} \rho &= \frac{a^-}{a^+} \\ &= \frac{a^-(0)e^{j\beta z}}{a^+(0)e^{-j\beta z}} \\ &= \rho_0 e^{j2\beta z} \end{aligned} \tag{8.66}$$

where

$$\rho_0 \equiv \frac{a^-(0)}{a^+(0)}$$

and ρ is a complex quantity which is a function of z. The value of ρ at $z = 0$, ρ_0, is not a function of z, but is complex. In terms of ρ, Eqs. (8.64) and (8.65) are

$$V = \frac{a^+(0)}{2} e^{-j\beta z}(1 + \rho) \tag{8.67}$$

$$I = \frac{a^+(0)}{2Z_0} e^{-j\beta z}(1 - \rho) \tag{8.68}$$

The impedance at a point z on the line is defined as $Z = V/I$. In terms of the V and I in Eqs. (8.67) and (8.68), Z is

$$Z = Z_0 \frac{1 + \rho}{1 - \rho} \tag{8.69}$$

The impedance Z is a function of z, because V and I are functions of z. In Eq. (8.69), ρ is a function of z.

Suppose that the value of Z is known to be the quantity Z_L at some point $z = l$, as indicated schematically in Fig. 8.9. For example, this would be the case when a transmission line is terminated in some lumped impedance. The impedance Z_L is called the *load impedance*. At the

Fig. 8.9 A transmission system with a known impedance Z_L at $z = l$.

point $z = l$, then, Eq. (8.69) becomes

$$Z_L = Z_0 \frac{1 + \rho_L}{1 - \rho_L} \tag{8.70}$$

where

$$\rho_L = \rho_0 e^{j2\beta l} \tag{8.71}$$

Since Z_L is known, ρ_L can be found from Eq. (8.70) as

$$\rho_L = \frac{Z_L - Z_0}{Z_L + Z_0} \tag{8.72}$$

Combining Eqs. (8.72) and (8.71) and solving for ρ_0 results in

$$\rho_0 = \frac{Z_L - Z_0}{Z_L + Z_0} e^{-j2\beta l} \tag{8.73}$$

Then putting Eq. (8.73) into Eq. (8.66) results in an expression for ρ in terms of Z_L, Z_0, β, and l,

$$\rho = \frac{Z_L - Z_0}{Z_L + Z_0} e^{-j2\beta(l-z)} \tag{8.74}$$

The *magnitude* of the reflection coefficient is seen to depend only on Z_L and Z_0. It is interesting to note in particular that $\rho = 0$ when $Z_L = Z_0$. When this is the case, the line is said to be *matched*, and no reflection occurs. When Z_0 is real, as for a lossless line, and when Z_L is passive (its real part is positive), it can easily be shown that $|\rho| \leq 1$. This is not necessarily true for a lossy line.

A convenient expression for $Z(z)$ in terms of Z_L is obtained by substituting Eq. (8.74) into Eq. (8.69). After some algebra, the following expression is obtained:

$$Z = Z_0 \frac{Z_L + jZ_0 \tan \beta(l - z)}{Z_0 + jZ_L \tan \beta(l - z)} \tag{8.75}$$

Equation (8.75) is a very important expression because it shows the variation of the impedance with z for a given load impedance Z_L. One interesting observation is that when $Z_L = Z_0$, $Z = Z_0$ at any point on the line. This is equivalent to saying that $\rho = 0$ when $Z_L = Z_0$, as indicated in Eq. (8.74). When $\rho = 0$, there are no waves traveling in the $-z$ direction [see Eqs. (8.67) and (8.68)]. The line is then said to be matched. The impedance in this case is the ratio of the $+z$ traveling voltage and current waves, which is just Z_0.

An important use of Eq. (8.75) is that of finding the input impedance of a line terminated in Z_L. The input impedance, Z_i, is the impedance at $z = 0$, as indicated in Fig. 8.9. From Eq. (8.75), the input impedance is

$$Z_i = Z_0 \frac{Z_L + jZ_0 \tan \beta l}{Z_0 + jZ_L \tan \beta l} \tag{8.76}$$

The input impedance depends on Z_L and the length of the line. For example, when $\beta l = \pi$ (which corresponds to $l = \lambda/2$, since $\beta = 2\pi/\lambda$), $Z_i = Z_L$, because $\tan \beta l = 0$. In this case, the input impedance is the same as the load impedance. For l such that $\tan \beta l \neq 0$, $Z_i \neq Z_L$. The relation of Eq. (8.76) can be thought of as a transformation of Z_L by the line; that is, Z_L at $z = l$ is transformed by the line to Z_i at $z = 0$. As indicated above, a line a half-wavelength long transforms Z_L back into Z_L.

Suppose that the line is shorted at $z = l$, so that $Z_L = 0$. Then

$$Z_i = jZ_0 \tan \beta l$$

For a quarter-wavelength line, $\beta l = \pi/2$ and $Z_i \to \infty$. Thus a quarter-wavelength line transforms a short circuit into an open circuit. As l varies, Z_i varies through all possible reactive values. Thus a short can be transformed into any reactance if the line length is chosen properly. The transformation is frequency sensitive, however, because $\beta = \omega \sqrt{LC}$.

Sometimes it is more convenient to use admittance instead of impedance. The admittance at a point z is defined as $Y = I/V$. From Eq. (8.75), the admittance is found to be

$$Y = Y_0 \frac{Y_L + jY_0 \tan \beta(l - z)}{Y_0 + jY_L \tan \beta(l - z)} \tag{8.77}$$

where $Y_0 = 1/Z_0$ and $Y_L = 1/Z_L$.

The variation of V along the line and some interesting relations between V and Z can be obtained by consideration of Eq. (8.67). It is convenient to write

$$\rho_0 = |\rho_0| e^{j\varphi}$$

where φ is the phase of ρ_0. Then the amplitude of V is given by

$$\begin{aligned} |V| &= \left| \frac{a^+(0)}{2} e^{-j\beta z} \right| |1 + |\rho_0| e^{j\varphi} e^{j2\beta z}| \\ &= \left| \frac{a^+(0)}{2} \right| |1 + |\rho_0| e^{j(\varphi + 2\beta z)}| \end{aligned} \tag{8.78}$$

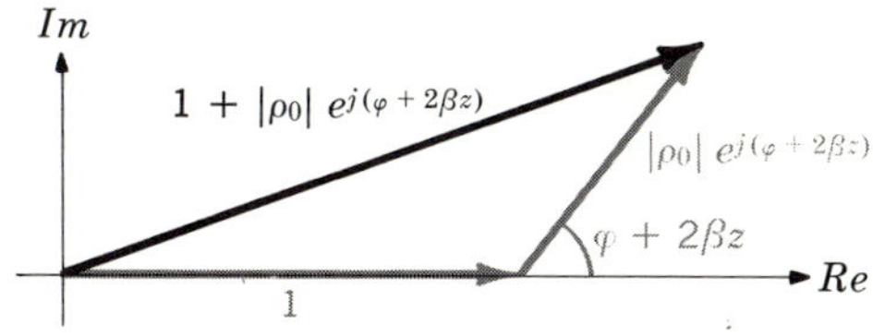

Fig. 8.10 The representation of $1 + |\rho_0|e^{j(\varphi+2\beta z)}$ in the complex plane.

The quantity $1 + |\rho_0|e^{j(\varphi+2\beta z)}$ can be represented in the complex plane as the sum of two phasors, as shown in Fig. 8.10. As z varies, the phasor $|\rho_0|e^{j(\varphi+2\beta z)}$ rotates as indicated in Fig. 8.10. From Fig. 8.10 and Eq. (8.78), it can be seen that $|V|$ has maxima and minima at certain positions on the line. The maxima are

$$|V|_{\max} = \left|\frac{a^+(0)}{2}\right|(1 + |\rho_0|) \tag{8.79}$$

which occur at

$$\varphi + 2\beta z = 2m\pi \qquad m = 0, \pm 1, \pm 2, \ldots$$

At these points

$$\begin{aligned}\rho &= |\rho_0|e^{j(\varphi+2\beta z)}\\ &= |\rho_0|e^{j2m\pi}\\ &= |\rho_0|\end{aligned}$$

and it can be seen from Eq. (8.68) that at these points $|I|$ is a minimum. The minima of $|V|$ are

$$|V|_{\min} = \left|\frac{a^+(0)}{2}\right|(1 - |\rho_0|) \tag{8.80}$$

which occur at the points

$$\varphi + 2\beta z = n\pi \qquad n = \pm 1, \pm 3, \pm 5, \ldots$$

At these points $|I|$ is a maximum.

The voltage described by Eq. (8.78) consists of part $+z$ and part $-z$ traveling components. When $|\rho_0| = 1$, $|V|_{\min} = 0$ and the wave is called a *standing wave*. As an illustration of the nature of the voltage wave, consider the case where $Z_L = 2Z_0$. From Eq. (8.73), $\rho_0 = \frac{1}{3}e^{-j2\beta l}$. Thus $|\rho_0| = \frac{1}{3}$ and $\varphi = -2\beta l$. Then the $|V|_{\max}$ positions occur at

$$\begin{aligned}\varphi + 2\beta z &= 2m\pi\\ 2\beta(z - l) &= 2m\pi \qquad m = 0, \pm 1, \pm 2, \ldots\\ z - l &= \frac{m\pi}{\beta}\end{aligned}$$

$$= \frac{m\pi\lambda}{2\pi}$$

$$= \frac{m\lambda}{2}$$

There is a maximum in voltage at $z = l$ and at multiples of $\lambda/2$ down the line. A plot of $|V|$ is shown in Fig. 8.11. The $|I|_{\min}$ occur at points of $|V|_{\max}$, as shown above. The current wave is also shown in Fig. 8.11.

A useful definition for characterizing the waves is the voltage standing-wave ratio S. S is defined as

$$S = \frac{|V|_{\max}}{|V|_{\min}}$$

Since $|V|_{\max}$ and $|V|_{\min}$ are given in terms of $|\rho_0|$ in Eqs. (8.79) and (8.80), S can be written as

$$S = \frac{1 + |\rho_0|}{1 - |\rho_0|} \tag{8.81}$$

The minimum value of S is $S = 1$, which is obtained when $|\rho_0| = 0$.

On transmission lines which are designed to transmit power to a load, it is usually desirable to have a low standing-wave ratio. The reason for this can be illustrated by considering the average power at some point on the line. The average power is

$$\langle P \rangle = \tfrac{1}{2} \operatorname{Re} VI^*$$

where V and I contain components from both the $+z$ and $-z$ traveling waves. Using Eqs. (8.67) and (8.68) results in

$$\langle P \rangle = \tfrac{1}{2} \operatorname{Re} \left[\frac{a^+(0)}{2} \frac{a^{+*}(0)}{2Z_0} (1 + \rho)(1 - \rho^*) \right]$$

$$= \tfrac{1}{2} \operatorname{Re} \left[\frac{a^+(0)a^{+*}(0)}{4Z_0} \left(1 - \rho\rho^* + \rho - \rho^* \right) \right]$$

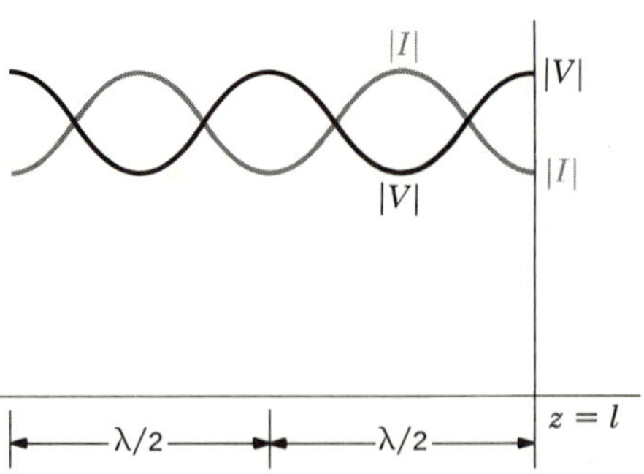

Fig. 8.11 Voltage and current waves on a line terminated in $Z_L = 2Z_0$.

For lossless lines, Z_0 is real. Hence

$$\langle P \rangle = \frac{1}{8} \frac{a^+(0)a^{+*}(0)}{Z_0} (1 - \rho\rho^*) + \frac{1}{8} \frac{a^+(0)a^{+*}(0)}{Z_0} \operatorname{Re} (\rho - \rho^*)$$

But since $\rho - \rho^* = 2 \operatorname{Im} \rho$, $\operatorname{Re} (\rho - \rho^*) = 0$; and since $\rho\rho^* = \rho_0\rho_0^*$,

$$\langle P \rangle = \frac{1}{8} \frac{a^+(0)a^{+*}(0)}{Z_0} (1 - \rho_0\rho_0^*) \tag{8.82}$$

The plus term in Eq. (8.82) is the power in the incident wave; the minus term represents power in the reflected wave. When $\rho_0 = 0$, all the power in the incident wave goes into the load, and maximum power transfer occurs. When $\rho_0 \neq 0$, a higher $a^+(0)$ is needed to get the same power into the load. We may not increase $a^+(0)$ indefinitely to get larger power transfer, because eventually the high voltage causes insulation breakdown. It then becomes important to reduce ρ_0 as much as possible in order to get maximum power into the load.

In some cases it is desirable to have a high standing-wave ratio. For example, when a transmission line is made into a resonant circuit by shorting both ends, the ideal situation is to have an infinite standing-wave ratio. The quantity S is especially useful because it is a physically measurable quantity. On all open transmission lines S can be measured by means of voltage probes or current-coupling coils.

Expressions for Z and Y in terms of S can be obtained from previously derived equations. As was explained in connection with Eq. (8.79), $\rho = |\rho_0|$ at a point of $|V|_{\max}$ (which is also a point of $|I|_{\min}$). Then, from Eq. (8.69), at that point,

$$\begin{aligned} Z &= Z_0 \frac{1 + |\rho_0|}{1 - |\rho_0|} \\ &= Z_0 S \qquad \text{(at points of } |V|_{\max}) \end{aligned} \tag{8.83}$$

Similarly, the admittance at that point is

$$Y = \frac{Y_0}{S} \qquad \text{(at points of } |V|_{\max}) \tag{8.84}$$

At a point of $|V|_{\min}$, $\rho = -|\rho_0|$, and

$$\begin{aligned} Z &= Z_0 \frac{1 - |\rho_0|}{1 + |\rho_0|} \\ &= \frac{Z_0}{S} \qquad \text{(at points of } |V|_{\min}) \end{aligned} \tag{8.85}$$

$$Y = Y_0 S \qquad \text{(at points of } |V|_{\min}) \tag{8.86}$$

The above expressions can be used to find Z_L when S and the position of $|V|_{\min}$ or $|V|_{\max}$ is known. Suppose $z = d$ is the position of $|V|_{\min}$. Then, from Eqs. (8.85) and (8.75),

$$\frac{Z_0}{S} = Z_0 \frac{Z_L + jZ_0 \tan \beta(l - d)}{Z_0 + jZ_L \tan \beta(l - d)}$$

Solving for Z_L results in

$$Z_L = Z_0 \frac{1 - jS \tan \beta(l - d)}{S - j \tan \beta(l - d)} \tag{8.87}$$

Similarly, combining Eqs. (8.85) and (8.77) results in

$$Y_L = Y_0 \frac{S - j \tan \beta(l - d)}{1 - jS \tan \beta(l - d)} \tag{8.88}$$

Equations (8.87) and (8.88) can be used to find the load impedance and admittance, respectively, when the standing-wave ratio and voltage minimum position are known. Similar expressions can be obtained in terms of the position of a voltage maximum, but since the voltage-minimum position can usually be measured more precisely, Eqs. (8.87) and (8.88) are generally more useful. When S is low, neither the $|V|_{\min}$ nor $|V|_{\max}$ position can be measured very precisely.

Example 8.6 Measurement of a lumped admittance on a lossless transmission line Figure 8.12*a* shows a terminated transmission line with a lumped element at a distance l from the input. The lumped element is called Y_1, because, as will soon be evident, it is easier to work in terms of admittance. Figure 8.12*b* shows an

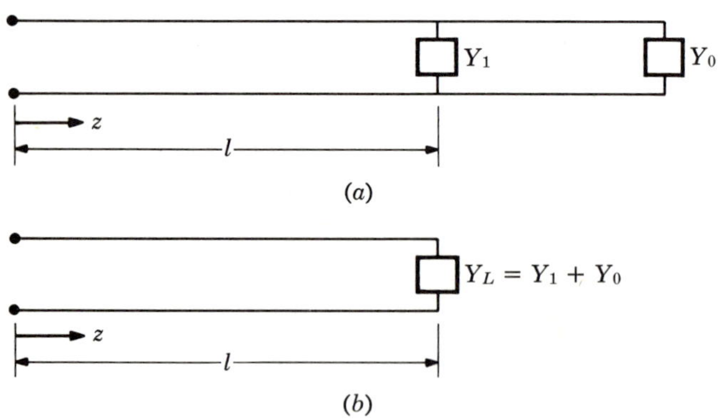

Fig. 8.12 (*a*) A lumped admittance on a transmission line; (*b*) an equivalent transmission line with the termination transformed to the lumped-admittance position.

equivalent transmission line, where the characteristic admittance terminating the line is transferred to the point $z = l$. This transformation was explained in the discussion following Eq. (8.76). The sum $Y_1 + Y_0$ is now considered to be the load admittance Y_L. It should be obvious now why it is easier to use admittance than impedance.

The characteristics of the line are

$$L = 10^{-6} \text{ h/m}$$

$$C = \tfrac{1}{4} \times 10^{-10} \text{ f/m}$$

$$f = 4 \times 10^6 \text{ Hz}$$

Measurements indicate that

$$|V|_{\min} \text{ occurs at } z = d$$

$$l - d = 27.5 \text{ m}$$

$$S = 2.0$$

The propagation constant is

$$\beta = \omega\sqrt{LC}$$

$$= 2\pi \times 4 \times 10^6 \sqrt{\tfrac{1}{4} \times 10^{-16}}$$

$$= \frac{2\pi}{50} \quad \text{m}^{-1}$$

and the wavelength is

$$\lambda = \frac{2\pi}{\beta}$$

$$= 50 \text{ m}$$

Therefore

$$\beta(l - d) = \frac{2\pi}{50} \times 27.5$$

$$= 0.55 \times 2\pi$$

and

$$\tan \beta(l - d) = \tan 1.1\pi$$

$$= 0.325$$

Substituting these values into Eq. (8.88) results in

$$Y_L = Y_0 \frac{2 - j0.325}{1 - j0.650}$$

$$= Y_0(1.555 + j0.684)$$

Since $Y_L = Y_1 + Y_0$,

$$Y_1 = Y_L - Y_0$$

$$= Y_0(0.555 + j0.684)$$

And

$$Y_0 = \frac{1}{Z_0}$$
$$= \sqrt{\frac{C}{L}}$$
$$= 1/500$$

Therefore

$$Y_1 = 1/500(0.555 + j0.684)$$

Although this method of measuring the admittance Y_1 is probably not a common one in practice, it is interesting because it shows the relations between standing-wave ratio, position of the voltage minimum, and admittance on the line.

Another useful parameter is the transmission coefficient, defined as the ratio of the voltage transmitted across a discontinuity to the incident voltage,

$$\tau_L = \frac{a_2^+(l)}{a_1^+(l)} \tag{8.89}$$

where a_2^+ and a_1^+ are as shown in Fig. 8.13. Since the voltage must be continuous at $z = l$,

$$a_1^+(l) + a_1^-(l) = a_2^+(l)$$

where V has been written in terms of a^+ and a^- by Eq. (8.37). Using Eq. (8.66), we have

$$a_1(l)(1 + \rho_{L1}) = a_2^+(l)$$

and hence

$$\tau_L = (1 + \rho_{L1}) \tag{8.90}$$

where ρ_{L1} is the reflection coefficient on line 1 at $z = l$.

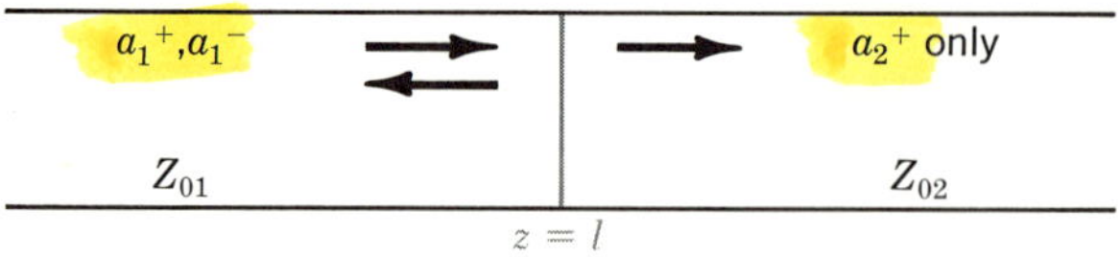

Fig. 8.13 The transmission across a discontinuity in Z_0. The line is assumed to be infinitely long, so there is no reflection of a_2^+.

The transmission coefficient can also be used to describe the ratio of the voltage across a load Z_L to the incident voltage. Then $a_2^+(l)$ is interpreted as proportional to the voltage across the load, and Eq. (8.90) still holds.

8.8 LOSSY-TRANSMISSION-LINE DISCONTINUITIES AND IMPEDANCES

For lossy lines, the solutions of the transmission-line equations corresponding to Eqs. (8.64) and (8.65) are

$$V = \frac{a^+(0)}{2} e^{-\Gamma z} + \frac{a^-(0)}{2} e^{\Gamma z} \tag{8.91}$$

$$I = \frac{1}{Z_0}\left[\frac{a^+(0)}{2} e^{-\Gamma z} - \frac{a^-(0)}{2} e^{\Gamma z}\right] \tag{8.92}$$

where Γ is as defined in Eq. (8.39). The reflection coefficient is defined similarly to the way it is in the lossless case,

$$\begin{aligned} \rho &= \frac{a^-}{a^+} e^{2\Gamma z} \\ &= \rho_0 e^{2\Gamma z} \end{aligned} \tag{8.93}$$

and

$$V = \frac{a^+(0)}{2} e^{-\Gamma z}(1 + \rho) \tag{8.94}$$

$$I = \frac{a^+(0)e^{-\Gamma z}}{2Z_0} (1 - \rho) \tag{8.95}$$

In the lossy case $|\rho|$ depends on z because Γ is complex, whereas in the lossless case it does not. A further complication is that Z_0 is complex in the lossy case.

The impedance is

$$\begin{aligned} Z &= \frac{V}{I} \\ &= Z_0 \frac{1 + \rho}{1 - \rho} \end{aligned} \tag{8.96}$$

and, as in the lossless case, ρ_L is given by Eq. (8.72),

$$\rho_L = \frac{Z_L - Z_0}{Z_L + Z_0} \tag{8.72}$$

When losses are present, it is possible for $|\rho_L|$ to be greater than 1, because both Z_L and Z_0 are complex.

Following the procedure used to derive Eq. (8.75) in the lossless case, we have an expression for impedance,

$$Z = Z_0 \frac{Z_L + Z_0 \tanh \Gamma(l - z)}{Z_0 + Z_L \tanh \Gamma(l - z)} \tag{8.97}$$

When $\Gamma = j\beta$, Eq. (8.97) reduces to Eq. (8.75). The impedance-transformation ideas discussed in connection with Eq. (8.75) also apply to Eq. (8.97). The transformation is different, of course, because Γ and Z_0 are complex.

It is not as easy to determine the variation of V with z in the lossy case as it was in the lossless case. The expression for V can be written as

$$V = \frac{a^+(0)}{2} \left[e^{-j\beta z} e^{-\alpha z} + \frac{a^-(0)}{a^+(0)} e^{j\beta z} e^{\alpha z} \right]$$

from Eqs. (8.91) and (8.42). This expression can be thought of as two counterrotating vectors, one growing and one decaying. A typical plot of $|V|$ versus z is shown in Fig. 8.14.

Reflections in lossy lines cause an increase in loss which can be very substantial. Physically, higher losses would be expected when reflections are present, because each time a wave travels down the line it is attenuated. If the load reflects part of the power, more power is dissipated in the lossy line than if no reflection occurred. This can be shown mathematically. The time-average power at $z = l$ is

$$\begin{aligned} \langle P_l \rangle &= \tfrac{1}{2} \operatorname{Re} VI^* \\ &= \tfrac{1}{8} a^+(0) a^{+*}(0) e^{-2\alpha l} \\ &\qquad \times \operatorname{Re} \frac{1 - \rho_0 \rho_0^* e^{4\alpha l} + (\rho_0 e^{2j\beta l} e^{-2\alpha l} - \rho_0^* e^{-2j\beta l} e^{-2\alpha l})}{Z_0^*} \end{aligned}$$

The average power at $z = 0$ is

$$\langle P_0 \rangle = \tfrac{1}{8} a^+(0) a^{+*}(0) \operatorname{Re} \frac{1 - \rho_0 \rho_0^* + \rho_0 - \rho_0^*}{Z_0^*}$$

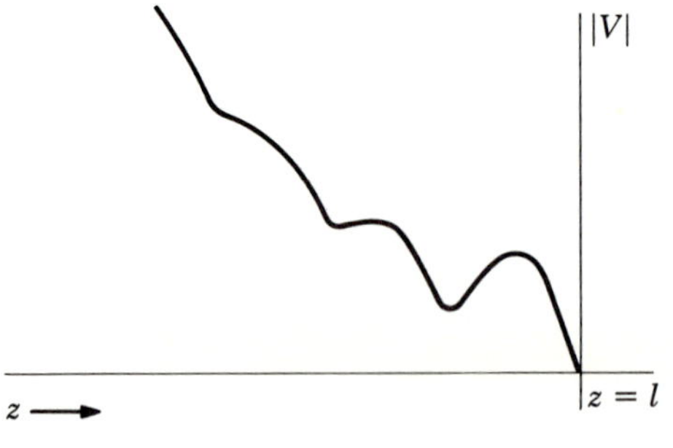

Fig. 8.14 Plot of $|V|$ versus z for a lossy line.

The average power dissipated in the length l is

$$\begin{aligned}\langle P_d\rangle &= \langle P_0\rangle - \langle P_l\rangle \\ &= \tfrac{1}{8}a^+(0)a^{+*}(0) \\ &\times \operatorname{Re}\frac{1 - e^{-2\alpha l} + \rho_0\rho_0^*(e^{2\alpha l} - 1) + \rho_0(1 - e^{2j\beta l}) - \rho_0^*(1 - e^{-2j\beta l})}{Z_0^*} \\ &= \tfrac{1}{8}a^+(0)a^{+*}(0) \\ &\times \operatorname{Re}\frac{1 - e^{-2\alpha l} + \rho_0\rho_0^*(e^{2\alpha l} - 1) + 2\operatorname{Im}\rho_0(1 - e^{2j\beta l})}{Z_0^*}\end{aligned}$$

where Im x and Re x denote the imaginary and real parts of x, respectively. Multiplying by Z_0/Z_0 and rearranging results in

$$\langle P_d\rangle = \frac{1}{8}\frac{a^+(0)a^{+*}(0)}{Z_0Z_0^*}[1 - e^{-2\alpha l} + \rho_0\rho_0^*(e^{2\alpha l} - 1)]\operatorname{Re}Z_0 - \frac{a^+(0)a^{+*}(0)}{4Z_0Z_0^*}\operatorname{Im}[\rho_0(1 - e^{2j\beta l})]\operatorname{Im}Z_0$$

We assume now that the losses are small enough that $\operatorname{Im}Z_0 \ll \operatorname{Re}Z_0$ and neglect the second term on the right. Then

$$\langle P_d\rangle = \frac{1}{8}\frac{a^+(0)a^{+*}(0)}{Z_0Z_0^*}[1 - e^{-2\alpha l} + \rho_0\rho_0^*(e^{2\alpha l} - 1)]\operatorname{Re}Z_0$$

When $\rho = 0$, there are no reflections, and the line is matched. The power dissipated in a matched lossy line is $\langle P_d\rangle_m$, given by

$$\langle P_d\rangle_m = \frac{1}{8}\frac{a^+(0)a^{+*}(0)}{Z_0Z_0^*}(1 - e^{-2\alpha l})\operatorname{Re}Z_0$$

The fraction of extra power dissipated by reflections is

$$\frac{\langle P_d\rangle - \langle P_d\rangle_m}{\langle P_d\rangle_m} = \rho_0\rho_0^*(e^{2\alpha l} - 1) \tag{8.98}$$

It is evident from Eq. (8.98) that the extra power dissipated through reflections can be substantial, especially when the line is long.

8.9 THE SMITH CHART

This section describes a convenient graphical method for solving many transmission-line problems, based on the Smith chart.†

† P. H. Smith, Transmission-line Calculator, *Electronics*, vol. 12, 1939, pp. 29–31; P. H. Smith, An Improved Transmission-line Calculator, *Electronics*, vol. 17, 1944, p. 130.

LOSSLESS LINES

The *Smith chart* is a graphical representation of Eq. (8.69), which is a relation between Z and ρ. It is convenient to normalize the impedance by dividing by Z_0; the resulting normalized impedances are denoted by lowercase script functions. Equation (8.69) can be written in the form

$$\begin{aligned}\mathfrak{z} &= \frac{Z}{Z_0} \\ &= \frac{1 + |\rho_0|e^{j(\varphi+2\beta z)}}{1 - |\rho_0|e^{j(\varphi+2\beta z)}}\end{aligned} \tag{8.99}$$

The normalized impedances written in terms of resistance and reactance are

$$\mathfrak{z} = \mathfrak{r} + jx \tag{8.100}$$

and ρ, which is also a complex variable, is written as

$$\begin{aligned}\rho &= |\rho_0|e^{j\theta} \\ &= u + jv \\ &= w\end{aligned} \tag{8.101}$$

where

$$\theta = \varphi + 2\beta z \tag{8.102}$$

The u and v variables are the rectangular representation of ρ, and $|\rho_0|e^{j\theta}$ is the polar representation of ρ. With the definitions of Eqs. (8.100) and (8.101), Eq. (8.99) becomes

$$\frac{1 + (u + jv)}{1 - (u + jv)} = \mathfrak{r} + jx$$

Rationalizing the left-hand side and equating real and imaginary parts results in

$$\frac{1 - (u^2 + v^2)}{(1 - u^2) + v^2} = \mathfrak{r}$$

$$\frac{2v}{(1 - u)^2 + v^2} = x$$

After some algebraic manipulation, these equations can be written in the forms

$$\left(u - \frac{\mathfrak{r}}{1 + \mathfrak{r}}\right)^2 + v^2 = \frac{1}{(1 + \mathfrak{r})^2} \tag{8.103}$$

$$(u - 1)^2 + \left(v - \frac{1}{x}\right)^2 = \frac{1}{x^2} \tag{8.104}$$

The Smith chart is a plot of these two equations in the complex plane $w = u + jv$. Equations (8.103) and (8.104) have the form

$$(u - u_0)^2 + (v - v_0)^2 = a^2$$

which is a circle with center at (u_0, v_0) and radius a. In uv space the constant r lines are circles with radius $1/(1 + r)$ and center at $(r/(1 + r), 0)$. The constant x lines are circles with radius $1/x$ and center at $(1, 1/x)$. Some representative circles are shown in Fig. 8.15. From inspection of Fig. 8.15, it appears that all the circles pass through the point (1,0). This is true, because $u = 1$, $v = 0$ satisfies both Eq. (8.103) and Eq. (8.104).

Also shown in Fig. 8.15 are the polar coordinates of ρ. From Eq. (8.102) we see that θ increases when z increases. Hence motion in the $+z$ direction along the transmission line is equivalent to motion in the counterclockwise direction on the chart in Fig. 8.15. When the generator is located at $z = 0$ and the load is at $z = l$, as shown in Fig. 8.9, motion in the counterclockwise direction on the chart corresponds to motion toward the load along the line. Motion in the clockwise direction on the chart corresponds to motion toward the generator along the line. These directions are indicated in Fig. 8.15.

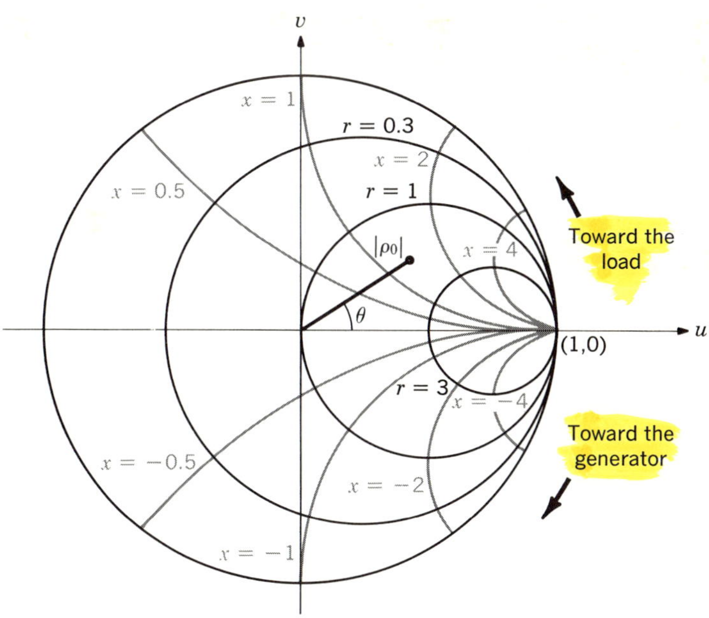

Fig. 8.15 Constant r and x lines in uv space (Smith chart)

At each point on the chart a value $\mathfrak{z} = \mathfrak{r} + jx$ and a value $\rho = |\rho_0|e^{j\theta}$ may be read. These values of $\mathfrak{z}$ and ρ are related by Eq. (8.99), since the chart is a plot of that equation. Thus, if ρ is known at a given value of z, the corresponding value of $\mathfrak{z}$ can be read from the chart. If $\mathfrak{z}$ is known, ρ can be read from the chart. Since $\rho = |\rho_0|e^{j\theta}$, and $|\rho_0|$ does not depend on z, ρ at one point on the line differs from the ρ at another point only by a difference in the angle θ. Suppose that $\rho = |\rho_0|e^{j(\varphi+\beta z_1)} = |\rho_0|e^{j\theta_1}$ at $z = z_1$. Then at $z = z_2$, $\rho = |\rho_0|e^{j(\varphi+2\beta z_2)} = |\rho_0|e^{j\theta_2}$ can be found by moving on the chart along a circle of radius $|\rho_0|$ through an angle

$$
\begin{aligned}
\Delta\theta &= \theta_2 - \theta_1 \\
&= \varphi + 2\beta z_2 - (\varphi + 2\beta z_1) \\
&= 2\beta(z_2 - z_1)
\end{aligned}
$$

This is illustrated in Fig. 8.16. Also, the values of $\mathfrak{z}$ at $z = z_1$ and $z = z_2$ can be read from the chart. Thus if either ρ or $\mathfrak{z}$ is known at one point on the line, ρ or $\mathfrak{z}$ at any point on the line can be found by moving along a circle of radius $|\rho_0|$ through the appropriate angle $\Delta\theta$. This is one of the features which makes the chart extremely useful, as illustrated in the examples that follow. Since $\beta = 2\pi/\lambda$, $\Delta\theta = (4\pi/\lambda)(z_2 - z_1)$, and going around the chart once is equivalent to moving a half-wavelength along the line. Thus $\mathfrak{z}$ and ρ are periodic; their values repeat every half-wavelength along the line. Most charts have a scale around the edge, showing the angle in terms of wavelength, as in Fig. 8.17, so the angle need not be computed separately.

The standing-wave ratio S can also be found from the chart. As pointed out previously, $|V| = |V|_{\max}$ when $\theta = \varphi + 2\beta z = 2\pi$. This corresponds to the $+u$ axis on the chart. Also, $\mathfrak{z} = Z/Z_0 = S$ when $|V| = |V|_{\max}$. Thus the value of $\mathfrak{z}$ on the $+u$ axis is equal to S. From the expression

$$
x = \frac{2v}{(1-u)^2 + v^2}
$$

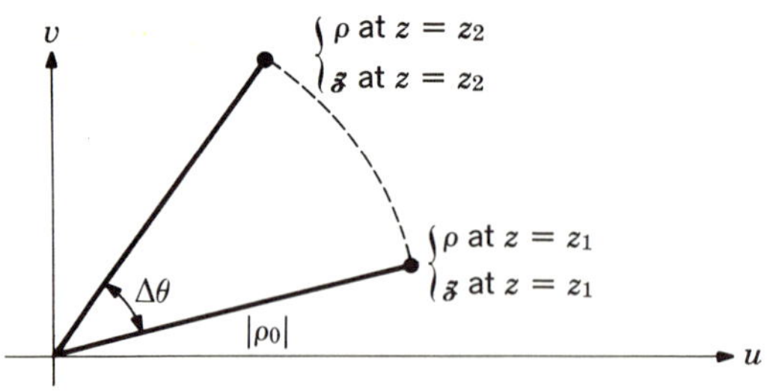

Fig. 8.16 The relation between ρ and $\mathfrak{z}$ at $z = z_1$ and ρ and $\mathfrak{z}$ at $z = z_2$.

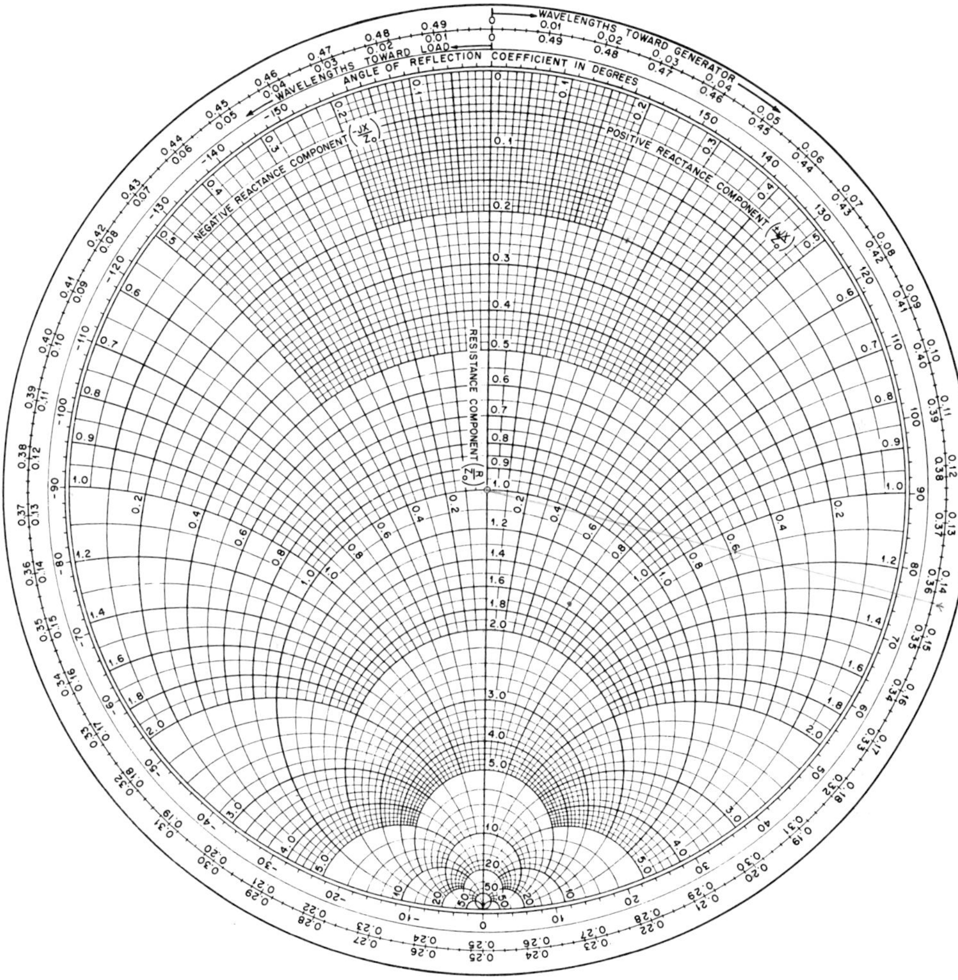

Fig. 8.17 The Smith chart.

it is apparent that on the $+u$ axis, where $v = 0$, $x = 0$. Therefore at the point where $|V| = |V|_{max}$, $z = r = S$. If z or ρ is known at one point on the line, S can be found from the chart simply by moving from the point on the chart where z or ρ is known along a circle of radius $|\rho_0|$ to the $+u$ axis. The value of r at that point is S. This is illustrated in Fig. 8.18. Similarly, the point of $|V|_{min}$ is the $-u$ axis, where $z = 1/S$. Since $x = 0$ on the $-u$ axis also, $S = 1/r$ on the $-u$ axis. If S and either the position of $|V|_{max}$ or $|V|_{min}$ is known, z and ρ can be found, as illustrated in Example 8.8 (page 359).

The Smith chart can also be used as an admittance chart. From Eqs. (8.67) and (8.68), the admittance I/V in terms of ρ is found to be

$$
\begin{aligned}
y &= \frac{Y}{Y_0} \\
&= \frac{1 - \rho}{1 + \rho} \\
&= \frac{1 - |\rho_0|e^{j\theta}}{1 + |\rho_0|e^{j\theta}}
\end{aligned}
$$

Since $e^{j\pi} = -1$, this equation can be rewritten as

$$
\begin{aligned}
y &= g + jb \\
&= \frac{1 + |\rho_0|e^{j(\theta+\pi)}}{1 - |\rho_0|e^{j(\theta+\pi)}}
\end{aligned}
$$

This equation is formally the same as Eq. (8.99), from which the Smith chart is plotted, if the θ in Eq. (8.99) is changed to $\theta + \pi$. Consequently, y can be found from z on the chart by moving at a constant radius through

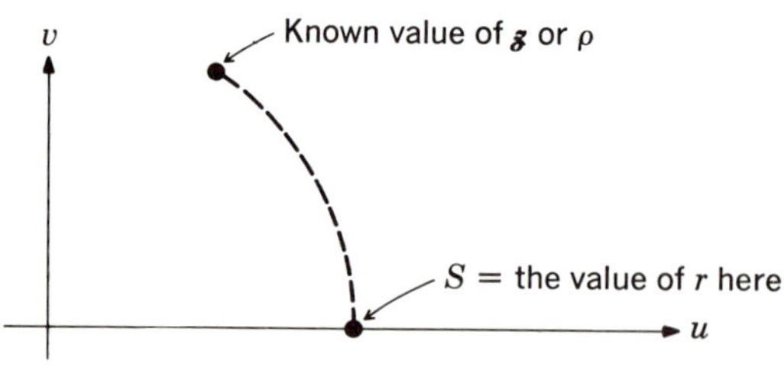

Fig. 8.18 Finding S when one value of z or ρ is known.

the angle π. Thus each number on the chart corresponds to an impedance and an admittance, but the impedance is at a different point on the transmission line from the admittance.

To find the admittance at a point z on the line, the value is read from the chart at the angle $\theta + \pi = \varphi + 2\beta z$, or $\theta = \varphi + 2\beta z - \pi$. Since it is usually the change in angle $\Delta\theta$ which is used in working with the Smith chart, the chart can be used as an admittance chart in the same way that it is used as an impedance chart. For example, suppose that the admittance at some point z is known and the admittance at another point z_2 is desired. The admittance at z_2 can be found by moving on the chart from the admittance at $\theta_1 + \pi = \varphi + 2\beta z_1$ along a circle of radius $|\rho_0|$ through the angle $(\theta_2 + \pi) - (\theta_1 + \pi) = 2\beta(z_2 - z_1)$. Since $(\theta_2 + \pi) - (\theta_1 + \pi) = \theta_2 - \theta_1$, this is exactly the same procedure used for impedance. For admittance, the numbers on the chart are read as admittance numbers.

There is a difference in the location of $|V|_{\max}$ and $|V|_{\min}$ on the chart when it is used as an admittance chart. $|V|_{\max}$ occurs at $\theta = 2\pi$, or $(\theta + \pi) = 3\pi$, which is the $-u$ axis. There $\mathscr{b} = 0$ and $y = \mathscr{g} = 1/S$ [see Eq. (8.84)]. $|V|_{\min}$ occurs at $\theta = \pi$, or $(\theta + \pi) = 2\pi$, which is the $+u$ axis. There $\mathscr{b} = 0$, and $y = \mathscr{g} = S$ [see Eq. (8.86)]. Thus the same Smith chart can be used either as an impedance chart or as an admittance chart, the main differences being that $|V|_{\max}$ occurs on the $+u$ axis when the chart is used as an impedance chart and on the $-u$ axis when the chart is used as an admittance chart. $|V|_{\min}$ is on the $-u$ axis when the chart is used as an impedance chart and on the $+u$ axis when the chart is used as an admittance chart.

These facts can easily be remembered by recalling that $|V|_{\max}$ and $|I|_{\min}$ occur at the same point, as explained in connection with Eq. (8.79), and $|V|_{\min}$ and $|I|_{\max}$ also occur at the same point. Thus at the point of $|V|_{\max}$ the impedance will be a maximum, and at the point of $|V|_{\min}$ the impedance will be a minimum. On the chart, the large values of $\imath$ occur on the $+u$ axis; hence $|V|_{\max}$ occurs on the $+u$ axis and $|V|_{\min}$ on the $-u$ axis. The opposite is true when the chart is used as an admittance chart. Since $\mathscr{g}$ is large on the $+u$ axis and small on the $-u$ axis, $|V|_{\min}$ occurs on the $+u$ axis and $|V|_{\max}$ on the $-u$ axis.

Example 8.7 Finding Z_i when Z_L is known Suppose a two-wire transmission line is terminated in a load impedance Z_L at $z = l$, as indicated in Fig. 8.9. The inductance and capacitance of the line are

$$L = 10^{-6}\ \text{h/m}$$

$$C = \tfrac{1}{9} \times 10^{-10}\ \text{f/m}$$

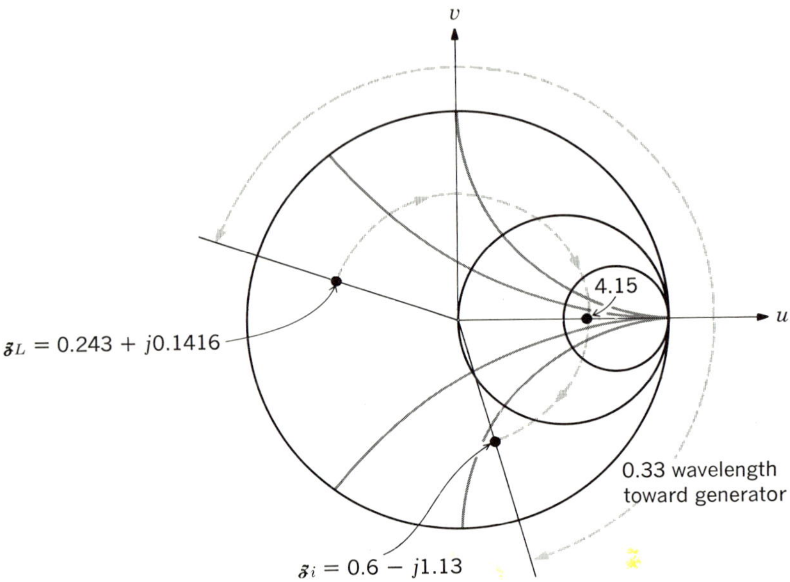

Fig. 8.19 Finding z_i when z_L is given, as explained in Example 8.7.

The load impedance, frequency, and line length are

$$Z_L = 73 + j42.5 \text{ ohms}$$
$$f = 10^7 \text{ Hz}$$
$$l = 10 \text{ m}$$

The R and G of the line are small enough to be neglected. From Table 8.1,

$$Z_0 = \sqrt{\frac{L}{C}}$$
$$= 300 \text{ ohms}$$
$$\beta = \omega \sqrt{LC}$$

The wavelength is

$$\lambda = \frac{2\pi}{\beta}$$
$$= \frac{2\pi}{\omega \sqrt{LC}}$$
$$= \frac{3 \times 10^8}{10^7}$$
$$= 30 \text{ m}$$

The line is $l/\lambda = 0.33$ wavelength long. The normalized load impedance is

$$\begin{aligned} z_L &= \frac{Z_L}{Z_0} \\ &= \frac{73 + j42.5}{300} \\ &= 0.243 + j0.1416 \end{aligned}$$

The input impedance z_i is obtained by entering the Smith chart at

$$z_L = 0.243 + j0.1416$$

and moving 0.33 wavelength clockwise toward the generator along a circle about the origin, as shown in Fig. 8.19. From the chart, $z_i = 0.6 - j1.13$. The unnormalized input impedance is $Z_i = Z_0 z_i = 180 - j339$. From the $+u$ axis, the standing-wave ratio is read as $S = 4.15$.

Example 8.8 Using the Smith chart to find the admittance of Example 8.6 From the data of Example 8.6, a point of $|V|_{\min}$ occurs a distance of $(l - d)/\lambda = 0.55$ wavelength from Y_1 toward the generator. The standing-wave ratio is given as $S = 2.0$. As in Example 8.6, it is easier to use admittances. As shown in Fig. 8.12, the admittance at $z = l$ is $y_1 + y_0$. Since $|V|_{\min}$ occurs on the $+u$ axis when the chart is used for admittance, the chart is entered at the point $g = 2.0$, $b = 0$. Recall that $g = S$ at the point where $|V| = |V|_{\min}$. y_L can be found by moving on the chart 0.55 wavelength counterclockwise toward the load. Since a distance of 0.50 wavelength means one rotation around the chart, moving 0.05 wavelength on the chart is the same as moving 0.55 wavelength. Hence y_L can be found by moving 0.05 wavelength toward the load, as illustrated in Fig. 8.20. The value of y_L read from the chart is $y_L = 1.55 + j0.7$. Since $y_L = y_1 + 1$, $y_1 = 0.55 + j0.7$.

Although y_1 could not be obtained with the same accuracy as the calculated

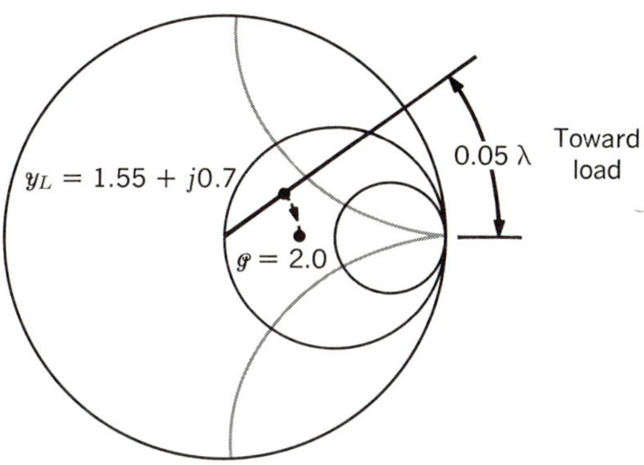

Fig. 8.20 The use of the Smith chart in Example 8.8.

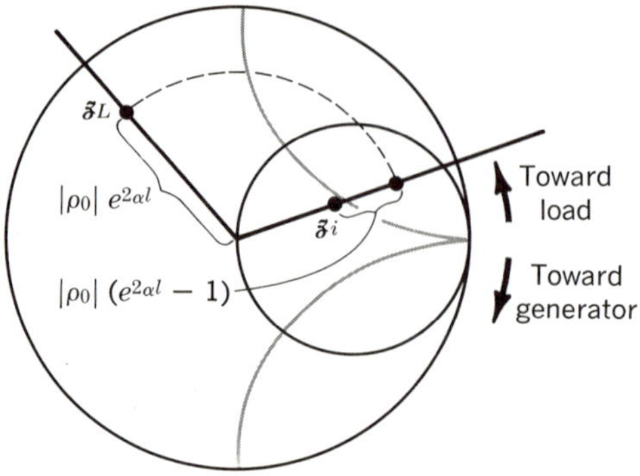

Fig. 8.21 A method of finding z_i when z_L is given and the line is lossy.

value in Example 8.6, the value obtained from the Smith chart can be obtained much more quickly and with less effort.

LOSSY LINES

From Eq. (8.96), the relation between z and ρ is still

$$z = \frac{1+\rho}{1-\rho} \tag{8.96}$$

for lossy lines, but from Eq. (8.93), for the lossy line,

$$\rho = |\rho_0| e^{2\alpha z} e^{j(\varphi + 2\beta z)}$$

and $|\rho|$ is a function of z because of the $e^{2\alpha z}$ factor. Since the Smith chart is based on Eq. (8.96), which is the same for lossy and lossless lines, the chart is valid for either case. However, since $|\rho|$ is a function of z, moving along a lossy line corresponds to moving in a spiral on the chart, instead of along a circle, as in the lossless case. Since $|\rho|$ increases as z increases, the spiral is outward for movement toward the load and inward for movement toward the generator.

In practice, we move along a circle and then inward or outward to account for the $e^{2\alpha z}$ factor. This is illustrated in Fig. 8.21, which shows how z_i is found when z_L is given and the line is lossy.

8.10 IMPEDANCE TRANSFORMATION AND MATCHING

It is often desirable to transform impedances and to match impedances. For example, the impedance of an antenna must be matched to its transmission line to get optimum power transfer. As indicated by Eq. (8.75), a transmission line transforms impedances in proportion to the length of the line. Thus a desired impedance can often be obtained by choosing the proper line length. The values of impedance for a given line length and load impedance can easily be found from the Smith chart. One disadvantage of using transmission lines to transform impedances, however, is that the transformation is frequency sensitive.

A common impedance-matching technique involves adding reactive elements in series or shunt with the transmission line at certain points to eliminate reflections and obtain an impedance match for optimum power transfer. Shorted or open sections of two-wire lines make good reactive elements for use with two-wire transmission systems, as explained in connection with Eq. (8.76). Reactive elements are introduced first, and then matching techniques are discussed.

REACTIVE ELEMENTS

From Eq. (8.76), with $Z_L = 0$, the impedance of a shorted stub is

$$\frac{Z}{Z_0} = j \tan \beta l \tag{8.105}$$

Theoretically, any value of reactance can be obtained by adjusting l. Practically speaking, precise values of some ranges of impedance would be difficult to obtain because of the sensitivity of $\tan \beta l$ to changes in l. For example, when βl is close to $\pi/2$, a very small change in l will cause a large change in Z.

The reactance of a shorted stub can be found by entering a Smith chart at the point $\mathfrak{z}_L = 0$, which is $\mathfrak{r} = x = 0$. This is the point $u = -1$, $v = 0$, as shown in Fig. 8.22. The impedance at the input of the shorted stub is found by moving from this point on a circle toward the generator a distance of l wavelengths. In this case the circle is the $\mathfrak{r} = 0$ circle, which is along the periphery of the chart.

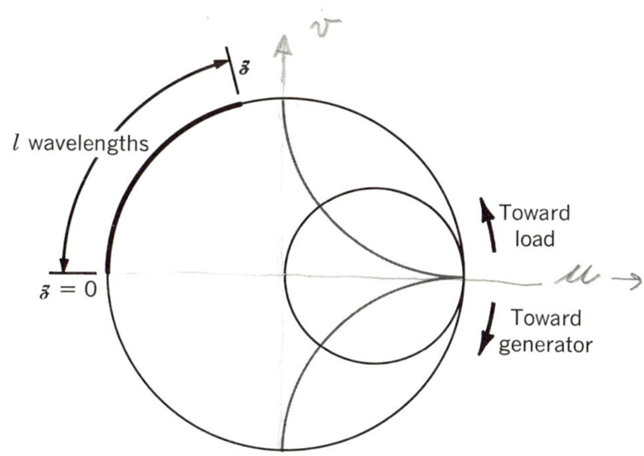

Fig. 8.22 Finding the reactance of a shorted stub.

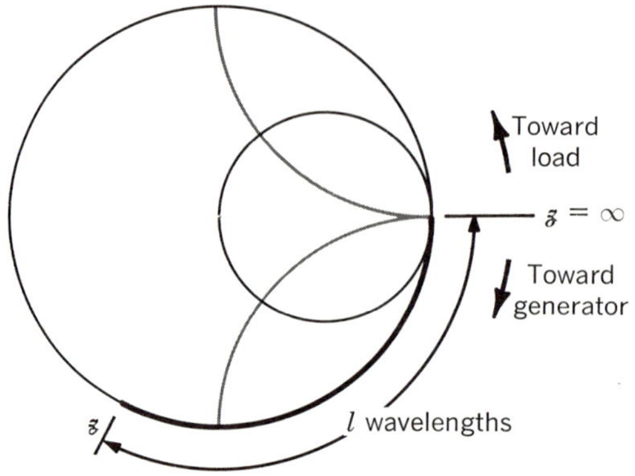

Fig. 8.23 Finding the reactance of an open stub.

For the open stub $Z_L = \infty$, and the input impedance as found from Eq. (8.76) is

$$\frac{Z}{Z_0} = -j \cot \beta l \tag{8.106}$$

This impedance may be found by entering the Smith chart at $\mathfrak{z} = \infty$, which is the point $u = 1$, $v = 0$, and moving toward the generator l wavelengths. This is illustrated in Fig. 8.23. In practice, good shorted stubs are easier to obtain than good open stubs.

MATCHING WITH SHUNT ELEMENTS

In using shunt elements for matching, it is usually easier to work in terms of transmission-line admittances. Matching with a shunt element can be illustrated by considering a transmission line terminated in a load admittance Y_L. A shunt element is added at some point on the line to make the input admittance of the line equal to Y_0.

From the Smith chart we see that $\mathcal{y}_L$ will be transformed into $1 + j\mathcal{b}$ at some point $z = d$ along the line. This is the point where the $|\rho_0|$ circle intersects the $\mathcal{g} = 1$ circle, as indicated in Fig. 8.24. If at this

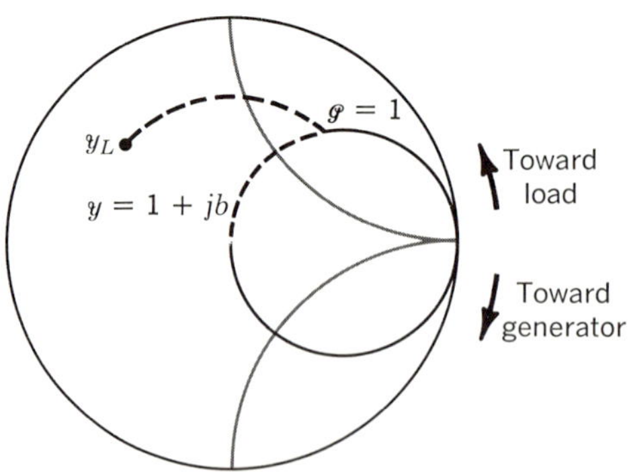

Fig. 8.24 Transformation of $\mathcal{y}_L$ to $1 + j\mathcal{b}$, and then the addition of a shunt admittance $\mathcal{y}_s = -j\mathcal{b}$ to arrive at the center of the chart.

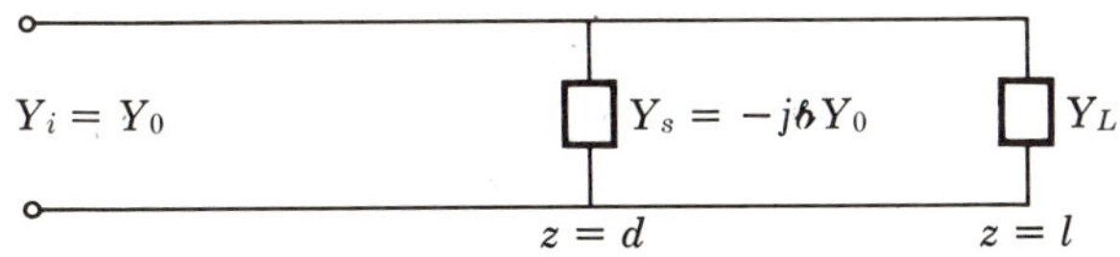

Fig. 8.25 Matching with a shunt element Y_s.

point a shunt susceptance of $y_s = -jb$ is added, the total admittance is

$$\begin{aligned} y &= 1 + jb - jb \\ &= 1 \end{aligned}$$

From this point on toward the generator, the line appears to be terminated in its characteristic admittance, and there are no reflections. Adding y_s is equivalent to moving along the $g = 1$ circle to the center of the chart, where the admittance is $1 + j0$. The line is then said to be matched. The resulting configuration is shown in Fig. 8.25. There are no reflections and no standing waves from $z = 0$ to $z = d$, but there are standing waves from $z = d$ to $z = l$. For this reason, it is usually desirable to put Y_s as close to the load as possible.

Example 8.9 Shunt stub matching Suppose $y_L = 0.5 - j0.9$. From the Smith chart, the admittance on the line is $y = 1 + j1.45$ at a point which is 0.303 wavelength from y_L. At this point a shunt element with susceptance $Y_s = -j1.45Y_0$ is added. If the Y_0 of the stub is the same as that of the line, the length of a shorted stub having the proper Y_s is 0.096 wavelength. If the characteristic admittance of the stub is not the same as that of the line, the normalized admittance of the stub must be $y_s = -j1.45Y_0/Y_{0s}$, where Y_{0s} is the characteristic admittance of the stub. Instead of using the Smith chart, Eq. (8.77), could be used to calculate the admittances and distances.

In practice, a variable-length shorted stub which can be moved along the line is often used to match the line. On many lines, however, it is not practical to move the stub along the line. Consequently, it is sometimes easier to match by using a combination of two variable-length stubs at fixed positions. This is called a *double-stub tuner*. A double-stub tuner is limited in that it cannot be used to match all values of y_L. A triple-stub tuner does not have this limitation and can be used to match any y_L.

Another element called a *stub stretcher* is used in coaxial lines. This element is a combination of a phase changer, which appears to "stretch" the line, and a shorted stub.

MATCHING WITH SERIES ELEMENTS

In using series elements, it is usually easier to work in terms of impedances. The same basic procedure as was used in matching with shunt elements is used here. A reactance of $-jb$ is added in series at the point on the line where $z = 1 + jb$.

Example 8.10 Series stub matching Suppose $z_L = 0.3 + j1.0$. From the Smith chart it is found that $z = 1 + j2.2$ at a distance of 0.063 wavelength from z_L. A series reactance of $Z_s = -jZ_0 2.2$ is added to make the net impedance at that point $z = 1 + j2.2 - j2.2 = 1$. The line is then matched. If the characteristic impedance of the stub is the same as that of the line, the proper shorted-stub length is 0.318λ.

QUARTER-WAVE TRANSFORMERS

Quarter-wave transformers are used primarily to match two transmission systems having different characteristic impedances. The configuration is shown in Fig. 8.26. The object of the quarter-wave transformer is to transform the impedance Z_{03} to Z_{01} at $z = l - \lambda_2/4$. The line on the right is assumed to be infinite or terminated in its characteristic impedance, so that the impedance at $z = l$ is Z_{03}. From Eq. (8.75), the impedance at $z = l - \lambda_2/4$, with Z_L at $z = l$ considered to be Z_{03}, is

$$Z = Z_{02} \frac{Z_{03} + jZ_{02} \tan \beta_2(l - l + \lambda_2/4)}{Z_{02} + jZ_{03} \tan \beta_2(l - l + \lambda_2/4)}$$

where β_2 and λ_2 are the propagation constant and wavelength in the line with characteristic impedance Z_{02}. Since $\beta_2 = 2\pi/\lambda_2$, $\beta_2\lambda_2/4 = \pi/2$, and Z becomes

$$Z = \frac{Z_{02}^2}{Z_{03}} \qquad \text{at } z = l - \frac{\lambda_2}{4}$$

If $Z_{02}^2 = Z_{03}Z_{01}$, then $Z = Z_{01}$, and the line is matched. Hence the quarter-wave transformer must be a quarter-wavelength long and have a characteristic impedance

$$Z_{02} = \sqrt{Z_{03}Z_{01}} \tag{8.107}$$

A disadvantage of the quarter-wave transformer is that the trans-

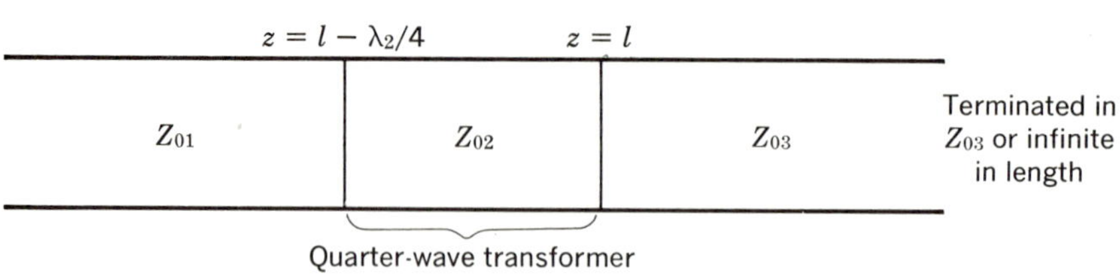

Fig. 8.26 Quarter-wave transformer used to match lines having characteristic impedances Z_{01} and Z_{03}.

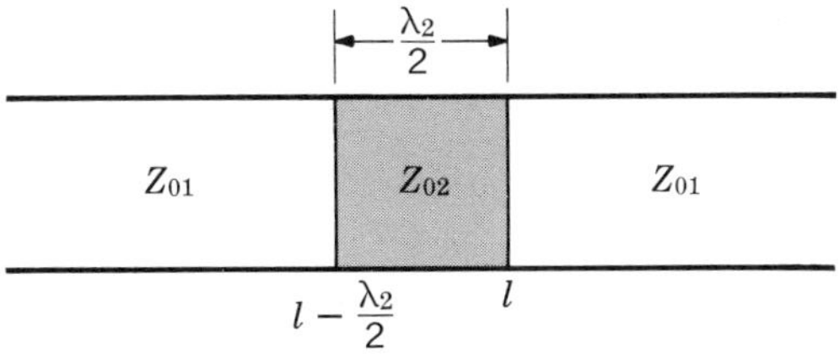

Fig. 8.27 A half-wave transformer.

formation is frequency sensitive. However, a combination of quarter-wave transformers can be used to obtain low reflections over a band of frequencies.

HALF-WAVE TRANSFORMERS

A half-wave transformer is useful in the configuration shown in Fig. 8.27, where two transmission systems having the same Z_0 are connected by a transmission system having a different Z_0. From Eq. (8.75) it is clear that Z_{01} at $z = l$ is transformed to

$$Z = Z_{02} \frac{Z_{01} + jZ_{02} \tan (\beta_2\lambda_2/2)}{Z_{02} + jZ_{01} \tan (\beta_2\lambda_2/2)}$$

$$= Z_{01}$$

at $z = l - \lambda_2/2$ because $\tan (\beta_2\lambda_2/2) = 0$. Thus the system on the left is matched if the intervening system is a half-wavelength long.

★8.11 Nonuniform and Tapered Transmission Lines

A nonuniform transmission line has a series impedance Z and a shunt admittance Y per unit length which vary with z. The analysis of nonuniform transmission lines is based on the transmission-line differential equations where the coefficients are variables instead of constants. This introduces some complications in solving for the modes of propagation, as two coupled-mode equations are obtained instead of two uncoupled equations. The nonuniformity in Z and Y couples the a^+ and a^- modes on the transmission line.

An important application of the nonuniform transmission line is for broadband impedance matching between two impedances of different value. For example, a transmission line of characteristic impedance Z_1 may be matched to another transmission line of characteristic impedance Z_2 by introducing between the two lines a tapered transmission line whose characteristic impedance varies from Z_1 to Z_2. This application is discussed in examples which follow.

When the dimensions of the transmission system are a function of z, the derivation of the transmission-line equations must be modified.

However, when the dimensions change slowly with z, that is, when the taper is very gradual, an approximation can be made which results in transmission-line equations having the form of Eqs. (8.18) and (8.19), with Z and Y being functions of z. When the taper is gradual, the transmission-line equations are

$$\frac{\partial V}{\partial z} = -Z(z)I \qquad \frac{\partial I}{\partial z} = -Y(z)V$$

where Z and Y are now functions of z, and V and I are functions of z with an $e^{j\omega t}$ time dependence. These equations were uncoupled in Sec. 8.5 by introducing the new variables

$$a^{\pm} = V \pm AI$$

where $A = \sqrt{YZ}$. The analysis proceeds in Sec. 8.5 under the condition that A is a constant, but for nonuniform lines A is variable.

Nevertheless, the transmission-line equations are combined as usual to obtain the mode equation

$$\frac{\partial V}{\partial z} + A\frac{\partial I}{\partial z} = -(ZI + AYV)$$

Since

$$\frac{\partial}{\partial z}(V + AI) = \frac{\partial V}{\partial z} + A\frac{\partial I}{\partial z} + I\frac{\partial A}{\partial z}$$

the mode equations become

$$\frac{\partial}{\partial z}a^{\pm} = \pm\sqrt{YZ}\,a^{\pm} \pm I\frac{\partial}{\partial z}\sqrt{\frac{Z}{Y}}$$

Both equations have been written at once, with the top signs for one equation and the bottom signs for the other equation. The coupling term involving I may be expressed in terms of the modes by the relation

$$I = \frac{a^{+} - a^{-}}{2\sqrt{Z/Y}}$$

and we obtain the two coupled-mode equations

$$\left(\frac{\partial}{\partial z} \pm \sqrt{YZ}\right)a^{\pm} = \pm\frac{(\partial/\partial z)\sqrt{Z/Y}}{2\sqrt{Z/Y}}(a^{+} - a^{-}) \tag{8.108}$$

Note that when the characteristic impedance $\sqrt{Z/Y}$ is a constant, the coupling term on the right-hand side of Eq. (8.108) vanishes, and the results of Sec. 8.5 are obtained. A variable characteristic impedance couples the a^+ mode to itself and to the a^- mode, and vice versa. Thus the presence of an a^+ mode generates an a^- mode through the coupling term.

Using the definitions of Eqs. (8.39) and (8.42), we have

$$\Gamma = \sqrt{YZ} = \alpha + j\beta \tag{8.39}$$

For convenience, a new parameter is defined as

$$K = \frac{1}{2}\frac{(\partial/\partial z)\sqrt{Z/Y}}{\sqrt{Z/Y}} = \frac{1}{2}\frac{(\partial/\partial z)Z_0}{Z_0} \tag{8.109}$$

where Eq. (8.45) has also been used. The remainder of the development in this section is restricted to the lossless case, where $\alpha = 0$. Then, with the definition of K just made, the coupled-mode equations are written in the form

$$\left(\frac{\partial}{\partial z} + j\beta - K\right) a^+ = -Ka^- \tag{8.110}$$

$$\left(\frac{\partial}{\partial z} - j\beta - K\right) a^- = -Ka^+ \tag{8.111}$$

These two first-order differential equations may be uncoupled by writing two second-order differential equations. The first equation is differentiated with respect to z, and terms involving a^- and $\partial a^-/\partial z$ are obtained. The term $\partial a^-/\partial z$ is obtained in terms of a^- and a^+ from the second equation, and a^- is obtained from the first equation such that an equation is obtained in terms of a^+ alone. A similar procedure gives an equation in terms of a^- alone,

$$\frac{\partial^2 a^\pm}{\partial z^2} - \left(2K + \frac{1}{K}\frac{\partial K}{\partial z}\right)\frac{\partial}{\partial z}a^\pm + \left[\beta^2 \pm j\left(\frac{\partial \beta}{\partial z} - \frac{\beta}{K}\frac{\partial K}{\partial z}\right)\right] a^\pm = 0$$

Solutions to these equations give the general results for a nonuniform transmission line. By applying the boundary conditions, the $a^\pm$ modes are obtained as a function of z. The solutions for $a^\pm$ are simplified if the coupling coefficient K is small, i.e., if the impedance change in a wavelength is small compared to the impedance. The assumption of small K is used in the rest of this section. This is consistent with the gradual-taper assumption stated at the beginning of the section.

Low-reflection Tapered Transmission Lines

Consider the case where a large-amplitude a^+ wave exists on a tapered nonuniform line, and only small values of a^- are generated. In this case the a^- term in Eq. (8.110) may be neglected to obtain a first approximation for a^+,

$$\frac{\partial}{\partial z} a^+ = -(j\beta - K)a^+$$

This expression is integrated to give

$$a^+ = B \exp\,[-\textstyle\int(j\beta - K)\,dz] \tag{8.112}$$

where B is an arbitrary constant. The small reflected mode a^- is obtained from a combination of Eqs. (8.112) and (8.111) as

$$\frac{\partial}{\partial z} a^- - (j\beta + K)a^- = -KB \exp\,[-\textstyle\int(j\beta - K)\,dz]$$

Multiplying both sides of this equation by $e^{-\int(j\beta+K)dz}$ gives an equation which can be written in the form

$$\frac{\partial}{\partial z}\{a^- \exp\,[-\textstyle\int(j\beta + K)\,dz]\} = -KB \exp\,[-2j\textstyle\int\beta\,dz]$$

which is integrated to give

$$a^- = -\exp\,[\textstyle\int(j\beta + K)\,dz]\int KB \exp\,[-2j\int\beta\,dz]\,dz + C \tag{8.113}$$

where C is an arbitrary constant. This result may now be used in the right-hand side of Eq. (8.110) to obtain a closer approximation to a^+, if desired. It is obvious that the complexity of the resulting equations increases rapidly as closer approximations are sought, and the results presented here in Eqs. (8.112) and (8.113) are good for $a^- \ll a^+$.

Exponential Impedance Taper for Matching

Suppose two transmission lines are to be broadband matched by means of an exponentially tapered transmission-line section, as shown in Fig. 8.28. An incident a^+ mode from line Z_{01} generates an $a^+(0)$ mode in the tapered section at $z = 0$. Coupling along the line generates an a^- mode of amplitude $a^-(0)$ at $z = 0$. Line Z_{02} is terminated such that no reflected wave exists at $z = l$; thus $a^-(l) = 0$. It is desired to find the reflection coefficient associated with this matching section,

$$\rho_0 = \frac{a^-(0)}{a^+(0)}$$

Many transmission lines maintain a constant β as their geometries

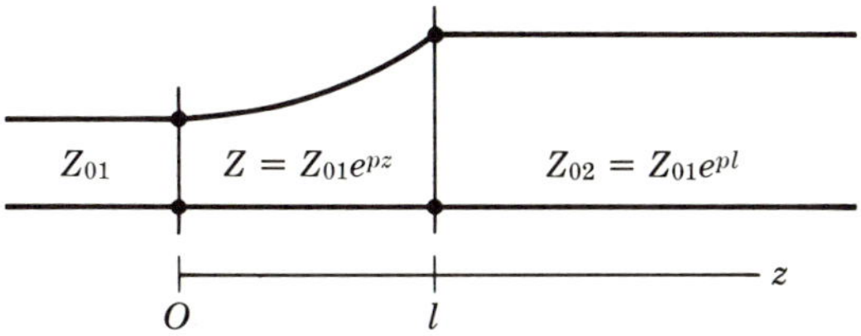

Fig. 8.28 An exponential impedance taper.

are altered to taper impedance. We shall assume this to be the case here and set $\beta = \beta_1$. The coupling coefficient K is

$$K = \frac{1}{2}\frac{\partial Z_0/\partial z}{Z_0} = \frac{1}{2}\frac{Z_{01}pe^{pz}}{Z_{01}e^{pz}} = \frac{p}{2}$$

and a^+ is obtained from Eq. (8.112),

$$a^+ = B \exp\left[-\int\left(j\beta_1 - \frac{p}{2}\right)dz\right] = B \exp\left[-\left(j\beta_1 - \frac{p}{2}\right)z\right]$$

Since

$$B = a^+(0)$$

we write

$$a^+ = a^+(0) \exp\left[-\left(j\beta_1 - \frac{p}{2}\right)z\right] \tag{8.114}$$

Equation (8.113) is written in the form

$$a^- \exp\left[-\left(j\beta_1 + \frac{p}{2}\right)z\right] = -\frac{p}{2}a^+(0)\int \exp(-2j\beta_1 z)\,dz + C = \frac{p}{4j\beta_1}a^+(0)\exp(-2j\beta_1 z) + C \tag{8.115}$$

The constant C is evaluated by setting $a^-(l) = 0$,

$$0 = \frac{pa^+(0)}{4j\beta_1}\exp(-2j\beta_1 l) + C$$

Equation (8.115) then becomes

$$a^- \exp\,[-\,(j\beta_1 + p/2)z] = \frac{pa^+(0)}{4j\beta_1}\,[\exp\,(-2j\beta_1 z) - \exp\,(-2j\beta_1 l)]$$

In order to find ρ_0, $a^-(0)$ is needed,

$$a^-(0) = a^+(0)\,\frac{p}{4j\beta_1}\,[1 - \exp\,(-2j\beta_1 l)]$$

The reflection coefficient is

$$\rho_0 = \frac{a^-(0)}{a^+(0)} = \frac{pl}{2}\exp\,(-j\beta_1 l)\,\frac{\sin\beta_1 l}{\beta_1 l}$$

Since $pl = \ln\,(Z_{02}/Z_{01})$,

$$\rho_0 = \tfrac{1}{2}\ln\frac{Z_{02}}{Z_{01}}\exp\,(-j\beta_1 l)\,\frac{\sin\beta_1 l}{\beta_1 l}$$

Of particular interest is the magnitude of the reflection coefficient versus the length of the tapered section. Figure 8.29 shows a plot of $|2\rho_0/\ln\,(Z_{02}/Z_{01})|$ versus $\beta_1 l$. This plot shows that if the taper is made long and gradual, low input reflections are obtained over a broad frequency band (β_1 varies linearly with frequency). Conversely, short lengths ($\beta_1 l = \pi$) may be used to obtain a perfect match at one frequency $\omega = \pi v_p/l$.

In some transmission lines β varies with z. The effects of variable β may be illustrated by considering an exponential β taper along with an

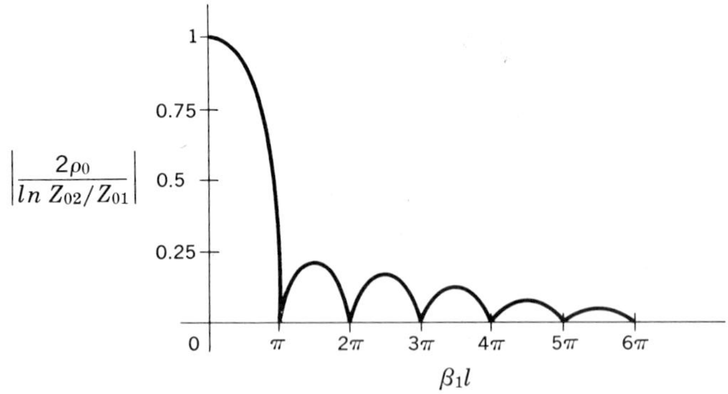

Fig. 8.29 The reflection coefficient for an exponential taper.

exponential Z taper. The phase constant for a^+ involves the integral $\int(j\beta - K)\,dz$ in Eq. (8.112). Using $\beta = \beta_1 e^{pz}$,

$$\int(j\beta - K)\,dz = \int(j\beta_1 e^{pz} - K)\,dz$$

where $K = p/2$ for the exponential impedance taper. The integral is evaluated to give

$$\int (j\beta - K)\,dz = \frac{j\beta_1}{p} e^{pz} - \frac{pz}{2}$$

and a^+ becomes

$$a^+ = a^+(0) \exp\left[-j\frac{\beta_1}{p}(e^{pz} - 1)\right] \exp\left(\frac{pz}{2}\right)$$

The reflected mode $a^-(0)$ may be evaluated in terms of $a^+(0)$ by setting $a^-(l) = 0$, as before. The reflection coefficient ρ_0 is then determined,

$$\rho_0 = \tfrac{1}{2} e^{2j\beta_1/p}\left[Ci\left(\frac{2\beta_1}{p}e^{pl}\right) - Ci\left(\frac{2\beta_1}{p}\right) - jSi\left(\frac{2\beta_1}{p}e^{pl}\right) + jSi\left(\frac{2\beta_1}{p}\right)\right]$$

For $p \ll 2\beta$ the large-argument approximation for the cosine and sine integrals Ci and Si may be used to obtain

$$\rho_0 = \frac{j}{4}\ln\frac{Z_2}{Z_1}\,\frac{\exp\left[-(2j\beta_1/p)(e^{pl} - 1) - pl\right] - 1}{\beta_1 l}$$

These results are similar in form to the results for the derivation for ★constant β, and ρ_0 versus $\beta_1 l$ looks very much like Fig. 8.29.

★8.12 Transmission-line Transients

The previous discussions of transmission-line theory have applied mostly to steady-state sinusoidal conditions. In this section the analysis of transients on transmission lines is developed in terms of the Laplace transformation. This discussion is limited to the two-conductor TEM waves. It is assumed here that the reader is familiar with Laplace transforms and their use in solving differential-equation problems.

The Laplace Transform of the Transmission-line Equations

Just as in circuit theory, the Laplace transform provides a convenient tool for analyzing transients in transmission-line theory, although the application of the Laplace transform to the transmission-line case is somewhat complicated by the dependence of voltage and current on the coordinate z as well as the time t.

The definition of the Laplace transform of $V(z,t)$ is

$$\mathcal{V}(z,s) = \int_0^\infty V(z,t)e^{-st}\,dt \tag{8.116}$$

A similar definition holds for the Laplace transform of $I(z,t)$. Script letters are used to denote Laplace transforms. The Laplace transforms of Eqs. (8.16) and (8.17) may be obtained by multiplying the equations by $e^{-st}\,dt$ and integrating.

$$\int_0^\infty \frac{\partial V(z,t)}{\partial z} e^{-st}\,dt + R\int_0^\infty I(z,t)e^{-st}\,dt + L\int_0^\infty \frac{\partial I(z,t)}{\partial t} e^{-st}\,dt = 0 \tag{8.117}$$

$$\int_0^\infty \frac{\partial I(z,t)}{\partial z} e^{-st}\,dt + G\int_0^\infty V(z,t)e^{-st}\,dt + C\int_0^\infty \frac{\partial V(z,t)}{\partial t} e^{-st}\,dt = 0 \tag{8.118}$$

From a text on Laplace transforms or by integration by parts, the Laplace transforms of $\partial I/\partial t$ and $\partial V/\partial t$ are found to be

$$\int_0^\infty \frac{\partial I(z,t)}{\partial t} e^{-st}\,dt = s\mathcal{I}(z,s) - I(z,0^+) \tag{8.119}$$

$$\int_0^\infty \frac{\partial V(z,t)}{\partial t} e^{-st}\,dt = s\mathcal{V}(z,s) - V(z,0^+) \tag{8.120}$$

where $I(z,0^+)$ and $V(z,0^+)$ are the values of $I(z,t)$ and $V(z,t)$ as t approaches zero from the positive side. We shall use the notation

$$I(z,0^+) = I_0(z) \tag{8.121}$$

$$V(z,0^+) = V_0(z) \tag{8.122}$$

Equations (8.117) and (8.118) can now be written as

$$\frac{\partial \mathcal{V}(z,s)}{\partial z} + R\mathcal{I}(z,s) + Ls\mathcal{I}(z,s) - LI_0(z) = 0 \tag{8.123}$$

$$\frac{\partial \mathcal{I}(z,s)}{\partial z} + G\mathcal{V}(z,s) + Cs\mathcal{V}(z,s) - CV_0(z) = 0 \tag{8.124}$$

Note that

$$\int_0^\infty \frac{\partial V(z,t)}{\partial z} e^{-st}\,dt = \frac{\partial}{\partial z}\int_0^\infty V(z,t)e^{-st}\,dt$$

$$= \frac{\partial}{\partial z}\mathcal{V}(z,s)$$

The notation $\mathcal{V}(z,s)$ and $\mathcal{I}(z,s)$ will often be abbreviated to $\mathcal{V}$ and $\mathcal{I}$ unless it is important to emphasize the functional dependence.

The next step is to solve the simultaneous partial-differential equations, Eqs. (8.123) and (8.124). One convenient way to solve the equations is by uncoupling them by the procedure used in Sec. 8.5. Equation (8.124) is multiplied by an arbitrary constant A and added to Eq. (8.123) to obtain

$$\frac{\partial}{\partial z}(\mathcal{V} + A\mathcal{I}) + A(G + Cs)\left[\mathcal{V} + \frac{R + Ls}{A(G + Cs)}\mathcal{I}\right] - AC\left(V_0 + \frac{L}{CA}I_0\right) = 0 \quad (8.125)$$

A is defined so that the quantities $\mathcal{V} + A\mathcal{I}$ and $\mathcal{V} + [(R + Ls)/A(G + Cs)]\mathcal{I}$ are equal. This requires that

$$A = \frac{R + Ls}{A(G + Cs)} = \pm\sqrt{\frac{R + Ls}{G + Cs}} \quad (8.126)$$

Since A has two values, Eq. (8.125) becomes two equations. Defining,

$$\sqrt{\frac{R + Ls}{G + Cs}} = Z_0(s) \quad (8.127)$$

$$\mathcal{V} \pm Z_0(s)\mathcal{I} = \mathcal{A}^{\pm}(z,s) \quad (8.128)$$

$$V_0 \pm \frac{L}{CZ_0(s)}I_0 = A_0^{\pm}(z,s) \quad (8.129)$$

$$\sqrt{(R + Ls)(G + Cs)} = \Gamma(s) \quad (8.130)$$

Equation (8.125) can be written as

$$\frac{\partial \mathcal{A}^{\pm}}{\partial z} \pm \Gamma\mathcal{A}^{\pm} = \pm CZ_0A_0^{\pm} \quad (8.131)$$

where the top sign in Eq. (8.131) results in one equation and the bottom sign results in the other equation.

Equation (8.131) is an inhomogeneous equation whose solution is the sum of the solution to the inhomogeneous equation and any one particular solution to the inhomogeneous equation. The solution to the homogeneous equation is, like Eqs. (8.40) and (8.41), $\mathcal{A}^{\pm}(0)e^{\mp\Gamma(s)z}$, which is abbreviated to $\mathcal{A}_0^{\pm}e^{\mp\Gamma(s)z}$. A particular solution may be obtained by using a trial solution of the form $\mathcal{A}^{\pm} = K^{\pm}(z)\mathcal{A}_0^{\pm}e^{\mp\Gamma(s)z}$, where $K^{\pm}(z)$ is some function of z yet to be determined. Putting this trial solution in

Eq. (8.131) results in

$$\frac{dK^\pm}{dz}\,\mathcal{V}_0^\pm e^{\mp\Gamma z} \mp \Gamma K^\pm \mathcal{V}_0^\pm e^{\mp\Gamma z} \pm \Gamma K^\pm \mathcal{V}_0^\pm e^{\mp\Gamma z} = \pm C Z_0 A_0^\pm$$

Since the second and third terms cancel,

$$\frac{dK^\pm}{dz} = \pm \frac{CZ_0}{\mathcal{V}_0^\pm}\, e^{\pm\Gamma z} A_0^\pm$$

Integrating this equation gives

$$K^\pm = \pm \frac{CZ_0}{\mathcal{V}_0^\pm} \int_0^z e^{\pm\Gamma z} A_0^\pm \, dz$$

Hence the particular solution is

$$\pm C Z_0 e^{\mp\Gamma z} \int_0^z e^{\pm\Gamma z} A_0^\pm \, dz \tag{8.132}$$

and the complete solution to Eq. (8.131) is

$$\mathcal{V}^\pm(z,s) = \mathcal{V}_0^\pm(s) e^{\mp\Gamma(s)z} \pm C Z_0(s) e^{\mp\Gamma(s)z} \int_0^z e^{\pm\Gamma(s)z} A_0^\pm(z,s)\, dz \tag{8.133}$$

When the initial conditions are known, $A_0^\pm$ is known, and the integral can be evaluated to obtain the complete solution for $\mathcal{V}^\pm$. In some cases it may be easier to find a particular solution to Eq. (8.131) directly, rather than by the integral expression in Eq. (8.133). This is the case in Example 8.11. The two equations contained in Eq. (8.128) can be added and subtracted to obtain

$$\mathcal{V} = \frac{\mathcal{V}^+ + \mathcal{V}^-}{2} \tag{8.134}$$

$$\mathcal{I} = \frac{\mathcal{V}^+ - \mathcal{V}^-}{2Z_0} \tag{8.135}$$

Formally, the transient solutions to the transmission-line equations can be obtained by substituting Eq. (8.133) into Eqs. (8.134) and (8.135) and taking the inverse Laplace transform. In practice this is often difficult to do, especially for lossy lines. In the examples which follow ★the lines are taken to be lossless for simplicity.

Example 8.11 A charged-line pulse generator A pulse generator can be made by periodically charging a transmission line and then discharging it into a load, preferably a matched load. The pulse produced by this kind of arrangement can be found by the formalism just developed.

Assume that an open-ended lossless line has been charged to a dc voltage of 1 volt and then disconnected from the dc source. Then $V_0(z) = 1$ and

$I_0(z) = 0$. Then, from Eq. (8.129),

$$A_0^\pm = 1$$

Since the line is assumed to be lossless, $R = G = 0$ and

$$Z_0 = \sqrt{\frac{L}{C}}$$

$$\Gamma = \sqrt{LC}\, s$$

We could use Eq. (8.133) to find the solutions to Eq. (8.131), but because of the simplicity of $A_0^\pm$ in this case, it is easier to return to Eq. (8.131) and find a particular solution directly. Since $A_0^\pm$ is independent of z, it is easy to see that a particular solution to Eq. (8.131) is

$$\begin{aligned}\mathcal{A}^\pm &= \frac{CZ_0A_0^\pm}{\Gamma} \\ &= \frac{C\sqrt{L/C}}{\sqrt{LC}\, s}1 \\ &= \frac{1}{s}\end{aligned}$$

which can be verified by direct substitution into Eq. (8.131). The complete solution is then

$$\mathcal{A}^\pm = \mathcal{A}_0^\pm e^{\pm\Gamma z} + \frac{1}{s}$$

From Eqs. (8.134) and (8.135), $\mathcal{V}$ and $\mathcal{I}$ are

$$\mathcal{V} = \frac{\mathcal{A}_0^+ e^{-\Gamma z} + \mathcal{A}_0^- e^{\Gamma z}}{2} + \frac{1}{s}$$

$$\mathcal{I} = \frac{\mathcal{A}_0^+ e^{-\Gamma z} - \mathcal{A}_0^- e^{\Gamma z}}{2Z_0}$$

We wish to find V and I after the switch shown in Fig. 8.30 is closed at $t = 0$. The values of $\mathcal{A}_0^\pm$ can be found from the boundary conditions at $z = 0$ and $z = l$. At $z = 0$, $\mathcal{I} = 0$, because the line is open. Hence

$$\frac{\mathcal{A}_0^+ - \mathcal{A}_0^-}{2Z_0} = 0$$

$$\mathcal{A}_0^+ = \mathcal{A}_0^-$$

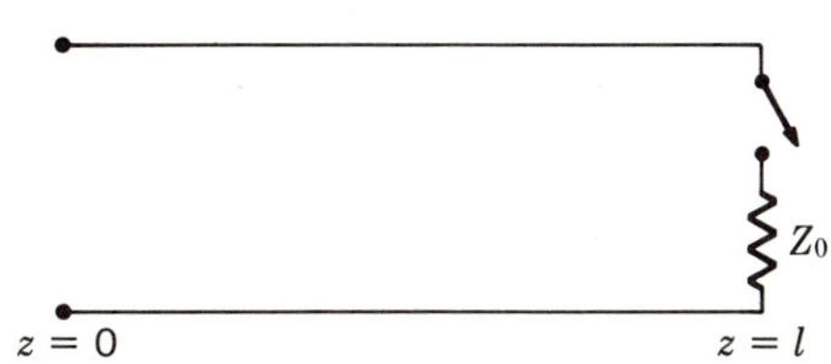

Fig. 8.30 A charged-line pulse generator.

At $z = l$, $\mathcal{V} = \mathcal{I}Z_0$. Then

$$\frac{\mathcal{A}_0^+ e^{-\Gamma l} + \mathcal{A}_0^+ e^{\Gamma l}}{2} + \frac{1}{s} = \frac{\mathcal{A}_0^+ e^{-\Gamma l} - \mathcal{A}_0^+ e^{\Gamma l}}{2}$$

and

$$\mathcal{A}_0^+ = -\frac{1}{s} e^{-\Gamma l}$$

Consequently,

$$\mathcal{V} = \frac{1}{s}\left[1 - \frac{e^{-\Gamma(l+z)} + e^{-\Gamma(l-z)}}{2}\right] \tag{8.136}$$

$$\mathcal{I} = \frac{1}{s}\frac{e^{-\Gamma(l-z)} - e^{-\Gamma(l+z)}}{2\sqrt{L/C}} \tag{8.137}$$

The voltage pulse and current pulse delivered to the load are found by evaluating $\mathcal{V}$ and $\mathcal{I}$ at $z = l$ and finding the inverse Laplace transforms,

$$\mathcal{V}(l,s) = \frac{1}{s}\frac{1 - e^{-2\Gamma l}}{2}$$

$$= \frac{1}{2s}\left(1 - e^{-2\sqrt{LC}\,ls}\right)$$

$$\mathcal{I}(l,s) = \frac{1}{2s}\frac{1 - e^{-2\sqrt{LC}\,ls}}{\sqrt{L/C}}$$

The inverse transforms are found to be

$$V(l,t) = \tfrac{1}{2}[u(t) - u(t - 2\sqrt{LC}\,l)]$$

$$I(l,t) = \frac{1}{2\sqrt{L/C}}[u(t) - u(t - 2\sqrt{LC}\,l)]$$

where $u(t)$ is a unit step function and $u(t - 2\sqrt{LC}\,l)$ is a shifted unit step function. The plots of V and I are shown in Fig. 8.31.

Since the phase velocity is given as $v_p = 1/\sqrt{LC}$, it can be seen from the

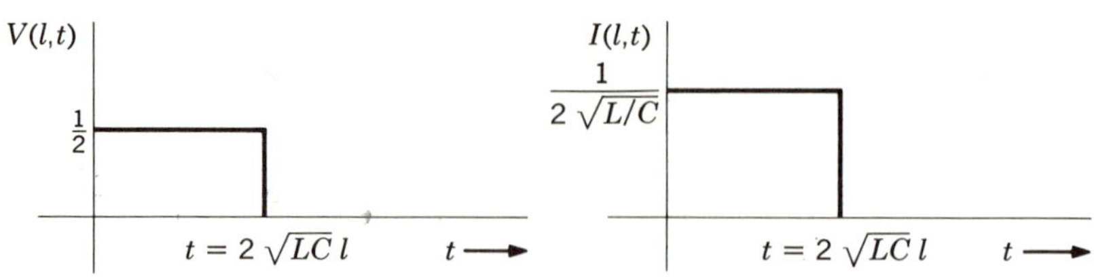

Fig. 8.31 Plots of the voltage and current pulses produced by the discharge of the charged line shown in Fig. 8.30.

plot that the length of both pulses is $2l/v_p$. The reason the current pulse width is $2l/v_p$ instead of l/v_p, as one might first suspect, can be understood from the waves propagating on the line. Taking the inverse Laplace transform of Eq. (8.137) results in

$$I(z,t) = \frac{1}{2\sqrt{L/C}}\left[u\left(t - \frac{l-z}{v_p}\right) - u\left(t - \frac{l+z}{v_p}\right)\right]$$

The first term in the brackets represents a wave traveling to the left, and the second represents a wave traveling to the right. Since $z \leq l$, $(l - z) \leq l$ and $(l + z) \geq l$. Thus the wave traveling to the right is zero until at least $t = l/v_p$ [recall that $u(t - a) = 0$ for $t < a$]. This wave is then the wave reflected by the open circuit at $z = 0$. When the switch is closed at $t = 0$, current begins to flow through the load impedance, and also a current wave begins to propagate to the left (the first term in the brackets). When this wave reaches the open circuit at $z = 0$, it is reflected, and a wave begins to propagate to the right. This occurs at $t = l/v_p$. The wave propagates to the right until it reaches $z = l$ at $t = 2l/v_p$. Since the load impedance is equal to Z_0, no further reflection occurs, and the current stops. This means that the line has been discharged. If the load impedance were not equal to Z_0, further reflections would occur, and the wave would travel back and forth down the line, decreasing in amplitude with each reflection. The current would not be zero until $t \rightarrow 0$, just as a capacitor discharging through a resistor does not completely discharge until $t \rightarrow 0$. The rate of decrease in amplitude of the current depends on the ratio of the terminating resistance to Z_0.

To get an idea of the pulse widths obtainable from a charged transmission line, suppose the line is a 20-cm length of coaxial cable with a permittivity of $2\epsilon_0$. From Eqs. (8.49), (8.61), and (8.62),

$$\begin{aligned} v_p &= \frac{1}{\sqrt{LC}} \\ &= \frac{1}{\sqrt{\mu\epsilon}} \\ &= \frac{1}{\sqrt{2}\sqrt{\mu_0\epsilon_0}} \\ &= \frac{3 \times 10^8}{\sqrt{2}} \text{ m/sec} \end{aligned}$$

Then the pulse width would be

$$\begin{aligned} \frac{2l}{v_p} &= \frac{2 \times 20 \times 10^{-2}}{3 \times 10^8/\sqrt{2}} \\ &= 1.89 \text{ nanosec} \end{aligned}$$

QUIESCENT LINES

When the initial current and voltage are zero, that is, $A_0^{\pm} = 0$, the line is said to be quiescent. In this case, $\mathcal{V}$ and $\mathcal{I}$ are

$$\mathcal{V}(z,s) = \frac{\mathcal{A}_0^+(s)e^{-\Gamma(s)z} + \mathcal{A}_0^-(s)e^{\Gamma(s)z}}{2} \tag{8.138}$$

$$\mathcal{I}(z,s) = \frac{\mathcal{A}_0^+(s)e^{-\Gamma(s)z} - \mathcal{A}_0^-(s)e^{\Gamma(s)z}}{2Z_0(s)} \tag{8.139}$$

which have the same form as Eqs. (8.64) and (8.65). The difference is that here $\mathcal{A}_0^{\pm}$, Γ, and Z_0 are functions of s. Since Eqs. (8.138) and (8.139) do have the same form as Eqs. (8.64) and (8.65), a reflection coefficient and impedance similar to those in Eqs. (8.67) and (8.68) can be defined. Thus

$$\begin{aligned} \rho(z,s) &= \frac{\mathcal{A}^-}{\mathcal{A}^+} \\ &= \frac{\mathcal{A}_0^-(s)}{\mathcal{A}_0^+(s)} e^{2\Gamma(s)z} \\ &= \rho_0(s)e^{2\Gamma(s)z} \end{aligned} \tag{8.140}$$

and

$$\begin{aligned} Z(z,s) &= \frac{\mathcal{V}(z,s)}{\mathcal{I}(z,s)} \\ &= Z_0(s)\,\frac{1+\rho(z,s)}{1-\rho(z,s)} \end{aligned} \tag{8.141}$$

Hence the impedance is a function of the complex variable s instead of $j\omega$ as in Sec. 8.8. Following the development of Sec. 8.8, the expression obtained for ρ in terms of $Z_L(s)$, the impedance at $z = l$, is

$$\rho = \frac{Z_L(s) - Z_0(s)}{Z_L(s) + Z_0(s)}\, e^{-2\Gamma(s)(l-z)} \tag{8.142}$$

The expression for the impedance in terms of $Z_L(s)$ is

$$Z(z,s) = Z_0(s)\,\frac{Z_L(s) + Z_0(s)\tanh\,[\Gamma(s)(l-z)]}{Z_0(s) + Z_L(s)\tanh\,[\Gamma(s)(l-z)]} \tag{8.143}$$

which describes the transformation of the complex-plane impedance along the transmission line. Note that when $Z_L = Z_0$ the impedance at any point on the line is Z_0, just as in the sinusoidal steady-state case. Complex-plane-impedance concepts are useful in transmission-line theory, just as they are in circuit theory.

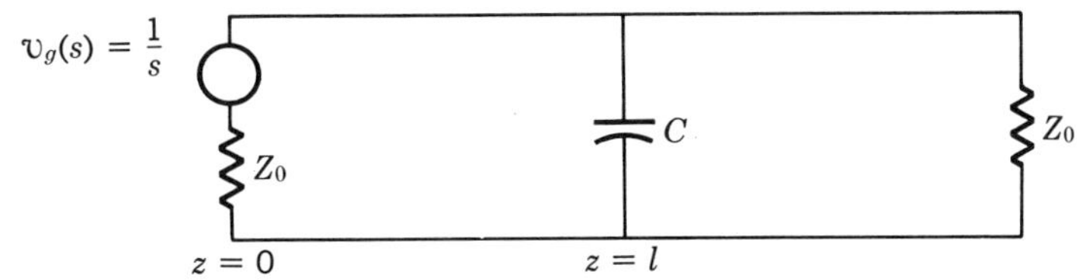

Fig. 8.32 The capacitive discontinuity discussed in Example 8.12.

Example 8.12 Time-domain reflectometry The response of a transmission-line to a voltage step-function input can be used to obtain information about discontinuities and impedances on the line. As a simple example of this, the capacitive discontinuity illustrated in Fig. 8.32 is discussed.

Since the line is terminated in Z_0, the impedance at $z = l$ is

$$Z_L = \frac{(1/Cs)Z_0}{Z_0 + 1/Cs} = \frac{Z_0}{1 + Z_0Cs}$$

From Eq. (8.142), the value of ρ is

$$\rho = -\frac{Z_0Cs}{2 + Z_0Cs} e^{-(2s/v_p)(l-z)}$$

where $\Gamma = \sqrt{LC}\, s$ and $\sqrt{LC} = 1/v_p$. Since

$$\mathcal{V} = \frac{\mathcal{A}_0^+ e^{-\Gamma z}}{2}(1 + \rho)$$

$$\mathcal{I} = \frac{\mathcal{A}_0^+ e^{-\Gamma z}}{2Z_0}(1 - \rho)$$

at $z = 0$,

$$\mathcal{V} = \frac{\mathcal{A}_0^+}{2}\left(1 - \frac{Z_0Cs}{Z + Z_0Cs} e^{-2sl/v_p}\right)$$

$$\mathcal{I} = \frac{\mathcal{A}_0^+}{2Z_0}\left(1 + \frac{Z_0Cs}{2 + Z_0Cs} e^{-2sl/v_p}\right)$$

But it can be seen from Fig. 8.32 that at $z = 0$,

$$\mathcal{V} = \mathcal{V}_g - \mathcal{I}Z_0$$

Thus

$$\frac{\mathcal{A}_0^+}{2}\left(1 - \frac{Z_0Cs}{2 + Z_0Cs} e^{-2sl/v_p}\right) = \frac{1}{s} - \frac{\mathcal{A}_0^+}{2}\left(1 + \frac{Z_0Cs}{2 + Z_0Cs} e^{-2sl/v_p}\right)$$

and

$$\mathcal{A}_0^+ = \frac{1}{s}$$
$$= \mathcal{V}_g$$

The voltage at $z = 0$ is then

$$\mathcal{V} = \frac{1}{2s}\left(1 - \frac{Z_0Cs}{2 + Z_0Cs}e^{-2sl/v_p}\right)$$

Taking the inverse transform results in

$$V(0,t) = \frac{1}{2}\left[u(t) - u\left(t - \frac{2l}{v_p}\right)e^{-(2/Z_0C)(t-2l/v_p)}\right]$$

A plot of $V(0,t)$ is shown in Fig. 8.33. It is apparent that the position of the capacitive discontinuity could be determined by displaying $V(0,t)$ on an oscilloscope and measuring $\Delta t = 2l/v_p$. When more than one discontinuity is present, there are multiple reflections separated by the travel time of the reflection. Because of the separation in the reflections, the reflections can be identified with the discontinuities which produce them. This allows not only detection of discontinuities, but also experimental adjustment of line parameters until the reflections are reduced or eliminated. The discontinuities can be manipulated one at a time until the desired results are obtained. When standing-wave measurements are used to detect discontinuities, the effects of all the discontinuities are included in the standing-wave ratio. Since the effect of one discontinuity cannot be isolated, it is much more difficult to adjust the line parameters experimentally until satisfactory results are obtained.

The minimum separations between discontinuities which can be resolved depends on the rise time of the pulse generator. With available equipment, separations of about 5 mm can be detected.†

† *Hewlett Packard Journal*, vol. 15, no. 6, p. 2, February, 1964.

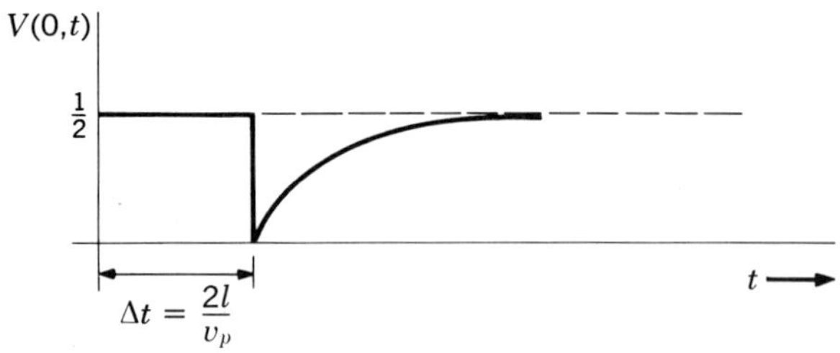

Fig. 8.33 The voltage at $z = 0$ for the situation shown in Fig. 8.32.

PROBLEMS

8.2-1 What is θ_n from Eq. (8.7) for the following cases:
(a) A microwave planewave at $f = 10^{10}$ of width 1 cm
(b) A millimeter planewave at $f = 3 \times 10^{11}$ of width 1 cm
(c) An infrared beam at $\lambda = 10\ \mu$ of width 1 mm
(d) A laser light beam at $\lambda = 0.6328\ \mu$ of width 1 mm

8.2-2 Prove that the first null of the diffraction pattern occurs at $x = a$ when $\lambda/a = 2a/z$ and $a \gg \lambda$.

8.2-3 A beam 1 m in diameter is to be transmitted 20 miles into a 10-m diameter receiving antenna such that the first null of the diffraction pattern is at the edge of the antenna. What wavelength is required, assuming that the slit relations apply?

8.2-4 Obtain from a numerical computer integration the ratio of the power carried in the main lobe of Fig. 8.2 (between $-\pi < ka \sin\theta < \pi$) to the total power for $ka = 1{,}000$.

8.3-1 Derive Eqs. (8.18) and (8.19) from the node and loop circuit equations for a cascade of series elements $Z\,\Delta z$ and shunt elements $Y\,\Delta z$ with section length Δz.

8.3-2 Show by direct substitution in rectangular coordinates that Eq. (8.23) satisfies Eq. (8.22) for any Φ.

8.5-1 A transmission line is excited such that a wave travels only in the $+z$ direction. The mode amplitude $a^+(0) = 10$. Solve for the peak V and I on the transmission line. The characteristic impedance of the transmission line is 100 ohms and $C = 10^{-10}$ f/m, with $f = 10^9$. Express the voltage and current on the transmission line as a function of t and z. What is the wavelength along the transmission line?

8.5-2 A wave travels on a transmission line in the $+z$ direction with $a^+(0) = 20$. A wave also travels in the $-z$ direction with magnitude $a^-(0) = 5$. Solve for V and I on the transmission line as a function of t and z. The transmission-line characteristic impedance is 50 ohms and $C = 10^{-10}$ f/m at $f = 10^8$.

8.5-3 A transmission line has one pair of terminals at the origin and extends to infinity in one direction. The transmission line is excited with a generator which generates a voltage $V_0e^{j\omega t}$ at the terminals. The characteristic impedance of the transmission line is Z_0 and the propagation constant is β. How much current is drawn from the generator by the transmission line? Find V, I, and the mode amplitudes a^+ and a^- as a function of t and z.

8.5-4 Differentiate Eq. (8.18) with respect to z and use Eq. (8.19) to obtain a second-order differential equation for the voltage V. Solve the equation and show that the result is the same as that obtained from Eqs. (8.37), (8.40), and (8.41).

8.6-1 Find the characteristic impedance and propagation constant for a distributed-circuit-element transmission line where the losses are small; that is, $R \ll \omega L$ and $G \ll \omega C$. Keep second-order terms of the order $(R/\omega L)^2$ and $(G/\omega C)^2$, but neglect higher-order terms.

8.6-2 If losses are present on the circuit-element transmission line, the propagation constant becomes complex. Show that for large losses, the real and imaginary values of the propagation constant are, respectively,

$$\alpha = \sqrt{RG}$$

and

$$\beta = \frac{1}{2}\omega\sqrt{RG}\left(\frac{L}{R} + \frac{C}{G}\right)$$

8.6-3 Solve for the impedance V^-/I^- for the $-z$ traveling wave. What does negative impedance mean?

8.6-4 Sketch the V and I waveforms $V^+(z)$ and $I^+(z)$ versus βz at $t = 0$ when $V^+(0) = 10e^{j\pi/4}$. Assume $Z_0 = 100e^{j\pi/2}$.

8.6-5 A two-wire transmission line with L and C values given by the equations in Example 8.2 is characterized by the small loss term R ohms/m and $G = 0$. Solve for the complex voltage and current at the end of a transmission line L meter long in terms of the voltage input $V^+(0)$.

8.6-6 Find the characteristic admittance, defined as the reciprocal of the characteristic impedance, for a transmission line with small but finite loss terms R and G.

8.6-7 Investigate the nature of wave propagation on a lumped-parameter transmission line with series capacitance elements and shunt inductance elements. Find β for this type of transmission line and compare it with the propagation characteristics of the series inductance and shunt capacitance transmission line. Discuss the variation of v_p with frequency.

8.6-8 It is desired to obtain an impedance match from a two-wire distributed-circuit-element transmission line to a lumped-circuit-element transmission line. The ratio d/a for the transmission line is 5, and the dielectric medium surrounding the wires is characterized by the parameters $\epsilon = 2\epsilon_0$ and $\mu = \mu_0$. It is necessary to use inductors in the lumped line of 1.0 μh. Solve for the capacitance-element values required for a match of the characteristic impedance between the two transmission lines. Solve for the ratio of the phase velocity on the lumped line to the phase velocity in the two-wire line when $\Delta z = 1$ cm.

8.6-9 Consider the lumped-parameter transmission line shown in Fig. P8.6-9. It is easily shown that the voltage and current at the nth terminal in terms of the voltage

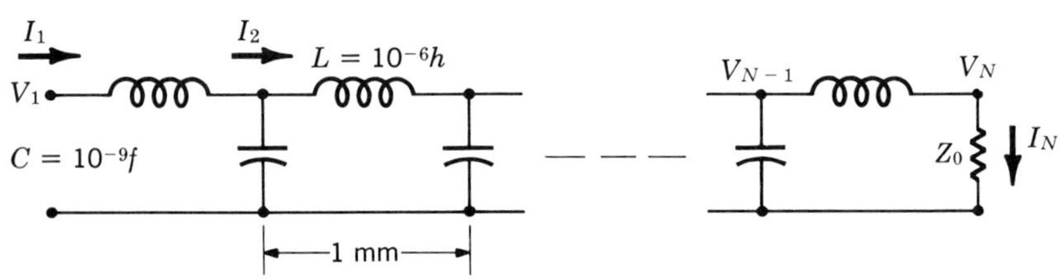

Fig. P8.6-9

and current at the $n - 1$ terminal are given in the equations

$$V_n = V_{n-1} - j\omega L I_{n-1}$$

$$I_n = I_{n-1} - j\omega C V_n$$

Ten volts is impressed at the left end of the transmission line, $V_1 = 10e^{j\omega t}$, with $\omega = 2\pi \times 10^5$, and a current I_1 flows in accordance with the characteristic impedance of the transmission line. Solve for the voltage V_N and current I_N at the output terminals of the transmission line, when $N = 100$. Write an appropriate computer program to solve the two equations above for each stage of the transmission line.

Compare the computer result obtained with a calculation based on the equivalent distributed-parameter transmission line.

8.7-1 Show that $|\rho| \leq 1$ when Z_0 is real and Z_L has a positive real part.

8.7-2 Show that $|\rho|$ can be greater than unity when Z_0 is complex and Z_0 and Z_L have positive real parts.

8.7-3 When $Z_L = (0.4 + j0.5)Z_0$, find βl for a lossless line such that the real part of the input impedance at $z = 0$ is $2Z_0$.

8.7-4 Show that $Z_0 = \sqrt{Z_{ioc}Z_{isc}}$, where Z_{ioc} is the input impedance for $Z_L = \infty$ and Z_{isc} is the input impedance for $Z_L = 0$.

8.7-5 Show that a quarter-wavelength line transforms an open circuit into a short circuit.

8.7-6 From Eq. (8.75) plot Z versus z when $Z_L = 0$ and $Z_0 = 100$ ohms. Make the plot over at least a half-wavelength.

8.7-7 Plot $|V|$ and $|I|$ versus z over at least a half-wavelength when $Z_L = 2Z_0$.

8.7-8 Plot $|V|$ and $|I|$ versus z over at least a half-wavelength when $Z_L = jZ_0$.

8.7-9 Find the position of the $|V|_{min}$ closest to Z_L when $Z_L = 2jZ_0$.

8.7-10 Find Z_L/Z_0 if $S = 4$ and $(l - d)/\lambda = 0.106$. d is the position of $|V|_{min}$.

8.7-11 Find the value of S and the position of the first voltage minimum when $Z_L = (0.5 + j0.9)Z_0$.

8.7-12 A transmission line of characteristic impedance Z_0 is connected to a transmission line of characteristic impedance $2Z_0$. Find the value of the reflection and transmission coefficients at the junction.

8.8-1 A thin half-wave antenna having an impedance of $73 + j42.5$ ohms is connected to a two-wire transmission line having the following parameters:

$$L = 10^{-6} \text{ h/m} \qquad G = 0$$

$$C = \tfrac{1}{9} \times 10^{-10} \text{ f/m} \qquad l = 2.7\lambda$$

$$R = 2 \text{ ohms/m} \qquad f = 10^{7} \text{ Hz}$$

Calculate Z_i, assuming $R = 0$. Then calculate Z_i including the R value given. Compare the correct result with the lossless approximation.

8.9-1 Show that all the circles corresponding to the constant r and x curves of Eqs. (8.103) and (8.104) pass through the point $u = 1$, $v = 0$.

8.9-2 From the Smith chart, find S and the position of the $|V|_{min}$ nearest the load when $z_L = 0.4 + j1.2$.

8.9-3 From the Smith chart, find S and the position of the $|V|_{min}$ nearest the load when $y_L = 0.2 + j0.25$.

8.9-4 From the Smith chart, find z_i when $z_L = 0.75 + j2.0$ and $l = 1.3\lambda$.

8.9-5 From the Smith chart, find y_i when $y_L = 0.3 + j0.5$ and $l = 1.2\lambda$.

8.9-6 If $S = 3.2$ and the $|V|_{min}$ nearest the load is 0.08λ from the load, find z_L.

8.9-7 Find $1/(0.3 + j0.5)$ by using the Smith chart to convert from impedance to admittance.

8.9-8 From the Smith chart, find the normalized input impedance of a shorted stub 0.09λ long.

8.9-9 From the Smith chart, find the normalized input admittance of a shorted stub 0.05λ long.

8.9-10 If $z_L = 0.3 + j0.4$, find the point nearest the load on the line where $z = 1 + jx$. What is x at this point?

8.9-11 If $z_L = 0.28 + j0.33$, and $\alpha l = 0.1$, and $l = 0.76\lambda$, find z_i.

8.10-1 Design a shunt shorted stub to match a load $z_L = 0.2 + j0.5$ to the line. Give the position of the stub and its length.

8.10-2 Design a shunt shorted stub to match a load $y_L = 0.1 + j0.5$ to the line. Use a stub which has a characteristic admittance which is one-half that of the line.

8.10-3 Design a series stub to match a load $z_L = 0.2 + j0.5$ to the line.

8.10-4 Design a series stub to match a load $y_L = 0.1 + j0.3$ to the line.

8.10-5 It is desired to connect a transmission line having $L = 10^{-6}$ h/m, $C = \frac{1}{9} \times 10^{-10}$ f/m to a transmission line having $L = 10^{-6}$ h/m, $C = \frac{1}{4} \times 10^{-10}$ f/m. Design a quarter-wave transformer to eliminate reflections at the junction at a frequency of $f = 10^7$ Hz.

8.10-6 Plot the magnitude of the reflection coefficient versus frequency for the configuration of Prob. 8.10-5 with the quarter-wave transformer connecting the two lines. Make the plot for a frequency band about 10^7 Hz of sufficient width to show the frequency characteristics of the match.

8.11-1 An exponential impedance taper is to be used to match a 50-ohm line to a 200-ohm line with $\rho_0 < 0.1$, over a 2:1 frequency band. What is the length of tapered section l required, in terms of wavelength at the lowest frequency? Find the d versus z required for a strip line in order to achieve the desired impedance taper.

8.11-2 A linear-impedance taper is used to match a line of characteristic impedance Z_{01} to a line of characteristic impedance Z_{02}, that is, $Z(z) = Z_{01} + \Delta Z_0\, z/L$, where $\Delta Z_0 = Z_{02} - Z_{01}$. The propagation constant is a constant, β_1.

(a) Show that $a^+ = a^+(0)e^{-j\beta_1 z}\sqrt{1 + \dfrac{z\,\Delta Z_0}{LZ_{01}}}$

(b) Derive the relation

$$\rho_0 = \tfrac{1}{2}e^{jX_0}[Ci(X_l) - Ci(X_0) + jSi(X_0) - jSi(X_l)]$$

where Ci and Si are the cosine and sine integrals and

$$X_l = \frac{2\beta_1 l Z_{02}}{\Delta Z_0}$$

$$X_0 = \frac{2\beta_1 l Z_{01}}{\Delta Z_0}$$

(c) Assume that $\Delta Z_0/Z_{01} \ll 2\beta_1 l$ and obtain the relation

$$\rho_0 = \frac{j\,\Delta Z_0/Z_{01}}{4\beta_1 l}\left(\frac{Z_{01}}{Z_{02}}e^{-2j\beta_1 l} - 1\right)$$

Plot $|\rho_0|$ versus $\beta_1 l$ and compare with Fig. 8.29.

8.11-3 We see from Eq. (8.114) that the a^+ mode grows exponentially with z for an exponential impedance taper. This implies an exponential increase in power along the line. Determine $\langle P \rangle$ and prove that the power is a constant with z.

8.11-4 A linear impedance taper is to be used to match a 50-ohm coaxial line to a 100-ohm coaxial line. The taper is limited to 10 cm in length. The permittivity of the material in all the lines is $5\epsilon_0$. Find ρ_0 versus λ in the wavelength range 10 cm $> \lambda >$ 5 cm. What is the b/a ratio required versus z in the tapered coaxial line?

8.11-5 For the exponential impedance taper with constant β, solve for a^- versus z, assuming that $a^-(l) = 0$. Discuss where on the line the greatest amount of a^- is generated.

8.12-1 Find the length of coaxial cable which would produce a pulse of length 10^{-9} sec when charged and discharged as in Example 8.11.

8.12-2 Find the current pulse produced in the load resistor if the load resistor in Fig. 8.30 were $R = 2Z_0$ and the line were initially charged to 1 volt. Plot the current against time including several reflections.

8.12-3 Repeat Prob. 8.12-2 with $R = \frac{1}{2}Z_0$.

8.12-4 A unit-step-function voltage generator with internal impedance Z_0 is connected at $z = 0$ to a lossless transmission line. The line is terminated at $z = l$ in a capacitance C. Find an expression for the voltage at $z = 0$. Plot this voltage against time.

8.12-5 Repeat Prob. 8.12-4 with the termination being an inductance L.

8.12-6 Repeat Prob. 8.12-4 with the termination being a resistor of resistance $2Z_0$.

8.12-7 Repeat Prob. 8.12-4 with the termination being a resistor of resistance $\frac{1}{2}Z_0$.

8.12-8 The line of length l in Fig. P8.12-8 is charged to 1 volt. The switch is closed at $t = 0$. Plot the current through R as a function of time.

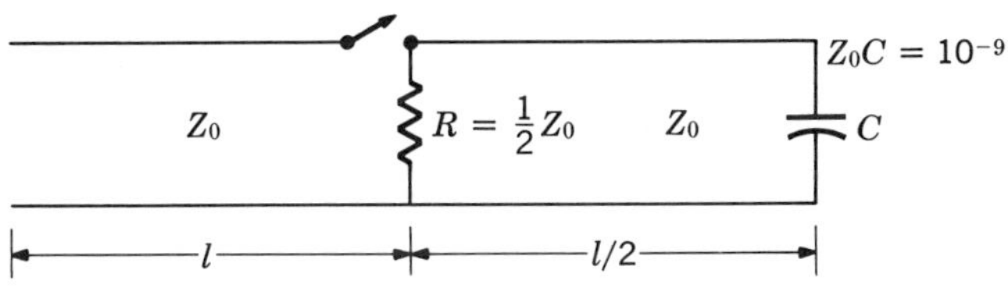

Fig. P8.12-8

CHAPTER

9

boundary-value problems

9.1 INTRODUCTION

Since Maxwell's equations are generally difficult to solve, many special techniques have been developed which apply to the solution of a limited class of problems. The purpose of this chapter is to develop the technique for a class of problems called *boundary-value problems.* In these problems a solution is to be found in a given region and is required to satisfy certain conditions at the boundaries of that region. The boundaries of the region usually coincide, at least piecewise, with constant-coordinate curves in some orthogonal coordinate system.

The solution of boundary-value field problems consists of solving the point form of Maxwell's equations, i.e., partial-differential field equations, in separate regions where the point solution can conveniently apply at all points in that region. The boundary conditions are then used to relate the solutions in the separate regions. For example, the regions might be divided according to values of dielectric constant; the solutions would be found in each region of like dielectric constant and then related by the boundary conditions at the interfaces between the dielectrics. Or the regions may consist of different conductors. Finding the potential between conducting plates is a special example of this type problem; the conductivity is zero between the plates and very high in the plates.

Much of this chapter is devoted to mathematical methods for solving the partial-differential field equations. Since it is usually better to reduce Maxwell's equations to wave equations (Laplace's or Poisson's equation in the static case), the methods of solution of the wave equation are stressed. As contrasted with the special planewave solution of Chap. 6, the general solutions to the field equations are developed in this chapter. For convenience, the usual exponential time dependence is assumed.

9.2 A ONE-DIMENSIONAL BOUNDARY-VALUE PROBLEM

The methods used in solving boundary-value problems can be illustrated with the problem of finding the fields between two concentric conducting spheres when there is a potential difference between them. The situation is shown in Fig. 9.1. The inner sphere is held at zero potential and the outer sphere is at a potential of V_0. This could be accomplished by connecting a battery between the two spheres.

In general, the fields between the spheres could be found by solving Maxwell's equations directly as given in Eqs. (5.85) and (5.86),

$$\nabla \times \mathbf{E} = -\frac{\partial \mathbf{B}}{\partial t} \tag{5.85}$$

$$\nabla \times \mathbf{H} = \mathbf{J} + \frac{\partial \mathbf{D}}{\partial t} \tag{5.86}$$

Or the fields could be found by solving the wave equations for **E** and **H**, Eqs. (6.12) and (6.13),

$$\nabla^2\mathbf{E} - \mu\epsilon\frac{\partial^2\mathbf{E}}{\partial t^2} = \mu\frac{\partial \mathbf{J}}{\partial t} + \nabla\left(\frac{\rho}{\epsilon}\right) \tag{6.12}$$

$$\nabla^2\mathbf{H} - \mu\epsilon\frac{\partial^2\mathbf{H}}{\partial t^2} = -\nabla \times \mathbf{J} \tag{6.13}$$

Or the fields could be found by solving the wave equations for Φ and **A**,

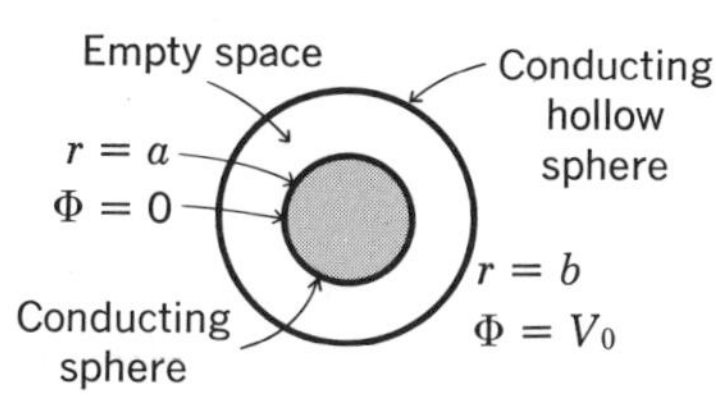

Fig. 9.1 Potential difference applied to two conducting concentric spheres.

Eqs. (6.19) and (6.17),

$$\nabla^2\Phi - \mu\epsilon \frac{\partial^2\Phi}{\partial t^2} = -\frac{\rho}{\epsilon} \tag{6.19}$$

$$\nabla^2\mathbf{A} - \mu\epsilon \frac{\partial^2\mathbf{A}}{\partial t^2} = -\mu\mathbf{J} \tag{6.17}$$

Then Eqs. (6.14) and (2.54) could be used to find **E** and **B**,

$$\mathbf{E} = -\nabla\Phi - \frac{\partial\mathbf{A}}{\partial t} \tag{6.14}$$

$$\mathbf{B} = \nabla \times \mathbf{A} \tag{2.54}$$

For the static case illustrated in Fig. 9.1, a convenient method is to solve Eq. (6.19) for Φ and then use Eq. (6.14) to find **E**. There is no magnetic field in this case because there is no current and no changing electric field. Hence **A** is zero.

In the static case, Eq. (6.19) becomes

$$\nabla^2\Phi = -\frac{\rho}{\epsilon}$$

which is called Poisson's equation. This equation is a point relation; it describes the relation between Φ and ρ at a point. Between the spheres, $\rho = 0$ because the space between the spheres is empty. Consequently, for points between the spheres, Poisson's equation reduces to

$$\nabla^2\Phi = 0 \tag{9.1}$$

which is called Laplace's equation. In spherical coordinates, Laplace's equation is (see the Appendix)

$$\frac{1}{r^2}\frac{\partial}{\partial r}\left(r^2\frac{\partial\Phi}{\partial r}\right) + \frac{1}{r^2 \sin\theta}\frac{\partial}{\partial\theta}\left(\sin\theta\frac{\partial\Phi}{\partial\theta}\right) + \frac{1}{r^2\sin^2\theta}\frac{\partial^2\Phi}{\partial\varphi^2} = 0$$

Because of the symmetry of the concentric spheres, Φ will not vary with θ or φ Hence Laplace's equation reduces in this special case to

$$\frac{1}{r^2}\frac{\partial}{\partial r}\left(r^2\frac{\partial\Phi}{\partial r}\right) = 0 \tag{9.2}$$

This can be solved easily by integrating twice,

$$\Phi = -\frac{K_1}{r} + K_2 \tag{9.3}$$

where K_1 and K_2 are constants of integration. The expression for Φ in Eq. (9.3) satisfies Eq. (9.2) for any values of K_1 and K_2. However, only for one value of K_1 and one value of K_2 will Φ have the proper values at $r = a$ and $r = b$, that is, 0 and V_0, respectively.

These values of K_1 and K_2 can be found by requiring Φ as given by Eq. (9.3) to satisfy the boundary conditions. Thus $\Phi = 0$ at $r = a$ and $\Phi = V_0$ at $r = b$ require that

$$0 = -\frac{K_1}{a} + K_2$$

$$V_0 = -\frac{K_1}{b} + K_2$$

Solving these two equations simultaneously results in

$$K_1 = \frac{V_0}{1/a - 1/b}$$

$$K_2 = \frac{V_0}{a(1/a - 1/b)}$$

and hence

$$\Phi = V_0 \frac{1/a - 1/r}{1/a - 1/b} \tag{9.4}$$

This expression for Φ is the only one of the infinite number of values for Φ given in Eq. (9.3) which satisfies *both* Laplace's equation *and* the boundary conditions. As shown in Sec. 9.6, any solution which satisfies both Laplace's equation and the boundary conditions is a unique solution.

Even though the mathematics involved in this example are simple, the procedure illustrates the general methods used in solving boundary-value problems. Partial-differential equations, either Maxwell's equations or the wave equations obtained from Maxwell's equations, are solved, and the solutions are made to satisfy the boundary conditions. In more complicated problems, the mathematics involved in obtaining the solutions to the partial-differential equations can be quite complicated, but the general procedure is still the same. A more complicated boundary-value problem is illustrated in the next section.

9.3 FIELDS BETWEEN INFINITE PARALLEL PLATES

In the last section a general method of solving boundary-value problems was illustrated by consideration of a very simple one-dimensional problem. In this section a more complicated problem is considered. The configuration is illustrated in Fig. 9.2. There are two parallel plates, each infinite in the y and z directions and each held at zero potential. Another plate, which is insulated from the first two by an infinitesimal

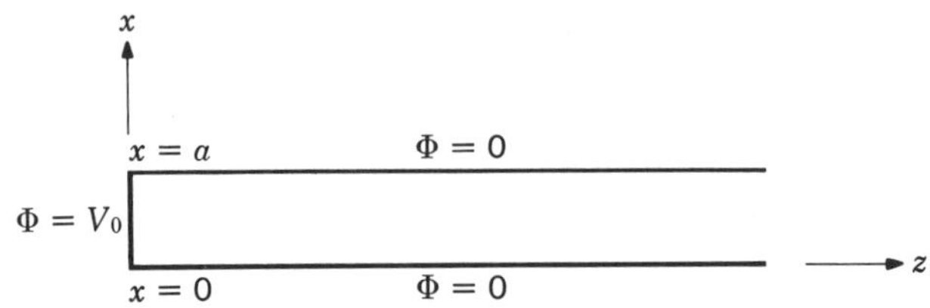

Fig. 9.2 The parallel-plate configuration considered in Sec. 9.3.

gap, is held at a potential V_0. This latter plate is in the $z = 0$ plane and is infinite in the y direction, as shown in Fig. 9.2. The problem is to find the fields between the parallel plates.

Since this is an electrostatic problem like the one in the last section except for the difference in configuration, the same procedure used there is appropriate here; that is, Laplace's equation is solved to obtain an expression for Φ involving arbitrary constants, and then that expression is made to satisfy the boundary conditions. Then $\mathbf{E}$ can be found from Eq. (6.14).

Because of the symmetry of the configuration, Φ will not vary with y. Hence $\partial\Phi/\partial y = 0$, and Laplace's equation in rectangular coodinates reduces to

$$\frac{\partial^2\Phi}{\partial x^2} + \frac{\partial^2\Phi}{\partial z^2} = 0 \tag{9.5}$$

This partial-differential equation is more difficult than the one in the last section, because two variables are involved. However, a technique called *separation of variables* can be used to reduce this equation to two ordinary differential equations, each involving functions of only one variable. The separation-of-variables technique is discussed in detail in the next section.

The first step is to *assume* that Φ can be written as the product

$$\Phi(x,z) = X(x)Z(z) \tag{9.6}$$

where $X(x)$ is a function of x only and $Z(z)$ is a function of z only. Substituting Eq. (9.6) into Eq. (9.5) results in

$$X''Z + XZ'' = 0$$

where $X'' = d^2X/dx^2$ and $Z'' = d^2Z/dz^2$. Dividing by XZ and rearranging gives

$$\frac{X''}{X} = -\frac{Z''}{Z} \tag{9.7}$$

Next comes a crucial argument. Since Eq. (9.7) must be true for all values of x and z, and since the left-hand side is a function of x only and the right-hand side a function of z only, each side must be constant; otherwise the equation could not be true for all values of x and z.

Since each side must be constant,

$$\frac{X''}{X} = -k_x^2 \tag{9.8}$$

$$\frac{Z''}{Z} = k_x^2 \tag{9.9}$$

where k_x^2 is a constant yet to be determined. The signs could have been chosen differently, but the ones used here are convenient. More will be said about this in the next section.

Equations (9.8) and (9.9) are both standard differential equations whose solutions are well known. Although the solutions can be written in several equivalent forms (see Sec. 9.4), appropriate forms here are

$$X = A_1 \cos k_x x + A_2 \sin k_x x \tag{9.10}$$

$$Z = B_1 e^{-k_x z} + B_2 e^{k_x z} \tag{9.11}$$

where A_1, A_2, B_1, and B_2 are arbitrary constants to be determined.

Now combining Eqs. (9.10) and (9.11) with Eq. (9.6) gives the solution as

$$\Phi = (A_1 \cos k_x x + A_2 \sin k_x x)(B_1 e^{-k_x z} + B_2 e^{k_x z}) \tag{9.12}$$

This expression must be made to satisfy the boundary conditions. At $x = 0$, Φ must be zero. Setting $x = 0$ and $\Phi = 0$ in Eq. (9.12) gives

$$0 = A_1(B_1 e^{-k_x z} + B_2 e^{k_x z})$$

Since this must be true for all values of z, A_1 must be zero. Also, at $x = a$, Φ must be zero for all z. Hence

$$0 = A_2 \sin k_x a(B_1 e^{-k_x z} + B_2 e^{k_x z})$$

Now either $A_2 = 0$ or $\sin k_x a = 0$. But if $A_2 = 0$, $\Phi = 0$ for all values of x and z. This is a solution, but a trivial one. Hence we choose $\sin k_x a = 0$, which requires

$$k_x a = m\pi$$

$$k_x = \frac{m\pi}{a} \qquad m = 1, 2, 3, \ldots \tag{9.13}$$

This determines k_x, which can be any one of an infinite number of values.

At this point the solution is

$$\Phi_m = A_{2m} \sin \frac{m\pi x}{a} (B_{1m}e^{-m\pi z/a} + B_{2m}e^{m\pi z/a})$$

where Φ and the remaining constants have been subscripted with m to indicate that there could be different expressions for each value of m. There are two more conditions which Φ must satisfy. One is that Φ must remain finite as z becomes infinite. This is based on physical reasoning. Since the potential on the parallel plates is zero, there is no reason that the potential should not be bounded at infinity. If Φ is to remain finite as $z \to \infty$, B_{2m} must be zero. Hence

$$\Phi_m = A_{2m}B_{1m}e^{-m\pi z/a} \sin \frac{m\pi x}{a} \tag{9.14}$$

The other condition which Φ must satisfy is that $\Phi = V_0$ when $z = 0$ for all values of x between $x = 0$ and $x = a$. However, it is easy to see that the expression for Φ_m in Eq. (9.14) cannot be made to satisfy this condition for any values of $A_{2m}B_{1m}$, because when $z = 0$,

$$\Phi_m = A_{2m}B_{1m} \sin \frac{m\pi x}{a}$$

which is not constant with x. But Φ must still have some kind of periodic variation, such as $\sin m\pi x/a$, or else the boundary conditions cannot be satisfied at $x = 0$ and $x = a$.

The way out of this dilemma is the Fourier series. An expression for Φ is constructed by summing the Φ_m as given by Eq. (9.14),

$$\Phi = \sum_{m=1}^{\infty} A_m e^{-m\pi z/a} \sin \frac{m\pi x}{a} \tag{9.15}$$

where the definition $A_m = A_{2m}B_{1m}$ has been made for convenience. This infinite series expression for Φ satisfies Laplace's equation because each term satisfies Laplace's equation. Similarly, the infinite series satisfies the boundary conditions at $x = 0$ and $x = a$ because each term does. The remaining boundary condition at $z = 0$ is satisfied if

$$V_0 = \sum_{m=1}^{\infty} A_m \sin \frac{m\pi x}{a} \qquad 0 \le x \le a \tag{9.16}$$

The coefficients A_m can be chosen so that the series in Eq. (9.16) converges to V_0, and then the last boundary condition will be satisfied, and the final solution will have been obtained.

Since Eq. (9.16) is a Fourier series, expressions for the coefficients

A_m can be found by looking in a book on Fourier series. However, there is a more general approach based on the *orthogonality* of the sine functions. Orthogonality is discussed in Sec. 9.5. The sine functions have the interesting property that

$$\int_0^a \sin \frac{m\pi x}{a} \sin \frac{l\pi x}{a}\, dx = \begin{cases} \dfrac{a}{2} & \text{if } l = m \\ 0 & \text{if } l \neq m \end{cases} \tag{9.17}$$

where l and m are any integers. The sin $(m\pi x/a)$ and sin $(l\pi x/a)$ are said to be orthogonal when $m \neq l$, because the integral in Eq. (9.17) is zero. As an illustration of how this property can be used to find the A_m values, both sides of Eq. (9.16) are multiplied by sin $(3\pi x/a)\, dx$ and then integrated. The result is

$$\int_0^a V_0 \sin \frac{3\pi x}{a}\, dx = A_1 \int_0^a \sin \frac{3\pi x}{a} \sin \frac{\pi x}{a}\, dx + A_2 \int_0^a \sin \frac{3\pi x}{a} \sin \frac{2\pi x}{a}\, dx + A_3 \int_0^a \sin^2 \frac{3\pi x}{a}\, dx + A_4 \int_0^a \sin \frac{3\pi x}{a} \sin \frac{4\pi x}{a}\, dx + \cdots$$

Evaluating the integrals gives

$$\frac{2a}{3\pi} V_0 = 0 + 0 + A_3 \frac{a}{2} + 0 \cdots$$

and thus

$$A_3 = \frac{4V_0}{3\pi}$$

In this manner each of the A_m can be found by multiplying both sides of Eq. (9.16) by the appropriate sine function and integrating. A general expression for A_l can be found by multiplying both sides by sin $(l\pi x/a)$ and integrating. Since l can stand for any integer, this results in a general expression for the A. Thus we have

$$\frac{a}{l\pi} V_0(1 - \cos l\pi) = A_l \frac{a}{2}$$

The only term on the right-hand side which is not zero is the one for which $m = l$. Since

$$1 - \cos l\pi = \begin{cases} 2 & \text{when } l \text{ is odd} \\ 0 & \text{otherwise} \end{cases}$$

then

$$A_l = \begin{cases} \dfrac{4V_0}{l\pi} & \text{for } l \text{ odd} \\ 0 & \text{otherwise} \end{cases}$$

Since l can be any integer, A_m can be written as

$$A_m = \begin{cases} \dfrac{4V_0}{m\pi} & \text{for } m \text{ odd} \\ 0 & \text{otherwise} \end{cases} \tag{9.18}$$

Now substituting Eq. (9.18) into Eq. (9.15) gives the solution to the problem,

$$\Phi = \sum_{\substack{m=1 \\ m \text{ odd}}}^{\infty} \frac{4V_0}{m\pi} e^{-m\pi z/a} \sin \frac{m\pi x}{a} \tag{9.19}$$

The expression for **E** can be found by using Eq. (9.19) in Eq. (6.14).

In summary, the problem was solved by solving Laplace's equation by the separation-of-variables technique and then requiring the solution to satisfy the boundary conditions. Satisfying the boundary condition at $z = 0$ required constructing a series solution of terms that individually satisfied Laplace's equation and all the other boundary conditions. The coefficients of the terms in the series were found by making use of the orthogonality properties of the terms in the series. In this particular case the series was a trigonometric Fourier series. However, when Laplace's equation is solved in other coordinate systems, other kinds of series are obtained, but the terms in the series are orthogonal, and hence the coefficients can be evaluated in the same way. We shall see in Sec. 9.6 that any solution which satisfies both Laplace's equation and the boundary conditions is a unique solution.

9.4 SEPARATION OF VARIABLES IN RECTANGULAR COORDINATES

The separation-of-variables technique was illustrated in the last section for one special case. In this section a more general discussion of the method is given. The discussion is based on the wave equation in rectangular coordinates for any scalar field function ψ,

$$\nabla^2\psi + k^2\psi = 0 \tag{9.20}$$

This equation is of the form of the wave equations given in Eqs. (6.12), (6.13), (6.17), and (6.19) for sinusoidal time variation and when **J** and ρ

are zero. Thus ψ stands for Φ or any one of the components of **A**, **E**, and **H**. Recall that $k^2 = \omega^2\mu\epsilon$.

$$\frac{\partial^2\psi}{\partial x^2} + \frac{\partial^2\psi}{\partial y^2} + \frac{\partial^2\psi}{\partial z^2} + k^2\psi = 0 \tag{9.21}$$

This equation is separated by *assuming* a solution of the form

$$\psi = X(x)Y(y)Z(z) \tag{9.22}$$

where $X(x)$ is a function only of x, $Y(y)$ is a function only of y, and $Z(z)$ is a function only of z. Substituting Eq. (9.22) into Eq. (9.21) results in

$$X''YZ + XY''Z + XYZ'' + k^2XYZ = 0 \tag{9.23}$$

where

$$X'' = \frac{d^2X}{dx^2}$$

$$Y'' = \frac{d^2Y}{dy^2}$$

and

$$Z'' = \frac{d^2Z}{dz^2}$$

The notation $X(x)$ has been abbreviated to X. Dividing Eq. (9.23) by XYZ gives

$$\frac{X''}{X} + \frac{Y''}{Y} + \frac{Z''}{Z} + k^2 = 0 \tag{9.24}$$

where the first term is a function only of x, the second term a function only of y, and the third a function only of z. Since each term is a function of only one variable, the terms can add to zero for *all values of x, y, and z* only if each term is equal to a constant. For example, suppose that y and z are held fixed at some value and x is allowed to vary. Under these conditions the Y''/Y and Z''/Z terms would remain constant, and Eq. (9.24) could be satisfied for all x only if X''/X remained constant as x varied.

Thus we write

$$\frac{X''}{X} = -k_x^2 \tag{9.25}$$

$$\frac{Y''}{Y} = -k_y^2 \tag{9.26}$$

$$\frac{Z''}{Z} = -k_z^2 \tag{9.27}$$

where k_x^2, k_y^2, and k_z^2 are called *separation constants* and are as yet undetermined. As will be seen later, these constants are determined by the boundary conditions, and they can be positive, negative, or zero. The minus sign in Eqs. (9.25) to (9.27) has been used for convenience. If Eq. (9.24) is to be satisfied, it must be true that

$$k_x^2 + k_y^2 + k_z^2 - k^2 = 0 \tag{9.28}$$

and the three-dimensional partial-differential wave equation, Eq. (9.21), reduces to an algebraic equation, Eq. (9.28), and three one-dimensional differential equations, Eqs. (9.25) to (9.27).

The solutions of Eqs. (9.25) to (9.27) are familiar, since the equations are linear second-order differential equations, which are often encountered in physical problems. When $k_x^2 > 0$, the solution to Eq. (9.25) is

$$X = A_1 \cos k_x x + A_2 \sin k_x x \tag{9.29}$$

or

$$X = A_3 e^{jk_x x} + A_4 e^{-jk_x x} \tag{9.30}$$

where A_1 and A_2 or A_3 and A_4 are arbitrary constants to be determined by the boundary conditions, as illustrated in Sec. 9.3. Even though Eqs. (9.29) and (9.30) are equivalent, one is sometimes more convenient than the other. Equation (9.29) or Eq. (9.30) is the general solution to the *second-order* differential equation because it is the sum of *two* independent solutions.

When k_x is an imaginary number, that is, $k_x^2 < 0$, the solution to Eq. (9.25) is

$$X = A_1 \cosh \gamma_x x + A_2 \sinh \gamma_x x \tag{9.31}$$

or

$$X = A_3 e^{\gamma_x x} + A_4 e^{-\gamma_x x} \tag{9.32}$$

where

$$k_x^2 = -\gamma_x^2$$

Again, Eqs. (9.31) and (9.32) are equivalent forms, but one form is sometimes more convenient than the other.

When $k_x^2 = 0$, the solution to Eq. (9.25) is

$$X = A_1 x + A_2 \tag{9.33}$$

This last form is sometimes required in special cases.

Since Eqs. (9.26) and (9.27) have the same form as Eq. (9.25), the solutions have the same form. These trignometric and hyperbolic forms are

$$Y = B_1 \cos k_y y + B_2 \sin k_y y \qquad k_y^2 > 0 \tag{9.34}$$

$$Y = B_1 \cosh \gamma_y y + B_2 \sinh \gamma_y y \qquad k_y^2 < 0,\ k_y^2 = -\gamma_y^2 \tag{9.35}$$

$$Y = B_1 y + B_2 \qquad k_y = 0 \tag{9.36}$$

and

$$Z = C_1 \cos k_z z + C_2 \sin k_z z \qquad k_z^2 > 0 \tag{9.37}$$

$$Z = C_1 \cosh \gamma_z z + C_2 \sinh \gamma_z z \qquad k_z^2 < 0,\ k_z^2 = -\gamma_z^2 \tag{9.38}$$

$$Z = C_1 z + C_2 \qquad k_z = 0 \tag{9.39}$$

Since, from Eq. (9.22), $\psi = XYZ$, the general solution for ψ consists of some combination of the various forms given above, depending on the values of k_x, k_y, and k_z. For example, suppose that

$$k_x^2 > 0$$

$$k_y^2 > 0$$

$$k_z^2 < 0 \qquad k_z^2 = -\gamma_z^2$$

Then the general solution is

$$\psi = (A_1 \cos k_x x + A_2 \sin k_x x)(B_1 \cos k_y y + B_2 \sin k_y y) \\ (C_1 \cosh \gamma_z z + C_2 \sinh \gamma_z z)$$

or

$$\psi = (A_1 \cos k_x x + A_2 \sin k_x x)(B_3 e^{jk_y y} + B_4 e^{-jk_y y})(C_3 e^{\gamma_z z} + C_4 e^{-\gamma_z z})$$

or one of the other equivalent forms. The particular solution used is determined by the boundary conditions of the problem, as illustrated in later examples. In any case Eq. (9.28) must always be satisfied. In the static case, where $k = 0$, k_x^2, k_y^2, and k_z^2 cannot all be positive or all negative. Consequently, the solutions cannot all be trigonometric in form; at least one must be hyperbolic. When $k \neq 0$, however, all the solutions can be trigonometric.

Generally speaking, the separation constants k_x, k_y, and k_z are determined by the boundary conditions, and they can have only certain values. These allowed values of the separation constants are called *eigenvalues*. The corresponding expressions for X, Y, Z, or ψ are called *eigenfunctions*. There may be an infinite number of eigenvalues and eigenfunctions allowed by the boundary conditions. The complete solution is then a sum of all the eigenfunctions.

9.5 ORTHOGONALITY AND EIGENFUNCTION EXPANSIONS

In Sec. 9.3 it was shown how the orthogonality of the sine functions made possible the evaluation of the coefficients A_m in the series in Eq. (9.15).

Since the series solution is a common one in boundary-value problems, orthogonality is an important property. It can be shown that the eigenfunctions of a certain class of differential equation called the *Sturm-Liouville equation*† are orthogonal for certain boundary conditions. The discussion here is limited to equations like Eq. (9.25).

Consider the equation

$$\frac{d^2\psi_m}{dx^2} + k_{xm}{}^2\psi_m = 0 \tag{9.40}$$

where ψ_m is an eigenfunction which satisfies the differential equation and the given boundary conditions, and k_{xm} is the eigenvalue. For example, in Sec. 9.3, $A_{2m} \sin (m\pi x/a)$ could be ψ_m and $m\pi/a$ could be k_{xm}. In addition, the same equation can be written with another eigenfunction and eigenvalue as

$$\frac{d^2\psi_l}{dx^2} + k_{xl}{}^2\psi_l = 0 \tag{9.41}$$

where the subscript l means that ψ_l is a different eigenfunction from ψ_m.

Now suppose that Eq. (9.40) is multiplied by ψ_l and Eq. (9.41) is multiplied by ψ_m, and the second is subtracted from the first. This results in

$$\psi_l \frac{d^2\psi_m}{dx^2} - \psi_m \frac{d^2\psi_l}{dx^2} + (k_{xm}{}^2 - k_{xl}{}^2)\psi_l\psi_m = 0 \tag{9.42}$$

but the first two terms on the left can be combined and written as

$$\psi_l \frac{d^2\psi_m}{dx^2} - \psi_m \frac{d^2\psi_l}{dx^2} = \frac{d}{dx}\left(\psi_l \frac{d\psi_m}{dx} - \psi_m \frac{d\psi_l}{dx}\right)$$

Hence Eq. (9.42) can be rearranged to

$$(k_{xl}{}^2 - k_{xm}{}^2)\psi_l\psi_m = \frac{d}{dx}\left(\psi_l \frac{d\psi_m}{dx} - \psi_m \frac{d\psi_l}{dx}\right)$$

Now, if both sides are integrated from x_1 to x_2, the result is

$$(k_{xl}{}^2 - k_{xm}{}^2) \int_{x_1}^{x_2} \psi_l\psi_m \, dx = \left[\psi_l \frac{d\psi_m}{dx} - \psi_m \frac{d\psi_l}{dx}\right]_{x_1}^{x_2} \tag{9.43}$$

If $k_{xl}{}^2$ and $k_{xm}{}^2$ are *not equal*, and if the right-hand side of Eq. (9.43) is zero, it must be true that

$$\int_{x_1}^{x_2} \psi_l\psi_m \, dx = 0 \tag{9.44}$$

† For example, see C. R. Wylie, Jr., "Advanced Engineering Mathematics," 3d ed., p. 320, McGraw-Hill Book Company, New York, 1966.

If Eq. (9.44) is true, ψ_l and ψ_m are said to be *orthogonal* over the interval x_1 to x_2. There are a number of combinations of boundary conditions which make the right-hand side of Eq. (9.43) zero. For example, when ψ_m and ψ_l are both equal to zero at x_1 and x_2, or when $d\psi_m/dx$ and $d\psi_l/dx$ are both equal to zero at x_1 and x_2, the right-hand side is zero; or combinations of the ψ and their derivatives could be zero at x_1 and x_2. Note that ψ_l and ψ_m must have some kind of periodicity to make the right-hand side go to zero at both x_1 and x_2.

The following examples illustrate the ideas of orthogonality.

Example 9.1 Orthogonality of the cosine functions Two eigenfunctions which satisfy Eq. (9.40) are

$$\psi_m = \cos\frac{m\pi x}{a}$$

$$\psi_l = \cos\frac{l\pi x}{a}$$

where l and m are integers. The corresponding eigenvalues are $k_{xm} = m\pi/a$ and $k_{xl} = l\pi/a$. In this case the right-hand side of Eq. (9.43) becomes

$$\left[-\frac{m\pi}{a}\cos\frac{l\pi x}{a}\sin\frac{m\pi x}{a} + \frac{l\pi}{a}\cos\frac{m\pi x}{a}\sin\frac{l\pi x}{a}\right]_{x_1}^{x_2}$$

This term will be zero if $x_1 = 0,\ x_2 = a;\ x_1 = a,\ x_2 = 2a;$ etc. Hence, since k_{xm} and k_{xl} are not equal,

$$\int_{x_1}^{x_2} \psi_l\psi_m\,dx = 0$$

and ψ_l and ψ_m are orthogonal over the intervals 0 to a, a to $2a$, etc. This can also be verified by direct integration.

Example 9.2 Nonorthogonality of real exponentials If $k_{xm}{}^2 = -\gamma_m{}^2$ and $k_{xl}{}^2 = -\gamma_l{}^2$, then two eigenfunctions which satisfy the differential equation, Eq. (9.40), are

$$\psi_l = e^{\gamma_l x}$$

$$\psi_m = e^{\gamma_m x}$$

For this case the right-hand side of Eq. (9.43) is

$$[\gamma_m e^{\gamma_l x}e^{\gamma_m x} - \gamma_l e^{\gamma_m x}e^{\gamma_l x}]_{x_1}^{x_2} = [(\gamma_m - \gamma_l)e^{\gamma_l x}e^{\gamma_m x}]_{x_1}^{x_2}$$

It is apparent that if γ_m and γ_l are different, the right-hand side is not zero for any values of x_1 and x_2. Hence the real exponentials are not orthogonal. This is to be expected, since real exponentials have no periodicity.

The usefulness of orthogonality lies in the series expansion of a function in terms of orthogonal functions; that is,

$$f(x) = \Sigma c_m\psi_m(x) \tag{9.45}$$

where c_m are constant coefficients and the $\psi_m(x)$ are an orthogonal set of functions. If the $\psi_m(x)$ are trigonometric functions, the series is a Fourier series, which is one special kind of orthogonal function.

The c_m can be found by multiplying both sides by ψ_l and integrating over the range of orthogonality, as illustrated in Sec. 9.3 in connection with Eq. (9.16):

$$\int_{x_1}^{x_2} f(x)\psi_l \, dx = c_l \int_{x_1}^{x_2} \psi_l^2 \, dx$$

$$c_l = \frac{\int_{x_1}^{x_2} f(x)\psi_l \, dx}{\int_{x_1}^{x_2} \psi_l^2 \, dx}$$

In Eq. (9.45) $f(x)$ can be any piecewise continuous function, but the set of orthogonal functions ψ_m must be *complete* for the series to converge to $f(x)$. The idea of completeness can be illustrated by supposing that the set of orthogonal functions consisted of the set of sin $(m\pi x/a)$, with $m = 1, 2, 3, \ldots$, except that sin $(4\pi x/a)$ is not included. Then suppose that $g(x) = \sin (4\pi x/a)$ were expanded as

$$g(x) = \sum_{\substack{m=1 \\ (m=4 \text{ not included})}}^{\infty} c_m \sin \frac{m\pi x}{a}$$

The series would not converge to $g(x)$ because the c_m would all be zero, since $g(x)$ is orthogonal to all the sin $(m\pi x/a)$. Thus the set of orthogonal functions used in this case is not complete. Fortunately, in solving the wave equations for physical problems, complete sets of orthogonal functions are usually obtainable.

Some of the orthogonality properties of the trigonometric functions are summarized as follows:

$$\int_0^{2a} \sin \frac{m\pi x}{a} \sin \frac{l\pi x}{a} \, dx = \begin{cases} a & \text{when } l = m \\ 0 & \text{when } l \neq m \end{cases}$$

$$\int_0^{2a} \cos \frac{m\pi x}{a} \cos \frac{l\pi x}{a} \, dx = \begin{cases} a & \text{when } l = m \\ 0 & \text{when } l \neq m \end{cases}$$

$$\int_0^{2a} \sin \frac{m\pi x}{a} \cos \frac{l\pi x}{a} \, dx = 0 \qquad \text{for all } m, l$$

9.6 UNIQUENESS OF SOLUTIONS FOR FIELD EQUATIONS

In Secs. 9.2 and 9.3 solutions to Laplace's equation were sought which satisfied the boundary conditions. When such solutions were obtained, they were considered to be the only solutions; i.e., they were considered to be *unique* solutions. But one might wonder just what determines whether a solution is unique, especially when there seemed to be a certain amount of cleverness involved in constructing the series solution which satisfied the boundary condition at $z = 0$ in Sec. 9.3. Could it happen that the wrong series would be picked and the wrong answer obtained?

The purpose of this section is to show that *if a solution satisfies both Laplace's equation in a region and the boundary conditions at the boundary of the region, it is a unique solution.* In addition, it has been shown,† but will not be shown here, *that if a solution satisfies Maxwell's equations in a region and if either the tangential electric fields or the tangential magnetic fields satisfy the boundary conditions at the boundary of the region, the solution is unique.*

Consider two solutions to Laplace's equation, Φ_1 and Φ_2, both of which satisfy the boundary conditions at the surface enclosing the region. Since both satisfy Laplace's equation,

$$\nabla^2\Phi_D = 0 \tag{9.46}$$

where

$$\Phi_D = \Phi_1 - \Phi_2$$

According to the divergence theorem,

$$\int_V \nabla \cdot \mathbf{F}\, dV = \oint_S \mathbf{F} \cdot d\mathbf{S} \tag{9.47}$$

where $\mathbf{F}$ is any vector. Let

$$\mathbf{F} = \Phi_D \nabla \Phi_D$$

Then, using a vector identity, $\nabla \cdot \mathbf{F}$ can be written as

$$\begin{aligned}\nabla \cdot \mathbf{F} &= \nabla \cdot (\Phi_D\, \nabla\Phi_D) \\ &= \Phi_D\, \nabla^2\Phi_D + \nabla\Phi_D \cdot \nabla\Phi_D\end{aligned}$$

Then

$$\nabla \cdot \mathbf{F} = \nabla\Phi_D \cdot \nabla\Phi_D \tag{9.48}$$

since $\nabla^2\Phi_D = 0$ from Eq. (9.46). Putting Eq. (9.48) into Eq. (9.47) gives

$$\int_V \nabla\Phi_D \cdot \nabla\Phi_D\, dV = \oint_S \Phi_D\, \nabla\Phi_D \cdot d\mathbf{S} \tag{9.49}$$

But since both Φ_1 and Φ_2 satisfy the boundary conditions, $\Phi_1 = \Phi_2$ on S and thus $\Phi_D = 0$ on S. Therefore the right-hand side of Eq. (9.49) is zero. Hence

$$\int_V \nabla\Phi_D \cdot \nabla\Phi_D\, dV = 0$$

† J. R. Stratton, "Electromagnetic Theory," pp. 486–488, McGraw-Hill Book Company, New York, 1941.

Since the integrand is always positive, the integral can be zero only if the integrand is zero. Therefore

$$\nabla\Phi_D = 0$$

and Φ_D = constant everywhere in V. But since $\Phi_D = 0$ on S, the constant must be zero. Then $\Phi_D = 0$ everywhere in the region, and consequently $\Phi_1 = \Phi_2$. This is the uniqueness property that we wished to show: any two solutions to Laplace's equation which satisfy the boundary conditions must be identical.

The uniqueness property allows considerable freedom in techniques for solving boundary-value problems. If a solution can be found by any means whatever which satisfies the appropriate field equations and the boundary conditions, that solution is the unique solution. Thus, even if a solution which satisfies the differential equations and the boundary conditions is "guessed," we can be assured that it is a unique solution. Consequently, ingenuity in guessing at solutions is sometimes a great help in solving boundary-value problems.

9.7 METHOD OF IMAGES

One class of boundary-value problems involving point charges and conducting boundaries can conveniently be solved by a technique known as the *method of images*. The method can be illustrated by consideration of Fig. 9.3, which shows a point charge Q and a conducting plane. The objective is to find the potential Φ produced by the point charge in the presence of the conducting plane.

Because of the uniqueness theorem discussed in the last section, any expression which satisfies Laplace's equation and the boundary conditions is a unique solution. The boundary condition for the situation illustrated in Fig. 9.3 is that Φ be constant on the conducting plane; that is, the conducting plane is an equipotential surface. The surface must be

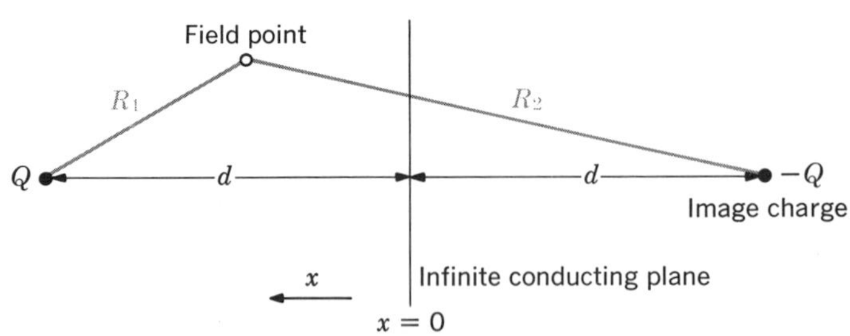

Fig. 9.3 A point charge and a conducting boundary used to describe the method of images.

equipotential, because in the static case **E** is zero inside a good conductor and has only a normal component at the surface, as explained in Chap. 5. Since the tangential component of **E** is zero, the potential difference between any two points on the surface, which is $-\int \mathbf{E} \cdot d\mathbf{l}$, is also zero because the path lies on the surface and hence involves only tangential **E**, which is zero on the surface. Hence the surface is equipotential.

An expression for Φ which satisfies the requirements mentioned above is the Φ produced by Q and by an image charge $-Q$ which is located symmetrically behind the conducting surface, as shown in Fig. 9.3. This expression is

$$\Phi = \frac{Q}{4\pi\epsilon_0}\left(\frac{1}{R_1} - \frac{1}{R_2}\right) \tag{9.50}$$

where R_1 and R_2 are shown in Fig. 9.3. The expression for Φ in Eq. (9.50) satisfies Laplace's equation because the term due to each charge satisfies Laplace's equation individually. Hence the sum of the two terms also satisfies Laplace's equation.

Now it must be shown that this Φ also satisfies the boundary condition at $x = 0$. The expressions for R_1 and R_2 are

$$R_1 = \sqrt{(x-d)^2 + y^2 + z^2}$$
$$R_2 = \sqrt{(x+d)^2 + y^2 + z^2}$$

When $x = 0$, $R_1 = R_2$ and $\Phi = 0$, for all y and z. Hence Φ is constant on the $x = 0$ plane. In this case the constant value of Φ is zero. If the boundary condition required that Φ be some nonzero constant at $x = 0$, a constant could be added to Eq. (9.50) to meet this condition. This expression for Φ would still satisfy Laplace's equation. The expression for **E** can be found from $\mathbf{E} = -\nabla\Phi$.

In summary, the method of images amounts to imaging the charge or charges in the plane of the conducting surface and calculating the potential due to both the charge and its image.

Example 9.3 A point charge in a corner The method of images can be used to find the potential due to the point charge Q in the corner between two conducting planes shown in Fig. 9.4. Q is imaged first in the vertical plane with the $-Q$ at point 1 and then in the horizontal plane with the $-Q$ at point 3. However, the combination of the two image charges and Q itself does not make Φ zero on the two planes. In order to make Φ zero, the image charges must also be imaged. Thus $-Q$ at point 1 is imaged by the $+Q$ at point 2. In this case the $+Q$ at point 2 is also the image of the $-Q$ at point 3. Thus both image charges are imaged by $+Q$ at point 2. Since the combination of all four charges makes Φ zero on the conducting planes, the imaging is complete.

If the angle of the corner were not a submultiple of 180°, an infinite number

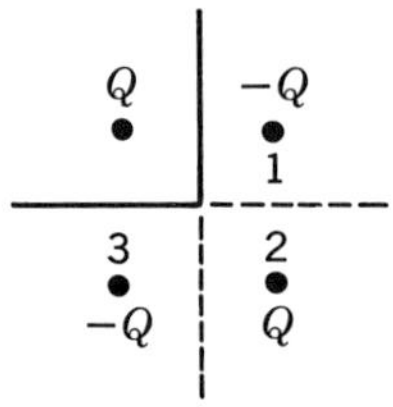

Fig. 9.4 A point charge in the corner between conducting planes and the image charges.

of image charges would be required to make Φ zero on the conducting planes. The reason an infinite number of image charges is not required for the 90° corner of Fig. 9.4 is that the $+Q$ at point 2 imaged the $-Q$ at both points 1 and 3 simultaneously. If the angle is not a submultiple of 180°, this will not happen, and an infinite number of image charges will be required.

A similar image technique can be used to find the potential due to a line charge and an infinitely long conducting cylinder and that due to a point charge and a conducting sphere. These situations are illustrated in Figs. 9.5 and 9.6, respectively. For the line-charge image,

$$\rho_{li} = -\rho_l \tag{9.51}$$

$$R_2 = \frac{a^2}{R_1} \tag{9.52}$$

and for the sphere at zero potential,

$$Q_i = -\frac{a}{R_1}Q \tag{9.53}$$

$$R_2 = \frac{a^2}{R_1} \tag{9.54}$$

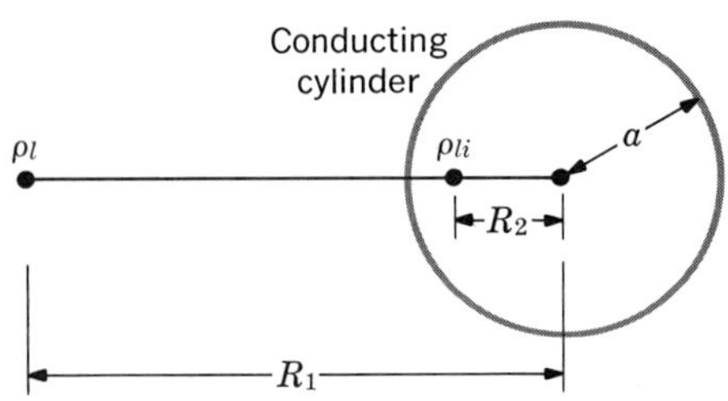

Fig. 9.5 Imaging a line charge in a cylinder of infinite length.

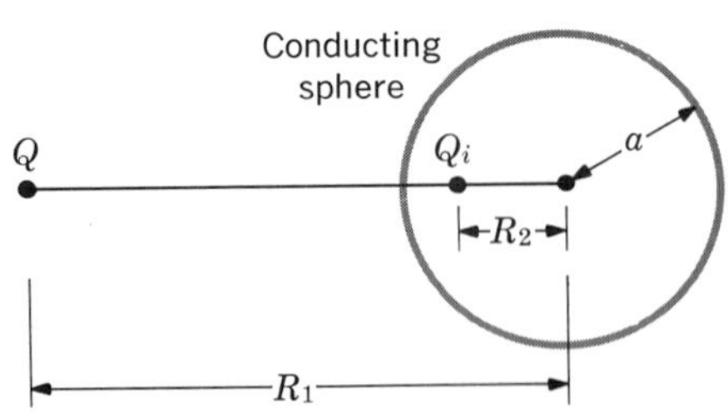

Fig. 9.6 Imaging a point charge in a sphere at zero potential.

9.8 THE PARALLEL–PLATE WAVE GUIDE

In Sec. 9.3 the electrostatic fields between two infinite parallel plates were found. The fields were found to decay in the z direction because the z dependence was $e^{-m\pi z/a}$. When the fields are time-varying, however, the z dependence can be of the form $e^{-j\beta z}$. As explained in Chap. 6, this means the fields have the form of traveling waves. In Example 6.6 a planewave solution for the fields in the parallel-plate wave guide was obtained. This is not the complete solution to the problem, however, as will be seen from the analysis presented in this section.

SOLUTION OF MAXWELL'S EQUATIONS

As discussed in Sec. 9.2, the fields can be found by solving Maxwell's equations or the wave equations in **E** and **H** or **A** and Φ. When $\mathbf{J} = 0$ and $\rho = 0$, it is just as easy to solve the wave equations for **E** and **H** as it is to solve the wave equations for **A** and Φ. Hence the problem will be approached by solving for **E** and **H** from the wave equations.

The orientation of the parallel plates in a rectangular coordinate system is illustrated in Fig. 9.7. The problem is to solve the wave equations for **E** and **H** and make the solutions satisfy the boundary conditions. For sinusoidal time variation, $\mathbf{J} = 0$ and $\rho = 0$, Eqs. (6.12) and (6.13) reduce to

$$\nabla^2\mathbf{E} + k^2\mathbf{E} = 0 \tag{9.55}$$

$$\nabla^2\mathbf{H} + k^2\mathbf{H} = 0 \tag{9.56}$$

Assuming that **E** and **H** do not vary with x because the plates are infinite in the x direction, Eqs. (9.55) and (9.56) become

$$\frac{\partial^2\mathbf{E}}{\partial y^2} + \frac{\partial^2\mathbf{E}}{\partial z^2} + k^2\mathbf{E} = 0 \tag{9.57}$$

$$\frac{\partial^2\mathbf{H}}{\partial y^2} + \frac{\partial^2\mathbf{H}}{\partial z^2} + k^2\mathbf{E} = 0 \tag{9.58}$$

From the two vector equations, six scalar equations can be written,

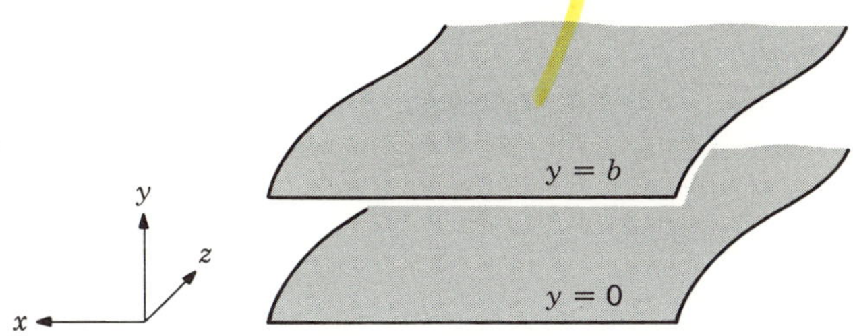

Fig. 9.7 The parallel-plate wave guide.

one for each component of **E** and one for each component of **H**. These scalar equations can be solved by the separation-of-variables method described in Sec. 9.4. The solution will consist of expressions for the components of **E** and **H**, each with a different set of arbitrary constants. These arbitrary constants are not all independent, however, because **E** and **H** are related by the curl equations

$$\nabla \times \mathbf{E} = -j\omega\mu\mathbf{H} \tag{9.59}$$

$$\nabla \times \mathbf{H} = j\omega\epsilon\mathbf{E} \tag{9.60}$$

These equations are obtained from Eqs. (5.85) and (5.86) with $\mathbf{J} = 0$ and sinusoidal time variation. Thus after Eqs. (9.57) and (9.58) are solved, the solutions must be related by Eqs. (9.59) and (9.60). One might wonder, then, if it would be just as easy to start with Eqs. (9.59) and (9.60), from which Eqs. (9.57) and (9.58) were obtained.

As it turns out, the most convenient method of solution consists of a combination of the two methods described above. E_z and H_z are found by solving the two scalar wave equations for E_z and H_z obtained from Eqs. (9.57) and (9.58). The expression for E_z contains one set of arbitrary constants. Then Eqs. (9.59) and (9.60) are combined in a manner that results in expressions for the other components of **E** and **H** in terms of derivatives of E_z and H_z. Thus expressions for all the fields are found in terms of the two sets of arbitrary constants, the set in E_z and the set in H_z. This eliminates four sets of arbitrary constants which would be obtained if the wave equations in E_x, E_y, H_x, and H_y were solved. This method is used now for the parallel-plate-wave-guide problem.

From Eq. (9.58), the wave equation in H_z is

$$\frac{\partial^2 H_z}{\partial y^2} + \frac{\partial^2 H_z}{\partial z^2} + k^2 H_z = 0 \tag{9.61}$$

To separate the variables, the definition is made that

$$H_z = Y(y)Z(z) \tag{9.62}$$

Then substituting in the wave equation and dividing by YZ results in

$$\frac{Y''}{Y} + \frac{Z''}{Z} + k^2 = 0 \tag{9.63}$$

According to the argument given in Secs. 9.3 and 9.4, each term must be equal to a constant. Hence we set

$$\frac{Y''}{Y} = \gamma^2 \tag{9.64}$$

$$\frac{Z''}{Z} = -\beta^2 \tag{9.65}$$

where the separation constants have been chosen to be γ^2 and β^2 because this notation is commonly used in connection with wave propagation. From Eqs. (9.63), (9.64), and (9.65) it can be seen that

$$\gamma^2 = k^2 - \beta^2 \tag{9.66}$$

Solving Eqs. (9.64) and (9.65) and using Eq. (9.62) results in

$$H_z = (A_1 \cos \gamma y + A_2 \sin \gamma y)(B_1 e^{-j\beta z} + B_2 e^{j\beta z}) \tag{9.67}$$

Following a similar procedure for E_z results in

$$E_z = (C_1 \cos \gamma y + C_2 \sin \gamma y)(D_1 e^{-j\beta z} + D_2 e^{j\beta z}) \tag{9.68}$$

In both cases the exponential form of the z solution has been used because this is convenient in describing propagation, as shown in Chap. 6.

Since the wave equations for the other components of **E** and **H** have the same form as Eq. (9.61), the z dependence of the other components will also have the same form. It is clear, therefore, that

$$\frac{\partial^2 E_y}{\partial z^2} = -\beta^2 E_y$$

and a similar relation can be written for each field component. This can be expressed by writing

$$\frac{\partial^2}{\partial z^2} = -\beta^2 \tag{9.69}$$

The expressions for the other components can now be found from the curl equations. Writing out Eqs. (9.59) and (9.60) in component form with $\partial/\partial x = 0$ results in

$$\frac{\partial E_z}{\partial y} - \frac{\partial E_y}{\partial z} = -j\omega\mu H_x \tag{9.70}$$

$$\frac{\partial E_x}{\partial z} = -j\omega\mu H_y \tag{9.71}$$

$$-\frac{\partial E_x}{\partial y} = -j\omega\mu H_z \tag{9.72}$$

$$\frac{\partial H_z}{\partial y} - \frac{\partial H_y}{\partial z} = j\omega\epsilon E_x \tag{9.73}$$

$$\frac{\partial H_x}{\partial z} = j\omega\epsilon E_y \tag{9.74}$$

$$-\frac{\partial H_x}{\partial y} = j\omega\epsilon E_z \tag{9.75}$$

Equations (9.71) and (9.73) may be combined to eliminate H_y and obtain

E_x in terms of H_z. The result is

$$E_x = \frac{j\omega\mu}{\beta^2 - k^2} \frac{\partial H_z}{\partial y} \tag{9.76}$$

where Eq. (9.69) has also been used. Similarly, Eqs. (9.70) and (9.74) may be combined to obtain an expression for E_y,

$$E_y = \frac{-1}{\beta^2 - k^2} \frac{\partial}{\partial z} \left(\frac{\partial E_z}{\partial y} \right) \tag{9.77}$$

Similar expressions may be obtained for H_x and H_y.

$$H_x = \frac{-j\omega\epsilon}{\beta^2 - k^2} \frac{\partial E_z}{\partial y} \tag{9.78}$$

$$H_y = \frac{-1}{\beta^2 - k^2} \frac{\partial}{\partial z} \left(\frac{\partial H_z}{\partial y} \right) \tag{9.79}$$

The equations have been combined in this particular way because this fits a more general set of expressions, which are valid when $\partial/\partial x \neq 0$. These expressions are given in Sec. 9.9.

Now all the components of the fields can be found by using the expressions for H_z and E_z from Eqs. (9.67) and (9.68) in Eqs. (9.76) to (9.79). The results are

$$E_x = \frac{j\omega\mu}{\gamma} (A_1 \sin \gamma y - A_2 \cos \gamma y)(B_1 e^{-j\beta z} + B_2 e^{j\beta z}) \tag{9.80}$$

$$E_y = \frac{j\beta}{\gamma} (C_1 \sin \gamma y - C_2 \cos \gamma y)(D_1 e^{-j\beta z} - D_2 e^{j\beta z}) \tag{9.81}$$

$$H_x = -\frac{j\omega\epsilon}{\gamma} (C_1 \sin \gamma y - C_2 \cos \gamma y)(D_1 e^{-j\beta z} + D_2 e^{j\beta z}) \tag{9.82}$$

$$H_y = \frac{j\beta}{\gamma} (A_1 \sin \gamma y - A_2 \cos \gamma y)(B_1 e^{-j\beta z} - B_2 e^{j\beta z}) \tag{9.83}$$

Before we proceed further, it is important to note that there is the possibility of a solution with E_z and H_z both zero but H_x and E_y not zero. This solution cannot be obtained from Eqs. (9.76) to (9.79), because it turns out also that $\beta = k$ for this solution, and the equations therefore have the indeterminate form 0/0. Expressions for H_x and E_y can be found, however, from Eqs. (9.70), (9.74), and (9.75), with $H_z = 0$ and $E_z = 0$. Combining Eqs. (9.70) and (9.74) results in

$$\frac{\partial^2 H_x}{\partial z^2} = -k^2 H_x$$

This, combined with Eq. (9.69), means that $\beta^2 = k^2$. From Eq. (9.75), $\partial H_x/\partial y = 0$. Hence H_x varies only with z and has the form

$$H_x = F_1 e^{-jkz} + F_2 e^{jkz} \tag{9.84}$$

Then, from Eq. (9.74),

$$E_y = \frac{k}{\omega\epsilon}\left(F_1 e^{-jkz} - F_2 e^{jkz}\right) \tag{9.85}$$

Similar expressions for E_x and H_y could be obtained from Eqs. (9.71) to (9.73), but since the E_x obtained would not vary with y, and since one of the boundary conditons is that $E_x = 0$ at $y = 0$ and $y = a$, E_x must be zero, and consequently H_y must be zero.

At this point, the field expressions which satisfy Maxwell's equations are Eqs. (9.67), (9.68), and (9.80) to (9.85). The next step is to require these expressions to satisfy the boundary conditions and thereby evaluate the arbitrary constant coefficients and the separation constants β and γ.

SATISFYING THE BOUNDARY CONDITIONS

Since the parallel plates are assumed to be perfectly conducting, the boundary conditions are

$$E_x = 0 \qquad \text{at } y = 0,\ y = b$$

$$E_z = 0 \qquad \text{at } y = 0,\ y = b$$

Requiring E_x to satisfy the first boundary condition requires that

$$A_2 = 0$$

$$\gamma = \frac{n\pi}{b} \qquad n = 1, 2, 3, \ldots \tag{9.86}$$

The second boundary condition requires, in addition, that $C_1 = 0$.

As indicated by Eq. (9.86), there are an infinite number of eigenvalues and hence an infinite number of eigenfunctions, just as there were in Sec. 9.3. In general, a sum over all these eigenfunctions is needed to satisfy the boundary conditions at $z = 0$ and $z = c$, just as in Sec. 9.3. Thus the general form for the field components is

$$H_z = \sum_{n=1}^{\infty} A_{1n} \cos \gamma_n y \left(B_{1n} e^{-j\beta_n z} + B_{2n} e^{j\beta_n z}\right) \tag{9.87}$$

$$E_x = \sum_{n=1}^{\infty} \frac{j\omega\mu}{\gamma_n} A_{1n} \sin \gamma_n y \left(B_{1n} e^{-j\beta_n z} + B_{2n} e^{j\beta_n z}\right) \tag{9.88}$$

$$H_y = \sum_{n=1}^{\infty} \frac{j\beta_n}{\gamma_n} A_{1n} \sin \gamma_n y \, (B_{1n}e^{-j\beta_n z} - B_{2n}e^{j\beta_n z}) \tag{9.89}$$

$$E_z = \sum_{n=1}^{\infty} C_{2n} \sin \gamma_n y \, (D_{1n}e^{-j\beta_n z} + D_{2n}e^{j\beta_n z}) \tag{9.90}$$

$$E_y = \sum_{n=1}^{\infty} -\frac{j\beta_n}{\gamma_n} C_{2n} \cos \gamma_n y \, (D_{1n}e^{-j\beta_n z} - D_{2n}e^{j\beta_n z}) + \frac{k}{\omega\epsilon}(F_1e^{-jkz} - F_2e^{jkz}) \tag{9.91}$$

$$H_x = \sum_{n=1}^{\infty} \frac{j\omega\epsilon}{\gamma_n} C_{2n} \cos \gamma_n y \, (D_{1n}e^{-j\beta_n z} - D_{2n}e^{j\beta_n z}) + (F_1e^{-jkz} + F_2e^{jkz}) \tag{9.92}$$

In wave-guide systems, an important consideration is the propagation characteristics, which are described in terms of the propagation constants, the β_n. The boundary conditions at $z = 0$ and $z = c$ are usually treated in terms of transmission-line theory, as discussed in Sec. 9.12. Consequently, the propagation characteristics will be discussed in this section, but the remaining boundary conditions will not be discussed. A transmission-line description of wave guides is given in Sec. 9.12.

PARALLEL-PLATE-WAVE-GUIDE MODES

The field components given in Eqs. (9.87) to (9.92) have purposely been written in two groups. The first group contains only the A_{1n}, B_{1n}, and B_{2n} constants which appear in H_z. The second group contains only the C_{2n}, D_{1n}, and D_{2n} constants which appear in E_z and the F_1 and F_2 which appear in the solution for which $E_z = H_z = 0$. Each of the two groups satisfies both Maxwell's equations and the boundary conditions independently. Furthermore, each set of eigenfunctions in the first group, i.e., one corresponding term in each series, also satisfies both Maxwell's equations and the boundary conditions. Consequently, each group is said to be a set of *wave-guide modes,* and each set of eigenfunctions in the group is said to be *one mode.* Since the first group has no E_z components, these modes are called transverse electric (TE) modes. Since the second group has no H_z components, these modes are called transverse magnetic (TM) modes. The terms for E_y and H_x containing F_1 and F_2 are called a transverse electromagnetic (TEM) mode because both H_z and E_z are zero for this mode.

The lowest-order mode is the one for which $n = 1$. For example, the lowest order TE mode is, from Eqs. (9.87) to (9.89),

$$H_z = A_{11} \cos \gamma_1 y \, (B_{11}e^{-j\beta_1 z} + B_{21}e^{j\beta_1 z})$$

$$E_x = \frac{j\omega\mu}{\gamma_1} A_{11} \sin \gamma_1 y \, (B_{11}e^{-j\beta_1 z} + B_{21}e^{j\beta_1 z})$$

$$H_y = \frac{j\beta_1}{\gamma_1} A_{11} \sin \gamma_1 y \, (B_{11}e^{-j\beta_1 z} - B_{21}e^{j\beta_1 z})$$

From Eqs. (9.86) and (9.66),

$$\gamma_1 = \frac{\pi}{b}$$

$$\beta_1 = \sqrt{k^2 - \gamma_1{}^2} = \sqrt{k^2 - \left(\frac{\pi}{b}\right)^2}$$

PROPAGATION CHARACTERISTICS OF THE MODES

In the expressions for the field components the $e^{-j\beta z}$ term represents a wave traveling in the $+z$ direction and the $e^{j\beta z}$ term represents a wave traveling in the $-z$ direction, as explained in Chap. 6. The propagation characteristics are determined by the nature of β. From Eqs. (9.86) and (9.66),

$$\beta_n = \sqrt{k^2 - \left(\frac{n\pi}{b}\right)^2} \tag{9.93}$$

When the frequency is such that $k^2 > (n\pi/b)^2$, then β_n is real and the $e^{-j\beta_n z}$ and $e^{j\beta_n z}$ terms represent traveling, or propagating, waves. However, when the frequency is such that $k^2 < (n\pi/b)^2$, then β_n is imaginary and the exponentials become real exponentials rather than imaginary exponentials. The waves then become decaying, or *evanescent*, waves, because the amplitude decreases with distance in the z direction. The *cutoff frequency* is the frequency at which the changeover from propagating to evanescent modes occurs. From Eq. (9.93) we see that this frequency corresponds to the value of k for which $\beta_n = 0$; that is,

$$k_{nco} = \frac{n\pi}{b}$$

where the subscript *co* stands for cutoff.

Note that each mode has a different cutoff frequency. With proper adjustment of the frequency with respect to the spacing b, it is possible

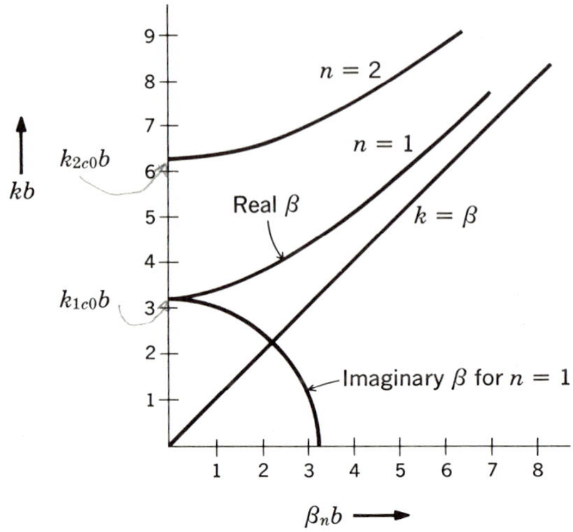

Fig. 9.8 The $k\beta$ diagram for the two lowest-order TE and TM modes of a parallel-plate wave guide.

to have just one TE and TM mode propagating while all the others are cut off. The cutoff modes, however, must generally be used in satisfying the z boundary conditions, even though they do not propagate.

The propagation characteristics are often displayed in a diagram called a $k\beta$ diagram, or sometimes in an $\omega\beta$ diagram. The $k\beta$ diagram is a plot of k versus β_n, as obtained from Eq. (9.93). Figure 9.8 shows a normalized plot of kb versus $\beta_n b$ for $n = 1$ and $n = 2$. The imaginary β is shown for $n = 1$ only. Below $k_{1co}b$, no propagation occurs because β is imaginary. Between $k_{1co}b$ and $k_{2co}b$, only the $n = 1$ modes can propagate. All the $k\beta$ curves approach the line $k = \beta$ as k gets very large. Further discussion of propagation characteristics and $k\beta$ diagrams is found in Sec. 9.13.

It can be shown by writing $\cos \gamma y = (e^{j\gamma y} + e^{-j\gamma y})/2$ that the modes described in this section are equivalent to planewaves bouncing back and forth between the plates in a way like that illustrated in Fig. 6.11 (see Prob. 9.8-8).

FIELD CONFIGURATION OF THE MODES

The configuration of the field lines is helpful in visualizing the characteristics of the modes. Since $e^{j\omega t}$ time variation has been assumed, the expressions for the real fields in terms of the phasors given in Eqs. (9.87) to (9.89) can be obtained by multiplying by $e^{j\omega t}$ and taking the real part (see Sec. 1.16). The result for the TE_1 mode traveling in the $+z$ direction is

$$H_{z1} = A_{11} \cos \gamma_1 y \cos (\omega t - \beta_1 z)$$

$$E_{x1} = -\frac{\omega\mu}{\gamma_1} A_{11} \sin \gamma_1 y \sin (\omega t - \beta_1 z)$$

$$H_{y1} = -\frac{\beta_1}{\gamma_1} A_{11} \sin \gamma_1 y \sin (\omega t - \beta_1 z)$$

where

$$\gamma_1 = \frac{\pi}{b}$$

$$\beta_1 = \sqrt{k^2 - \left(\frac{\pi}{b}\right)^2}$$

Since the fields are traveling waves, it is convenient to look at the spatial variation of the fields at one instant of time and then think of this pattern moving in the z direction as time changes. A convenient time to choose is $t = 0$, and a convenient frequency is the one which corresponds to $k^2 = \frac{5}{4}(\pi/b)^2$ so that $\beta_1 = \sqrt{\frac{5}{4}(\pi/b)^2 - (\pi/b)^2} = \pi/2b$. For this case the field expressions are

$$H_{z1} = A_{11} \cos \frac{\pi}{b} y \cos \frac{\pi}{2b} z$$

$$E_{x1} = \frac{\omega\mu}{\gamma_1} A_{11} \sin \frac{\pi}{b} y \sin \frac{\pi}{2b} z$$

$$H_{y1} = \frac{\beta_1}{\gamma_1} A_{11} \sin \frac{\pi}{b} y \sin \frac{\pi}{2b} z$$

The qualitative nature of the field patterns can be easily determined from these equations. The field pattern is illustrated in Fig. 9.9 in a view toward the $+x$ direction. At $z = 0$, H_y is zero and H_z is not; hence the magnetic field lines are in the z direction. Since H_z varies as $\cos (\pi/b)y$, the magnetic field is in the $+z$ direction near the bottom and the $-z$ direction near the top. At $z = b$, H_z is zero and H_y is not. Then at $z = 2b$, H_y is zero again, etc. Also, H_z is maximum at the top and bottom, and H_y is zero there. The result of all of this is that the magnetic field lines have the general nature shown in Fig. 9.9.

The electric field has only an x component, which goes to zero at the top and bottom. Also, E_x is zero at $z = 0, 2b$, etc. Thus the electric field is as shown in Fig. 9.9 by the circles. The crosses represent E_x in the $+x$ direction and the dots E_x in the $-x$ direction.

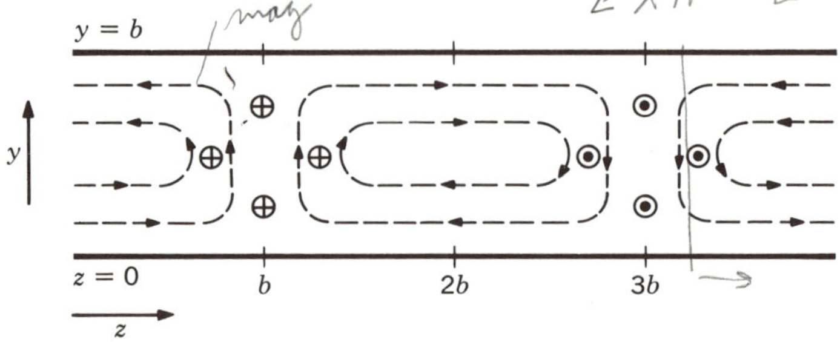

Fig. 9.9 Field patterns of the parallel-plate TE_1 mode. Dotted lines represent magnetic fields and circles represent electric fields. $\gamma_1 = \pi/b$, $\beta_1 = \pi/2b$.

The pattern shown in Fig. 9.9 is repeated at intervals of $4b$ in the z direction. Thus in this case the *wave-guide wavelength* is $\lambda_g = 4b$. The relation between λ_g and β is

$$\lambda_g = \frac{2\pi}{\beta}$$

As time increases, the field pattern shown in Fig. 9.9 moves in the $+z$ direction.

9.9 SEPARATION OF MAXWELL'S EQUATIONS

In Sec. 9.8 it was shown that Maxwell's equations, Eqs. (9.59) and (9.60), could be written in component form in such a way that all the other field components could be found in terms of H_z and E_z. This was shown, however, only for the special case of rectangular coordinates and when $\partial/\partial x = 0$.

The technique is more general, as we might expect, and it can be used with any coordinate system which has a z axis. In our case this means rectangular coordinates and cylindrical coordinates, since the discussions in this book have been limited to the three most commonly used coordinate systems, rectangular, cylindrical, and spherical.

The derivation, which will not be given here, consists of writing Eqs. (9.59) and (9.60) in terms of z components and components transverse to the z direction and then combining these components. In terms of curvilinear coordinate systems, the derivation is based on three assumptions, where u_3 has been taken as equal to z:

1. $h_3 = 1$.
2. h_1 and h_2 do not depend on u_3.
3. $\partial^2/\partial u_3{}^2 = -\beta^2$.

The results are

$$\mathbf{E}_t = \frac{1}{k^2 - \beta^2} \boldsymbol{\nabla}_t \frac{\partial E_z}{\partial z} + \frac{j\omega\mu}{k^2 - \beta^2} \hat{\mathbf{z}} \times \boldsymbol{\nabla}_t H_z \tag{9.94}$$

$$\mathbf{H}_t = \frac{1}{k^2 - \beta^2} \boldsymbol{\nabla}_t \frac{\partial H_z}{\partial z} - \frac{j\omega\epsilon}{k^2 - \beta^2} \hat{\mathbf{z}} \times \boldsymbol{\nabla}_t E_z \tag{9.95}$$

$$(\nabla_t^2 + k^2 - \beta^2)H_z = 0 \tag{9.96}$$

$$(\nabla_t^2 + k^2 - \beta^2)E_z = 0 \tag{9.97}$$

In these equations the operator $\boldsymbol{\nabla}_t$ means the part of the gradient operator which contains no z derivatives. In curvilinear coordinates,

$$\boldsymbol{\nabla}_t E_z = \frac{\hat{\mathbf{u}}_1}{h_1} \frac{\partial E_z}{\partial u_1} + \frac{\hat{\mathbf{u}}_2}{h_2} \frac{\partial E_z}{\partial u_2} \tag{9.98}$$

The ∇_t^2 operator is the part of the laplacian operator which contains no z derivatives. Thus

$$\nabla_t^2 E_z = \frac{1}{h_1 h_2} \left[\frac{\partial}{\partial u_1} \left(\frac{h_2}{h_1} \frac{\partial E_z}{\partial u_1} \right) + \frac{\partial}{\partial u_2} \left(\frac{h_1}{h_2} \frac{\partial E_z}{\partial u_2} \right) \right] \tag{9.99}$$

Note that h_3 has been set equal to 1, which is consistent with the assumptions on which the derivation is based.

Equations (9.94) to (9.97) are very useful because the two wave equations, Eqs. (9.96) and (9.97), can be solved for H_z and E_z by separation of variables, and then all the other field components can be found by using Eqs. (9.94) and (9.95). This technique was illustrated in a simple case in Sec. 9.8. The same method will be used in the next section in a more complicated situation.

9.10 THE RECTANGULAR WAVE GUIDE

The separated Maxwell's equations given in the previous section provide a very convenient method for finding the electromagnetic fields inside the hollow rectangular conductor illustrated in Fig. 9.10. Since waves can propagate in this structure, it is called a *rectangular wave guide*. The field expressions for the rectangular wave guide are like those for the parallel-plate wave guide, modified to include the x variation which results from the walls at $x = 0$ and $x = a$.

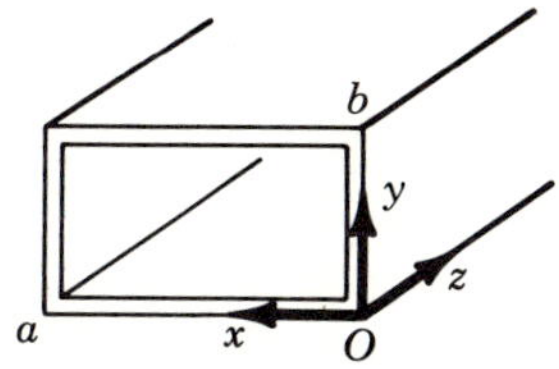

Fig. 9.10 A rectangular wave guide.

From the expressions for the fields of the parallel-plate wave guide, Eqs. (9.87) to (9.92), we can see that each nth field mode consists of the sum of a wave traveling in the $+z$ direction and one traveling in the $-z$ direction. Since the two waves have the same variation with x and y and differ only in their z variation and the arbitrary constant multipliers, it is convenient to consider only the wave traveling in the $+z$ direction. Notice that the expressions for the wave traveling in the $-z$ direction can be obtained from the expressions for the wave traveling in the $+z$ direction simply by changing the sign of β and changing the arbitrary constant multiplier. Then the two waves can be added. This procedure will be used here.

First, consider the TE modes. The expressions for H_z can be found by solving Eq. (9.96),

$$(\nabla_t^2 + k^2 - \beta^2)H_z = 0 \tag{9.96}$$

To separate the variables for $+z$ traveling waves, H_z is assumed to have the form

$$H_z = XYe^{-j\beta z}$$

Putting this in Eq. (9.96) gives

$$\frac{X''}{X} + \frac{Y''}{Y} + k^2 - \beta^2 = 0$$

The separated equations are

$$X'' = -k_x^2 X$$

$$Y'' = -k_y^2 Y$$

where

$$-k_x^2 - k_y^2 + k^2 - \beta^2 = 0 \tag{9.100}$$

The solutions to the equations result in

$$H_z = (A_1 \cos k_x x + A_2 \sin k_x x)(B_1 \cos k_y y + B_2 \sin k_y y)e^{-j\beta z}$$

Since $E_z = 0$ for TE modes, the transverse electric field is found from Eq. (9.94) to be given by

$$\mathbf{E}_t = \frac{j\omega\mu}{k^2 - \beta^2}\,\hat{\mathbf{z}} \times \nabla_t H_z$$

Consequently,

$$\begin{aligned}\mathbf{E}_{t\text{TE}} = {} & \frac{j\omega\mu k_y}{k^2 - \beta^2}(A_1 \cos k_x x + A_2 \sin k_x x)(B_1 \sin k_y y - B_2 \cos k_y y)e^{-j\beta z}\hat{\mathbf{x}} \\ & - \frac{j\omega\mu k_x}{k^2 - \beta^2}(A_1 \sin k_x x - A_2 \cos k_x x)(B_1 \cos k_y y + B_2 \sin k_y y)e^{-j\beta z}\hat{\mathbf{y}}\end{aligned}$$

Assuming that the walls are perfectly conducting, the boundary conditions that the fields must satisfy (see Chap. 5) are

$$E_x = 0 \qquad \text{at } y = 0,\ y = b$$

$$E_y = 0 \qquad \text{at } x = 0,\ x = a$$

From the boundary conditions on E_x it is found that a nontrivial solution requires that

$$B_2 = 0$$

$$k_y = \frac{n\pi}{b} \qquad n = 1, 2, \ldots \tag{9.101}$$

Similarly, the boundary conditions for E_y require that

$$A_2 = 0$$

$$k_x = \frac{m\pi}{a} \qquad m = 1, 2, \ldots \tag{9.102}$$

Now that k_x and k_y are known, β can be found from Eq. (9.100),

$$\beta_{mn}{}^2 = k^2 - \left(\frac{m\pi}{a}\right)^2 - \left(\frac{n\pi}{b}\right)^2 \qquad \text{TE and TM modes} \tag{9.103}$$

Equation (9.103) is very important, as it gives the propagating characteristics of all the TE modes.

The expressions for the fields of the mnth mode (designated TE_{mn}) are

$$H_{zmn} = H_{0mn} \cos \frac{m\pi x}{a} \cos \frac{n\pi y}{b} e^{-j\beta_{mn}z} \tag{9.104}$$

(where H_0 replaces A_1B_1)

$$\mathbf{E}_{t\mathrm{TE}_{mn}} = \frac{j\omega\mu(n\pi/b)}{k^2 - \beta_{mn}{}^2} H_{0mn} \cos \frac{m\pi x}{a} \sin \frac{n\pi y}{b} e^{-j\beta_{mn}z}\hat{\mathbf{x}} - \frac{j\omega\mu(m\pi/a)}{k^2 - \beta_{mn}{}^2} H_{0mn} \sin \frac{m\pi x}{a} \cos \frac{n\pi y}{b} e^{-j\beta_{mn}z}\hat{\mathbf{y}} \tag{9.105}$$

$$\mathbf{H}_{t\mathrm{TE}_{mn}} = \frac{j\beta_{mn}(m\pi/a)}{k^2 - \beta_{mn}{}^2} H_{0mn} \sin \frac{m\pi x}{a} \cos \frac{n\pi y}{b} e^{-j\beta_{mn}z}\hat{\mathbf{x}} + \frac{j\beta_{mn}(n\pi/b)}{k^2 - \beta_{mn}{}^2} H_{0mn} \cos \frac{m\pi x}{a} \sin \frac{n\pi y}{b} e^{-j\beta_{mn}z}\hat{\mathbf{y}} \tag{9.106}$$

The TE_{00} mode is a trivial solution; all the fields are zero. However, the TE_{10}, TE_{01}, and all other modes are nontrivial solutions.

From Eq. (9.103) it is evident that the cutoff frequency is the frequency corresponding to

$$k_{mnco}^2 = \left(\frac{m\pi}{a}\right)^2 + \left(\frac{n\pi}{b}\right)^2 \qquad \text{TE and TM modes} \tag{9.107}$$

The TE_{0n} cutoff frequencies are identical to those of the parallel-plate wave guide of Sec. 9.8. This is to be expected, for when $m = 0$, there is no variation of the rectangular wave-guide fields with x, just as in the parallel-plate wave guide.

The TM modes are easily found by following the same procedure used to obtain the TE modes, starting with the wave equation for E_z. The derivation is left as a problem, but the results are

$$E_{zmn} = E_{0mn} \sin\frac{m\pi x}{a} \sin\frac{n\pi y}{b} e^{-j\beta_{mn}z} \tag{9.108}$$

$$\mathbf{E}_{t\mathrm{TM}_{m}} = \frac{-j\beta_{mn}}{k^2 - \beta_{mn}{}^2}\frac{m\pi}{a} E_{0mn} \cos\frac{m\pi x}{a} \sin\frac{n\pi y}{b} e^{-j\beta_{mn}z}\hat{\mathbf{x}} - \frac{j\beta_{mn}}{k^2 - \beta_{mn}{}^2}\frac{n\pi}{b} E_{0mn} \sin\frac{m\pi x}{a} \cos\frac{n\pi y}{b} e^{-j\beta_{mn}z}\hat{\mathbf{y}} \tag{9.109}$$

$$\mathbf{H}_{t\mathrm{TM}_{mn}} = \frac{j\omega\epsilon}{k^2 - \beta_{mn}{}^2}\frac{n\pi}{b} E_{0mn} \sin\frac{m\pi x}{a} \cos\frac{n\pi y}{b} e^{-j\beta_{mn}z}\hat{\mathbf{x}} - \frac{j\omega\epsilon}{k^2 - \beta_{mn}{}^2}\frac{m\pi}{a} E_{0mn} \cos\frac{m\pi x}{a} \sin\frac{n\pi y}{b} e^{-j\beta_{mn}z}\hat{\mathbf{y}} \tag{9.110}$$

The expressions for β and k_{co} are the same for both TE and TM modes. The TEM mode cannot exist in a rectangular wave guide, because it cannot satisfy the boundary conditions at the walls.

It is interesting to note that for the TE modes either m or n may be zero, but not both; otherwise, all the fields would be zero except H_z, which would be constant. This would be a trivial solution. However, for TM modes, neither m nor n may be zero; otherwise, all the fields would be zero. Hence the lowest-order TM mode is the TM_{11} mode. This means that for a given frequency range the TE_{10} mode is the only mode which is not cut off (for $b < a$). This single-mode propagation is usually desirable. If more than one mode is propagating, power fed into the wave guide is divided among the modes. Since the modes have different field configurations, it is difficult to couple the power back out of the modes at the other end of the wave guide. In addition, multimode propagation complicates the problems involved in impedance matching, etc.

From Eq. (9.107) it can be shown that $b = a/2$ provides the maximum separation between k_{co} for the TE_{10} mode and the next highest mode. The results are summarized in Fig. 9.11. Since the TE_{10} mode has the lowest cutoff frequency, it is the one commonly used in wave-guide systems.

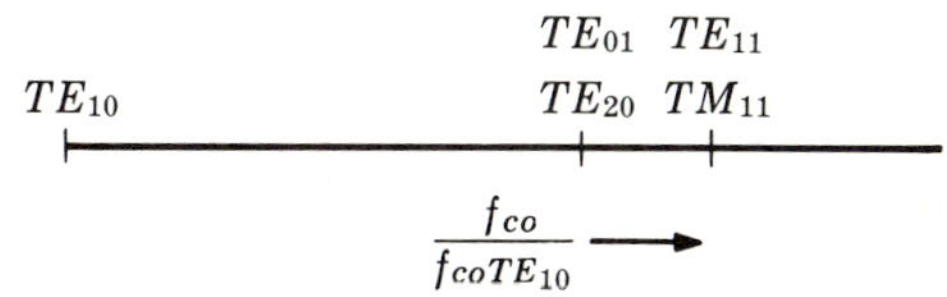

Fig. 9.11 Locations of the cutoff frequencies of the lower-order modes for rectangular wave guide with $b = a/2$.

Example 9.4 Field configuration of the TE$_{10}$ rectangular-wave-guide mode From Eqs. (9.104) to (9.106) the expressions for the fields in the TE$_{10}$ mode are obtained by setting $m = 1$ and $n = 0$. They are

$$H_z = H_0 \cos \frac{\pi x}{a} e^{-j\beta_{10}z}$$

$$\mathbf{E}_t = -\frac{j\omega\mu}{k^2 - \beta_{10}^2} \frac{\pi}{a} H_0 \sin \frac{\pi x}{a} e^{-j\beta_{10}z} \hat{\mathbf{y}}$$

$$\mathbf{H}_t = \frac{j\beta_{10}}{k^2 - \beta_{10}^2} \frac{\pi}{a} H_0 \sin \frac{\pi x}{a} e^{-j\beta_{10}z} \hat{\mathbf{x}}$$

As indicated by $n = 0$, there is no variation of these fields with y.

A schematic illustration of the field configuration is given in Fig. 9.12. The configuration can be determined by the same kind of procedure used in Sec. 9.8 for the parallel-plate wave guide. The view shown in Fig. 9.12 is what would be seen by looking down the wave guide at one instant of time. The E_y lines are shown as solid lines and the H_x are shown as dotted lines. H_z is shown going into the paper on the right and coming out of the paper on the left. The magnetic field lines are thus seen to encircle the electric field lines. The electric field lines begin and terminate on surface charges on the top and bottom walls. The surface charge density is given by Eq. (5.113). There are also surface currents in the walls, which are given by Eq. (5.116).

This field pattern is reversed a half-wavelength down the wave guide at the same instant of time. As time changes, the pattern propagates down the wave guide.

An interesting characteristic of the TE$_{10}$ mode is that E_y and H_x are related by

$$\frac{E_y}{H_x} = -\sqrt{\frac{\mu}{\epsilon}} \frac{k}{\beta_{10}}$$

This is almost like the relation between E and H for a planewave, as given in Eq. (6.7). In fact, it reduces to that result when $\beta_{10} = k$, which would

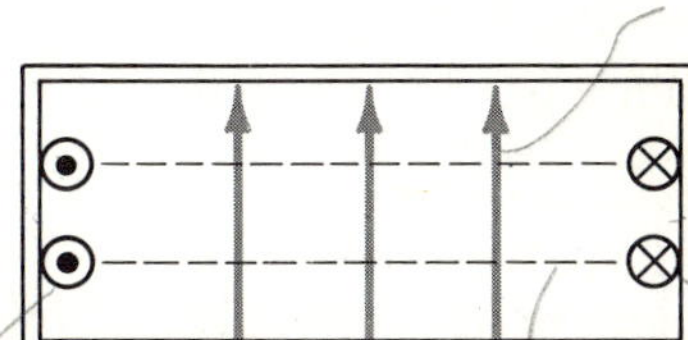

Fig. 9.12 The field configuration for the TE$_{10}$ mode.

be true for a planewave. It is also interesting to note that there is a striking similarity between planewave propagation, wave-guide propagation, and the transmission-line propagation described in Chap. 8. In the planewave and wave-guide case, components of **E** and **H** are related by impedances, while in the transmission-line case V and I are related by impedances. In each case the solutions can be described in terms of traveling waves. The connection between field theory and circuit theory was pointed out by Schelkunoff.†

Since the transmission-line equations were derived from Maxwell's equations, the similarity is perhaps not too surprising. This similarity can be put to good use, because transmission-line theory is a very convenient and useful method of describing wave propagation on two-conductor systems. The impedance concepts and the Smith chart were seen to be very useful tools in Chap. 8. Hence it would seem desirable to be able to describe wave-guide transmission systems in terms of the same concepts and to be able to use tools like the Smith chart. This can be done, as shown in the next section.

In the next section we shall see how a partial separation of variables in Maxwell's equations can lead to expressions for Maxwell's equations which are in the same form as the transmission-line equations in Chap. 8. This derivation shows the connection between Maxwell's equations and the transmission-line equations and hence shows how wave-guide systems can be treated in terms of transmission-line theory.

★9.11 Derivation of Transmission-line Equations for Wave Guides

In Sec. 9.4 was shown how partial-differential equations could be solved by assuming a product solution. For example, to solve a partial-differential equation in E_z, we assumed E_z to be $E_z = X(x)Y(y)Z(z)$, which allowed separation of the partial-differential equation into three ordinary differential equations, one in x, one in y, and one in z. In Sec. 9.9 we saw that Maxwell's equations could be separated in terms of vector components; that is, **E** was separated into two components, $\mathbf{E}_t$ transverse to the z direction and E_z. The same thing was done with **H**, and this allowed separation of the equations into two sets, one for E_z and H_z and the other giving $\mathbf{E}_t$ and $\mathbf{H}_t$ in terms of E_z and H_z.

In this section a combination of the two techniques is used. The vectors are separated into transverse and z components, as in Sec. 9.9, and a partial separation of variables is made as in Sec. 9.4. The derivation is carried out in two parts, one for TEM modes and another for TE and TM modes.

† S. A. Schelkunoff, Transmission Theory of Plane Electromagnetic Waves, *Proc. IRE*, vol. 25, pp. 1457–1492, November, 1937.

In order to keep the derivation independent of a specific coordinate system, curvilinear coordinates are used, but it is assumed that the coordinate system has a z direction. The first step is to separate the curl equations into transverse and z components. The expression for **curl E** is

$$\nabla \times \mathbf{E} = \frac{1}{h_1h_2}\begin{vmatrix} h_1\hat{\mathbf{u}}_1 & h_2\hat{\mathbf{u}}_2 & \hat{\mathbf{z}} \\ \dfrac{\partial}{\partial u_1} & \dfrac{\partial}{\partial u_2} & \dfrac{\partial}{\partial z} \\ h_1E_1 & h_2E_2 & E_z \end{vmatrix}$$

This expression can be written as the sum of three terms,

$$\nabla \times \mathbf{E} = \frac{1}{h_1h_2}\begin{vmatrix} h_1\hat{\mathbf{u}}_1 & h_2\hat{\mathbf{u}}_2 & \hat{\mathbf{z}} \\ \dfrac{\partial}{\partial u_1} & \dfrac{\partial}{\partial u_2} & 0 \\ h_1E_1 & h_2E_2 & 0 \end{vmatrix} + \frac{1}{h_1h_2}\begin{vmatrix} h_1\hat{\mathbf{u}}_1 & h_2\hat{\mathbf{u}}_2 & \hat{\mathbf{z}} \\ 0 & 0 & \dfrac{\partial}{\partial z} \\ h_1E_1 & h_2E_2 & 0 \end{vmatrix} + \frac{1}{h_1h_2}\begin{vmatrix} h_1\hat{\mathbf{u}}_1 & h_2\hat{\mathbf{u}}_2 & \hat{\mathbf{z}} \\ \dfrac{\partial}{\partial u_1} & \dfrac{\partial}{\partial u_2} & 0 \\ 0 & 0 & E_z \end{vmatrix} \quad (9.111)$$

Now the definitions are made that

$$\nabla_t \times \mathbf{E}_t = \frac{1}{h_1h_2}\begin{vmatrix} h_1\hat{\mathbf{u}}_1 & h_2\hat{\mathbf{u}}_2 & \hat{\mathbf{z}} \\ \dfrac{\partial}{\partial u_1} & \dfrac{\partial}{\partial u_2} & 0 \\ h_1E_1 & h_2E_2 & 0 \end{vmatrix} \quad (9.112)$$

$$\nabla_t \times \mathbf{E}_z = \frac{1}{h_1h_2}\begin{vmatrix} h_1\hat{\mathbf{u}}_1 & h_2\hat{\mathbf{u}}_2 & \hat{\mathbf{z}} \\ \dfrac{\partial}{\partial u_1} & \dfrac{\partial}{\partial u_2} & 0 \\ 0 & 0 & E_z \end{vmatrix} \quad (9.113)$$

$$\nabla_z \times \mathbf{E}_t = \frac{1}{h_1h_2}\begin{vmatrix} h_1\hat{\mathbf{u}}_1 & h_2\hat{\mathbf{u}}_2 & \hat{\mathbf{z}} \\ 0 & 0 & \dfrac{\partial}{\partial z} \\ h_1E_1 & h_2E_2 & 0 \end{vmatrix} \quad (9.114)$$

$$\mathbf{E}_t = E_1\hat{\mathbf{u}}_1 + E_2\hat{\mathbf{u}}_2$$

$$\mathbf{E}_z = E_z\hat{\mathbf{z}}$$

The subscript t stands for transverse, or perpendicular to $\hat{\mathbf{z}}$.

From the definitions we see that $\nabla_t \times \mathbf{E}_t$ has only a $\hat{\mathbf{z}}$ component, and $\nabla_z \times \mathbf{E}_t$ and $\nabla_t \times \mathbf{E}_z$ have no $\hat{\mathbf{z}}$ components. Thus the **curl E** equation, Eq. (9.59), can be written as

$$\nabla \times \mathbf{E} = \nabla_t \times \mathbf{E}_t + \nabla_z \times \mathbf{E}_t + \nabla_t \times \mathbf{E}_z$$
$$= -j\omega\mu\mathbf{H}_t - j\omega\mu\mathbf{H}_z$$

Since transverse components on the left must equal transverse components on the right, and z components on the left must equal z components on the right,

$$\nabla_t \times \mathbf{E}_t = -j\omega\mu\mathbf{H}_z \tag{9.115}$$

$$\nabla_t \times \mathbf{E}_z + \nabla_z \times \mathbf{E}_t = -j\omega\mu\mathbf{H}_t \tag{9.116}$$

In a similar way, Eq. (9.60), the **curl H** equation, can be written as

$$\nabla_t \times \mathbf{H}_t = j\omega\epsilon\mathbf{E}_z \tag{9.117}$$

$$\nabla_t \times \mathbf{H}_z + \nabla_z \times \mathbf{H}_t = j\omega\epsilon\mathbf{E}_t \tag{9.118}$$

Equations (9.115) to (9.118) are Maxwell's equations separated into transverse and z components.

Transmission-line Equations for TEM Modes on Guiding Structures

TEM modes consist of **E** and **H** fields which are transverse to the z direction. These are labeled $\mathbf{E}_t$ and $\mathbf{H}_t$. The z components, H_z and E_z, are zero. This being the case, Eq. (9.115) becomes

$$\nabla_t \times \mathbf{E}_t = 0$$

and hence $\mathbf{E}_t$ can be written as

$$\mathbf{E}_t = -\nabla_t\Phi \tag{9.119}$$

where Φ is a scalar potential. Because Eq. (9.119) is the same as Eq. (2.8) when $E_z = 0$, the TEM fields have the same spacial distribution as static fields, even though they are not static. It follows, then, that capacitance and inductance, which are quasi-static parameters, can also be legitimately defined for high-frequency TEM modes on guiding structures. Consequently, the TEM modes are equivalent to the quasi-static transmission-line modes, and the same transmission-line equations may be obtained either from the quasi-static approach or from Maxwell's equations. The quasi-static approach was outlined in Sec. 8.3, where it was shown that TEM waves propagate on a two-wire transmission line. The derivation which follows is based on Maxwell's equations with no quasi-static restriction.

A *partial* separation of variables of the type made in Sec. 9.4 is made by defining

$$\mathbf{E}_t = V(z,t)\boldsymbol{\mathcal{E}}_t(u_1,u_2) \tag{9.120}$$

$$\mathbf{H}_t = I(z,t)\boldsymbol{\mathcal{H}}_t(u_1,u_2) \tag{9.121}$$

The script functions $\boldsymbol{\mathcal{E}}_t$ and $\boldsymbol{\mathcal{H}}_t$, called *normalized field functions,* are functions only of the variables transverse to z. At this point the relative magnitudes of V, I, $\boldsymbol{\mathcal{E}}_t$, and $\boldsymbol{\mathcal{H}}_t$ are arbitrary. As the derivation develops, the $\boldsymbol{\mathcal{E}}_t$ and $\boldsymbol{\mathcal{H}}_t$ will be normalized. The z and t dependence is contained in V and I, which will be shown to be voltage and current for TEM waves on transmission lines.

The procedure is to substitute Eqs. (9.120) and (9.121) into Eqs. (9.116) and (9.118), respectively, while at the same time setting $E_z = H_z = 0$. The result is

$$\nabla_z \times V\boldsymbol{\mathcal{E}}_t = -j\omega\mu I\boldsymbol{\mathcal{H}}_t$$

$$\nabla_z \times I\boldsymbol{\mathcal{H}}_t = j\omega\epsilon V\boldsymbol{\mathcal{E}}_t$$

Since $\boldsymbol{\mathcal{E}}_t$ and $\boldsymbol{\mathcal{H}}_t$ do not depend on z, these equations can be written (by expanding the vector product) in the form

$$\frac{\partial V}{\partial z}\hat{\mathbf{z}} \times \boldsymbol{\mathcal{E}}_t = -j\omega\mu I\boldsymbol{\mathcal{H}}_t \tag{9.122}$$

$$\frac{\partial I}{\partial z}\hat{\mathbf{z}} \times \boldsymbol{\mathcal{H}}_t = j\omega\epsilon V\boldsymbol{\mathcal{E}}_t \tag{9.123}$$

It has been assumed that h_1 and h_2 are not functions of z. Equation (9.114) was used to evaluate $\nabla_z \times V\boldsymbol{\mathcal{E}}_t$, etc.

The next step is to take the cross product of $\boldsymbol{\mathcal{E}}_t^*$ and both sides of Eq. (9.122). This results in

$$\frac{\partial V}{\partial z}\boldsymbol{\mathcal{E}}_t^* \times (\hat{\mathbf{z}} \times \boldsymbol{\mathcal{E}}_t) = -j\omega\mu I\boldsymbol{\mathcal{E}}_t^* \times \boldsymbol{\mathcal{H}}_t$$

By a vector identity,

$$\begin{aligned}\boldsymbol{\mathcal{E}}_t^* \times (\hat{\mathbf{z}} \times \boldsymbol{\mathcal{E}}_t) &= \boldsymbol{\mathcal{E}}_t \cdot \boldsymbol{\mathcal{E}}_t^*\hat{\mathbf{z}} - \boldsymbol{\mathcal{E}}_t^* \cdot \hat{\mathbf{z}}\boldsymbol{\mathcal{E}}_t \\ &= \boldsymbol{\mathcal{E}}_t \cdot \boldsymbol{\mathcal{E}}_t^*\hat{\mathbf{z}}\end{aligned}$$

since $\boldsymbol{\mathcal{E}}_t^*$ and $\hat{\mathbf{z}}$ are orthogonal. Thus

$$\frac{\partial V}{\partial z}\boldsymbol{\mathcal{E}}_t \cdot \boldsymbol{\mathcal{E}}_t^*\hat{\mathbf{z}} = -j\omega\mu I\boldsymbol{\mathcal{E}}_t^* \times \boldsymbol{\mathcal{H}}_t \tag{9.124}$$

In order to take into account the transverse configuration of the transmission system, we integrate Eq. (9.120) over the cross section. Then

$$\frac{\partial V}{\partial z}\int_S \boldsymbol{\mathcal{E}}_t \cdot \boldsymbol{\mathcal{E}}_t^* \, dS = -j\omega\mu I \int_S \boldsymbol{\mathcal{E}}_t^* \times \boldsymbol{\mathcal{H}}_t \cdot d\mathbf{S}$$

or

$$\frac{\partial V}{\partial z} = -j\omega\mu \frac{\int_S \boldsymbol{\mathcal{E}}_t^* \times \boldsymbol{\mathcal{H}}_t \cdot d\mathbf{S}}{\int_S \boldsymbol{\mathcal{E}}_t \cdot \boldsymbol{\mathcal{E}}_t^* \, dS} I \tag{9.125}$$

Up to this point, no restriction has been placed on V, I, $\boldsymbol{\mathcal{E}}_t$, and $\boldsymbol{\mathcal{H}}_t$ except that they are functions of certain variables only. It is convenient now to stipulate that the time-average power propagating down the system be given by

$$\begin{aligned}\langle P \rangle &= \tfrac{1}{2} \operatorname{Re} VI^* \\ &= \tfrac{1}{2} \operatorname{Re} V^*I\end{aligned} \tag{9.126}$$

In terms of the fields, the time-average power is obtained by integrating the z component of the time-average of Poynting's vector over the cross section of the transmission system,

$$\begin{aligned}\langle P \rangle &= \tfrac{1}{2} \operatorname{Re} \int_S \mathbf{E}_t \times \mathbf{H}_t^* \cdot d\mathbf{S} \\ &= \tfrac{1}{2} \operatorname{Re} \int_S \mathbf{E}_t^* \times \mathbf{H}_t \cdot d\mathbf{S}\end{aligned} \tag{9.127}$$

The substitution of Eqs. (9.120) and (9.121) gives

$$\langle P \rangle = \tfrac{1}{2} \operatorname{Re} VI^* \int_S \boldsymbol{\mathcal{E}}_t \times \boldsymbol{\mathcal{H}}_t^* \cdot d\mathbf{S} \tag{9.128}$$

If Eq. (9.126) is to be valid, it is necessary, as indicated by Eq. (9.128), to set

$$\begin{aligned}\int_S \boldsymbol{\mathcal{E}}_t \times \boldsymbol{\mathcal{H}}_t^* \cdot d\mathbf{S} &= \int_S \boldsymbol{\mathcal{E}}_t^* \times \boldsymbol{\mathcal{H}}_t \cdot d\mathbf{S} \\ &= 1\end{aligned} \tag{9.129}$$

Equation (9.129) is one normalizing relation which affects the amplitudes of $\boldsymbol{\mathcal{E}}_t$ and $\boldsymbol{\mathcal{H}}_t$.

With Eq. (9.129), Eq. (9.125) becomes

$$\frac{\partial V}{\partial z} = \frac{-j\omega\mu}{\int_S \boldsymbol{\mathcal{E}}_t \cdot \boldsymbol{\mathcal{E}}_t^* \, dS} I \tag{9.130}$$

Similarly, if the cross product of $\boldsymbol{\mathcal{H}}_t^*$ and Eq. (9.123) is taken, and Eq.

(9.129) is used, a companion equation is obtained,

$$\frac{\partial I}{\partial z} = \frac{-j\omega\epsilon}{\int_S \mathcal{H}_t \cdot \mathcal{H}_t^* \, dS} V \tag{9.131}$$

Equations (9.130) and (9.131) can be put in the form of Eqs. (8.16) and (8.17) by evaluating the integrals in terms of inductance and capacitance. The validity of the use of inductance and capacitance here was discussed at the beginning of this section. From Eq. (7.51), the time-average energy stored in the electric fields of a capacitor is

$$\langle W_e \rangle = \tfrac{1}{4} \operatorname{Re} VV^* C \tag{7.51}$$

The time-average energy stored per unit length in the electric fields of a TEM mode can be obtained by taking the time average of Eq. (5.118) and integrating. The result is

$$\langle \mathcal{W}_e \rangle = \tfrac{1}{4} \operatorname{Re} \int_S \epsilon \mathbf{E}_t \cdot \mathbf{E}_t^* \, dS \tag{9.132}$$

where the integration is taken over a constant z plane. Substituting Eq. (9.120) in Eq. (9.132) results in

$$\langle \mathcal{W}_e \rangle = \tfrac{1}{4} \operatorname{Re} VV^* \int_S \epsilon \boldsymbol{\mathcal{E}}_t \cdot \boldsymbol{\mathcal{E}}_t^* \, dS \tag{9.133}$$

Because of the similarity between Eqs. (9.133) and (7.51), it makes sense to normalize $\boldsymbol{\mathcal{E}}_t$ according to

$$\int_S \boldsymbol{\mathcal{E}}_t \cdot \boldsymbol{\mathcal{E}}_t^* \, dS = \frac{C}{\epsilon} \tag{9.134}$$

where C is the capacitance per unit length of the transmission system.

Similarly, since the time-average energy stored in the magnetic fields of an inductor is

$$\langle W_m \rangle = \tfrac{1}{4} \operatorname{Re} II^* L \tag{7.33}$$

and the time-average energy stored per unit length in the magnetic field of a TEM mode is

$$\langle \mathcal{W}_m \rangle = \tfrac{1}{4} \operatorname{Re} II^* \int_S \mu \mathcal{H}_t \cdot \mathcal{H}_t^* \, dS \tag{9.135}$$

$\mathcal{H}_t$ is normalized according to

$$\int_S \mathcal{H}_t \cdot \mathcal{H}_t^* \, dS = \frac{L}{\mu} \tag{9.136}$$

where L is the inductance per unit length of the transmission system.

With the normalizations of Eqs. (9.134) and (9.136), Eqs. (9.130) and (9.131) become

$$\frac{\partial V}{\partial z} = -\frac{j\omega\mu\epsilon}{C} I \tag{9.137}$$

$$\frac{\partial I}{\partial z} = -\frac{j\omega\mu\epsilon}{L} V \tag{9.138}$$

Equations (9.137) and (9.138) can be put in a more standard form by combining them with Eqs. (9.122) and (9.123). Substituting Eq. (9.137) into Eq. (9.122) and Eq. (9.138) into Eq. (9.123) results in

$$\hat{\mathbf{z}} \times \boldsymbol{\mathcal{E}}_t = \frac{C}{\epsilon} \boldsymbol{\mathcal{H}}_t \tag{9.139}$$

$$\hat{\mathbf{z}} \times \boldsymbol{\mathcal{H}}_t = -\frac{L}{\mu} \boldsymbol{\mathcal{E}}_t \tag{9.140}$$

From Eqs. (9.139) and (9.140) it is easily seen that

$$LC = \mu\epsilon \tag{9.141}$$

Combining Eq. (9.141) with Eqs. (9.137) and (9.138) yields the same kind of transmission-line equations obtained from the circuit approach in Sec. 8.3

$$\frac{\partial V}{\partial z} = -j\omega LI \tag{9.142}$$

$$\frac{\partial I}{\partial z} = -j\omega CV \tag{9.143}$$

Since these equations are the same as Eqs. (8.18) and (8.19) (for the lossless case), the $V(z,t)$ and $I(z,t)$ parameters are voltage and current. The capacitance and inductance of the transmission system can be found by the methods described in Chap. 7.

Thus it has been shown that for TEM modes the same transmission-line equations obtained from the quasi-static approximations in Sec. 8.3 may be obtained directly from Maxwell's equations with no quasi-static approximation. Although quasi-static and high-frequency TEM modes on two conductor lines are equivalent, there is a difference between the transmission characteristics of a two-wire line at low and high frequencies. The difference is that modes other than TEM modes can propagate at higher frequencies, and therefore the TEM mode is not a complete description of propagation effects at higher frequencies.

Transmission-line Equations for TEM Modes in Free Space

The principal differences between the derivation of the transmission-line equations for TEM modes in free space and TEM modes on guiding structures is one of normalization of $\mathcal{E}_t$ and $\mathcal{H}_t$. As was pointed out earlier, the relative amplitudes of V and $\mathcal{E}_t$ and I and $\mathcal{H}_t$ are arbitrary and can be chosen to be any convenient values. For example, Eqs. (9.120) and (9.121) can be written as

$$\mathcal{E}_t = \frac{V}{P} P\mathcal{E}_t$$

$$\mathcal{H}_t = \frac{I}{Q} Q\mathcal{H}_t$$

without changing the values of $\mathbf{E}_t$ and $\mathbf{H}_t$. The quantities P and Q are arbitrary constants. Changing the normalization of $\mathcal{E}_t$ (multiplying $\mathcal{E}_t$ by an arbitrary constant P) is seen to be equivalent to changing the normalization of V accordingly (dividing V by P). Thus changing the normalization of $\mathcal{E}_t$ and $\mathcal{H}_t$ results in different normalization for V and I. In the previous section the normalization of $\mathcal{E}_t$ and $\mathcal{H}_t$ in terms of capacitance and inductance resulted in V and I being voltage and current in the quasi-static sense. This was obviously a very convenient normalization. But capacitance and inductance have no meaning for planewaves in free space because there is no guiding structure present. Consequently, another normalization for $\mathcal{E}_t$ and $\mathcal{H}_t$ may be chosen which is more convenient. As will be seen, a normalization is chosen such that the equivalent transmission-line impedance is the planewave intrinsic impedance $E_t/H_t = \sqrt{\mu/\epsilon}$ [see Eq. (6.7)]. Later, in the normalization for TE and TM modes in a wave guide, the normalization is chosen such that the equivalent transmission-line impedance is the wave-guide wave impedance. The wave-guide wave impedance is defined in a way analogous to the intrinsic impedance for planewaves and will be discussed in Sec. 9.12. It is expected that the V and I parameters resulting from these other normalizations would not be voltage and current in the quasi-static sense, because the concept of voltage is not valid in a non-quasi-static analysis.

The derivation for the planewave case is the same as that of the previous section up to Eqs. (9.130) and (9.131). The remainder of the derivation involves a different normalization. Substituting Eqs. (9.130) and (9.131) into Eqs. (9.122) and (9.123), respectively, results in

$$\hat{\mathbf{z}} \times \mathcal{E}_t = \mathcal{H}_t \int_S \mathcal{E}_t \cdot \mathcal{E}_t^* \, dS \tag{9.144}$$

$$\hat{\mathbf{z}} \times \mathcal{H}_t = -\mathcal{E}_t \int_S \mathcal{H}_t \cdot \mathcal{H}_t^* \, dS \tag{9.145}$$

Solving Eq. (9.144) for $\mathcal{H}_t$ and substituting into Eq. (9.145) results in

$$\int_S \mathcal{E}_t \cdot \mathcal{E}_t^* \, dS \int_S \mathcal{H}_t \cdot \mathcal{H}_t^* \, dS = 1 \tag{9.146}$$

The normalization of Eq. (9.129) and the relations between $\mathcal{E}_t$ and $\mathcal{H}_t$ indicated in Eqs. (9.122) and (9.123) thus require the relation between $\mathcal{E}_t$ and $\mathcal{H}_t$ shown in Eq. (9.146), but otherwise, the normalization of $\mathcal{E}_t$ and $\mathcal{H}_t$ is not yet specified. The simplest normalization which satisfies Eq. (9.146) is

$$\int_S \mathcal{E}_t \cdot \mathcal{E}_t^* \, dS = 1 \tag{9.147}$$

$$\int_S \mathcal{H}_t \cdot \mathcal{H}_t^* \, dS = 1 \tag{9.148}$$

and as we shall see, this sets the transmission-line characteristic impedance equal to the planewave impedance E/H.

Since $\mathcal{E}_t$ and $\mathcal{H}_t$ do not vary with u_1 and u_2 for a TEM wave in free space, the integrals in Eqs. (9.147) and (9.148) would be infinite if they were evaluated over an infinite cross section. Consequently, the surface S is taken to be a unit surface.

With the normalization of Eqs. (9.147) and (9.148), the transmission-line equations, Eqs. (9.130) and (9.131), are

$$\frac{\partial V}{\partial z} = -j\omega\mu I \tag{9.149}$$

$$\frac{\partial I}{\partial z} = -j\omega\epsilon V \tag{9.150}$$

for a TEM wave in free space.

Transmission-line Equations for TE and TM Modes

For TE and TM modes, the separation of variables indicated in Eqs. (9.120) and (9.121) for TEM modes can be made, but like the TEM wave in free space, the V and I are not voltage and current. Nevertheless, the same kind of transmission-line equations can be obtained for TE and TM modes, and the resulting V and I, which are analogous to the quasi-static voltage and current, are useful parameters.

In the following derivation, the TE equations are written on the left side of the page and the TM equations are written on the right. The derivations for the two cases are parallel. The derivation is much like that for the TEM wave in free space, the difference being that an E_z or H_z is present here. The same normalization procedure used for the TEM wave in free space is used here.

The field quantities are defined by

TE	TM	
$\mathbf{E} = V(z,t)\boldsymbol{\varepsilon}_t(u_1,u_2)$	$\mathbf{E} = V(z,t)\boldsymbol{\varepsilon}_t(u_1,u_2) + \mathbf{E}_z$	(9.151)
$\mathbf{H} = I(z,t)\boldsymbol{\mathcal{H}}_t(u_1,u_2) + \mathbf{H}_z$	$\mathbf{H} = I(z,t)\boldsymbol{\mathcal{H}}_t(u_1,u_2)$	(9.152)

E_z and H_z need not be separated at this point. Substituting Eqs. (9.151) and (9.152) into the appropriate forms of Eqs. (9.116) and (9.118) results in

TE	TM	
$\frac{\partial V}{\partial z}\hat{\mathbf{z}} \times \boldsymbol{\varepsilon}_t = -j\omega\mu I\boldsymbol{\mathcal{H}}_t$	$\frac{\partial V}{\partial z}\hat{\mathbf{z}} \times \boldsymbol{\varepsilon}_t = -j\omega\mu I\boldsymbol{\mathcal{H}}_t - \boldsymbol{\nabla}_t \times \mathbf{E}_z$	(9.153)
$\frac{\partial I}{\partial z}\hat{\mathbf{z}} \times \boldsymbol{\mathcal{H}}_t = j\omega\epsilon V\boldsymbol{\varepsilon}_t - \boldsymbol{\nabla}_t \times \mathbf{H}_z$	$\frac{\partial I}{\partial z}\hat{\mathbf{z}} \times \boldsymbol{\mathcal{H}}_t = j\omega\epsilon V\boldsymbol{\varepsilon}_t$	(9.154)

As for the TEM wave in free space, the normalization is taken to be

$$\int_S \boldsymbol{\varepsilon}_t \times \boldsymbol{\mathcal{H}}_t^* \cdot d\mathbf{S} = \int_S \boldsymbol{\varepsilon}_t^* \times \boldsymbol{\mathcal{H}}_t \cdot d\mathbf{S} = 1 \tag{9.155}$$

$$\int_S \boldsymbol{\varepsilon}_t \cdot \boldsymbol{\varepsilon}_t^* \, dS = \int_S \boldsymbol{\mathcal{H}}_t \cdot \boldsymbol{\mathcal{H}}_t^* \, dS = 1 \tag{9.156}$$

where the integration is over the cross section S of the transmission system.

Taking the cross product of $\boldsymbol{\varepsilon}_t^*$ and Eq. (9.153) for TE modes and of $\boldsymbol{\mathcal{H}}_t^*$ and Eq. (9.154) for TM modes results in

TE	TM	
$\frac{\partial V}{\partial z}\boldsymbol{\varepsilon}_t \cdot \boldsymbol{\varepsilon}_t^* = -j\omega\mu I\boldsymbol{\varepsilon}_t^* \times \boldsymbol{\mathcal{H}}_t$	$\frac{\partial I}{\partial z}\boldsymbol{\mathcal{H}}_t \cdot \boldsymbol{\mathcal{H}}_t^* = j\omega\epsilon V\boldsymbol{\mathcal{H}}_t^* \times \boldsymbol{\varepsilon}_t$	(9.157)

These equations are integrated over the cross section, and Eqs. (9.155) and (9.156) are used to obtain

TE	TM	
$\frac{\partial V}{\partial z} = -j\omega\mu I$	$\frac{\partial I}{\partial z} = -j\omega\epsilon V$	(9.158)

which are the first transmission-line equations.

From Eqs. (9.158), (9.153) (left), and (9.154) (right), a relation between $\mathcal{E}_t$ and $\mathcal{H}_t$ can be obtained,

TE	TM
$\hat{\mathbf{z}} \times \mathcal{E}_t = \mathcal{H}_t$	$\hat{\mathbf{z}} \times \mathcal{H}_t = -\mathcal{E}_t$

(9.159)

Note that Eqs. (9.159) are the same relation for TE and TM modes.

Equations relating $\mathcal{E}_t$ to $\mathbf{H}_z$ and $\mathcal{H}_t$ to $\mathbf{E}_z$ can be obtained by combining Eq. (9.153) (right) and (9.154) (left) and Eqs. (9.159),

TE	TM
$\mathcal{E}_t = \dfrac{\nabla_t \times \mathbf{H}_z}{j\omega\epsilon V + \partial I/\partial z}$	$\mathcal{H}_t = \dfrac{-\nabla_t \times \mathbf{E}_z}{j\omega\mu I + \partial V/\partial z}$

(9.160)

Another useful relation is obtained by substituting Eqs. (9.151) and (9.152) into Eqs. (9.115) and (9.117),

TE	TM
$V\nabla_t \times \mathcal{E}_t = -j\omega\mu\mathbf{H}_z$	$I\nabla_t \times \mathcal{H}_t = j\omega\epsilon\mathbf{E}_z$

(9.161)

Substituting Eqs. (9.160) into (9.161) results in the wave equations

TE	TM
$\left[\nabla_t^2 + \left(k^2 - \dfrac{j\omega\mu}{V}\dfrac{\partial I}{\partial z}\right)\right] H_z = 0$	$\left[\nabla_t^2 + \left(k^2 - \dfrac{j\omega\epsilon}{I}\dfrac{\partial V}{\partial z}\right)\right] E_z = 0$

(9.162)

where

$$\nabla_t \times \nabla_t \times \mathbf{H}_z = -\hat{\mathbf{z}}\nabla_t^2 H_z + \nabla_t(\nabla_t \cdot \mathbf{H}_z)$$
$$\nabla_t \times \nabla_t \times \mathbf{E}_z = -\hat{\mathbf{z}}\nabla_t^2 E_z + \nabla_t(\nabla_t \cdot \mathbf{E}_z)$$

and

TE	TM
$\nabla_t \cdot \mathbf{H}_z = 0$	$\nabla_t \cdot \mathbf{E}_z = 0$

have been used. It is convenient now to make the definitions

TE	TM	
$\gamma^2 = k^2 - \frac{j\omega\mu}{V}\frac{\partial I}{\partial z}$	$\gamma^2 = k^2 - \frac{j\omega\epsilon}{I}\frac{\partial V}{\partial z}$	(9.163)

so that

TE	TM	
$(\nabla_t^2 + \gamma^2)H_z = 0$	$(\nabla_t^2 + \gamma^2)E_z = 0$	(9.164)

These wave equations can be put into a more convenient form by writing $\mathbf{H}_z$ and $\mathbf{E}_z$ in terms of normalized field functions $\boldsymbol{\mathcal{H}}_z$ and $\boldsymbol{\mathcal{E}}_z$. This can be done by combining Eqs. (9.163) with Eqs. (9.160) to get

TE	TM	
$\boldsymbol{\mathcal{E}}_t = -\frac{j\omega\mu}{\gamma^2 V}\nabla_t \times \mathbf{H}_z$	$\boldsymbol{\mathcal{H}}_t = \frac{j\omega\epsilon}{\gamma^2 I}\nabla_t \times \mathbf{E}_z$	(9.165)

It is apparent from the expression on the left that H_z must be proportional to V, because $\boldsymbol{\mathcal{E}}_t$ is not a function of t or z, and yet there is a V in the denominator which is a function of both z and t. Similarly, it is apparent from the expression on the right that E_z must be proportional to I. Hence we set

$$\mathbf{H}_z = V\boldsymbol{\mathcal{H}}_z \tag{9.166}$$

$$\mathbf{E}_z = I\boldsymbol{\mathcal{E}}_z \tag{9.167}$$

where $\boldsymbol{\mathcal{H}}_z$ and $\boldsymbol{\mathcal{E}}_z$ are normalized field functions which are like $\boldsymbol{\mathcal{H}}_t$ and $\boldsymbol{\mathcal{E}}_t$; they are functions only of u_1 and u_2.

Substituting Eqs. (9.166) and (9.167) into Eqs. (9.164) results in

TE	TM	
$(\nabla_t^2 + \gamma^2)\mathcal{H}_z = 0$	$(\nabla_t^2 + \gamma^2)\mathcal{E}_z = 0$	(9.168)

Substituting Eqs. (9.166) and (9.167) into Eqs. (9.165) results in

TE	TM	
$\boldsymbol{\mathcal{E}}_t = -\frac{j\omega\mu}{\gamma^2}\nabla_t \times \boldsymbol{\mathcal{H}}_t$	$\boldsymbol{\mathcal{H}}_t = \frac{j\omega\epsilon}{\gamma^2}\nabla_t \times \boldsymbol{\mathcal{E}}_t$	(9.169)

The quantity γ is an eigenvalue which is determined solely by the transverse boundary conditions. It is shown in Sec. 9.12 that when the boundaries are perfect conductors, all the boundary conditions are satisfied if

TE	TM
$\hat{\mathbf{n}} \cdot \nabla_t \mathcal{H}_z = 0$	$\mathcal{E}_z = 0$

(9.170)

at the boundaries, where $\hat{\mathbf{n}}$ is the unit normal to the boundary. Therefore γ can be found by requiring $\mathcal{H}_z$ and $\mathcal{E}_z$ to satisfy the above boundary conditions. Hence the transmission characteristics can be found without ever finding $\boldsymbol{\mathcal{E}}_t$ and $\boldsymbol{\mathcal{H}}_t$. All that is required is that the wave equations, Eqs. (9.168), be solved for $\mathcal{H}_z$ and $\mathcal{E}_z$, and γ be evaluated by requiring $\mathcal{H}_z$ and $\mathcal{E}_z$ to satisfy transverse boundary conditions.

In general, there is a doubly infinite set of values of γ, which is designated by γ_{mn}. Corresponding to each eigenvalue γ_{mn} there is a set of propagating fields, which is called a mode. Thus there is a V_{mn} and an I_{mn} which, according to Eq. (9.163), must satisfy the relations

TE	TM
$\gamma_{mn}{}^2 = k^2 - \dfrac{j\omega\mu}{V_{mn}} \dfrac{\partial I_{mn}}{\partial z}$	$\gamma_{mn}{}^2 = k^2 - \dfrac{j\omega\epsilon}{I_{mn}} \dfrac{\partial V_{mn}}{\partial z}$

(9.171)

A rearrangement of Eq. (9.171) results in the second set of transmission-line equations,

TE	TM
$\dfrac{\partial I_{mn}}{\partial z} = \dfrac{k^2 - \gamma_{mn}{}^2}{j\omega\mu} V_{mn}$	$\dfrac{\partial V_{mn}}{\partial z} = \dfrac{k^2 - \gamma_{mn}{}^2}{j\omega\epsilon} I_{mn}$

(9.172)

The corresponding transmission-line equations obtained from Eqs. (9.158) are

TE	TM
$\dfrac{\partial V_{mn}}{\partial z} = -j\omega\mu I_{mn}$	$\dfrac{\partial I_{mn}}{\partial z} = -j\omega\epsilon V_{mn}$

(9.173)

Equations (9.172) and (9.173) are transmission-line equations for the *mn*th TE and TM modes. Each of the TE_{mn} and TM_{mn} modes is thus represented by a different transmission-line equation. We know this must be true because the propagation constant is determined by the transmission-line equations (they contain the z variation), and from the results of Sec. 9.10 we know that the TE_{mn} and TM_{mn} modes have different propagation constants. Equations (9.172) and (9.173) are in the form of Eqs. (8.18) and (8.19) with the impedances and admittances given by

TE	TM	
$Z_{mn} = j\omega\mu$	$Z_{mn} = j\omega\mu - j\dfrac{\gamma_{mn}{}^2}{\omega\epsilon}$	(9.174)
$Y_{mn} = j\omega\epsilon - j\dfrac{\gamma_{mn}{}^2}{\omega\mu}$	$Y_{mn} = j\omega\epsilon$	(9.175)

Thus it has been shown that a rigorous separation-of-variables technique can be used to obtain equations having the form of transmission-line equations which describe the propagation characteristics of TE and TM modes. Consequently, the transmission-line theory and techniques developed in Chap. 8 can be applied to wave-guide systems.

Transverse Boundary Conditions on $\mathcal{H}_z$ and $\mathcal{E}_z$

Because of the relations between the transverse fields, $\mathbf{E}_t$ and $\mathbf{H}_t$, and the fields $\mathcal{E}_z$ and $\mathcal{H}_z$, it can be shown that in the case of perfectly conducting boundaries, all the boundary conditions are satisfied if the boundary conditions in $\mathcal{H}_z$ and $\mathcal{E}_z$ given in Eqs. (9.170) are satisfied. First consider the TE modes. The boundary conditions are that the tangential $\mathbf{E}$ fields and the normal $\mathbf{H}$ fields are zero at the perfectly conducting boundaries. From Eqs. (9.151) and (9.152) it is apparent that $\boldsymbol{\mathcal{E}}_t$ and $\boldsymbol{\mathcal{H}}_t$ must satisfy the same transverse boundary conditions as $\mathbf{E}_t$ and $\mathbf{H}_t$ because V and I are not functions of u_1 and u_2. Then the boundary condition on $\boldsymbol{\mathcal{E}}_t$ is that its component parallel to the wall is zero, or

$$\hat{\mathbf{n}} \times \boldsymbol{\mathcal{E}}_t = 0 \tag{9.176}$$

where $\hat{\mathbf{n}}$ is the unit normal at the boundary (see Table 5.3). Substituting Eq. (9.169) (left) into Eq. (9.176) results in

$$\hat{\mathbf{n}} \times (\boldsymbol{\nabla}_t \times \boldsymbol{\mathcal{H}}_z) = 0 \tag{9.177}$$

But, as can be shown by direct expansion,

$$\boldsymbol{\nabla}_t \times \boldsymbol{\mathcal{H}}_z = -\hat{\mathbf{z}} \times \boldsymbol{\nabla}_t \mathcal{H}_z \tag{9.178}$$

Hence Eq. (9.177) becomes

$$\hat{\mathbf{n}} \times (\hat{\mathbf{z}} \times \boldsymbol{\nabla}_t \mathcal{H}_z) = 0$$

and by a vector identity this relation becomes Eq. (9.170) for TE modes,

$$\hat{\mathbf{n}} \cdot \boldsymbol{\nabla}_t \mathcal{H}_z = 0 \tag{9.170}$$

since $\hat{\mathbf{n}} \cdot \hat{\mathbf{z}} = 0$. Thus the boundary condition on $\mathcal{H}_z$ given in Eq. (9.170) is equivalent to the boundary condition on $\mathbf{E}_t$. Taking the cross product of $\hat{\mathbf{z}}$ and Eq. (9.159) (left) and using a vector identity results in

$$\boldsymbol{\mathcal{E}}_t = -\hat{\mathbf{z}} \times \boldsymbol{\mathcal{H}}_t$$

Substituting this into Eq. (9.176) and using a vector identity gives

$$\hat{\mathbf{n}} \cdot \boldsymbol{\mathcal{H}}_t = 0$$

which is the boundary condition on $\boldsymbol{\mathcal{H}}_t$ (see Table 5.3). Hence the boundary condition on $\boldsymbol{\mathcal{H}}_t$ is satisfied if that on $\boldsymbol{\mathcal{E}}_t$ is satisfied, and therefore all the boundary conditions for TE modes are satisfied if the boundary condition on $\mathcal{H}_z$ given in Eq. (9.170) is satisfied.

Next let us consider TM modes. Since $\boldsymbol{\mathcal{E}}_z$ is tangential to the transverse boundary, one of the boundary conditions for TM modes is that $\mathcal{E}_z = 0$ at the boundary. It is easy to show that when $\mathcal{E}_z = 0$ at the boundary, tangential $\boldsymbol{\mathcal{E}}_t$ and normal $\boldsymbol{\mathcal{H}}_t$ are also zero. From Eqs. (9.159) and (9.169),

$$\boldsymbol{\mathcal{E}}_t = \frac{j\omega\epsilon}{\gamma^2} \hat{\mathbf{z}} \times (\boldsymbol{\nabla}_t \times \boldsymbol{\mathcal{E}}_z)$$

Since $\boldsymbol{\nabla}_t \times \boldsymbol{\mathcal{E}}_z = -\hat{\mathbf{z}} \times \boldsymbol{\nabla}_t \mathcal{E}_z$,

$$\boldsymbol{\mathcal{E}}_t = \frac{j\omega\epsilon}{\gamma^2} \boldsymbol{\nabla}_t \mathcal{E}_z \tag{9.179}$$

Let $\hat{\mathbf{n}}$ be a unit vector normal to the transverse boundary and $\hat{\boldsymbol{\tau}}$ be a unit vector tangential to the transverse boundary such that

$$\hat{\mathbf{n}} \times \hat{\boldsymbol{\tau}} = \hat{\mathbf{z}} \tag{9.180}$$

Then the normal and tangential components of $\boldsymbol{\mathcal{E}}_t$ are

$$\hat{\mathbf{n}} \cdot \boldsymbol{\mathcal{E}}_t = \frac{j\omega\epsilon}{\gamma^2} \hat{\mathbf{n}} \cdot \boldsymbol{\nabla}_t \mathcal{E}_z$$

$$= \frac{j\omega\epsilon}{\gamma^2} \hat{\mathbf{n}} \frac{\partial \mathcal{E}_z}{\partial n}$$

$$\hat{\boldsymbol{\tau}} \cdot \boldsymbol{\mathcal{E}}_t = \frac{j\omega\epsilon}{\gamma^2} \hat{\boldsymbol{\tau}} \cdot \boldsymbol{\nabla}_t \mathcal{E}_z$$

$$= \frac{j\omega\epsilon}{\gamma^2} \hat{\boldsymbol{\tau}} \frac{\partial \mathcal{E}_z}{\partial \tau}$$

Now, if $\mathcal{E}_z = 0$ at the boundary, $\partial \mathcal{E}_z/\partial \tau = 0$ because $\mathcal{E}_z$ is constant (zero) on the boundary. Hence $\hat{\boldsymbol{\tau}} \cdot \boldsymbol{\mathcal{E}}_t = 0$, and the boundary condition on the tangential component of $\boldsymbol{\mathcal{E}}_t$ is satisfied. However, $\partial \mathcal{E}_z/\partial n$ is not necessarily zero if $\mathcal{E}_z = 0$, so the normal component of $\boldsymbol{\mathcal{E}}_t$ is not necessarily zero.

Using Eq. (9.159), we have

$$\hat{\boldsymbol{\tau}} \cdot \boldsymbol{\mathcal{E}}_t = -\hat{\boldsymbol{\tau}} \cdot \hat{\mathbf{z}} \times \boldsymbol{\mathcal{H}}_t$$

which can be rearranged to

$$\hat{\boldsymbol{\tau}} \cdot \boldsymbol{\mathcal{E}}_t = -\boldsymbol{\mathcal{H}}_t \cdot \hat{\boldsymbol{\tau}} \times \hat{\mathbf{z}}$$

From Eq. (9.180),

$$\hat{\boldsymbol{\tau}} \times \hat{\mathbf{z}} = \hat{\mathbf{n}}$$

Hence

$$\hat{\boldsymbol{\tau}} \cdot \boldsymbol{\mathcal{E}}_t = -\hat{\mathbf{n}} \cdot \boldsymbol{\mathcal{H}}_t$$

and when $\hat{\boldsymbol{\tau}} \cdot \boldsymbol{\mathcal{E}}_t = 0$, then $\hat{\mathbf{n}} \cdot \boldsymbol{\mathcal{H}}_t = 0$. Thus when $\mathcal{E}_z = 0$ at the transverse boundary, all the transverse boundary conditions on $\boldsymbol{\mathcal{E}}_t$ and $\boldsymbol{\mathcal{H}}_t$ are satisfied.

Thus γ can be found by solving the wave equations, Eqs. (9.168), and satisfying the boundary conditions on $\mathcal{H}_z$ and $\mathcal{E}_z$, Eqs. (9.170). All the other boundary conditions are automatically satisfied.

Example 9.5 TE_{10} transmission-line parameters The expressions for the normalized field functions and the transmission-line impedance for the TE_{10} rectangular-wave-guide mode are worked out in this example to illustrate the use of the results derived in this section.

For TE modes, the wave equation is

$$(\nabla_t^2 + \gamma^2)\mathcal{H}_z = 0 \tag{9.168}$$

which, in rectangular coordinates, is

$$\frac{\partial^2 \mathcal{H}_z}{\partial x^2} + \frac{\partial^2 \mathcal{H}_z}{\partial y^2} + \gamma^2 \mathcal{H}_z = 0$$

Separating the variables according to the methods of Sec. 9.4 by letting

$$\mathcal{H}_z = XY \tag{9.181}$$

results in

$$\frac{X''}{X} = -k_x^2$$

$$\frac{Y''}{Y} = -k_y^2$$

$$k_x^2 + k_y^2 = \gamma^2$$

$\mathcal{H}_z$ must satisfy the boundary conditions of Eq. (9.170),

$$\hat{\mathbf{n}} \cdot \boldsymbol{\nabla}_t \mathcal{H}_z = 0 \qquad \text{at the boundaries}$$

Substituting Eq. (9.181) into this boundary condition results in

$$\hat{\mathbf{n}} \cdot (X'Y\hat{\mathbf{x}} + XY'\hat{\mathbf{y}}) = 0 \qquad \text{at the boundaries}$$

For the orientation of the wave guide shown in Fig. 9.10, the boundary conditions are

$$X' = 0 \qquad \text{at } x = 0,\ x = a$$

$$Y' = 0 \qquad \text{at } y = 0,\ y = b$$

Hence the eigenfunctions and eigenvalues are

$$X = A_m \cos \frac{m\pi x}{a}$$

$$Y = B_n \cos \frac{n\pi y}{b}$$

$$k_x = \frac{m\pi}{a}$$

$$k_y = \frac{n\pi}{b}$$

and

$$\gamma_{mn}{}^2 = \left(\frac{m\pi}{a}\right)^2 + \left(\frac{n\pi}{b}\right)^2$$

which are the same as the results obtained in Sec. 9.10 from a more traditional approach.

The TE_{10} mode means $m = 1$ and $n = 0$. Hence

$$\gamma_{10} = \frac{\pi}{a} \tag{9.182}$$

$$\mathcal{H}_{z10} = AB \cos \frac{\pi x}{a} \tag{9.183}$$

From Eqs. (9.174), (9.175), and (9.182),

$$Z_{10} = j\omega\mu \tag{9.184}$$

$$Y_{10} = j\omega\epsilon - j\frac{(\pi/a)^2}{\omega\mu} \tag{9.185}$$

From the definition in Eq. (8.45), the characteristic impedance is

$$Z_0 = \sqrt{\frac{Z_{10}}{Y_{10}}}$$

$$= \frac{\omega\mu}{\sqrt{k^2 - (\pi/a)^2}}$$

$$= \sqrt{\frac{\mu}{\epsilon}} \frac{k}{\sqrt{k^2 - (\pi/a)^2}} \tag{9.186}$$

and the propagation constant as defined in Eqs. (8.39) and (8.42) is

$$\begin{aligned}\beta_{10} &= \sqrt{Z_{10}Y_{10}} \\ &= \sqrt{k^2 - (\pi/a)^2}\end{aligned} \tag{9.187}$$

The constants AB in Eq. (9.183) can be evaluated by finding $\mathcal{E}_t$ from Eq. (9.169) and using the normalization of Eq. (9.156),

$$\begin{aligned}\mathcal{E}_t &= -\frac{j\omega\mu}{\gamma^2}\nabla_t \times \mathcal{H}_z \\ &= -\frac{j\omega\mu}{\pi/a} AB \sin\frac{\pi x}{a}\,\hat{\mathbf{y}}\end{aligned}$$

The normalization is

$$\int_S \mathcal{E}_t \cdot \mathcal{E}_t^*\,dS = \int_0^b \int_0^a \left(\frac{\omega\mu}{\pi/a}\right)^2 |AB|^2 \sin^2\frac{\pi x}{a}\,dx\,dy = 1$$

from which

$$|AB| = \sqrt{\frac{2}{ba}}\,\frac{\pi/a}{\mu\omega}$$

Then

$$\mathcal{E}_t = -j\sqrt{\frac{2}{ba}}\sin\frac{\pi x}{a}\,\hat{\mathbf{y}} \tag{9.188}$$

From Eqs. (9.188) and (9.159),

$$\mathcal{H}_t = j\sqrt{\frac{2}{ba}}\sin\frac{\pi x}{a}\,\hat{\mathbf{x}} \tag{9.189}$$

★This completes the transmission-line description of the TE_{10} mode.

9.12 TRANSMISSION-LINE CHARACTERISTICS OF WAVE GUIDES

It was shown in Sec. 9.11 that TE and TM modes can be described by the transmission-line equations

$$\frac{\partial V_{mn}}{\partial z} = -Z_{mn}I_{mn} \tag{9.190}$$

$$\frac{\partial I_{mn}}{\partial z} = -Y_{mn}V_{mn} \tag{9.191}$$

where for TE modes

$$Z_{mn} = j\omega\mu \tag{9.192}$$

$$Y_{mn} = j\left(\omega\epsilon - \frac{{\gamma_{mn}}^2}{\omega\mu}\right) \tag{9.193}$$

and for TM modes

$$Z_{mn} = j\left(\omega\mu - \frac{\gamma_{mn}^2}{\omega\epsilon}\right) \tag{9.194}$$

$$Y_{mn} = j\omega\epsilon \tag{9.195}$$

The γ_{mn} are eigenvalues, as explained in Sec. 9.11 and Example 9.5. For rectangular wave guides,

$$\gamma_{mn} = \sqrt{\left(\frac{m\pi}{a}\right)^2 + \left(\frac{n\pi}{b}\right)^2} \qquad \text{rectangular TE and TM modes} \tag{9.196}$$

where a and b are the dimensions of the wave guide, as in Fig. 9.10.

The V_{mn} and I_{mn} in Eqs. (9.190) and (9.191) are not actually voltage and current, as in the quasi-static case, but they are analogous to voltage and current. They contain all the z and t variation of the wave-guide fields and hence describe all the propagation characteristics of the wave guide. The transverse dimensions of the wave guide are accounted for in this transmission-line description by the γ_{mn}.

It was also shown in Sec. 9.11 that TEM modes in free space can be described by the transmission-line equations,

$$\frac{\partial V}{\partial z} = -ZI \tag{9.197}$$

$$\frac{\partial I}{\partial z} = -YV \tag{9.198}$$

$$Z = j\omega\mu \tag{9.199}$$

$$Y = j\omega\epsilon \tag{9.200}$$

where V and I again are analogous to, but not equal to, voltage and current.

Since Eqs. (9.190) and (9.191) are of the same form as the transmission-line equations given in Eqs. (8.18) and (8.19), the transmission-line theory and techniques developed in Chap. 8 can be applied to wave-guiding systems. Thus the powerful tools and methods developed for two-conductor quasi-static transmission systems can be applied with equal advantage to wave-guide systems. Some of these applications are discussed in this section.

CHARACTERISTIC IMPEDANCE AND PROPAGATION CHARACTERISTICS

From Eq. (8.45), the characteristic impedance is defined as

$$Z_0 = \sqrt{\frac{Z}{Y}} \tag{8.45}$$

For the TE and TM modes

$$Z_{0mn} = \sqrt{\frac{Z_{mn}}{Y_{mn}}} \tag{9.201}$$

From Eq. (9.196), the expression for γ_{mn} for the TE_{10} mode is found to be

$$\gamma_{10} = \frac{\pi}{a} \tag{9.202}$$

Hence the characteristic impedance for the TE_{10} mode as found from Eqs. (9.192), (9.193), and (8.45) is

$$Z_0 = \sqrt{\frac{\mu}{\epsilon}} \frac{k}{\sqrt{k^2 - (\pi/a)^2}} \tag{9.203}$$

The propagation constant, as defined by Eqs. (8.39) and (8.42), is given by β where

$$\begin{aligned} \Gamma &= \sqrt{ZY} \\ &= \alpha + j\beta \end{aligned}$$

For the TE_{10} mode, Eqs. (9.202), (9.192), and (9.193) can be combined to give

$$\beta = \sqrt{k^2 - \left(\frac{\pi}{a}\right)^2} \tag{9.204}$$

which is the same result as that obtained in Sec. 9.10 by the other approach.

The phase velocity for the TE_{10} mode can now be found from Eq. (8.48) to be

$$\begin{aligned} v_p &= \frac{\omega}{\beta} \\ &= \frac{\omega}{\sqrt{k^2 - (\pi/a)^2}} \\ &= \frac{1}{\sqrt{\mu\epsilon}} \frac{k}{\sqrt{k^2 - (\pi/a)^2}} \end{aligned} \tag{9.205}$$

This phase velocity differs from the phase velocity of a planewave by the factor $k/\sqrt{k^2 - (\pi/a)^2}$.

The wavelength of the propagating wave in a wave guide is called λ_g. As defined in Chap. 6, λ_g is the longitudinal distance along the axis corresponding to one cycle of field variation and is given by $\lambda_g = v_p/f$. For the TE_{10} mode, Eq. (9.205) can be used to obtain

$$\lambda_g = \frac{1}{f\sqrt{\mu\epsilon}}\frac{1}{\sqrt{1-(\pi/a)^2/k^2}} = \frac{\lambda}{\sqrt{1-(\pi/a)^2/k^2}} \tag{9.206}$$

where $\lambda = (1/\sqrt{\mu\epsilon})/f$ is the wavelength of a planewave. Since $k_{co} = \pi/a$ for the TE_{10} mode (see Sec. 9.10), k must be greater than π/a for propagation to occur, and hence λ_g is greater than λ.

WAVE-GUIDE TRANSMISSION-LINE DISCONTINUITIES AND IMPEDANCES

In the quasi-static transmission systems, lumped-element impedances and changes in line parameters introduce discontinuities. In wave guides, similar discontinuities are introduced by placing obstacles, such as irises, in the wave guide, and also by abruptly changing ϵ or μ or the dimensions of the wave guide. *Irises* are simply thin conductors placed in the wave guide. Other commonly used obstacles are posts. Some typical posts and irises are illustrated in Fig. 9.13. The slide-screw tuner is an adjustable post. These discontinuities all produce reflections, which can be taken into account by impedances, as discussed in Chap. 8.

A significant difference between wave guides and the quasi-static system is that wave guides propagate an infinite number of modes. Each mode is described by a different set of transmission-line equations, as indicated in Eqs. (9.190) and (9.191) by the subscripts m and n. However, in many practical wave-guide systems, only one of the modes is propagating, and all the rest are evanescent. The evanescent modes can be taken into account in terms of lumped-element impedances, as a consideration of boundary conditions will show.

From a circuit point of view, the boundary conditions on V and I at a discontinuity are obtained from Kirchhoff's laws. At a discontinuity in Z_0, V and I must be continuous. When a lumped impedance is present, V and I may be discontinuous, depending on whether the impedance is in series or shunt with the conductors. This kind of discontinuity is usually handled by finding the combined impedance of the lumped element and the rest of the line, as described in Chap. 8.

From a fields point of view, the boundary conditions on **E** and **H** at a discontinuity are those given in Chap. 5. In general, satisfying these boundary conditions requires an infinite summation of both TE and TM modes.

When the boundary conditions at the discontinuity cannot be satisfied by one mode, evanescent modes must be present (assuming only

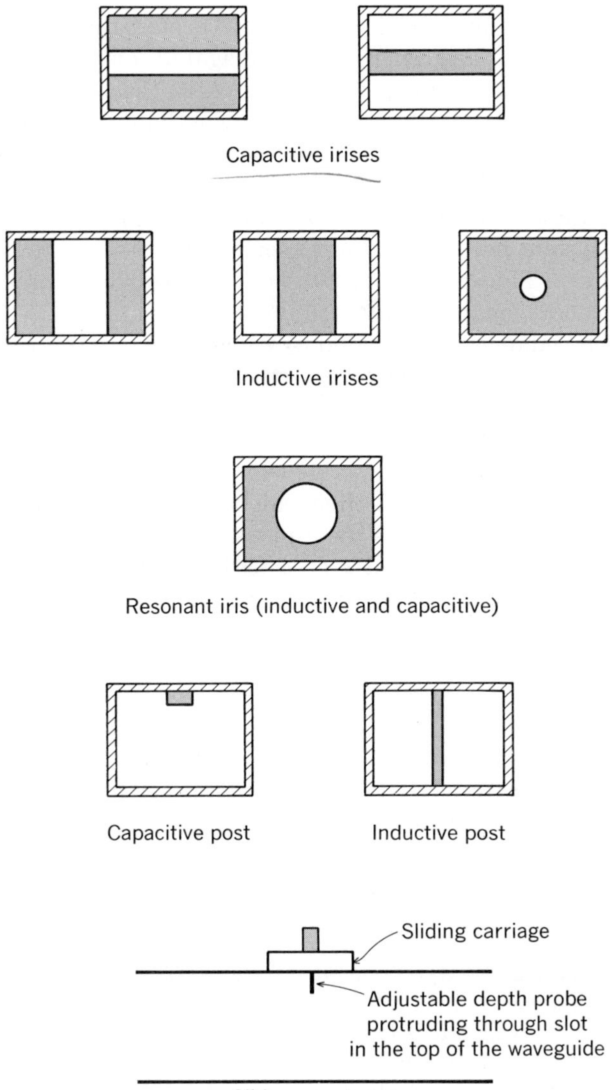

Fig. 9.13 Some wave-guide elements used to produce impedance discontinuities in wave guides.

one mode propagates). This would be the case when the discontinuity involves a change in wave-guide dimensions, or when an obstacle is present in the wave guide. The evanescent modes do not contribute to the energy propagating in the wave guide because they exist only near the discontinuity. The energy is propagated only by the propagating mode. There is, however, energy stored in the fields of the evanescent modes. Since this energy is localized near the discontinuity, the presence of the evanescent modes has the same effect that the presence of a lumped impedance would have on a two-wire transmission system; that is, the lumped-element impedance affects the propagation of energy along the system because it stores energy.

Thus wave-guide discontinuities which produce evanescent modes can be treated as lumped impedance elements. The value of the lumped impedance can be found by its effect on the propagating mode. Example 9.6 illustrates the measurement of the impedance of an iris in a wave guide. Since that particular iris has the effect of a lumped inductor, it is called an *inductive iris*. When the obstacle in a wave guide is thin, its effect can be described in terms of a shunt impedance. When the obstacle is thick, its effect can be described by an equivalent π or T section.

In some cases the dimensions of the cross section of the wave guide are continuous and ϵ or μ is discontinuous, resulting in a discontinuity in Z_0. If only one mode is not cut off, and if the boundary conditions can be satisfied by the one mode, then since

$$\mathbf{E}_t = V\boldsymbol{\mathcal{E}}_t$$

$$\mathbf{H}_t = I\boldsymbol{\mathcal{H}}_t$$

as defined in Eqs. (9.151) and (9.152), V and I must be continuous because $\boldsymbol{\mathcal{E}}_t$ and $\boldsymbol{\mathcal{H}}_t$ are continuous if the dimensions of the wave guide are continuous. Then the boundary conditions on V and I are the same as those of the quasi-static case.

In many cases, then, discontinuities in quasi-static transmission systems and wave guides can be treated on a common basis.

Example 9.6 Measurement of the admittance of a thin inductive iris in a wave guide Figure 9.14*b* illustrates a wave guide with a thin inductive iris at the point $z = l$. The wave guide is terminated in its characteristic impedance, and only the TE_{10} mode is propagating. Figure 9.14*c* shows the equivalent transmission line with the characteristic admittance transformed to the point $z = l$. This transformation was explained in the discussion following Eq. (8.76). The sum $Y_I + Y_{10}$ is considered to be the load admittance Y_L.

The measured quantities are

$$S = 3.6$$

$$f = 10 \text{ GHz}$$

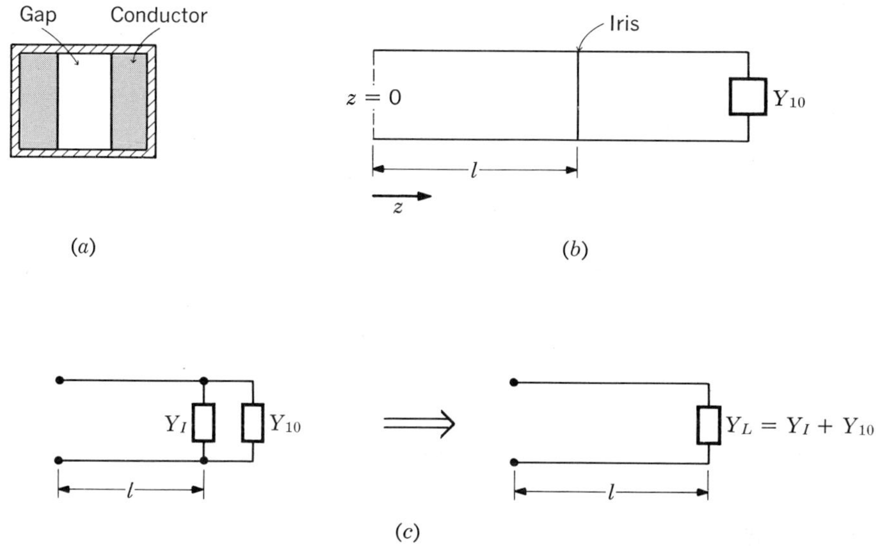

Fig. 9.14 (*a*) A thin inductive iris. (*b*) The thin inductive iris in a wave guide terminated in its characteristic admittance; the TE_{10} mode is the only propagating mode. (*c*) An equivalent transmission line with the termination transformed to the iris position.

Wave-guide dimensions are 0.900 by 0.400 in.

$|V|_{min}$ at $z = d$

$$l - d = 17.559 \text{ cm}$$

The objective is to calculate the admittance of the iris, Y_I, by means of the Smith chart. From Eq. (9.202),

$$\gamma_{10} = \frac{\pi}{a}$$

From Eq. (9.206) λ_g is found to be

$$\lambda_g = 3.97 \text{ cm}$$

The point of $|V|_{min}$ occurs a distance of $(l - d)/\lambda_g = 4.423$ wavelengths from the iris toward the generator. As shown in Fig. 9.14*c*, the admittance at $z = l$ is $y_I + 1$, where y_I is the admittance of the iris. Since $|V|_{min}$ occurs on the $+u$ axis when the chart is used for admittance, the chart is entered at the point $\mathscr{G} = 3.6$, $\mathscr{b} = 0$. Recall that $\mathscr{G} = S$ at the point where $|V| = |V|_{min}$. y_L can be found by moving on the chart 4.423 wavelengths toward the load. Since a distance of four complete wavelengths means eight complete rotations around the chart, moving 0.423 wavelength on the chart is the same as moving 4.423 wavelengths. Hence y_L can be found by moving 0.423 wavelength toward the load, as illustrated in Fig. 9.15. The value of y_L read from the chart is $y_L = 1 - j1.37$.

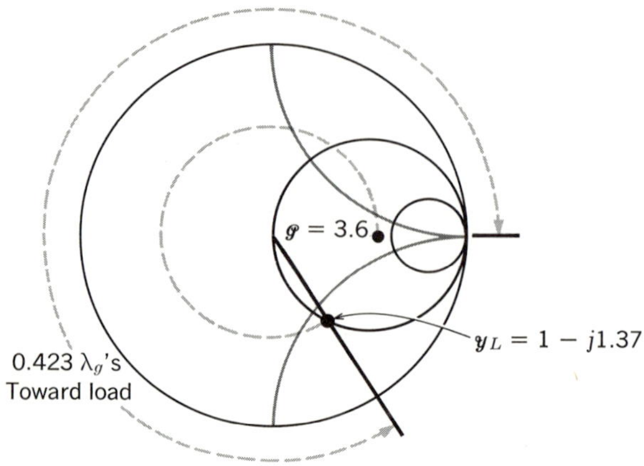

Fig. 9.15 The use of the Smith chart in Example 9.6.

Since $y_L = y_I + 1$, $y_I = -j1.37$. The iris is called an *inductive iris* because the admittance y_I is an inductive susceptance.

Example 9.7 Dielectric quarter-wave transformer matching Consider the case of a planewave normally incident upon a dielectric interface; this is the case described in Sec. 6.14 with $\theta_i = 0$. The reflections at the interface can be eliminated by means of the quarter-wave transformer illustrated in Fig. 9.16. Since the wave is normally incident, it can be treated by the TEM transmission-line equations, Eqs. (9.197) and (9.198). From Eqs. (9.199) and (9.200), $Z = \sqrt{Z/Y} = \sqrt{\mu/\epsilon}$. Hence, from Eq. (8.107),

$$Z_{02} = \sqrt{\sqrt{\frac{\mu_0}{\epsilon_3}}\sqrt{\frac{\mu_0}{\epsilon_0}}}$$

$$= \frac{\sqrt{\mu_0}}{(\epsilon_3\epsilon_0)^{1/4}}$$

$$= \sqrt{\frac{\mu_0}{\epsilon_2}}$$

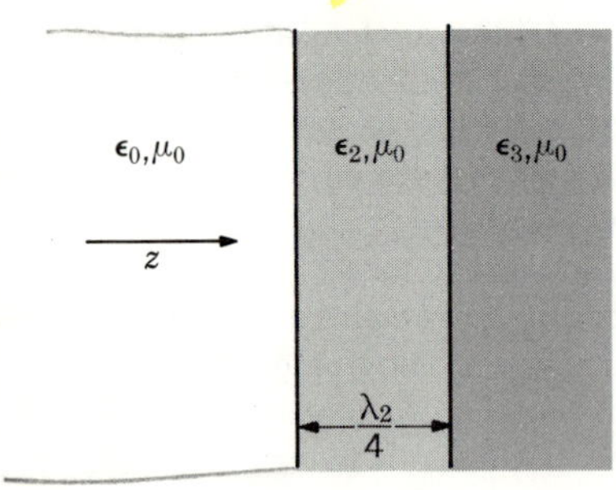

Fig. 9.16 A dielectric quarter-wave transformer for eliminating normally incident planewave reflections.

and $\epsilon_2 = \sqrt{\epsilon_o \epsilon_3}$ is the required permittivity of the dielectric transformer. The length of the transformer must be $\lambda_2/4$. Since $\beta = \sqrt{ZY} = \omega\sqrt{\mu\epsilon}$ and $v_p = \omega/\beta$, $\lambda = v_p/f = (\omega/\beta)/f = 2\pi/\beta$. Hence the length is

$$l = \frac{\lambda_2}{4}$$

$$= \frac{2\pi}{4 \times 2\pi f \sqrt{\mu_0 \epsilon_2}}$$

$$= \frac{1}{4f\sqrt{\mu_0 \epsilon_2}}$$

This shows the dependence of the transformation on frequency.

The principles of impedance matching illustrated here are used in the design of antireflection coatings for lenses. Another use is in connection with light emitters such as injection lasers, in which the light is generated inside a dielectric material. It is possible to increase the amount of light getting out of the dielectric by applying dielectric coatings which improve the impedance match.

★9.13 Transmission-line Power and Energy

It is of great interest to know the power carried by a wave-guide line in terms of the mode amplitudes a^+ and a^- or the V and I parameters. The calculation of electromagnetic power carried by a wave guide or plane-wave is based on an evaluation of the Poynting vector. In terms of the transverse fields for a given mode, $\mathbf{E}_t$ and $\mathbf{H}_t$, the time-average power density or Poynting vector in the z direction is

$$\langle \mathcal{P} \rangle = \tfrac{1}{2} \operatorname{Re} \mathbf{E}_t \times \mathbf{H}_t^*$$

Equations (9.151) and (9.152) are used to obtain

$$\langle \mathcal{P} \rangle = \tfrac{1}{2} \operatorname{Re} VI^* \boldsymbol{\mathcal{E}}_t \times \boldsymbol{\mathcal{H}}_t^*$$

The total power is obtained by integrating the z component of $\langle \mathcal{P} \rangle$ over a cross section (constant z plane) which includes all the fields,

$$\langle P \rangle = \tfrac{1}{2} \operatorname{Re} VI^* \int_S \boldsymbol{\mathcal{E}}_t \times \boldsymbol{\mathcal{H}}_t^* \cdot \hat{\mathbf{z}}\, dS$$

Using Eq. (9.129), we obtain the simple relation

$$\langle P \rangle = \tfrac{1}{2} \operatorname{Re} VI^* \qquad (9.207)$$

as a direct consequence of the power normalization used in Eq. (9.129).

Equation (9.207) is derived right from the field equations and therefore must hold for circuit-element transmission systems as well as for the wave guide. However, the use of the Poynting vector for circuit transmission lines may appear unjustified, since the variables used are voltage and current instead of fields. A simple argument shows that Eq. (9.207) must also hold for a circuit transmission line. Suppose that the line is broken at some constant z plane, and a resistor is attached across the conductors of resistance $R = Z_0 = V^+/I^+$ such that it supports the correct V^+/I^+ ratio. The resistor would experience a voltage V^+ and carry a current I^+, and it would accept all the power flowing along the line. Therefore the power dissipated in the resistor would equal the power flowing along the transmission line. The time-average power dissipated in the resistor is just Eq. (9.207), and thus Eq. (9.207) gives the power flow in the transmission line.

A corresponding relation for $\langle P \rangle$ in terms of a^+ and a^- is obtained by using Eqs. (8.37) and (8.38) in Eq. (9.207) to give

$$\langle P \rangle = \tfrac{1}{2} \operatorname{Re} \left(\frac{a^+ + a^-}{2} \frac{a^{+*} - a^{-*}}{2Z_0^*} \right)$$

where

$$Z_0 = \sqrt{\frac{Z}{Y}}$$

is the characteristic impedance of the transmission line. The multiplications are carried out to give

$$\langle P \rangle = \tfrac{1}{8} \operatorname{Re} \frac{1}{Z_0^*}(a^+a^{+*} - a^-a^{-*} + a^-a^{+*} - a^+a^{-*})$$

For a lossless line Z_0 is real, and $Z_0^* = Z_0$. It is easily seen that

$$\operatorname{Re}(a^-a^{+*} - a^+a^{-*}) = 0$$

since the difference of a complex number and its complex conjugate is imaginary. Thus the time-average power carried in the $+z$ direction on a lossless line is

$$\langle P \rangle = \frac{1}{8Z_0}(a^+a^{+*} - a^-a^{-*}) \tag{9.208}$$

Notice that the power carried by a mode is proportional to the mode amplitudes squared. Since the a^+ mode travels in the $+z$ direction, it carries power in the $+z$ direction, whereas the a^- mode traveling in the $-z$ direction carries power in the $-z$ direction.

The electric and magnetic energy stored on a transmission line per unit length may be calculated from the field energy density equations developed in Chap. 5. The time-average electric and magnetic energy densities obtained from Eqs. (5.118) and (5.119) are

$$\langle \mathcal{W}_e \rangle = \tfrac{1}{4}\epsilon \text{ Re } \mathbf{E} \cdot \mathbf{E}^* \qquad \text{joules/m}^3$$

$$\langle \mathcal{W}_m \rangle = \tfrac{1}{4}\mu \text{ Re } \mathbf{H} \cdot \mathbf{H}^* \qquad \text{joules/m}^3$$

The energy densities per unit length along the transmission line are found by integrating the above equations over the cross section in a constant z plane,

$$\langle \mathcal{W}_e \rangle = \tfrac{1}{4}\epsilon \text{ Re} \int_S \mathbf{E} \cdot \mathbf{E}^* \, dS \qquad \text{joules/m}$$

$$\langle \mathcal{W}_m \rangle = \tfrac{1}{4}\mu \text{ Re} \int_S \mathbf{H} \cdot \mathbf{H}^* \, dS \qquad \text{joules/m}$$

The notation $\langle \mathcal{W} \rangle$ will now be used to denote joules per meter, not joules per cubic meter. In the script field notation, these equations may be written in terms of the V and I parameters and surface integrals of the script fields which are known from Eqs. (9.134), (9.136), (9.147), and (9.148).

For a TEM mode

$$\langle \mathcal{W}_e \rangle = \tfrac{1}{4}\epsilon \text{ Re } VV^* \int_S \boldsymbol{\mathcal{E}}_t \cdot \boldsymbol{\mathcal{E}}_t^* \, dS$$

$$= \tfrac{1}{4}\epsilon \text{ Re } VV^*$$

$$\langle \mathcal{W}_m \rangle = \tfrac{1}{4}\mu \text{ Re } II^* \int_S \boldsymbol{\mathcal{H}}_t \cdot \boldsymbol{\mathcal{H}}_t^* \, dS$$

$$= \tfrac{1}{4}\mu \text{ Re } II^*$$

A single mode, the $+z$ traveling mode a^+ (which will be written as a), will be considered. In terms of a the above relations become

$$\langle \mathcal{W}_e \rangle = \tfrac{1}{16}\epsilon \text{ Re } aa^*$$

$$\langle \mathcal{W}_m \rangle = \frac{1}{16} \frac{\mu}{Z_0^2} \text{ Re } aa^*$$

where Z_0^2 is μ/ϵ. The total electric and magnetic energy per unit length along the TEM mode transmission line is

$$\langle \mathcal{W} \rangle = \tfrac{1}{8}\epsilon \text{ Re } aa^* \tag{9.209}$$

For a TE wave an additional term is required in the magnetic energy expression for the H_z field. The magnetic energy per unit length is obtained from the equation

$$\langle \mathcal{W}_m \rangle = \tfrac{1}{4}\mu \text{ Re} \left(II^* \int_S \boldsymbol{\mathcal{H}}_t \cdot \boldsymbol{\mathcal{H}}_t^* \, dS + \int_S \mathbf{H}_z \cdot \mathbf{H}_z^* \, dS \right)$$

The integral involving H_z can be evaluated in terms of $\mathcal{H}_t$ by using Eq. (9.165). Since $\nabla_t \times \mathbf{H}_z = -\hat{\mathbf{z}} \times \nabla_t H_z$ [see Eq. (9.178)], Eq. (9.165) can be written as

$$\mathcal{E}_t = \frac{j\omega\mu}{\gamma^2 V} \hat{\mathbf{z}} \times \nabla_t H_z \tag{9.210}$$

Equation (9.210) and some vector manipulation can be used to write

$$\int_S \mathcal{E}_t \cdot \mathcal{E}_t^* \, dS = \int_S \frac{(\omega\mu)^2}{\gamma^4 V V^*} \nabla_t H_z \cdot \nabla_t H_z^* \, dS$$

Because of the normalization of Eq. (9.156), the term on the left is unity. Hence

$$\begin{aligned} \int_S \nabla_t H_z \cdot \nabla_t H_z^* \, dS &= \frac{\gamma^4 V V^*}{(\omega\mu)^2} \\ &= \frac{\gamma^4 \epsilon}{k^2 \mu} V V^* \end{aligned} \tag{9.211}$$

By a vector identity known as *Green's identity*,

$$\int_S \nabla_t \mathbf{H}_z \cdot \nabla_t H_z^* \, dS = - \int_S H_z^* \, \nabla_t^2 H_z \, dS + \oint_l H_z^* \, \nabla_t H_z \cdot \hat{\mathbf{n}} \, dl$$

where $\hat{\mathbf{n}}$ is a unit outer normal to the path l bounding S. Because of the boundary condition of Eq. (9.170), the line integral is zero. Using Eq. (9.164) in the other term on the right results in

$$\int_S \nabla_t H_z \cdot \nabla_t H_z^* \, dS = +\gamma^2 \int_S H_z H_z^* \, dS \tag{9.212}$$

Combining Eqs. (9.212) and (9.211) results in

$$\int_S H_z H_z^* \, dS - \frac{\gamma^2}{k^2} \frac{\epsilon}{\mu} V V^* \tag{9.213}$$

The stored magnetic energy is therefore

$$\langle \mathcal{W}_m \rangle = \tfrac{1}{4}\mu \, \text{Re} \left(I I^* + V V^* \frac{\gamma^2}{k^2} \frac{\epsilon}{\mu} \right)$$

and by adding this magnetic energy term to the transverse electric energy, the total energy per unit length is obtained.

$$\langle \mathcal{W} \rangle = \tfrac{1}{4}\epsilon \left(1 + \frac{\gamma^2}{k^2} \right) \text{Re} \, V V^* + \tfrac{1}{4}\mu \, \text{Re} \, I I^*$$

For a single mode traveling in the $+z$ direction the above equation becomes

$$\langle \mathcal{W} \rangle = \tfrac{1}{16}\epsilon \left(1 + \frac{\gamma^2}{k^2}\right) \operatorname{Re} aa^* + \frac{1}{16} \frac{\mu}{Z_0{}^2} \operatorname{Re} aa^*$$

The characteristic impedance Z_0 for TE modes is found from Eqs. (9.203). Inserting this into the above relation gives the final result,

$$\langle \mathcal{W} \rangle = \tfrac{1}{8}\epsilon \operatorname{Re} aa^* \tag{9.214}$$

Note the rather unexpected result that the total time-average energy stored per unit length for the TE mode is the same as that for the TEM mode.

A TM mode requires consideration of the electric energy stored in E_z. The magnetic energy is the same as that for a TEM wave. The electric energy equation is

$$\langle \mathcal{W}_e \rangle = \tfrac{1}{4}\epsilon \operatorname{Re} \left(VV^* \int_S \boldsymbol{\mathcal{E}}_t \cdot \boldsymbol{\mathcal{E}}_t^* \, dS + \int_S \mathbf{E}_z \cdot \mathbf{E}_z^* \, dS \right)$$

The integral involving E_z can be evaluated in a way similar to that used in evaluating the integral involving $\mathbf{H}_z$ in $\langle \mathcal{W}_m \rangle$. From Eqs. (9.165) and (9.178),

$$\boldsymbol{\mathcal{H}}_t = -\frac{j\omega\epsilon}{\gamma^2 I} \hat{\mathbf{z}} \times \boldsymbol{\nabla}_t E_z \tag{9.215}$$

Then

$$\begin{aligned} 1 &= \int_S \boldsymbol{\mathcal{H}}_t \cdot \boldsymbol{\mathcal{H}}_t^* \, dS \\ &= \frac{k^2}{II^*\gamma^4} \frac{\epsilon}{\mu} \int_S \boldsymbol{\nabla}_t E_z \cdot \boldsymbol{\nabla}_t E_z^* \, dS \end{aligned}$$

Using Green's identity, we have

$$\frac{\gamma^4}{k^2} \frac{\mu}{\epsilon} II^* = -\int_S E_z^* \nabla_t{}^2 \, dS + \oint_l E_z^* \boldsymbol{\nabla}_t H_z \cdot \hat{\mathbf{n}} \, dl$$

The line integral is zero because $E_z = 0$ on the boundary, according to Eq. (9.170). Using Eq. (9.164) in the other term results in

$$\int_S E_z E_z^* \, dS = \frac{\gamma^2}{k^2} \frac{\mu}{\epsilon} II^* \tag{9.216}$$

Thus the stored electric energy is

$$\langle \mathcal{W}_e \rangle = \tfrac{1}{4}\epsilon \operatorname{Re} \left(VV^* + II^* \frac{\gamma^2}{k^2} \frac{\mu}{\epsilon} \right)$$

and by adding the magnetic energy to this expression, we obtain the total energy per unit length,

$$\langle \mathcal{W} \rangle = \tfrac{1}{4}\mu \left(1 + \frac{\gamma^2}{k^2}\right) \operatorname{Re} II^* + \tfrac{1}{4}\epsilon \operatorname{Re} VV^*$$

In terms of the mode amplitude a, this becomes

$$\begin{aligned}\langle \mathcal{W} \rangle &= \tfrac{1}{16}\mu \left(1 + \frac{\gamma^2}{k^2}\right) \frac{\epsilon k^2}{\mu(k^2 - \gamma^2)} \operatorname{Re} aa^* + \tfrac{1}{16}\epsilon \operatorname{Re} aa^* \\ &= \tfrac{1}{16}\epsilon \operatorname{Re} aa^* \left(\frac{k^2 + \gamma^2}{k^2 - \gamma^2} + 1\right)\end{aligned}$$

But since $k^2 - \gamma^2 = \beta^2$ for TM modes, this reduces to

$$\langle \mathcal{W} \rangle = \frac{\epsilon}{8} \frac{k^2}{\beta^2} \operatorname{Re} aa^* \tag{9.217}$$

The result obtained is different from that for either TEM or TE waves. The energy stored for TEM and TE waves is independent of frequency, whereas Eq. (9.217) shows that as the frequency is reduced from above cutoff frequency toward cutoff, the energy increases.

Energy-flow Velocity (Group Velocity)

The transmission line carries power and stores energy. Power is transferred by a movement of stored energy, and the velocity of energy flow may be determined, since both the power and stored energy are known from the results of this section. It is clear that the appropriate relation for power, energy, and velocity is $\langle P \rangle = \langle \mathcal{W} \rangle v_g$, where v_g denotes the velocity of energy flow. The dimensions of the variables are $\langle P \rangle$, watts; $\langle \mathcal{W} \rangle$, joules per meter, and v_g, meters per second. The relation is correct dimensionally, as watts = joules/sec.

For one mode Eq. (9.208) gives $\langle P \rangle = \operatorname{Re} aa^*/8Z_0$ for the real power flow. This expression is combined with Eqs. (9.209), (9.214), and (9.217) successively, to obtain the energy flow velocity for TEM, TE, and TM modes,

$$v_g = \frac{1}{\sqrt{\mu\epsilon}} \frac{\beta}{k} \tag{9.218}$$

For TEM modes $\beta = k$, and v_g is simply $v_g = 1/\sqrt{\mu\epsilon}$.

A convenient expression for v_g is found by taking the differential of the basic propagation equation $\beta^2 = k^2 - \gamma^2$,

$$\begin{aligned}2\beta\, d\beta &= 2k\, dk \\ &= 2k\, d\omega \sqrt{\mu\epsilon} \\ \frac{d\omega}{d\beta} &= \frac{1}{\sqrt{\mu\epsilon}} \frac{\beta}{k}\end{aligned}$$

and thus

$$v_g = \frac{d\omega}{d\beta} \tag{9.219}$$

This important relation will bc used in the next section in the discussion of the $k\beta$ diagram.

The $k\beta$ Diagram

The nature of wave propagation on the wave-guide transmission line is conveniently described in a plot of the propagation constant on a $k\beta$ diagram. The phase velocity of propagation has been derived previously for the TE_{10} mode in Eq. (9.205). Using $\beta = \sqrt{ZY}$ and Eqs. (9.192) to (9.195) results in the phase velocity for the more general case of TE and TM modes,

$$\begin{aligned} v_p &= \frac{\omega}{\beta} \\ &= \frac{\omega/k}{\sqrt{1 - \gamma^2/k^2}} \\ &= \frac{v_{p0}}{\sqrt{1 - (f_{co}/f)^2}} \end{aligned} \tag{9.220}$$

where $v_{p0} = \omega/k$, and the ratio γ/k is identified as the frequency ratio f_{co}/f. Observe that the phase velocity approaches the phase velocity of planewave propagation in the medium, v_{p0}, when $f \gg f_{co}$, and increases to infinity as f approaches f_{co}.

The variation of v_p with k is easily seen in a plot of k versus β, as shown in Fig. 9.17, where it is recognized that the normalized phase velocity v_p/v_{p0} is simply the slope of the line OP at the frequency corresponding to k_1. The slope of the line increases from unity to infinity as k_1 is lowered from values much greater than γ to γ. The velocity of energy flow, called group velocity, is also easily determined from the $k\beta$ diagram. From Eq. (9.219) we have the definition

$$v_g = \frac{d\omega}{d\beta} \tag{9.219}$$

from which we may write

$$\frac{v_g}{v_{p0}} = \frac{dk}{d\beta} \tag{9.221}$$

The normalized group velocity v_g/v_{p0} at a frequency corresponding to k_1 is the slope of the $k\beta$ plot at $k = k_1$, as shown in Fig. 9.17. In contrast

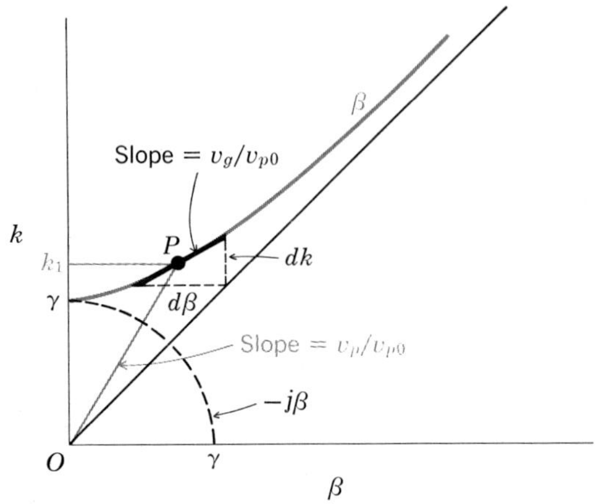

Fig. 9.17 The $k\beta$ diagram for a general wave-guide transmission line. Only the $+z$ traveling wave is shown.

to the phase velocity, which increases to infinity as f approaches γ, the ★group velocity decreases to zero.

PROBLEMS

9.2-1 Find **E** between the spheres in Fig. 9.1.

9.2-2 Find Φ and **E** between the spheres when $\Phi = V_0$ on the inner sphere and $\Phi = 0$ on the outer sphere.

9.3-1 Show that the X given in Eq. (9.10) satisfies the differential equation, Eq. (9.8).

9.3-2 Show that the Z given in Eq. (9.11) satisfies Eq. (9.9).

9.3-3 Verify Eq. (9.17) when $m = 1$, and $l = 2$; when $m = 3$, and $l = 3$.

9.3-4 Find Φ between the parallel plates in Fig. 9.2 if a conducting plane is placed at $z = c$ and the additional boundary condition $\Phi = 0$ at $z = c$ is imposed. This will require a relation between B_{1m} and B_{2m} which makes $\Phi = 0$ at $z = c$.

9.4-1 Show that Eq. (9.29) is equivalent to Eq. (9.30) and give the relations between A_1, A_2, A_3, and A_4 which make them equivalent. Note that these constants can be complex.

9.5-1 Following the procedure used in Example 9.1, find the orthogonality properties of e^{jlx}, where l is an integer. Verify the orthogonality by direct integration.

9.5-2 Following the procedures used in Example 9.1, show that

$$\int_0^{2a} \sin\frac{m\pi x}{a} \cos\frac{l\pi x}{a}\, dx = 0 \qquad \text{for all } m, l$$

9.7-1 Find the potential due to a point charge Q in a 60° corner between conducting planes.

9.8-1 Show that Eqs. (9.71) and (9.73) may be combined to obtain Eq. (9.76).

9.8-2 Show that Eq. (9.77) may be obtained by combining Eqs. (9.70) and (9.74).

9.8-3 Derive Eq. (9.78).

9.8-4 Derive Eq. (9.79).

9.8-5 Derive Eqs. (9.80) to (9.83).

9.8-6 Write down the field expressions for the second lowest TE mode. Show that these expressions satisfy Maxwell's equations and the boundary conditions.

9.8-7 Make a normalized $k\beta$ diagram for the $n = 3$ TE and TM modes. Identify k_{co}.

9.8-8 Show that the TE_1 mode for the parallel-plate wave guide can be considered to be planewaves bouncing back and forth between the plates.

9.8-9 Sketch the field configurations for the lowest-order TM mode for the parallel-plate wave guide.

9.9-1 Show that Eq. (9.94) reduces to Eqs. (9.76) and (9.77) for the special case $\partial/\partial x = 0$.

9.9-2 Show that Eq. (9.95) reduces to Eqs. (9.78) and (9.79) for the special case $\partial/\partial x = 0$.

9.10-1 Show that the TE_{00} mode is a trivial solution.

9.10-2 Derive the TM field expressions, Eqs. (9.108) to (9.110).

9.10-3 Show that a TEM mode cannot satisfy the boundary conditions in the rectangular wave guide.

9.10-4 Show that the TM_{10} and TM_{01} modes are trivial.

9.10-5 Derive expressions for the cutoff frequencies of the TE_{10}, TE_{01}, TE_{20}, TE_{11}, and TM_{11} rectangular-wave-guide modes. Show that the maximum separation between the TE_{10} mode and the next lowest one is obtained when $b = a/2$. Verify Fig. 9.11.

9.10-6 Make a $k\beta$ diagram for the TE_{10} and TE_{20} rectangular-wave-guide modes when $b = a/2$.

9.10-7 Find the expressions for the rectangular-wave-guide TE_{mn} modes which travel in the $-z$ direction.

9.11-1 Verify Eq. (9.111).

9.11-2 Show that Eq. (9.141) follows from Eqs. (9.139) and (9.140).

9.12-1 A wave-guide mode is characterized by $\gamma = 100$. Find λ_g and v_p at $f = 10^{10}$ when $\mu = \mu_0$ and $\epsilon = \epsilon_0$.

9.12-2 An iris in a wave guide terminated in its characteristic impedance produces a standing-wave ratio $S = 3.1$ and a $|V|_{\min}$ at a point 0.082 wavelength from the iris. What is the normalized admittance of the iris?

9.12-3 Find the position and admittance of a slide-screw tuner which would match the iris-termination combination of Fig. 9.14b. The admittance of the iris is given in Example 9.6.

9.12-4 A 10-GHz TEM wave is normally incident on a dielectric having a permittivity of $3\epsilon_0$. Design a quarter-wave transformer which would eliminate reflections.

9.12-5 Plot the magnitude of the reflection coefficient against frequency for the reflection coefficient resulting from the TEM wave of Prob. 9.12-4 incident on the matching dielectric layer. Make the plot for a frequency band about 10 GHz of sufficient width to show the frequency characteristics of the match.

9.12-6 Design a series combination of two quarter-wave transformers to replace the quarter-wave transformer of Prob. 9.12-4. Compare the bandwidth of the series combination and the single transformer.

9.12-7 Verify the results of Example 9.7 by writing the field equations in the three regions and matching the boundary conditions at the two boundaries.

9.12-8 Derive Eq. (9.218).

9.12-9 Prove that $v_p v_g = \dfrac{1}{\mu\epsilon}$.

APPENDIX

vector relations

Vector Identities

$$\mathbf{A} \cdot \mathbf{B} \times \mathbf{C} = \mathbf{B} \cdot \mathbf{C} \times \mathbf{A} = \mathbf{C} \cdot \mathbf{A} \times \mathbf{B}$$

$$\mathbf{A} \times (\mathbf{B} \times \mathbf{C}) = (\mathbf{A} \cdot \mathbf{C})\mathbf{B} - (\mathbf{A} \cdot \mathbf{B})\mathbf{C}$$

$$\begin{aligned}(\mathbf{A} \times \mathbf{B}) \cdot (\mathbf{C} \times \mathbf{D}) &= \mathbf{A} \cdot [\mathbf{B} \times (\mathbf{C} \times \mathbf{D})] \\ &= (\mathbf{A} \cdot \mathbf{C})(\mathbf{B} \cdot \mathbf{D}) - (\mathbf{A} \cdot \mathbf{D})(\mathbf{B} \cdot \mathbf{C})\end{aligned}$$

$$(\mathbf{A} \times \mathbf{B}) \times (\mathbf{C} \times \mathbf{D}) = [(\mathbf{A} \times \mathbf{B}) \cdot \mathbf{D}]\mathbf{C} - [(\mathbf{A} \times \mathbf{B}) \cdot \mathbf{C}]\mathbf{D}$$

$$\nabla(\psi + \Phi) = \nabla\psi + \nabla\Phi$$

$$\nabla(\Phi\psi) = \Phi\,\nabla\psi + \psi\,\nabla\Phi$$

$$\nabla(\mathbf{A} \cdot \mathbf{B}) = (\mathbf{A} \cdot \nabla)\mathbf{B} + (\mathbf{B} \cdot \nabla)\mathbf{A} + \mathbf{A} \times (\nabla \times \mathbf{B}) + \mathbf{B} \times (\nabla \times \mathbf{A})$$

$$\nabla \cdot (\mathbf{A} + \mathbf{B}) = \nabla \cdot \mathbf{A} + \nabla \cdot \mathbf{B}$$

$$\nabla \cdot (\psi\mathbf{A}) = \mathbf{A} \cdot \nabla\psi + \psi\nabla \cdot \mathbf{A}$$

$$\nabla \cdot (\mathbf{A} \times \mathbf{B}) = \mathbf{B} \cdot \nabla \times \mathbf{A} - \mathbf{A} \cdot \nabla \times \mathbf{B}$$

$$\nabla \times (\mathbf{A} + \mathbf{B}) = \nabla \times \mathbf{A} + \nabla \times \mathbf{B}$$

$$\nabla \times (\psi\mathbf{A}) = \nabla\psi \times \mathbf{A} + \psi\nabla \times \mathbf{A}$$

$$\nabla \times (\mathbf{A} \times \mathbf{B}) = \mathbf{A}\, \nabla \cdot \mathbf{B} - \mathbf{B}\, \nabla \cdot \mathbf{A} + (\mathbf{B} \cdot \nabla)\mathbf{A} - (\mathbf{A} \cdot \nabla)\mathbf{B}$$

$$\nabla \times (\nabla \times \mathbf{A}) = \nabla(\nabla \cdot \mathbf{A}) - \nabla^2 \mathbf{A}$$

$$\nabla \cdot \nabla \psi = \nabla^2 \psi$$

$$\nabla \times \nabla \psi = 0$$

$$\nabla \cdot \nabla \times \mathbf{A} = 0$$

$$\int_V \nabla \psi \, dV = \oint_S \psi \, d\mathbf{S}$$

$$\int_V \nabla \cdot \mathbf{A} \, dV = \oint_S \mathbf{A} \cdot d\mathbf{S}$$

$$\int_V \nabla \times \mathbf{A} \, dV = \oint_S \hat{\mathbf{n}} \times \mathbf{A} \, dS$$

$$\int_S \hat{\mathbf{n}} \times \nabla \psi \, dS = \oint_l \psi \, d\mathbf{l}$$

$$\int_S \nabla \times \mathbf{A} \cdot d\mathbf{S} = \oint_l \mathbf{A} \cdot d\mathbf{l}$$

See Sec. 1.8 for definitions of $\hat{\mathbf{n}}$ and $d\mathbf{S}$.

Orthogonal Curvilinear Coordinates

$$\nabla \Phi = \frac{1}{h_1} \frac{\partial \Phi}{\partial u_1} \hat{\mathbf{u}}_1 + \frac{1}{h_2} \frac{\partial \Phi}{\partial u_2} \hat{\mathbf{u}}_2 + \frac{1}{h_3} \frac{\partial \Phi}{\partial u_3} \hat{\mathbf{u}}_3$$

$$\nabla \cdot \mathbf{A} = \frac{1}{h_1 h_2 h_3} \left[\frac{\partial}{\partial u_1} (h_2 h_3 A_1) + \frac{\partial}{\partial u_2} (h_3 h_1 A_2) + \frac{\partial}{\partial u_3} (h_1 h_2 A_3) \right]$$

$$\nabla \times \mathbf{A} = \frac{1}{h_1 h_2 h_3} \begin{vmatrix} h_1 \hat{\mathbf{u}}_1 & h_2 \hat{\mathbf{u}}_2 & h_3 \hat{\mathbf{u}}_3 \\ \dfrac{\partial}{\partial u_1} & \dfrac{\partial}{\partial u_2} & \dfrac{\partial}{\partial u_3} \\ h_1 A_1 & h_2 A_2 & h_3 A_3 \end{vmatrix}$$

$$\nabla \times \mathbf{A} = \frac{\hat{\mathbf{u}}_1}{h_2 h_3} \left[\frac{\partial}{\partial u_2} (h_3 A_3) - \frac{\partial}{\partial u_3} (h_2 A_2) \right]$$
$$+ \frac{\hat{\mathbf{u}}_2}{h_1 h_3} \left[\frac{\partial}{\partial u_3} (h_1 A_1) - \frac{\partial}{\partial u_1} (h_3 A_3) \right] + \frac{\hat{\mathbf{u}}_3}{h_1 h_2} \left[\frac{\partial}{\partial u_1} (h_2 A_2) - \frac{\partial}{\partial u_2} (h_1 A_1) \right]$$

$$\nabla^2 \Phi = \frac{1}{h_1 h_2 h_3} \left[\frac{\partial}{\partial u_1} \left(\frac{h_2 h_3}{h_1} \frac{\partial \Phi}{\partial u_1} \right) + \frac{\partial}{\partial u_2} \left(\frac{h_3 h_1}{h_2} \frac{\partial \Phi}{\partial u_2} \right) + \frac{\partial}{\partial u_3} \left(\frac{h_1 h_2}{h_3} \frac{\partial \Phi}{\partial u_3} \right) \right]$$

Rectangular Coordinates

$$u_1 = x \qquad u_2 = y \qquad u_3 = z$$
$$h_1 = 1 \qquad h_2 = 1 \qquad h_3 = 1$$

Derivatives of all unit vectors are zero.

$$\nabla\Phi = \hat{\mathbf{x}}\frac{\partial\Phi}{\partial x} + \hat{\mathbf{y}}\frac{\partial\Phi}{\partial y} + \hat{\mathbf{z}}\frac{\partial\Phi}{\partial z}$$

$$\nabla\cdot\mathbf{A} = \frac{\partial A_x}{\partial x} + \frac{\partial A_y}{\partial y} + \frac{\partial A_z}{\partial z}$$

$$\nabla\times\mathbf{A} = \hat{\mathbf{x}}\left(\frac{\partial A_z}{\partial y} - \frac{\partial A_y}{\partial z}\right) + \hat{\mathbf{y}}\left(\frac{\partial A_x}{\partial z} - \frac{\partial A_z}{\partial x}\right) + \hat{\mathbf{z}}\left(\frac{\partial A_y}{\partial x} - \frac{\partial A_x}{\partial y}\right)$$

$$\nabla^2\Phi = \frac{\partial^2\Phi}{\partial x^2} + \frac{\partial^2\Phi}{\partial y^2} + \frac{\partial^2\Phi}{\partial z^2}$$

Cylindrical Coordinates

$$u_1 = r \qquad u_2 = \varphi \qquad u_3 = z$$

$$h_1 = 1 \qquad h_2 = r \qquad h_3 = 1$$

$$\frac{\partial\hat{\mathbf{r}}}{\partial\varphi} = \hat{\boldsymbol{\varphi}} \qquad \frac{\partial\hat{\boldsymbol{\varphi}}}{\partial\varphi} = -\hat{\mathbf{r}}$$

All other partial derivatives of unit vectors are zero.

$$\nabla\Phi = \hat{\mathbf{r}}\frac{\partial\Phi}{\partial r} + \frac{\hat{\boldsymbol{\varphi}}}{r}\frac{\partial\Phi}{\partial\varphi} + \hat{\mathbf{z}}\frac{\partial\Phi}{\partial z}$$

$$\nabla\cdot\mathbf{A} = \frac{1}{r}\frac{\partial}{\partial r}(rA_r) + \frac{1}{r}\frac{\partial A_\varphi}{\partial\varphi} + \frac{\partial A_z}{\partial z}$$

$$\nabla\times\mathbf{A} = \hat{\mathbf{r}}\left(\frac{1}{r}\frac{\partial A_z}{\partial\varphi} - \frac{\partial A_\varphi}{\partial z}\right) + \hat{\boldsymbol{\varphi}}\left(\frac{\partial A_r}{\partial z} - \frac{\partial A_z}{\partial r}\right) + \hat{\mathbf{z}}\left[\frac{1}{r}\frac{\partial}{\partial r}(rA_\varphi) - \frac{1}{r}\frac{\partial A_r}{\partial\varphi}\right]$$

$$\nabla^2\Phi = \frac{1}{r}\frac{\partial}{\partial r}\left(r\frac{\partial\Phi}{\partial r}\right) + \frac{1}{r^2}\frac{\partial^2\Phi}{\partial\varphi^2} + \frac{\partial^2\Phi}{\partial z^2}$$

Spherical Coordinates

$$u_1 = r \qquad u_2 = \theta \qquad u_3 = \varphi \qquad h_1 = 1 \qquad h_2 = r \qquad h_3 = r\sin\theta$$

$$\frac{\partial\hat{\mathbf{r}}}{\partial\theta} = \hat{\boldsymbol{\theta}} \qquad \frac{\partial\hat{\boldsymbol{\theta}}}{\partial\theta} = -\hat{\mathbf{r}} \qquad \frac{\partial\hat{\boldsymbol{\varphi}}}{\partial\varphi} = \frac{-\mathbf{r}_\parallel}{\sin\theta}$$

See Sec. 1.6 for $\mathbf{r}_\parallel$.

$$\frac{\partial\hat{\mathbf{r}}}{\partial\varphi} = \sin\theta\,\hat{\boldsymbol{\varphi}} \qquad \frac{\partial\hat{\boldsymbol{\theta}}}{\partial\varphi} = \cos\theta\,\hat{\boldsymbol{\varphi}}$$

All other partial derivatives are zero.

$$\nabla\Phi = \hat{\mathbf{r}}\frac{\partial\Phi}{\partial r} + \frac{\hat{\boldsymbol{\theta}}}{r}\frac{\partial\Phi}{\partial\theta} + \frac{\hat{\boldsymbol{\varphi}}}{r\sin\theta}\frac{\partial\Phi}{\partial\varphi}$$

$$\nabla\cdot\mathbf{A} = \frac{1}{r^2}\frac{\partial}{\partial r}(r^2A_r) + \frac{1}{r\sin\theta}\frac{\partial}{\partial\theta}(\sin\theta\, A_\theta) + \frac{1}{r\sin\theta}\frac{\partial A_\varphi}{\partial\varphi}$$

$$\nabla\times\mathbf{A} = \frac{\hat{\mathbf{r}}}{r\sin\theta}\left[\frac{\partial}{\partial\theta}(A_\varphi\sin\theta) - \frac{\partial A_\theta}{\partial\varphi}\right] + \frac{\hat{\boldsymbol{\theta}}}{r}\left[\frac{1}{\sin\theta}\frac{\partial A_r}{\partial\varphi} - \frac{\partial}{\partial r}(rA_\varphi)\right] + \frac{\hat{\boldsymbol{\varphi}}}{r}\left[\frac{\partial}{\partial r}(rA_\theta) - \frac{\partial A_r}{\partial\theta}\right]$$

$$\nabla^2\Phi = \frac{1}{r^2}\frac{\partial}{\partial r}\left(r^2\frac{\partial\Phi}{\partial r}\right) + \frac{1}{r^2\sin\theta}\frac{\partial}{\partial\theta}\left(\sin\theta\frac{\partial\Phi}{\partial\theta}\right) + \frac{1}{r^2\sin^2\theta}\frac{\partial^2\Phi}{\partial\varphi^2}$$

bibliography

Electromagnetic Theory

1. Dekker, A. J.: "Solid-state Physics," Prentice-Hall, Inc., Englewood Cliffs, N.J., 1957.
2. Ehrenreich, Henry: The Optical Properties of Metals, *IEEE Spectrum*, pp. 162–170, March 1965.
3. Hayt, William H., Jr.: "Engineering Electromagnetics," 2d ed., McGraw-Hill Book Company, New York, 1967.
4. Harrington, R. F.: "Time-harmonic Electromagnetic Fields," McGraw-Hill Book Company, New York, 1961.
5. Jackson, John David: "Classical Electrodynamics," John Wiley & Sons, Inc., New York, 1962.
6. Johnson, Curtis C.: "Field and Wave Electrodynamics," McGraw-Hill Book Company, New York, 1965.
7. Jordan, Edward C.: "Electromagnetic Waves and Radiating Systems," Prentice-Hall, Inc., Englewood Cliffs, N.J., 1950.
8. Kittel, Charles: "Introduction to Solid-state Physics," 3d ed., John Wiley & Sons, Inc., New York, 1966.
9. Kraus, John D.: "Electromagnetics," McGraw-Hill Book Company, New York, 1953.
10. Langmuir, R. V.: "Electromagnetic Fields and Waves," McGraw-Hill Book Company, Inc., New York, 1961.

11. Panofsky, Wolfgang K. H., and Melba Phillips: "Classical Electricity and Magnetism," 2d ed., Addison-Wesley Publishing Company, Inc., Reading, Mass., 1962.
12. Plonsey, Robert, and Robert E. Collin: "Principles and Applications of Electromagnetic Fields," McGraw-Hill Book Company, New York, 1961.
13. Ramo, Simon, John R. Whinnery, and T. Van Duzer: "Fields and Waves in Communication Electronics," John Wiley & Sons, Inc., New York, 1965.
14. Reitz, J. R., and F. J. Milford: "Foundations of Electromagnetic Theory," Addison-Wesley Publishing Company, Reading, Mass., 1960.
15. Schelkunoff, S. A.: Transmission Theory of Plane Electromagnetic Waves, *Proc. IRE*, vol. 25, pp. 1457–1492, November, 1937.
16. Schelkunoff, S. A.: "Electromagnetic Fields," Blaisdell Publishing Company, New York, 1963.
17. Smith, P. H.: Transmission Line Calculator, *Electronics*, vol. 12, no. 1, pp. 29–31, 1939.
18. Smith, P. H.: An Improved Transmission Line Calculator, *Electronics*, vol. 17, no. 1, p. 130, 1944.
19. Stratton, J. A.: "Electromagnetic Theory," McGraw-Hill Book Company, New York, 1941.
20. Time Domain Reflectometry, *Hewlett Packard J.*, vol. 15, February, 1964.
21. Von Hippel, A. R. (ed.): "Dielectric Materials and Applications," Technology Press of M.I.T. and John Wiley & Sons, Inc., New York, 1954.

Mathematics

22. Jahnke, Eugene, and Fritz Emde: "Tables of Functions," 4th ed., Dover Publications, Inc., New York, 1945.
23. Kaplan, Wilfred: "Advanced Calculus," Addison-Wesley Publishing Company, Inc., Reading, Mass., 1952.
24. Lindgren, B. W.: "Vector Calculus," The Macmillan Company, New York, 1964.
25. McQuistan, R. B.: "Scalar and Vector Fields," John Wiley & Sons, Inc., New York, 1965.
26. Wylie, C. R., Jr.: "Advanced Engineering Mathematics," 3d ed., McGraw-Hill Book Company, New York, 1966.

index